GROW
ORGANIC
COOK
ORGANIC

GROW ORGANIC
COOK ORGANIC

NATURAL FOOD FROM GARDEN TO
TABLE, WITH OVER 1700 PHOTOGRAPHS

**Christine & Michael Lavelle,
Ysanne Spevack**

LORENZ BOOKS

This edition is published by Lorenz Books,
an imprint of Anness Publishing Ltd,
Hermes House, 88–89 Blackfriars Road, London SE1 8HA
tel. 020 7401 2077; fax 020 7633 9499
www.lorenzbooks.com; www.annesspublishing.com

If you like the images in this book and would like to investigate using them for
publishing, promotions or advertising, please visit our website
www.practicalpictures.com for more information.

UK agent: The Manning Partnership Ltd; tel. 01225 478444;
fax 01225 478440; sales@manning-partnership.co.uk
UK distributor: Grantham Book Services Ltd; tel. 01476 541080;
fax 01476 541061; orders@gbs.tbs-ltd.co.uk
North American agent/distributor: National Book Network; tel. 301 459 3366;
fax 301 429 5746; www.nbnbooks.com
Australian agent/distributor: Pan Macmillan Australia; tel. 1300 135 113;
fax 1300 135 103; customer.service@macmillan.com.au
New Zealand agent/distributor: David Bateman Ltd; tel. (09) 415 7664;
fax (09) 415 8892

Publisher: Joanna Lorenz
Managing Editor: Linda Fraser
Editor: Clare Gooden
Designers: Nigel Partridge and Lisa Tai
Recipes by: Catherine Atkinson, Alex Barker, Mary Banks, Jacqueline Clarke,
Patrizia Diemling, Joanna Farrow, Jenni Fleetwood, Justine France, Brian Glover,
Nicola Graimes, Christine Ingram, Emi Kazuko, Lucy Knox, Sara Lewis, Christine
McFadden, Lesley Mackley, Kathy Man, Sally Mansfield, Maggie Mayhew, Jane
Milton, Sallie Morris, Jennie Shapter, Anne Sheasby, Marlena Spieler, Kate
Whiteman and Jeni Wright
Additional text: Richard Bird and Jonathan Edwards
Photography: Peter Anderson, Jonathan Buckley, Nicki Dowey, Gus Filgate,
Michelle Garrett, Amanda Heywood, William Lingwood, Steve Moss,
Thomas Odulate, Craig Robertson and Simon Smith
Illustrator: Liz Pepperell
Production Controller: Claire Rae

ETHICAL TRADING POLICY
Because of our ongoing ecological investment programme, you, as our
customer, can have the pleasure and reassurance of knowing that a tree is
being cultivated on your behalf to naturally replace the materials used to
make the book you are holding. For further information about this scheme,
go to www.annesspublishing.com/trees

Previously published as *Organic Kitchen and Garden*

NOTES
• Bracketed terms are intended for American readers.
• For all recipes, quantities are given in both metric and imperial measures and, where appropriate, in
standard cups and spoons. Follow one set of measures, but not a mixture, because they are not interchangeable.
• Standard spoon and cup measures are level. 1 tsp = 5ml, 1 tbsp = 15ml, 1 cup = 250ml/8fl oz.
• Australian standard tablespoons are 20ml. Australian readers should use 3 tsp in place of 1 tbsp for
measuring small quantities of gelatine, flour, salt, etc.
• American pints are 16fl oz/2 cups. American readers should use 20fl oz/2.5 cups in place of 1 pint when
measuring liquids.
• Electric oven temperatures in this book are for conventional ovens. When using a fan oven, the
temperature will probably need to be reduced by about 10–20°C/20–40°F. Since ovens vary, you should
check with your manufacturer's instruction book for guidance.
• Medium (US large) eggs are used unless otherwise stated.

CONTENTS

INTRODUCTION

More and more people are discovering the benefits of an organic lifestyle, either growing their own crops or enjoying the many organic products now available in supermarkets and health food stores. This book aims to make organic living even more accessible, with step-by-step guides to successful chemical-free gardening, followed by delicious seasonal recipes to make the most of your fresh, home-grown produce. The emphasis is firmly on quality, wholesome ingredients and natural processes, and the results make a convincing case for adopting the organic way of life.

THE ORGANIC GARDEN

The aim of this section is to show that organic gardening is
gardening at its best. The most successful organic gardeners learn
that the use of artifical chemicals for short-term gains leads to
long-term losses and also that nature makes the best model.
Whether you want to grow organic produce for your table, enjoy a
dazzling display of summer colour or create a wildlife paradise,
the organic garden is for you. Many techniques may already be
familiar to you, and the change will be less difficult than you think.
Going organic may not change the world immediately, but it
will certainly make a difference.

WHAT IS ORGANIC GARDENING?

The term organic means of living origin. When applied to gardening, organic has come to mean the systematic use of techniques that mirror naturally occurring systems. Put simply, it is about finding environmentally friendly ways to cultivate the land, working with rather than against nature. Organic gardening refers not just to a system of techniques, however, but also to a whole philosophy of life.

Above: *The organic garden uses a range of natural materials, including by-products such as chicken manure.*

THE ORIGINS OF ORGANIC GARDENING

From the point of view of gardening, the "modern" organic movement began in the late1940s as a reaction to the increased use of pesticides and synthetic fertilizers in the years after the Second World War. In many respects, however, the principles of organic gardening have been practised for centuries. Ancient writers, among them Pliny and Virgil, commented on the importance of "good husbandry to the health of the land". Thomas Tusser, in his classic work of 1580 entitled *Five Hundred Points of Good Husbandry*, recommends crop rotation to maintain good health. The 17th-century English garden writer John Evelyn begins his *Kalendarium Hortense* with a section describing how to enrich the ground in mid-winter with "horse and sheeps dung especially, that you may have some of two years preparation".

Above: *Many of the plants that benefit wildlife also make showy and decorative additions to beds and borders.*

ORGANIC GARDENING IN THE 21ST CENTURY

Much of the current interest in organic gardening began in the 1960s, when there was increasing concern about the growing levels of environmental damage caused by pesticides and other agrochemicals. If they were causing so much damage to the natural world, then surely they must ultimately affect human beings?

The organic approach aims to reduce the effects that our gardens, farms and cities have upon the wider natural environment. Activities such as recycling, using sustainably produced materials and avoiding pesticides and other harmful agrochemicals all help in this. Organic gardening is often described as being a more natural way to garden. This can make it appear to be somehow revolutionary. In many ways, however, organic gardening could be said to be counter-revolutionary. It aims to avoid artificial inputs and gains. Instead it draws from a vast resource of wisdom and experience amassed over 10,000 years. Much of the so-called conventional wisdom is, in fact, very recent. We only have to look back as far as our grandparents to see that they were naturally organic gardeners. Organic gardening then is the marriage of good horticultural practice to an awareness of our impact upon our surroundings.

IS IT POSSIBLE TO BE WHOLLY ORGANIC?

The short answer to this would probably have to be … with great difficulty. But the purpose of this book is not to promote difficulty or set unattainable goals. The aim should always be to aspire to the ideal solution. Almost all of us face compromise on a daily basis and understand that practicalities outweigh personal ideals. With perseverance and practice, however, it is possible to become less compromised in the confines of your own garden. Simple planning and the observance of good

Left: *Organic gardens can be beautifully designed and can include a mixture of ornamental and edible plants.*

Above: *A well-designed and properly maintained organic garden can be both attractive and productive.*

gardening practice can steadily improve your organic credentials and, with time, a natural balance will be established in your garden. Ultimately, the aim of all organic gardeners, be they landscaping a city garden, tending a country estate or growing home-produced vegetables, is to make choices appropriate to their situation. It is better to move a few steps towards the organic way than to ignore it completely.

Above: *Vegetables need not be planted in rows. Here, the beds are arranged in an attractive geometric pattern.*

ORGANIC STANDARDS

Organic standards are set out to explain the requirements that farmers, growers, processors and others must meet in order for their products or services to be marketed as organic. The standards can be extensive and cover a wide range of farming, growing and food manufacturing practices.

Are organic standards the same worldwide? No. Different countries may stipulate their own standards. IFOAM is the International Federation of Organic Agricultural Movements that represents the worldwide body of organic agriculture and provides a platform for the global exchange of information and co-operation.

Are any chemicals allowed in organic production? Yes. In line with the legal framework of the country, a very limited number of chemicals are allowed on a restricted basis. Organic standards do not allow the use of artificial herbicides or fungicides. By comparison, in non-organic farming as many as 450 chemicals can be routinely used.

If organic gardening severely restricts the use of artificial chemical fertilizers and pesticides, then how do I keep my garden healthy? Organic gardeners rely on developing a healthy fertile soil and growing a mixture of crops. By following these basic practices, organic gardeners work in harmony with nature and aim to achieve a healthy natural balance within their gardens.

Do I have to achieve any standards to become organic? No. Commercial standards are very strict and not necessarily easy to achieve for the amateur. Everyone must make choices appropriate to their own situation.

Is the organic movement just concerned with growing food? No. Going organic is not just about organic food – it should become a way of life. Today, organic wood, clothing, gardening products and even restaurants can all be found. This means that other areas of your life can be organic as well as your garden. It does not always mean completely changing your life, but it can change lives.

WHY GO ORGANIC?

This commonly asked question is easy to answer. The primary reason to embrace the organic approach is health. This means the well-being of the individual as well as the health of the environment. Many pesticides can accumulate over time, both in our own bodies and in the wider environment, a poisonous legacy that can persist for decades. Organic gardening seeks to redress this damage by working with and encouraging nature. It is a long-term investment in the health and wellbeing of us all.

Above: *Butterflies are just one of the many different types of wildlife that can benefit from a pesticide-free garden.*

GREEN CUISINE

Hardly a day seems to go by without some new revelation about the benefits or detrimental effects of some food or other. Recent concerns about the "goodness" of the things that we eat have been a major incentive to supermarkets to supply a growing demand for organic produce. There can be little that equals the satisfaction to be derived from eating home-produced food, gathered fresh from the garden. What better than garden-fresh vegetables that are produced naturally and cleanly?

A GREENER, SAFER GARDEN

Although we think of our gardens as places of safe retreat we have used a cocktail of pesticides and agrochemicals on them that has stripped them of their natural diversity. Many of these poisons no longer control the beasts that they were intended to. All that suffers in this noxious onslaught is the garden, its wild occupants and ultimately

the plants. This cycle of pesticide use eventually turns your personal paradise into a potential health hazard.

HELPING THE ENVIRONMENT

For many of us it can seem that there is little that we can do to change the degradation of our environment. But the truth is that the actions of all of us have both positive and negative impacts upon the land. If every individual reduces his or her own negative impact upon the environment, then collectively we can make a difference. By changing the way you garden to a more organic way, you can begin the healing process, literally in your own backyard.

PROTECTING AND ENCOURAGING WILDLIFE

Be it a bird on a feeder or brightly coloured butterflies on a flower, most of us enjoy seeing visitors from the wild in our gardens. But many of the unsung heroes of our gardens – the insects, worms, amphibians

and mammals that crawl, slither and scurry out of sight – are equally important and may even be the reason why some of the larger visitors come. Organic gardening helps many of these and promotes a balance of wildlife that is both interesting and beautiful to look at.

SO WHAT IF I DO NOT GO ORGANIC?

While the intention of this book is not to dwell upon negative points, the cost of not adopting an organic approach may be seen all around us. This is most frequently noticed as fields and open spaces bereft of butterflies, bees, birds and other wildlife with very little diversity of plant species. It is unthinkable that we could hand this planet to successive generations in a denuded and impoverished state. Perhaps a garden free of "bugs" may sound attractive to some, but the long-term cost to the environment may be felt for generations and in the worst case may even be permanent.

Above: *Organic flower gardens, with their wide range of wildlife-friendly plants, can provide a balanced habitat for birds and insects that is diverse, interesting and beautiful to look at.*

Above: *Imaginative planting designs can result in beautiful contrasts of flowers and foliage, while also providing a wealth of flavourful, home-grown food for your table.*

IT'S A SOLUTION AND IT'S FUN!

Organic gardening is not the solution to all humankind's problems. However, it is a positive and valuable step that you as an individual can take. What's more, you can contribute positively to the wellbeing of your surroundings and to that of your wider environment by doing something that is also fun and rewarding.

WILL "GOING ORGANIC" MEAN THAT MY WHOLE LIFESTYLE HAS TO CHANGE?

Organic gardening is often presented as part of a more general "organic movement". This movement owes its origins to a range of social philosophies, some of which are more fundamentalist than others. The aim of organic gardening is to change the way that you garden and not your whole life. People frequently get confused about the meaning of words that are used as part of the wider organic movement. Four of these terms are explained below. Of these, three describe a whole philosophy that affects practitioners far beyond the confines of their own gardens. An understanding of the philosophies of others can help inspire your own lifestyle changes and all have their own points of interest. In the end, however, it is a matter of choice for you alone and it is best to decide just how organic you (and your family) wish to be.

Biodiversity literally means "the variety of life". It includes all the different plant, animal, fungus and microscopic species in the world. It also considers the genes they contain and the ecosystems of which they form a part. Biodiversity has been seen as the total complexity of all life, including not only the great variety of organisms but also their varying behaviour and interactions. An organic garden aims to maximize all these many different things which are vital to every part of the garden, but especially important when considering the soil. Soil biodiversity is the "lifeblood" of the organic garden and demands investment in order to yield a return.

Biodynamics is described by its practitioners as a science of life forces, recognizing the basic principles at work in nature and taking into account how our actions can bring balance and healing to the world. It is based upon the work of Rudolf Steiner and is said to offer an account of the spiritual history of the Earth as a living being. Its enthusiasts advocate a

Above: *The foliage and form of many types of vegetables can provide striking contrasts in the vegetable garden.*

broadening of personal perspective that includes an understanding of cosmic rhythms, natural healing, a respect for life forces and ultimately a shift away from centralized economic strategies.

Permaculture is a concept that was originally developed in the 1970s by Australians Bill Mollinson and David Holgreen. It was conceived as a response to increasing concerns over the deteriorating natural environment. They attempted to answer the question "how do we, as the human species, sustain ourselves and provide for the needs of the environment for an indefinite period of time?". The answer to this question is the basis for creating a permanent culture (Perma-Culture). This philosophy aims to unite practical, ecological design philosophies by incorporating natural systems and materials into human habitats. Permaculture rejects short-term gains in favour of long-term stability for the environment and those who live in it.

Self-sufficiency is an ideal rather than a reality for most that attempt it, as modern living usually dictates some degree of trade, even if it is limited. Advocates of self-sufficiency aim to produce everything that they need in order to support themselves. The only imports are those that cannot be produced by an individual.

UNDERSTANDING YOUR GARDEN

Plants, like all living things, flourish when given the right conditions. Certain plants will only thrive in a hot, sunny and dry garden, for example, while others may need cool, moist and shady conditions to prosper. If you are to have healthy plants, you need to choose those that are best suited to your garden and this means understanding exactly what conditions prevail and taking into account a range of environmental factors.

Above: *A hot, sunny spot is ideal for growing pretty summer flowers such as argyranthemums and verbenas.*

CLIMATE
The climate causes a variety of responses, depending upon the plant's location, its stage of maturity, the length of exposure and the intensity of the type of weather. Climate may have a dramatic effect on plant growth and development, especially when extreme weather conditions prevail.

TEMPERATURE
All plant species have their own maximum and minimum temperature tolerances, beyond which the life processes of the plant cease. As a general rule, the maximum temperature that most plants can tolerate is around 35°C (95°F), while the minimum is highly variable. The air and soil temperatures are also crucial in influencing dormancy within plants and this, in turn, largely dictates the length of the growing season.

Air temperature is affected by the degree of energy received from the sun. A sheltered site that benefits from the warming effects of the sun may be used for growing plants that are indigenous to warmer climates.

Soil temperature influences a plant's root development and the rate at which water and nutrients can be absorbed. Sandy soils warm up quicker and earlier in the season than clay soils, mainly because they are relatively free draining and do not hold as much water. Sites that receive a lot of sun, or with a slight incline towards it, will also warm up quicker than shady ones.

WATER
This is the major constituent of all plants. In most gardens, rainfall is the principal source of water for plants and it can be lost through evaporation or surface run-off, although much of it is soaked up by soil particles. This water may then be absorbed by the root hairs of the plant. A steady supply of water is essential for the plant to sustain itself and for optimum growth.

Water may also be held in the air and is referred to as humidity. The amount of water vapour in the atmosphere at any one time is referred to as the relative humidity and is measured as a percentage of the saturation point (100 per cent humidity). In areas that receive heavy rainfall, relative humidity is also higher. Many plants, such as ferns and mosses, thrive in such conditions. But high relative humidity can have undesirable effects on plants, often encouraging disease.

Waterlogging refers to the build-up of water that may occur in badly drained soil with poor structure. The roots of plants that are not adapted to these conditions will suffer and probably die through asphyxiation.

Left: *A bog garden provides ideal conditions for a range of decorative moisture-loving plants.*

Right: *Blossom is both pretty and essential for good fruit-set. A sheltered site will also encourage pollinating insects.*

LIGHT LEVELS
Sunlight enables photosynthesis (the method by which plant food is made) to occur. As a result, it is vital to new growth as well as sustaining existing growth. Seasonal changes in light levels may also trigger different stages in the plants' development.

AIR CIRCULATION
Even moderate winds can increase a plant's transpiration rate. However, a light wind can also have beneficial effects, providing relief from extreme heat and cooling the foliage. It will also "change the air" around the plant, and thus help to alleviate a stagnant atmosphere that could promote disease.

ASSESSING THE CLIMATE
A range of climatic information is generally available for your local region. Weather forecasts are an obvious source, but long-term records are sometimes available. From these you should be able to get a picture of the average rainfall, snow, frosty days, wind direction and monthly temperatures.

A TYPICAL GARDEN AND ITS MICROCLIMATES

Even a small garden can contain a wide variety of microclimates, ranging from cool, shady corners to hot, dry areas. A proper assessment of the growing conditions that prevail in your garden allows you to choose the right plants for the right place.

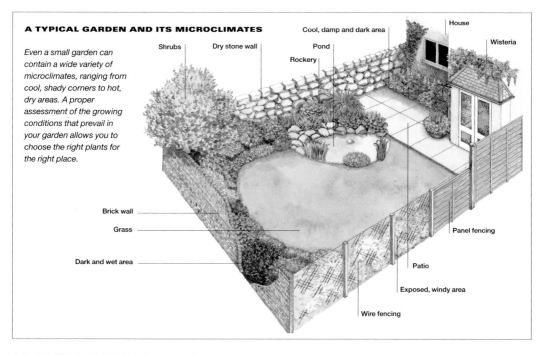

Cool, damp and dark area
House
Wisteria
Shrubs
Dry stone wall
Pond
Rockery
Brick wall
Grass
Dark and wet area
Panel fencing
Patio
Exposed, windy area
Wire fencing

A GARDEN'S MICROCLIMATE

The prevailing weather conditions in confined or discrete areas are termed the microclimate. For example, there will be a range of environments within a small domestic garden that may be very different from those weather conditions prevailing elsewhere in the locality. Observe what is going on in your own garden and keep a careful record of the position and influence of the following features.

Walls, hedges and fences may cause wind turbulence and dryness, depending upon their height and density. They may cause cold air to build up on sloping sites by preventing it from "draining away" downwards. This can create frost pockets that may have a crucial effect on the type and range of plants that may be grown.

Shadow projections from permanent features, such as buildings, walls, hedges and large trees, may create a range of dense shadow resulting in dark, dry and often cool conditions that will only suit certain plant species.

Hot spots may occur with aspects that are subject to high and prolonged levels of sunlight. Plants may struggle in the dryness created by such strong sunlight.

Damp areas may be anticipated where the ground is low-lying, especially on very heavy soils. During heavy rainfall you should also note the direction of water flow, including where necessary the route taken by excess surface water, which may in extreme cases be the cause of soil erosion.

Soil type and pH play an important role in the ability of a site to support particular plant species. The relative acidity or alkalinity can affect the availability of certain essential nutrients, leading to either shortage or toxicity in plants not ideally suited to the pH of a soil. It is always better to choose plants that thrive in the particular pH of a soil. Attempts to alter the pH by acidifying or adding lime are rarely satisfactory and neither are long-term solutions.

Existing habitat types on and around the garden indicate what plants are likely to thrive. Notes should be made on the range of species and the likely wildlife value.

The garden topography (the shape and aspect of the land) may also affect what you are able to do. If a garden slopes toward the

Right: A shady corner of the garden provides the perfect place for shade lovers such as these foxgloves (Digitalis).

direction of the midday sun, for instance, it will be warmer than a flat site. Sloping or uneven gardens have their own problems, particularly if you wish to site a greenhouse.

RIGHT PLANT, RIGHT PLACE

Once you have assessed your garden environment, you will be able to choose the right plants for your site. Every garden has its own unique set of advantages and limitations, and these take time to evaluate, so trial and error is ultimately the most reliable method.

THE ORGANIC CYCLE

Plants produce their own food using carbon dioxide from the air, water from the soil and energy from the sun in a process known as photosynthesis. The energy in this sugar powers all the growth, development and life-giving processes within the plant. Plants must also produce a range of other substances, including proteins, fats, oils and cellulose, for which they need nutrients such as nitrogen, phosphorus, and potassium. These are almost always taken up through the roots.

Above: *Plant leaves are remarkable structures because they are the factories in which a plant makes its food.*

WHAT PLANTS NEED

In natural systems, nitrogen, phosphorus and potassium are repeatedly taken up by the plant, used and returned to the soil when the plant dies, drops its leaves or is eaten by an animal. This process is known as nutrient cycling. Plant nutrients are covered in more depth later. For now we need only look at three of the most important cycles: water, carbon and nitrogen.

THE WATER CYCLE

The movement and endless recycling of water between the atmosphere, the surface of the land and under the soil is called the water cycle and is driven by the energy of the sun and the force of gravity.

Water vapour in the atmosphere condenses into clouds, which fall as snow, rain, sleet or hail. This water may be taken up by plants, stored in lakes, enter the soil or flow over the surface in streams. The sun causes water to evaporate back into the atmosphere, or gravity may pull it down through the pores of the soil to be stored as slow-moving ground water. Water can also return to the atmosphere indirectly through plants' leaves – a process known as

transpiration – this being highest during periods of high temperatures, wind, dry air and sunshine.

THE CARBON CYCLE

The movement of carbon, in its many forms, between the total living content of the earth, the atmosphere, oceans, and the rocks and

Above: *Plants rely on water, taken up through the roots, to support their life processes and facilitate growth.*

soils covering the surface, is termed the carbon cycle. It is complex and far reaching. The same carbon atoms in your body today have been used in countless other molecules since time began. Plants absorb carbon dioxide from the atmosphere during photosynthesis (food production) and release it back into the atmosphere during respiration (food use). This process is the great natural recycler of carbon atoms.

THE NITROGEN CYCLE

Nitrogen is used by living organisms to produce a number of complex organic molecules such as amino acids, proteins and nucleic acids, the "building blocks" of life. The largest store of nitrogen is in the atmosphere, where it exists as a gas. This store is about one million times larger than the total nitrogen contained in living organisms.

Right: *Left to develop naturally, grassland will become a rich and diverse habitat for a wealth of both plants and wildlife.*

NUTRIENT CYCLES IN A TYPICAL GARDEN

Even small gardens contain natural cycles. Elements and nutrients are cycled repeatedly both within the environment and as a result of the complex food chains and webs. This cycle of nature is essential in creating a balanced and healthy habitat.

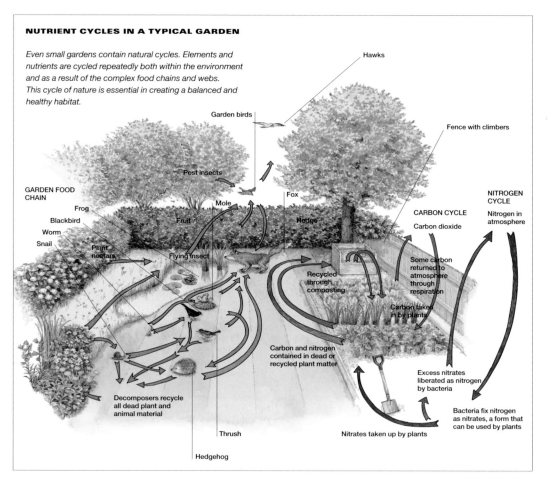

Hawks

Garden birds

Fence with climbers

Pest insects

GARDEN FOOD CHAIN

Frog

Blackbird

Worm

Snail

Plant nectars

Fruit

Mole

Fox

Hedge

Flying insect

NITROGEN CYCLE

Nitrogen in atmosphere

CARBON CYCLE

Carbon dioxide

Some carbon returned to atmosphere through respiration

Recycled through composting

Carbon taken in by plants

Carbon and nitrogen contained in dead or recycled plant matter

Excess nitrates liberated as nitrogen by bacteria

Decomposers recycle all dead plant and animal material

Bacteria fix nitrogen as nitrates, a form that can be used by plants

Thrush

Nitrates taken up by plants

Hedgehog

Despite its abundance in the atmosphere, plants can only take up nitrogen in two solid forms: ammonium and nitrate. Most plants fulfil their needs using nitrate from the soil. Ammonium is used less frequently because it is toxic in large concentrations. Most ecosystems have nitrogen stored in living and dead organic matter, which re-enters the cycle via decomposition. Decomposers in the soil, such as bacteria and fungi, chemically modify the nitrogen found in this organic matter.

Almost all of the nitrogen found in any terrestrial ecosystem originally came from the atmosphere and is biochemically converted ("fixed") into a useful form within the soil by specialized bacteria. Members of the bean family (legumes) and some

other kinds of plants form relationships with nitrogen-fixing bacteria. In exchange for nitrogen, the bacteria receive food from the plants and special root structures (nodules) that provide protection.

WHAT ARE ECOSYSTEMS?

Short for ecological systems, ecosystems are communities of plants and animals that consist of a given habitat (the place where an organism lives) and its community (all the plants and animals that live in it). Any group of living and non-living things interacting with each other (including those found in gardens) can be considered an ecosystem.

The chemical materials that are extracted from the environment and changed into living tissue by plants and

animals are continually recycled within the ecosystem. These nutrient cycles are at their most efficient when an ecosystem has a good diversity of species. Such diversity tends to make a community stable and self-perpetuating.

FOOD CHAINS AND WEBS

The energy necessary for life reaches the earth as sunlight. This is made into food and stored in plants. Animals acquire some of the stored energy by eating the plants or by eating other plant-eating animals. Such sequences, called food chains, overlap at many points, forming food webs which show "who eats whom" in an ecosystem. If one animal or plant is affected, then the entire food web can be changed.

DESIGNING YOUR GARDEN

Whether urban or rural, large or small, all gardens benefit from careful planning and design. Having great ideas about what you want to put in the garden is all very well, but they should always have direction. Modern gardens are essentially outdoor rooms, although, like so many aspects of modern living, they often fulfil several functions. Working out what you want beforehand will help you to get the very most from your garden.

Above: *A well-planned wildlife garden can attract a wealth of birds, insects and even mammals to feed and take shelter.*

PLANNING YOUR GARDEN

Measure and draw a plan of your garden as it is now (a base plan). This should ideally include the house, boundaries, shrubs, services (water, gas, sewerage, electricity and telephone cables) and other features. This is worth doing carefully and if surveyor's drawings exist already then these can form a useful starting point. Use graph paper and choose a scale such as 1cm (⅖in) equals 1m (3ft). Everything on your plan should then be drawn as close to scale as possible. Trees, for example, should be drawn as circles showing the width of the canopy and a small dot or circle in the centre for the trunk. Note where the midday sun appears and indicate the position of features such as shaded areas, suntraps, slopes, damp areas and existing vegetation.

If you have recently bought a new home you can start planning now, but it is best to see your garden through every season before making changes. What seems like a dull spot in winter could be a mass of flowers in spring.

WHAT DO YOU WANT FROM YOUR GARDEN?

Make a list of any essential features – a vegetable plot, path or shed, perhaps? Then draw up a "wish list" of things you'd like to have – a water feature, a climbing rose, an apple tree – arranging these things in order of preference. Add to them and alter them. All the items on your list should be grouped under either open spaces – planting and paths – or features such as pergolas and arches.

Once you have a base plan of your garden, and you know what you want, place a piece of tracing paper over it and draw another plan with all unwanted plants and structures removed. On this sheet you can also "zone" your garden into the following areas.

Public area This is the area visible from the front of the house. You may wish to conform to the style of the neighbourhood or use this area to make a statement.

Service area This houses utilitarian items such as bins, clotheslines, compost heap etc. This area is usually best located to the rear or side of the property and may benefit from some form of screening.

Private (living) area This is the most important expanse to develop as it provides a space for family activities and extends the living area of the house.

HOW MUCH TIME WILL YOU SPEND IN THE GARDEN?

While some garden enthusiasts would be content to spend almost every spare working hour tending their plot, others have less time that they can (or are willing to) spend maintaining their garden. For these people, high-maintenance features, such as lawns or a vegetable garden, may not be the best option. But by the same token, do not just avoid something because you think it sounds complicated. Many aspects of organic growing such as no-dig systems and mulching will actually save you time in the long run.

HOW MUCH SPACE WILL YOU NEED FOR DIFFERENT FEATURES?

The simple answer to this is as much space as you have in relation to the time you have available. You should think carefully about what you want the feature for. A large, time-consuming vegetable plot, for instance, might not be the right option for a busy single person. Remember, too, that your garden may change and evolve to mirror your needs and lifestyle. This is part of the beauty of having a garden.

ORNAMENTAL GARDENS

The choice as to how ornamental your garden will be is a matter of taste. A garden is a place where you should be able to relax and enjoy yourself and can be a reflection of

Left: *Bold, architectural plant forms can be used to excellent decorative effect in ornamental garden displays.*

your own personality. You must be able to create a space that you wish to spend time in. Ornamental gardens can be broadly characterized by those that are either largely formal or informal. Even informal gardens will need to be kept tidy, although their character may allow a certain degree of flexibility. The choice ultimately is yours.

KITCHEN GARDENS

Even a small space can be used to raise a range of fresh fruit, herbs and vegetables. The most important point is to ensure that you have the right conditions for the crops that you would like to grow. Each crop has its own requirements. Fruit, for example, needs appropriate sun exposure for it to ripen properly and develop flavour. Designs need to consider the difference between annual and perennial crops as these may well merit their own distinct areas and may need to be rotated. Lastly, you may also wish to consider how difficult a particular plant (or the produce it offers) is to grow. It may be easier to simply buy certain items and concentrate on those that you can grow easily.

WILDLIFE GARDENS

All gardens are habitats for some species or other; even the most desolate plot will support a few species. The aim of the wildlife garden should be to increase the number of all species, both the beautiful ones and the host of less attractive ones that make up this diversity. The best wildlife gardens are a mosaic of habitat types and will usually include a water feature, long grass, shrubs, trees and lots of flowers and

fruit. In addition, a variety of height is needed to create the most diverse habitat. Trees, shrubs and grasses of varying height will all help to provide the three-dimensional medley that is crucial to wildlife gardens.

DEVELOPING THE FINAL PLAN

First, sketch in roughly those items on your list of essentials and wishes. This will show how much space there is and whether you can fit it all in. If there is not enough room for all the items listed, then those with low priority will have to be dropped.

Next, determine more accurately how much space will be required for each feature and fit them more precisely on to the plan. Balance and scale are essential here. Try to visualize how it will feel to stand in the garden.

Think carefully about the planting schemes and where they are to go. You may wish to hide boundaries or block out eyesores with either climbers where space is limited or taller plants in larger areas. Position small plants where they will be seen, either at the front of a bed or the edge of a path. Group plants with similar growing requirements. Use plants to add mystery and create bold drifts. Incorporate meandering paths and naturally flowing shapes in order to create visual interest. Consider also the view of the garden from inside the house. Will certain planting schemes link the house and garden?

Paths should be placed where the most-travelled routes pass through – a worn track in the lawn is often a good indicator of where a path is needed. Paths can be used to link different areas of the

Above: *Vegetable gardens can provide an ornamental display if they are well planned as these red and green lettuces show.*

garden, using materials that are in keeping with the style of your house. By using the same types of material, you will give a sense of uniformity and "oneness" throughout the space. If paths are on a slope, you may wish to consider adding steps.

You should also think about any ornamental features that you would like to include. Items such as pots, urns, archways, pergolas, bird tables, water features and seats make interesting focal points and help to bring an individual touch to the garden. Ornaments can be placed at the end of a path or at intersections, and arches can be used to separate different parts of the garden. Always consider using small detail features such as pots and window boxes, as well as trellises, archways, pergolas, seats, bird feeders, and ponds. Make decisions after you have explored everything available to you, and what would suit your garden.

Left: *This charming, traditional kitchen garden has been well planned and carefully organized in order to utilize every available area of space.*

SOIL AND SOIL MANAGEMENT

Soil is the most precious resource in your garden. Some inherit a well-tended soil, while others, particularly those moving into new homes, inherit a rubble-filled mass. However, any soil can be improved through time and effort. If you regard your soil as a living entity, you will see that essential plant nutrients are cycled by a microscopic army of inhabitants and larger worms, insects and grubs. All these creatures need air, moisture and food. Using manure, garden compost and other sources of organic matter is the key to sustaining this soil life and keeping the soil healthy.

TYPES OF SOIL

Soil is probably the most important constituent of any organic garden because it is vital for successful plant growth. Understanding your soil and knowing how this can help you to create a healthy, fertile growing environment for your plants should be a priority. The starting point in this process is an understanding of the different soil types and how they affect the plants you can grow. Once you understand the soil in your own garden, then you will be able to create a successful organic garden.

Above: *All soil types benefit greatly from the addition of organic matter such as this green manure.*

WHAT ARE SOILS MADE OF?

Both natural soils and some potting mixes for container-grown plants usually have five main components. These are mineral particles (the inorganic fraction), organic matter (the remains of living organisms), water (the "soil solution"), air (which fills the spaces between solid particles that are not filled with water) and living organisms. The proportions of these components vary widely according to the soil type, or the growing medium.

The proportions of water, air and organic matter can be readily changed by soil cultivation and other horticultural practices. A good topsoil will continuously supply plant roots with water, air and nutrients. Subsoil (the largely inert soil layer that lies beneath the thin layer of "living" topsoil) has less organic matter than topsoil. Plant growth will suffer when the proportions of water and air in the medium are out of balance. Too much air will have the same effect upon plant roots as a drought, whereas too much water causes waterlogging. Growth will also suffer if nutrient levels are too low, too high or if there is an imbalance in supply between different nutrients. In addition, soil that is too compacted for roots to grow will also adversely affect growth.

SAND AND SILT

Sandy and silty soils originate from river deposits, windblown sediments or from the erosion of sandstone outcrops. Their general properties are that they do not provide or retain plant nutrients; they are not cohesive and therefore possess a weak structure; and in most cases they are free draining.

Silts, unless well structured, will be waterlogged. Sand, on the other hand, is naturally free draining. The structure and texture of sandy soils means that they are only able to hold a very small reserve of water. Organic matter can improve the available water content but the real trick in avoiding drought-stress lies in ensuring that plants root deeply into the soil. Nutrient shortage can also be a problem on sandy soils which have a tendency to become acidic over time. Liming and the regular addition of organic matter will help alleviate these problems.

Sandy soils do have the advantage of "warming up" quickly in spring due to their lower water content and are easier to work early in the year. This means that you can grow a wider range of plants in a sandy soil. Planting or transplanting is also easier in the autumn.

Organic material is broken down very quickly in sandy soils due to good aeration and a temperature that favours rapid bacterial action. Many light soils naturally have less than two per cent organic matter and it is vital that organic matter be added regularly to sustain healthy plant growth.

PLANTS SUITABLE FOR DIFFERENT SOIL TYPES

Many plants have a type of soil in which they grow best. The list below gives a few examples of the soil preferences of some common species.

Plants suitable for acid soils
Rhododendron (all species)
Camellia (all cultivars)

Plants suitable for alkaline soils
Butterfly bush (*Buddleja* spp.)
Sage (*Salvia*)

Plants suitable for hot dry soils in sun
Yucca (all species)
Broom (*Cytisus*)
Lavender (*Lavandula*)

Plants suitable for damp or wet soils
Willow (*Salix*)
Dogwood (*Cornus*)
Plantain lily (*Hosta*)

Plants suitable for heavy clay
Weigela (all cultivars)
Crocosmia (all cultivars)
Daffodil (*Narcissus*)

Plants suitable for dry shaded soils
Flowering currant (*Ribes sanguineum*)
Pachysandra terminalis
Elephant's ear (*Bergenia cordifolia*)

COMMON TYPES OF SOIL

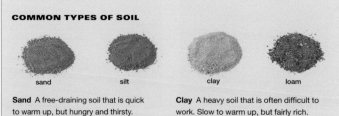

sand   silt   clay   loam

Sand A free-draining soil that is quick to warm up, but hungry and thirsty.
Silt River deposits can be sticky, but not as sticky as clay. Rich and easy to work.

Clay A heavy soil that is often difficult to work. Slow to warm up, but fairly rich.
Loam A moisture-retentive soil that warms up quickly and works perfectly.

HAND-TEXTURING METHOD

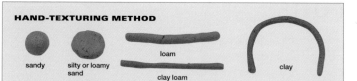

sandy   silty or loamy sand   loam   clay loam   clay

Finding out what type of soil you have is easy and does not require any specialist equipment. This test is ultimately a matter of judgement and will only give you a relative picture of the sort of soil you have. However, it is surprisingly accurate. Simply take a small amount of soil – about a teaspoonful will do – in the palm of your hand. Moisten with a little water (not too much but enough to make it just workable). Once moistened, try to form the soil into one of the shapes shown above.

1 Begin by forming a ball. If it stays together, then proceed to the next shape. If it does not form a ball, then you have a sandy soil.
2 If you can flatten the ball without it breaking up, then you have a silty sand or a loamy sand.
3 If you can roll the flattened ball into a thick sausage shape, then you have a loam.
4 A soil that can be rolled into a thin "sausage" is a clay loam.
5 If you can bend the soil into a horseshoe or ring shape, then you have a clay soil.

Above: *Plants such as alliums and eryngiums like well-drained soil and so will thrive together in the same site.*

CLAY

The particles found in clay are extremely small and are able to interact with, and directly affect, the chemistry of the soil. The individual clay particles are so tiny that they are actually bonded together by electrical charges which produce the characteristic plasticity of this type of soil. Clay is both water retentive and rich in nutrients. It has few pore spaces and those that are there have a tendency to become waterlogged. Clay is prone to swelling when waterlogged and shrinkage when dry. As a result, clays heave (swell outward and upward) when wet and crack when dry. They can also be subject to frost action which causes an increase in tiny, almost microscopic, airspaces (micro pores). Pure clay soils are rare, although some soils may be very rich in clay. They have the potential to be extremely fertile soils if they are well managed.

LOAMS

Loams are a mixture of sand, silt and clay that results in a blend of the characteristics of each constituent part. They are usually characterized by their clay content. Heavy loams are about 24–30% clay, whereas light loams contain about 12–18% clay. Heavy loams behave and should be treated like clay soils. Light loams should be treated like sandy soils. Medium loams are potentially the ideal mixture, exhibiting the advantages of both heavy and light soils without many of the disadvantages of either.

HUMUS

This is a stable form of partially decomposed plant material that gives topsoil its characteristically dark colour. Humus has a high nutrient-reserve potential

SOIL PROFILE
A typical soil profile usually consists of three main elements: an upper layer of dark, fertile topsoil; a middle layer of lighter, infertile subsoil; and a lower layer of bedrock, which ranges from a few to hundreds of metres (yards) deep.

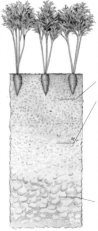

Topsoil is the dark layer of soil that contains organic material. Keep as deep as possible, although usually only one spit (spade) deep.

Subsoil is usually lighter in colour and contains little or no organic material or nutrients. It should be broken to one spit depth, but not mixed with the topsoil.

Bedrock is usually below the level of cultivation.

(2½ x better than clay), retains water, increases the friability (suitability for cultivation) of heavy soils and its darker colour encourages soils to warm up more rapidly.

MANAGING YOUR SOIL
Any soil has the potential to be a fertile growing medium in which plants will thrive if it is managed correctly.

Management of light/sandy soils
• Maintain levels of organic matter.
• Lime when required. (N.B. It is often easier to select species tolerant of the site conditions in the long term.)
• Fertilize well as light soils are usually infertile. (N.B. Some exotic and native plant species actually thrive under relatively poor nutrient conditions.)
• Irrigate frequently in the first year after planting, less so once deeper roots are established.

Management of clay soils
• Drainage is essential.
• Maintain lime status.
• Maintain levels of organic matter and fertilize when needed.
• Wise cultivation is needed to conserve winter or summer tilth produced by natural weathering, i.e. cracking due to wetting/drying cycle and breakdown by frost action.

SOIL STRUCTURE

Soils are made up of mineral and rock particles that give them their natural properties. The character of the mineral fraction cannot be changed but the way that these building blocks are organized within the soil can. Creating and maintaining soil structure is a key aspect of maintaining the fertility of the soil and supporting healthy plant growth. Even the most difficult soils can be modified to create a fertile growing medium for plants.

Above: *Even "difficult" soils can be transformed into a good growing medium by careful cultivation.*

WHAT IS MEANT BY SOIL STRUCTURE?

Soil structure is quite simply the way soils are organized. To use a simple analogy: if we see the soil particles (sand, silt or clay – the mineral fraction) as the building materials – like the bricks and mortar of a house, for instance – then the structure is the architecture. The building materials themselves cannot be altered, but the architecture can vary considerably from home to home. This is the key. It is possible to improve a soil's structure even if the mineral fraction remains unchanged. It is perfectly feasible to have a well-structured clay soil for instance. It all depends upon how well you manage it.

WHY IS SOIL STRUCTURE IMPORTANT FOR PLANT GROWTH?

In order to survive, plant roots need water, nutrients and air. Plant roots breathe in the soil, taking in oxygen and expelling carbon dioxide. A poorly structured soil may have too little airspace. This can have two negative effects. Fresh air (containing oxygen) may not be able to penetrate the soil very easily and the soil will tend to become waterlogged following rain. Waterlogging will also reduce the air available in the soil.

Below: *A rotavator is a useful and labour-reducing method of breaking up the soil to prepare it for planting.*

Structure is therefore very important in terms of maintaining the health of plant roots. Plant shoot development is directly linked to root health. A healthy root system ensures healthy shoots and will ultimately result in better growth and crop yields.

HOW DOES SOIL STRUCTURE DEVELOP IN NATURAL SYSTEMS?

Soil structure naturally develops in soils through the effect of weather cycles. Wetting causes soils to swell while drying causes shrinkage. This naturally causes soils to crack. The action of freezing and thawing is also important on clay soils in areas where frosts occur. They form particles known commonly as crumbs. The "crumb structure" of any soil develops over time and is important in terms of allowing the free passage of water through the soil and air that must be able to move in and out of the soil. In this way soils do not become habitually waterlogged and natural nutrient cycles – oxygen, carbon and nitrogen, for example – are not impeded. Plant roots and soil organisms, such as worms, naturally help to maintain soil structure, as does the natural addition of decaying plant material each autumn.

HOW TO ALTER SOIL STRUCTURE

Humans have learned over time that even an infertile area can be worked – and the structure of the soil improved – by cultivation. This is covered in more detail later but it is essential to understand now that cultivation is a way of rapidly accelerating the natural cycles that promote good structure. Digging and breaking down "clods" helps to introduce air and creates new pores in the soil. Adding organic matter helps to maintain these pore spaces, retains moisture (in dry soils) and encourages the action of soil-dwelling creatures such as worms. No-dig

Above: *If you need to work on wet soil, work from a plank of wood to ensure the soil is not compacted and its structure destroyed.*

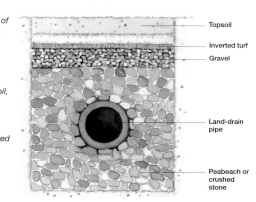

SECTION THROUGH A LAND DRAIN

This cross-section of a typical land drain shows the various layers of materials from which it is constructed, including the topsoil, an inverted turf or perforated plastic membrane, gravel, peabeach or crushed stone, and the land-drain pipe.

Topsoil

Inverted turf

Gravel

Land-drain pipe

Peabeach or crushed stone

systems aim to harness this natural cycle more closely, but the goal is the same – a rich, fertile and well-structured soil.

IMPROVING DRAINAGE

Soils that tend to become waterlogged often do so as a result of poor structure and because there is nowhere for the water to go. The vast majority of soils do not actually need (or benefit from) the installation of land drains. Often it is enough to dig over a site because much of the drainage problem may be due to surface compaction. Surface compaction severely reduces the passage of water into the soil and can result in a sticky surface that is prone to "puddling". Installing land drains is usually only done where the water table is very near to the surface or the consequences of flooding are severe (if they threaten housing or use of the area for instance). Land drainage using pipes or "tiles" is a complex undertaking and may be best left to a contractor.

If you have a sloping site you can dig a "soak away" drain at the base of the slope and improve the structure of the soil to encourage the rapid dispersal of water following rain. If you have a fairly flat site, then you should consider making a raised bed for growing crops. Raised beds are easy to manage and avoid the inconvenience of installing (and maintaining) a drainage system.

IMPROVING SOIL STRUCTURE

1 *One of the best ways to improve the structure of the soil is to add as much organic material as you can, preferably when the soil is dug. For heavy soils, this is best done in the autumn.*

2 *If the soil has already been dug, then well-rotted organic material can be worked into the surface of the soil with a fork. The worms will complete the task of working it into the soil.*

Above: *A well-prepared soil that is kept free of weeds and dug regularly will result in healthier, more vigorous crops throughout the growing season. A healthier crop will be more resistant to pest and disease attack.*

SOIL CHEMISTRY

While for many of us the word chemistry can be extremely off-putting, the truth of the matter is that everything in life is made up of chemicals. While the pure science of chemistry can be very complex, the chemistry of soil that organic gardeners must master is mercifully simple. A rudimentary knowledge of the chemicals that affect plant growth and how soil chemistry can be controlled and managed is all you need to grow healthy plants in an organic garden.

Above: *You can reduce the acidity of the soil by adding lime some weeks before planting. Test the soil first to see how much is needed.*

OXYGEN

The amount of oxygen in a healthy soil controls the type of life it will support. Nearly all organisms need oxygen to survive. Soils without oxygen are described as anaerobic. Most organisms can survive for short periods under anaerobic conditions, but this causes the accumulation of poisons that can become toxic at high concentrations.

A typical soil has about 50 per cent of its pore space filled by air and 50 per cent by water. Only certain bacteria can remain in anaerobic conditions for long periods of time, although some species of bacteria can readily switch from oxygen-rich to oxygen-poor conditions quickly to adapt to local conditions. Microbes use about 70 per cent of the oxygen in the soil and plant roots use the remaining 30 per cent. Under anaerobic conditions, the efficiency of microbes is poor and decomposition rates are much slower.

WATER

Soil water is vital for all soil life. Without it, microbes cannot grow or remain active and many will go into "hibernation" until water

returns. Fungi, on the other hand, are more resistant to water stress than bacteria. With too much water, oxygen levels drop and the lack of air tends to slow down the nutrient cycles driven by microbes. Water is also the medium by which essential nutrients are able to enter the plant.

SOIL pH

The pH scale is an abbreviated form of "Potential of Hydrogen". It is a measure of the degree of acidity or the alkalinity of a solution as measured on a scale (pH scale) of 0 to 14. The midpoint of 7.0 on the pH scale represents neutrality. A "neutral" solution is, therefore, neither acid nor alkaline. Numbers below 7.0 indicate acidity; numbers greater than 7.0 indicate alkalinity.

The level of acidity or alkalinity (pH) of a soil can significantly affect the nutrient availability. Many nutrients become "unavailable" to plants when the soil is either too acid or too alkaline. Microbial activity in soil is also largely controlled by pH. Fungi tend to predominate in acid soils, bacteria in neutral or alkaline soils.

Soil pH is essentially a measure of the acidity of the soil water, although the soil itself is the deciding factor in respect of what this will be.

Most plants prefer or are tolerant of a specific pH range. Some plants, such as the hydrangea, exhibit a different flower colour depending upon the prevailing pH. Most garden plants, especially vegetables, thrive within a range of 6–7 which happens to be where the majority of nutrients are available. It is best to maintain this pH in order to optimize the availability of nutrients. Many garden plants, however, are not too fussy about the pH levels, so if you choose plants carefully, it will not usually be necessary to alter the soil acidity.

ACIDIFYING SOIL

Lowering the pH of a naturally limy soil is difficult because the soil often contains a reserve of calcium that is released immediately upon acidification. Lowering the pH involves the use of flowers of sulphur and is only usually successful over a short period of time.

TAKING A pH TEST

1 *Place the soil in a test tube until it reaches the mark on the side. For the most accurate results, dry the sample first, grind it into a powder and ensure it is free from stones.*

2 *Put a layer of barium sulphate powder into the tube level with the mark. This compound helps the solution to clear rapidly and makes the pH reading clearer.*

3 *Pour in a little of the indicator solution up to the mark shown on the tube. Be careful not to put in too much because this can make the solution dark and difficult to read.*

MAKING A NUTRIENT TEST

1 *Place a small sample of the soil into the test tube up to the mark on the side.*

2 *Add a test solution (in this case one for nitrogen) up to the mark on the test tube.*

3 *Filter the solution to remove soil particles and leave just a liquid solution.*

4 *Decant the resulting filtered solution into another container for the final stage of the nutrient test.*

5 *Add a small amount of indicator powder. This will react with the solution and enable a colour reading to be taken.*

6 *Shake for about 10 seconds and compare with the chart. Here, the low reading indicates that a nitrogen-rich fertilizer will benefit this soil.*

LIMING SOIL

It is generally easier to raise the soil pH than to lower it. Lime neutralizes soil acidity and is commonly applied as ground limestone, chalk or dolomitic limestone (dolodust). Lime requirement cannot be determined from soil pH because it is influenced by soil texture and organic matter content. Clay and humus act as a "buffer" because of their complex chemistry. If soil is known to be acidic, regular light application is preferable to heavier, more infrequent, doses.

HIGHLY ALKALINE SOILS

Soils that are too alkaline suffer trace element deficiencies of manganese, copper, iron, zinc and boron. Phosphates are also less available, their maximum availability being between pH 6–7. Disease organisms can be more of a problem in calcium-rich soils, as many disease-causing fungal agents prefer alkaline conditions. Some plants, such as rhododendrons, are intolerant of high pH and only grow on acid soils, while others, like helianthemums, thrive in highly alkaline soils.

GROWTH RESTRICTIONS IN EXTREMES OF PH

Many vital nutrients that are essential for healthy plant growth become unavailable in extremes of soil pH.

Nitrogen deficiency Most nitrates are released from organic matter and a low soil pH limits the rate of decomposition severely.

Phosphate deficiency Phosphate becomes unavailable outside the 6.5–7.5 pH range. Some plants form relationships with soil-borne fungi that release phosphates in acid conditions.

Trace-element toxicity and deficiency Trace elements, especially aluminium, iron and manganese, are generally more soluble in acidic conditions. Extreme acidity can lead to excessive quantities of trace elements and to plant death. Other trace elements, such as copper, boron and molybdenum, become less available at low soil pH. Molybdenum deficiency affects legumes, which will not grow in acid soils.

4 *Add distilled water to the mark on the tube and shake the container vigorously for about a minute. Ensure the contents are mixed thoroughly and leave to settle.*

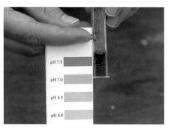

5 *Once sufficiently cleared, compare the colour against those on the chart, choosing the one that most closely matches that of the solution.*

DIGGING AND CULTIVATION

Every organic gardener's goal should be a healthy soil to support plant growth and development. Digging is one of the commonest ways to create a rich, fertile and ultimately productive soil. It can be hard work at the outset, particularly on sites not cultivated for some time, but the results – in the form of healthier, more productive plants – are worth it. Quite simply, what you get out of your soil will depend upon what you put into it.

Above: *After a winter exposed to the weather, most soils can be easily broken into a fine tilth with a rake.*

THE BENEFITS OF DIGGING

Winter is the commonest time to dig, but soil can be dug at any time of the year if the conditions are right. Avoid working the soil when it is too dry and impenetrable, or too wet and sticking to your tools and boots. Clay soils may be best dug in mid- to late autumn to allow the action of frost to make the soil more suitable for final cultivation. Lighter soils are best dug in the spring or immediately prior to planting the site. Done properly, digging increases the amount of air space in the soil, which in turn benefits soil-dwelling organisms and plant roots due to the increase in oxygen available. It also lets you add organic matter that will feed these vital denizens of the soil and aid nutrient cycling. Calculate how much organic matter you will need before you start. You should aim to add about 30 per cent of the volume cultivated. A 20m^2 (220ft^2) plot cultivated to one spade's depth will need 2.5 cubic metres (88 cubic feet) of manure or garden compost.

SINGLE DIGGING

This method involves digging down to the depth of one spade (this is called a spit). Single digging suffices on light free-draining soil as long as there is no layer of compacted stones in the topsoil. Much of the procedure is the same as for double digging, but the subsoil is left undisturbed. Mark out the position of the bed. Remove any turf or vegetation from the surface, put to one side and then bury it in the bottom of the bed as you proceed. Work across the bed, digging out a trench that is two spits wide and a single spit deep, and place the soil to one side. Remove stones and perennial weeds as you go. Fork well-rotted manure or compost into the trench. Begin digging a new trench behind the first. Throw the soil forward into the first trench, burying the organic matter. Repeat this process of trenching down the bed until the last trench has been dug. Add organic matter to the base and fill the trench with the soil dug from the first trench.

DOUBLE DIGGING

This is a method for deeply digging the soil, in which the soil is broken up to a depth of approximately 70cm (28in) or more. The method usually involves digging a quantity of soil and setting it aside while aerating and sometimes adding an amendment to the subsoil below, then returning the topsoil. There are several methods of double digging, all of which have their advocates. Two methods for double digging are described here.

First, define the area where the digging will take place, making an estimate of the area to be dug. Dig a trench, 30cm (12in) wide and a spit deep, across half the width of the bed. Place the excavated soil next to the other half, placing it on to a tarpaulin or similar covering if the surface needs protection.

When the trench is complete, fork the subsoil, rocking it back and forth, to loosen it down to a depth of about 30cm (12in). Then, spread a layer of garden compost over

---

SINGLE DIGGING

Single digging is the simplest method of cultivation. It is well suited to light soils or those soils that have been well worked for a number of years. It simply involves digging and inverting the soil to a single spade's depth, leaving the subsoil below undisturbed.

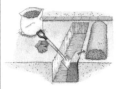

1 *Start by digging a single trench across the width of the plot. Put the soil from the first trench to one side because you will need to use it later in the final trench.*

2 *Put a layer of manure in the bottom of the trench. Dig out the next trench and cover over the manure in the first trench with the earth taken from the second trench.*

3 *Repeat this process of adding manure to each trench and filling in with earth from the next, breaking up the soil as you go and keeping the surface as even as possible.*

4 *Continue down the length of the plot until you reach the final trench. This should be filled in with the earth taken from the first trench, which was set to one side.*

DOUBLE DIGGING, METHOD ONE

Double digging is a good method for compacted, heavy or poor soils that are in need of rejuvenation. It involves a deep cultivation *of both the topsoil and subsoil and is well worth the hard work, producing a wonderful soil in which plants will thrive.*

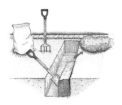 

1 *Dig a wide trench, placing the soil to one side to be used later when filling in the final trench.*

2 *Break up the soil at the bottom of the trench with a fork, adding manure to the soil as you proceed.*

3 *Dig the next trench in the bed, turning the soil over on top of the broken soil in the first trench.*

4 *Continue down the plot, ensuring that subsoil from the lower trench is not mixed with topsoil of the upper.*

DOUBLE DIGGING, METHOD TWO

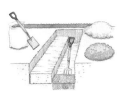  

1 *Keeping soil from each level separate, dig the first trench two spits deep and fork over. Dig the second trench one spit deep.*

2 *Add organic material to the first double trench and dig the lower spit of the second trench into it.*

3 *Dig an upper third trench one spit deep, and place the soil on top of that already placed in the first trench.*

4 *Continue, ensuring that the topsoil and subsoil do not mix. Fill in remaining trenches with soil taken from the first one.*

the exposed subsoil. Move over one spit's width in the bed, and begin to dig out another trench, moving and inverting the excavated soil into the adjacent trench that was just dug. When you get to the end of the bed replace the soil which was set aside.

When the digging is finished, level the site prior to planting. More garden compost (approximately 8cm/3in) can be spread over the surface and forked in at this stage.

You do not have to dig the entire garden all at once. Instead, work on small areas, say, one metre (yard) square, whenever you wish. Once you double-dig a bed, it is important not to walk on it. After all, the whole point of double digging is to loosen the topsoil and the subsoil to a sufficient depth so that the roots of the plants can grow unrestricted and water can readily percolate through the soil. Walking on the soil will simply pack it down again.

There is a second method of double digging that is less commonly used, which enriches the soil to a greater depth.

SECONDARY CULTIVATION

This normally involves the nourishing of the soil after it has been cultivated by digging and usually entails the addition of some form of organic matter during, or immediately after, its completion. Secondary cultivation also describes light digging used to control weeds or incorporate green manures. The tool generally used for this is a fork. Light forking is often the best method to use in areas with permanent plantings of perennial plants or shrubs.

USING A ROTAVATOR

A rotavator is a useful labour-saving device for breaking down dug clods and creating a fine, free-running "tilth" that can easily be levelled for planting or seed-bed preparation.

NO-DIG GARDENING

As the name suggests, no-dig gardening is a method of growing plants without cultivating the ground they occupy. While this may seem unnatural to some confirmed tillers of the soil, it is actually the most natural method available. No-dig gardening mimics the natural cycle. After all, plants have grown on the earth's surface for over 400 million years without people digging the soil for them. This approach also has the advantage of being less labour-intensive.

Above: *In nature, organic matter accumulates on the soil surface, breaks down and is worked into the soil by worms.*

ESTABLISHING A NATURAL CYCLE

Essentially no-dig gardening relies upon natural soil processes combined with the action of soil organisms to produce a good soil structure and natural nutrient cycles. There are numerous ways that this can be done, but all rely upon inputs from the top down. A thick top-dressing of organic matter is placed on the surface to be absorbed by the soil itself. Less laborious than digging, the no-dig method does need planning and careful input in order to be successful, although a properly prepared no-dig bed will be every bit as effective as a conventionally cultivated one.

Left: *Many organic gardeners grow crops such as potatoes quite successfully without ever resorting to digging.*

WHAT ARE THE BENEFITS?

Assuming weeds can be controlled, most vegetable crops can be grown with reduced tillage. The key features of a no-dig vegetable-growing system are to keep the soil covered with organic mulch as much of the time as possible and to keep off the soil. The beds are left permanently in place, and there is no cultivation.

Plants grown without tillage use water more efficiently, the water-holding capacity of the soil increases, and water loss from run-off and evaporation are reduced. For crops grown without irrigation in drought-prone soils, this more efficient use of water can translate into higher yields.

In addition, the organic matter in soil and populations of beneficial insects are maintained, as are earthworm populations and microbial activity. Soil and nutrients are less likely to be lost from the ground, less time is required to prepare the soil for planting, and, since there is less bare soil, there will be fewer opportunities for weeds to get established. The mulch of organic matter also helps to keep weeds down.

WHAT ARE THE DISADVANTAGES?

Potential problems associated with the no-dig method are compaction, flooding and poor drainage. However, if the water-holding capacity of a soil improves, no-till systems may produce higher yields. Soil temperatures under organic mulch can be several degrees lower than bare soil or soil under a plastic mulch. Although the lower temperature can be an advantage, especially in the summer when soil temperatures under plastic can be excessive, it can delay crop development.

MAKING A NO-DIG BED

A bed system which includes permanent paths is essential if digging is to be eliminated from gardening tasks. Planning the area so that all parts of the bed can be reached from the paths means that you can grow your crops closer together (you do not need to leave extra space for access) and you will be able to harvest more from a smaller area.

Mark out the beds on the ground or build simple raised beds with wooden sides. Alternatively, those wishing to make a more permanent edge could consider a low brick wall. By raising the bed it is possible to create a deep bed of good-quality soil that will warm up more quickly than the surrounding soil. A raised bed also means you do not have to bend down so far to carry out routine tasks and the method is tailor-made for disabled gardeners. Raised edging is also useful for attaching supporting hoops, crop covers and cloches. Edges such as these are also ideal

for providing barriers for pests. Devices such as water traps or copper paper are easily attached to them to prevent slugs and snails from entering the bed.

Beds should be no more than 1.2m (4ft) wide and paths at least 30cm (12in) wide with every other path double this width to allow for easy wheelbarrow access. Individual beds should be no longer than 3.5m (12ft) otherwise you will waste a lot of time walking around them. The beds can be of any design, from a simple series of parallel rectangles to a more complex design of interlocking shapes. Whatever design you choose, try to follow the same recommended bed and path widths, remembering that narrow angles and very small beds are more difficult to construct and use space less efficiently.

Right: *Green manures are usually dug into the soil, but they can still be used in a no-dig system. The manure can be cut down and left as a mulch.*

PLANTING POTATOES IN A NO-DIG BED

1 *Place a thick layer of well-rotted manure or garden compost on the bed to be planted. This should be quite deep – at least 15–20cm (6–8in) – as it will quickly decompose during the growing season. Early planting is possible by manuring in winter and covering with plastic sheeting to warm the soil. The potatoes are planted directly into this and may be more closely spaced than those planted in soil, perhaps as close as 30cm (12in) apart.*

2 *Apply a generous mulch of straw once the bed is planted to give cover to the tubers and to suppress weed growth on the manure or compost. Spread a second layer of composted organic material over the straw. Add another layer of straw and composted material. Water the bed well. Once the potato plants begin to emerge, more straw can be laid down on to the bed, as the material put down earlier in the season will begin to compost down.*

3 *As the potato stems grow, mulch heavily in order to ensure that no light reaches the developing tubers. The potato crop will mature at the same rate as potatoes grown in ordinary soil. The no-dig system is possibly the best method for heavy clay soils that are prone to waterlogging. Potatoes grown in this way are also easy to harvest as there is no digging and the potatoes are cleaner once they are ready for harvesting.*

SOIL CONDITIONERS

There is quite a range of conditioners available to the organic gardener for improving the soil. Some are free (if you do not count the time taken in working and carting them), others are relatively cheap, while those bought by the bag can be quite expensive. The best option for the organic gardener begins with using the materials that are closest to hand. Smaller gardens or those that are newly established may require soil conditioners to be brought in. This section looks at some of the options.

Above: *A well-conditioned soil will pay dividends in terms of enhanced plant growth and development.*

FARMYARD MANURE

This is usually freely available, although these days it comes increasingly from stables rather than farms. It contains a small amount of nutrients although it usually makes the soil more acidic as it decomposes and should always be well rotted before use. It can also contain lots of weed seeds, which often come from the bedding used for the animals. Occasionally there can be problems if the straw used has been sprayed with pesticides, so always be sure of your source. Farmyard manure is usually cheap or occasionally free for the taking.

Left: *Spent mushroom compost is an ideal material for improving the structure of many types of soil.*

BURYING GREEN WASTE

If you have space, you can simply open a trench in the soil and bury your green waste 20–30cm (8–12in) deep under the soil. It will take perhaps two to three months during the warm season to break down. Avoid planting crops in the soil above until the material has decomposed properly.

Left: *Animal manures can provide both nutrients and valuable organic matter when added to your garden soil.*

LEAF MOULD

Many gardeners believe leaf mould to be the finest addition to any soil. The product itself forms naturally under the closed canopy of forest trees. It is, as the name suggests, the rotted product of fallen leaves. It is not particularly rich in nutrients but it has an extremely good ability to condition a soil and encourages natural nutrient cycles in your soil. It is usually made by the gardeners that wish to use it and is rarely sold on. Anyone who has a ready supply of leaves will find this an easy material to make.

Start by gathering up leaves in the autumn and stack in a chicken-wire cage to prevent them being blown back over the garden. Do not add any greens or other materials to the pile. The heap will rot down slowly and be ready for use in one to two years. It can be sited in a dark corner where nothing else will grow, but you must ensure that you keep the pile moist all year round. The wire cage can be removed after two months or so and used again the following

autumn. Alternatively, two permanent pits, sited side by side, can be filled (or emptied) in alternate years. Smaller quantities of leaves can be pushed into black plastic sacks with the top closed and with holes pierced by a garden fork around the sides and bottom of the bag to allow some airflow.

SPENT MUSHROOM COMPOST

This is one of the few types of organic matter to have a slightly alkaline effect on the soil. It is a uniform and friable mixture of stable organic materials that is a waste product of the mushroom-growing industry. It is usually quite inexpensive. The composting and growing processes that produce this material bind nutrients to the organic matter, resulting in a substance that holds on to nutrients more readily than fresh or non-composted organic wastes. In addition, the compost has good moisture-holding abilities.

Spent mushroom compost is slightly alkaline with a pH ranging from 7–8 but generally around 7.3. There are few weed seeds, insects or pathogens because the compost is pasteurized before it is removed from the mushroom house. The addition of spent compost to garden soil can result in a

BUILDING A LEAF MOULD PIT

1 *Drive in four 1.5m (5ft) posts to form the four corners of a square on the ground. The posts should be spaced about 1m (3ft) apart and there should be just over 1m left above ground once the posts are driven in.*

2 *Attach chicken wire – a 1m (3ft) wide roll is needed for this – to the stakes using "U"-shaped fencing staples, hammered in firmly. Pull the wire tight across the length of the roll before attaching it to the next post.*

3 *Once the wire has been securely stapled to the posts all the way around, cut it with wire cutters, folding the sharp ends under the attached mesh so that they cannot cut you.*

4 *Place fallen leaves into the "pit" until it is full. Firm the leaves lightly in layers as you go, so that the pit is completely packed with leaves but still contains a little air.*

5 *After a year or two, the leaf mould is ready and should be applied to the soil in late winter or early spring in order to gain the most benefit.*

6 *It is a good idea to build two or more pits and rotate their use as a single pit will not be emptied in time to receive the new lot of leaves in the following autumn.*

Left: *Beans and other leguminous plants are an important part of a successful organic vegetable garden, "fixing" their own nitrogen and so helping to raise levels of soil fertility.*

or sickly cocoa, is often enough to put people off. They are sometimes marketed commercially although they may be available as a local by-product of industry. Whatever product you use, it should be well rotted before it is used as a soil conditioner.

WORM COMPOST

Worms can be used to compost your kitchen waste both indoors and outdoors, although both methods have their limitations and advantages.

The materials that are being composted are consumed by the worms and then excreted as worm casts. This process binds the nutrients consumed into a form that can be used by plants and reduces the volume of the original materials. These worm casts are covered with slow-dissolving, semi-permeable mucus that acts as a time-release mechanism for the nutritional content of the worm casts and also gives the finished compost good water-retentive qualities.

higher pH, increased nutrient-holding capacity and better soil structure. The main disadvantage occurs when the compost is first mixed with soil, as bacteria convert the proteins in the compost to ammonia, which can be toxic to young plants. Always ensure the source of your compost is an organic mushroom grower where possible.

VEGETABLE INDUSTRIAL WASTE

Some by-products of the food industry, such as spent hop waste and cocoa shells, can be beneficial as soil conditioners in the organic garden. They are useful in terms of their ability to improve soil structure. However, their smell, which may be described as rancid ale or beer with hops,

Above: *Brandling or tiger worms readily reduce vegetable matter into a useful compost material within a wormery.*

A WORMERY

Worms are an effective way to break down kitchen waste such as vegetable scraps. They will eventually eat their bedding as well as the kitchen waste. The resulting worm casts are a nutrient-rich soil conditioner.

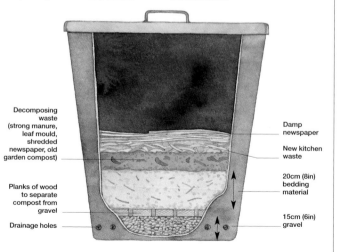

Decomposing waste (strong manure, leaf mould, shredded newspaper, old garden compost)

Planks of wood to separate compost from gravel

Drainage holes

Damp newspaper

New kitchen waste

20cm (8in) bedding material

15cm (6in) gravel

Worm colonies can be built in a similar way to a cold pile compost heap, with materials added as they become available. Excessive heat and frequent pile turning are not needed. Too much heat will actually kill the worms. Alternatively, a purpose-built wormery can be used. Both methods require materials to be placed in a shaded, cool and moist location. The worm colony must not become heated by the microbial action that takes place in normal composting. If the colony does get hot, it may cause the loss of the worms if they do not have cooler areas to which they can escape.

For an indoor worm colony, the wormery (a sealed, ventilated box with a close-fitting lid) is filled with bedding materials (usually damp shredded newspaper or similar) and the worms are added. Vegetable waste from the kitchen is placed on top or a few inches under the bedding where the worms can find and devour it. Eventually, the worms eat their bedding as well as the vegetable scraps. The finished worm castings can be removed and used. New bedding and kitchen scraps are then placed

in the container and the worms returned to make a new batch of compost. Many purchased wormeries have the facility to collect the liquid by-product of the worms' activities, which makes an excellent liquid plant food.

It is advisable to check the pH level of the wormery every now and then. Thin, white, thread-like cotton worms are usually

Above: *Leafy crops benefit from the addition of organic matter because it encourages nitrogen-fixing bacteria to do their all-important work in the soil.*

an indication that the pH is too low. Adding some calcified seaweed can help to counter this acidity, as can a regular addition of eggshells.

Above: *Place a thick layer – about 8–10cm (4–5in) – of well-rotted organic matter into the base of a trench dug to a spit's depth (the depth of a spade blade). Use a fork to break up the material and to ensure that there is plenty of air space in the soil to aid the breakdown of the material and help soil organisms to cycle the nutrients.*

THE BENEFITS OF ADDING ORGANIC MATTER

Using organic matter as a mulch or soil conditioner will help to warm up the soil earlier in the spring. This in turn will allow for the earlier planting of some types of plant.

- Organic matter inoculates the soil with vast numbers of beneficial microbes and provides the food source that soil-dwelling microbes need to live. These microbes are able to extract nutrients from the mineral part of the soil and eventually pass the nutrients on to plants.
- Adding organic matter to your soil improves the way in which water interacts with the soil and improves the overall soil structure. All soils can benefit from the regular addition of organic matter.

To sandy soils
- Organic matter acts as a sponge to help retain water that would otherwise drain down below the reach of plant roots. This has the benefit of protecting plants against drought.

To clay soils
- Organic matter helps to increase the air space within the soil, making it drain more quickly. This ensures that the soil does not become waterlogged or dry out into a brick-like substance.

MAKING GARDEN COMPOST

Every organic garden should have at least one compost heap, where garden and kitchen waste can be broken down by microbes and other soil-dwelling creatures to produce a good medium-fertility soil improver. Making compost is not difficult and is an excellent way to recycle waste. Many gardeners take great pride in their home-produced compost and all gardens can benefit from this sustainable approach to soil improvement.

Above: Even a stack of old tyres can be recycled and used to make an effective compost heap.

THE SITE

A position in full sun will give the compost heap additional heat, allowing the contents to decompose more rapidly. If time is not a key factor, partial shade or even full shade will do. Compost is easily made in a freestanding pile in a sunny or partially

shaded area in the garden. Alternatively, a simple structure can be used to contain the pile. A variety of materials can be used to make these structures, including wood, bricks, pallets, a wire cage or even a stack of used tyres. Whichever method you use, you must provide good drainage. An average heap should be around a cubic metre (10 cu. ft). It can be much larger, but any smaller and it will not be as effective.

When adding waste materials to the heap, the items should be as small as you can make them. The more surface area that is exposed, the quicker it will decompose. A chipper or shredder is a big help. Many gardeners are keen advocates of adding a small amount of good topsoil in order to introduce microorganisms that will kick-start the process of decomposition. Compost heaps in containers can be built

Left: Composting your garden and kitchen waste ensures that you return essential nutrients to the soil.

up with successive layers of "green" and "brown" materials, separating these with thin layers of topsoil.

Sifting the pile is the final stage of the process, with any large pieces of residue being returned back to the new heap.

COMPOST INGREDIENTS

The potential ingredients for your compost heap will be either "brown" or "green". Browns are dry and dead plant materials, such as straw, hay, dry brown weeds, autumn leaves, nutshells, shredded paper, pine needles, tough plant stems and wood chips or sawdust. Because they tend to be dry, browns often need to be moistened before they are put into a compost system.

Greens are fresh (and often green) plant materials, such as green weeds from the garden, fruit and vegetable scraps, green leaves, grass clippings, tea bags, coffee grounds, seaweed, eggshells, fish scraps, green manures and fresh horse manure. Compared with browns, greens contain

MAKING A HOT PILE COMPOST HEAP

1 *Starting with an empty compost bin, place a layer of "browns" – straw, old leaves and chipped wood are ideal – in the base of the bin. If the bin is positioned over bare soil, include some fine twiggy material to help to circulate air to the base of the pile.*

2 *Add a layer of brown compost materials, such as autumn leaves, plant stems and wood chips, which should be approximately 15cm (6in) deep, and ensure that it is of an even thickness. The material should be lightly firmed in.*

3 *Add a new layer of "greens" to the compost bin. Most plant material can be used for this, although you should avoid too much fibrous or woody material such as plant stems. Never include weed seeds if possible.*

Above: *It is often advisable to have two or more compost heaps at any one time in order to ensure a steady supply.*

more nitrogen. Nitrogen is a critical element in amino acids and proteins, and can be thought of as a protein source for the billions of multiplying microbes.

A good mix of browns and greens is the best nutritional balance for microbes. This mix also improves the aeration and level of water in the pile.

THE "COLD PILE" METHOD

Make a pile of "browns", such as autumn leaves, moisten them well and then slowly incorporate "greens" such as kitchen waste or lawn clippings over the next year (this method can take a full year to finish the compost). If it gets very cold in winter, cover

the heap with cardboard or old carpet and peel this back to stir in any greens. In this type of composting, there are never enough high-nitrogen greens to get the pile really hot. Turn the pile a minimum of once a month if you have not recently added any greens, thereby breaking up the decaying mass and making it friable. If you do use this method, be sure you always have at least as much browns as added greens, as too many greens will just create a slimy, smelly mess. Some compost heaps (those with lots of greens added) may reach very high temperatures, some even reaching 70°C (158°F), thereby killing weed seeds. Cold piles, on the other hand, do not and it is best not to add any weed wastes that will contain seeds. If you do, you could risk spreading weed seeds across your garden in their own growing mix when you come to use the compost.

THE "HOT PILE" METHOD

Wet the ground under the pile and add twigs or other un-shredded browns to provide some aeration at the base. Layer the rest of your materials, alternating green and brown layers of about 15cm (6in) thickness, and add water as you go. Topsoil can also be added as a 2cm (¾in) layer between each cycle of green and brown materials. Finish the pile with a layer of browns. Cover the pile with a lid or piece of carpet to keep out rain and conserve heat. Check to see that your pile becomes hot within a few days. Turn the pile to decrease composting time. This action allows all the material to be exposed to the

COMPOSTING MATERIALS

Many items can be composted into valuable soil conditioners. Whether because of toxins, plant or human diseases or weed problems, some things should never be used.

Good compost materials
Animal manure
Fallen leaves
Grass/lawn clippings
Hay and straw from organic farms
Kitchen waste
Prunings from the garden
Sawdust
Shredded browns
Soot and charcoal
Spent hops or cocoa shells
Spent mushroom compost
Weeds and other garden wastes

What not to compost
Chemically treated wood products
Diseased plants
Human and pet waste
Meat, bones and fatty food wastes
Pernicious weeds

hot centre, thereby increasing aeration. Do this once a week in the warmer season, and once a month in cooler periods. The pile's heat should peak every time you turn it, although the peak temperature will be lower with each turn. Always make sure that the pile remains moist, but avoid over-wetting.

4 *Continue adding greens until you have a layer about 15cm (6in) thick, the same depth as the browns below. Lawn clippings should be placed in layers of about 10cm (4in) or mixed with other green waste to avoid the layer becoming slimy and airless.*

5 *Kitchen refuse, such as vegetable waste, can also be added and is usually classed as a "green". You can include a thin layer of soil to add microorganisms before the next layer of "browns". Continue layering until the bin is full, then water and cover.*

6 *After two to three months, you should have well-rotted garden compost, which, due to the heat of the pile, will be largely free from weed seeds, pests and diseases. Once the bin has been emptied, it can be refilled in the same way.*

GREEN MANURES

Sometimes referred to as "cover crops", green manures are plants that are grown to benefit the soil rather than for consumption or display. Green manures replace and hold nutrients, improve the structure of the soil and increase its organic material content. They also smother the soil and so prevent weed growth. Green manures also "fix" atmospheric nitrogen. They are easy to grow and can be used to improve the soil when manures are not readily available.

Above: *Growing a green manure is an easy and effective way in which to add some organic matter to the soil.*

BENEFITS OF GREEN MANURES

At any time of year, but especially in winter, the soil loses nutrients if it is bare for six weeks or more. Green manures help to counteract this and maintain a more even soil temperature and moisture content. Many green manures grow deep roots to tap resources unavailable to some crops. Others produce a fibrous root system to help build structure in the soil, while many have flowers that attract pollinating insects.

TYPES OF GREEN MANURE

Some green manures are nitrogen-fixers, using bacteria that colonize the nodules on their roots. These microbes take nitrogen out of the air and convert it into a form that plants can use. Green manures are usually divided into two groups: legumes and non-legumes. Leguminous manures include clover, peas, fava beans and alfalfa. Despite their nitrogen-fixing abilities, legumes have slow autumn growth and add less organic content. They can also be less winter hardy.

Winter rye is the most commonly grown non-leguminous cover crop, but oats, wheat, oilseed rape and buckwheat are also used. Although they do not add nitrogen to the soil, they help maintain levels and have the additional advantage over legumes of growing faster through the autumn, thereby giving better weed suppression. They also tend to break down more slowly than legumes and add more organic matter to the soil. You may wish to use a combination of green manures in order to balance the benefits of the different types.

DEEP-ROOTED GREEN MANURES

The roots of certain green manure "crops" work through the soil, holding it together as they grow. Once dug in, however, they help to make it crumbly and friable as they rot. Some green manures have very deep roots that reach down into the subsoil and can harvest nutrients that are unavailable to other garden plants. In this respect they are a form of biological double digging.

PLANTING GREEN MANURES

Winter green manures should be planted early enough to give about four weeks of growth before cold weather stops their growth. Spring or summer crops must be given sufficient time to develop before they are dug in. After preparing the soil, plant large-seeded cover crops in shallow, closely spaced furrows. Smaller seeds can be broadcast over the surface and covered with a light raking, watering if needed until they germinate. Dig the crop in once it is ready, allowing at least three weeks before you intend to plant to give time for the material to rot down. It is best not to allow green manures to go to seed as they all have the potential to become weeds.

Gardens are traditionally dug over and manured in autumn, then left bare over winter. Many nutrients can be lost during this time due to the leaching action of rain. A hardy green manure sown in the autumn can be dug in the following spring, yielding nutrients to a newly sown or planted crop.

USING GREEN MANURES

1 *Sow the seed evenly across the area where you plan to grow the green manure. Either broadcast the seed or sow larger seed thinly in shallow drills and close rows.*

2 *Lightly rake in the seed so that it is covered and will germinate quickly. Water the area thoroughly if there is no rain due or if it does not rain for the following 48 hours.*

3 *Once the seed germinates, allow it to grow a little before digging it into the soil. Never let green manure crops set seed or they will become a weed in later crops on the site.*

TYPES OF GREEN MANURE

Green manure for growing over winter

These species can withstand moderate to hard frost for a long period and can be cut down in the spring, prior to cultivation. The shorter types can also be used as catch (cover) crops around winter vegetables or biennial crops for harvest in the early spring. This protects bare soil, prevents nutrient leaching and creates a more stable soil environment.

GREEN MANURE	SOWING TIME AND METHOD	HEIGHT	WINTER HARDY?	NITROGEN-FIXING ABILITY	TERMS OF GROWTH	DIGGING IN	OTHER NOTES
Alfalfa *Medicago sativa*	Early spring to mid-summer; broadcast at 3g ($\frac{1}{10}$oz) per square metre (yard).	100–150cm (3–5ft)	Yes	Yes but poor	Perennial. Grow for several months or more than one season.	Any time. Medium effort if young. Hard if left for more than one season.	Very deep rooting. Will grow on most soils. Dislikes acid or waterlogged soils, but drought resistant.
Asilke clover *Trifolium hybridum*	Mid-spring to late summer; broadcast at 3g ($\frac{1}{10}$oz) per square metre (yard).	30cm (12in)	Yes	Yes	Several months	Any time. Medium effort.	Will withstand wetter soils than other clovers but more prone to drought. Shallow rooted.
Essex or red merviot clover *Trifolium pratense*	Mid-spring to late summer; broadcast at 3g ($\frac{1}{10}$oz) per square metre (yard).	40cm (16in)	Yes	Yes	Several months	Any time. Easy, little effort.	Prefers good loamy soil. Can be mown or cut several times per season and used for compost.
Grazing rye *Secale cereale*	Late summer to late autumn; broadcast at 30g (1oz) per square metre (yard) or thinly in rows 20cm (8in) apart.	30–60cm (12–24in)	Yes	No	Autumn to spring	Before flowering. Hard work.	Grows in most soils. Keep watered during germination, else yield is poor. Sow thickly to smother weeds.
Phacelia *Phacelia tanacetifolium*	Early spring to early autumn; broadcast at 3g ($\frac{1}{10}$oz) per square metre (yard) or thinly in rows 20cm (8in) apart.	60–90cm (12–36in)	Yes	No	2 months in summer; 5–6 months over winter	Before flowering. Easy, little effort.	Grows in most soils. Quick to grow in summer. If left, will produce mauve flowers that bees love.
Trefoil *Medicago lupulina*	Early spring to late summer; broadcast at 3g ($\frac{1}{10}$oz) per square metre (yard).	30–60cm (12–24in)	Yes	Yes	Several months to a year	Any time. Medium effort.	Will grow in most soils but dislikes acid. Can be used for undersowing. Dense foliage.

Green manure for warm-season growing

Plants for use in the spring and summer have to be quick growing in order to cover the ground and yield benefit within a short period of time. They are generally slightly tender, although lower-growing species can actually be used as a catch crop around other seasonal crops.

GREEN MANURE	SOWING TIME AND METHOD	HEIGHT	WINTER HARDY?	NITROGEN-FIXING ABILITY	TERMS OF GROWTH	DIGGING IN	OTHER NOTES
Bitter lupin *Lupinus angustifolius*	Early spring to early summer 4cm (1$\frac{1}{2}$in) deep; 3cm (1$\frac{1}{4}$in) apart; in rows 15cm (6in) apart.	50cm (20in)	Mild winters	Yes	2–3 months	Before flowering. Easy, little effort.	Prefers light slightly acidic soil. Foliage not very dense. Deep rooted.
Buckwheat *Fagopyrum esculentum*	Early spring to late summer; broadcast at 10g ($\frac{1}{3}$oz) per square metre (yard) or thinly in shallow rows 20cm (8in) apart.	80cm (32in)	No	No	2–3 months	Before or during flowering. Easy, no effort.	Grows on poor soils. If allowed to flower, attracts hoverflies to aid pollination of crops.
Crimson clover *Trifolium incarnatum*	Early spring to late summer; broadcast at 3g ($\frac{1}{10}$oz) per square metre (yard).	30–60cm (12–24in)	Mild winters only	Yes	2–3 months or over winter	Before flowering. Medium effort.	Prefers sandy loam soil but will tolerate heavy clay. Large red flowers attract bees.
Fenugreek *Trigonella foenum-graecum*	Early spring to late summer; broadcast at 5g ($\frac{1}{6}$oz) per square metre (yard) or thinly in 15cm (6in) shallow rows.	30–60cm (12–24in)	Mild winters	No	2–3 months	Any time before flowering. Easy, little effort.	Prefers good drainage but will tolerate heavy or light soil.

BASIC TECHNIQUES

Most gardening techniques, from weeding and feeding to pruning and propagation, are straightforward and and easy to achieve if you plan and organize the task in hand. The procedures described here will help you to master the basics of organic gardening. You may well develop your own methods in time, based upon the techniques shown here as well as those that you learn from other gardeners. Always make sure that you are clear about what you want to do and approach a task positively. Gardening should bring enjoyment as well as a sense of satisfaction that comes from creating a thriving organic paradise in your own garden.

WEEDING AND WEED CONTROL

Many people are put off organic gardening because they do not like the idea of weeding. Not having the "quick fix" of weed-killing chemicals can make this task seem daunting. It is, however, worth considering that a well-maintained garden has less weeding to do than you might think. In addition, it can be a relaxing, even therapeutic, task and there is very little that is more satisfying in the garden than a freshly weeded plot.

Above: Hoeing is an effective way of keeping a garden plot free of weeds. Pull a draw or swan-neck hoe towards you in a series of chopping movements.

WHAT PROBLEMS DO WEEDS PRESENT?

Weeds compete with garden plants of all types for essential nutrients, light and water. Uncontrolled weed growth may kill plants that are less vigorous or seriously inhibit their development. Weeds also act as "host" plants for animal pests or diseases that may, in turn, affect the desired plants. Finally, weeds are controlled because they often look unsightly.

CAN WEEDS BE TOLERATED?

There is no easy answer to this question. It depends upon what exactly you want out of your garden. Aesthetic considerations aside, most gardens can survive quite healthily with some weeds. The majority only become a real nuisance when they start to take over or if they set seed. The simple rule is the fewer weeds in the garden the better.

Left: *Weed-free plots can be attractive to crop pests. Here, plant collars have been used to prevent root flies attacking the crop.*

GOOD CULTIVATION

The secret of organic weed control is good cultivation. This begins with thorough ground preparation to reduce the build-up of weeds and weed seeds before planting. Fallowing is commonly used to do this. After the ground has been prepared, it is left bare for a period of a few weeks to a few months. The weed seeds are allowed to germinate and are then removed as they appear. This method will never remove all the seeds because they can survive for several years in a dormant state. But the majority of them will have germinated and the task of weed control made easier for the future.

Vigilance is important throughout the growing season, but never more so than in spring and early summer. Tackle weed seedlings as they appear. Some methods of control, such as hoeing, may damage garden plants, so use a hand fork for close work or in areas where hoeing is difficult. A hoe, for example, can sever the roots of surface-rooting shrubs such as rhododendrons. These weeding methods are relatively slow and labour-intensive. The trick is to do it little and often.

Flails, brush cutters, mowers, rollers, burning and other mechanical means are occasionally used. Although strimmers can be used in shrub borders, those that cut using nylon cords can damage woody stems.

MINIMAL CULTIVATION

Many weeds are plants of cultivation, thriving in disturbed ground. Minimal cultivation reduces disturbance and relies on creating a ground-covering layer of vegetation. The plants literally out-compete the weeds, which can be removed as they appear.

COMMON WEEDS

Weeds can be divided into three groups. Annual weeds germinate, grow, flower and set seed in one growing season. Certain annuals, which are known as ephemerals, complete their lifecycle well within this period and can produce several successive generations within the space of one season. The third type of weeds are perennial species. Perennial weeds initially establish from seed, but tend to persist for several seasons, sometimes dying down during adverse seasons only to re-emerge as conditions improve. They are much more difficult to eradicate once established than annual weeds and many are a serious problem in gardens.

Ephemeral and annual weeds
- Annual meadow grass
- Bittercress
- Chickweed

Perennial weeds
- Blackberry (in Australia)
- Dock
- Ground elder
- Couch grass
- Groundsel
- Creeping buttercup
- Nettle

Meadow grass   Chickweed

Creeping buttercup   Dandelion

DIFFERENT TYPES OF MULCH

Mulches provide a physical barrier to weed seeds that would otherwise land on the soil surface. The materials that can be used for mulching are varied in their composition and the effects they have. They are generally classified into synthetic and natural types.

Bark chippings

Newspaper

Dried bracken

Gravel

Old carpet

Sawdust

Woven plastic

Cocoa shells

MULCH

This is a layer of material that is laid over the surface of a soil or other growing medium. While often cited as a means of weed control, applying mulch has other functions that are beneficial to growth. Mulches help to keep the plants' roots warm in winter and cool in summer, greatly assisting new growth in the spring. They also reduce water loss from the soil in two main ways: by shading the soil surface and by slowing down evaporation of water from the soil.

In general, most mulches reduce the number of weeds growing in a planted area. They act by inhibiting the germinating weed seedling from reaching the sunlight or by "drawing up" the weed so that it is spindly and can be easily removed or "pulled". Mulches should be laid on a bare surface, as they will not inhibit established weeds, especially vigorous perennial ones.

If a mulch is laid to an even depth of around 5cm (2in), it will develop a dry dusty surface that will deter the germination of weed seeds that land on it. This is only a temporary measure, but can help reduce weeding at the busiest times of the year.

TIMING AND APPLICATION

Mulches should be laid on warm, moist soil. Autumn is the ideal time, but they can be applied in the spring after the soil has warmed up. Applied too thickly (over 10cm/4in), they may affect water infiltration into the soil. Materials containing an excessive amount of fine humus or soil-like material ("fines") may encourage weed seedlings to establish. In poor-draining soil, mulch may keep the soil waterlogged and this will be detrimental to plant growth. Synthetic materials, especially if they are impermeable such as black plastic, will inhibit oxygen and water infiltration into the soil. Some materials, such as grass clippings, can "pack down" on the surface and form a water-shedding layer.

As mulches encourage surface-rooting, application must be continued once started, otherwise the plants will suffer later. Many ornamental plants, such as rhododendrons, are naturally very shallow-rooting and thus need the protection of mulch for good growth. They benefit from an organic mulch that conserves soil moisture. Some mulches, such as manure and compost, also aid plant development by supplying nutrients.

MULCHING TO CONTROL WEEDS

1 Grass clippings are a cheap, effective mulch. Apply them at a maximum depth of 5cm (2in) or the heat they create as they decompose may harm the stems. Do not use mowings from grass that has gone to seed.

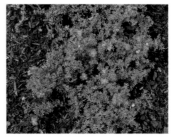

2 Chipped bark should be composted or stored for several months to let it release any resin and start to decompose. Some gardeners worry that it introduces fungal diseases, but the spores are already in the air.

WATERING

In order to cultivate a successful organic garden, it is crucial to recognize the water requirements of different plants. It is of vital importance that you know when and how to provide the right amount of water as well as how to avoid either drought or waterlogging. Conserving the water in the soil as well as storing and recycling this valuable commodity are of key importance in the organic garden, especially in areas where rainfall is seasonal and droughts are common.

Above: *Water that runs off the roof can be collected in a custom-made rainwater butt, and stored for later use.*

PRINCIPLES OF WATER MANAGEMENT

After rainfall or irrigation, all the soil pore spaces are filled with water. The air is displaced and the soil saturated. If the rain or irrigation were to continue, then surface pooling or runoff would occur. The rate at which a soil can absorb water is influenced by its texture and structure.

Water drains from the soil through the pore system and is replaced to some extent by air. After draining has removed the excess water, the remaining water may be lost either through evaporation or taken up by the plant and lost through its leaves.

All sands and loamy sands tend to have a low available water capacity. Loams and clay have a medium capacity while very fine sandy loam, silt loams, peats and any soil with a high water table have high available water capacity. Clay soils often have a large amount of water within them, but it is held so tightly that plants are not able to obtain it.

WATER AND THE PLANT

All plants are largely made of water and it is critical that water levels are maintained if the plant is to grow and develop. Soft fleshy subjects, such as many bedding plants and some vegetables, use large quantities of water, particularly during establishment. Plants with large leaves or with extensive branch systems, such as large trees, will remove gallons of water from the soil in the course of a hot sunny day.

WATERWISE GARDENING

Since water supplies are limited, we need to do all we can to conserve soil moisture. As the top layer of soil dries out, the dry soil acts as an insulation to further rapid moisture loss. Take advantage of this by avoiding over-cultivation, particularly during the summer, as this may bring moist soil to the surface to dry out. Always try to maintain a well-structured soil and avoid capping (a hard, partially compacted surface layer) as this can prevent the absorption of rainfall by the soil, leaving puddles that quickly evaporate. Mulches help to conserve moisture either by holding water or acting as insulation provided that they are deep enough. Keep the soil surface weed-free and provide shelter from drying winds. Maintain drainage, as poor drainage leads to limited root growth of the plant and poor soil structure.

STORING AND RECYCLING WATER

Water is a precious resource that is sometimes in short supply. Plants in open ground may acclimatize to the soil conditions, but those growing in pots are more susceptible to drought. Mains water can provide an answer but there is a cost involved and supplies can be restricted. Saving water from rainfall or recycling waste water (which is sometimes called "grey water") can overcome the worst ravages of summer drought.

METHODS OF WATERING

1 *When watering by hand, be patient and give the ground around the plant a good soaking. If in doubt, dig a small hole in the soil and check that the water has soaked through to the roots.*

2 *Turning on a sprinkler allows you to leave it and get on with something else. Place a jar under the spray to gauge how much has fallen. There should be at least 2.5cm (1in) of water for the sprinkler to have done any good.*

3 *A spray attached to a garden hose delivers at a greater rate than a sprinkler but it must be held in place until the ground is soaked. It is easy to under-water using this method. Spray the leaves to wash away dirt or dust.*

4 *A seep hose with holes in it is snaked around plants that need to be watered and left in position. When connected, it provides a gradual but steady flow of water that penetrates deeply into the soil.*

AUTOMATIC WATERING SYSTEMS

1 *You can bury a pipeline beneath the surface and plug in various watering devices. A sprinkler can be pushed on to this fitting, which lies flush with the turf.*

2 *Control systems can be fitted to the hose system so that you can alter the pressure of the water. These can also act as a filter.*

3 *Drip-feed systems can be used for beds, borders and containers. "T"-joints allow tubes to be attached for individual drip heads.*

4 *The delivery tube of the garden hose can be held firmly in position with a pipe peg that is inserted into the ground, if this is necessary.*

Storing and recycling household water is a relatively complicated undertaking that is usually best left to specialist contractors. The potential health risks mean that it is not usually wise to store this type of water for any length of time, but it can be used fresh to water non-food plants. Try keeping your bath water and using it to water ornamental plants. It can be used to fill watering cans and is ideal for watering outdoor pot specimens or plants in open ground.

Rainwater may be a viable alternative and some contractors will be able to install large underground tanks to contain seasonal rainfall. The quicker and easier alternative is to install water butts to collect water from downspouts from roof drains. This method will rarely provide enough water for your whole garden, but is often plenty to water (or supplement the watering of) plants in containers, particularly edible plants such as herbs. Rainwater is naturally acidic and is, therefore, not likely to contain many harmful bacteria. Its acidity also makes it the ideal choice for misting plants under glass on hot days (as it will not mark the leaves with lime) and suits many species sensitive to domestic water additives. Rainwater is also a must for people wishing to grow "acid-loving" specimens in pots.

WATERING PLANTS

In areas where seasonal water shortage is a regular problem, choose drought-tolerant species where possible. Seasonal crops (such as vegetables) and displays (summer or spring bedding) tend to suffer the most from drought due to the limited time that they have to develop extensive root systems. If you wish to grow these seasonal plants in drier areas, they will need to be watered

regularly to survive prolonged dry periods. Perennials, on the other hand, may actually become more drought-tolerant if they are watered less. This is because they will have to root deeper to find water. Perennials will need to be watered in their first season following planting to ensure their long-term survival. Remember that applying a good drench on a more occasional basis allows the water to penetrate more deeply and have a better long-term effect because it encourages deeper rooting. Watering little and often can prove detrimental in drier climates by encouraging surface roots that may become very drought-prone. After the first growing season following planting, they are better able to cope if not watered at all.

WATERING METHODS

Plants can be watered in many ways, but all generally fall into two categories: hand watering or automatic systems.

Hand watering The commonest "tool" here is the watering can. Numerous designs exist but they all rely upon a gradual delivery through a spout. A rose ensures that a fine spray is delivered that will not wash away soil or damage plants. Hoses can also be used for hand-watering and many nozzles have been designed to deliver a shower of water rather than a jet.

Automated systems There is an array of devices to choose from, some of which can deliver doses of water at set times of the day or week. Even the most complex of these use relatively simple water-delivery methods such as seep or drip hoses and sprinklers. Seep and drip hoses are essentially "leaky pipes" that gradually release water into the soil. Sprinklers shower an area of garden repeatedly until

the ground is well soaked. There are many designs for both and the amount of time they need to be left on depends upon the manufacturer's recommendations and the available water pressure. Both hoses and sprinklers offer the benefit of gradual delivery over a large area and both can be operated manually from a mains water supply. A good watering every few days can be extremely beneficial to most plants, especially if recently planted.

WATERING PROBLEMS

These are usually the result of either too much or too little water being applied to the plant. Both over- and under-watering have similar symptoms because both are related to root death. An over-watered plant's root system begins to die off due to a lack of oxygen. The plant becomes short of water and wilts. Other problems can result from the wetting of foliage and flowers. Watering in full sunlight can give plants a scorched appearance, so it is best not to water in hot sunny conditions.

RECYCLING WATER

The suitability of the water left over from washing, bathing and other household activities depends on how much waste matter it contains. Ordinary bath water, for instance, is useful for watering a variety of plants, but the main problem lies in its storage. Waste water always carries the risk of bacterial infestation. Specialist storage methods and filtration can be used, but it is easier to use it immediately (once cooled), and to avoid using it on houseplants or edible crops.

FEEDING

In order for plants to grow and sustain their life processes, they require water and air as well as a range of naturally occurring elements. At least sixteen different elements are needed by all plants for successful growth and development. Three of these elements – carbon, hydrogen and oxygen – are obtained from the carbon dioxide in the air and from the water and oxygen in the soil. In addition to these, plants also need a selection of other important nutrients, which are described here.

Above: *Top-dressing with organic matter provides the soil with nutrients and encourages nutrient cycles.*

IMPORTANT PLANT NUTRIENTS

In addition to carbon, hydrogen and oxygen, plants need other important nutrients, which they obtain directly from the soil or compost. These nutrients are commonly divided into two groups, depending upon whether they are found in plants in high or low concentrations. When they are found in high concentrations and are needed in large amounts, they are known as macro or major nutrients. There are three of these: nitrogen (N), phosphorus (P) and potassium (K). Every organic gardener must be fully aware of the functions of the "essential three". Nitrogen is essentially the shoot and leaf maker and is especially important early in the growing season; phosphorus is important in the formation of roots; and potassium plays a vital role in flower and fruit formation and is also important in promoting hardiness in overwintering plants. Elements that are needed in relatively small amounts are the micro or trace elements, of which there are ten. Among the most important of these are calcium, magnesium and sulphur, although all play a vital role in the growth and development of the plant.

SYMPTOMS OF DEFICIENCY

Plants exhibit varying symptoms to a nutrient deficiency. General ones are stunted growth, discoloured leaves, including mottling and inter-veinal coloration, and the premature death of leaves or other parts of the plant. Plants may also display twisted or distorted growth as well as poor root growth and development. In many cases, the symptoms are often seen first in the plant's extremities, such as the tips of the shoots, as these are furthest away from the nutrient source. If a plant cannot obtain enough of any nutrient from a soil it will be because there is either little or no nutrient present in the soil, or the nutrient is not "available" to the plant.

Any element can also be toxic to the plant if it is present in sufficiently high amounts or out of balance with other elements in the growing medium.

FEEDING PLANTS ORGANICALLY

Numerous organic nutrient supplements are available. All have their relative advantages, but they should be used only as part of a combined strategy that aims to harness natural nutrient cycles. This usually involves top-dressing the soil with well-rotted organic matter. This is the catalyst to nutrient cycling in the soil as it feeds the

---

ORGANIC FERTILIZERS

A wide variety of organic substances can boost nutrient levels. They should be used in addition to composts and manures.

Animal manure Bird manure is a good source of nitrogen. Use in pellet form, as the fresh substance will burn plant roots.

Bonemeal Promotes strong root growth due to its high phosphate content. Use it as a base dressing prior to planting perennials.

Bonemeal

Calcified seaweed This raises the pH of the soil and adds calcium, like limestone, but also contains magnesium.

Fish, blood and bone A general fertilizer that is normally applied in the spring to promote root and shoot growth.

Fish, blood and bone

Ground limestone This raises the pH and supplies calcium where there is a deficiency. It is applied as a powder when it is needed.

Gypsum This supplies calcium to soils where there is a deficiency, but does not alter the pH. It is added in a 4:1 ratio to "lighten" clay soils.

Hoof and horn This material gives a slow release of nitrogen where strong growth is needed and is applied in the spring or early summer.

Hoof and horn

Rock phosphate Used mostly to counter phosphate deficiency and as an alternative to bonemeal.

Seaweed meal Helps to build up humus levels in the soil and is used on a wide range of plants.

Wood ash An excellent source of potassium that can be added directly to the soil or to a compost heap.

Calcified seaweed

MAKING COMFREY TEA

1 *Cut a large bundle of comfrey leaves from the patch in your garden. Choose good, green, leafy growth. Remove the leaf and stem, but avoid using the crown.*

2 *Place in a plastic container with holes in the base. Weigh down the leaves. Line a second larger container with a plastic bag and place the first container inside. Tie the bag at the top.*

3 *The thick dark liquid from the decomposing comfrey leaves collects in the bag below. The lower bucket allows this to drip down and stores it until the process is complete.*

4 *Decant the finished liquid into a jam jar for later use. The liquid feed must be diluted before it is applied to plants at a ratio of about 10 parts water to 1 part concentrate.*

vast array of soil organisms that naturally make use of essential plant nutrients. The majority of garden composts do not contain especially large amounts of the major plant nutrients; it is their long-term ability to feed soil life that makes them so valuable.

Despite the best intentions, plants can become short of a certain type of nutrient. This is usually avoided by giving the plant a supplement of a "plant food" that is rich in that particular nutrient. This can be applied to the soil as a top-dressing, lightly worked in with a fork, or applied as a foliar feed. Foliar feeding involves spraying a fine mist of a low-strength solution of the feed. The exact concentrations vary according to the feed being used, but a rough guide would be to use a quarter strength of that which you would apply as a liquid feed to the soil. The nutrient will be taken up quickly and the residue is best washed off after a couple of days because any soil-applied fertilizer will have been taken up by then. Applying a weak solution of Epsom salts as a foliar or liquid feed is an example of applying such a tonic.

LIQUID FEEDS AND TEAS

Compost tea is easy to make. Comfrey is ideal for this, but stinging nettles are also very good. You could also use sheep or goat manure, or finely sifted compost from the heap. Simply fill an old pillowcase or burlap bag with your chosen material (comfrey, nettles, compost or manure) and sink it into a large bucket or barrel of water. Cover the container and let it steep for a few days. Remember, the longer you steep, the stronger the tea will be. You may use the final "brew" as a light liquid feed. It can also be used as a foliar feeding medium, provided that it is well diluted. Use the residue in the bag as mulch. An alternative method is shown above.

Worm colonies in containers also produce a liquid feed that is a tonic for your plants. It should be diluted to a ratio of about 10 parts water to 1 part liquid feed. It is generally high in potassium and phosphorus.

OTHER FEEDING METHODS

1 *An alternative method of feeding is to use a liquid feed. This is most useful for plants that are growing in containers. Add the organic fertilizer of your choice to one of the waterings, according to the manufacturer's instructions.*

2 *Organic granular fertilizer can be applied by hand, spreading it over the area covered by the roots below. Follow the manufacturer's instructions. You may wish to protect your hands when applying the fertilizer by wearing a pair of gloves.*

3 *Apply a layer of well-rotted organic material, such as farmyard manure or garden compost, to the surface of the soil around the plant. If the plant is not shallow-rooted, lightly fork the material into the top layer of the soil.*

PLANT NUTRIENTS

The following table highlights the characteristics of the soil nutrients. Symptoms of deficiency may be seen on different parts of the plant at different stages of growth, although it may not always be immediately obvious that a plant is suffering from a nutrient deficiency. Some of the more important symptoms that can be seen on plants are listed below.

PLANT NUTRIENT	NATURAL ORGANIC SOURCE	PLANTS MOST IN NEED	SOILS MOST IN NEED	SIGNS OF SHORTAGE	HOW TO AVOID SHORTAGE	TOXICITY CAUSE
Major plant nutrients						
Nitrogen (N) The "leaf maker"	Bird manure, blood and bone, grass clippings	Grass, vegetables grown for their leaves, and root-bound plants	Sandy soils in rainy areas	Stunted growth; small pale green leaves; weak stems	Apply a base dressing before sowing or planting. Top-dress in spring and summer with organic matter.	Excessive use of nitrogen-rich fertilizer
Phosphates (P_2O_5) The "root maker"	Comfrey, seagrass, horse manure, blood and bone	Young plants, root vegetables, and fruit and seed crops	Sandy soils	Stunted roots and stems; small leaves with a purplish tinge; low fruit yield	Apply a base dressing of bonemeal. Use fish, blood and bone when top-dressing plants.	Excessive use of fertilizer
Potash (K_2O) The "flower and fruit maker"	Comfrey, horse manure, seagrass	Fruit, flowers and potatoes	Sandy soils	Leaf edges turn yellow, then brown; low fruit yield; fruit and flowers poorly coloured	Apply a compound organic fertilizer or wood ash as a base dressing or top-dressing.	Excessive use of fertilizer; lack of magnesium
Minor plant nutrients						
Boron (B)	Beetroot leaves, horse manure, compost, seagrass, untreated sawdust	Root vegetables, top fruit (apples, pears etc.)	Sandy soils	Brown heart (roots); narrow leaves; corky patches on fruit	Top-dress with compost or apply borax in severe cases.	Irrigation water
Calcium (Ca)	Dandelion, lucerne hay, comfrey, horse manure, compost, blood and bone	Fruit, flowers, vegetables	Acid and potash-rich soils	Similar to nitrogen shortage – stunted growth and pale green leaves	Apply lime or use gypsum or calcified seaweed.	High pH causes toxicity for some acid-loving plants
Copper (Cu)	Nettles, yarrow, horse manure, dandelion, chickweed, compost, untreated sawdust	Fruit, vegetables	Sandy soils	Dieback; brown spots on leaves	Top-dress with compost.	Copper-based fungicides
Iron (Fe)	Stinging nettle, compost, dandelion, horse manure, spinach and seaweed	Rhododendrons, azaleas, camellias	Chalky soils	Yellowing of younger leaves	Trouble can occur on chalky, peaty, very light and acid soils. Iron shortage in chalky soils is due to lock-up by calcium and difficult to avoid.	Rare
Magnesium (Mg)	Grass clippings, seagrass	Roses, tomatoes	Sandy, peaty and potash-rich soils	Yellow or brown patches between veins of older leaves	Apply a mulch of compost or Epsom salts if deficiency is severe.	None
Manganese (Mn)	Chickweed, compost, untreated sawdust	Rhododendrons, azaleas, camellias	Chalky soils	Yellowing between the veins of older leaves	Shortage in chalky soils is due to lock-up by calcium (see iron). Acidification for some plants.	None
Molybdenum (Mo)	Cornstalks, compost, grass clippings	Brassicas	Acid soils	Narrow leaves	Apply lime and top-dress with compost.	None
Sodium (Na)	Seaweed	Root vegetables, fruit	Sandy soils	Very rare except in a few seaside-loving plants	Not usually warranted.	Land reclaimed from sea
Sulphur (S)	Cabbage leaves	All plants	Soils in rural areas	Stunted growth and pale green leaves	A light dusting of flowers of sulphur during the year.	Industrial sites and acid rain
Zinc (Zn)	Horse manure, corn stalks, garden compost, untreated sawdust	Fruit, vegetables	Sandy soils	Dieback	Top-dress with compost.	Leaching from containers

BASIC PRUNING

The task of pruning can seem a daunting prospect to some gardeners, but there is, in fact, no great mystery surrounding pruning and a few basic rules are all you need to get started in most cases. At its simplest level, pruning should be regarded as a way of introducing some order to your garden, giving your plants space to grow and look their best, while also controlling them within a set space. The following section provides some basic advice to enable you to prune with confidence.

Above: *Regular dead-heading keeps shrubs tidy and promotes further flowering. Cut flowering stems back to a bud or stem division.*

WHY IS PRUNING NECESSARY?

Pruning is usually carried out to control the growth of stronger subjects that may otherwise damage those of a weaker habit growing alongside; it also ensures plants do not outgrow their allocated space and cause an obstruction. Pruning is also used to train a plant to a specific shape or form; to maintain or improve flowering; and to improve the shape or "balance" of an individual shrub or tree. Finally, it is used to remove dead, damaged, diseased or pest-infected growth. This last type of pruning is referred to as hygienic pruning and helps maintain plant health and vigour.

Constant pruning, however, is not always necessary for the good cultivation of plants. Once a plant has become established and the initial framework has been formed, pruning is often reduced to a minimum. The major exceptions to this include plants that are pruned annually in order to improve flowering, fruiting or quality of foliage. Apples, peaches and other fruit trees and bushes are regularly pruned to increase the yield of fruit. Roses are a good example of an ornamental shrub that benefits from regular pruning, having more vigorous and prolific flowering as a result of cutting back on a yearly basis.

SUCCESSFUL PRUNING

There are arguably two hallmarks of good pruning: a well-planned, careful and methodical approach to the work undertaken and a good working knowledge of the requirements of the plants that are to be pruned. The real results may not always be apparent for months and, in the case of trees, for years.

With secateurs (hand pruners), always try to place the thin blade on the trunk/ branch side of the cut. This will result in a short stub and will also prevent a layer of damaged cambium tissue being left immediately under the line of the cut.

GOOD AND BAD PRUNING

1 *A good pruning cut is made just above a strong bud, about 3mm (⅛in) above the bud. It should be a slanting cut, with the higher end above the bud. The bud should generally be outward bound from the plant rather than inward.*

2 *If the stem has buds or leaves opposite each other, make the cut horizontal, about 3mm (⅛in) above the buds.*

3 *Always use a sharp pair of secateurs (hand pruners). Blunt ones will produce a ragged or bruised cut, which is likely to introduce disease into the plant.*

4 *Do not cut too far above a bud. The piece of stem above the bud is likely to die back and the rest of the stem may well die back even further, causing the loss of the whole stem.*

5 *Do not cut too close to the bud otherwise the bud might be damaged by the secateurs or disease might enter. Too close a cut is likely to cause the stem to die back to the next bud.*

6 *It is bad practice to slope the cut towards the bud as this makes the stem above the bud too long, which is likely to cause dieback. It also sheds rain on to the bud, which may cause problems.*

HARD PRUNING SHRUBS

1 *There are a few shrubs – buddleias are the main and most obvious example – which benefit from being cut hard back each spring. This treatment improves the development of the foliage. Elders (Sambucus) and the purple smoke bush (Cotinus) should also be treated in this way. Rosa glauca also responds very well to this type of hard pruning.*

2 *Cut the shoots right back almost to the ground. It is important to ensure that you make the cuts just above an outward-facing bud. Cutting back will leave little more than a stump. It may seem a little drastic, but the shrubs will quickly grow again in the spring. If they are not cut back, they become very leggy and do not make such attractive bushes.*

3 *Several plants that have attractive coloured bark in the winter are best cut to the ground in the spring. So, by the following winter, attractive new shoots will be displayed. The various coloured-stemmed Rubus, such as R. cockburnianus, as well as some of the dogwoods (Cornus) and willow (Salix), are good candidates for this treatment.*

Cuts should always be made immediately above a bud and should be done as cleanly as possible. Use well-maintained secateurs that are regularly sharpened. Make sure that you do not position your blade too close to the bud or the tissue that connects the bud to the main plant body could be damaged. As a guide, you should cut 3mm (⅛in) above a bud and always ensure the bud is not damaged when cutting.

Be careful when using a saw close to a trunk or stem to remove heavier thicker branches. The weight of the branch can sometimes cause splitting and tearing to the main stem wood or bark. These injuries can allow the entry of disease-causing organisms and damage the plant.

The typical order of cuts to follow when pruning any tree is to remember the D's. These are: dead, dying, diseased,

displaced or deformed branches. All of these must be removed as the first stage of any pruning work. Then add to this list the C's: criss-crossing branches and crowded growth.

The next stage is to remove any unwanted growth. Care must be applied at this critical stage to ensure that you do not remove too much growth. Finally, once you have cleared this material, it is possible to

Above: *When cutting out crossing stems, cut out the stems while they are still young and free from damage and disease. Using secateurs (hand pruners), cut the stem at its base where it joins the main branch.*

Left: *Tips of stems often die back, especially those that have carried bunches of flowers. Another cause is the young growth at the tip of shoots being killed by frost. If this dieback is not cut out, it can kill off the whole shoot. Even if dieback proceeds no further, the bush looks tidier without these dead shoots. Cut the shoot back into good wood, just above a strong bud.*

PRUNING OUT DEAD WOOD ON A CLIMBER

1 *Most climbers produce a mass of dead wood that has to be removed so that the plant does not become congested. Dead wood is normally quite clearly differentiated from live wood by its colour and lack of flexibility.*

2 *Thin out all of the dead wood that the climber has produced, removing it very carefully in sections, if this is necessary, so that the remaining stems are not damaged when the dead stems are eventually pulled out.*

see what further work needs to be done. Many species have specific pruning requirements, which need to be carried out if the plant is to reach its full potential. Creating balance, form and a pleasing shape in the pruned specimen requires a keen eye, as well as an understanding of the plant's growth habits and tolerances. It is worth taking a little time over this and planning what you are going to do before

starting. Acting too hastily now can easily spoil the job. Pruning is one of a few tasks in the garden that are best viewed intermittently from a distance. Remember, you can only cut a branch once. If you cut the wrong branch, you cannot rejoin it effectively to the plant from whence it came. Always check that you know the full extent of a branch and what effect its removal will have prior to making the cut.

Above: *Up to a third of the old wood should be removed to encourage the climber to produce new growth. If possible, cut some of this out to the base; also remove some of the upper stems, cutting them back to a strong growing point.*

Above: *Remove any wood that has become diseased, cutting it back to a point on the stem where the wood of the climber is healthy. If the cut end shows that the wood is still diseased on the inside of the stem, cut back further still.*

PLANT PROPAGATION

Despite the large variety of methods employed, there are really only two basic types of plant propagation: vegetative – taking cuttings, for example – and sowing seed. All of the techniques used fall into one or other of these categories. Raising your own plants is one of the most rewarding activities that any gardener can do. It can also be particularly beneficial for the organic gardener because, unlike with bought-in plants, you can be assured that self-raised stock will be pesticide-free.

Above: *Collecting your own seed can be very rewarding and ensures that your new plants are free of any pesticide residues.*

POTTING MIX FOR PROPAGATION

Seed and cutting potting mix should be almost free of nutrients – the plants do not need soil-derived nutrients until they have rooted. Numerous proprietary brands are available for organic propagation. Alternatively, you can make your own potting mix using finely sifted compost or leaf mould mixed with equal parts of sharp sand or grit. Mixing this is comparatively easy but problems can arise if the organic matter is not thoroughly sterilized. Unless you are able to do this, there is always the possibility of fungal diseases affecting the plants. Worm compost can be good for making potting mix but the easiest way to get sterilized potting mix is to use compost that was made in a hot pile. Use material from near the middle of the pile to get the most sterilized matter.

PROPAGATION FROM SEED

Seeds are nature's way of introducing variety into plant material. Fertilizing the female part of a flower with pollen from the male part produces a seed. Seeds are a resting and survival stage in the plant's life that help it survive adverse conditions in nature. Seeds can survive conditions that kill plants. A seed consists of three things: an embryo (a young plant at its most immature stage); a food supply (to maintain the embryo and provide energy after germination); and a protective seed coat. The embryo consists of a young root system (radicle); the young shoot system (plumule), which carries the seed leaves (cotyledons); and the hypocotyl, which is the junction between the root and shoot systems.

Some seeds need special treatment to germinate. One such treatment is stratification. To stratify seeds, cover them in some damp material, such as damp compost, and keep them in a refrigerator at about 4.5°C (40°F) for up to three months. After this treatment, the seeds are ready to germinate. Seeds that germinate better after stratification are oaks and hellebores.

Seeds require moisture, warmth and oxygen to germinate. Because a seed needs oxygen as well as moisture, it is important not to keep the seeds too wet.

On the other hand, the seeds must not dry out. Most seeds germinate best between 18.5–24°C (65–75°F). Most seeds will germinate well in light; however, some seeds, such as those of periwinkle, pansy and verbena, germinate best in the dark.

Many seeds have specific germination requirements that require knowledge of the particular species. Certain generalizations are possible and although it is always advisable to follow the instructions on packets you buy, self-collected seed may require a bit of guesswork. If it is a small dust-like seed (thyme and basil, for example), it probably needs light to germinate. Make sure the seed is well pressed into the moist mixture, but do not cover. Larger seed should be covered to twice its thickness in the soilless mixture. If the seed packet says to scarify, make a scar in the seed by nicking the seed coat in some way. Lightly rubbing the seeds with sandpaper usually accomplishes this. The reason for scarification is to speed up the lengthy process of letting the water past the waterproof seed coat.

MAKING ORGANIC PROPAGATION POTTING MIX

1 *Take equal quantities of an organic material, such as coir or finely sieved leaf mould, and a free-draining material such as vermiculite or perlite.*

2 *Mix the organic material and vermiculite or perlite together thoroughly, ensuring that there are no lumps and that the mixture is open and "free running".*

3 *This organic potting mix for propagation is now ready for use and does not need any additional fertilizer. It can be used to propagate seeds and cuttings.*

SOWING SEEDS IN CONTAINERS

1 *First gather together the basic equipment. You will need pots, potting mix, labels, a pencil, a firming board and a plastic bag.*

2 *Fill the container with the potting mix, gently tapping the pot to ensure that there are no air spaces in the mix.*

3 *Gently firm and flatten the potting mix with the firming board. Take care not to over-firm the potting mix.*

4 *Sow the seed evenly over the potting mix surface. Large seed can be placed, but smaller seed must be scattered.*

5 *With larger seed, lightly cover the seed with finely sieved potting mix. Sieved vermiculite or perlite can also be used.*

6 *Water the pot using a fine rose on a watering can. If the seed is small, water the potting mix prior to sowing.*

VEGETATIVE PROPAGATION

The vegetative parts of the plant (stem, root or leaf) can also be used to produce a new plant. Most fruit trees are propagated asexually, using a bud or a twig from a tree that produces exceptionally good fruit. When this bud or twig becomes an adult tree, it has the same qualities as the "mother" tree. By propagating asexually (cloning), we reproduce the "mother" plant.

PROPAGATING PLANTS FROM SPECIALIZED ORGANS

Plants may be propagated from many different plant parts. Specialized roots, stems and leaves that occur naturally make asexual propagation easy.

Bulb This consists of swollen leaves on a short stem. Bulbs can be propagated by removing small bulblets or offsets that form at the base of the parent bulb. These small bulbs take two or three years to mature into plants that flower. Place offsets in rich light soil. Certain bulbs, such as lilies, can be propagated by removing individual scales from the dormant bulb and placing them in a bag of damp moss. After a few months the scale will develop into a small bulb (a bulbil), which can be potted as if it were a large seed and grown on. Certain lilies (tiger lilies, for instance) produce bulbils in their leaf axils (where the bulb leaf joins the stem) that can also be propagated. Examples of bulbs are tulips, onions and lilies.

Corm This is similar to a bulb and often confused with one. Structurally, however, a corm is different, consisting of a stem that is swollen as a food store. It is shorter and broader than a bulb. The leaves of the stem are modified as thin dry membranes that enclose the corm and protect it against injury and drying. Examples of corms are crocus and gladiolus. The procedure for propagating these is the same as for taking offsets from bulbs.

Rhizome This is a stem that grows horizontally near the soil surface. A rhizome usually stores food, but, as it grows, it develops buds along its length. Rhizomes can be cut into sections with at least one eye or bud. Plants propagated in this way include iris.

Runner This is a stem that arises from a crown bud and creeps over the ground. The plantlet that forms at the tip is easily rooted and forms a new plant. Plants with runners include strawberries and spider plants.

Tuber This is a swollen underground stem or root that stores food. Tuberous plants, such as potatoes and dahlias, can be dug up and the tubers separated. Each section must have a segment of the crown that contains at least one eye or bud.

PROPAGATING TUBERS

1 *Take a sharp knife and cut the tuber (in this case a begonia tuber) through the middle so that each part has a shoot.*

2 *Dust the open cuts with a fungicide such as sulphur or Bordeaux mixture. Prepare two small pots with moist potting mix.*

3 *Plant both halves so that they sit firmly on top of the potting mix. Keep the potting mix moist and plant on when new growth appears.*

ROOT CUTTINGS

To produce a new plant from a root cutting, there must be a shoot bud present or it must be possible for the cutting to form one. The ability of root cuttings to form these buds depends on the time of year. The dormant (resting) season is usually the best time to take root cuttings and it is best to take them from newer root growth.

Make cuttings 3–10cm (1¼–4in) long from roots that are 1–1.5cm (⅜–⅝in) in diameter. Ensure the roots are from the chosen plant and not neighbouring plants. Cuttings are best taken during the winter, when roots have large carbohydrate supplies, but they may also be taken throughout the growing season. Cut straight through the end of the root closest to the stem. Cut the other end on a slant.

This will help you to remember which end is the top (the straight cut) and which is the bottom (the diagonal cut).

Store cuttings from dormant roots for three weeks in moist rooting medium at 5°C (41°F). After this, remove from storage and plant upright in the growing medium. Keep moist and warm in a bright location until the plant has grown large enough to pot on or plant out. This will, of course, vary depending upon the vigour of the plant and slow-growing plants may be best potted up and grown on for a season before finally planting out the following spring.

If root cuttings are taken during active growth, miss out the period of storage and place the cuttings directly in the rooting medium. Phlox and euphorbias are propagated from root cuttings.

STEM CUTTINGS AND LAYERING

Many trees, shrubs and herbaceous plants are propagated from stem cuttings. A root system must be formed on a stem either before or after the stem is removed. Roots can be formed on stems in two ways: by layering and by taking stem cuttings. With layering, the stem is allowed to produce roots before it is cut from the parent plant.

Stem cuttings form roots after the stem is removed. The main difficulty with stem cuttings is keeping the stems alive while they form new roots. Some plant stems root better when the wood is soft and actively growing, others root best from mature wood. Cuttings taken from plants that are actively growing are called softwood cuttings, while those taken after the wood is mature are known as hardwood cuttings.

TAKING ROOT CUTTINGS

1 *Dig up a small section of root from a suitable species with thick fleshy roots. The section must either have a shoot bud or be capable of forming one – in which case the cutting should be taken in the dormant season – if it is to be successful.*

2 *Remove as much of the soil as possible from the root cutting before slicing off the small side roots. Using a sharp knife, remove these as well as dead and damaged portions and any side shoots to leave a section of healthy root.*

3 *Cut the remaining sections of the root into small pieces, approximately 5cm (2in) in length, cutting the bottom end at an angle. Insert the root cutting into propagation potting mix, with the angled end pointing down.*

TAKING HARDWOOD CUTTINGS

1 *Select healthy, blemish-free pieces of wood about the thickness of a pencil. Cut each of these into sections about 20–25cm (8–10in) long, angling the top cut.*

2 *Stand the cut stems in a jar of water until you are ready to plant them out. Ideally, stand the jar in a cool moist place out of direct sunlight.*

3 *Dig a narrow trench that is deep enough for the cuttings. About 2.5–5cm (1–2in) should emerge above ground. The length of the row will depend on the number of cuttings.*

4 *Loosely fill the trench to about two-thirds full with sharp sand or fine grit. This is essential as it will allow the passage of air around the bases and prevent rotting off. It will also encourage rooting.*

5 *Insert the cuttings about 10–15cm (4–6in) apart, making sure that the angled cut is uppermost. If you place any cuttings in upside down – i.e. with the buds facing downward – rooting will not occur.*

6 *Gently firm the soil, making sure that the cuttings are firm but that the soil surface is not over-compacted. Leave the cuttings for the whole of the growing season before lifting and planting out next winter.*

TAKING STEM TIP CUTTINGS

1 *Take cuttings from the tips of the stems and put them in a plastic bag. The length of the cuttings will vary, depending on the subject, but take about 10cm (4in).*

2 *Trim the cuttings to just below a leaf joint and then remove most of the leaves and side shoots, leaving just two at the top. This will help to prevent stem rot.*

3 *Place up to twelve cuttings in a pot of potting mix that is specially formulated for cuttings or a 50:50 mixture of sharp sand and peat substitute such as coir or leaf mould mix.*

4 *Water well, and cover with the cut-off base of a soft-drinks bottle, a perfect substitute for a propagator. A heated propagator will speed up the rooting process. Place several pots in the same unit.*

Layering is a useful way of increasing some shrubs and climbers that cannot readily be propagated from cuttings. Simple layering is a method of getting a growing shoot to produce roots while it is still attached to the "parent" plant. There are several variations on the technique, and the one you use will depend on the plant and the type of growth it produces.

Softwood cuttings are taken from first-year branches that have not yet become woody. Flowering shrubs are often propagated by softwood cuttings. Late spring and early summer are the best times for success with this method. Take cuttings 5–10cm (2–4in) long. Larger cuttings produce larger plants sooner, but they are prone to more rapid water loss. Make cuts slightly below a leaf node. Remove any leaves on the lower section and insert them into potting mix, making sure that no leaves are touching each other or the potting mix. Remove any cuttings immediately from the tray or pot if they die or appear diseased. Pot healthy cuttings up promptly once they recommence growth following rooting.

Hardwood cuttings are taken once the tissue becomes woody and the plant is dormant. Cuttings can be taken two weeks after leaf fall and before bud burst. Select healthy wood that was produced the previous summer. The wood should be about pencil thickness and cut into sections of approximately 20–25cm (8–10in). Several cuttings can be made from the same branch of some shrubs.

To take hardwood cuttings, make basal cuts just below a node, and upper cuts slightly above a bud. The upper cut should be slanted and the lower cut straight, so that a cutting is less likely to be inserted into the potting mix upside down. Once inserted all the tops of the cuttings should be slanted cuts. Bury cuttings vertically in moist sandy topsoil or sand.

The cuttings should not freeze, but must remain cool. In spring, remove the cuttings from storage and plant in a hotbed or other protected site with exposure to morning sun or filtered light. Leave 2.5–5cm (1–2in) of cutting above ground. Keep cuttings moist until a root system forms. Transplant the cuttings the following spring while they are still dormant.

LAYERING SHRUBS

1 Choose a stem that will reach the ground without breaking and prepare the soil beneath it. In most cases, the native soil will be satisfactory, but if it is heavy clay, add some potting mix to improve its texture.

2 Trim off any side shoots or leaves. Dig a shallow hole and bend the shoot down into it.

3 To help hold the shoot in place, peg it down with a piece of bent wire.

4 Fill in the hole and cover it with a stone. In many cases, the stone will be sufficient to hold the layer in place and a peg will not be required. The stone will also help to keep the area beneath it moist.

5 It may take several months or even years for shrubs that are hard to propagate to layer but, eventually, new shoots will appear and the layer will have rooted. Sever it from its parent and pot it up into a container.

6 If the roots are well developed, transfer the layer directly to its new site.

SIMPLE DIVISION

1 *Water the plant that is to be divided during the previous day. Carefully dig up a clump of the plant using a spade, in this case a Michaelmas daisy (Aster novi-belgii).*

2 *Insert two garden forks back-to-back into the plant and lever apart by pushing the handles together. Keep on dividing until the pieces are of the required size.*

3 *The pieces of the plant can then be replanted in the bed, but dig over the soil first, removing any weeds and adding some well-rotted organic material.*

4 *Alternatively, small pieces of the plant can be potted up individually. After watering, place these in a closed cold frame for a few days before hardening off.*

DIVISION

Division is the cutting or breaking up of a crown or clump of suckers into segments. Each segment must have a bud and some roots to propagate successfully. These segments are replanted and grow into new plants identical to the parent. Most perennials should be lifted and divided when they become overgrown and begin to lose vigour. Vigorous growth in most perennials occurs on the outer segments of the clump. Old growth in the centre of the clump is discarded.

Carefully dig up the plant, loosening the roots and lifting it from the soil. Split apart the main clump with two spades or forks, or chop with a shovel or large knife if the clump is firmly massed. It is advisable to divide autumn-flowering perennials in spring, while those that flower in spring and summer are best divided in autumn.

GRAFTING AND BUDDING

Grafting and budding involve inserting or attaching a part of one plant on to another so that both parts continue to grow. In grafting, you attach a short twig from a desirable variety with two or more buds (called a scion) to a seedling. This seedling is called the stock and forms the root system for the new plant, while the scion becomes the top growth. Budding involves inserting the bud from a desirable variety into a cut or slit in the bark of the stock. The bud develops into the whole top of the plant. You must match scions and buds with stocks according to their ability to grow together.

CHIP BUDDING

1 *Select good bud wood that is free from blemishes and obvious damage, pests or diseases. If you are doing this in the summer, then you must first remove the leaves.*

2 *Remove the bud using a very sharp, flat-edged knife. Cut out the bud with a thin shaving of the wood below the bark and leave a "V" shape at the base.*

3 *Prepare the stock plant by cutting a "church window" shaped notch from the stem that is the same thickness as the chipped bud and leave a small notch cut into the base.*

4 *Place the bud into the notch, fitting the "V"-shaped base into the notch at the base of the "window cut".*

5 *Make sure that the bud fits snugly, with the edges of the bud-wood in contact with the edge of the "window" notch.*

6 *Secure the graft firmly with grafting tape to ensure that the join does not dry out. The graft will usually take in about 4–6 weeks in the summer but winter grafts can take longer.*

THE GREENHOUSE ENVIRONMENT

Greenhouses provide an environment in which levels of light and shade, temperature and moisture, and protection from the elements can be closely controlled and monitored. You can propagate plants to grow outside, protect tender plants from frosts and grow certain crops out of season. A basic understanding of the ways that the greenhouse environment can be controlled will help you on your way to a bumper harvest.

Above: *Shading helps to keep temperatures down in the summer and also protects the plants from sun scorch.*

LIGHT INTENSITY

Natural light has all the right wavelengths that plants need to function and grow successfully. Light intensities vary considerably during the year and gardeners often try to compensate for this by giving extra light to the plant. The quality of this light must be correct for the growth of plants, and light bulbs used to supplement natural light must be of a suitable daylight quality. Natural winter light intensity is often insufficient for certain crops. Conversely, summer light levels, especially when combined with elevated temperatures, can cause problems for other crops. Balanced growth requires good greenhouse design and proper planning for the light requirements of the crop. As a general rule, the ridge that runs along the middle of your

greenhouse (if yours is a traditional "A"-shaped one) should always be orientated so that it runs east to west.

LIGHT READINGS WITH A METER

These should be taken inside the greenhouse and then compared with an outside reading. The difference between the two readings will indicate the percentage of available light transmitted into the greenhouse. A good tip here for those without a professional light meter is to use the automatic aperture reading on an SLR camera or a photographic light meter. It will not give actual figures, but will indicate to a certain extent just how much of the available light is getting through.

ADDITIONAL LIGHTING

Supplementary lighting can be used to "top-up" existing daylight, especially in winter. You should always buy bulbs that give a full spectrum of light (the same quality as daylight – often sold or described as "grow lights"). Almost all bulbs for household use are short of the particular light wavelengths that plants need to produce food and grow successfully. Grow lights tend to use a lot of electricity and it may be cheaper to provide additional light for just a part of the greenhouse, suspending the lights above a crop that really needs the light. Grow lights are available as bulbs or strip lights and can sometimes be bought as special enclosed units.

SHADING

This controls temperature and light. Shading is usually put in place in order to reduce summer temperatures (if they are excessive) or to protect young plants and shade-loving ones from very intense sunlight. Blinds, netting or white shade paint can all be effective.

TEMPERATURE

Almost all plants like a fall in night-time temperature of about 4–6°C (7–10°F) below that in the day. Many commonly grown species have a relatively wide range of tolerances, but most grow best between about 16–24°C (60–76°F). All plants have maximum and minimum temperature tolerances that should never be exceeded.

You can take an average temperature reading inside the greenhouse using a maximum and minimum thermometer. Compare it with one taken outside. You should note, however, that more than just the outside temperature influences that of a greenhouse. The action of the sun, even on a relatively cold day, can result in temperatures being much higher inside than out. Wind is also a factor to consider that can cause a chilling effect far below the temperature average, rapidly cooling the glass and air nearby.

HEATING SYSTEMS

Most heaters depend upon a hotbox or burner. These work by heating the air directly. They are more generally used

Above: *A maximum/minimum thermometer is an essential tool in helping you to judge the conditions in your greenhouse.*

Above: *Some automated systems measure air temperature, and then turn on heat and open vents as necessary.*

Left: *Even a relatively small greenhouse can vastly increase the range of plants that you can grow in your garden.*

CHECKING THE CONDITIONS

The greenhouse microclimate differs from the garden chiefly because the light intensity is lower, the temperature is higher and air turbulence is less. How you modify the environment largely depends on what you intend to grow. Winter salad crops need some additional heat, particularly on cold winter nights. Slightly tender, overwintering perennials may not need any heat unless the temperature drops very low. You must know what the environment will be even on cold winter nights. The only really accurate way to assess the suitability of an environment for plant growth is to take regular readings. Many devices exist to monitor the internal conditions within protected structures. These include thermostats for heating and automatic ventilators, although a seemingly endless array of humidification, automatic shading and watering devices are now available for small greenhouses.

GREENHOUSE HYGIENE

Practising good hygiene is important in maintaining the health of the plants. Dead leaves and debris left lying about can harbour pests and diseases, as can badly affected plants if they are not removed promptly. Once a year, thoroughly clean all surfaces, including glass and glazing bars, with hot soapy water. This will pay dividends during the growing season by reducing the number of annually re-occurring pests and diseases. Where plants are grown in open borders, rotate crops or replace the soil with fresh topsoil every two or three years.

where there is no need to provide heat on a regular basis – in cold greenhouses, for example, or in polytunnels used for raising early hardy stock. Some enterprising gardeners link hot water pipes to their domestic heating systems to provide heating for the greenhouse. The disadvantage here is that the heat tends to be applied at times to suit the household but not the plants within the greenhouse.

INSULATION

It is possible to insulate a greenhouse by providing additional layers within the structure to trap air. Bubble-wrap plastic is a popular method as it is easy to place in position and allows for the transmission of light. Such methods always reduce the amount of light transmitted, but will save upon heating costs. In addition to this, careful siting of the greenhouse can help to reduce the chilling effects of high winds.

HUMIDITY

Most plants thrive in about 40 to 60 per cent humidity. Plants that are grouped together often set up their own small microclimate where the humidity is higher in the immediate vicinity. Much of the humidity requirement for a plant depends upon where it comes from. Rainforest plants often need 85 per cent or more humidity, whereas cacti need as little as 15 per cent (in cultivation). The humidity is also affected by other factors, notably temperature. Warm air can hold much more moisture than cooler air.

The need to increase humidity rises during the hotter months when it is harder to keep down the temperature in protected structures. Increasing the humidity also helps to slow down the water loss from leaves and may also help to prevent wilting or scorch.

Humidity should be raised by damping down (spraying a hose on hard surfaces, paths or under benches) on hot dry days. If there are only certain plants, such as young seedlings, that require elevated humidity, then these are best covered with a thin layer of clear plastic.

AIR CIRCULATION

All plants need a constant supply of clean fresh air around them in order to grow healthily. Outdoors, normal wind movements would supply this, but in a greenhouse you will need to make provision for this.

Ventilators help control temperature and air flow. Roof vents should normally occupy the equivalent of 15 per cent of the floor space in order to be fully effective. They are normally a single structure that opens "window fashion" with a safety catch to keep them open to the required width. As with greenhouse design in general, there are many designs, most being simple variations on a theme. Side ventilators are also occasionally seen in some greenhouses. These are usually arranged in a "louvre type" fashion, with several overlapping strips that can be opened or closed with a small lever.

Above: *Bubble-wrap plastic is an ideal material with which to insulate the greenhouse in the winter.*

GREENHOUSE CULTIVATION

In a greenhouse you can hasten the arrival of spring by forcing hyacinths, tulips, azaleas and a whole variety of spring crops. You can also lengthen summer, with roses that bloom far into the autumn, and brighten winter with carnations, camellias and rare tropical flowers. You may also harvest tomatoes in mid-winter and vegetables or greens at any time of the year.

Above: *Early crops and flowers can be raised in pots ready for planting out when the weather is warmer.*

METHODS OF GROWING

Think carefully about how you plan to use your greenhouse and what plants you would like to grow there. The true art of greenhouse gardening lies in using every available area of space. This will involve planning the layout of the growing areas in the greenhouse and making a cropping plan to ensure that you not only use all of the available space, but also every "time space" within the growing calendar.

GROWING IN OPEN GROUND

Many greenhouse plants will grow well in open soil borders. The soil can be prepared in a similar way to that used for borders outside. Remember that much of what benefits outdoor soil (digging and adding organic matter) is also good for indoor soil. The advantage is that the system is sustainable over a long period and can even be serviced as a small raised bed system to help maintain steady soil temperatures. Taller crops, such as tomatoes, are particularly well suited to growing in open borders in the greenhouse, but a whole

range of both ornamentals and edible crops can also be grown in this way. Remember that if you intend to grow certain crops indoors – salad crops, tomatoes, legumes or cucumbers, for example – then you may need to rotate these, or in smaller spaces avoid growing them in open ground every second or third year. This is done for the same reasons that outdoor crops are rotated.

Above: *Staging can provide extra space in the greenhouse as well as a comfortable surface on which to work.*

GROWING IN POTS ON STAGING

Staging is essentially a shelf or shelves on which plants in pots are arranged. It enables the gardener to work at a comfortable height and is particularly useful for those who wish to raise seedlings and propagate plants. The area beneath the staging is somewhat shaded but by no means wasted as it can be used for overwintering dormant plants, growing ferns and other shade-lovers, and for some forms of propagation (lilies propagated from scales, for instance). It also provides the perfect place for propagators and can easily be adapted to become a propagating tent.

USING GROW BAGS

Grow bags offer a good alternative to open beds in smaller greenhouses, where space is limited and no open beds exist. These can be purchased or you can easily make your own by filling a large plastic potting-mix bag with a mixture of garden compost and a little grit. Each bag will support four tomato plants and even greater numbers of smaller plants. Grow bags are ideal for raising sweet peas (*Lathyrus odoratus*) for use on patios or roof gardens where the rich deep soil in which they thrive is unavailable. They can equally be used to raise garden peas or beans.

GROWING CLIMBING PLANTS

The last dimension in the greenhouse is the vertical one, ultimately to the roof. Lean-to greenhouses are especially useful for this, their back walls being well suited for growing such things as vines or kiwi. Even freestanding "apex" houses (those shaped like an "A" with a central ridge) can be used to raise climbing crops, such as cucumbers or melons, to say nothing of the thousands of delightful and colourful ornamental climbers that thrive in the greenhouse.

Left: *You can grow crops in soil beds as well as in pots in the greenhouse.*

A YEARLY GREENHOUSE CROPPING PLAN

The plan shown below is a sample of how a greenhouse can be used to be productive all year round. The essential point is that you plan what you want to grow. Once you have decided on this it is a relatively simple matter to make your greenhouse a productive space.

GREENHOUSE TASK	MID-WINTER	LATE WINTER	EARLY SPRING	MID-SPRING
Edible crops	Sow seeds for early crops. Interplant with radishes. Sow early cabbage and cauliflower in pots. Bring strawberries in from frames. Top-dress vines and fruiting climbers.	Sow broad beans. Pot on early vegetable seedlings. Reduce young shoots of vines to one to two per spur and raise lowered rods back to the greenhouse side.	Sow the seeds of Brussels sprouts. Sow indoor tomato seed and make sowings of calendula, tagetes or similar in order to encourage beneficials and pollinators. Prick out seedlings.	Sow seed of outdoor tomatoes, celery, celeriac, melons and cucumbers. Harden off early vegetable plants. Tie new growth from vine rods on to wires. Remove side shoots of early tomatoes.
Ornamentals	Take cuttings of plants such as chrysanthemums. Bring bulb pots in for forcing. Pot on autumn-sown sweet peas into "long" pots.	Start off dahlia cuttings. Cut back and re-pot fuchsias and pelargoniums. Sow sweet peas (*Lathyrus odoratus*). Pot up cuttings of herbaceous plants. Sow herbaceous seed and begin sowing bedding plants.	Harden off early sweet peas. Pot up cuttings and sow seed of half-hardy annuals. Take cuttings. Prick out seedlings. Pot up summer bedding tubers and corms.	Finish sowing half-hardy bedding. Pot up cuttings and prick out seedlings. Make up summer tubs and hanging baskets for growing on.
General	Wash glass panes of greenhouse and frames. Keep conditions on the dry side. Be vigilant for winter pests and diseases. Provide heat as necessary.	Keep an eye on ventilation. Watch for pests and diseases. Keep conditions on the dry side. Remove dead or dying material from plants. Provide heat as necessary and ventilate.	Damp down on hot days and ventilate. Watch for pests and diseases. Begin to feed plants as growth increases. Dig, manure and top-dress borders ready for planting.	Damp down at least twice daily when hot and ventilate. Continue to watch for pests and diseases. Dig borders and manure if you have not already done so.

GREENHOUSE TASK	LATE SPRING	EARLY SUMMER	MID-SUMMER	LATE SUMMER
Edible crops	Plant greenhouse tomatoes into prepared borders or large pots of loam-based potting mix. Interplant with calendula and tagetes to encourage bees into the crop. Prick out celery and celeriac cuttings.	Thin grape trusses using vine scissors. Thin fruit if necessary on peaches growing under glass. Pick tomatoes regularly as they ripen. Pinch out and tie in melons and cucumbers as they reach their intended size.	Hand pollinate melons and cucumbers. Perform last thinning on grape trusses. Feed tomatoes with dried blood to develop uppermost trusses.	Remove lower leaves of tomatoes as fruit ripens. Support melons, removing leaves that shade the fruit. Harvest cucumbers. Sow seeds of winter leaf crops and companion plants.
Ornamentals	Harden off bedding plants. Place winter-flowering cyclamen in shade and allow to partially dry out.	Take cuttings of deciduous shrubs. Propagate houseplants. Sow seeds of spring bedding plants in frames.	Take cuttings of evergreen shrubs and deciduous species. Propagate houseplants. Sow seeds of biennials in frames. Re-start rested cyclamen corms.	Take cuttings of pelargoniums and fuchsias to act as "mother plants" for cuttings the next season.
General	Provide shade over sensitive crops. Feed plants regularly with a liquid "tea". Watch for pests and diseases and introduce biological control.	Water regularly. Continue potting on developing cuttings and seedlings of all plants.	Water regularly (twice daily in hot weather) and damp down two or three times daily to maintain humidity.	Continue potting on developing cuttings and seedlings. Continue to watch for pests and diseases and introduce biological control if necessary.

GREENHOUSE TASK	EARLY AUTUMN	MID-AUTUMN	LATE AUTUMN	EARLY WINTER
Edible crops	Cut melons as soon as they are ripe. Clear tomatoes as they finish.	Plant up winter leaf and salad crops, interplanting these with an appropriate companion planting.	Lift crowns of rhubarb for forcing and leave them on the surface for a week.	Sow seed of early onion varieties. Lift further crowns of rhubarb for forcing. Prune peach trees that are growing under glass.
Ornamentals	Take last semi-ripe cuttings and softwood cuttings.	Harden off spring bedding plants ready for planting.	Move bulbs for forcing into a frame to encourage top growth. Lift and pot up lily-of-the-valley for spring display.	Bring in bulbs for forced flowers. Stool back "mother" plants for early cuttings.
General	Decrease watering as days shorten. Pot on developing cuttings and seedlings of all plants. Remove shading and provide gentle heat on cold nights.	Pot on any remaining cuttings and seedlings. Pick over plants on a regular basis in order to remove dead or dying material. Provide gentle heat on cold nights.	Keep conditions on the dry side. Be vigilant for winter pests and diseases, as plants become more stressed due to low light levels. Provide heat as necessary.	Repair any damage to glass panes immediately it is noticed. Order seed for the coming season if you have not done so already.

COLD FRAMES AND CLOCHES

Individual and multiple plant protectors are useful for covering the transplants or seedlings of warm-weather vegetables or flowers that are set out ahead of the normal planting season. These usually take the form of low plastic tunnels, cloches or individual bell jars. The colder the area in which you live, the greater their usefulness because they effectively extend the length of the normal growing season.

Above: *This is a sturdy brick cold frame with a soil bed for growing winter and early spring vegetables.*

COLD FRAMES

These enable you to sow summer flowers and vegetables some weeks before outdoor planting and may even allow for an extra crop within a season. They are relatively inexpensive, simple structures, providing a favourable environment for growing cool-weather crops in the very early spring, the autumn and even into the winter.

Cold frames have no outside energy requirements, relying on the sun as a source of heat. They collect heat when the sun's rays penetrate the light (the top cover) which is made from plastic, glass or fibreglass. The ideal location for a cold frame is facing the direction of the sun with a slight slope to ensure good drainage and maximum solar absorption. A sheltered spot against a wall or hedge is best. Sink the frame into the ground to provide extra protection, using the earth for insulation. Put a walkway to the front and adequate space behind the frame to help when removing the light.

Designs for cold frames vary. For example, some contain barrels that are painted black and filled with water. These absorb heat during the day and release it at night. Some cold frames are built with a very high back and a steep glass slope. Others are insulated very well and may also include moveable insulation. A simple method of providing insulation is to use sacks filled with leaves over the top of the frame and bales of straw or hay stacked against the sides at night in order to protect against freezing.

There is no standard-sized cold frame. The inside depth of the frame should be determined by the height of the plants that you plan to grow. Spring annuals, perennial seedlings or low over-wintering stock may need as little as a 30cm (12in) backboard and a 20cm (8in) front board. Potted plants may need a 38cm (15in) front board and a 45cm (18in) back board. A standard glass frame light is usually about 1 x 1.8m (3 x

6ft). Do not make the structure too wide for weeding and harvesting; a width of 1.2–1.5m (4–5ft) is convenient to reach across.

Cold frames are useful for hardening-off seedlings that were started indoors or in a greenhouse. This hardening-off period is important because seedlings can suffer serious setbacks if they are moved directly from the warmth and protection of the greenhouse to the garden. It is also possible to start cool-weather crops in the cold frame and either grow them to maturity or transplant them in the garden. Cold frames may also be useful for rooting the cuttings of deciduous and evergreen shrubs and trees, and the softwood cuttings of chrysanthemums, geraniums and fuchsias during the warmer months. Ventilation is most critical in late winter, early spring, and early autumn on clear, sunny days when temperatures may rise above 45°C (113°F). The light should be raised partially to prevent the build-up of extreme temperatures inside the frame. Lower or replace the light early each day in order to conserve some heat for the evening.

In summer, extreme heat and intensive sunlight can damage plants. You can avoid this by shading with a lath (a slatted wooden frame) or old bamboo window blinds. Water plants early so that they dry before dark; this helps to reduce disease problems.

CLOCHES

Traditionally a bell-shaped glass cover, a cloche is a moveable structure that serves as a mini-greenhouse. Cloches can be used to protect transplanted tender plants from spring frosts. They also help to warm up the soil for crops sown directly in the soil.

Left: *When the seedlings are fully acclimatized and ready to be planted out, the lights or lids can be left off altogether.*

Above: *A rigid plastic cloche is easy to use. The sections butt up against each other and can be pegged into the soil. Endpieces are also available.*

Above: *Glass bell jars are simple cloches for covering one plant. They are expensive, but large plastic jars make a good, if not as attractive, alternative.*

The traditional or European cloche is usually built in 60cm (24in) sections that vary in height from 20–60cm (8–24in) and 40–65cm (16–26in) in width. It is made of four panes of glass held together with heavy galvanized wire fittings. It has a handle for ease in carrying and for operating the ventilation system. Several cloches placed end to end make a miniature greenhouse.

Plastic bottles with the bottoms cut out can provide protection for small individual plants. These will last a season or two, but will become brittle over time. Flexible fibreglass sheets held in an inverted "U"-shape by stiff wire hoops or small wooden stakes can be used to cover rows of plants.

A tunnel-like plant protector can be made with a 1.5m (5ft) strip of plastic or fleece laid over 1.8m (6ft) wire hoops placed 1m (3ft) apart. Elastic tiedowns over the top near each hoop will hold the plastic.

Temporary cloches can also be made by arching black, semi-rigid, plastic piping over the row or bed and sticking it into the ground on each side. Lay clear plastic over the arches. If the beds are enclosed with wood, attach brackets to the inside edges of the boxes or sink short pieces of pipe with a larger inside diameter along the sides to hold the arches. The arches can be used to support fleece or shade cloth to ward off both frost and bright sunlight. When this

cloche is no longer needed, simply remove the plastic sheet and pipe ribs and store them until the following season.

THE BOTTLE RADIATOR
In areas prone to late air frosts, this simple method can protect outdoor crops such as bush tomatoes. Fill a glass or plastic bottle with water and place it next to the plant. The sunlight will warm the water in the bottle, which will in turn release a gentle heat at night. This is sufficient to prevent cold shock to the plant and will ensure good growth and cropping. It can also be used in conjunction with a fleece covering to enhance the warming effect.

Left: *Old-fashioned cloches are particularly good for decorative vegetable gardens. However, they are also very expensive.*

Far left: *Upturned, clear plastic bottles with the bottoms cut out are ideal for using as mini-cloches, protecting individual plants. This is also an environmentally friendly technique.*

PLANT HEALTH

The main concern for new organic gardeners is that their plants
will be attacked by pests and diseases. There are various
techniques used to control these undesirables, although the
organic gardener must first learn to recognize signs of distress.
However, you are unlikely to experience more than a handful of the
problems described, all of which are relatively easy to solve. Pests,
for example, are eaten by creatures known as beneficials and so
the ecology of the garden, once stabilized, will be enough to keep
most problems at bay. There is always a technique to control more
persistent problems and so ensure the health of your plants.

WHY PLANTS GET SICK

Plants are prone to numerous ailments, some of which can be a serious threat to their survival. Pests and diseases are only one of the potential pitfalls that you will meet during a normal growing season. A basic knowledge of the other main factors that can affect plant health are all you will need to help your garden to flourish. While the sight of your plants suffering can be alarming, there are, in general, only a few potential health threats that you are likely to encounter.

Above: *Large blocks of the same type of plant are easy for pests to locate and are therefore prone to attack.*

FROST

This can cause serious problems and is actually more critical than average minimum temperatures. Most harmful are unexpected frosts that can cause severe damage even to hardy subjects, especially when they may have produced "soft" new growth.

While warm air rises, cold air will settle and collect in hollows and depressions. Cold air is laden with water vapour and is therefore heavier. Any valley or low-lying area is, therefore, a potential frost pocket. Cold air will accumulate in a depression and then back up the sloping sides as the build-up increases. Any barrier, such as a hedge or a wall, will obstruct the passage of the cold air and a frost pocket will form. Any plants growing in the vicinity will be exposed to the frost and may be damaged by it.

When the soil is frozen, water is no longer available to the plant and shallow-rooted plants are not able to access any water to replace that which they are losing through transpiration. The plant will dehydrate and the foliage will brown and shrivel. Ground frosts may also cause the soil to "heave" and plants will be lifted out of the ground.

Alternate freezing and thawing is often more damaging to the plant than the initial frost itself, especially for tender or half-hardy subjects such as bedding plants. Severe frost can split the bark on woody subjects and may also distort leaves.

The damage caused by frost is directly related to its duration. A temperature of -4°C (25°F) for one hour may cause little or no damage, while the same temperature for four hours may be disastrous.

WATERLOGGING AND DROUGHT

The build-up of water in the soil, particularly where this occurs over a prolonged period of time, can be highly detrimental to the health of your plants. This is of greatest concern with plants that are not adapted to such waterlogged conditions. As a result, the roots of the plants will suffer and probably die from asphyxiation.

Water shortage or drought only tends to occur during the summer months when temperatures and light intensity are at their peak. The most obvious sign of the effects of water shortage on a plant is when it wilts and loses its turgidity. Water shortage also causes plant functions to slow down dramatically and prolonged drought can result in permanent cell damage.

WIND

The effects of wind damage to plants, especially woody trees and shrubs, are sometimes only too obvious. Wind often worsens extremes of temperature and drought. In severe cases of wind damage, trees can be broken and shrubs uprooted. The stronger the wind, the more damage is likely to occur.

LIGHT IMBALANCES

A plant's growth is always directed towards the available light. Plants growing in shade often become drawn and etiolated. Conversely, strong sunlight damages plants by scorching the foliage. To prevent such problems it is best to select plants that will grow well in the prevailing site conditions.

NUTRIENT IMBALANCES

Plants exhibit varying symptoms to a nutrient imbalance depending, in general, upon the severity of the problem. Symptoms of deficiency may include stunted growth, discoloured leaves (including mottling and interveinal coloration), the premature death of leaves and parts of the plant, twisted and distorted growth and poor root growth and development.

Left: *Planting crops among companion plants will make it more difficult for pests to locate them.*

Right: *A healthy, flourishing border, which is free of pests and diseases, is the ultimate aim of all organic gardeners.*

The symptoms are usually noticed first on the shoot tips, although problems may appear on any part of the plant and in different stages of growth. Determining a cause may involve an analysis of the soil.

Any nutrient can be toxic to the plant if it is present in sufficiently high amounts or is out of balance with other elements in the growing medium.

POLLUTION

Specific symptoms of pollution may include leaves turning brown at the tips and margins, leaf discoloration or premature leaf fall. Growth may also be stunted.

Soil pollutant damage can be very severe and rapid in its effects on a plant and its growth. Common problems that you may encounter include extreme soil acidity or alkalinity, chemical toxicity, salt toxicity or pesticide residues. Of these, only soil acidity is relatively easy to cure. If serious pollution is suspected, then this requires specialist help. Such situations, however, are thankfully rare.

PESTS AND DISEASES

It is important to bear in mind that a certain level of pest and disease invasion is normal even on healthy crops. However, it is also true to say that healthy vigorous plants are more resistant to serious attack than plants that are growing under stress. The best form of pest and disease control is obviously prevention. You will need to be able to find and recognize a range of pests and diseases in order to prevent outbreaks of them in your garden and, if necessary, take prompt action.

Left: *Healthy plants are often the result of careful selection according to the site conditions.*

Right: *It is very important to recognize potential problems before your plants suffer too much damage.*

PREVENTING PROBLEMS

Organic gardening is about working with nature to create an environment in which plants can withstand attack from pests and diseases, without you resorting to the use of harmful insecticides. If plants become infested with pests or diseases, they may fail to give a good display and crop yields can suffer. Prevention is better than cure, and a keen eye and regular checks will help you to anticipate and prevent the worst of any potential problems.

Above: *A planting combination of roses and daisies will help to attract beneficial predators to the garden.*

GOOD CULTURAL PRACTICE AND HYGIENE

Many pests and diseases can survive without a susceptible host even under the most unfavourable conditions. Myriad plant diseases survive from one growing season to the next on plant debris, in the soil, on seeds or on alternate hosts (some pests and diseases affect different plant species at different times of the year e.g. peach-potato aphid). This means it is vital to remove and properly dispose of any infected plant materials. It is also important for the organic gardener to be aware of the diseases that can threaten an individual crop and recognize the conditions in which these potential threats to plant health can thrive.

GROW DISEASE-RESISTANT CULTIVARS

Plant varieties and cultivars were mostly chosen for other reasons than their disease-resistant qualities. Often they become so commonly grown that their diseases become widespread. Many plants have disease-resistant strains or cultivars, but this does not necessarily guarantee that they will be immune to a disease. However, they will be better able to resist the worst of its ravages.

Above: *Place straw under growing strawberries in order to protect them from rot and soil-dwelling pests.*

Above: *The regular washing down of the glass panes in a greenhouse can reduce the build-up of disease-causing organisms.*

Right: *Regular deadheading of old or damaged blooms will help to reduce the spread of some fungal diseases.*

AVOID PLANT STRESS

A plant that is stressed – by drought or an unfavourable temperature, for example – will be predisposed to pest or disease attack. Plants that are not subjected to higher levels of stress than they can cope with will remain healthy and better able to deal with potential attackers.

Stressed plants often show signs of physical disorders (e.g. being tall, drawn and pale due to lack of light). These can be due to the weather, being wrongly sited, nutrient imbalance or the presence of a toxic substance in the air or soil. Physically stressed plants may become sicker than if a pest- or disease-causing organism actually had invaded them. Stress can kill a plant if the problem is not quickly remedied.

RIGHT PLANT, RIGHT PLACE

Plants all have their preferred locations and the occurrence or lack of a particular environmental factor or factors will ultimately determine whether a plant will prosper in the position in which it has been

planted. Ferns, for example, need a cool moist site. Placing one in a hot sunny site will lead to its death as it struggles to keep its moisture. Plants that become stressed will neither grow as well, nor be as disease-resistant, as they would otherwise. Choosing an appropriate site in the first place will at least help to ensure the initial health of your plants and will render them more able to resist other potential threats to their health.

RECOGNIZING THE PROBLEM

Organic gardeners who understand pest life-cycles and behaviour are better able to determine when control will be most effective. Insects living in your garden are all part of nature's complex ecosystems and food chains. Less than one per cent of species that you are likely to encounter are considered pests. Since few insects are actually harmful, organic gardeners must learn which are pests, which are beneficials, and which ones will have no effect on the garden whatsoever.

Left: *Always choose plants that are suited to the site. Alkaline soils – indicated here by the pink flower of this hydrangea – will not suit certain plant species.*

damage to the plant begins to appear. Symptoms may be seen on any plant parts and include mottling, dwarfing, distortion, discoloration, wilting, shrivelling or holes and notching in the margins of leaves. The first signs of pest infestation may not appear until well after the insect has laid its eggs and disappeared.

Seeds or cuttings from infected plants will also transmit disease. Certified organic seed guarantees that at the time of sale the seeds are free of all diseases. Always try to obtain disease-free stock as this should guarantee that the plant is not infected and will not introduce disease into your garden. This is particularly important with plants such as roses as well as crop plants like raspberries and other small fruits.

Pest insects and mites may carry diseases that infect plants. Organic gardeners use the term "pest management" rather than pest control or pest eradication. It is impossible to eradicate pests from your garden completely. The best option is to try to keep pest numbers low in order to minimize the damage that they can cause in your garden.

ADOPT AN INTEGRATED STRATEGY

Organic gardeners must learn how to use a range of pest management techniques, such as introducing beneficial predators into their gardens (often referred to as biological controls), making gardens less attractive to harmful pests, and encouraging conditions in the garden that favour beneficial predators of all types (cultural controls).

Despite the fact that they are not always popular, insects play an important role in our gardens. Beneficial insects, such as bees, are necessary in the organic garden to pollinate fruit and some vegetable crops. Others, such as springtails, also help to break down dead plant tissue, while wasps and ground beetles capture and eat other pest insects and are called predators. Wasps and midges have larvae that attack pests by living inside their bodies and are called parasitoids. Organic gardeners must learn to cherish this "willing army" of helpers in their gardens.

PEST AND DISEASE CYCLES

Often gardeners believe that their plants have been attacked overnight. This may be true in the case of damping-off disease or with larger pests such as rabbits. More often, however, much has occurred before the symptoms are actually visible.

The pathogen (the pest- or disease-causing organism) must be introduced (inoculated) to the host plant. Most pathogens either move by themselves (as with most pests) or must be carried to the host plant (as with the vast majority of diseases). Rain, wind, insects, birds and people usually spread plant diseases.

Splashing rain carries spores of apple scab fungus from infected apple leaves to uninfected leaves. Wind blows fungal spores from plant to plant, while aphids and whiteflies transmit many common plant diseases. Believe it or not, smokers can transmit tobacco mosaic virus from a cigarette to tomato plants.

Once the pathogen has been transferred to the host plant, it begins to multiply, change or grow into a form that can then enter the host. In many fungal diseases, the pathogen arrives on the plant as a spore, which must germinate before it can begin to grow and invade the plant. Once the fungal spore germinates, it sends out thread-like tubes called hyphae. These penetrate the plant through wounds or natural pores in the outer skin of leaves, stems and roots. The roots of bedding plants that have been damaged during transplanting are a common entry point for root-rotting fungi. A single aphid that lands on a plant can give birth to a clone every twelve hours and can eventually form a small thriving colony within a few days, leaving the gardener with the impression that it suddenly appeared.

Once established, pests or diseases can grow or increase in number and begin damaging plant tissue. As they consume nutrients or plant tissue, evidence of the

Left: *Composting is the best way of recycling garden waste, but you must never compost material that is diseased.*

PLANT PESTS

Pests can be described as those creatures that harm your garden plants and, if left unchecked, they can quickly cause a great deal of damage. There is a huge army of these pests, but most organic gardeners are unlikely to encounter the vast majority of them. A basic knowledge of the commonest types that occur in domestic gardens is all that you should need to be familiar with in order to protect your plants and guarantee their health and successful growth.

Above: *Pests may well be present before symptoms appear. Close examination may reveal them before the plants start to suffer.*

HOW CAN YOU TELL IF A PEST IS A PROBLEM OR NOT?

Deciding whether a pest is a problem or not is very much a matter of opinion. Commercial growers assess the importance of a pest in terms of their financial losses. Domestic organic gardeners, however, tend to grow fewer plants or crops and mainly grow these for their beauty or for the pleasure of eating home-grown produce. The final decision as to the importance of a pest will rely upon the circumstances and experience of individual gardeners. All organic gardeners must be willing to accept a certain number of pests in their garden as these form part of the intricate food webs that result in natural control. If there are no pests, then the animals that eat them will disappear and open the door to future, potentially serious, pest outbreaks.

RECOGNIZING PESTS

It is important that you are able to accurately identify a pest that has been attacking your plants so that you can take the appropriate action. Just because an insect is seen walking on an affected plant does not mean that it is the one causing the damage. The only real way to control pests

involves getting to know them. Many pests produce characteristic symptoms that make it possible to diagnose the cause with relative certainty. Some have a wide range of host plants, and symptoms may not always be as conspicuous on all affected plants. Close examination – perhaps with a hand lens – may be necessary for the final diagnosis. With careful observation and experience, it is possible to keep one step ahead of the pests in your garden.

CONTROL OPTIONS

It is important to control pests before they become a problem. A single black bean aphid (*Aphis fabae*) that lands on a broad bean at the start of the summer could theoretically give rise to 2,000,000,000,000,000 aphids by the start of the autumn. This would be about a million tons of aphids. Numbers such as this are impossible but it does go to show that early control is essential. Quantities such as those quoted in the aphid example cannot occur as the food supply would run out before this can happen. In addition, a whole host of predators eat them. In just a few days, however, pests can cause considerable damage and quick action is

needed if you are to save your plants. Organic gardeners must employ a full range of control measures to ensure their plants survive this seasonal invasion, including cultural practices (crop rotation, good hygiene and encouraging biodiversity), physical controls (hand picking, traps, repellents and barriers) and biological control (using other animals that naturally eat pests). These are covered more extensively later in this section but for now it is important to stress that pests can only really be controlled by an integrated strategy that uses a variety of techniques.

CAN PESTS BE TOLERATED?

It is worth pointing out that we tend to be unduly concerned with pests damaging our plants. Supermarkets have conditioned us to expect blemish-free produce. We need to judge the overall health of a plant rather than react when we see a pest. If there were no pests in the garden, then there would be no predators. Step back and look at the whole picture and remember that everything, even pests, has its place in nature. They all add to the interest and diversity that is the most unique quality of an organic garden.

Above: *Birds can be serious pests in the garden. Here, large bites have been taken out of a brassica.*

Above: *Rabbits can devastate a garden overnight, leaving nothing but chewed off stumps as a result of their visit.*

Above: *Although fascinating to watch, squirrels are a garden pest and are closely related to rats.*

COMMON PESTS

There is a seemingly endless array of garden creatures that are waiting to devour and attack your garden plants. The most common pests are almost worldwide in their distribution, but they can be controlled relatively easily. It can be discouraging to see how many potential pests may attack your garden, but it is important to bear in mind that you will only encounter a handful of these in your gardening career.

PEST		PLANTS AT RISK	TREATMENT
Ants and termites		Ants are not really pests, but they "farm" aphids for sticky sugar. Termites can attack some woody species.	Few organic treatments, but baits based on borax are useful. Use a herbal spray of essential oil (citronella and lavender) or lukewarm water as a repellent.
Aphids		Most cultivated plants growing in the open, under glass or indoors.	Encourage beneficial insects to feed on them. Organic insecticidal soap can also be useful, particularly if the aphids are being "farmed" by ants.
Birds		Some birds will attack fruit and brassicas as well as brightly coloured flowers, including blossom.	Bird scarers may be employed as a deterrent and netting will also provide cover for individual crops and plants.
Cabbage root fly		The small maggots grow and develop on and within the roots of the developing cabbage plant.	Place a collar around newly planted seedlings, sinking it into the ground to prevent the newly hatched maggot from reaching the plant roots.
Carrot fly		These root-feeding maggots feed on carrots.	Try companion planting and avoid large monocultures of carrots. Erect plastic or fleece barriers, about 45–50cm (18–20in) high and 2–3m (6½–10ft) apart.
Caterpillars		Many different species of plant, especially those in the cabbage family.	Birds and other predators will reduce populations. Biological control, using a bacterial agent, and pesticides such as derris. Hand-pick off individual plants.
Chafers		Raspberries, strawberries, potatoes, lettuce, young trees, lawns and some herbaceous perennials.	Keep the ground weed-free, and well cultivated in order to reduce the number of bugs. Roll lawns in late spring.
Deer		Browse on garden plants. Male deer rub their antlers against trees, causing damage to the bark.	Notoriously difficult to control, often best kept out by fencing. Repellents are available, based upon formulae such as bear or even lion droppings.
Fruit flies		Troublesome on softer fruits in warm conditions, especially tomatoes.	Cover the fruit with a small piece of rag. Paper bags are also good to use, but can be difficult to get around a truss of tomatoes.
Gall mites and wasps		These pests affect a wide range of trees and shrubs, especially oak trees.	Generally not problematic or life-threatening. They are a good indicator of healthy biodiversity in a garden.
Leaf hoppers		There are many different types, affecting a wide range of plant species.	Difficult to control. Remove dead leaves to reduce overwintering eggs and nymphs. Encourage predators such as lacewings.
Leaf miners		There are many hundreds of species that all have their preferred host species.	Hand-picking of severely affected leaves. Biological controls exist but the problem is rarely serious enough to warrant their artificial introduction.
Leather-jackets		Can be a nuisance, especially of turf grass. They feed on roots just below the soil surface.	Can be difficult to control. Damp sacking over the soil can lure them up to the surface where they can be hand-picked or left for birds to eat.

PEST		PLANTS AT RISK	TREATMENT
Mealy bugs		Suck the sap of many species and produce a sticky honeydew that supports the growth of sooty moulds.	Biological controls are available. Cultural control is more difficult and involves drenching with an organic soap solution and then rinsing.
Mites		A common pest of many plants, especially those growing in hot dry conditions.	Biological controls are available. For a cultural control, improve humidity or spray foliage with an organic soap solution and then rinse.
Moles		Damage roots by lifting small newly planted trees. Tunnel under lawns, making them a serious pest.	Best controlled by trapping or using repellents. Sonic repellent devices are rarely effective. Removing one mole can simply "open the door" to another.
Nematodes (eelworms)		A few species cause disease-like symptoms. A problem when the same plants are grown in the same place.	Regular crop rotations can help to reduce damage. If numbers build up or plants become badly affected, avoid growing the affected species.
Rabbits and hares, squirrels, voles and mice		Rabbits gnaw shoots. Mice and voles eat small bulbs and corms in winter. They all ring-bark young trees.	They may be trapped or a variety of repellents are available. Tree and shrub shelters are useful against voles and mice as is fencing for rabbits and hares.
Sawflies		Developing larvae eat plant tissue. Fruit sawflies are notorious. Slugworm sawfly attack ornamentals.	Control slugworm by applying insecticidal soap. Control fruit sawfly larvae with derris. Both these treatments reduce numbers of beneficial insect predators.
Scale insects		Several species, some of which have specific host plants.	A cultural control consists of swabbing woody stems with a strong organic soap solution or pruning and removing affected parts.
Sciarid fly (fungus gnat)		Tiny flies that feed on soil fungus. The larvae attack the roots of young plants in water-logged potting mix.	Control by preventing the potting mix becoming too wet, although biological controls of nematodes are also available.
Slugs and snails		Common pests of a wide variety of plants. Snails, in particular, cause damage and defoliation of plants.	Often difficult to control although they can be caught in traps containing beer. A variety of barriers and deterrents are also available.
Thrips		Small insects suck the sap of soft foliage and attack flowers. Rarely a problem outside in cooler climates.	Remove seriously damaged foliage. Several natural predators (usually mites) are available for use against thrips.
Weevils		Larvae attack roots, stems or flowers and fruit of a range of plants. Adults feed on affected plants.	Wet acidic composts favour ground-living types such as vine weevil. Biological control possible with parasitic nematodes if temperatures sufficiently high.
Whiteflies		A greenhouse pest in cooler climates that may occur outside in warmer areas.	Biological controls are available but the best option can be to avoid growing susceptible species.
Woodlice (pill bugs)		Usually a pest indoors of crops like cucumbers. May chew through young seedlings.	Often more of an indication of poor hygiene than a problem in itself. A sign that you must clean up the greenhouse.

PLANT DISEASES

The early detection of plant disease can help to halt the widespread infestation of your crop. Try to establish a routine of regularly checking your plants and crops. Look closely for any telltale signs, using a hand lens if necessary. Remember that the first or most obvious symptom may not always be the only one or even the most important. Always check to see if there are other symptoms to ensure that you get the full picture before making your final diagnosis.

Above: *Modern rose varieties are highly susceptible to diseases such as blackspot and mildew.*

RECOGNIZING PLANT DISEASES

Vigilance is the key to success in controlling plant disease. Carefully inspect leaves, stems, roots, flowers and fruits for any sign of disease. You may even find it useful to cut open a branch or stem to look for problems such as discoloration of the tissue, which may explain leaf or stem wilting and sudden wilting of a section of or a whole plant.

Stand back and look at the overall picture. Consider the whole environment. This will include the weather, soil, the stage of development of the plant (and any pathogens present), cultural practices and the condition of other plants in the area. All of this information can help to indicate what may be wrong with the plant. Remember that a plant growing in the wrong location may be stressed.

Try to determine when the symptoms became apparent. The onset of a problem may be due to a cultural practice, the seasonal appearance of a disease or insect, or a weather-related event. Remember that long-term stress is slow to appear, taking a year or more at times.

Try to determine whether the problem is spreading, as this may indicate that it is a disease. Check whether plants of other species have been affected, as diseases are usually (but not always) species-specific. Problems caused by environmental factors do not spread, although the symptoms may become more severe.

You must know what the plant should look like in order to be able to recognize any abnormalities. Reading up a little on the species that you are growing in your garden can help you to make a more accurate diagnosis of the problem.

Remember that there is usually no single cause of a disease infestation. The primary cause may be associated with cultural or environmental conditions. And just as there is probably no single cause, there is usually no single symptom.

When you are attempting to diagnose the cause of plant illness, always inspect symptoms that appear on parts that are still alive (or at least partially alive). Dead plants are often invaded by secondary infestations of decomposer fungi, which may hide the original problem. If possible, make an examination of the entire plant, including roots, although this may not be possible for large specimens such as trees.

Left: *Although a plant may be in obvious distress, closer examination may be needed to properly determine the cause.*

Right: *Disease-causing organisms can enter a plant each time it is cut or pruned.*

CONTROL OPTIONS

Ultimately, where a serious disease is suspected, it may be advisable to avoid growing susceptible species altogether, or, in the case of fruit and vegetables, to rotate the crop as part of a regular cycle. Make notes that provide details on disease occurrence (the type of disease and when it appeared), the plants affected, the weather and environmental conditions in your garden each year. By doing this you can better anticipate what problems are likely to occur in your garden during the growing season.

Finally, remember that even the best gardeners lose plants to disease. This is only serious when large numbers of plants are affected. A diverse garden will contain other highlights, and diseases will claim only a fraction of the planting.

COMMON DISEASES

There are all kinds of diseases that can affect your plants. Most of these are mercifully rare, but every garden will suffer from its share of diseases during the growing season. Most of these conditions are relatively easy to deal with, but a correct diagnosis is essential. As always, it is preferable to try to prevent these diseases taking hold and spreading in the first place rather than treating them when they occur.

DISEASE	PLANTS AT RISK AND THE SYMPTOMS	TREATMENT
Bacterial canker	Many trees and shrubs. Reduces vigour and the rate of growth of the affected plant. Branches become girdled and die back. A sticky secretion will ooze from cracks or welts in the bark.	Difficult to control once a plant is infected. Confine the problem to one specimen by cleaning pruning tools between cuts and before moving on to another specimen of the same type.
Blackspot	A common fungal disease of roses, which is most prevalent on modern hybrid tea and floribunda types. Black spots appear, primarily on the leaves and sometimes on the stems as well.	Prune bush roses into a goblet shape. Use disease-resistant cultivars. Dust affected plants with sulphur early and intermittently throughout the growing season.
Bracket fungus	This disease can affect all types of tree. Bracket fungi are the fruiting bodies of fungi that either parasitize healthy heart wood or, more commonly, decay heart wood that is already dead.	Many affected trees live for many years and need only be felled if they present a risk of collapse.
Common scab of apple	A bacterial disease that causes the formation of large (albeit harmless) scabs on the surface of the apples. Commonly encountered in damp weather and on trees with crowded branches.	Rake up and dispose of affected leaves. Prune out cracked or scabby shoots to remove places for the fungus to overwinter.
Coral spot	A common fungus affecting many woody plant species. Appears as pink or bright red, raised pustules on wood that is showing signs of dieback.	Prune out infected tissue and destroy it. Regular "hygienic pruning" can help to prevent it taking hold in the first place.
Downy mildew	A group of fungal diseases that affects a wide range of plants. Appears as a white coating over leaves that display distended growth, browning and wilting. Thrives in warm moist conditions.	Dust with sulphur or spray with Bordeaux mixture to form a protective barrier against the spores. Note that these are both easily washed off by watering or rain.
Fireblight	Attacks plants of the Rosaceae family, notably apples, pears, plums, cherries, pyracanthas, cotoneasters and roses. The affected plant dies back rapidly from the branch tip.	Remove and destroy all affected material, cutting back to at least 50cm (20in) below the point of infection. Best to remove diseased plants, replacing them with a non-susceptible tree or shrub.
Fungal canker	Affects many woody plants. The bark tissue begins to peel and flake away around the affected tissue in concentric rings.	Prune out the affected material, about 15cm (6in) below the point of infection, and burn it. Clean tools with disinfectant between cuts and especially between pruning individual plants.
Honey fungus	A soil-dwelling fungus that parasitizes the roots of woody plants. Leaves tend to discolour and wilt and fail to develop in the spring. Ultimately, this can weaken and kill the plant.	Difficult to control organically. It may be best to grow herbaceous plants in affected areas for two to three years before attempting to replant woody plants there.
Mosaic virus	This group of viruses affects a very large number of species and is characterized by an irregular, angular mottling or streaking of the leaves.	Winged insects that feed on plants, then migrate to another, can rapidly spread the virus. Control the pests themselves where possible.
Phytophthora	A soil-borne fungal disease that affects many species of woody plants, particularly conifers. Branches die back, often very quickly. Serious infection may cause death for a large proportion of the root system and severe dieback of top growth.	There is no cure for this condition and the removal of badly affected plants may be the only answer. The disease is often restricted to damp or heavy soils, although prolonged wet weather can result in outbreaks.
Powdery mildew	Affects many plant species, with asters being especially prone. The leaves become covered with white powdery patches that may distort growth or even cause leaf drop in severe cases. Thrives in warm, humid or wet conditions.	Sulphur and Bordeaux mixture can provide protection, but these are easily washed off in wet conditions. Avoid growing susceptible species if conditions favour the spread of the disease.
Rust	A common fungal disease affecting many species. Characterized by rusty coloured patches or spots, known as pustules, on leaves. Tissue around the pustules yellows and dies, and this, in turn, may distort growth or cause leaf drop in severe cases.	Commonly seen on soils rich in nitrogen. It may have a noticeable effect on seasonal crops or those grown for their leaves. Bordeaux mixture can reduce its spread but it is difficult to control completely. Avoid susceptible crops and varieties if the problem is persistent.
Silverleaf	Affects both fruiting and ornamental species of *Prunus*. The leaves on some branches gain a silvery sheen, gradually dying back a year or two later. A purple fungal growth appears on the dead tissue.	The affected wood should be pruned out below the point of infection and disposed of in late summer after fruit has set. Badly infected specimens should be removed completely and disposed of, preferably by burning.
Stem rot	Attacks trees and larger woody plants. Stems and branches gradually become hollow.	Smaller trees or shrubs may be much more seriously affected and may be best removed if their condition deteriorates too much.

PLANT DISORDERS

Many external factors can affect garden plants. Weather seldom does what we want it to – there is either too little or too much rain or it is too cold or too hot. If you combine these climatic disappointments with other factors that can affect your plants, such as pollution or nutrient deficiencies, you will see why these difficult conditions can produce a number of disease-like symptoms. They can all put severe stress on an ornamental plant or crop and so precipitate attack from living organisms.

Above: *Nutrient deficiencies can cause discoloration of the leaves. This plant is short of magnesium.*

RECOGNIZING DISORDERS

Plants can be susceptible to a long list of outside forces. Extremes of weather, nutrient deficiencies and physical damage can all take their toll on the health and vigour of a plant. Other environmental factors, such as too much or too little water or pollutants in the soil, can also encourage disease-like symptoms.

Soil pollution can be caused by nutrient deficiency, misapplied fertilizer (resulting in too much nutrient and, therefore, toxicity), spilt lawnmower fuel (perhaps due to careless filling) or buried inert material. Airborne pollution can be more insidious and more difficult to determine or detect.

Weather events such as high winds or frost may go unnoticed if you are not there to witness them. A huge storm will leave evidence in its wake. The effect of a sharp early morning frost, however, or a steady drying wind on a sunny afternoon may not show the damage caused until several days have passed. Often frost occurs in the hours just before daybreak and quickly disappears to leave a fine sunny morning.

Disease can result from a combination of factors, affecting growing conditions and actual disease-causing organisms. Plants may initially be placed under stress – by high winds or frost, for example – making them vulnerable to attack by living agents. For instance, drought may damage roots, which in turn renders them more liable to infection by fungal diseases.

It is important to determine whether the distress that your plant is suffering is the result of a pathogen or due to a problem in the environment. In order to work out which of these is responsible, look to see if the occurrence of ill health is random or uniform in terms of its distribution. As a general rule of thumb, randomly distributed symptoms on injured plants are usually caused by a living factor, such as infectious diseases or a pest. In addition to this, infestations, particularly those caused by diseases, tend to radiate out from central points. Uniform patterns are generally associated with non-living or non-infectious agents such as poisons, fertilizers, environmental stress or mechanical damage.

Above: *Drought is a common cause of stress in potted plants, damaging both roots and shoots.*

CONTROL OPTIONS

If the cause of the problem is physical, you will need to find out whether it is due to a recurring environmental factor inherent in the site, such as constant buffeting by strong winds, or whether it is caused by "one-off" events such as unseasonable frosts or contamination from a careless neighbour's weedkiller spray. Some factors can be removed, such as polluted soil, and windbreaks can be planted and fleece draped over tender specimens on cold nights. If plants continue to be affected, it could be that the plant is in the wrong place and you may have to try it elsewhere.

Left: *Plants sometimes show unusual growth patterns in response to environmental conditions. Here, the growth of a tree has been affected by the wind.*

COMMON DISORDERS

Disorders are the result of either an imbalance of essential nutrients or of a range of stresses that are caused by adverse or difficult environmental conditions. Many of the disorders and conditions described here can resemble diseases. This means that is very important for you to diagnose the cause of the distress in the plant before taking any remedial action. A plant disorder will call for a different response to a plant disease.

CONDITION		PROBABLE CAUSE	TREATMENT
Bare patches or areas of poor plant establishment		The patchy establishment of cover crops or turf can be due to soil compaction or underground obstructions. Soil can easily become compacted if it is walked on a lot, particularly when it is wet. Buried obstructions such as rubble can also cause similar growth distortions.	Remove all buried rubble prior to planting or replanting. Relieve compaction by cultivating and replant if required.
Blackening of leaf tips		Usually the result of overwatering, particularly with container-grown plants. The waterlogged soil or potting mix forces oxygen out of the soil, thereby suffocating the roots which suffer a form of drought-stress.	Do not water until the soil or potting mix dries out a little. Check to see if plants need watering before doing so.
Etiolation		Sun-loving plants kept in low light conditions quickly become starved and will be significantly weakened. If kept in these conditions for any length of time, the plant will eventually die.	Choose specimens that are appropriate for the light levels in the garden.
Leaf blackening		Frost damage on buds and leaves in early spring, even to hardy specimens, is usually noticed on new growth that has not yet become acclimatized. It is the sudden shock that often causes the problem, not the actual temperature itself.	Cover slightly tender plants with fleece in the winter. Lightly spray plants with water in the evening to help protect against late frosts.
Leaf scorch		High winds and bright sunlight, especially on shade-loving species. Some plants can also be damaged by watering in bright sunlight, by providing too little or too much water or by applying too much fertilizer to the soil. Hail can also cause leaf spotting or holes.	Water in the evening. Choose wind-resistant species, if appropriate. Apply fertilizer at recommended rates. Do not over- or under-water plants.
Mechanical or physical damage		High winds, which are especially damaging to deciduous woody plants in full leaf. Herbaceous plants can easily break if not adequately staked, as may newly planted trees and shrubs. Snow can snap the branches of conifers and evergreens. Visiting animals can also flatten or snap garden plants.	Stake plants firmly and ensure that animals are excluded from areas where plants could be damaged.
Nutrient deficiency		A lack of or too much of a particular nutrient. Nutrients can also become in short supply if other nutrients are present in large amounts.	Deficiencies are best treated with the application of fertilizer or choose plants that are adapted to deal with the site conditions.
Poisoned ground		Leaked fuel or lubricants used in construction work can leave the ground contaminated. This is usually more of a problem in gardens attached to modern houses. Underground gas pipes can leak, flooding the ground with gas that is lethal to plant roots. Other chemical spillages could come from machinery such as a lawnmower.	Remove all affected soil and replace with fresh topsoil. If pipes are leaking, make sure that they are fixed before replacing soil. Fill lawnmowers with fuel over a plastic sheet.
Root girdling		This can cause instability and the collapse of larger trees and shrubs. Tree and shrub roots become woody following the first year's growth and, if these are constrained in round pots, they tend to grow in spirals.	Try to use bare-rooted stock whenever possible. Tease out roots from the rootball immediately prior to planting.
Wilting		A normal response in many plants to either a lack of water or high temperatures, and not necessarily a cause for great concern. Ligularias habitually wilt on hot summer afternoons, even when planted in wet ground, only to "pick up" and show no ill effects later.	Treatment may not always be necessary. Check the soil first to see if it is dry. If not, wait until the evening to see if the plant shows any signs of improvement.

BENEFICIAL PREDATORS

A thriving population of natural predators and parasites can significantly help to keep pest populations down. The organic gardener must strive to create and maintain an environment in which these welcome visitors to the garden or greenhouse can prosper. Above all, this means avoiding pesticides, which can wipe out beneficial predators and so upset the natural balance in the garden or greenhouse.

Above: *Creating a diverse range of habitats, including a pond, in your garden will encourage beneficial predators.*

BIOLOGICAL CONTROLS

Nearly every species of plant-feeding insect has another insect that is its predator or parasite. Some pests, such as aphids, are eaten by ladybirds (ladybugs), hoverflies and midge larvae, parasitized by wasps and infested by fungal diseases. Large pest populations are a food larder for many "natural enemies", including carnivorous animals, parasites and diseases.

Biological methods of control use these natural enemies of pest insects to keep their populations under control. It is like having an army of insects and other creatures doing the work for you. Biological controls can be encouraged into the garden by creating a suitable habitat. Ironically, this means that the pests must be present first. They must also be present in sufficient numbers to support a viable population of the beneficial predator. This can be a complex area and the easiest way is to encourage the conditions that will favour a balanced food web to develop. Purchasing beneficials is only generally recommended for use in greenhouses although a few (particularly microbes) are suitable for use outdoors.

Above: *Biological controls are a successful way to fight pests. They are mainly used in greenhouses, but others are now becoming available for the open garden. The control insects are released, here from a sachet, in order to attact the pests.*

CREATING SUITABLE HABITATS

The easiest way to achieve this is to get a mixture of habitats. The more variety your garden has, the more biodiversity it will support. Ponds, long grass, log piles, and food plants for animals with varied tastes all encourage a stable garden ecosystem where pests are kept at relatively low levels.

Many birds and bats eat insects. Bats need a roosting site, so place a purpose-made bat box on the shady side of a tree. Position the box at least 3m (10ft) high with a clear airspace in front. Night-scented flowers encourage the moths that bats feed upon. This is the key. The predators must be able to live in your garden or they will go and find a more suitable habitat elsewhere.

The longer you garden organically, the more balance will appear in your garden. This is simply because your garden ecosystem begins to stabilize and diversify over time.

BENEFICIAL INSECTS

Predators (those that devour pests directly) and parasitic insects (those whose young hatch inside and devour pests) are often termed "beneficials". Predators include lacewings and wasps. Parasitic insects

Above: *Log piles encourage beneficial predators such as beetles to colonize and take shelter in your garden.*

(more correctly termed parasitoids) are less well known than predators, but equally effective. They lay their eggs in a pest species. When the eggs hatch, the larvae feed on the pest insect, killing it. The majority of these insects are tiny wasps, although some flies and mites also fall under this category. Learning to recognize beneficial insects is crucial if you want to avoid killing your army of garden helpers.

BENEFICIAL PREDATORS IN THE GARDEN

There are many beneficial predators that will willingly take up residence in your garden and help to control populations of pests in a natural way.

- Anthocorid bug or red kneed capsid
- Bats
- Birds (robin, blue tit and thrush)
- Centipedes
- Earwigs
- Frogs, toads and newts
- Ground beetle

- Harvestman
- Hedgehogs
- Hoverflies
- Lacewings (adult or larva)
- Ladybirds (ladybugs)
- Mites e.g. *Phytoseiulus*
- Nematodes e.g. *Heterorhabditis*

- Parasitic wasps (*Encarsia* or *Aphidoletes*)
- Slow worm
- Spider on web or wolf spider
- Tachinid flies
- Wasps (solitary and social)

BIOLOGICAL CONTROLS IN THE GREENHOUSE OR GARDEN

The application of biological controls in the greenhouse or garden involves using predatory insects or other beneficial animals to control commonly occurring pests. Many pests are only a problem because their natural predators are missing from the garden. Introducing a biological control usually results in the rapid control of the pest.

NAME	PREFERRED TEMPERATURE RANGE	WHAT THEY CONTROL
Amblyseus cucumeris (predatory mite)	25°C (77°F)	The nymphal forms and adults consume large quantities of immature thrips.
Aphidoletes aphidimyza (predatory midge larva)	21°C (70°F); needs 80%+ humidity	Tiny mosquito-like midge larvae that control substantial populations of more than 60 species of aphids.
Cryptolaemus montrouzieri (predatory beetle)	20–25°C (68–77°F); needs 70%+ humidity	This ladybird is effective in controlling mealybugs on houseplants and in greenhouses.
Encarsia formosa (parasitic wasp)	18–25°C (64–77°F)	Minute, flying parasitic wasps, which lay their eggs inside whitefly scales (the pupa stage) and eat them in two to four weeks
Heterorhabditis megidis (parasitic nematode)	Minimum soil temperature of 14°C (57°F). If temperature drops below 20°C (68°F), they become less effective.	Patrol the soil to a depth of about 18cm (7in) and quickly take care of the slow-moving grubs, like vine weevil grubs and chafers. Very effective in pots and containers. Soil must be moist.
Metaphycus helvolus (parasitic wasp)	20–30°C (68–86°F)	These tiny, black and yellow wasps are effective against several soft-scale species, including brown scale. The females lay their eggs under the body of first- and second-stage scales. The grubs feed on scales and develop into adults within two weeks. Adults also provide control by feeding on non-parasitized scales. *Metaphycus* are most effective in semi-tropical conditions.
Phasmarhabditis hermaphrodita (parasitic nematode)	Minimum soil temperature of 5°C (40°F)	Useful for slug control. Should be applied during the early growing stages of vulnerable plants. Needs moist soil.
Phytoseiulus persimilis (predatory mite)	Use once temperature is regularly above 15°C (60°F). Best at 18–25°C (64–77°F); needs 60%+ humidity	Predator mites, slightly larger than the two-spotted mites (also known as red spider mites) upon which they feed.
Steinernema feltiae (parasitic nematode)	Minimum temperature of 10°C (50°F), although they remain effective when the soil temperature drops below this.	Aggressive predators used to control fungus gnats, mushroom flies and leatherjackets. They can be used on lawns as well as in flower and vegetable gardens, fields, orchards and greenhouses.

Above: *Ladybirds (ladybugs) are just one of the many beneficial insects that will help to keep garden pests in check.*

MICROBES

Bacteria, fungi, viruses, protozoans and parasitic nematodes are microorganisms that attack insects. These microscopic hordes are generally effective against very specific pests and present little risk to humans and the environment. Many organic gardeners may well be familiar with a popularly known, microbial-based insecticide known as Bt or *Bacillus thuringiensis*. This commonly available product, which is used to kill many different kinds of moth and butterfly larvae, is a bacterium. It produces a toxin that kills specific caterpillars. The larval pest usually dies within four to seven days. There are many strains of Bt, each type controlling specific pests.

Parasitic nematodes are also very effective against certain pests that live in the soil. However, the nematodes require moist conditions in order to survive and their temperature requirements further limit their use to greenhouses in many cases.

Despite their potential, very few fungi, viruses and protozoa are commercially available because these living organisms are difficult to raise, store and apply. The best way to encourage these willing and tiny helpers into your garden is to maintain a healthy soil that is rich and diverse in terms of the life it contains.

Above: *Providing convenient shelter, such as this lacewing hotel, for beneficial insects can help to increase their numbers.*

OTHER CONTROL METHODS

There are many ways of dealing with the different pests that appear in the garden. Some of these methods have been tried and tested for generations, others are individual to the gardener and are often the result of a happy accident. As an organic gardener, you must learn to use as many different tricks as possible to manage the pests in your garden and to protect your plants.

Above: *Companion plants such as these marigolds confuse or deter pests that would otherwise attack garden plants.*

GOOD GARDENING PRACTICE

The selection and culture of plants can reduce the potential for pests and diseases. Cultural practices are methods the organic gardener can use to change environmental factors that affect plants and their pest populations. It is essential, therefore, that gardeners know the cultural or growing requirements of each plant. Providing the correct conditions results in a vigorous plant that is less likely to be attacked by pests and diseases and can tolerate some damage.

ASSESSING THE DAMAGE

When problems do arise, you must decide whether a pest is causing enough damage to warrant control. In other words, you will

Left: *Slugs and snails are notorious garden pests that are easily kept at bay using a water trap.*

Above: *Compact discs are an unusual and amusing way of scaring away marauding birds from your crops.*

need to assess how far the problem can be tolerated before action is necessary. Some form of pest damage is inevitable with any crop, but you will need to establish limits. To do this, you will need to take into consideration the amount of damage that can be tolerated, the numbers of an individual pest that can cause significant damage and the plants' stage of development. The health and vigour of the plant can also have a direct bearing on when or if you need to take action. A few holes on a leaf may not require control, but, if most of the leaf has been eaten, the plant may die.

TAKING ACTION

Monitor your plants to determine when action is necessary. A thorough inspection of the plant allows you to identify a problem before major damage occurs. You should also inspect the plant's entire environment for clues to the problem. Observing and keeping records of weather conditions, for example, can help provide clues to growth patterns and problems.

TYPES OF CONTROL

Control options can be arranged by their mode of action and their impact on the environment. These methods of control can be grouped from least to highest impact: cultural and mechanical controls; and "permitted" chemical controls (soaps, oils and botanical insecticides).

Cultural control includes hand removal of larger pests, the use of screens, barriers, and traps, freezing and crushing. These methods generally have little or no negative effect on the environment and are particularly suitable for smaller gardens.

COMPANION PLANTING

This is commonly used to protect plants from pest attack. The theory is that the companion plants – flowers growing next to a food crop, for example – disrupt the searching pattern of the pests looking for host plants. They literally smell these hosts but become confused with the more diverse planting style. Separating rows of cabbages, broccoli or other brassicas with rows of onions has always been a popular combination, possibly because the onion's strong scent confuses cabbage pests. Tomato plants also grow well next to cabbages and seem to deter caterpillars while growing leeks near carrots repels carrot flies.

SCREENS AND BARRIERS

Any material that is fine enough to keep pests out can be used as a barrier. A variety of screens of different mesh sizes can keep out large insects, birds and rabbits, but they can also prevent pollinating insects from reaching a plant, resulting in lack of fruit. Cardboard and metal collars will prevent cutworms from reaching young transplants. Sticky bands placed on tree trunks trap beetles and soil-hibernating pests. Copper strips are available for slug control. These supposedly react with the slugs' slime to shock them. Sharp particles, such as crushed eggshells, are also used to control slugs.

TRAPS

Certain insect pests can be monitored by using traps. Sticky coloured traps, pheromone traps and pitfall traps (like beer traps for slugs) can all be used to monitor the occurrence of some pests. Whiteflies and aphids are attracted to bright yellow, and this colour is used for sticky cards upon which they become trapped.

You may want to apply a control and then enclose the plants in netting to keep further infestation from occurring – perhaps putting up netting and then releasing predators.

Traps usually serve as a monitoring system, warning of the presence or

increase in undesirable pest numbers. Traps can also be useful in timing control measures by showing the presence of migrating or emerging adults. The control measure can then be introduced at the best time to control the particular pest. Codling moth traps for use in orchards are a good example of this. They are sometimes used to control numbers, but most types are limited in their real effectiveness. Yellow, sticky traps attract whiteflies, aphids, thrips, leafhoppers and other small flying insects. Traps that use pheromones or attractive scents to tantalize adult insects are best used as a way to check presence and numbers. Pitfall traps can be cups or jars placed into the ground filled with yeast and water or beer to trap slugs.

WATER

A jet of water from a hose washes aphids, spider mites and other small insects from plant foliage. This must be done frequently since it does not kill insects or eggs and it does not prevent some insects from crawling back on to plants.

INSECTICIDAL SOAPS

These are made from the salts of fatty acids. Fatty acids are components of the fats and oils found in plants and animals. These soaps should not be confused with ordinary cleaning soaps. Insecticidal soaps kill only what they touch and are effective against soft-bodied pests such as aphids, thrips, crawler stage scales, whiteflies, leafhoppers and mites. Insecticidal soaps may cause burning on some plants, particularly those with hairy leaves. Test

Above: *Birds can be dissuaded from attacking your plants by stretching string and shiny foil over the crops.*

insecticidal soap on a single leaf if you are unsure – burning will usually occur within 24 hours.

BOTANICAL INSECTICIDES

Derived from plants, botanical insecticides include pyrethrum, citrus oil extracts and the extract of the neem tree. They act rapidly to stop feeding by insects, although they may not kill the pest for hours or days. There are also disadvantages to the use of botanicals. They must be applied frequently, may be difficult to obtain, and, although generally less toxic than many pesticides, they are still toxic and may harm other beneficial garden residents.

Above: *Sticky traps are another form of pest control in greenhouses. Here, pheromones attract pests to the trap where they get stuck. Other traps consist of sheets of plastic covered with a non-drying glue.*

Above: *Horticultural fleece, which is stretched over developing young plants, can provide a physical barrier against smaller pests such as flying insects.*

TRAPS, BARRIERS AND DETERRENTS

The prevention of pest and disease attacks is an essential part of organic gardening. Plants that are infected by pests or diseases are weaker specimens that are difficult to treat and never quite recover their former vigour. Many garden pests can be trapped or kept at bay using relatively inexpensive materials and sometimes recycled household items. Put the barriers in place when the plants are young and always ensure that pests are not trapped inside the barrier.

CONTROL METHOD	HOW IT WORKS
Beer traps and deterrents (granules, copper strips and greasebands)	Traps are effective ways of both controlling pests, such as slugs, and finding out which ones you actually have. Deterrents are physical barriers over which the pest cannot or will not pass. There are many types and their effectiveness can vary.
Bug nets in the greenhouse	Greenhouse vents are problematic in terms of pest control in that they allow both pests in and purchased biological controls out. Bug nets are put in place to avoid this happening.
Fleece on frames	Frames covered in horticultural fleece can be used over outdoor crops to help keep pests out and control the temperature.
Fleece stretched over a crop	Fleece can be used to create a favourable microclimate around young plants. It also acts as a barrier to airborne pests. On the downside, however, it can also keep out airborne predators from pests that overwinter in the soil.
Fruit nets over fruit	Fruit nets are especially useful for summer soft fruit crops that can quickly be devastated by birds.
Individual cloches	Cloches can act as barriers to a wide variety of airborne pests. Any pests that are sealed into this environment may, however, find the perfect environment within which to thrive.
Mesh cages for trees	Mesh cages are usually used to keep rabbits and hares at bay. They are usually simple constructions formed from three or more stakes driven into the ground with chicken wire (or similar) attached to them.
Rabbit fencing	A continuous barrier to prevent rabbits entering areas where plants are growing. The base of the wire should be buried below ground level to prevent the rabbits burrowing a passage beneath it.
Bird scarers (e.g. scarecrows)	Bird scarers have the drawback of a limited lifespan before the birds learn that they are not a real threat. They can, of course, be changed and most bird scarers are only needed on a seasonal basis.
String or wire netting stretched over seedlings (e.g. peas)	Aerial barriers can protect against bird attack. They may only be needed for the duration of the crop's life or even less.
Traps (sticky, coloured traps used in the greenhouse)	Sticky traps can provide a certain degree of control against the flying adults of insect pests. However, they are not as effective as they are sometimes thought to be and are, in fact, of more use for showing whether a particular pest is present or not, thereby allowing appropriate control measures to be put in place.
Traps (pheromone)	Pheromone traps are used to detect the presence of insects. The pheromones attract members of the opposite sex and the appearance of the target species allows you to begin looking for and controlling the young that cause the damage.
Tree guards (spiral)	Spiral guards are useful for protecting the bark of newly planted trees from rabbits and hares, especially in winter and early spring. These guards expand as the tree develops, but they are best removed completely after about a year.
Tree shelter	These protect newly planted trees from vertebrate pests and from the worst rigours of the environment by providing a favourable microclimate around them. They naturally degrade under the action of sunlight, but are best removed after two to three years.
Twiggy branches over plants	Arched over young plants, these can be an effective deterrent to pests such as birds and cats. They do not prevent the migration of beneficial predators to the plants.

Above: *Slugs and snails can be caught in a trap that is filled with stale beer, or water that has been mixed with yeast.*

Above: *Ring tunnels that are covered in a fine mesh will prevent flying insects from attacking your crops.*

Above: *Plastic netting, stretched over the crop and carefully secured, provides an effective barrier against birds.*

Above: *Old plastic bottles make an ideal barrier to protect young plants from pests. These are cheaper than traditional cloches.*

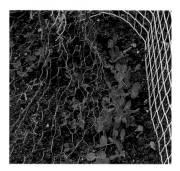

Above: *Chicken wire, stretched over young plants, will prevent birds from reaching and eating them.*

ORGANIC PESTICIDES

While most pesticides are not used in organic gardens, some naturally occurring substances can be used to protect your plants from pests and diseases. The pesticides which you are allowed to use in an organic garden should only be applied when necessary and not on a regular basis.

ORGANIC PESTICIDE	HOW IT WORKS
Bacillus thuringiensis	These are bacterial spores that produce a toxic protein that is useful against caterpillars but will not cause any harm to beneficials. *Bacillus thuringiensis* works quickly, paralysing the caterpillar and so preventing any further damage, although it quickly degrades in sunlight and needs frequent re-application throughout the growing season.
Bordeaux mixture	A compound containing copper and sulphur used to control various fungal diseases including apple scab and potato blight. It is harmful to fish and livestock, and frequent use can lead to a build up of copper in the soil that can be harmful to worms.
Derris	A chemical extracted from the roots of the derris and longocarpus plants. It is useful against a variety of insects including aphids, caterpillars, sawflies and plant-eating beetles. It can prove harmful to beneficials, although it is not a threat to bees.
Insecticidal soap	This is not soap, like the domestic washing soap, but is made from the salts of fatty acids, extracted from plant material. It can be effective against a wide variety of insect pests, although it can damage sensitive plant species.
Plant oils	Their effectiveness varies but most depend upon coming into contact with the pest itself and suffocating it, although some, like neem tree oil, do appear to have insecticidal properties.
Pyrethrum	This organic pesticide is extracted from the flower-heads of *Chrysanthemum cinerariifolium* and is especially effective in controlling aphids. However, it does not persist for long and can also cause harm to beneficial insects.
Sulphur	An effective fungicide against a variety of plant fungi, including powdery mildew, greymould and blackspot. Sulphur can also prove harmful to predatory mites and can cause damage to certain sensitive species.

Above: *Tree shelters and quills protect trees from rabbits and voles, and also provide an ideal growing environment for the tree.*

Above: *Scarecrows are an attractive method of deterring birds and occasionally large pests away from your vegetable garden. They should be moved around the garden and redressed so that the birds do not get too accustomed to them.*

THE ORNAMENTAL GARDEN

Unlike the more fleeting nature of crops in the kitchen garden, the plants in the ornamental garden are usually permanent, which means that a stable ecology may be set up very easily. In fact, lawns, shrubs, trees and flower beds can all be adapted to organic culture. The ornamental garden needs flair and imagination, not only in its design and construction, but also in the types of materials it uses; there is little point in creating an organic garden with materials that have been treated with toxic chemicals and wood that was logged from a tropical rainforest.

THE GARDEN FRAMEWORK

It would be a great shame if we spent a lot of time and effort creating an organic garden, only to find that we had done so at the expense of another habitat or the wider environment. A truly organic approach to gardening should extend beyond the way we grow the plants and maintain the beds and borders to include all the elements of the garden, from the hardscaping materials to the furniture.

Above: *A natural dry-stone wall – assembled without mortar – can quickly become colonized with showy flowers.*

ECOLOGICALLY SOUND MATERIALS

Pictures of logged rainforests, eroded soils and drought-ravaged landscapes are all too familiar. So familiar, in fact, that we run the risk of becoming immune to their shocking truth. Many habitats around the world face increasing pressure from human activities. While there is often little we can do as individuals, we can at least try not to contribute to the demise of such habitats. Rainforests, the source of much of the wood used for garden furniture, are often clear felled, resulting in the loss of much of the biodiversity that they contain.

For this reason, it is important that we use ecologically sound materials. Numerous suppliers claim that they offer ecologically sound products, gathered from sustainable sources. You should check the ecological credentials of the items you buy wherever possible. Buying materials from local sources can help. Always ask who the supplier is, where the materials come from and how their extraction impacts upon the environment. Rocks for alpine gardens, wood for posts and fences, mulch material and potting mixes can all be detrimental to the environment if not carefully sourced.

It is also worth finding out what chemical treatments the material has undergone. Some wood is treated with preservative that may leach out into the soil given time. Potting mixes that are purchased may also contain chemical additives.

Even when products are environmentally sound, it is always worth finding out if the same material (or one that is sufficiently similar) is available from a local source. Transporting materials over great distances, particularly those that are bulky or heavy, involves the use of a considerable amount of fossil fuel. One of the cornerstones of sustainability is to think globally while acting locally. It may even be possible to see the products being made if you do buy from local sources.

Ultimately, of course, the closest source is that which you produce yourself in your own garden. Any organic gardener should, therefore, aim to be as self-sufficient as possible.

PLANTS SUITABLE FOR COPPICING

Most broadleaved trees can be used for coppicing, although some are more suitable than others as the rate of growth varies so widely.

In general, most conifers are not suitable for coppicing because they do not readily re-grow from a stump.

PLANT SPECIES	SITE	POTENTIAL USES
Wattle (*Acacia*)	Warm dry situations with good drainage. Especially tolerant of low fertility.	Hurdles and barriers (wattlework). Excellent in warmer climates where other weaving species will not prosper.
Gum (*Eucalyptus*)	Hot dry situations especially where soil is well drained and seasonally dry.	Durable fence posts, stakes and young ornamental growth.
Willow (*Salix*)	Tolerant of wet situations and heavy soils. The roots are notoriously aggressive and may damage nearby drains or foundations.	Weaving work, building and fencing. In a small garden, dogwood is a good substitute for weaving work.
Hazel (*Corylus avellana*)	Any garden soil with good drainage and a pH over 6.5. Tolerates frost, shade, and exposure.	Wattle work, weaving, pea and bean sticks.
Sweet chestnut (*Castanea sativa*)	Light, slightly moist, acid garden soils. Protect from frost and exposure.	Wattlework and fence construction.
Dogwood (*Cornus*)	Most garden soils but dislikes exposure and can sucker aggressively.	Red, orange or lime-green shoots suitable for basketry and other fine rustic weaving work.
Elder (*Sambucus*)	An adaptable species that will thrive in a variety of situations.	Twigs are useful for a number of garden projects and the berries and flowers can be used to make wines and cordials.
Honeysuckle (*Lonicera*)	Likes most soils and thrives with the roots in shade and the topgrowth in full sun.	Stems are a traditional basketry material.

USING RECYCLED MATERIALS

Recycling plays an important role in the organic garden. Waste materials from the kitchen and garden are added to the compost heap; plastic bottles can become mini cloches; and old carpet makes a useful protective cover. Old building materials, such as bricks, slabs, quarried stone and wooden railway sleepers (ties), can all be re-used in the garden.

SUSTAINABLE DESIGN

The more self-sustaining your garden is the better. Gardens that rely heavily upon recycled material – compost, leaf mould and pea sticks, for example – produced within their own confines are naturally self-sustaining. Some external input will always be needed but the garden's long-term success is assured. In short, you will have a sustainable organic garden.

BIO-ENGINEERING YOUR PLOT

This term describes the use of living material to construct the garden framework. It ensures that you make the most of the natural capabilities of some plant species, such as willow, that have been used for centuries for building and fencing. Other examples include using grass for stabilizing soil on slopes or woody plants for hedging. Living barriers do not rot and are self-sustaining.

WILLOW WEAVING

1 *Willow comes in various lengths. The shorter lengths are finest and suited for fine-quality work. This 2.1m (7ft) bundle of "weavers" is the best length for fencing. Thicker uprights are also needed to form the vertical columns to weave around.*

2 *Place the uprights in the ground about 10–20cm (4–8in) apart, ensuring that they are firmly secured. Use a metal spike to make the holes if the ground is hard. The stakes at each end must be the largest and need to be firmly secured.*

3 *Groups of four weavers are used together. Place two in the first gap (between the uprights) and the second pair in the next gap along. Take the back pair of weavers in front of the vertical upright, behind the next upright and to the front again.*

4 *Pick up the other set of weavers and do the same again. Add more weavers as they become thinner and slot these into the uprights to anchor them in. This will give the cross-over effect to the previous weavers.*

5 *Use successive groups of four weavers and continue to weave. Work from the front in order to ensure that the willow fence is neatly finished. Cut off any stubs as you progress.*

6 *At the end of the panel, wrap all four weavers round the post and begin weaving in the other direction. Ensure the weave is tight here and avoid making joins in the weave on the end posts.*

7 *The panels can be solid and used to form a garden boundary. They may also contain spaces, as shown, and act as dividers, while not obstructing the view beyond.*

8 *The finished willow fence will last for many years, especially if it is adorned with climbers such as ivy. Willow fencing encourages wildlife as well as making an attractive feature.*

ORNAMENTAL LAWNS

In spite of the growth in popularity of hard surfaces, such as decking and paving, a well-tended ornamental lawn is still regarded by many as the quintessential feature of a beautiful garden. The lawn provides a safe surface on which children can play as well as an area for relaxing. In the organic garden, the lawn also provides a unique habitat for a wide range of wildlife. There is no reason why you should not have a fully organic lawn that looks pleasing while also contributing to the garden's diversity.

Above: *A well-manicured lawn is the result of regular care and maintenance. Mowing stripes in the lawn is a finishing touch.*

WHAT MAKES A GOOD LAWN?

Some gardeners believe that a good lawn is the product of time, patience and effort, which is true of highly manicured lawns. Others believe that an attractive, but low-maintenance, lawn is the ideal. Neither of these lawns is an impossible dream in the organic garden, but consider whether a lawn can withstand the wear and tear it is likely to receive in a small garden. In this case, it might be better to consider an alternative such as paving or gravel.

You should also consider how much time you are willing to spend maintaining the lawn. Short, highly ornamental lawns need more regular maintenance than longer grass areas, but all lawn areas require some degree of maintenance.

CAN I HAVE AN ORGANIC LAWN?

Lawns, like any community of plants, can be grown quite successfully the organic way. The key to success lies in keeping the grass plants healthy. Lawn grasses are naturally very resilient and competitive plants, well able to withstand a great deal of abuse when they are healthy. Provided they get sufficient light, water, nutrients, air and space, you will be rewarded with an attractive lawn.

CARING FOR AN ORGANIC LAWN

Each grass plant occupies just enough space to grow and closely "knits in" with its neighbours. The taller the plants grow, the lower the number of plants in any one space becomes. As they grow taller, their needs increase and the most competitive plants win. Regular cutting results in a dense coverage with short green leaves and a high number of plants in a given area. The more regularly you cut grass, the more vigorously it grows. Irregular cutting means fewer plants in the area. Less frequent removal of the green material at the top of the plants makes the leaf bases white or yellow and also results in a patchy lawn.

A lawn that is cut regularly will be greener and more attractive than one that is cut more infrequently. In addition, short-cut lawns are an ideal habitat for many garden creatures, particularly birds such as starlings and thrushes. Short grass can even be flower-rich and benefit bees and butterflies.

However, tall grasses favour visiting wildlife and can become an attractive feature in their own right, but they are not ideal for sitting out or for children to play on.

CHOOSING GRASS PLANTS

Once you know what sort of lawn you want, then you must choose the right grass species for your site and what you want to use it for. Some grass species, such as ryegrass, are hardwearing, while others, like the fescues, are drought-tolerant and need less mowing. Trying to grow the wrong grass species for your garden environment will only work if you go to great lengths to tend it and, even then, it will probably be extremely susceptible to damage. Heavy clay soil that becomes wet in winter will not support a close-mown community of fescues, but would be ideal for a ryegrass and bent mixture.

TYPES OF LAWN GRASSES

The grasses below, if present in seed mixes or turf, should prosper in the given conditions. Common names of grasses, while frequently used, are not the same in all countries and the Latin names are given as a definitive reference.

Coarse-leaved species
Large-leaved timothy (*Phleum pratense*)
Meadow grass (*Poa pratensis*)
Perennial ryegrass (*Lolium perenne*)
Rough-stalked meadow grass (*Poa trivialis*)
Small-leaved timothy (*Phleum bertolonii*)
Tall fescue (*Festuca arundinacea*)
Wavy hair grass (*Deschampsia flexuosa*)

Drought-tolerant species
Chewing's fescue (*Festuca commutata*)
Hard fescue (*Festuca longifolia*)
Meadow grass (*Poa pratensis*)
Red fescue (*Festuca rubra*)
Sheep's fescue (*Festuca tenuifolia*)
Slender creeping red fescue (*F. rubra litoralis*)

Fine-leaved species
Browntop bent (*Agrostis tenuis*)
Chewing's fescue (*Festuca commutata*)
Hard fescue (*Festuca longifolia*)

Red fescue (*Festuca rubra*)
Sheep's fescue (*Festuca tenuifolia*)
Slender creeping red fescue
(*F. rubra litoralis*)

Shade-tolerant species
Chewing's fescue (*Festuca commutata*)
Hard fescue (*Festuca longifolia*)
Red fescue (*Festuca rubra*)
Wavy hair grass (*Deschampsia flexuosa*)

Species for damp conditions
Large-leaved timothy (*Phleum pratense*)
Rough-stalked meadow grass (*Poa trivialis*)
Small-leaved timothy (*Phleum bertolonii*)

Wear-tolerant species
Browntop bent (*Agrostis tenuis*)
Hard fescue (*Festuca longifolia*)
Sheep's fescue (*Festuca tenuifolia*)
Tall fescue (*Festuca arundinacea*)

HOW TO SOW A NEW LAWN

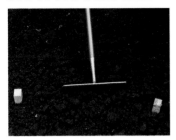

1 *Dig the ground thoroughly, removing deep-rooted perennial weeds. Rake the soil level. Use pegs marked with lines drawn 5cm (2in) down from the top as a guide, having checked with a spirit (carpenter's) level on a straightedge that the pegs are level.*

2 *Allow the soil to settle for a week or so, and then consolidate it further by treading it evenly in order to remove large air pockets. The best method by which to do this is to shuffle your feet methodically over the whole area, first in one direction, then at right angles.*

3 *Rake the consolidated soil in order to produce a fine, crumbly structure that is suitable for sowing seeds. If you can, leave the area for a couple of weeks to allow any weed seeds to germinate. Hoe off the weed seedlings and leave them to die before you apply the grass seed.*

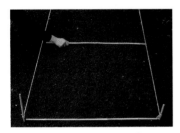

4 *Use string to divide the area into clearly demarcated strips. The strips should be approximately a metre (yard) wide. Divide the strips into squares with bamboo canes or stakes. Move the canes along the strips as you sow.*

5 *Use a small container that holds enough seed for a square metre (yard). Make a mark on it if the amount only partly fills the container. Scatter the seeds as evenly as possible with a sweeping motion of the hand.*

6 *Hire or buy a calibrated granular fertilizer spreader to sow large areas quickly. Check the delivery rates over sheets of paper first and adjust the spreader until the correct amount is being applied per square metre (yard).*

HOW TO LAY A LAWN WITH TURFS

1 *Dig and consolidate the soil as for seed. There is no need to leave it for a few weeks to allow weed seeds to germinate; the turf will prevent them from sprouting. Start by laying the turf along a straightedge.*

2 *Stand on a plank while you lay the next row, as this will distribute your weight. Stagger the joints between rows to create a bond like brickwork. Turf in a long roll will have fewer joints, but these should not align.*

3 *Tamp down each row of turf to eliminate air pockets with the head of a rake, then roll the plank forwards to lay the next row. Brush sandy soil, or a mixture of peat substitute and sand, into the joints to bind the turfs.*

LAWN MAINTENANCE

A rich green lawn is coveted by many gardeners, but a certain amount of maintenance is needed to achieve this. The secret of a healthy and attractive lawn lies in adopting a regular routine. Applying systematic care will also make the lawn relatively easy to maintain. Mowing is the most important and frequent operation carried out, but other practices, including watering, feeding, aerating and top-dressing, will also need to be done to keep your lawn in good condition.

Above: *Mowing will help to keep your lawn both green and healthy but it must be done frequently for the best results.*

MOWING

Where mowing is concerned there is a simple rule that you should always remember. The more grass that you remove by mowing, the more rapid its regrowth will be. The cutting height should be higher during late autumn, winter and early spring when little growth is taking place, but may be lowered in the warmer growing season. Raising the cutting height can also alleviate drought-stress and can help lawns stay green during hot dry summers. As a general rule, you should never remove more than a third of the leaf at any one mowing (unless of course you are cutting down an area left deliberately long for wildlife).

Grass can produce 2–3mm (½–⅛in) of growth over a 24-hour period in ideal conditions. The single most important factor is that you should mow regularly. Mowing will need to be less frequent when growth is slow, as in periods of dry or cool weather. Remember that lawns may need cutting in mild periods during the winter.

LAWN CLIPPINGS

Grass clippings contain up to 3% nitrogen, 0.7% phosphorus and 2% potassium by dry weight. Returning clippings directly to the grass surface during mowing promotes the recycling of nutrients and "feeds" the lawn. Clippings also add organic matter to the soil, which will retain water, thus making the lawn more drought-resistant and helping to conserve water. On the downside, grass clippings can make turf more susceptible to disease and soil-borne pests and lead to a build up of "thatch" (a mat of partially decomposed grass leaves above the soil surface). Grass clippings should always be removed if they are excessively thick and will restrict future growth. This is especially true if the grass has not been cut regularly enough.

CONTROLLING THATCH

Thatch is the general term used to describe the layers of organic fibrous material found in turf. It is a perfectly natural component of turf and is desirable to a certain extent because it increases resilience to wear and drought tolerance. Too much thatch, however, can cause an increase in disease, localized dry spots, leaf yellowing, proneness to scalping (during mowing) and a soft spongy surface. It may also affect the tolerance of grass plants to heat, cold and drought.

Top-dressing and avoiding the over-application of nitrogen can help to reduce the build up of thatch, as can liming on acidic soils. Thatch can also be physically removed. This activity is commonly referred to as scarification but is also known as vertical mowing, power-raking or de-thatching. Scarification not only removes thatch, but also removes or controls moss and creeping weeds. It can also help air and

TURF PROBLEMS

Numerous problems periodically affect turf. The organic approach emphasizes the importance of maintaining strong healthy grass and removing the causes of ill health.

Organic control of turf diseases
- Maintain a vigorous growing sward.
- Control moisture to avoid humid surface conditions, e.g. by brushing.
- Ensure free movement of air.
- Regular aeration treatments.
- Reduce thatch.
- Box off clippings where possible.
- Avoid excessive nitrogen combined with cool conditions (in autumn).
- Avoid lime where possible (test water and top-dressings for lime).
- Adopt a balanced fertilizer regime.
- Sterilize loams and top-dressings.

Organic control of turf weeds
- Aerate to improve surface drainage and enhance grass vigour.
- Hand-dig persistent weeds.
- Mow and collect clippings regularly.
- Scarify the lawn surface.
- Remove earthworm casts.

Above: *Grass clippings, leaves and other debris form a thatch at the base of grasses which can stifle them. Remove it with a spring-tine rake. Raking also removes moss.*

Above: *In autumn, rake fallen leaves into piles and scoop them up with a pair of boards. Choose a still day when the leaves are dry to make the job pleasant.*

water to enter the soil. Scarification must only be carried out when the grass is actively growing.

TURF AERATION

Aeration, put simply, means allowing air to get into the soil. In a lawn, it can improve surface drainage, improve soil air supply and relieve compaction. It also makes the lawn more drought-resistant because of improved, deeper grass root growth. Thatch will be reduced due to the increased microbial activity that is the result of better-aerated soil. Improved drainage leads to a warmer soil that will stimulate root growth and will help release unwanted chemicals and gases from the soil.

You should aerate the turf when the soil is moist, but not wet because it will then damage the soil structure. Aerating the lawn when it is too dry can be difficult if the soil is hard. Small areas can be done by hand, with the traditional garden fork proving very effective for relieving localized compaction.

ROLLING THE LAWN

Rolling a lawn gives a smooth, flat and level surface, but it is frequently overdone and invariably leads to soil compaction, loss of structure, poor drainage, poor aeration and reduced root growth. It is important never to roll a lawn when it is wet.

TOP-DRESSING MATERIALS

Numerous materials can be used as bulky top-dressing and each has its own benefits for both soil and grass plants.

Charcoal Sometimes used to improve surface drainage and ventilation.

Garden compost and leaf mould Improves the moisture-holding capacity of a rootzone while being relatively sterile. Often best used in mixtures. Homemade compost should be left for sufficient time to decay. Rich in trace elements.

Sand Porous and compaction-resistant, sand is used as a component for most top-dressing mixes and on its own.

Topsoil Used in "composts" for top-dressing and on its own for fine-turf areas if it contains sufficient sand.

AERATING THE LAWN

1 *Poor grass growth could be because the soil is poorly drained. You can aerate the lawn by pushing the prongs of a fork into the ground.*

2 *Gently brush a soil improver, such as sharp sand or a mixture of soil and sand, into the holes made by the fork.*

TOP-DRESSING THE LAWN

1 *Scatter dry topsoil or top-dressing mix evenly over the surface of the lawn using a shovel. As you throw the shovel outwards in a wide arc, twist it through 180° by rotating the handle. This will help you to spread the mix evenly.*

2 *Using either the flat side of a rake or a stiff broom or besom, work the top-dressing into the surface with short, even strokes. Only apply a top-dressing when the grass is actively growing.*

BRUSHING

Brushing scatters worm casts, grass clippings and other debris on the surface. It also disperses dew and "dries" the surface of the lawn, making it easier to obtain a clean cut with the mower. Frequent brushing can also act as a mild scarifier, lifting the grass blades ready for mowing. Brushing is also used to "work in" bulky top-dressing into the turf surface. A stiff broom or a besom is the most commonly used tool for brushing turf.

TOP-DRESSING

This is the application of a bulky material to the surface of the lawn and usually has no or only minor nutritional value. It is carried out to help level the surface or to improve the nature of the soil. It may also help to reduce the build up of thatch.

Top-dressing should be applied when both it and the surface are dry. It must be thoroughly incorporated into the turf using a brush or besom. Top-dress during the growing season so that the grass has a chance to grow through it and never apply so much that it smothers the grass.

Top-dressing is easier to work into the sward if the area has been mown and scarified first. If it is being carried out as part of autumn renovation work you can mow the area closer than normal. Make sure that you use the same type of material each time you apply top-dressing.

FERTILIZING YOUR LAWN

Organic fertilizers are applied to turf to ensure that there are sufficient nutrients available for healthy, sustained grass growth. The nutrient reserve within the soil is continually being diminished by plant uptake and removal of clippings. Nitrogen is the most important nutrient as it has the most effect upon growth and development. In most situations only nitrogen and potassium will need supplementing by fertilizer application. Most soils have adequate reserves of phosphorus and micronutrients. Organic fertilizers are available as pre-formulated dressings, although fine fertilizers such as fish, blood and bone are quite suitable for early-season application.

Soluble forms of fertilizer (compost teas or worm liquid for instance) should never be applied when grass is not actively growing. The first application of fertilizer in the spring helps to boost grass growth and recovery

Above: *Feed lawns using an organic fertilizer mix formulated for the season: spring and summer feeds have more nitrogen than autumn ones.*

HOW TO REMOVE WEEDS

1 *Use a special weeding tool or knife to prise out weeds. Push the tool in next to the plant and lever out as you pull. Even deep-rooted plants can be removed like this.*

2 *Make any necessary lawn repairs. If you have had to lift a lot of weeds growing close together, leaving a bare patch in your lawn, sprinkle grass seeds over the area.*

from winter and quickly improves the appearance of the turf for summer. Closely cut lawns need regular applications every four to six weeks through the growing season. Fertilizer dressing for use in late summer must be low in nitrogen, as an excess will invariably lead to soft growth that is prone to frost damage.

Apply lawn fertilizer evenly over the area to ensure uniform turf grass growth. Poor distribution may lead to scorching in areas that receive too much fertilizer. The best time to apply fertilizer is during a dry interval in a showery weather period when rainfall will wash it into the sward. Water the lawn if there is no rain for 24 hours.

WATERING LAWNS

Grass becomes dormant during prolonged dry weather. This may lead to invasion by weed species, but the main concern of

most gardeners is that the lawn keeps its colour. Raising the height of cut may reduce this problem, but, in prolonged dry periods, the only real solution is to water. Well-aerated lawns often allow the quickest entry of moisture and lose less water to evaporation. Hand watering may be feasible for smaller areas, but it can be time-consuming. If you live in a drought-prone area, the best option is to choose drought-resistant species.

TURF GRASS DISEASES

Fungi cause the majority of diseases. The best way of controlling diseases is to keep the grass growing strongly by choosing the right species for the conditions and ensuring that the lawn is well maintained. Not all turf and soil fungi are harmful, however. Many are beneficial, aiding the decomposition of plant materials and organic matter and so releasing nutrients.

HOW TO CREATE A MOWING EDGE

1 *An edge of bricks or paving slabs prevents flowers smothering the lawn. Mark out the area to be lifted, using the paving as a guide. To keep the edge straight, use a half-moon edger. Lift the grass by slicing it with a spade.*

2 *Remove enough soil to allow for the depth of the slab or brick and a few blobs of mortar. Make a firm base by compacting gravel or a mixture of sand and gravel. Use a plank of wood to make sure it is level.*

3 *Bed the edging on mortar for stability. As it will not be taking a heavy weight, just press the slabs on to blobs of mortar and tap level. Lay the slabs evenly and flush with, or very slightly below, the lawn. Check levels.*

REPAIRING A LAWN

1 *Lift the area of damaged turf using a large shovel to beyond the point of wear or damage.*

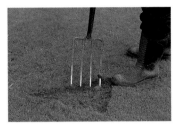

2 *Cultivate the soil beneath in order to remove compaction or, alternatively, remove all the contaminated soil.*

3 *Add a layer of new, good-quality topsoil using the shovel.*

4 *Lightly firm down the topsoil with the back of a rake.*

5 *Sow grass seed over the newly added soil and gently rake in the seed.*

6 *Water in the seed and keep the patch moist until the new grass is established.*

REMOVING MOSS

Moss readily establishes on areas where grass growth is weak. Moss growth is favoured by a moist surface, mowing too close, surface compaction, shade, low soil fertility and excessive pH. Removing moss is palliative and moss soon returns unless the health of the grass is restored. The best solution is to find the cause and remedy it.

LAWN REPAIRS

There are two methods for repairing turf areas: seeding and turfing. Turf has an instant effect, but seeding is more economical over larger areas. Grass established from seed is usually more hard-wearing.

Repairing with turves Mark out the area and use a half moon and turfing iron or a spade to remove the worn/damaged area of turf. Fork over the soil to relieve surface compaction and add a suitable pre-seeding fertilizer. Firm the area by treading. Rake to obtain a tilth. Lay new turves on prepared soil, ensuring all joints are staggered and leaving the turves about 6mm (¼in) proud of the surrounding area to allow for future soil settlement. Top-dress and ensure the area is irrigated when necessary.

Repairing with seed Mark out the affected area and break up the soil by forking. Rake to produce a suitable tilth and "top up" soil levels if need be. Consolidate the surface by treading and apply a suitable pre-seeding fertilizer. Rake to a tilth and sow the seed in two (or more) directions. Rake in the seed, ensuring the area is level with the surrounding turf. Firm by rolling, if required.

Overseeding This method is used to thicken an existing lawn. Seed is scattered over the lawn, where the seed will then germinate, grow and fill-in the turf surface. Overseeding can be done by hand, broadcasting and scratching in the seed. When overseeding grassy areas, lower seed rates are used than those for new lawns. When soil conditions are dry, ensure that the seed is covered and in contact with the soil underneath. Keep the soil moist until the seed germinates and establishes.

Repairing damaged edges Mark out and lift an area of turf around the damaged edge. Fork over the soil in order to prepare a tilth and relieve surface compaction. Incorporate a suitable pre-seeding fertilizer and firm the area by treading. Rake to obtain a suitable tilth. Re-lay the turf with the damaged edge

innermost. Top-dress the newly laid turves, working the top-dressing into the joints. Pay particular attention to the damaged zone. The top-dressing should ideally have a small quantity of seed mixed into it. Alternatively, the area may be overseeded once the turf is laid and top-dressing applied. Ensure the area is irrigated when necessary.

Above: *Insert a half-moon edging tool into the soil. Lever forwards to form a gulley with one vertical side against the lawn and one curved side against the border.*

WOODY PLANTS

Woody plants maintain permanent living structures above ground. They are unique in that their stems repeatedly thicken and strengthen, as is easily seen in the familiar growth rings in wood. Woody plants take many forms: they can be small ground-hugging shrubs or forest giants, and both the largest and oldest living things on our planet today are woody plants. They are the backbone of many gardens, providing height and structure as well as a feeling of permanence.

Above: *Woody plants, such as this flowering quince (Chaenomeles), often have very decorative and colourful flowers.*

BUYING WOODY PLANTS

Woody plants may be bought bare-rooted or rootballed, or in containers. All plants should be vigorous, healthy and suitable for the site conditions and intended use. Check that bare-rooted specimens are properly wrapped so as to prevent their roots drying out and ensure that trees and shrubs are free from any obvious pest or disease.

PREPARING THE GROUND

Organic matter is best incorporated across the whole area as a mulch after planting. This encourages the development of a healthy root system. Apply across the whole site during digging if the soil is sandy.

Adding fertilizer is only generally recommended when analysis reveals the soil to be deficient in particular nutrients. Woody plants set up mutually beneficial relationships with soil fungi and gain much of their nutrients as a result of natural nutrient cycles. Often, the best floral displays occur on soils of low fertility, making fertilizer unnecessary.

The key to woody plant growth usually lies in applying organic mulch on an annual basis. Leaf mould is arguably the best substance to use, but well-rotted compost or manure is almost equally useful. An application of bonemeal or similar organic base dressing before mulch is applied can prove to be beneficial when shrubs are newly planted.

PLANTING OUT BARE-ROOTED OR ROOTBALLED TREES

The soil should ideally be moist and friable, not frozen or excessively dry or waterlogged. Bare-rooted or root-balled specimens are usually planted during the dormant season. For deciduous broad-leaved species, this is in winter. An early planting results in better establishment in the following season, and often makes the

PLANTING A SHRUB

2 *If the soil has not been recently prepared, fork it over, removing any weeds. Add a slow-release fertilizer, such as bonemeal, wearing rubber or vinyl gloves if required, and fork this in.*

4 *Remove the plant from its pot, taking care not to disturb the rootball. If it is in a plastic bag, cut away the bag rather than trying to pull it off. Place the shrub in the hole and draw the earth around it. Firm the soil down with the heel of your boot and water in well.*

1 *Never plant a shrub that is stressed. Before you start planting, check that the plant has been watered. If not, give it a thorough soaking, preferably the night before planting. If this is not possible, ensure that the shrub is watered at least an hour before you plant. This allows the water to be absorbed thoroughly by the potting mix and will help the plant to establish.*

3 *Dig a hole wider than the rootball. Put the plant in the hole and check it is deep enough by placing a stick across the top of the pot. It should align with the top of the soil. Adjust the depth of the hole accordingly.*

5 *Finally, mulch all around the shrub, covering the soil with an 8–10cm (3–4in) layer of bark or a similar material. This will not only help to preserve moisture but will also help to prevent any weed seeds from germinating.*

PLANTING A CLIMBER

1 *Dig over the proposed site, loosening the soil and removing any weeds. If the ground has not recently been prepared, work some well-rotted organic material into the soil to improve soil texture and fertility.*

2 *Add a general or specialist shrub fertilizer, if necessary, to the soil at the dose recommended on the packet. Work into the soil around the planting area with a fork. A slow-release organic fertilizer is best.*

3 *Water the plant in the pot. Dig a hole that is much wider than the rootball. The hole should be at least 30cm (12in) from the wall or fence. The free-standing canes will be angled towards the wall or fence.*

4 *Stand the plant in its hole and place a cane across the hole to check that it is at the same level. Take the plant from the pot or cut the bag away. Holding the plant steady, fill in the soil. Firm as you go with your hands.*

5 *Train the stems up individual canes. Tie in with string or plastic ties. Even twining plants or plants with tendrils will need this help. Spread them out, so that they will ultimately cover the whole of their support.*

6 *Water the climber thoroughly. Put a layer of mulch around the plant to help preserve the moisture and prevent weed growth. Do not pile mulch up against the stems of the climber, however.*

---

plants more resistant to spring drought. Evergreen specimens establish more readily if planted during early autumn or late spring in conditions in which enough moisture is available for rapid root growth.

Mark out the positions of the plants and dig each pit, allowing ample space to accommodate the roots, rootball or container size. This is usually a quarter to half the diameter again of the rootball. Take care not to smear the sides of a pit dug in heavy soil as this will effectively cause it to fill up with water during the wetter months, resulting in root dieback, subsequent shoot dieback and in extreme cases, the death of the whole plant.

Remove protection from the roots and place the tree into the hole. Prune any damaged tissue with a sharp knife or secateurs (hand pruners). Position the plant in the pit with roots well spread. Where

trees require staking, the stake should be hammered into the ground before planting the tree to avoid damaging the roots. Position the stake on the side from which the wind most commonly blows.

PLANTING OUT CONTAINER-GROWN PLANTS

Container-grown specimens may be planted throughout the year, provided that the ground is sufficiently moist and adequate water supplies are available and used to irrigate the newly planted area. Other site-related stresses, such as high wind and hot conditions, may also have to be minimized where plants are planted outside of the optimum winter period. Preparation of the planting pit, and staking, are the same as for bare-rooted or rootballed trees, but the positioning of the rootball and treatment of the roots differs

slightly. Remove the tree from the container and lightly shake out the rootball over the hole of excavated soil. Check the root collar area for girdling roots. These are roots that spiral around and may eventually damage the developing stem. Where present sever these cleanly with a knife and remove carefully out of the rootball. Tease out the lower roots using a fork. Place the rootball in the hole so that the roots are spread out and the surface of the potting mix is level with the ground. Tease out the circling roots at the edges of the rootball with a fork or by hand especially where plants are pot bound. Fill in and firm, staking where required.

Immediately after planting, remove any damaged, diseased or untidy growth. Do not remove excessive amounts of top growth, however, as this will reduce the plant's ability to produce food.

STAKING TREES AND SHRUBS

Large shrubs and trees larger than about 1.2m (4ft) may require staking. Low stakes are now recommended as they allow the top growth to move in a circular motion. This motion encourages rapid lower-stem thickening and the development of fibrous root systems that are essential for quick establishment and support of the plant.

PROTECTING NEWLY PLANTED SPECIMENS

Plants unused to cold or hot drying winds may suffer from drought stress. Cold drying winds may damage foliage, buds and branch tips, as well as the bark of thin-barked tree species unused to such exposure. Tree shelters protect trees from adverse conditions, providing an extremely suitable environment for the rapid growth and development of the tree. They are also useful in protecting plants from voles, rabbits and sometimes deer attack. They are usually designed to last three to five years before the material starts to degrade under the action of sunlight. Shrub shelters are similar in most respects to those for trees but are generally shorter.

STAKING A STANDARD ROSE

1 For a standard shrub, make sure you use a strong stake. It should be of a rot-resistant wood. Firmly place the stake in the planting hole, knocking it into the soil so that it cannot move.

2 Plant the shrub, pushing the rootball up against the stake, so that the stem and stake are approximately 8–10cm (3–4in) apart.

3 Firm the soil down around the plant with the heel of your boot.

4 Although you can use string, a proper rose or tree tie provides the best support. Fix the lower one 15cm (6in) above the soil.

5 Fix the second tie near to the top of the stake, but just below the head of the standard shrub.

6 Water the ground around the plant thoroughly and mulch with chipped bark or a similar material.

Spiral guards, designed to protect larger trees from rabbits, can act as tree shelters for smaller plants. When used on larger trees, they are designed to expand as the stem diameter increases, thereby not constricting growth. Open-mesh guards, which are mesh rolls supported with two or more canes or stakes, provide alternative rabbit protection.

Re-firm roots of all newly planted trees and shrubs after wind or frost, using the heel of your boot, to exclude air pockets around the roots.

Irrigation should only be applied on very dry soils during the first year of establishment. Water is best applied only when absolutely necessary using a sprinkler to thoroughly drench the soil.

All shrub and tree bases should be kept weed-free during the first year. Mulching may help to achieve this, but some hand weeding may be necessary.

RENOVATING OLDER SHRUBS

Shrubs that become overgrown look unsightly and will often have a poor display of flowers. Many shrubs can, however, be rejuvenated by pruning. In certain cases the pruning programme can be staggered over a period of two or more years. Deciduous species, such as lilacs (*Syringa*), may be pruned after flowering, or more commonly during the dormant season. Evergreen shrubs, such as *Viburnum tinus*, are best treated in mid-spring. Remove all weak spindly growth and any badly placed branches or crossing stems. Remove stems to leave a balanced framework by cutting them back to around 30–45cm (12–18in), depending on the species and its vigour. Mulch using leaf mould or compost to 5–10cm (2–4in) in depth. Ensure that the plant is never short of water in the summer.

The following season the shrub will have produced a mass of new shoots. These should be thinned as necessary. After renovation, all shrubs should be pruned according to their normal requirements.

RENOVATING HEDGES

If hedges become overgrown or too wide through neglect or incorrect maintenance, they may respond to drastic pruning methods. The method is similar to that which is carried out on shrubs. Instead of cutting hard back to the base, however, only one side of the hedge is pruned back hard to the main stems of the hedge plants.

One side of the hedge is left alone so there is enough foliage area left to stimulate new growth and recovery on the pruned side. This can also prove useful in providing cover for wildlife, especially nesting birds.

The process is repeated on the other side of the hedge the following year or, perhaps, two years later. Evergreen subjects (but not conifers) should be pruned in this way during early to mid-spring and deciduous subjects when they are dormant in late winter.

PROVIDING PROTECTION

1 *Many shrubs need some winter protection. This shrub is in a pot but the same principles can be applied to free-standing shrubs. Insert a number of canes around the plant. Cut a piece of horticultural fleece, hessian (burlap) or bubble plastic to size, allowing room for overlap. Wrap around the plant, using a double layer for very tender plants.*

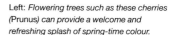
Left: Flowering trees such as these cherries (Prunus) can provide a welcome and refreshing splash of spring-time colour.

Feed using an organic mulch, such as farmyard manure, and water during the following season to ensure that the hedge survives such drastic pruning. This technique can be very successful for many evergreen plants as well as most deciduous plants.

RENOVATING WOODY CLIMBERS

Climbers that have not been pruned or trained properly often degenerate into a tangled mass of woody stems which look unsightly and give poor foliar or floral displays. Hard pruning will often rejuvenate the plant. In most cases, the plant will tolerate close pruning in early spring to within 30–60cm (12–24in) of the ground or its main framework of branches. Plants in poor health may not survive this treatment, in which case you may need to carry out the work over a period of two or more years.

Water the base of the plant well and apply bulky organic material. New growth must be trained and pruned according to the species. New growth can initially be trained as if it were a newly planted climber.

2 *Tie the protective cover around the pot or lightly around the shrub if it is in the ground. Horticultural fleece can be tied at the top because moisture can penetrate, but, if you are using bubble plastic, then leave it open for ventilation and watering.*

FLOWERS FOR BEDS AND BORDERS

Flowers are an essential part of the ornamental garden and there can be few sights that can rival a flower border at the height of summer. Understanding the lifecycles and horticultural needs of these plants is essential if you are to use them to their best effect in flower beds and borders. This section looks at planting and caring for herbaceous perennials, bulbs and annuals.

Above: *Few sights in the ornamental garden can rival that of a flower border in full bloom in mid-summer.*

HERBACEOUS PLANTS

The strict definition of a herbaceous plant is one that dies down to or near to ground level each year in order to avoid harsh and extreme weather conditions. In the garden this includes herbaceous perennials as well as grasses – which may not actually die down but never exceed a certain height – and bulbs.

Herbaceous perennials are non-woody plants that live for more than one year. They usually grow, flower and set seed before dying down to ground level in the autumn. They remain there until the next season when the cycle begins again. Herbaceous perennials may form sizeable clumps which are best divided every three to five years to maintain vigour and promote flowering.

Ornamental grasses contrast superbly with broad-leaved plants and narrow-leaved forms and are ideally suited for creating "dry" gardens.

The maintenance requirements for the vast majority of these plants are the same and they form the backbone of the ornamental garden by providing colour which, if planned properly, may benefit the garden all year round.

Planting out Herbaceous plants may be planted in either autumn or spring. The advantage of autumn planting is usually noticed on drier soils as the plants establish and are potentially more drought resistant. Those planted on heavier soils may benefit from spring planting, as heavy soils may be wet and cold – conditions that may cause the newly planted specimen to rot. Grasses are planted in the same way as "true" herbaceous plants. Bulb planting is different and is dealt with separately.

Pot-grown specimens should be watered at least an hour before planting. The ground should be dug and manured before being levelled ready for planting.

A base dressing of bonemeal or fish, blood and bone may also be applied. Plant only when the soil is moist, but not waterlogged or frozen. Dig a pit larger than the rootball and ensure that the plant is well firmed, taking care not to compact the soil when it is returned around the rootball. Care should be taken immediately after to ensure that slugs and snails do not damage the crowns. Set traps and barriers around them to avoid this.

Thinning Removing weak shoots allows the plant to divert its energy into the remaining shoots, which will be sturdier and produce larger flowers. Thinning is carried out when the plant has reached one-quarter to one third of its eventual height and is useful for plants such as as delphiniums, phlox and Michaelmas daisies.

Stopping This is the removal of the growing tip of a stem in order to encourage the side shoots to develop. The tips may be

HOW TO PLANT PERENNIALS

1 *Always prepare the soil first. Dig it deeply, remove weeds, and incorporate a fertilizer and well-rotted compost if the soil is impoverished. Most perennials are sold in pots, so arrange them to create pleasing associations.*

2 *Water thoroughly at least an hour before knocking the plant from its pot, then dig a hole. If the rootball is congested, tease out a few roots first. Work methodically from the back of the border or from one end.*

3 *Carefully firm the soil around the roots with the heel of your boot. This helps to remove any large pockets of air.*

4 *It is important that you always remember to water thoroughly after planting and keep the new plants well watered in dry weather for the first few months.*

pinched out when the plant has attained a third of its ultimate height. This encourages the buds on the leaf axils to develop and leads to more flowers being produced, although these will be smaller than if the one terminal bud had been allowed to flower. This technique is successful for a range of plants including *Helenium*, *Rudbeckia*, *Dahlia* and *Chrysanthemum*.

Dead-heading Unless the plant produces decorative seed heads or seed is to be collected for propagation purposes, it is often best to remove all flowers as they begin to fade. Further side shoots will then often develop and the flowering period will be extended. Notable exceptions to this are those plants that produce seed heads that are valuable food sources for overwintering birds. Examples of this include teasels, *Echinops* and many of the ornamental grasses.

Cutting back Some shrubby perennials (often referred to as sub-shrubs), such as *Chrysanthemum*, *Phygelius* and *Penstemon*, benefit from being pruned annually in early spring. This is especially true of sub-shrubs that are somewhat tender. The older twiggy and unproductive growth is cut hard back in order to promote the growth of new shoots that will flower in summer and autumn.

Feeding Few perennials require more than an annual fertilizer application if initial soil preparation has been thorough and included the addition of bulky organic matter. An organic fertilizer, such as bonemeal or fish, blood and bone, may be added to the soil in spring, preferably after rain.

Above: *When dead-heading, snip off the flowers cleanly where they join the stem. Cut back to the first set of leaves if a whole head of flowers has to be removed.*

CUTTING BACK

1 *Some herbaceous plants remain green throughout winter. Cut back to sound growth, removing dead and leggy material.*

2 *Here, the old stems have been cut off so that they are level with the emerging growth, so as not to damage it.*

Bulky organic material, such as leaf mould or compost, applied in spring before shoot growth is also beneficial. Care must be taken not to apply this too thickly and not to cover the crowns of plants resting at the soil surface as these may rot off.

Renovating Herbaceous perennial plants should be lifted, divided and replanted every three to five years. Some fast-growing and vigorous plants, such as *Ajuga* and *Stachys*, may need to be divided every year. Herbaceous plants can become woody towards the centre and may lose vigour.

Lifting the plants for dividing will not only rejuvenate them but also allows for other border maintenance operations to be carried out. The site can be cleared of any weeds and organic matter such as compost or manure dug into the border. The process of division is beneficial to the whole border. In addition, it keeps the plant healthy and will prevent the over-vigorous growth of fast-growing species. Lifting and dividing is normally done while the plants are dormant in late autumn or early spring.

Transplanting Most perennials can be transplanted relatively easily. This should be done during the dormant season, which is usually in autumn or early spring. Some plants dislike cold wet conditions and these should be moved once the soil has warmed sufficiently to encourage growth. This is particularly true for any plants that are not fully hardy. Some plants that are relatively long-lived, such as peonies, resent being disturbed and will take two or more years to establish again after transplanting.

Plant replacement If possible, all planted areas should be designed to contain plants that have similar life spans and respond to rejuvenation techniques. Some species are relatively short lived and will die out before others within a bed. It is possible to rejuvenate beds on a set cycle, say every three to four years, and avoid gaps appearing in the periods between.

Plant losses can occur in severe winters when those that are normally regarded as hardy are exposed to very low temperatures. Half-hardy or tender perennials are even more susceptible. Some perennials are probably best lifted and stored over winter until the worst weather has passed, when they can be planted out again.

Above: *Lightly dig over the soil around the plants, removing any weeds. Avoid digging around plants such as asters which have shallow roots.*

ANNUALS AND BIENNIALS

As the name suggests, annuals are plants that grow, set seed and die, completing their lifecycle within one growing season. Some garden annuals may actually be perennials in nature, but are treated as annuals for ease of cultivation. Many half-hardy and summer bedding annuals fall into this category. Almost all spend a maximum of one calendar year in the ground before dying off.

Biennials are similar to annuals as they flower once and die, but differ in that they grow and establish in the first season before resting in a similar manner to herbaceous perennials over winter. They grow, flower and die the following season. Some plants that are grown as biennials (especially as bedding) are perennials. They are treated as biennials, however, because they tend to weaken during their second year and are therefore better re-started in order to maintain vigorous plants.

Annuals are used as displays in their own right or as small groupings of colour among more established plantings. Groups of annuals strategically placed together in, for example, containers can have a greater

visual impact than if they were spread throughout the garden. Many annuals, especially those with composite flower heads, attract beneficial insect species into the garden and some are used as companion planting for vegetable crops. Annuals can also be a useful infill in new borders as they are easily removed or thinned out later when the perennials have grown and become established.

PLANTING ANNUALS

1 *Remove the plants from the pack. If they are attached to each other, try not to tear off too many roots when removing. Dig a hole wider and slightly deeper than the rootball.*

2 *Fill in the hole around the plant with soil and gently firm down with your hands. Water the plant with a watering can fitted with a fine rose.*

Planting annuals, biennials and tender perennials Hardy annuals can be sown *in situ* and then thinned. Some may self-seed freely through borders. If annuals are to be grown in pots or trays prior to planting, the planting is much the same as for herbaceous plants. Always ensure that the risk of frost has passed before planting out tender specimens and that these plants are acclimatized thoroughly beforehand.

SPLITTING CONGESTED PLANTS

1 *Some perennials need splitting every few years to keep them flourishing. In spring, lift the whole of the clump from the ground.*

2 *Clean the ground thoroughly, removing any weeds, particularly perennial ones that have appeared since the border was last dug.*

3 *Incorporate some well-rotted organic material such as farmyard manure in order to rejuvenate the soil.*

4 *Remove the earth from the plant and divide. Use the new growth around the edge, and discard the woody centre.*

5 *Replant some of the divisions, making certain that the roots are well spread out. Firm them in and then water.*

6 *Keep the plants watered until they have re-established themselves. They will soon fill out the gaps in the border.*

SOWING SEED IN OPEN GROUND

1 *Dig over the ground and break it down into a fine tilth using a rake. Do not work the soil when wet or it will become compacted.*

2 *Using a garden line as a guide, draw out a shallow drill. Use the corner of a hoe, a stick or a trowel.*

3 *If the soil is very dry, water the drill using a watering can and leave to drain. It should not be muddy for sowing.*

4 *Identify the row with a clearly labelled marker. This is important because when the row is backfilled it will be impossible to see where the seed is until it germinates.*

5 *Sow the seed thinly by hand along the length of the drill. Sowing thinly will reduce the amount of thinning that is required at a later stage.*

6 *Rake the soil back over the drill and lightly tamp it down with the back of the rake. When the seedlings emerge, thin them out in order to prevent overcrowding.*

Many hardy annuals thrive in poorer soils, and are undemanding and easy to grow. Dry banks are ideal for a whole range of species including poppies and nasturtiums, both of which flower more abundantly on slightly poorer soils.

The only "pruning" required for annual plants is dead-heading to promote new shoot and flower development, or stopping to promote side shoot development and multiple flower production as opposed to large single flowers.

BULBS, CORMS AND TUBERS

These rest below the surface and are modified buds, stems or roots. They emerge, often for only a short time to grow and flower, before retreating back down underground to escape harsh weather conditions.

Planting and maintenance Bulbs, corms and tubers can be lifted during their dormant period and transported and stored easily. Generally speaking, bulbs are planted in a hole that has been dug to about two to three times their length deep. Bulbs have a base plate, which is where the

roots appear. This must always be placed in the hole roots down and should be in contact with the soil in the base of the hole. Placing fine sand in the base will ensure this. The top of the bulb (the neck) should

Above: *The rule is that bulbs should be planted at a depth of three times their own size. Exceptions include nerines, crinums and some lilies, which prefer to be planted with the top of the bulb at soil level.*

always point upwards. Fill the hole firmly once the bulb is in the hole. After this the bulbs need little care and attention, although tall varieties may need staking and all should be dead-headed after flowering.

Above: *Dig a large hole, according to the requirements of the individual bulbs or corms. These gladioli corms are placed, base down and nose up, about 10cm (4in) apart. Gladioli corms need to be lifted in autumn.*

BEDS AND BORDERS

Whether you are creating a flower border from scratch or updating an existing design, there are a number of important factors that you will need to consider before you start planting the scheme. Begin by looking very carefully at the site and its conditions. This initial planning and preparation will help you in your choice of plants. Hardiness and suitability to the soil type, as well as the aspect of the site, are also factors that will determine which plants will thrive.

Above: *Flowers are not only decorative, but will also encourage pollinators and other insects into your garden.*

PLANNING AND SITING

Ideally, the bed or border should be positioned in a sunny site away from the shade of trees or buildings unless you intend to plant a border with shade-loving species. A hedge, wall or fence can provide valuable protection for your plants, and will create a warm microclimate for more tender plants. A sheltered spot will also extend the planting season. These structures may also provide a backdrop for climbers.

When you begin planning the border, ask yourself what you hope to achieve. Borders that are to be viewed from a distance will benefit from larger groupings of each plant type. Larger specimens can also appear very striking from further away. These can be used as character plants and provide a recurring theme through your border.

Borders may have a particular theme. They may be planted with fruiting shrubs, plants to create a "tropical" look or fragrant plants such as philadelphus and lavender for rich summer fragrance. Colour also provides interesting themes. A golden border of yellow flowers in association with plants that have variegated or yellow leaves is striking. Remember that you can leave gaps in the planting for seasonal features

Above: *Combining strong colours such as orange and blue can produce striking planting associations.*

such as bedding plants and bulbs. Decide what look you would like to achieve before buying any plants.

SEASONAL CONSIDERATIONS

Ask yourself when you want the border to look its best. Perhaps you would like a bright display of bulbs in spring followed by a colourful selection of annuals and bedding plants in summer. Alternatively, you may want to plan for a bed or border that provides year-round interest, in which case you will need to consider a selection of hardy shrubs or perennials that are appropriate for your garden conditions.

Make a list of all the plants that you would like to include and when they will look their best. Many plants have more than one season. For example, shrubs such as *Viburnum opulus* flower in early summer and have bright red berries in autumn. If you intend to use winter-stem shrubs such as *Cornus alba*, then choose varieties with interesting foliage, such as the golden form 'Aurea'.

Left: *Herbaceous borders are easy to create and maintain, and can provide year-round interest if they are properly planned.*

COLOUR CONTRASTS

Once you have your list of desired plants, consider their colours. Contrasting colours can look effective. Try plants that have blue, purple or pink flowers, and choose as many examples of these as you can find with bronze foliage. A much brighter combination would call for hot vibrant colours such as yellow, orange and red.

Cottage gardens throw all caution to the wind, including a riot of contrasting and clashing colours to provide unexpected and beautiful combinations of hue and form. Alternatively, you might prefer a monochrome scheme, using flowers of one colour – white or cream, say, offset by a display of green foliage.

FOLIAR AND TEXTURAL EFFECTS

Placing plants with contrasting foliage next to each other can create great interest in a border. This is also true where evergreens are used in conjunction with winter-stem colour. *Cornus sibirica*, for example, has striking red stems in winter and is best shown off against a carpet of weed-suppressing variegated ivy. Textural contrasts can also be striking. For example, the bold leaf forms of plants such as *Rheum* contrast well with the more feathery forms of astilbes and *Aruncus* in summer.

THREE-DIMENSIONAL STRUCTURE

When you plan out a border on paper, it can sometimes be difficult to envisage just how it will look when it is established and growing. In order to get a better idea of the final result, it can be helpful to draw a sketch relief of the border. This should always be done as a projection into the future, based upon the lifespan of the plant. This will be the following year in the case of herbaceous plants but may be five years or more in the case of shrub beds.

PLANTING OUT A PERENNIAL BED

1 *If the bed was dug in the autumn, winter weather should have broken down the soil. In spring, rake over the soil and remove any weeds that have reappeared.*

2 *Although well-rotted organic material should have been added at the time of digging, a sprinkling of bonemeal will ensure the plants get off to a good start.*

3 *Draw a grid on a plan and then mark out a scaled-up version on the bed, using sand or potting mix. Alternatively, use string between canes to mark out the plan.*

4 *Using your planting plan and grid as a guide, lay out the plants, still in their pots, on the ground. Stand back, try to envisage the border as it will be, and make any necessary adjustments.*

5 *Dig a hole and, with the plant still in its pot, check that the depth and width is right. Adjust if necessary. Remove the plant from the pot and place in the planting hole. Fill in the hole with soil and then firm the plant in.*

6 *When the bed is completely planted, water in all the plants. They should be kept watered until they have become established, especially throughout dry periods.*

7 *Go over the border with a fork, or use a rake if there is room. This will loosen any compacted areas, as well as level the soil.*

8 *Cover the soil between the plants with a layer of mulch like composted bark to keep weeds down and preserve moisture.*

9 *Mark each plant with a label. The finished border should need little attention, apart from removing the odd weed.*

PLANTING GROUPS

When designing and planning your border, always remember to set out and plant the herbaceous plants in groups of three, five, seven or nine. In this way, you can create a more natural and informal effect because this approach does not show the rigid lines or geometric shapes that often appear when you plant even numbers of plants.

Larger planting groups than this need not adhere to this number rule because an overall random effect is created by the shape of the drift alone. Larger shrubs, such as *Deutzia* or *Buddleja*, can make stand-alone specimens. Smaller shrubs, such as rosemary or potentillas, may well have greater impact if they are positioned in groups.

CREATING BORDERS WITH HERBACEOUS PLANTS

The popularity of herbaceous plants has meant that they are used in a wide variety of different situations in the garden. However, they are primarily used in the herbaceous border where they can be shown to great effect. Three important categories of this kind of border are usually recognized.

One-sided borders These were extremely popular in Victorian and Edwardian gardens and are the very essence of the English "gardenesque" style. The design usually involves creating a border along one side of a pathway, with the plants arranged in order of ascending height from the path edge. The border is usually positioned in front of a solid backdrop beyond which the eye cannot see.

The backdrop may be living, such as a hedge, or man-made, taking the form of a wall or fence. These beds, while pretty, are often limited by their lack of perspective. The relative proximity of the backdrop often draws attention away from the nearer plants and destroys any illusion of distance. This drawback can be rectified by planting mainly red-flowered plants at one end of the border, gradually changing to blue-flowered plants at the other end. This makes the border seem longer than it actually is. Such schemes are only really effective, however, in borders that are 10m (35ft) or more in length.

Island beds These differ from one-sided borders in that the plants can be viewed from all sides by walking around the whole bed. This kind of planting does not have a backdrop and relies, therefore, on the strategic placement of groups of large plants in the centre of the feature. Island borders allow the onlooker to view the plants from a number of different angles, thus enhancing the interest of the border as a whole.

Mixed borders These designs use many types of plant, including trees, shrubs, herbaceous plants, annuals and bulbs. In a mixed border, one group of plants should complement and enhance the other. For example, the trees provide the shelter and backdrop for the shrubs and flowers in a woodland garden. Rock gardens can also be regarded as mixed borders, with a rich (if diminutive) array of dwarf trees, creeping shrubs and ground-hugging herbaceous plants and bulbs.

ROSE BEDS

A well-tended, healthy and pest-free rose bed has long been, and indeed continues to be, the desire of many gardeners. However, roses can be at risk from pests and diseases. This risk is increased when too many roses are grown in one bed. Most modern cultivars are also too highly bred to resist the range of diseases that can affect them, having been chosen for flower size rather than disease immunity. Choose old-fashioned varieties or modern cultivars that offer resistance to disease.

Most rose pests are common garden pests that are easily controlled by natural predators. The trick with roses is to indulge them with plenty of colourful companion planting, especially daisy-type plants – *Argyranthemum* is ideal – which will encourage those beneficial insects into your garden. It can yield wonderful results and makes the bed even more colourful. Old-fashioned roses need less work in general than modern cultivars and are often more suitable for pollinating insects like bees.

GROUNDCOVER PLANTING

This is a way of exploiting the competitive abilities of plants that grow by spreading sideways and smothering their neighbours. An obvious example of a plant type that is good for this is turf grass, but many herbaceous and shrubby species are also able to fulfil this function. These include conifers, roses, heathers, and both broadleaved evergreens and deciduous

A PARTLY SHADED BORDER

A shady spot in the garden can provide the right growing conditions for a dazzling array of flowers. This mixed border in heavy shade is shown in summer to late autumn.

1 *Aconitum napellus* (poisonous)
2 *Digitalis purpurea* (poisonous)
3 *Anemone sylvestris*
4 *Hyacinthoides non-scripta*
5 *Astilbe* 'Aphrodite'
6 *Primula bulleyana*
7 *Aconitum napellus vulgare* 'Albidum' (poisonous)
8 *Cardiocrinum giganteum*
9 *Lilium regale*
10 *Convallaria majalis*
11 *Primula vialii*
12 *Anemone nemorosa*
13 *Digitalis purpurea* var. *alba* (poisonous)
14 *Campanula alliariifolia*
15 *Aquilegia vulgaris stellata* 'Nora Barlow'
16 *Aster novi-belgii*
17 *Digitalis ferruginea* (poisonous)
18 *Galax urceolata*
19 *Primula japonica* 'Millers' Crimson'
20 *Acer*
21 *Mahonia* 'Charity'
22 *Cotinus coggygria*

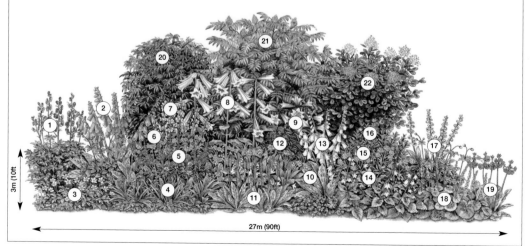

3m (10ft)

27m (90ft)

plants. Their main characteristic is a close, compact and low-growing form that suppresses the underlying weeds. The same effect can, of course, be achieved by planting closely. This method is especially useful with herbaceous plants that grow up quickly and suppress the weeds below. No groundcover will suppress all weeds, however, and you may have to weed among them while they become established.

There are numerous groundcover roses available that offer a colourful carpet of flowers. If you opt for roses as a groundcover, you should be aware that some are covered with thorns and it can be difficult to weed between them. Mulching the bed following planting can help to suppress weeds until the plants achieve full cover. All groundcover can take two to three years (or more) to become fully established and so should be considered as a long-term, labour-saving feature.

BORDER MAINTENANCE

It is possible to plan a border to be low maintenance, but there is no such thing as a maintenance-free border. Decide how much time you can spend caring for the

TIDYING UP

1 *Some edging plants spread out over the grass, possibly killing it or creating bald patches, as has this poached egg plant (Limnanthes douglasii).*

2 *If the plant is an annual and has finished flowering, it can be removed. Otherwise, just cut back the part that is encroaching on the grass.*

border and choose your plants accordingly. A close planting, particularly one that uses ground-covering shrubs or closely planted herbaceous plants, will certainly cut down on the weeding as can mulching the border regularly. Any border will need at least one seasonal tidy up in late winter. Shrub beds are also best mulched at this time before bulbs and other flowers have fully emerged. Choose shrubs that will grow into the space

available and avoid very vigorous varieties or ones that need pruning on a regular basis. Even large herbaceous borders need not be too difficult to maintain. Delay your winter clear up for as long as possible and choose species that do not need staking. Do not worry if the plants grow among each other, it will just add to the effect. The less labour a border needs, the less disturbance there will be to the wildlife it contains.

A SPRING BORDER FOR AN OPEN, SUNNY SITE

A sunny spot can provide the ideal conditions for a wide range of showy blooms in the early part of the year. The plants in this border prefer a neutral to slightly alkaline soil.

1 *Lupinus* 'The Page'
2 *Aster novi-belgii* 'Fellowship'
3 *Lobelia* 'Bees Flame'
4 *Heuchera micrantha* 'Palace Purple'
5 *Aquilegia skinneri*
6 *Primula* 'Gold Lace'
7 *Aquilegia chrysantha* 'Yellow Queen'

8 *Lupinus arboreus* 'Mauve Queen'
9 *Iris* 'Blue Eyed Brunette'
10 *Heuchera* 'Leuchtkäfer'
11 *Campanula latifolia* 'Brantwood' (deep blue) and *C. latifolia* 'Gloaming' (light blue)
12 *Iris chrysographes*
13 *Sidalcea* 'Party Girl'

14 *Physostegia virginiana* 'Vivid'
15 *Geranium macrorrhizum* 'Ingwersen's Variety'

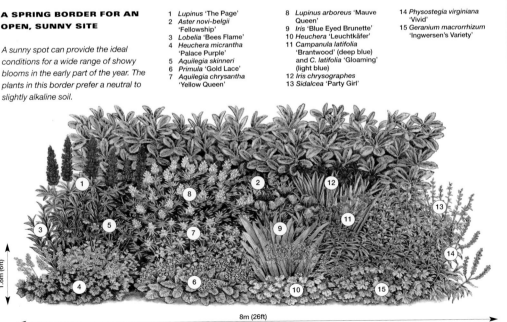

1.8m (6ft)

8m (26ft)

CONTAINERS

These are an attractive feature in any garden and are very useful when there is no soil at all for planting, as is the case with patios and roof gardens. They are also easy to maintain. There are many types of container available, which means that you can create a theme of your own choice: Mediterranean or perhaps lush and tropical in style. You can also plant up seasonal containers to create different effects through the year or you can change the style from year to year.

Above: A wooden barrel makes an attractive container in which to grow a profusion of plants.

TYPES OF CONTAINER

Always choose containers that fit in with the general garden style and with each other. Terracotta and wooden planters are easy to fit into almost any garden scheme, but shiny metal containers may be more difficult to place. Hanging baskets usually take the form of a basket of wire, but they can also be made of wicker. This is lined with a permeable material such as wool, hay, coir matting or even conifer cuttings. You can buy purpose-made lining material which is made from recycled materials or you can make your own. Hanging baskets are an excellent way of covering a wall or post and can even increase the growing space in your greenhouse. They are best planted with a selection of trailing plants (placed around the edge of the basket) and upright types (placed in the centre). They are extremely prone to drying out and should be watered at least once a day and even twice in hot dry conditions. Window boxes should be treated in a similar way to hanging baskets.

The size of a container will influence the kind of plant that you can grow. Any container must be at least 15–20cm (6–8in) deep, although most plants will be happier in a deeper one than this. Be wary of putting a small plant in a very large pot, as this can lead to very wet potting mix that the plant will not want to root into. Large pots with arrangements of several plants are ideal and much easier to look after than several smaller pots.

MATERIALS AND FINISHES

Containers are available in a range of different materials and finishes. Glass fibre and resin containers are extremely strong and lightweight but they tend to be expensive because they are hand-made. They are available as extremely realistic stone-look containers, but can also be found in almost any other finish, including wood and glazed ceramic. Plastic containers are very cheap, lightweight and often last a long time. The finish on some may be poor, but they are very easy to paint and customize. Metal containers are available as pots, "manger-style" window boxes or hanging baskets. There are many different designs and the best quality ones have a properly lacquered finish.

PLANTING A CONTAINER

1 The materials you need include a suitable container, your choice of plants (in this case, the central plant is a striking cordyline), some stones to place at the bottom of the container for drainage and potting mix.

2 Cover the bottom of the container with small stones or some pieces of tile or pottery, so that water can drain freely from the container.

3 Partly fill the container with a good-quality potting mix.

Above: *Hanging baskets can help to provide colour and interest at eye-level throughout the year.*

Above: *Using a watering can is one of the easiest ways to keep the soil moist. It allows you to deliver the right amount of water.*

Above: *You can create a stunning display with a range of different containers, including an old wheelbarrow.*

Stone and terracotta pots offset the shades of flowers and foliage beautifully. The main problem with terracotta is that it is water permeable and requires more frequent watering than plastic, resin or metal pots. Both stone and terracotta containers can be very heavy, so plant them up *in situ*. Look out for frost-resistant types that will not crack in winter. Glazed ceramic pots need less watering than plain terracotta pots, and can be chosen in almost any colour to suit the theme of the garden.

Wooden or wicker planters have a very natural look and can easily be home-made. Oak, cedar and chestnut are the best woods

to use because they do not need preservative and planed wood – of any type – can easily be painted. Wicker is an excellent material for making hanging baskets, while wood can be used for window boxes. Wicker or wooden planters benefit from being lined with plastic or a non-permeable paint. The paint can be plastic resin or bitumen based, but make sure that it does not contain fungicides or preservative. Alternatively, plastic sheeting can be stapled firmly inside the pot. Wooden and wicker pots should be raised off the ground slightly to prevent the base rotting. There are many different designs,

ranging from half-barrels to wheelbarrows. However, take care with wooden items for outdoor use because many of them have been chemically treated. A wide variety of recycled objects can be used as containers. An old boot, bucket or watering can, painted if you wish, can all be used.

DRAINAGE

All containers must have drainage holes in the base. To ensure that the potting mix drains freely, place a layer of gravel – about 4cm (1½in) deep for most pots – over the base of the pot before putting in the mix. Terracotta and stone pots may need as

4 *Scoop out a hole in the potting mix and insert the plant, positioning it so that the top of the rootball will be level with the surface of the potting mix.*

5 *Place any extra plants around the edge of the main plant. Add more potting mix in order to fill in any gaps, and firm down. Water the container thoroughly.*

6 *The plants will soon grow away and fill out the container to create a stunning year-round feature.*

much as one-fifth of their total depth filled with gravel to help protect them from frost damage. Standing pots on bricks or purpose-made "feet" also helps them to drain freely.

ORGANIC POTTING MIX

The best potting mixes contain sufficient air space to allow the roots to breathe, while retaining enough water and nutrients to support plant growth. Potting mix must also be heavy enough to support the weight of the top growth of the plant if it is to remain upright. You can buy a general-purpose potting mix, although some gardeners prefer to mix their own.

Potting mix can be loam-based or soilless. Loam-based potting mix is a "heavy-weighted" mix that provides good anchorage for tall or heavy specimens. It

also holds on well to nutrients. It is ideal for plants that will stay in containers for several years or more as it will not degrade or become structureless.

Soilless potting mixes do not contain loam. They have the advantage of being free-draining and relatively lightweight, although some grit or sand is usually added to give them weight. Coir-based potting mixes are made with a natural fibre that is a by-product of the coconut-growing trade. It has been hailed as a peat substitute and is equally good in containers. However, it is expensive and can be difficult to re-wet once dry. Composted fine bark is cheap and readily available. There have been some advances in its use in recent years and it has even been suggested that bark-based potting mix increases a plant's resistance to pest and disease attack.

MAKING ORGANIC POTTING MIX

You can make your own potting mix with ingredients such as well-rotted compost, leaf mould and worm compost; loamy garden soil; and clean, coarse sand or fine grit. The organic matter and loam should be thoroughly sieved. A slow-acting, balanced fertilizer may also be added along with ground limestone to bring the mixture's pH to around 6.5 which is suitable for the majority of plants. Containers for seasonal displays such as bedding will not need loam.

PLANTS FOR CONTAINERS

Fruit, herbs and even vegetables can all be grown in containers, as well as a wide range of ornamental plants. A flowering shrub such as an azalea can act as a focal point and enliven a shadier part of the garden. Pots of fresh herbs and salad crops can provide a welcome addition to summer meals and a window box can even be used as a miniature wildlife garden. Seasonal bedding can transform a patio into a riot of colour and be changed regularly to reflect the seasons. Containers also enable you to grow a range of plants that would not otherwise grow in your soil. For example, if your garden soil is alkaline, you can still enjoy the spring and summer delights of acid-loving rhododendrons, blue poppies (*Meconopsis*) and Himalayan primulas.

CARE AND MAINTENANCE

There are a number of tasks that you will need to perform in order to keep your container plants in peak condition.
Watering Knowing when and how much water a plant needs is one of the most important aspects of container gardening. Often a look at the surface of the potting mix may give the impression that it is dry. If you dig down with your finger, however, you quickly discover moist potting mix. If the mix feels wet, then do not water it.
Feeding Container plants need more fertilizer than plants grown in the open garden because frequent watering washes out the nutrients. For the best results, start feeding container plants six to eight weeks after planting. Use a liquid tea, worm liquid or a purchased soluble food such as seaweed extract or liquid manure every two to three weeks. Apply fish emulsion or garden compost once or twice a season to add trace elements to the mix. Do not add more than the recommended rate of any fertilizer as too much can harm plant roots.

PLANTING A HANGING BASKET

1 *Line the hanging basket with a suitable organic material. Conifer branches are an ideal material, as is shown here.*

2 *Fill the lined basket with a suitable soilless organic potting mix to about one-third of its depth.*

3 *Position the plants first to see how they will look. Fill in the spaces between the plants with more potting mix.*

4 *Any gaps between the plants can be filled with small bulbs or bedding in order to provide a riot of spring colour.*

PLANTING A WINDOW BOX

1 *Assemble all the necessary materials. These include the window box, crocks, a good organic potting mix and the plants. If the box is light, assemble it on the ground. If not, then assemble it in position.*

2 *Holes in the bottom are essential to allow good drainage. Stop the potting mix from being washed out by placing crocks over these. If very good drainage is needed, then a layer of gravel can also be added.*

3 *Partially fill the box with potting mix, gently tapping the sides to make sure that no air gaps remain. Never over-firm soilless potting mixes as they will become waterlogged and airless, and the plants will suffer.*

4 *Place the plants in position and check these positions before finally planting. Make sure that they are planted in the potting mix at the same depth that they were in their pots or trays. Plant them fairly close for an instant effect.*

5 *A selection of bulbs makes a useful additional display for the window box. The bulbs can be planted in among the main plants and are best planted in groups of three so that they give a fuller display. Water the basket once it is planted.*

6 *Window boxes that are planted for seasonal display will quickly use up all the available nutrients. This is less of a problem with baskets planted for winter interest, such as this, but summer boxes will need regular feeding.*

Monitoring plant health Containers are best placed where they will receive maximum sunlight and good ventilation. During periods of high temperatures and bright sunshine, many containers may benefit from shade during the hottest part of the day. Shelter plants from severe rain, hail and wind storms. Also watch out for and control insect pests.

Pinch pruning When young, the growth of many ornamentals is readily shaped by the pinching out of young shoots. Many specimens treated in this way yield impressive results. This pinching out, or stopping as it is sometimes called, stimulates the development of side shoots and, if carried out regularly, results in dense bushy growth. The selective use of this method of pruning allows for considerable freedom in the shaping of plants.

MAKING ORGANIC POTTING MIX

Mixing your own organic potting mix is relatively easy. You can use a combination of a variety of materials, including loam, leaf mould, garden compost and worm compost.

INGREDIENTS	RATIO BY VOLUME	ADDITIONAL INFORMATION
Loam : Leaf mould : Garden compost	1 : 1 : 1	A basic mix that is well drained, fertile and suited for longer-term plantings.
Leaf mould : Worm compost	3 : 1	Very nutrient rich. Add extra grit for better drainage. Best for short-term pots of vegetables, herbs and flowers.
Loam : Manure : Leaf mould	3 : 1 : 1	A rich mix for heavy feeding plants such as pot-grown tomatoes and peppers.
Leaf mould : Loam	1 : 1	Ideal for long-term plantings such as trees and shrubs. Use acidic loam for lime-haters.
Loam : Leaf mould or Coir	1 : 1	Enrich with 225g (8oz) seaweed meal; 110g (4oz) bonemeal; 85g (3oz) hoof and horn; 55g (2oz) ground limestone per 30 litres (63 pints) base potting mix.

THE WILDLIFE GARDEN

Wildlife gardening involves providing food, shelter and a habitat for creatures as well as relying on native plants that are suited to the climate and soils in the locality. A single plant species may directly and indirectly serve species of insects, invertebrates, fungi and other organisms, which in turn become a meal for larger wildlife such as birds. In time you will have a functioning ecosystem on your doorstep. In fact, creating a garden of this kind can help break up the "grass desert" responsible for reducing the variety of birds, insects and other wildlife.

WHAT IS A WILDLIFE GARDEN?

The organic garden can provide a welcome refuge for a wide range of wildlife, from birds and butterflies to creatures such as frogs and hedgehogs. The basic requirements for any visitor to the garden are food, water and shelter. You may also want to consider organizing some, or all, of your planting schemes around species that will attract a diversity of fascinating wildlife.

Above: Wildlife gardens such as this grassland area can be attractive as well as providing useful habitats.

WHAT ARE THE BENEFITS OF A WILDLIFE GARDEN?

Domestic gardens cover a huge area around our towns, cities and urban fringes. This is a potentially fantastic resource for an otherwise denuded habitat. Keeping your garden free of harmful chemicals gives you a head start in attracting wildlife and, with a little planning, you can create a habitat that will welcome a diverse range of creatures. The visitors in turn will repay you by acting as predators, helping to control the level of problem-causing pests in your garden. Knowing that your patch, no matter what its size, is providing a haven for wildlife will give you a closer connection with the natural world. Just to be able to enjoy watching birds feeding can lift the spirits and improve your sense of wellbeing.

Encouraging natural cycles in your garden will promote biodiversity. The more soil life there is, the more insects will come to feed on it. Birds will come to feed on the insects, as will amphibians and mammals. In this way, food webs will gradually recover in the absence of pesticides.

Making your own garden compost, instead of using peat, for instance, prevents damage to a fragile habitat that cannot be re-created. Collecting rainwater and using this in the garden will reduce the consumption of mains water. Huge amounts of energy are wasted on cleaning and transporting this precious resource and it is often extracted from rivers at levels that threaten the local wildlife. The careful gardener can encourage the creation of wildlife habitats in their own backyard and prevent habitat destruction somewhere else.

CREATING THE RIGHT HABITAT

Much of the wildlife that thrives in a garden does so under the care of a gardener who is not unduly tidy. The best wildlife gardens

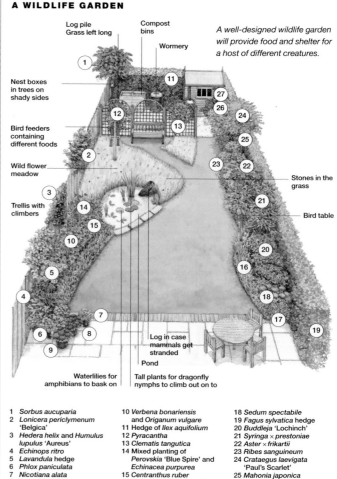

A WILDLIFE GARDEN

Log pile
Grass left long

Compost bins

Wormery

A well-designed wildlife garden will provide food and shelter for a host of different creatures.

Nest boxes in trees on shady sides

Bird feeders containing different foods

Wild flower meadow

Trellis with climbers

Stones in the grass

Bird table

Log in case mammals get stranded
Pond

Waterlilies for amphibians to bask on

Tall plants for dragonfly nymphs to climb out on to

1 *Sorbus aucuparia*
2 *Lonicera periclymenum* 'Belgica'
3 *Hedera helix* and *Humulus lupulus* 'Aureus'
4 *Echinops ritro*
5 *Lavandula* hedge
6 *Phlox paniculata*
7 *Nicotiana alata*
8 *Phacelia campanularia*
9 *Heliotropium* in pots

10 *Verbena bonariensis* and *Origanum vulgare*
11 Hedge of *Ilex aquifolium*
12 *Pyracantha*
13 *Clematis tangutica*
14 Mixed planting of *Perovskia* 'Blue Spire' and *Echinacea purpurea*
15 *Centranthus ruber*
16 *Nepeta* 'Six Hills Giant'
17 *Eschscholzia californica*

18 *Sedum spectabile*
19 *Fagus sylvatica* hedge
20 *Buddleja* 'Lochinch'
21 *Syringa* × *prestoniae*
22 *Aster* × *frikartii*
23 *Ribes sanguineum*
24 *Crataegus laevigata* 'Paul's Scarlet'
25 *Mahonia japonica*
26 *Cotoneaster horizontalis*
27 *Jasminum officinale*

leave room for decay. This approach – and it is one that is good for organic gardens in general – involves piling up old logs and autumn leaves in a quiet shady corner to create a home for insects and hibernating hedgehogs. Do not confuse this with making leaf mould pits; these stay in place and gradually rot down. Log piles can also be overplanted with ivy to enhance both their appearance and attractiveness to insects such as stag beetles.

Consider planting native trees, shrubs and flowers so that native creatures will have a familiar food source or nesting site. Plant as many suitable flowers as possible to attract bees, butterflies and other insects that will enhance your wildlife garden. Many beneficial species are attracted to a garden that is effectively a feeding station for them. For the larger visitors, such as small mammals and birds, you can plant flowering and berrying trees and shrubs.

Ponds provide a rich habitat for a variety of wildlife. Many familiar creatures, such as frogs, toads, newts and dragonflies, depend upon ponds to breed. Many urban gardens have become havens for these creatures. Even a small pool will provide somewhere that birds and other visitors can come to drink. If you have no space for a pond, try introducing a suitable container that can be utilized as a drinking or bathing area for birds, mammals and even insects.

Just leaving the lawn uncut for a few weeks in mid-summer will give many of the plants you do not normally see the opportunity to flower. An area of longer grass also benefits butterflies, moths and many other insect species by providing food and shelter. Many of these insects will

Above: Wildlife thrives in natural wetlands, many of which are threatened by domestic water use.

fall prey to larger garden occupants such as songbirds and hedgehogs, so diversifying and enhancing the food web in the garden.

The barriers and structures in your garden also provide very useful habitats. Hedges are a sanctuary for all sorts of wildlife, where they can breed, feed and take shelter. These hedges are easy to maintain, as they should only be cut once in the winter to avoid interfering with spring and summer nesting birds. Cutting is done on alternate sides in alternate winters. If one side is cut this winter, then the opposite side is cut the next. This ensures that only one side is clipped before the growing season. The unclipped side flowers and provides nectar and fruit for wildlife. Dry-stone walls

Above: Recycling organic material through composting reduces the need to use substances such as peat.

Above: Looking at natural habitats such as woodlands can provide inspiration for your own garden.

are another garden feature that can provide homes for hibernating amphibians, lizards, insects and bees and are best left undisturbed throughout the winter.

If you are lucky enough to have a few trees in your garden, you could try to re-create a woodland habitat. Larger gardens may actually contain a small area of woodland but most are more likely to have a shady patch under a few trees. Choose plants that mimic a woodland floor: bluebells, anemones and sorrel are just a few of the handsome plants that will thrive in these conditions. Planting a few understorey shrubs (those that grow below the trees) such as holly and hazel will complete the effect and may well tempt the shyer woodland birds into your garden.

WILDLIFE CORRIDORS

A wildlife garden is often likened to an oasis in an urban desert. Gardens are the only chance of cover that many creatures have to migrate between larger blocks of suitable habitat such as parks or a greenbelt. If these important habitats become totally isolated then they begin to lose much of their diversity. Town gardens play a vital role in protecting the health of the wider urban habitat, while rural gardens play a similar role in areas denuded by intensive farming. Try putting up a few bird or bat nest boxes and providing nesting areas for insects and mammals. The greater the year-round diversity, the more useful your garden will be.

WOODLAND GARDENS

Woodland can be one of the most interesting and diverse natural habitats. Those with smaller gardens may think that such a feature would be too large for them to create. However, even a few trees in the corner of the garden can provide ample opportunity for the creation of a small wooded area and provide a rich and diverse habitat for a range of visiting wildlife. Try to select native trees or species that have nectar-rich flowers or berries.

Above: *Woodlands are home to many of our favourite garden flowers such as these primroses (*Primula vulgaris).

WHAT IS WOODLAND?

Woodland is a very variable habitat and its exact character will mostly depend upon the prevailing climate. It is often a more open environment than that of a forest, having clearings, glades, pools and streams that break up the monotony of tree cover.

Large trees such as oak (*Quercus*), beech (*Fagus*) or plane (*Platanus*) are known as the woodland canopy. Beneath the canopy are smaller trees such as holly (*Ilex*) and hazel (*Corylus*), known as understorey species. They are often shade-tolerant trees, but grow best under gaps in the canopy. Beneath this, a shrubby layer develops in more open woodland, possibly consisting of bushes such as hawthorn (*Crataegus*) and elder (*Sambucus*).

The floor of the woodland is called the herb layer. The plants that live here tend to be seasonal, taking advantage of early spring sunshine to grow and flower, although some, such as mosses and ferns, grow through the summer. It is also where all seedlings grow and is mulched each year with the falling leaves of the trees.

CREATING A WOODED AREA

Gardeners who have a few trees (even if they do not provide a continuous canopy) can easily make a small woodland area. Visit some woods in your area to gain some inspiration and emulate natural growth if possible. Think how the existing tree cover can be linked, maybe by planting more canopy species and some understorey trees.

Woodland environments are often havens for plants and animals, with many containing an enormous diversity of species. This is most pronounced where there is a "mosaic" of open ground and trees. This is because it increases the "marginal areas" – the point between woodland and more open habitat. The places where two habitats meet are always the most diverse. Layered woodland (one with canopy, understorey, scrub and ground herbs) is beneficial for wildlife as it provides ample feeding and shelter for a range of creatures. Any additional planting should always be aimed at achieving or maintaining this layered structure and providing the highest number of habitats.

You can think of woodland as a collection of diverse habitats. Even those that have only a few types of tree are capable of supporting a great number of species that live on or within these trees. Oak trees in Britain, for instance, are known to provide homes for over 400 insect and other invertebrate species. This does not mean, however, that simply planting an oak tree in your organic garden will guarantee all 400 will appear at once. If you aim to create a woodland that is similar to others in your area, then species will be able to migrate from these to the one in your garden.

You may need to provide additional help for wildlife if it is to establish successfully in the woodland area. Nesting boxes, log piles, rocks and a long grass area linked to your pond can all help to encourage wildlife to use your planting as a habitat. Make sure that you include plants that provide food and be prepared to give additional sustenance, especially in the winter for non-hibernating foragers such as blue tits and other woodland birds. As the woodland develops, so will the diversity it contains. Let nature do its work and give a helping hand from time to time.

PLANTING WOODLAND FLOWERS

In most deciduous woodland, the ground is a riot of colour from late winter until early summer as showy woodland species grow, flower and set seed before the leaves in the canopy cast too much shade. As a consequence, most "woodland gardens" are at their best from late winter to early summer. The edges and clearings provide the chance for later colour, of course, but

Left: *Shady and partly shaded wooded areas can provide the perfect habitat for a host of creatures.*

Above: *Foxgloves (*Digitalis*) thrive in shady woodland corners and are very easy to grow from seed.*

Above: *Bluebells (*Hyacinthoides*) naturally grow and flower in the spring before the trees shade them.*

these boundaries are as long as possible. Fashioning them into "scalloped" or bay shapes will usually achieve this and each scallop or bay may contain different plants or shrub species. The clearings inside your woodland (if it is large enough) are also important. When you create these clearings, ensure that they are sufficiently long to allow plenty of sunshine into each one. Woodland glades should not be less than 7m (23ft) across and are best if they are irregular in shape.

Remember that the direction of the sun in your garden will affect the type of plants that you can grow at the woodland edge, and butterflies, for example, will prefer a sunny aspect. If the bays or clearings in your woodland area are mainly intended for long grass, then this may only need cutting every two to five years unless, of course, you wish to have a secluded seating area that may need more frequent mowing to maintain access.

some of the showiest species are to be found among the spring flowers. Choose species that grow in your own area, where possible, because these will be of most benefit to wildlife.

Primroses (*Primula vulgaris*), bluebells (*Hyacinthoides*), snowdrops (*Galanthus*) and wake robin (*Trillium grandiflorum*) are all guaranteed to give a good display, especially at a time when there are fewer colours in the rest of the ornamental garden. Later flowers such as foxgloves (*Digitalis*) should be planted at or near the edge, where they will still get sunlight once the leaves have appeared on the trees. Climbers such as honeysuckle (*Lonicera*) or clematis are also best situated at the woodland edge where you can appreciate the plants as they bloom. It is advisable to always obtain your seed or plants from a reputable source that does the propagation themselves. Never buy bulbs or plants that have been collected from the wild. Your aim is to create a habitat, but not by destroying another.

ASSOCIATED PLANTING
Perhaps the easiest way to mimic a woodland habitat in a smaller garden is to link a few trees with shrubs and understorey trees in order to provide the shelter and food plants that wildlife needs. These shrubs – particularly if they are deciduous – can provide a larger space in which to plant "woodland herb layer" species. Doing this

will also widen the edge of the habitat and provide extra coverings around the base of trees. There is, of course, no problem in having a few decorative species in or around your woodland. Try a few rhododendrons, mahonias, lilacs and hydrangeas to provide additional colour and interest if you have enough space. They will all provide shelter and look attractive when they are in flower.

EDGE ENHANCEMENT
Woodland edges are often the most valuable area in many types of woodland for a variety of wildlife and plants. The trick with any wildlife-friendly area is to make sure that

Above: *Hellebores and* Anemone blanda *make an ideal under-planting for trees, providing colour in early spring.*

Left: *Hornbeam (*Carpinus*), grown as a decorative hedge, can be underplanted with a selection of woodland flowers for added interest in the spring.*

WILD FLOWER LAWNS

Compared with a closely mown pristine lawn, an area of rough grass with flowers growing in it can provide a rich haven for a diverse range of wildlife. In nature, many attractive and species-rich habitats develop over time but in the garden, things may need a helping hand. You do not have to let the whole of the turfed area go untouched. Simply leave an area of grass uncut for some of the year and plant it up with your own choice of wild flowers to create a rich habitat.

Above: Lawns and areas of long grass can easily be transformed into a stunning display of summer flowers.

PLANTING AND MAINTAINING A WILD FLOWER MEADOW

Small areas of flowery grassland seem to work best when co-ordinated with hedges, shrubs or trees. They are not necessarily spectacular from a distance and need close inspection to appreciate the detailed tapestry of colour and form. Think carefully about where you would like to site such a feature. Always choose a simple mix of species that are well adapted to the conditions in your garden. Take a walk around your home area to see which local or well-adapted species thrive in similar soil types and aspects to your own.

ANNUAL FLOWERS OR PERENNIALS?

Many annuals have attractive flowers and seem ideal for flower-rich lawns but most require yearly soil disturbance and open ground. Poppies and cornflowers are good examples of showy annual plants that benefit from such conditions. Annuals are usually better treated as a separate display. Try planting some wheat or other grain along with the annuals and leave this for foraging birds and mammals. Don't try and harvest the wheat, just cut it down in late autumn and rotavate the plot ready for the spring.

Wild flower meadow species are perennials, which are adapted to life in permanent grassland. The easiest way to make a wild flower lawn is to plant small wild flower plants, directly into an existing lawn. Many wild flowers are easily raised from seed that is available from specialist suppliers. Sowing and growing this is generally the same as for any other herbaceous plant but you should use potting mix that is low in nutrients for the best results. A late autumn or early spring sowing will provide plants that are large enough to plant out in early to mid-summer.

HOW TO SOW WILD FLOWERS

1 The most satisfactory way to create a wild flower meadow is to sow a special mixture of wild flower seeds. Remember to completely clear the ground of all perennial weeds before you start.

2 To bury the seeds, simply rake in one direction and then in the other. It does not matter if some seeds remain on the surface. Keep the area well watered until the seeds germinate. Protect from birds if necessary.

ADDING INTEREST TO NATIVE GRASSLAND

1 For a very small area, wild flower plants may be more convenient. You can raise your own from seed or buy them. Plant into bare ground or in an existing lawn.

2 Keep the plants well watered until they are established. Several years of successional planting may be needed to fully establish your wild flower lawn.

Plant these out about 10–20cm (4–8in) apart in groups of 9–15 to ensure that the group can compete with the grass. Mark where you plant them so that you can see which ones have succeeded later.

If your plants do not establish the first time around, then it is worth trying again. Two failures should tell you that they are not suited for your conditions. You can always try a few non-native plants that have proven wildlife value. Prairie plants such as *Echinacea* are very useful in long grass. Try to avoid rare species, as they are likely to be particular in their habitat requirements, and always consider the attractiveness of plants to insects, birds or other wildlife when deciding what to grow.

NATURALIZING BULBS IN GRASS

Bulbs are potentially one of the easiest plants for flowery lawns. Many early-flowering species are suitable, including crocus, iris and snowdrops. Others, such as *Narcissus*, *Puschkinia*, fritillaries and *Leucojum*, provide good displays later in the spring. Planting bulbs is quite simple. Planting holes can be dug singly with a trowel or spade to the required depth – usually two to three times the height of the bulb. Bulbs should be placed with the base plate firmly in the bottom of the hole. An alternative method for large groupings of small bulbs like crocus and snowdrops is to cut an "H" shape in the grass surface and

Above: *Daffodils (Narcissus) are an ideal bulb to naturalize in lawns, giving spectacular early-spring interest in the wildlife or ornamental garden.*

HOW TO NATURALIZE BULBS IN A LAWN

1 *Lift an area of turf to create an H-shaped cut. Slice beneath the grass until you can fold back the turf for planting. Loosen the ground, as it will be very compacted. If you want to apply a slow-acting fertilizer, such as bonemeal, work it into the soil at the same time. Scatter the bulbs and plant them where they fall for a natural effect.*

2 *Use a trowel or a bulb planter for large bulbs, making sure that the bulb will be covered with twice its own depth of soil when the grass is returned. Firm down the soil and then return the grass. Firm once again if necessary to make sure that the grass is flat, and water well. Water the grass again in dry weather.*

3 *Special bulb planters can be used for large bulbs. The planters remove a cylindrical core of soil.*

4 *Place the bulb at the bottom of the hole on a bed of gravel to improve drainage, if necessary, and replace the plug of earth.*

peel the grass back in two "flaps". Place the bulbs underneath with the top uppermost and gently replace the flaps, firming them carefully. Any group of bulbs should be denser at the centre, gradually becoming wider spaced toward the outside, as this will give a natural appearance. Bulbs such as *Narcissus* may survive for many years but some smaller types – crocus being a prime example – may be eaten by rodents.

CARE AND MAINTENANCE

The time of year that you mow your meadow will influence the species you can grow and also when it will look good. If bulbs are not being grown in the grass then a spring cut can help keep a summer wild flower area tidy, especially after a mild winter. A high cut is best, especially if wild flowers have started to produce leafy growth. Cutting in mid-spring will produce a flowering peak in mid-summer. A slightly later cut in late spring will delay the peak of flowering by a few weeks.

Once flowering has finished, the long grass should be cut down. Spring-flowering meadows are best not cut until after flowering. If bulbs are included then the area should not be cut for six weeks after they have flowered. A second cut in mid-autumn will tidy the area ready for the winter. Summer meadows are usually cut from late summer to mid-autumn. All cuts must stress the grasses but minimize damage to wild flowers. Cuts should be between 30–70mm (1¼–2¾in) in order to achieve this.

Cuttings should be removed to help reduce fertility (as this will help your wild flowers) and to prevent long cuttings smothering the plants below. The cuttings should be left on the ground for three to five days, though, to allow insects to move back into the cut grass below. A portion of lawn may be left completely uncut to protect over-wintering insects, but the portion left must be rotated each year to make sure that the wild flowers survive.

WILDLIFE PONDS

Water is a key element in a wildlife garden. Garden ponds attract an enormous range of living creatures, such as dragonflies, newts and birds, to name just a few of the insects and animals that will visit the garden. Some will come to drink or bathe, others will set up permanent residence there, adding to the beauty and diversity of your garden. A pond not only provides an attractive feature in your garden, but also has far-reaching benefits to wildlife.

Above: *Pond plants are essential to the health and balance of the habitat as well as being highly attractive.*

CREATING A HEALTHY ENVIRONMENT FOR A POND

There are a number of points that you must be aware of if you want to provide a safe and healthy environment for wildlife. A pond is always best sited in a sunny position. This is because many pond plants will not prosper in shade, while the water may also be rather cold until the early summer. Shade within the pool is best achieved by surface vegetation, although a pond may have up to a third of the surface in shade if the remainder is well lit. You should also avoid a site near to overhanging trees whose shade can cause the water to be colder for longer in the spring. Falling leaves can cause a build-up of nutrients and increase the potential for toxic tannins in the water. The roots of some species may also interfere with the lining of the pond and can, in extreme cases, cause serious damage.

WATER FOR THE POND

Never fill your pond with tapwater, which often contains many additives, most notably chlorine. Much tapwater can have a high pH and may contain phosphates or nitrates. These can raise the pond's nutrient levels and promote algal growth. Water runoff from nearby lawns or borders can have much the same effect. If the water level becomes very low during the summer it is possible to use solarized mains water to top up your pond. This involves filling large containers with tap water, partially covering the tops and leaving them to stand in the sun for a couple of days. It removes chemicals like chlorine and, although not as good as rainwater, it will stop your pond from drying out. The majority of pool life requires a still environment, so avoid introducing pumps, fountains or filters.

POND SIZE

Even small-scale ponds can support an amazing diversity of life. The shallows are the most important areas for wildlife but a depth of at least 60cm (24in) must be reached in some parts to give creatures a place to which they can escape in extreme heat, cold or drought. The greater the surface area of a pool, the deeper it has to be (at its deepest point) to maintain an even temperature throughout the year. The average pool will need to be about 1m (3ft) deep.

STOCKING A POND

Ponds that are designed to attract wildlife should be colonized naturally within a couple of years. This is the best method for stocking your new pond in the first instance as it is providing a breeding place or hibernating area for those creatures already established in your area. Introducing frog (or other amphibian) spawn can sometimes spread diseases such as red leg that can devastate populations of frogs and other amphibians. Never attempt to introduce adult amphibians to your pond. They have an amazingly strong homing instinct and can die in the process of finding their way back.

A CROSS-SECTION OF A WILDLIFE POND

Displayed below are some of the more common inhabitants of the garden pool which go towards forming a healthy and balanced ecosystem.

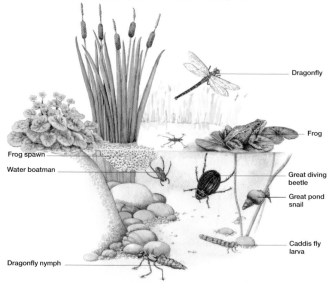

Dragonfly

Frog

Frog spawn

Water boatman

Great diving beetle

Great pond snail

Caddis fly larva

Dragonfly nymph

A WILDLIFE POND

Wildlife ponds depend upon correct planning. Ponds must be both deep enough and possess the right balance of plant types.

These plants will provide habitats, shelter, and maintain a balanced environment for the wildlife in the pond.

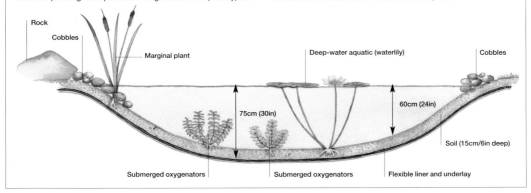

Rock
Cobbles
Marginal plant
Deep-water aquatic (waterlily)
Cobbles
75cm (30in)
60cm (24in)
Soil (15cm/6in deep)
Submerged oxygenators
Submerged oxygenators
Flexible liner and underlay

Avoid introducing fish to small wildlife ponds, as they can exclude other wildlife. Sticklebacks can wipe out the tadpoles of frogs and newts. Fish also eat valuable water-living crustaceans that help to control the growth of water algae and their droppings promote algal bloom.

PLANTING

Bank-side vegetation provides cover for animals entering or leaving the pond. Choose a selection of marginal plants, submerged plants and plants with floating leaves. Leaving long grass around a pond will also provide important cover for wildlife. Gently sloping sides make it easier for creatures to climb in and out of the pond.

Pond dwellers, such as dragonflies and caddis flies, need vegetation to climb out of the water so that the adult may emerge. Small reeds such as the lesser bulrush are ideal but any plants that grow about 40cm (16in) or more above the normal water surface will do.

A log pile nearby will provide a place for hibernating frogs and toads, as well as being a habitat for many other creatures. Add an escape log to help small mammals get out of the pond if they fall in.

Ideally the water surface should have a third or more covered with plant leaves such as water lilies, water soldier, frog-bit or even

Right: Even a small garden will benefit from a tranquil wildlife pond where animals can come to drink.

duckweed. These help keep the water cool, provide shelter and breeding cover for wildlife and help to prevent the development of algae in the water.

Plants that are to form part of your pond habitat should always be grown in a nutrient-poor potting mix. Slow-release fertilizers effectively act as an algal "time bomb", steadily releasing a supply of nutrients that encourage green water and blanket weed development.

Oxygen is essential for the growth and development of pond-dwelling creatures and can easily be boosted by the inclusion of plants that release it directly into the water. These are plants that are entirely aquatic and do not emerge above the water

surface. Plants such as milfoil and Canadian pondweed are often used for this purpose.

Native plants should be a first choice for a pond. Many are showy and often rare or endangered in the wild. If you decide to use natives, never take them from the wild. Always buy them from a reputable nursery or take small offsets from a friend's pond.

Some plants are just too vigorous to be included and will rapidly outgrow their situation. Reedmace (*Typha latifolia*), reeds such as phragmites, floaters such as duckweed (*Lemna*) and the *Azolla* fern are all potentially problematic and should only be included where space permits. They are the equivalent of aquatic weeds and may cause maintenance problems.

PROVIDING SHELTER

As well as needing water and food, wildlife occupants and passing visitors to the garden need a secure place in which to shelter, where they can feed, nest, breed or escape from predators. Almost every part of the garden can potentially shelter wildlife and the key is not only to provide the right kind of cover but also to make sure that it is not disturbed once it is occupied. These sites can take the form of natural plantings or man-made shelters.

Above: *Providing winter cover such as this lacewing hotel for beneficial insects ensures a healthy population for next season.*

TYPES OF SHELTER

In nature, evergreen trees and shrubs provide year-round cover from weather and predators, while deciduous ones give summer cover for nesting and protection. Dead trees provide habitats for owls, woodpeckers and bats, while fallen logs are host to a wide array of ground dwellers such as wood-boring beetles and other insects.

Centipedes and ground and rove beetles that are active all year round need undisturbed soil, stones and logs. Frogs, toads and newts hibernate through the coldest months, often overwintering in damp hidden sites. Place stones and logs near to a pond and ensure that it has shallow edges and sloping sides. Newts prefer overhanging vegetation to shield them on entering and leaving.

Think about where specific creatures live in nature and aim to mimic these habitats. Sometimes this will involve using the natural landscape or erecting a purpose-built shelter.

Left: *Logs and branches, left over from pruning or tree felling, can be left as a habitat or winter shelter for wildlife.*

LOG PILES

These are an essential part of any wildlife garden because they offer shelter and food for a wide range of different organisms and insects that will in turn provide food for other visiting animals.

Log piles make an excellent place for frogs, toads, lizards, hedgehogs and other wildlife species to shelter, find food, and raise their young. Build a permanent log pile in a shaded area, and let it decay naturally. The logs form food for fungi and insects, while providing shelter for reptiles and small mammals. Dead wood on the ground and especially up in the trees is a very important source of nourishment for insect-feeding birds, such as woodpeckers and tree creepers.

Left: *A shady part of the garden, under the cover of trees, is the ideal place for a log pile. Log piles are both useful for hibernating animals and as a food source for beetles.*

TIDINESS

You should not be in too much of a hurry to clear and tidy up your garden in the autumn, as this will provide shelter during the winter months for a wide variety of garden wildlife. Always be selective, preferably removing only piles of diseased debris. The later you can leave your winter clearance, say until early spring, then the greater the numbers of animals there will be successfully overwintering.

WHICH SPECIES SHOULD YOU SHELTER?

There is a wide range of species that can benefit from cover in your garden. However, you should always try to assess the likelihood that these creatures will actually visit your garden in the first place. There is little point in putting up luxury accommodation for creatures that will never even see it, much less shelter within. The following are some of the creatures that may benefit from a shelter in your garden.

Above: *It is advisable to position shelters for beneficial insects near to a suitable habitat or to a source of food so that they can find them easily.*

Above: *Pollinating insects such as bees need both shelter and protection. Bees are very important inhabitants of a wildlife garden; honeybees pollinate plants in the garden.*

Bats These are probably the most elusive of our garden visitors and because of their nocturnal lives we know very little about them and often, rather unfairly, fear them. Bats roost during the day in tree hollows, in dense shrubs or climbers, and in buildings, although during winter they hibernate, often in deeper, solid places with an even, cool temperature. These fascinating mammals are declining in number due mainly to the loss of roosts and feeding areas, and the increasing use of pesticides. One of the easiest ways to help bats is by putting up bat boxes. These should be located in a sheltered position that gets morning sun and afternoon shade.

Birds The lively activity around your bird table or feeders shows that it can be easy to attract more birds into your garden. Birds need more than just a source of food, though, and suitable nesting sites can be essential for some common garden species. Trees, shrubs and climber-covered walls and fences will provide shelter and nest sites.

Though the term nesting box implies birds may nest in them, only a few species use natural or man-made cavities. Most look for shelter in vegetation, with shrubs being perhaps more valuable than trees for this purpose. You should note that regular close pruning of shrubs might cause growth that is too dense for birds to navigate easily. Try to use native species where possible. Hedges that also produce berries are a good source of food for birds in the colder months.

Butterflies These also require shelter from the elements and a place to roost. The foliage of shrubs is useful as an overnight roost, as are patches of tall grass. You can also provide a place for butterflies to roost, perch, or even hibernate by building a log pile and stacking the logs crosswise to create as many open spaces as possible. The ideal log pile size is about 1.5m (5ft) tall and 2m (6½ft) long. You can also buy a butterfly hibernation house, although there is little evidence that these are ever actually used by butterflies.

Hedgehogs If you lean a sheet of wood at an angle against a wall and stuff it with dry leaves, this will provide a suitable nest for hedgehogs. They will also nest under raised sheds and beneath hedgerows, as long as there are plenty of dry leaves for bedding. You can also provide a winter box in an old compost heap or leaf pile for hibernation.

Above: *You can encourage butterflies into your garden by planting wildlife-friendly plants such as these purple verbenas.*

Reptiles and amphibians Rocks, logs, and leaf piles offer cover for small mammals, reptiles, amphibians and insects. In the autumn, try constructing small rock piles that can provide lizards, reptiles and amphibians with a warm winter retreat. If you have a pond, leave brushwood and leaves or rock piles near the bank to provide shelter for amphibians as many of these hibernate in damp areas on the land.

Pollinators Bumble-bees can overwinter in a small terracotta pot filled with moss or finely shredded newspaper. Bury the filled pot upside down and protect the hole from rain with stones, but leave a tiny gap for the bee to get in and out. Masonry bees can be encouraged to take up residence by tying a bundle of bamboo canes together – lengths of about 25cm (10in) are ideal – and then placing them inside a length of old plastic pipe that is about 5–7.5cm (2–3in) longer than the canes. They will make nests inside the hollow bamboo canes and lay eggs within these that will hatch out the following spring. Always place the pipe in a sunny sheltered position where rain will not reach it. You can also buy purpose-built masonry bee shelters.

Predators Lacewings will shelter in a similar construction to that used for masonry bees. Ready-made lacewing hotels are available and are impregnated with a pheromone that attracts the adults in the autumn. Ladybird (ladybug) shelters are also marketed commercially for the same purpose. You can also buy the pheromone with which to impregnate your own home-made shelters.

PLANTS TO ATTRACT WILDLIFE

Plants are the single most important factor when it comes to attracting wildlife into your garden. They provide a food source and shelter for visiting bees, butterflies, moths and a whole host of beneficial insects. Even if your garden is tiny, you can still introduce a selection of useful plants by planting tubs of brightly coloured and nectar-rich summer flowers and pots of sweet-smelling herbs such as lavender and rosemary.

Above: *Beneficial predators such as ladybirds (ladybugs) will be attracted to the garden if you include the right species of plant.*

PLANTS FOR FOOD AND SHELTER

Planting colourful, nectar-rich plants attracts butterflies and other beneficial insects. Choose plants that will provide the visitors with nectar from early spring to late autumn. This of course has the added benefit that your flower beds will be brimming with colour for most of the year. Combine selected species of herbs, wild flowers and cottage garden plants in a herbaceous border to create a butterfly or bee border.

To encourage breeding insects, allow a few nettles and grasses to grow in a secluded corner of the garden or let ivy trail up your fence. These will provide sites for female butterflies to lay eggs and a food source for caterpillars.

Wild or single-flowering varieties of plants are often best for wildlife. You should not be too eager to dead-head plants in autumn.

Many birds feed on spent flower heads such as those of forget-me-nots and pansies. Leave perennial flower stems in autumn, as birds will be attracted to them, searching for seeds and hiding insects. Nesting birds need insects to raise young, so try early-flowering plants such as aubrietia that attract aphids and provide a source of food.

Left: *Plants with composite flower-heads, such as thistles and daisies, readily attract insects to the garden.*

A hedge that is left relatively undisturbed by the gardener can prove a rich habitat for a diverse range of wildlife. Dense hedges give birds protection from predators and provide windbreaks. The thick undergrowth encourages many species of small bird to take shelter and unclipped hedges of all types have more chance of bearing flowers and fruit.

If your garden is large enough to have at least one large tree then this will provide perches and nesting sites for many birds. Native trees are valuable to insects, birds and other animals as they provide better shelter and food than introduced species. The best trees are those that produce

Above: *Choose plants such as roses that have berries or edible fruits for birds and mammals to feed on.*

Above: *Sunflowers* (Helianthus annuus) *provide food for insect pollinators as well as late seeds for overwintering birds.*

Above: Knautia macedonica *can be used in flower borders or in wild flower lawns in order to attract insects such as bees.*

seeds or fruit, as these are often a valuable source of food for many birds in autumn or winter.

Shrubs provide shelter for birds, enabling them to nest safely. Choose shrubs such as *Pyracantha*, *Cotoneaster* and *Viburnum* that produce a good crop of berries for the birds to feed on. Climbers are attractive to birds, especially if they are late flowering or bear fruit and seeds for winter food.

Annual species, planted on vacant patches where quick reliable displays of colour are required, will produce an outstanding array of colour, and their nectar and seeds provide valuable food for many types of insect.

Meadow-plant species will provide colour while the foliage of naturalized bulbs withers down. A fine early display can be created under deciduous trees before the soil becomes too dry and shaded, and grassy banks provide a marvellous opportunity for creating a mini meadow. An informal lawn is the intermediate step between a formal lawn and a meadow and is often created adjacent to a formal lawn and sown at the same time. It contains species tolerant of close cutting and if mowing is relaxed in summer, an enchanting display of flowers can be enjoyed for many weeks. When mowing is recommended no harm will come to the plants, and the practice can be repeated annually.

Shaded areas of the garden often present a problem for gardeners, but there are many varieties of woodland plants – often including some of the most beautiful wild flowers such as anemones and foxgloves (*Digitalis*) – that will thrive in these conditions. A woodland area planted with native trees and shrubs is the ideal backdrop for bulbs and woodland wild flowers. This habitat provides a continual source of interest throughout the year and attracts insects, birds and mammals.

Above: *Encouraging beneficial insects into your garden by including insect-friendly plants can help to create a natural balance.*

Plants growing along and in hedgerows are particularly useful to attract wildlife, especially if the hedge is made up of native species. Plants for sun, shade or semi-shade should be selected depending on the aspect of the hedgerow. New hedgerows should be allowed to establish free of competition for two to three years before associated plants are introduced. Hedges provide corridors for wildlife and sources of interest throughout the year, with attractive foliage in spring, flowers in summer and berries, hips or leaf colour in autumn and winter.

Plants that grow in or around ponds act as a magnet to surrounding wildlife. Damp soil borders and marshy areas are the ideal habitat for many species of wild flower.

Dry-stone walls can also be exploited by planting up nooks and crannies with wild flowers adapted to the conditions, adding interesting foliage and colour.

Combinations of wild flowers can also make excellent subjects for patio tubs, pots and hanging baskets, as many of them are tolerant of drought and have a spreading habit, making them ideal for low-maintenance containers.

Left: *As its common name of butterfly bush suggests, buddleia is a particularly excellent source of nectar for butterflies.*

TOP 20 GARDEN PLANTS TO ATTRACT WILDLIFE

There are literally thousands of plants that all have the potential to attract various forms of wildlife to the garden. Some plants, however, are more effective at this than others. Twenty of the best plants for attracting wildlife that are easy to grow are listed below.

PLANT		WILDLIFE ATTRACTED	BENEFITS TO THE GARDEN
Achillea millefolium **(Yarrow)** A vigorous herbaceous perennial that grows to a height of 60cm (2ft). Flower colour ranges from white through to reds and oranges.		An abundance of hoverflies can be found nectaring on the flowers in summer. Also attracts bees and bumble-bees.	Hoverfly larvae are an excellent addition to the garden, providing efficient control of aphids. The larvae can eat vast amounts of aphids during this part of the life-cycle.
Angelica archangelica **(Angelica)** A tall, upright, herbaceous perennial, more often grown as a biennial, which grows to 1.8m (6ft). The architectural flower-heads bloom in early to mid-summer.		Bees, butterflies, hoverflies, insects and birds all congregate around the huge flower heads of this garden bloom.	This plant can be likened to a supermarket where many species gather to stock up on food. Count the number of species on one bloom, it is amazing.
Aster novi-belgii **(Michaelmas daisy)** The flowers of this herbaceous perennial provide a rich source of late nectar. A full range of sizes and colours are available.		In late summer and autumn butterflies and bees visit the flowers. Birds eat the seed after ripening.	This plant provides a valuable late source of nectar. Butterflies will use this food to strengthen them up for winter hibernation or to produce eggs to overwinter.
Aurinia saxatilis **(Golden alyssum)** Also known as *Alyssum saxatile*, this herbaceous perennial forms a carpet of yellow flowers in spring.		Butterflies, bees and early flying hoverflies are attracted to the bright yellow flowers of this popular rock garden plant.	A very useful source of nectar for all early insects, especially early season or overwintering butterflies.
Buddleja davidii **(Butterfly bush)** This deciduous shrub is often quoted as the saviour of the British butterfly population due to the high quantities of nectar it produces.		As the name suggests, this is an excellent plant for attracting butterflies. Also useful for a variety of nectar feeders, including bees and moths.	Like asters, this is an excellent feeding stop for migratory and resident butterflies. The caterpillars are a good source of protein for birds.
Centranthus ruber **(Red valerian)** A herbaceous perennial that grows to 60cm (2ft). It performs well in poor dry soils and does especially well in seaside locations.		One of the best flowers for butterflies, providing nectar for small tortoiseshells, peacocks, red admirals and white and yellow butterflies.	Butterflies are a good indicator of the health of the environment. Their caterpillars are a good source of protein for nesting songbirds.
Cerinthe major 'Purpurascens' A small herbaceous perennial that flowers in spring. Produces fantastic blue flowers with lilac bracts. It self-seeds freely.		Bees love the blue flowers and congregate in vast numbers while the plant is in flower.	This early flowering perennial gives a boost of nectar to resident bee populations, which are good pollinators.
Eryngium giganteum **(Miss Willmott's ghost)** A short-lived herbaceous perennial that reaches a height of 90cm (3ft) and has beautiful steel-blue flowers.		This plant hums with bees and bumble-bees during its long summer-flowering period.	An outstandingly beautiful plant that attracts bees which will pollinate your plants. Good for naturalizing in wild areas.
Eschscholzia californica **(Californian poppy)** An annual that produces striking orange, cream, red or yellow flowers which will bloom all summer. This is a small plant, reaching 45cm (18in) in height.		Hoverflies, bees and bumble-bees are attracted to this plant. Once it is sown, it will self-seed freely round the garden.	The bright orange flowers attract hoverflies, the larvae of which are extremely voracious predators of aphids.
Eupatorium cannabinum A tall plant that produces large heads of fluffy pink flowers in late summer. This herbaceous perennial is a must for the wildlife garden.		Attracts butterflies and bees. As well as looking fantastic, this plant is one of the best for providing nectar to adult butterflies.	From mid-summer onwards, this decorative plant offers a rich and steady source of nectar and is a firm favourite with visiting butterflies.

PLANT		WILDLIFE ATTRACTED	BENEFITS TO THE GARDEN
Helianthus annuus (Sunflower) If you want to make a statement, grow a few of these in your garden. They have enormous yellow, red or orange heads with some tall varieties easily reaching 2m (6½ft).		Birds such as greenfinches and bullfinches will eat the seeds. Also visited by honeybees and bumble-bees when in flower.	The seeds provide a late-summer boost to the diet of birds and some small mammal species. Good for encouraging birds into your garden.
Humulus lupulus 'Aureus' (Golden hop) A vigorous climber with twining stems. It is unusual in that it dies down every year. The female plants produce hops that are used in flavouring beer.		Caterpillars of the beautiful comma butterfly and button snout moth feed on the golden foliage.	Food plants for caterpillars and larvae are an invaluable part of a wildlife garden, otherwise we would not be graced with the adult butterflies.
Lavandula angustifolia (Lavender) A compact bushy shrub that sports many varieties to choose from. It produces fragrant pink to purple flowers in early summer.		The fragrant blooms attract many different species of bees, bumble-bees and also white and blue butterflies.	Insect-eating birds are attracted to feast on the insects drawn to nectar on these fragrant bushes.
Lonicera periclymenum (Honeysuckle) A climber with twining stems reaching up to 6m (18ft). It bears sweetly scented, pink and cream flowers in early summer, with red berries appearing later.		Nectar provides food for bumble-bees, bee hawk moths as well as elephant, lime and privet hawk moths. Fruit-eating birds will feast on the berries.	A superb plant for night-flying moths that should be placed next to the house so you can enjoy both the fragrance and watch these night-flying beauties. The moths are also a good source of protein for birds and bats.
Nymphaea alba (Waterlily) An aquatic plant that has large round floating leaves with beautiful white flowers in the summer months.		Adult frogs and dragonflies use the floating leaves of this aquatic plant for basking on. The leaves also provide cover for tadpoles of newts and frogs.	Adult frogs eat slugs and snails. The tadpoles help to control algae in the pond, as it is part of their diet.
Phlox paniculata The lovely, sweetly scented flower heads provide a colourful display in late summer. This 90cm (3ft) herbaceous perennial prefers a moist soil in light shade.		This plant will attract adult butterflies and moths, which will appreciate the nectar from the flower heads in late summer to early autumn.	The moths nectaring on this plant will provide a tasty meal for wandering bats. Butterflies flying during the day will provide a meal for hungry birds.
Rosmarinus officinalis (Rosemary) A dense bushy shrub with aromatic foliage growing up to 1.5m (5ft) tall. It bears purple to blue flowers in mid-spring to early summer.		Almost unrivalled in its ability to attract honeybees, butterflies and hoverflies to its nectar-rich flowers.	Honeybees pollinate many garden plants and trees. They are welcomed by farmers into fruit orchards.
Sedum spectabile (Ice plant) This small herbaceous plant is one of the best butterfly plants. It has thick succulent leaves and stems that are well suited to growing in hot well-drained positions.		An old favourite for the herbaceous border, Sedum is extremely useful to butterflies, bees and hoverflies as a late summer source of nectar.	Provides a good source of nectar late in the season that is a positive benefit for overwintering butterfly species to build up their energy.
Sorbus aucuparia (Mountain ash) A wonderful tree for the small garden. It has attractive white flowers in the spring and bears red fruit in the autumn. It can reach heights of 12m (36ft).		The flowers are excellent for feeding bees and other insects in the spring whereas the berries are consumed by many species of birds.	The tree can attract up to 30 different species of insect, not including the birds and small mammals it feeds, providing a meal for many.
Verbena bonariensis (Tall verbena) This versatile plant can be grown as an annual or short-lived perennial, reaching up to 1.8m (6ft). The purple-flowering spikes bloom in late summer until the first frosts.		This is a fantastic plant for nectaring butterflies such as the small tortoiseshell, peacock, red admiral and comma. It is perhaps more effective than the more well-known buddleia.	Good for planting in large groups throughout the garden to attract large numbers of butterflies and bees to pollinate plants and to provide food for garden birds.

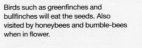

THE KITCHEN GARDEN

The kitchen garden is a paradise for gardener and cook alike.
Few pleasures in life can compare with the satisfaction of
harvesting and eating fresh produce from your own garden.
There are many design possibilities when planning a kitchen
garden. Some gardeners prefer to lay out their vegetable plot in
neat rows; others choose an edible landscape that is ornamental
as well as functional. There is also a seemingly endless choice
of varieties in seed and nursery catalogues which can be
confusing, but merely reflects the popularity of home-growing.

PLANNING A KITCHEN GARDEN

Growing your own vegetables, herbs and fruit ensures that the food you eat is fresh, tasty and chemical-free. The healthiest food is found closest to its source, so freshly picked produce from your garden is both tastier and better for you than that which has travelled long distances by air, sea or road. Your garden will also be more appealing when it is planted with a wide selection of plants that will attract an equally diverse range of wildlife.

Above: *A well-planned kitchen garden, with companion planting, can be a feast for the eyes as well as the table.*

WHAT DO YOU WANT FROM YOUR KITCHEN GARDEN?

An ideal starting point is to make a list of all the vegetables and fruit that you eat on a regular basis, adding in a few that you are curious about and would like to try. The next stage is to look at the size of your garden and consider if there is enough room to grow everything that is on your list. Think about the quantity needed to feed your family. There is no point in planting ten apple trees for a family of four. It is a good idea to start with a few easy crops to build your confidence and progress from there.

Many edible plants, especially vegetables and herbs, are easy to grow and can be ready for harvesting in a short space of time. Children love to sow and grow less difficult crops, such as spring onions (scallions), radishes, carrots and lettuce. Growing fruit is usually a longer-term investment, as many types, such as apples, pears and blackcurrants, for example, will take several years to crop. Once they start to produce fruit, however, your investment will pay off, as they will continue to crop for many years to come and are less time-consuming than vegetables.

Furthermore, you do not need acres of space to enjoy growing your own fresh fruit and vegetables. In fact, even a small garden will support an edible crop or two. You could grow potatoes in barrels, herbs in pots and fruit trees in ornamental containers. If you live in an apartment, you can use window boxes and containers to grow fresh herbs and vegetables. Try planting hanging baskets with trailing tomatoes, herbs or fruits such as strawberries to overcome space difficulties. Edible gardening involves using any space that is conveniently available. It also promises a colourful garden and unusual ways to feed your family.

DESIGNING THE GARDEN

There are a number of points that you will need to consider in order to get the most out of your kitchen garden and to ensure that the food you produce is safe and fresh. Siting your crops next to a busy road, for instance, can mean eating produce that is polluted by cars. When siting the crops, think carefully about your own garden environment. Each garden is different and

Left: *Peas and beans can easily be trained up supports, giving height and structure to the kitchen garden.*

has specific requirements for growing various crops. Check the pH of your soil before getting underway as vegetables such as cauliflowers and cabbages will not grow well if the soil is too acidic (under pH of 6.5). As well as testing the pH level, test the soil for nutrients. The results will indicate if there is any need to improve the soil before planting.

The aspect of your garden is also critical in the siting of your plants. Fruit, for example, needs plenty of sun exposure in order to ripen properly and develop flavour. Fruit trees are also often best sited over a lawn to facilitate fruit collection.

Any design needs to consider the difference between annual and perennial crops. Annual vegetable crops, such as potatoes, carrots, cabbages and beetroot, need to be rotated within the vegetable garden to deter soil-borne pests and diseases from attacking them. Strawberries are a good example here, as they are effectively an annual, needing to be divided every year. A strawberry bed that you rotate with flowers and annual herbs (such as basil or dill) is useful for avoiding soil-borne pest problems.

Perennial crops, such as asparagus and rhubarb, may well merit their own distinct areas and are not rotated like annual crops. Raspberries and blackberries, which are both perennial, are best sited permanently on a wire trellis. Avoid putting them in a huge expanding clump that can take over your garden.

Consider, too, how difficult a particular plant (or the produce it offers) is to grow. Peaches, for example, can be challenging. They are disease-prone and require lots of care and attention. Unless you are a committed gardener with time on your hands, it may be best to purchase a few organically grown fruits from a local shop.

PLANTING THE KITCHEN GARDEN

If you have recently moved into a new home, then you will have the luxury of starting your kitchen garden from scratch. If your garden is already established, there is no need to uproot everything to grow your own produce. Gardens need not be exclusively made up of just edible or ornamental plants. You may wish to start by planting a few annual vegetables and herbs among your ornamental plants. Indeed, you can easily incorporate edible plants into the garden, even mixing fruit, vegetables and herbs in ornamental beds. This planting arrangement avoids crops grown in visually uninspiring mono-cropped rows.

If you are planting vegetables in new beds, then they can be interplanted with ornamentals and herbs. Fragrant plants such as English marigolds (*Calendula*), French marigolds (*Tagetes patula*) and oregano (*Origanum*) are excellent choices for attracting beneficial insects, and interplanting with plants such as these will help to keep pests to a minimum. Large blocks of the same vegetable are likely to attract high concentrations of pests, whereas interplanting tends to confuse and dissuade them.

If you need to remove an ornamental tree or shrub that has died or outgrown its site, consider replacing it with a fruit-bearing tree or shrub. There are many possibilities, including apples, currants, raspberries, crab apples, plums and cherries, which can all provide valuable colour and texture in the garden as well as a source of food. Apart from feeding the household, excess fruit from these trees will also provide food for a range of birds and insects.

It is worthwhile researching the eventual height of plants in the planning stages. Some will simply look out of place if they are grown in the wrong location, such as planting tall plants in front of smaller ones. Many large ones will also need some form of staking or support.

Lettuce, chives, pansies and parsley create excellent borders along the edges of raised beds. Tall plants such as dill, sunflowers, daylilies, fennel, valerian, peas and beans are best grown at the back of beds or at the centres of containers. Provide trellises and other supports where needed. Choose edible flowers such as nasturtiums and chives wherever possible because they are a natural addition to gardens and make salad bowls look and taste wonderful.

You may wish to consider an edible lawn, in which some (or even all) of the lawn is given over to a groundcover such as strawberries. Strawberries are a very attractive crop because they produce fruit for most of the summer and tolerate marginal soils and light shade. However, large patches are likely to attract pests, so they should be interplanted with strong-smelling herbs like thyme and oregano which also form good groundcover. It may be an idea to keep a permanent cover of herbs and rotate the strawberry crop on a two- or three-year cycle.

PLANTS USED AS FENCES, SCREENS AND BARRIERS

Plants can be used in a number of imaginative ways. Instead of erecting plain wooden fencing or mesh barriers why not consider planting a living one?

Above: *Onions, with their tall stems, can be grown for their decorative appearance in ornamental beds and borders.*

Gooseberries, raspberries or currants are readily trained along a fence and apples can be trained as an espalier cordon or fan along a wall. Climbing plants, such as hardy kiwi fruits, trailing nasturtiums, broad beans, or sugar snap peas, can all be grown over a fence or trellis work to provide an ornate screen. Hedges can also form useful and attractive edible barriers. Shrub roses, such as *Rosa rugosa*, create an attractive, but impenetrable barrier, producing large red rose hips that contain 60 times the vitamin C of an orange. The hips can be used to make tea, jam, syrup or jelly. Currants and other fruit can also be included on the sunny side.

When designing your kitchen garden, bear in mind that the garden is for everyone in the household. Hold family discussions to involve everyone in the planning and design stage. It is worthwhile taking everyone's needs and tastes into consideration when undertaking this extremely important stage of development.

Right: *Cloches and low tunnels can increase the range of early crops that can be grown in the kitchen garden.*

CROP VARIETIES

There is a seemingly endless array of seeds available to the home gardener. Each supplier makes claims that their variety is better than all those that went before and any others currently available. Others claim to have older, more choice varieties saved from extinction and representing a time when everything was purer and more wholesome. Personal preference usually decides the best varieties for you, but an understanding of what you can expect from the seed in a packet can be very useful.

Above: *Onions come in a range of attractive colours and can be grown for their ornamental value in beds and borders.*

WHAT ARE HYBRIDS?

Often when we purchase seed, we respond more readily to the picture on the front of the packet. We may not notice whether it is marked with the terms "F1" or "hybrid". A hybrid is the result of a cross between one variety with pollen from another specific variety. The breeder chooses parent varieties that will produce first generation offspring (F1 hybrids) with known characteristics. The crossing is done in a very controlled manner so that no pollen from another variety is able to pollinate the flowers. As a result, all of the plants that are grown from the hybrid seed will be genetically identical.

Hybrids may be bred to be more widely adapted to environmental stresses such as heat, cold, disease or drought than non-hybrids. They also have more uniform characteristics, making crops more predictable in their qualities. They also have

"hybrid vigour" and may grow faster or be more disease-resistant than either of the parents. They may also give better yields than open-pollinated varieties. They will not breed true, however, meaning that seed collected will not produce plants that are the same as the parent (F1 hybrids). For this reason, seed cannot be saved from F1 hybrid plants by the home gardener. Seed for hybrid varieties must be purchased year after year from the seed companies or nurseries, unless you want to gamble and grow an array of offspring.

WHAT ARE OPEN-POLLINATED VARIETIES?

Open-pollinated varieties are traditional varieties that have (in some cases) been grown and selected for desirable traits such as taste, yield or disease-resistance for many years. They often grow well in organic kitchen gardens as many were originally selected under organic conditions. These plants can mutate and adapt to the local ecosystem, as the seed is often collected and re-used by the organic gardener.

If a seed packet is labelled "heirloom", "open-pollinated" or has no special markings, then it is most likely a standard or traditional variety. The majority of lettuce, bean and pea varieties for domestic use are open-pollinated, while most cabbages, broccoli, tomatoes, cucumbers, melons and Brussels sprouts are hybrids.

Right: *Allowing a few of your crops to flower will also provide you with seed for growing next year's crop.*

Left: *Unusual crop varieties can often be grown from seed that you have collected yourself each year. This is a striking variety of kohl rabi.*

Hybrid seeds can dominate the garden seed market, but open-pollinated varieties are more or less stabilized in their characteristics, remaining fairly consistent and producing seed that will grow into plants that are more or less like the parent plants. They are a little less uniform than hybrids, but the home gardener can safely collect seed and grow plants from them that will be essentially the same as the original plants. Open-pollinated varieties either self-pollinate or are pollinated by wind or insects and they usually produce viable seed.

There have been various claims that open-pollinated varieties do not taste as good as hybrids. It is also claimed that they are smaller and not as uniform and, in many cases, this may be true. However, where matters of taste in varieties are concerned, the only real answer is to try them and see for yourself.

Right: *Old varieties of tomato tend to have varying sizes of tastier fruits that crop over a long period of time.*

WHAT ARE HEIRLOOM VARIETIES?

In the 1970s the European Community brought in regulations to encourage the breeding of new vegetable cultivars and the standardization of older ones. This resulted in a list of approved cultivars being drawn up and it became illegal to sell any cultivar that was not included on this list. It is very expensive to have a single cultivar tested in order to then register it on the list. This meant that many old cultivars were put in grave danger of being lost forever, as the funds to test each variety were not available. It was due to this legislation that HDRA, the Organic Organisation, in England, a society which was established to promote organic issues, founded the Heritage Seed Library (HSL). This seed library ensures that old or "heirloom varieties" are kept safe for posterity by distributing its seed. Although HDRA grow some of the seeds themselves, they also employ contract growers and seed guardians to make up the bulk of the seeds that are supplied.

Each year a catalogue is sent to HSL members from which they can select up to six varieties free of charge. This distribution set-up overcomes the clause of selling only approved cultivars. This service is also available to members in the United States.

The best heirloom cultivars can be traced back fifty years or longer. Many of these early varieties have been lost already, making those that remain all the more precious. A number of these cultivars have been collected and saved by families and ethnic groups dating back many years. This practice protected the genetic make-up that made each variety successful within a given environment. These base characteristics have become invaluable and the genetic strains of these vegetables are the backbone of modern disease- and drought-resistant hybrids. It is this that makes the collection and preservation of these cultivars so important.

Left: *Many heirloom varieties have been selected for the way they perform in local garden conditions, rather than for crop size or uniformity.*

CROP ROTATION

This is the practice of grouping and growing related plants together and rotating them around different areas of land in a regimented fashion from year to year. Rotating your crops in this way has many advantages, including helping to prevent pest and disease problems from arising in the first place. This method of gardening is fundamental to successful organic growing. It has been practised for thousands of years and developed into a system that is easy to follow.

Above: *The secret to achieving a thriving and healthy kitchen garden is to rotate the crops on a regular basis.*

WHY ARE CROPS ROTATED?

Continuous cropping in the same area puts both plants and soil at risk. It not only allows large numbers of soil-borne pests and diseases to build up, but, because crops require the same nutrients from the soil year after year, the practice can deplete nutrient levels. A poor infertile soil produces weak unhealthy plants, which, in turn, will be more prone to pest and disease attacks. All these problems amount to reduced yields and even complete crop failure.

When crops are rotated, the groups are divided up into closely related plants that are prone to similar pests and diseases. For example, carrots, parsnips, beetroot and potatoes are members of one group and prone to carrot fly, whereas cabbage, kale, broccoli and Brussels sprouts, which are members of another group, can be prone to clubroot and cabbage root fly. If the groups are grown in different areas on a rotational basis, it can help to prevent the establishment of soil-borne pests and diseases.

Combined with regular additions of compost and manure, crop rotation will make the soil richer, replace certain nutrients and help prevent pH imbalances that can result from repeated crops of the same type of vegetable. Companion planting will also aid a rotational plan, particularly if the species improve pest control.

MAKING A ROTATIONAL PLAN

The basic rules of crop rotation are simple. If you are planning a four-year crop rotation, the plants you have selected are split up into five groups. Group one contains the legumes (peas and beans); group two contains the brassicas (cabbages, Brussels sprouts, broccoli, kale etc); group three contains the onion family and others (onions, lettuce, garlic, sweetcorn etc); group four includes root crops (potatoes, parsnips,

---

BENEFITS OF CROP ROTATION

There are many benefits to be gained from rotating your crops regularly.

- Prevents the build-up of soil pests and diseases
- Helps to prevent nutrient depletion from heavy-feeding crops
- Rotated crops produce higher yields
- Results in a healthier soil

---

carrots, beetroot etc); and finally group five houses permanent crops such as asparagus and rhubarb.

The vegetable plot is then divided into five sections. The permanent crops are given a specific area and are not moved or included in the rotational cycle. The remaining four groups are allocated an area in which to grow. Every year each group is moved on to the next plot, making it four years before the crops are grown on the same area of land again; hence the name crop rotation.

If space is limited, crops can be grown on a three-year rotation. Quite simply, the crops are split into three groups, plus the permanent ones. The plant groups are divided up as before except group three is incorporated into group one.

There is no need to grow each crop in every year of a cycle. Remember that it is the vegetable groups that dictate the cropping cycle according to their soil needs and any associated problems. Rotating the crops helps provide the correct soil requirements for certain crops. For example, cabbages and the rest of the group grow well in soil that has been manured the previous autumn, whereas carrots and other root crops (not including potatoes) do not. Where carrots are to be grown, then the plot will need to be dug deeply in readiness for them.

It is important that you plan where the crops are to be every year, so that you know their position for the following year. A comprehensive cropping plan can help you to maximize the yield on a year-round basis by working out successional sowings and intercropping and catch cropping. The plan needs to include not only the crops that will be grown but also the companion plants and the soil amendments that are needed to support the best possible growth of your plants.

COMMON DIFFICULTIES

When planning the cycle, you may encounter certain problems. Careful planning will show that potatoes often take up more space in a vegetable bed than any other crop and finding enough room to grow them in their allocated area may prove difficult. Other problems you may come across include overwintering brassicas or plants left in the ground for seed collection. This is when you find that practising crop rotation in a small garden is difficult and that you may not be able to practise a strict rotation.

If space is proving a problem, consider some of the following strategies. Keep brassicas together as a group and never plant them in the same ground two years running. Keep potatoes together every year; if you have planned a lot of potatoes, move all the other members from group four into group three. Also bear in mind that some root crops, such as potatoes, are manure-friendly, while others, like parsnips, are not. Finally, alternating shallow-rooted plants like cabbages or lettuce with deep-rooted plants like tomatoes or squash will allow the plants' roots to do much of the soil loosening that would otherwise have to be done by hand. This will help to preserve the health of the soil, while causing minimal disturbance to its ecosystem.

FOUR-YEAR CROP ROTATION

Divide the vegetables you have decided to grow into the five groups (plots 1–5) shown in the table. Draw a plan to indicate which group of crops goes where, using a different colour for each group. (Remember plot 5 is for the permanent crops.) Next year, move the crops in each group on to the next plot.

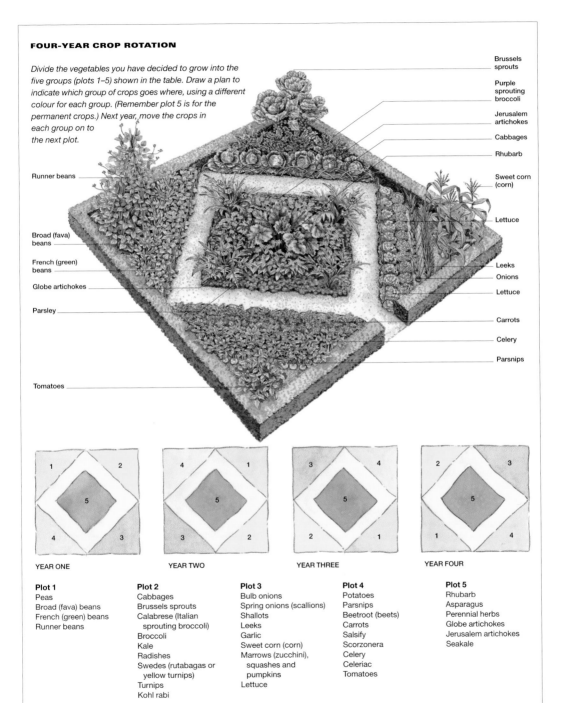

Runner beans

Broad (fava) beans

French (green) beans

Globe artichokes

Parsley

Tomatoes

Brussels sprouts

Purple sprouting broccoli

Jerusalem artichokes

Cabbages

Rhubarb

Sweet corn (corn)

Lettuce

Leeks

Onions

Lettuce

Carrots

Celery

Parsnips

YEAR ONE

YEAR TWO

YEAR THREE

YEAR FOUR

Plot 1
Peas
Broad (fava) beans
French (green) beans
Runner beans

Plot 2
Cabbages
Brussels sprouts
Calabrese (Italian sprouting broccoli)
Broccoli
Kale
Radishes
Swedes (rutabagas or yellow turnips)
Turnips
Kohl rabi

Plot 3
Bulb onions
Spring onions (scallions)
Shallots
Leeks
Garlic
Sweet corn (corn)
Marrows (zucchini), squashes and pumpkins
Lettuce

Plot 4
Potatoes
Parsnips
Beetroot (beets)
Carrots
Salsify
Scorzonera
Celery
Celeriac
Tomatoes

Plot 5
Rhubarb
Asparagus
Perennial herbs
Globe artichokes
Jerusalem artichokes
Seakale

GROWING METHODS

There are many different ways to grow your crops. You can try the traditionally practised method of sowing crops in rows or be more adventurous and grow them in blocks. The crops you have chosen to grow can be planted into a number of different types of vegetable bed: flat beds, raised or edged beds and no-dig beds. Each method and type of bed has its own advantages and disadvantages, which are described here, so choose the one that best suits your needs.

Above: *Twiggy sticks provide an ideal support for young climbers such as peas. They also look very decorative.*

PLANTING IN ROWS

This is the most traditionally practised and popular form of vegetable growing. It is an effective method because the spacing of the plants allows the crop to grow without excessive competition. In addition, it is relatively easy to add supports and protection such as cloches to the crops. However, this type of planting does have the disadvantage of needing relatively high maintenance. Due to the large amounts of bare earth left between the rows, the conditions are ideal for weed growth. Rows are spaced according to the optimum growth of the plants and so rows of pumpkins need to be much wider than those for carrots. Setting out rows in this way allows free movement of air along the rows. This results in fewer disease problems which can occur with more closely grown methods such as block plantings.

The rows are quite easily maintained by regular hoeing but can be wasteful of space, particularly in smaller gardens. They will produce sizeable vegetables, but this is offset by the actual yield per unit area being smaller than more intensive systems.

BLOCK PLANTING

In this method plants are grown in squares or rectangles rather than in straight rows. Blocks of plants are grown next to each other, for example in dimensions such as five plants by five plants. The numbers of plants grown can be larger or smaller than this. Block plantings use space efficiently, producing many more plants in an area than if grown in rows.

Well-tended soil can support planting that forms a close network of foliage over the soil. The soil will retain moisture extremely well underneath the canopy. It also stops weed seeds from germinating, resulting in a less weedy environment than other growing methods. However, a close canopy of leaves can have disavantages, resulting in poor air flow and high humidity which are ideal for attracting diseases such as botrytis. During dry spells watering is essential for the health of the crops. Double check all watering that has been done because water easily runs off the dense cover of the leaves and never reaches much of the root system.

Blocks can be planted and managed at ground level or in slightly raised beds. They suit modestly sized vegetables, such as root and salad crops, that are usually grown in rows. You may have to be inventive with crop protection for early-sown crops, as cloches and low polythene tunnels do not cover the area well. The blocks are edged with permanent paths for easy access to the centre from any side so you need never walk on freshly cultivated soil. As a result, the soil does not get compacted and the closely grouped plants make maintenance and cultivation easier.

Seeding a block involves sowing the furrows thinly along close rows. For example, instead of the usual 30–40cm (12–16in) distance between carrot rows, this can be reduced to 20–25cm (8–10in). Further space savings can result from growing as much as you can vertically, rather than sprawled over the ground. Wire fencing, netting or poles and tepees take up less space than blocks of climbing vegetables. This will also keep the climbing plants dry and free of disease.

FLAT BEDS

As the name suggests, flat beds are constructed at the natural ground level of your garden. They are the traditional way of cultivating ground for growing vegetables and are most suitable for gardens that have good soil. Flat beds will naturally raise the level of the soil, especially where organic matter is added on a regular basis as part of the cultivation regime, but the bed remains effectively at ground level. This form of gardening is relatively labour-intensive because all of the bed is cultivated, with large areas then being used as paths between the vegetables. With raised beds, there are no paths and only the growing areas are dug.

Left: *The close planting of crops in rows or blocks helps to retain soil moisture as well as reduce the growth of weeds.*

Above: *Plants such as beans can be trained over an arch in order to provide an ornamental and productive feature.*

RAISED AND EDGED BEDS

These can be freestanding garden beds or beds with wooden or brick walls constructed several inches above the normal ground level. Raised bed gardens not only look good but they also can help solve many problems associated with soils that are difficult to manage. Problems with soil are often aggravated in urban and suburban settings, where topsoil and vegetation may have been removed or the surface level changed during building work.

Raised bed gardens improve the environment for plants by lifting their roots above poor soil. The growing medium can

be amended by the incorporation of manure and/or garden compost. Soil in these beds warms up earlier in the spring, allowing the seed sown to germinate quicker than if it is grown in flat beds. Beds should be located where they will receive full sun and with protection from prevailing winds. Do not site the beds in frost pockets or where air circulation is poor.

Drainage is important. Build the beds so that the crops will not become waterlogged, as good drainage is especially important when growing vegetables. If the bed contains clay soil, incorporate sand, grit or organic matter to improve drainage. Construct the bed so that it slopes about 2cm (¾in) per metre (yard) of horizontal distance away from any structures, or away from the centre of the bed.

NO-DIG BEDS

As the term suggests, no digging is involved in this method, which is a good way to retain good soil structure within a vegetable garden. Weeding is kept to a minimum and because the soil is not disturbed it will be alive with worms and other organisms. The bed is made on top of the ground and can be built over existing beds, lawns and even hard or rocky ground. Situate the bed in a sunny area that receives morning sun and has good drainage. It can be any size or shape, depending on your space. Start with a small bed – about 2 x 1.5m (6½ x 5ft) – but with a view to expanding in time.

When preparing the site it is not necessary to pull up the lawn or existing garden if the soil conditions are good, but if the ground is very poor, compacted or the drainage is bad, initial digging may be necessary.

Above: *Containers are an ideal way to grow a variety of crops where space is limited. These pots contain courgettes (zucchini).*

The outside wall of a no-dig bed is formed using logs, old planks, tiles, bricks or stones. Line the bed with a layer of plain wet newspaper, at least 6mm (¼in) thick. This layer should cover the enclosed area completely and overlap slightly, so as to kill off any weeds and stop new ones growing. Spread out a thin layer of hay or straw, ensuring that there are no gaps. Place a layer of good organic fertilizer, such as chicken manure, 20mm (¾in) thick, on top. Cover with a 20cm (8in) thick layer of loose bedding straw. Follow this with a 2cm (¾in) layer of good organic fertilizer and complete the bed with a top layer of garden compost, about 10cm (4in) thick. Make sure the bed is watered in well. Once it is settled you can plant out seedlings, but not seeds. Sowing seeds can begin when the bed has matured and the soil has become fine and crumbly.

No-dig beds that have been recently created are best for growing crops such as potatoes, lettuce, brassicas and cucurbits, whereas root crops grow better when the bed is mature. No-dig beds are best suited to planting vegetables in small blocks of different varieties rather than in long rows.

Left: *Vegetable beds need not be rectangular to be functional. This kitchen garden uses simple geometric shapes to provide interesting effects.*

COMPANION PLANTING

This is when two or more crops are grown together for the benefit of one or all. This technique creates a colourful landscape, made up of different species, which mirrors nature itself. Plants are grown together for several reasons, including to attract beneficial insects or to give off odours that deter or confuse pests. This is so different from large fields planted with only one crop, a monoculture that allows large numbers of pests and diseases to build up rapidly.

Above: Nasturtiums have edible leaves and flowers as well as being a colourful companion plant.

HOW COMPANION PLANTING WORKS

Plants have natural affinities with others of their kind. The smell of volatile oils from many plants discourages certain pests, making them excellent companion plants. A good example of this is the well-known relationship between the tomato plant and the French marigold (*Tagetes patula*). The scent of the French marigold is said to deter whitefly from entering the greenhouse and therefore avoids a whitefly attack on the tomato plant.

Plants such as yarrow (*Achillea*) and hyssop (*Hyssopus*) are just a couple of plants from a list of many that attract beneficial insects like hoverflies. The hoverflies will lay their eggs around these plants and, after hatching, the larval stage of the insect will start to eat adult aphids. So greedy are these larvae that they can eat up to 800 aphids before pupating. Many organic gardeners grow trays of single-flowered French marigolds to dot around their gardens, both in the vegetable and

BENEFITS OF COMPANION PLANTING

A mosaic of plants offers many benefits to the organic garden, some of which are outlined below.

• Creates a colourful landscape.
• Plants can attract benefical insects.
• Plant odour can deter harmful insects.
• A variety of plants together confuses pests from locating host plants.
• Plants attract birds that prey on pests.
• Flowers attract pollinators.

ornamental areas, in order to encourage these eating machines. This is both very effective and quite stunning to look at.

Certain distinct qualities of a plant have a proven benefit to others, such as fixing nitrogen in the soil. Clover in grass will fix nitrogen, offering the excess nitrogen produced to the surrounding grass which improves the yield. By the same token,

others are less suited as partners. It is never wise, for example, to plant two vegetables side by side that attract the same pests, as this effectively doubles the chances of attack. It is advisable to practise crop rotation or use companion planting in between them.

BENEFICIAL COMBINATIONS

There is little scientific evidence of these associations working, but if you talk to any organic practitioner, they will certainly provide plenty of anecdotal evidence. Tomatoes, for instance, like to be grown near basil and parsley plants. This is, of course, useful for cooks as well as gardeners. Separating rows of cabbages, broccoli or other brassicas with rows of onions has always been a popular combination, possibly due to the onion's strong scent confusing cabbage pests. Tomato plants also grow well next to cabbages and seem to deter caterpillars. Other beneficial combinations include leeks near carrots as they repel carrot flies, while Swiss chard thrives near carrots and beetroot. Never plant carrot and dill close by each other. This makes the carrots woodier and stronger-flavoured, and the dill milder and with weaker stems.

DECORATIVE COMPANION PLANTS

Certain flowers and flowering herbs offer potential benefits for a variety of vegetables. French marigolds (*Tagetes patula*) are cited as a wonder flower by many organic gardeners and the bright flowers make a colourful companion crop. They deter many pests, and seem to spur growth in roses. They are also said to reduce the number of soil nematodes, while attracting hoverflies and their larvae which eat aphids. French marigolds are frequently planted with pot marigolds (*Calendula officinalis*).

Right: Companion plants can provide welcome splashes of colour in the kitchen garden.

CROPS AND THEIR COMPANION PLANTS

While it is not an exact science, any practitioner of companion planting will tell you that individual crops have their "preferred companions". Experience is the best guide, but the list below outlines some plant combinations that work well in most situations.

Apples Chives, foxgloves, wallflowers, nasturtiums, garlic, onions

Apricots Basil, tansy, wormwood

Asparagus Tomatoes, parsley, basil

Beans Carrots, cucumbers, cabbages, lettuce, peas, parsley, cauliflower, spinach, summer savory

Beans (broad/fava) Potatoes, sweetcorn (corn).

Beans (dwarf) Beetroot, potatoes

Beetroot Onions, kohl rabi, lettuce, cabbage, dwarf beans

Brussels sprouts Nasturtiums

Cabbages Beans, beetroot, celery, mint, thyme, sage, onions, rosemary, dill, potatoes, chamomile, oregano, hyssop, wormwood, nasturtiums, tansy, coriander (cilantro)

Carrots Peas, radishes, lettuce, chives, sage, onions, leeks

Cauliflowers Celery, beans, tansy, nasturtium

Celery Tomatoes, dill, beans, leeks, cabbage, cauliflowers

Chives Parsley, apples, carrots, tomatoes

Courgette (zucchini) Nasturtiums

Cucumbers Potatoes (early crop only), beans, celery, lettuce, sweetcorn, Savoy cabbages, sunflowers, nasturtiums

Kohl rabi Beetroot, onions

Garlic Roses, apples, peaches

Grapevines Geraniums, mulberries, hyssop, basil, tansy

Leeks Carrots, celery

Lettuce Carrots, onions, strawberries, beetroot, cabbages, radishes, tagetes

Onions Carrots, beetroot, lettuce, chamomile, kohl rabi, courgettes

Parsnips Peas, potatoes, peppers, beans, radishes, garlic

Peaches Tansy, garlic, basil, wormwood

Peas Potatoes, radishes, carrots, turnips

Potatoes Peas, beans, cabbage, sweetcorn, broad beans, green beans, nasturtium, marigolds, foxgloves, horseradish, aubergine (eggplant)

Pumpkin Sweetcorn

Radishes Lettuces, peas, chervil, nasturtium

Raspberries Tansy

Spinach Strawberries

Squash Sunflowers

Strawberries Borage, lettuce, spinach, sage, pyrethrum

Sunflowers Squash, cucumber

Sweetcorn (corn) Broad beans, potatoes, melons, tomatoes, cucumber, squash, tansy

Tomatoes Asparagus, celery, parsley, basil, carrots, chives, marigolds, foxgloves, garlic, sweetcorn

Turnips Peas, nasturtiums

White alyssum (*Lobularia maritima*), by reseeding frequently, helps to break up the soil and adds to its organic content, while chrysanthemums reduce nematodes, making for healthier soil. Mint almost always works with various types of squashes and brassicas to aid plant growth, although it can become invasive. Tansy (*Tanacetum*

*Left: Foxgloves (*Digitalis*) make excellent companion plants for growing under apple trees.*

vulgare) is said to repel ants, aphids and plant beetles although this, too, can become invasive if not regularly checked.

Chamomile (*Chamaemelum nobile*) is known as the "plant doctor" by some organic gardeners because of its alleged ability to encourage other plants to increase their production of essential oil, making plants such as rosemary and lavender taste and smell stronger. Chamomile is easy to grow and looks beautiful anywhere, although it should be kept well trimmed to avoid a straggly look. It is also thought that chamomile can help to activate the composting process if it is added to the compost heap.

Lavender (*Lavandula*) is a general insect repellent and makes an excellent small hedge. It is a great addition to the garden, attracting bees and numerous white and blue butterflies.

Plants that produce berries such as cotoneaster and the rowan tree (*Sorbus*) will attract birds into the garden. Birds, in turn, eat many pests, such as protein-rich

aphids, caterpillars and various flies. Thrushes are the unsung heroes of the garden because they decrease the snail population quite considerably.

Be prepared to experiment before committing to a companion species. Nasturtiums have been cited as an effective aphid control, although many wonder if they do this by attracting all the aphids to themselves. What works in one area may not always work elsewhere and experimentation is the key to success in this interesting yet uncertain area of organic gardening.

CROPS AND THEIR ANTAGONISTS

Some plants are highly antagonistic to one another. You should always avoid planting the following combinations.

Asparagus Onion and potato

Beans Chives, fennel or garlic

Carrots Dill

Carrots, cauliflower or potatoes Tomatoes

Peas Onion, garlic and shallots

Potato Pumpkin and summer squash

MAKING THE MOST OF YOUR SPACE

There are three basic growing techniques that you can use to make the most of your space. These are known as intercropping, catch cropping and successional sowing. By adopting the latter two practices, you will extend the cropping season instead of harvesting a crop all at once. You will also make use of the available space, therefore increasing yields. All that is needed is careful planning to work out which crops to sow and when.

Above: *Close planting in blocks makes the most of available space and allows more crops to be raised in a season.*

INTERCROPPING

This kitchen-garden technique increases productivity and also helps to keep the numbers of weeds down. It refers to the practice of planting a fast-growing crop, such as carrots, radishes and lettuce, between main crops that are slower growing. These include vegetables such as cabbages, peas and potatoes.

Intercropping involves harvesting the quicker-growing crop first before the slower-growing one achieves total foliage cover of the soil or shades out the area. A good example of intercropping is to grow a crop of spring onions or lettuce between tomatoes. Similarly, spinach or radishes can easily be planted out early between sweetcorn or, alternatively, radishes can be planted between cabbages.

Intercropping can also be used to increase productivity. It ensures that no space is left unused and makes the most efficient use of light, nutrients and moisture. It will also reduce the amount of weeds in the vegetable patch by maintaining a continuous plant canopy over the soil.

One slight variation on the theme is to combine the benefits of a green manure with a crop. This can be useful in the case of winter crops because the green manure doubles up as a cover crop, protecting the soil from erosion and leaching as well as stabilizing soil temperatures. If a leguminous green manure is planted in late summer or early autumn in a bed along with leafy crops such as Brussels sprouts, it can provide nitrogen throughout the remaining growing season. It will also provide a boost for early

crops that will be planted out after the green manure crop has been dug into the soil. While intercropping requires careful planning, it can increase the productivity of even a relatively small vegetable plot.

CATCH CROPPING

This technique is when fast-maturing vegetables, such as radishes and lettuce, are grown in an area of ground that has just been cropped and has a vacancy until the next crop is either sown or planted. The sowing of the catch crops can be done in between the main ones or after harvesting at the end of the season if there is time. It is important to know how long a crop takes to mature when planning catch cropping so that you do not sow anything that takes too long to mature in between the main crops.

Left: *Successional sowing in rows allows the same space in the vegetable plot to be kept productive throughout the growing season.*

ADVANTAGES OF INTERCROPPING AND CATCH CROPPING
Making the most of your space is not only productive, but it also has environmental advantages.

- Suppresses weed growth in the kitchen garden
- Increases the productivity of the vegetable patch
- Planting green manures enriches the soil with nitrogen
- Helps to protect against the erosion of the soil
- Helps prevent leaching

SUCCESSIONAL SOWING

This is the practice of sowing the seeds of fast-maturing vegetables at regular intervals several times during the growing season. This practice will ensure that you have a continuous supply of crops such as lettuces, carrots and spinach throughout the season. Successional sowing is also useful where crops are sown directly outdoors early in the season where they may be prone to frost damage. Early crops

Above: *The close spacing of rows and successional sowing of new rows allows the maximum use of space on your plot.*

such as lettuce and radish can be sown under the cover of, for example, a cloche where they will begin to develop earlier than would otherwise be possible. Subsequent sowings outdoors will mature later, thus extending the growing season for harvesting.

Gardeners with small plots can use this method by sowing only a half a row at any one time. This process is then repeated a week or so later, with further sowings as often as you like. This way you will have fresh vegetables for several weeks and will avoid a sudden glut.

Above: *Sweetcorn (corn) is a late-maturing crop that can be intercropped with fast-growing, early salad crops. This enables you to make the most of your growing space.*

SOWING IN THE OPEN

There can be nothing more satisfying than sowing seeds and watching in anticipation for them to germinate. Watching the seedlings grow in your kitchen garden, making it come alive with leaves, flowers and insects is a fantastic experience. One of the drawbacks of sowing out in the open is that you are at the mercy of the weather, but you can manipulate your garden environment by using cloches, small plastic bottles and polythene tunnels to increase your chances of success.

Above: *A dibber (dibble) is a very helpful tool to use when you are transplanting seedlings outside.*

SITE REQUIREMENTS

If you are a novice kitchen gardener, be assured that sowing seed is easier than you may think. In order to germinate successfully seeds need water, air, a suitable temperature and a place into which they can root in order to support the top growth that will follow. For this reason, good soil preparation is everything to organic success. Most garden soils are able to supply all the necessary elements and only slight modifications are usually necessary. However, it is important that the ground is prepared in a way that will enable the seed to germinate evenly and grow in a uniform environment. The prior preparation of a seedbed can provide the seed with the environment that it needs and has the added bonus of making the task of seed sowing easier.

Preparing a seedbed is simple. Following cultivation, the ground is levelled using a rake, held at a shallow angle, to break down any large clods. The art of levelling is to keep the rake angle shallow and move the high spots over into the low spots with even strokes. Hold the rake firmly at the rear and let the shaft run smoothly through the front hand. All stones and large objects, including organic matter such as twigs or previous crop debris, should be removed by combing them out with the teeth of the rake, while holding the tool in a near vertical position. The soil is then firmed with light treading. A light shuffle across the bed is best. Once firmed, lightly rake the soil again at a shallow angle to produce a light "fluffy" surface that runs freely through the teeth of the rake. This is the perfect environment for sowing and growing seeds.

SEED REQUIREMENTS

The conditions that seeds require to germinate are easy and straightforward to create. A well-aerated moist soil environment is almost all that the seed needs. Most seeds will germinate quite successfully once the temperature gets above 7°C (45°F). Seeds carry their own food supply that provides them with everything they need for those first crucial days following germination. Once the plant begins to establish and grow, it needs soil-borne nutrients. This means that the soil in which it is growing needs to be of the right fertility for the plant. Poorer soils can benefit from the addition of a base dressing with fish, blood and bone prior to sowing to give the boost that the developing plant needs, although loamier soils need only be properly dug and prepared to support germination.

SOWING SEEDS OUTDOORS

1 *Set a tight string line where you intend your crop row to be and make a shallow drill with the edge of a swan-necked hoe.*

2 *Water dry soil using a watering can fitted with a fine rose about an hour before sowing and allow to drain.*

3 *Sow the seed thinly along the length of the row. Larger seed may be station sown at regular intervals.*

Some seeds can benefit from being soaked for a short period in tepid water just before planting to help them take on the water they need for germination. This is especially true of beets, but other large seeds also benefit from this treatment.

SOWING IN ROWS

Seed is usually sown in rows. Using a tightly drawn garden line as a guide, draw the corner of a swan-necked hoe along the line to create a shallow drill of about 1–2cm (⅜–¾in) depth, depending upon the seed's individual requirements. Dry ground can be watered after the drill is made. Sow the seed thinly and mix fine seed with silver sand to make it easier to distribute evenly. Mark the end of each row with a label before moving on to the next.

STATION SOWING

Seeds of larger growing plants, particularly those with seed that is large enough to handle, benefit from station sowing. This involves sowing two or three seeds at intervals that will be the eventual crop spacing. If all three germinate, then the two weaker ones are removed or transplanted to gaps where none has germinated.

WIDE ROWS

Certain seeds, particularly peas and beans, benefit from being planted in wide rows. Two rows are effectively station sown at

once, one on each side of a drill that is 15cm (6in) across. The drill is made with the flat of the hoe and after sowing the soil is carefully raked back. Make sure that you do not disturb the seeds from their stations.

BROADCASTING (BLOCKS)

Broadcasting is an ancient method of seed sowing that was used to sow large areas of crops. It involves a "broadcasting" action that separates the seed to an even spacing. The easiest way to do this in small vegetable plots is to split the seed into two halves, mixing small seed with fine sand. Scatter the seed carefully, letting it run from your hand in even arcs as you move your arm from side to side. Sow each half of the

Left: Station sowing is ideal for larger seeds or seedlings that resent disturbance. Use a marked stick to set the spacing of the seed.

seed at a 90-degree angle to the other, thereby assuring an even distribution. Gently rake the seed in once sown and lightly water if needed.

PROTECTING SEEDLINGS

Seedbeds, with their fine "fluffed" earth, act as magnets to birds and animals. Some may take the seed from the ground, but, in truth, most will find it more attractive as a dust bath or litter tray. Once the seedlings emerge, however, some birds find them irresistible. They must be kept out with some form of barrier. One of the easiest methods is to form a low tunnel of chicken wire, supporting this on hoops. For larger areas, a series of stakes in the ground can be covered with netting to keep birds at bay. Sticks with thread or string stretched between them are also effective, but less easily removed for you to tend the crop.

LABELLING

When you sow a row or area of seeds, label it straightaway. Re-usable plastic labels are the best option. Each label should have the name and variety of the plant sown. You may also wish to record the sowing date and if the seed was pre-treated.

4 *Place a label at the end of each row, showing the crop name, variety and the sowing date, before you start a new one.*

5 *Gently cover the seed using a rake. Take care not to disturb or move the seed in the row when you cover it.*

6 *Alternatively, seed can be covered using a soil and potting mix. This is useful on heavy soils and avoids capping (surface hardening).*

SOWING UNDER GLASS

Sowing seed under glass extends the growing season and enables you to raise tender crops that only survive outside in warmer months. It is also ideal for rapidly establishing plants to use as catch crops and as early companion plants. In short, it offers variety and choice for your cropping regimes. Plants raised under glass can be grown on until they reach a size where they are better able to resist pest attack. They can also be planted out at their final spacing, thereby avoiding thinning or gaps in rows.

Above: *A propagator is a useful piece of equipment for raising your seed in ideal growing conditions.*

HEAT REQUIREMENTS

Most seeds have a preferred temperature range within which they will grow. A heated greenhouse, a conservatory or even a warm living room will often provide this, although seeds needing a constant high temperature may need a propagator. Such seeds are mercifully rare among vegetables, although cucumbers, tomatoes and peppers are good examples of crops that will benefit if they are first started off in a propagator.

CHOICE OF CONTAINER

There are a variety of containers that may be used to sow seed under glass. The most common form is the plastic seed tray which has now largely replaced the wooden seed tray. Although more attractive, wooden trays are difficult to keep clean and may harbour plant diseases. Plastic trays can be made of durable polyurethane or sometimes a more flimsy, thin, moulded plastic which is intended for single use. They are available in a variety of sizes, although small 9cm (3½in) pots may be more suitable when you are raising only a few plants.

Modular seed trays are another option. These are made up of individual cells, and a single seed is sown into each one. Seeds that are sown in these trays have the advantage of not suffering any root disturbance when they are planted out in their eventual position. The same is true of some biodegradable pots, which are formed out of paper and coir. These are better (environmentally speaking) than those made from peat, but any recycled material used for these trays is acceptable in the organic kitchen garden.

Inventive recycling can also provide an array of useful sowing containers. Re-using plastic cups, vegetable packing trays and

any other throw-away items that might otherwise end up on a landfill site are all possibilities worth exploring. Old plastic bottles make good individual propagation cowls for small pots and plastic bags can also be used to cover the tops of pots and trays in order to maintain humidity.

PROPAGATORS

These are, in effect, mini-hothouses that help to keep the seed in a warm, moist, stable environment both above and below the soil line. Expensive propagators involve the use of electric soil-warming cables and some have thermostats to control the soil temperature. Many are designed for use in the greenhouse, but

Left: *Many propagators have ventilators on the top in order to aid the flow of fresh air to the seedlings.*

some models are narrow enough for use on a windowsill inside the house. Alternatively, instead of buying the whole propagator, you can purchase a heating mat on which the seed trays can stand in order to receive heat at the bottom. This system has the advantage of being mobile and easily moved about from area to area. Another cheaper method is to buy soil-heating cables to bed into sand. The seed trays sit on the bed of heated sand to receive an even supply of bottom heat.

AFTERCARE OF SEEDLINGS

Once seeds begin to germinate, they can be moved gradually into a less humid environment. The trays are freed of plastic covers, or the propagator vents or lids are opened and, after a few days, the lid is removed completely. As soon as the seedlings reach a size at which they can be handled, they are carefully pricked out into individual pots or larger boxes and trays. Always handle the seedlings by the leaves,

Above: *Modular trays are ideal for planting large seeds and avoid disturbance to roots when planting out or potting on.*

Above: *Individual pots can be used for large seeds. Plant two seeds per pot and remove the weaker seedling.*

SOWING IN TRAYS

1 *Fill a seed tray with propagation potting mix that has been thoroughly mixed. Fill the tray to overflowing and do not firm in the potting mix.*

2 *Using a straightedged piece of board, level the surface of the potting mix by carefully moving the board across the top of the tray.*

3 *Water the tray and leave to drain for about 20 minutes before sowing the seed on the moist surface of the potting mix.*

4 *Larger seed can be placed on the surface of the potting mix at regular intervals. Regular spacing will prevent overcrowding.*

5 *Once the seed has been sown, use a sieve to cover the surface with a fine layer of potting mix.*

6 *Do not cover the seeds of plants that require light for germination. Always check the growing requirements of plants before sowing the seed.*

gently lifting each one from beneath, using a dibber (dibble). Never hold them by the stems because this can cause a great deal of damage to the developing plant. They should be spaced at least 5cm (2in) apart to allow for subsequent development. Water

Above: *Growing vegetables in pots under glass can extend the growing season and also provide a colourful greenhouse display.*

the transplanted seedlings with a fine upturned rose attached to a watering can that has been filled with water overnight, thus bringing it up to room temperature and not giving the transplants a shock of cold water. Keep the seedlings on a warm and sheltered windowsill or in a greenhouse or conservatory. A constant temperature will promote healthy growth.

HARDENING OFF

Plants that have been grown in a greenhouse cannot be put straight outside because their growth is too soft to withstand the cold. They must be gradually hardened off and acclimatized to outdoor conditions. The young plants are hardened off by moving them from the greenhouse and into a cold frame, planted out under cloches, low polythene tunnels or horticultural fleece. Open up the cloches and cold frames or remove the fleece

during the day and replace at night for a week or two before planting out or removing the cloches completely. Remove low polythene tunnels after a couple of weeks depending on the weather conditions. If these are severe, leave in place for longer.

Above: *Watering from below by pouring the water into the base of the seed tray will prevent damage to newly emerging seed.*

THINNING AND TRANSPLANTING

Thinning seedlings not only allows the plants left in the soil to develop and mature into their natural shape and habit, but it is an essential process for good plant health. Thinned seedlings can be transplanted into bare areas or more often special seedbeds are set up or crops are grown under glass and the whole batch of seedlings are transplanted into their final destination within the vegetable garden.

Above: *Growing plants from seed is one of the most satisfying ways of producing new stock for the kitchen garden.*

WHY THIN SEEDLINGS?

All plants need space to develop and grow. Plants that are growing too closely compete not only for space, but also for light, water and important nutrients. In addition to this competitive stress, they also become prone to a variety of fungal diseases, as the air is not able to move around them. Thinning the seedlings helps to counteract these problems and will result in larger, stronger and healthier plants.

HOW TO THIN SEEDLINGS

Thinning is essentially two processes in one. Firstly, you are removing all the plants that are excess to requirements and at the same time you are selecting the biggest, healthiest and strongest plants that will be retained to form the crop.

Before starting to thin, dry ground must be watered, preferably the night before you intend to thin. A measuring stick, marked with the appropriate crop distance, can be used to show the approximate position of

Left: *Seedlings grown elsewhere in the garden can be lifted and replanted in their eventual positions. This method is good for crops that need wide spacing.*

stressed if their roots are disturbed. The alternative, in this case, is to snip off the seedlings at ground level with a pair of sharp scissors, thereby avoiding root disturbance.

Above: *Rows of seedlings are often too crowded and need to be thinned when the plants are young.*

the individual plants. Remove all the plants in between each of the markers, selecting the healthiest plant at or near the mark on the stick. If there are no plants at the marked point, then you can transplant one of the seedlings that is excess to requirements into this position. When you are removing the excess plants, place a finger on the soil at either side of the seedling that is being kept. This protects it from root disturbance. Once you have finished, water the remaining seedlings with a fine rose on a watering can to re-firm the soil around the plants. The seedlings that have been removed can be put on the compost heap.

Avoid thinning with this method on hot dry days or in windy conditions, as the remaining seedlings may become water-

THINNING DISTANCES

The following measurements are the distances that need to be left between thinned seedlings.

Beetroot	7.5–10cm (3–4in)
Broad beans	
(fava beans)	23cm (9in)
Carrots	7.5cm (3in)
Dwarf French beans	
(bush green beans)	20cm (8in)
Florence fennel	25cm (10in)
Kohl rabi	20cm (8in)
Lettuce	23cm (9in)
Parsley	15cm (6in)
Peas	5cm (2in)
Parsnips	15–20cm (6–9in)
Radishes	2.5–5cm (1–2in)
Runner beans	25–30cm (10–12in)
Salsify	15cm (6in)
Scorzonera	15cm (6in)
Spinach	15cm (6in)
Spring onions	
(scallions)	5cm (2in)
Swedes (rutabaga	
or yellow turnip)	30cm (12in)
Swiss chard	30cm (12in)
Turnips	15–20cm (6–8in)

TRANSPLANTING SEEDLINGS

1 *Water your row of seedlings at least an hour before transplanting and preferably the night before if no rain has fallen.*

2 *Using a fork to loosen the soil, gently lift the seedlings. Take care to handle them by their leaves and never touch the stems.*

3 *Using a tight line, straight edge or notched planting board, replant the seedlings at the appropriate spacing for that crop.*

4 *Gently water the seedlings immediately after sowing. Never let roots dry out at any stage during transplanting.*

TRANSPLANTING SEEDLINGS

The most common way of transplanting seedlings involves planting container-grown plants into open ground. Early vegetable crops can easily be raised in this way. The other method is to raise seedlings in open ground near to where they are to be planted out. Transplanting outdoor seedlings means that a smaller area of the vegetable plot is needed for sowing and, in consequence, a smaller seedbed is required. Transplanting seedlings is a good way of growing plants such as lettuce that are to be used in catch-cropping beds or where plants are to be planted out in no-dig beds.

The ideal time for transplanting outdoor seedlings is during damp overcast weather because this helps to prevent the seedlings' roots drying out. As is the case when thinning the plants, the seedlings will need watering the evening before. It is best to dig up only a few plants at a time, discarding any that are weak, damaged or appear to be sick. Seedlings can be placed in a plastic bag to maintain humidity around them while they are out of the ground.

A garden line can be set out in the vegetable patch in a similar manner to the way in which it is placed for preparing a seed drill. The position of the plants can then be determined using a measuring stick. Use a dibber (dibble) or thin trowel to plant the seedlings, firming lightly around the base before moving on to the next transplant. Once the row is completed, it is important that you water them in.

For catch cropping or planting among other plants, the surrounding crop may well determine the spacings between the transplants, although the procedure remains exactly the same.

AFTERCARE

The aftercare that your crops require is essential to ensure healthy plants that produce high yields. There are a number of different techniques that are listed below to help you on your way. Just remember that the more effort you put in then the better they will taste. As well as judicious watering and feeding, you will also have to weed the vegetable plot and provide some form of plant protection and support. But the reward of such care and attention is delicious home-grown produce.

Above: *Regular cropping of vegetables such as this ruby chard will encourage the development of new growth.*

WATERING

Vegetables need watering if there is no significant rainfall. This is especially true when the crops are young and only have shallow roots. Having a soil that is rich in organic matter is an advantage because it conserves water in the soil, particularly if the soil is sandy. You can enrich the soil by digging in organic matter, growing green manures or by continuous mulching.

If you have a large garden, mulching around the crop with straw, farmyard manure, garden compost or another similar substance can help to limit water loss. When you water, it is best to give the plants a thorough soaking, allowing the water to penetrate deeply. Giving a light watering will just encourage shallow surface roots that are easily damaged by prolonged drought. Prolonged dry periods also encourage plants to bolt, thus ruining the crop.

Certain plants such as cabbages and lettuces are naturally shallow rooted, whereas others such as tomatoes and squash are naturally deep rooted. Shallow rooters especially benefit from mulching and may need watering often in hot summers.

FEEDING

This is generally only necessary for heavier feeding plants such as pumpkins and marrows, but can provide a tonic for any crop during the growing season. Specific nutrient deficiencies are rare in the garden if a regular crop rotation and soil enrichment programme is followed, but if specific shortages are noticed, they must be countered immediately. Good liquid feeds can be made in your back garden. Try making compost tea or "worm liquid", as these are an excellent choice for actively growing plants.

Above: *The effort you put into protecting and caring for your crops will be rewarded at harvest time.*

Apply these feeds once every week or two. Many plants are given their main feed annually. This type of feeding is normally applied to fruit trees and bushes in the spring and is best applied in the form of a slower-release fertilizer such as bonemeal.

WEEDING

Check your plants regularly and try to keep them as weed-free as possible. Remember that weeds compete with your plants for light, space, water and nutrients. It is better to weed a little and often than to weed irregularly. Even areas that have been mulched or have close cropping regimes need regular checks and weeds removed.

PLANT PROTECTION

Pests and diseases come in many different forms. Over time you will learn which specific problems your garden is prone to. Keep a yearly notebook of all the things that affect your crop each season, noting what control measures you used and how effective they were. In time you will have a record of how and when to manage pests and other problems in your own garden.

Above: *The careful harvesting of crops is essential if they are to store well. Here, carrots are being lifted with a garden fork.*

Above: *The regular harvesting of peas and beans will help to extend the length of the harvest period.*

Above: *Taller plants and climbers will need some form of support. Canes or sticks with twine tied between them provide ideal temporary supports.*

PROVIDING SUPPORT

Plants may need supporting, especially climbers such as peas and beans. This support must begin at an early age, using twiggy pea sticks or hazel sticks, both of which can look ornate. Bamboo canes can be used for a host of climbing plants, but it is more ethically correct to use local materials rather than to use a product that has been transported thousands of miles. Squashes can be grown up fancy supports made from stakes and strong string or rope, making a curious garden feature. Other plants such as globe artichokes and Florence fennel can benefit from individual supports for their stems.

Above: *Marrows and pumpkins are easily stored in trays that should then be kept in a cool dark place.*

HARVESTING AND STORING

When harvesting, it is tempting to pick the good specimens and leave the rest, but remember to pick and compost poor or rotten ones as well as the best of the crop. Diseased or damaged crops can begin to rot and may infect the remaining harvest.

Freshly picked vegetables are higher in nutritional value than stored ones. So, during the growing season, pick what you need and store the surplus. Choosing when to pick a certain vegetable is a matter of taste. Some prefer to pick produce such as beans when they are young, small and succulent, whereas others prefer the beans to be more mature.

Crops can be stored in a number of ways. Root crops can be left in the ground in all but the coldest winters, lifting them as they are needed. Some crops, such as parsnips, actually develop a better taste after they have been subjected to frost. Alternatively, root crops can be stored in a cool dark place. They should be cleaned and stored in sand and a sterile organic substance such as coir, untreated sawdust, fine leaf mould, fine bark or sterilized soil.

Store other vegetables on shelves or boxes, ensuring that they do not touch. Onions and garlic are best kept in open sacks or in strings. Cabbages can be kept in nets until needed for up to two to three months. Other brassicas such as Brussels sprouts and swedes are best kept outside in the ground, harvesting them as needed.

Freezing is another storage option. Some vegetables, such as asparagus, beans and cauliflowers, are best blanched in boiling water for a couple of minutes before freezing. Alternatively, you can cook the vegetables and then freeze them, as is the case for marrows and Jerusalem artichokes.

Above: *Store root crops such as carrots in a cool dark place and cover them in sterile sawdust, leaf mould or coir.*

CROPS FOR STORING OVER WINTER

Harvest time often brings the problem of a crop glut. Storage can enable you to enjoy this bounty for longer.

Asparagus Best consumed fresh. Cook or blanch before freezing
Aubergines (eggplant) Cook before freezing
Beetroot (beets) Shelf storage or pickling
Broad (fava) beans Freezing or drying
Brussels sprouts Freezing. Leave on plant until needed
Cabbages Freezing or shelf storage. Leave in ground in mild conditions
Carrots Leave in ground in mild conditions. Shelf storage
Cauliflowers Blanch before freezing. Shelf storage if hung upside down in dark and misted
Celery Cook before freezing. Limited shelf storage
Courgettes (zucchini) Cook before freezing. Limited shelf storage
Dwarf French beans (bush green beans) Freezing
Garlic In sacks or strung
Kale Harvest through winter
Kohl rabi Leave in ground if mild or protected, medium shelf storage
Leeks Freezing, leave in ground in mild conditions, shelf storage
Marrows (zucchini) Cook before freezing, shelf storage
Onions In sacks or strung
Parsnips Leave in ground until needed or late winter
Peas Freezing or drying on plant
Peppers Blanch before freezing. Pickle or dry
Potatoes Store in paper sacks once cleaned and dried
Pumpkins Cook before freezing. Good shelf storage if fully ripe
Rhubarb Cook before freezing
Runner beans Freezing
Shallots In sacks or strung
Spinach Cook then freeze
Swedes (rutabaga or yellow turnip) Leave in ground until needed (may go woody by late winter)
Sweetcorn (corn) Freezing or pickling
Tomatoes Cook before freezing. Pickle
Turnips Leave in ground until needed

GROWING HERBS

Herbs are valued for their culinary, medicinal, decorative and aromatic properties. They come in a diverse range of sizes, shapes and habits, ranging from ground-creeping thyme through to the tall architectural stems of angelica. The choice of herbs is so great that there is always something to offer a gardener with only a window box, hanging basket or a small space. A herb garden offers a treat for the senses and these fragrant plants are also easy to grow in the organic garden.

Above: *Herbs are easy to grow given the right growing conditions. They provide an attractive, often fragrant, display.*

WHERE TO GROW HERBS

Herbs can be grown in a range of settings, such as custom-designed herb gardens and ornamental borders. They can also be grown as companion plants in the vegetable garden and are eminently suited to growing in containers, hanging baskets and window boxes. They are especially useful if grown near the kitchen.

Herbs range from tall showy herbaceous plants such as fennel (*Foeniculum vulgare*) and tansy (*Tanacetum vulgare*) to ground-hugging cushion plants such as thyme (*Thymus vulgaris*). The majority of herbs originate from dry sunny environments and so need sunshine to help them develop their essential oils. It is best to site herbs in an open, sunny spot in the garden where they will thrive.

SOIL PREPARATION

Drier sites suit most herbs, and the sunnier and hotter the site the better they will taste. The taste and smell of herbs is usually due to the production of essential oils within the plants. If they are grown in hot conditions, then the concentrations of essential oils will be greater. Growing herbs in very moist rich soils can accelerate their growth, but will result in a milder flavour. They will also look better and flower less than their "hot-site" counterparts and be easier to harvest.

Herbs are, however, best grown in a soil that is loamy with some added organic matter. The ideal pH is 6.5 to 7.0, which means that herbs can easily be planted among vegetables in the kitchen garden.

SOWING HERB SEED

Herbs may be sown directly in the soil outdoors, just like vegetables. The preparation of the seedbed and the sowing techniques are exactly the same, and they can easily be interplanted or block planted among other vegetables.

Alternatively, herb seeds may be planted under cover, raising them in the same way as early vegetables and bedding plants and then hardening them off before planting out in the garden. This method is especially useful for more tender, leafy herbs such as basil or coriander (cilantro).

Left: *Herbs are an important element in both ornamental and kitchen gardens, being decorative as well as useful.*

Above: *You can restrict the spread of invasive plants such as mint (*Mentha*) by planting them in pots or buckets that are then buried in the ground.*

Above: *Pinching out newly planted herbs such as this bay (*Laurus*) will encourage bushy, leafy growth.*

Basil (*Ocimum basilicum*), for example, associates well with outdoor tomatoes, both in the garden and in the kitchen. These can be planted out together from an indoor sowing and the crop will be mutually complementary. Indoor sowing can also provide you with herbs that can be cropped earlier in the season, effectively extending the useful life of your organic herb garden.

PLANTING HERBS

1 *Excavate a planting hole that is about a quarter to half as big again as the plant's rootball. Make sure it is deep enough.*

2 *Ensure that the top of the compost is the same level as the surrounding soil. Refill the gap around the rootball and firm the soil.*

3 *Water the plant immediately after planting. Keep the plant well watered until it is fully established into the surrounding soil.*

PLANTING HERBS IN THE GARDEN

Herbs can be sited anywhere in the garden as long as it is sunny. They have a range of forms and colours and often make valuable additions to the ornamental garden. Foxgloves (*Digitalis*), sage (*Salvia officinalis*) and the curry plant (*Helichrysum italicum*) are a few examples of herbs that can be used in annual and herbaceous borders as well as in the kitchen garden. Some herbs, such as mint (*Mentha*) and lemon balm (*Melissa officinalis*), can become very invasive if they are not contained in a pot or sunken sink when growing among other plants in an ornamental border. Remove the flower-heads from the mint before they have had a chance to seed, as the seed will germinate all over your border.

PLANTING HERBS IN CONTAINERS

Herbs make excellent subjects for use in pots and containers and are wonderful for patio gardens that catch plenty of summer sun, although you need to make sure that the potting mix never dries out. Raised beds, which provide good drainage, are also good areas for growing herbs. Always plant them in a free-draining potting mix that will not become waterlogged. There are numerous cultivars of culinary herbs that can be used for ornamental purposes, and groups of pot-grown herbs can be extremely decorative as well as supplying you with a range of fresh flavourings. Thyme, rosemary, lavender and sage are all good choices to grow in pots, either outdoors or on your windowsill.

Above: *Herbs are easily grown in a container which will provide an excellent focal point in the kitchen garden.*

Herb pots require little maintenance, save for watering and the occasional feed during the growing season. Most are rarely long term and are best restarted yearly or every other year. Herbs that are permanently in pots, such as bay trees, will need repotting every year. Spreading subjects like thyme can be lifted and both top-pruned and root-pruned prior to repotting.

Mint and other spreading herbaceous subjects may need dividing and repotting from time to time. This is done by splitting the crown of the plant into smaller pieces and then repotting one of these back into the container with some fresh potting mix. Dividing in this way is best performed annually for very vigorous herbs. Harvesting on a regular basis is often enough to control the growth of many potted herb arrangements (where a number are planted in one container), but a light trim may also be necessary from time to time.

Potted herbs may also be grown in the greenhouse to ensure a supply both earlier and later in the season. Try growing basil (*Ocimum basilicum*), coriander (cilantro; *Coriandrum sativum*), chives (*Allium schoenoprasum*) and dill (*Anethum graveolens*) in pots because this will save money if you spend a lot on fresh herbs. Pots raised under glass can be brought into the kitchen for ease of use. A series of successional sowings under glass will ensure that you have fresh herbs for most or even all of the year, both indoors and out.

Above: *Planting spreading herbs such as thyme (*Thymus*) in pots will help to control them and can also be decorative.*

HARVESTING AND STORING HERBS

Many commonly used culinary herbs such as basil, coriander (cilantro), chives and parsley can be grown indoors on a windowsill or conservatory during the cooler winter months if you have space. If you are not able to spare growing room for these, most are easily stored for use later. Herbs are easily harvested and most of the storage techniques are simple and straightforward.

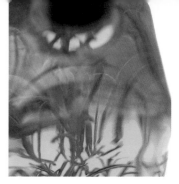

Above: *Aromatic herbs such as rosemary (Rosmarinus officinalis) can be used to flavour bottles of olive oil.*

HOW TO HARVEST HERBS

Various parts of herbs, including the leaves, flowers, fruits and seeds, are gathered at different times, depending upon the plant and the part that provides the desirable properties. Annual leafy herbs such as basil (*Ocimum basilicum*) and parsley (*Petroselinum crispum*) should be carefully picked, never taking more than about 10 per cent of the growth in a single picking.

The same is true of perennials such as sage (*Salvia officinalis*), thyme (*Thymus vulgaris*) and rosemary (*Rosmarinus officinalis*) because severe pruning or over-stripping of the leaves will weaken the plant. It is important that you not remove more than one-third of the growth at any one time. If you harvest carefully, you will get a more vigorous leaf growth that will result in healthier plants.

Above: *The best time to harvest herbs is usually just before they flower. This is when they have their strongest flavour.*

As a general rule, pick herbs just before the plant is about to flower, which is when they have the strongest flavour. Pick the leaves when they are fresh and at their sweetest, selecting blemish-free, upper leaves. Collect the leaves in early morning or late evening, provided they are dry, rather than in bright afternoon sun when the plant's sap is rising. This is when the aroma of herbs is at its strongest and is easily lost if picked during this time of day. Flowers such as borage (*Borago officinalis*) and lavender (*Lavandula*), however, are best picked just before they reach full bloom and once they begin to open in the heat of the day.

Rhizomes, like ginger and turmeric, are collected in autumn, just as the leaves begin to change colour and the maximum amount of nutrition has been stored. Use a fork to gently free the roots from the soil and always avoid "hand-pulling" them. Choose only the best ones and use a vegetable brush to gently loosen any dirt. If you do need to wash them, do so quickly in cold water and avoid soaking them, as this can result in lost flavour.

Harvesting seeds tends to vary from plant to plant. Some seeds, like those of borage, simply fall to the ground as soon as they are ripe. Thyme seeds are very small and hard to see. Parsley and coriander seeds shake off very easily, and frequently the plants will have sown next year's crop for you before you realize they have gone to seed. One method of harvesting any seed that is difficult to collect is to tie a small paper bag over the flower head when the seeds start to form, ensuring that you can collect the seed without losing any. It would be advisable to use this method for collecting from plants with small seed as they can drop off when ripe or sometimes spring from the plant.

Above: *Herbs can be dried for later use by hanging them in bunches in a dry place out of direct sunlight.*

DRYING HERBS AND FLOWERS

Store herbs in a cool, dry place with minimum exposure to air and sunlight. One of the most popular methods of preserving them for use during the winter months is drying. This method can actually improve the flavour of some herbs, particularly the leaves of bay trees (*Laurus nobilis*). Herbs may be dried in bundles secured with a rubber band or string and hung upside down from a rack in a dry location such as an airing cupboard or shed.

When drying the herbs, the temperature of the area should not exceed 30°C (86°F) because the plants' essential oils will evaporate at or above this temperature. Do not dry your herbs in the kitchen where they will be spoiled by the humidity caused by cooking.

Fresh herbs can also be placed in brown paper bags. Remember to label the bags because it will be hard to distinguish between the herbs once they have dried. Store in a dry, dark, cool place until the herbs inside are dry, shaking the bags occasionally so that the plants dry evenly. Remove any stems and store the dried herbs in airtight jars. Keep the jars away from light to protect the colour and flavour of the herbs. Roots are best chopped into small pieces and dried in an oven. In general, you can expect those that you have grown and dried yourself to last at least two years.

STORING HERBS

Herbs can also be preserved in other ways, so that you can use them in cooking throughout the year.

Herb salts In a cool oven, spread a layer of ground salt on a sheet of greaseproof (waxed) paper. Sprinkle the chopped fresh herbs on top of the salt and bake for 10–20 minutes. When the herbs are dry, let them cool and place in a jar. Chives, oregano, thyme, lemon balm, lemon thyme, parsley, rosemary and basil can all be treated this way.

Puréeing This method involves mixing approximately 60ml (4tbsp) of olive oil with 2l (8 cups) fresh basil leaves which have been washed and dried. These are blended in a processor until puréed before being transferred to a jar. Stir each time you use it and top with a thin layer of oil afterwards. The purée should keep for up to one year in a refrigerator.

Above: *After herbs have been hung up to dry, separate the seeds from the dry flower heads before storing in tightly sealed jars.*

Freezing herbs Herbs such as dill, fennel, basil and parsley freeze well. The herbs should be cleaned and put into separate, labelled freezer bags. Alternatively, chop the leaves and freeze them with a little water in ice-cube trays. Chop the herbs finely, filling each cube, half with herbs and half with water, before freezing. Transfer the frozen cubes to plastic bags and label. Frozen herbs are best used within six months.

HERBAL INFUSIONS

You can also make a hot infusion of leafy herbs by placing the herb and any fine-quality olive oil in a glass bowl. This is then placed over a pan of gently simmering water and heated gently for about three hours, ensuring that the water in the pan does not dry out. The strained oil, once it has cooled, should be stored in airtight bottles or jars.

A cool infusion of flowery herbs involves using fresh herbs such as chamomile which are ground with a pestle and mortar and packed into a large jar and covered with oil. The sealed jar is then left in a warm, sunny place for two to three weeks and shaken occasionally. It is then strained and placed into airtight jars or bottles where it can be stored for up to a year.

A simple way of creating aromatic olive oil is to simply add a large sprig of your chosen herbs – rosemary and mint are good choices – to a bottle of olive oil. Store the bottle in a cool dark place for about ten days before using.

You can also make your own herbal vinegars by adding fresh herbs such as tarragon or rosemary or cloves of garlic, slices of ginger, chillies or peppercorns and all-spice powder to white vinegar. Crush about a quarter litre volume (1 cup) of loosely packed fresh herbs for each litre of vinegar. If you are using dried herbs, use half the amount of herb stated above. It is important that you use only commercially prepared vinegars, as homemade vinegar may not have a low enough pH to prevent bacterial growth. Place the vinegar in a pot on the stove and heat, but do not boil. Place the herbs in a clean, sterilized jar and slightly crush them. Pour the vinegar over the herbs and cover the jar tightly. Let the herb-vinegar mixture steep in a dark place at room temperature, shaking the jar every couple of days. After a week, strain the vinegar and place in bottles and store for up to six weeks.

DRYING AND FREEZING HERBS

1 *Pick seed just as it is ripening. Place the seeds on a tray or in a paper or muslin bag. Leave in a cool, dark place for a few days until the seed is completely dry.*

2 *Herb seeds that have been dried can be stored in old glass jars with an airtight lid. Store the jars in a cool, dry, dark place and label them for future reference.*

3 *Herbs can be frozen in ice-cube trays. Fill the trays with water after you have added the herbs to make ready-to-use cubes. Herbs can also be packed into freezer bags.*

GROWING FRUIT TREES AND BUSHES

Freshly picked fruit from the organic garden tastes absolutely delicious. The warm taste of a juicy sweet raspberry or the crisp flavour of a tree-ripened apple would tempt many a gardener into growing their own fruit produce. The tastes can be quite different from shop-grown produce where storage, handling, packing and off-the-tree ripening all take their toll on the quality and taste of the fruit.

Above: *A sunny wall provides an ideal location for growing fruit trees, such as this pear, that need warmth.*

WHERE CAN FRUIT BE GROWN?

Fruit trees and bushes can be grown wherever there is space. Strawberries can be used in hanging baskets or tubs, dwarf apple trees can be planted in ornamental containers and a number of fruits, such as cherries, white and red currants and figs, can all be grown against walls. Fruits not only provide produce for the kitchen table but many of them have ornamental qualities and can blend well with other plants in the decorative garden.

CHOOSING A SITE

The best site for fruit, both indoors and out, is a sunny one. Sunlight is essential, not just for the ripening of the fruit itself but also for flower bud formation and flowering. In addition, fruit trees and bushes often appreciate a sheltered spot where even exotic fruit can be raised. Within the garden a sheltered sunny wall can provide the ideal place to grow peaches, apricots or figs. If cold winters are a problem, then provide winter protection in the form of a portable frame or, alternatively, grow the plants in a greenhouse. It is worth noting that providing your plants with the ideal conditions for healthy growth will reap its rewards in the

end. Not only will you harvest heavier yields, but, more importantly, your plants will be less prone to pest and disease attacks, which is an obvious advantage when growing organically.

SELECTING THE RIGHT PLANTS

Variety selection should not be based purely on hardiness but on personal preference. You may also wish to consider how easy the fruit tree or bush is to grow, fruit size, taste and the time of harvest. Selecting more than one variety can result in having fresh fruit over a longer period due to a succession of ripening.

Some fruit trees combine the best qualities of two plants. Grafting utilizes the qualities of the variety as top growth (scion) and other desirable qualities from a rootstock that may be absent from the variety. The scion is the fruiting variety that is budded or grafted on to the rootstock which is selected for certain characteristics such as dwarfing, nematode insect resistance, soil type, cold hardiness and disease resistance.

The most commonly grown rootstocks for amateur gardeners are the apple semi-dwarfs and dwarfs. Grapes are also grafted on to clonal rootstocks, although they are often supplied on their own roots. Figs, olives and various types of berry are also usually supplied as plants on their own roots.

Dwarf apple trees are very useful in small gardens and are eminently suited to container growing. They produce fruit of the same size, colour and quality as larger standard trees and require the same pruning, nutritional and care regimes as a standard-size tree.

Left: *Most fruit bushes will benefit from a generous application of well-rotted manure or compost early in the year.*

Dwarf trees fruit much sooner after planting and bear less fruit per tree. When harvesting the fruit, you can reach all parts of the tree from the ground without using a ladder and the trees are easier to train and prune on an annual basis. Grafting the desired variety on to special clonal rootstocks "dwarfs" apples. The most popular dwarfing rootstocks for apple were developed in England and are designated as either EM or M (for East Malling) or MM (for Malling Merton). Dwarfed trees must be pruned annually or size control may be lost. In addition, loss of fruit by frost or pests will also increase growth so necessitating summer pruning.

PLANTING FRUIT TREES AND BUSHES

As with any other type of tree, good ground preparation and careful handling are essential steps to successfully establishing your fruit trees and bushes. The cheapest option when buying fruit trees is to purchase bare-rooted plants. The disadvantage is that they are only available during the dormant season. The most important factor in handling bare-rooted plants is not to let the roots dry out. When you buy trees always check the condition of the roots and packing material. Heel in plants by covering the roots with moist soil in a cool environment outdoors if they are not to be planted immediately.

Dig a hole slightly wider and deeper than the spread and length of the root system, making sure the sides of the hole are not "glazed" over as this will result in a root girdling. After trimming diseased, dead, broken or extra long roots, place the tree in the hole and spread out the roots. For larger trees, place the stake in the hole and drive it in (remembering to first remove the tree and cover the roots). Place the tree back into

PLANTING A FRUIT TREE

1 *Dig a hole in the ground that is at least half as large again as the rootball of the fruit tree. Loosen the sides and the base of the planting hole with a garden fork.*

2 *Remove the pot and check the rootball for girdling roots. Tease these out by hand or with a garden fork.*

3 *Use a straightedge to make sure that the plant is at the right depth in the hole. Fill around the roots with soil, firm it down and water well.*

4 *Hammer in a stake at an angle of about 60° in order to avoid the rootball and place a tie on the tree. Saw off the end of the stake. Nail the tie to the stake to secure it.*

5 *The tree should remain staked for approximately one year. As the diameter of the tree stem increases, loosen the tree tie as required.*

the hole and return the soil, firming in layers of about 30cm (12in) as you go. This avoids large air spaces being left around the roots and ensures that it is set firmly. Trees should be planted at the same depth as they were grown in the nursery. Make sure the bud union (for trees on rootstocks) is about 5–7cm (2–2¾in) above the soil line. Do not place fertilizer in the planting hole as this can be added later. Mulch the newly planted tree with well-rotted manure or compost to suppress weeds. Container-grown nursery stock can be transplanted any time of the year. Site preparation is the same as for bare-rooted stock. Make sure that you check the roots as they can become distorted or root bound if they are

grown in containers for a long period of time. Teasing these roots out can help avoid root girdling, but the best way to do this is to use field-grown (bare-rooted) stock.

PRUNING NEWLY PLANTED STOCK

Fruit trees must be pruned when they are planted for a number of reasons. If planting bare-rooted stock, the top of the tree must be pruned to counter-balance the loss of the root system which would have been severed in the nursery during lifting. Pruning also forces the growth of laterals from which the future framework of the fruit tree will be selected. Branches that are desirably located can be retained as part of the framework whereas undesirable branches are removed.

FRUIT TREE POLLINATION

Pollination is the transfer of pollen from the male part of the flower to the female part of the flower (the stigma) to allow fruit to set and seeds to develop. Seeds cause the fruit to develop properly. If both the pollen and stigma are from the same flower or from another flower from the same variety, the process is called self-pollination. Fruit trees that set fruit as the result of self-pollination are called self-fruitful, whereas those relying on pollen from a different variety are called self-unfruitful. The latter needs two varieties near to each other for fruit set to occur. This is called cross-pollination.

Apples Apples generally need two varieties for good fruit set. This can be another apple variety or a crab apple that blooms with the edible crop.
Apricots Self-fruitful
Berries (all types) Self-fruitful
Cherries Sweet cherry is self-unfruitful and needs two varieties for good crop set. Sour cherry varieties are self-fruitful.
European plums Self-fruitful
Figs Self-fruitful
Japanese plums Self-unfruitful as a rule with the exception of Santa Rosa which will set fruit fairly well without cross-pollination.
Nectarines Self-fruitful
Peaches Self-fruitful with the exception of 'J.H. Hale' which has to be pollinated by another variety.
Pears These always need two varieties to ensure good fruit set.

SUPPORTING FRUIT TREES AND SHRUBS

Many of the fruits that we grow, such as free-standing apple or plum trees, require support only in the early stages, whereas other fruits, like the raspberry, need this throughout their lives. Supports benefit the plants in a number of different ways. They help in establishing strong roots and can prop up trained specimens such as cordons and espaliers. This helps to maintain healthy vigorous growth and increase fruit yields.

Above: *Apples can easily be grown in rows as cordons that are supported by a framework of stakes and wires.*

WALL AND FENCE FRUIT

The training of fruit on a wall or a fence is carried out to gain the maximum production of high-quality fruit in a limited space. As well as being ideal for a small garden, this can also look extremely decorative. Numerous training systems, based on the art of espalier which originated in France and Italy about 400 years ago, have been devised. The most useful training systems used in gardens today are the fan, espalier and cordon. Apples, pears and plums are all suited to this method of training, which is usually supported by a wall, fence or wire trellis. The plants are normally held to the wall or fence using wires which are held in place by vine eyes, positioned 60–90cm (2–3ft) apart. The wire is led through the holes in the vine eyes and secured at both ends. The wires should be no more than 30–45cm (12–18in) apart.

FREESTANDING WIREWORK

Raspberries, blackberries and other hybrid berries are all grown on a permanent framework. They are usually grown on a freestanding structure that supports the loose growth of the plants. To build such a structure, insert a post at least 60cm (24in) into the ground at the end of each row. Brace each end post with another post set at a 45-degree angle. Insert intermediate posts between the two end ones at a distance of every 2m (6½ft). They are set in at the same depth as the end posts, but no bracing posts are needed. Fix the wires on to the posts so that they run the length of the support. Place the first wire 60cm (24in) from the ground, pull tight and attach to the posts using staples or eye-bolts. The other wires are attached at 30cm (12in) intervals until they reach the top of the support. The final height depends on the height of the fruit.

INDIVIDUAL SUPPORT

When they are first planted, all free-standing trees require support to help them to establish a strong healthy root system. You can use a stake to support a fruit tree, ensuring that the stake is placed on the windward side of the tree. The stake is inserted before the tree is planted and is driven well into the ground. The general rule is to have a stake that is one-third the height of the tree showing above the ground. The tree is then tied to the stake using a tree tie. Do not use string or rope because this can damage the bark. A low stake such as this will allow the top part of the tree to move about freely and so help the tree to thicken and strengthen its trunk. For most fruit trees the stake should only be left in the ground for approximately one year and not for several years as is commonly practised.

STAKING A FRUIT BUSH

1 *Using a large mallet, drive a strong wooden post into the ground at the end of a row of the fruit bushes to a depth of about 60cm (2ft).*

2 *Fix another strainer post at a 45-degree angle in order to support the upright. Place this on the side the wire is to run and nail it firmly.*

3 *Fix the wires to one of the posts and then stretch these tightly along the row, stapling them at each post along the row as you go.*

4 *The fruit bushes can be fastened to or trained along these wires. Take care not to tie stems too tightly as this will damage them.*

PROTECTING FRUIT

There can be few more frustrating events in the kitchen-garden calendar than losing your fruit crop (or a fair portion of it) to birds. However, we have to remember that birds are a strong ally in the fight against pests in an organic garden and should be encouraged into fruit-growing areas when the bushes are not fruiting. Protection for the fruit crops will therefore need to take the form of moveable cloches or fruit cages where the netting can be removed after fruiting has taken place.

Above: *Cloches can be used to protect young strawberries from bad weather and also to keep pests at bay.*

FRUIT CAGES

This is perhaps the easiest way to protect tall fruit crops such as blackcurrants, raspberries and gooseberries because these plants can all be grown under the one structure. This makes it easy to maintain and harvest the fruit.

A permanent fruit-cage structure with removable netting is the ideal scenario because the netting can be put in place just before the crop ripens and then is taken down again after fruiting has occurred. This allows the birds to roam freely around the area at all other times, but without jeopardizing the crop at fruiting time. Alternatively, a series of small cages can be constructed over crops that ripen at different times, netting each of them individually as the fruit begins to ripen. This is a wildlife-friendly way of protecting the fruit, but it is also time-consuming.

Above: *A tunnel of wire netting is ideal for protecting ripening strawberries from pests such as birds.*

LOW-LEVEL PROTECTION

Smaller- or lower-growing crops, such as strawberries, can also benefit from a barrier to protect them from birds. This is easily achieved, as the structure does not need to be large, permanent or even particularly sturdy. One simple method is to form a low tunnel of chicken wire, supported on hoops that are bent into an inverted U-shape. For larger areas, a series of stakes hammered into the ground can be covered with netting to keep the birds at bay. Plants growing on wire trellises can be protected with netting draped over the stakes and top wires and weighted at the base with stones.

Left: *Fruit trees growing against a wall can easily be protected with a cost-effective frame that is covered with netting.*

Right: *Fleece stretched over a frame can help protect the blossom of wall specimens from late frosts.*

Larger bush fruit can be covered with netting and weighted down with stones. A little of the crop may be accessible to birds, but most will be protected.

PROTECTION WITHOUT BARRIERS

Most bird deterrents depend upon shocking the birds or mimicking something that they are naturally afraid of. Scarecrows are an age-old favourite. Other deterrents mimic the shape of hawks or make noises that will startle the birds. A relatively recent "innovation" has been to hang compact discs from wires stretched through the crop. Most of these deterrents tend to work very well at first until the birds get used to them. However, the only drawback is that when the birds get used to them, they resume their onslaught with a vengeance. The only way to overcome this is to keep changing the deterrents every few days.

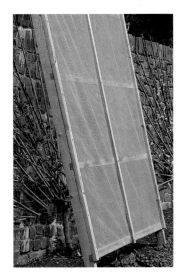

PRUNING FRUIT TREES AND SHRUBS

The general purpose of pruning fruit trees is to regulate growth, increase crop yields and to improve fruit size and quality. The fruit trees also need to have all the dead, diseased and damaged wood removed as well as overcrowded areas thinned out. Pruning is also performed in order to establish a tree with a strong framework that is capable of supporting heavy crops without causing damage to the plant.

Above: *The careful pruning of trained specimens, such as this pear, will result in good blossom and improve fruit yields.*

WHEN TO PRUNE FRUIT TREES

If a fruit tree is pruned in spring, all the effort that the tree has put into bud production is wasted. The best time to prune is in winter when the plants are dormant and the sap has not yet started to rise. This applies to all fruit except for plums and cherries which are susceptible to silverleaf disease at this time and are best pruned in summer.

Summer pruning is also recommended if you wish to control vigorous growth in formally trained fruits such as fans, cordons and espaliers.

When pruning is underway, older fruit-bearing trees should be pruned first. Young, non-bearing apple trees and stone fruits can be pruned later to minimize the risk of winter injury.

BASIC PRUNING CUTS

Although there are different methods of pruning and training, the pruning cuts are the same. Always make the pruning cut just above a bud, ensuring that the cut is angled away from the bud. This will allow rainwater

---

BENEFITS OF PRUNING

Pruning fruit trees and bushes has many advantages, some of which are outlined below.

- Increased fruit yields.
- Can aid ripening of the fruit.
- Maintains healthy growth.
- Regulates growth.
- Improves fruit size and quality.
- Controls the spread of diseases.

---

to drip down the other side of the stem and away from the bud, thus protecting the top of the cut from rotting.

Larger branches will need to be cut with a saw. If the branch is very heavy, you will need to remove the branch in three separate stages. Cut underneath the branch first, 20–25cm (8–10in) away from where the final cut will be. Make the second cut on the top of the branch just behind the first undercut. Follow this through until the

weight of the branch makes the wood split and it falls off cleanly at the undercut. You will then need to make a third cut at the branch collar, cutting straight from the top to the bottom of the branch as there is no weight left to tear the bark.

Above: *Training can give rise to a variety of ornamental shapes. These pear trees have been trained into a cylindrical shape.*

PRUNING LARGE BRANCHES

1 *Make a cut about 20–25cm (8–10in) out from where the final cut will be on the underside of the branch. Cut about a third of the way into the branch.*

2 *Make a cut about 10cm (4in) nearer the position of the final cut, cutting until the branch snaps. The initial undercut prevents the wood splitting or bark from stripping.*

3 *Position the saw for the last cut to avoid damaging the swollen area at the base of the branch. The cut will heal in a couple of seasons. No wound painting is necessary.*

SUCCESSFUL FRUIT TREE AND SHRUB PRUNING

Pruning fruit trees is a very complex subject and, like so many areas of organic gardening, is the subject of opinion and hot debate. Despite this it is possible to apply certain guiding principles that can enable you to prune your fruit trees and bushes successfully.

1 **Remove root suckers arising at the base of the tree**
These compete with the upper growth for water and essential nutrients and their dense habit can harbour pests.

2 **Always cut out dead, dying, damaged or diseased limbs first**
Helps to maintain the plant's health and enables you to see precisely what needs doing next.

3 **Remove low, drooping limbs**
These will not bear fruit and will often be heavily shaded by growth above. They are an unproductive drain on the tree.

4 **Remove upright growth or outward growth in the case of wall-trained bushes**
Upright growth will produce a flush of growth at the end and will not fruit well. Branches growing away from the wall will shade the fruit behind causing poor ripening.

5 **Remove crossing or dense parallel growth**
Crossing growth will rub and can cause bark damage that will allow disease entry. Dense growth will also shade the developing fruits. This will slow and limit the ripening of the fruit.

6 **Freestanding trees should have upper limbs cut back further than lower limbs**
This will result in the development of a conical shape that will allow light penetration all the way down the side. Fruit will ripen more evenly.

7 **Remove water sprouts as they develop**
Water sprouts can quickly develop and cover the developing fruits, causing poor ripening and harvesting difficulties. They can be easily removed by hand. This is best done early in the season when the growth is soft and is therefore easily removed. Carry out regular inspections throughout the season to control the water sprouts.

8 **Once the larger cuts have been made, thin out the smaller branches**
Removing thick branches first allows you to see what remains to be done and also makes it easier to get to the remaining pruning work. Removing older wood encourages young growth to fill the gap. Remember to stand back and view what you have pruned as you go along.

9 **Always make clean cuts above a leaf bud or close to the stem**
Pruning cuts that are not performed cleanly or that leave a long stub will damage the plant tissue and encourage the entry of pests and diseases.

10 **Avoid feeding with nitrogen for a season before and following heavy pruning**
Both pruning and high nitrogen fertilizers promote the development of rapid growth flushes that can result in the poor development of the crop.

Above: *This well-established pear tree has been trained into an espalier on wire supports. Many fruit trees can be grown and supported in this way.*

Above: *This pear tree has been grown as a fan. Fans are an ideal way to train many species of fruit tree and are well suited for growing against a wall.*

HARVESTING AND STORING FRUIT

When harvesting your fruits, you will find that there is only so much you can eat fresh or give away. There is always surplus fruit left over and you are faced with the question of what to do with it. Leaving some on the plant to help feed the wildlife in your organic garden is a good idea, but storing the rest of the excess fruit using a variety of methods will ensure that you can eat your home-grown produce over a longer period of time.

Above: *An apple is ready to be picked if it can be removed from the tree with only a single twist of the fruit.*

HARVESTING

The key to successfully storing fruit begins well before harvesting commences. Your first objective should be to grow fruit that is as healthy as possible because it will be the best for storage. Harvesting immature crops or attempting to save those that are in poor condition – due perhaps to a lack of water or nutrients or to pest and disease damage – can lead to many storage losses.

There are several ways that fruit can be stored and the condition of the picked crop will usually be the deciding factor as to which of these you should use. Top fruit such as apples and pears can often be stored fresh through most of the winter, whereas stone fruits and berries, such as peaches, strawberries and raspberries, must be quickly consumed, turned into a preserve or frozen.

Careful handling, both during and following harvesting, is essential because, from the moment they are harvested (and in many cases well before), crops have no

means of repairing any physical damage that they may suffer. Even firm, strong-looking fruit such as apples can easily be bruised, although the damage may well not show up immediately.

As well as good handling, a careful selection of the fruits during harvesting is essential for successful storage. You should inspect the picked fruits and select only those of the best quality for fresh storage. Reject any that have a broken skin or show any sign of pest or disease damage. Do not throw them on the compost heap yet, however, because damaged fruit may well be useful for making preserves such as jellies and jams or for freezing.

It is also a good idea to leave a small percentage of mature fruit on the plants when you are harvesting to help feed the wildlife in your organic garden.

STORING

In general, the storage area for fruit must be frost-free, safe from pests, rainproof and ideally kept at a constant temperature.

STORING FRUIT

To store surplus fruit and avoid the risk of rotting, make sure that you use the appropriate method.

Apples, pears and quinces
Store in a cool place for up to 12 months, depending on the variety.
All other fruit Eat immediately or freeze. Alternatively, preserve fruit by bottling or making into jam. Fruit can be kept for up to 12 months, depending on the method of preservation that has been used.

The long-term storage of any fruit calls for cool conditions with adequate ventilation. If you have space, consider having a separate refrigerator specifically for fruit storage, or choose an area with a low temperature that does not go below freezing. A garden shed or garage can be ideal, in many cases, but even these

Far left: *Pick soft fruits, such as strawberries, raspberries and gooseberries, carefully to avoid bruising the fruit.*

Left: *Pears can last for up to 12 months, depending upon the variety. Lay them in a recycled box, ensuring that the fruits do not touch and air can circulate around the fruit.*

Above: *Fruit trays, recycled from supermarkets, make ideal storage boxes for surplus fruit. The trays should be kept in a cool dry place such as a garage or shed.*

Above: *Soft fruit is best placed in small individual containers as it is picked to prevent it being squashed and spoiling. Store in a refrigerator or other cool place.*

spaces may need extra insulation if winter weather conditions become severe. Some houses have a basement, cellar or unheated room that may be ideally suited for the task. Attics are not recommended for fruit storage because of their wide temperature fluctuations and variable humidity.

It is worthwhile trying out a variety of different storage methods. This can be done by splitting the crop up and then trying out different locations in your home. You will soon find which are the best places to store fruit, and what areas are best for storing a particular kind of fruit.

Ensure that you check the stored fruit regularly, at least weekly, removing any that show signs of decay. Remember the old adage that "one bad apple spoils the whole barrel"? This can be true for your crop too unless you prevent rots from spreading. The unblemished parts can often still be used for eating or cooking. If lots of fruits begin to rot simultaneously, it could be that the storage conditions are not suitable, the crop has reached its maximum "shelf-life" or the fruit was not of sufficiently good quality to start with.

FREEZING AND PRESERVING

Freezing is an excellent way of storing all the surplus fruit that has been produced in your garden. Unfortunately, fruit tends to lose its firmness once it has been frozen,

although the taste will remain more or less the same. Raspberries, for example, are best used for making pies or flans after they have been frozen and will be of very poor quality if they are eaten raw. Most fruits can be frozen after they have been stewed or puréed; this is true of fruits such as apples and plums.

Fruits like strawberries and blackcurrants that are not suited to long-term storage can be made into jams, pickles and chutneys. You can find recipes for these in good cookbooks.

Above: *One of the simplest ways of preserving fruit is to freeze it, although once frozen most fruits are only good for cooking.*

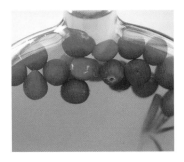

Above: *Adding a favourite fruit such as these cranberries to good wine vinegar can produce interesting flavours.*

Right: *Bottling fruit in alcohol is an ideal way to preserve soft fruits such as peaches, nectarines and apricots.*

DIRECTORY OF VEGETABLES

Growing concern over the use of agrochemicals and the safety of our food has been a major incentive to farmers and suppliers to meet an increasing demand for organically grown produce. Although we think of our gardens as places of retreat, a cocktail of pesticides has gradually left them bereft of much of their natural diversity. Couple disquiet with the quality of commercially produced food with the pleasure of eating home-grown fruit and vegetables that have been cultivated naturally, and it is easy to understand the growing popularity of organic kitchen gardening.

BULB VEGETABLES

ONIONS

Allium cepa

Onions are available in a wide range of shapes, sizes and colours: oval, cylindrical, red, white and golden brown. They are easy to grow and need little care throughout their growing period. By using different growing methods to obtain a fresh supply, and through careful storage, it is possible to achieve an all-year-round supply of home-grown onions.

SOIL
Grow in fertile soil with good drainage. Do not plant in ground that has been freshly manured. Dig and manure the previous autumn. Add compost to the ground to improve the soil structure. Crop rotation can prevent a number of pests and diseases.

ASPECT
An open, sunny site, but sets will tolerate some shade.

PLANTING SETS
The majority of onion sets are planted out in early spring. Plant in rows, with 10cm (4in) between each set and 25cm (10in) between the rows, so that the tip of the bulb peeks above the surface. Firm around the sets to remove any air pockets. To harvest an early crop, plant out Japanese onion sets in early autumn. These will be ready for lifting in mid-summer of the following year.

Above: *The leaves of these onions have been moved over to one side to help ripen the bulbs.*

SOWING SEEDS OUTSIDE
If you have room, sow directly outside in rows in late summer. Sow thinly, as there will be less waste when thinning. The odour, which is exuded when the stems are crushed during thinning, will not be too strong, so there will be less chance of attracting onion fly. Thin out when the soil is moist. The onions will not be ready for harvesting until late summer to autumn of the following year. To spread out the maturing of the onions, sow direct outside in rows in late winter and early spring. This will produce a crop ready to harvest in early autumn. Protection may be given in colder areas.

SOWING SEEDS UNDER GLASS
Sow seeds in trays in mid-winter. Harden off the seedlings in a cold frame and in mid-spring plant out in rows, 10cm (4in) apart, leaving 25cm (10in) between each row.

AFTERCARE
A weed-free area enhances the yield. Hand weeding is preferable to hoeing as hoes can cut into the bulbs. Water the maturing crop only if the season is dry and stop watering after the onions have swollen. Mulching with compost helps to retain moisture in the soil and suppress weed growth.

HARVESTING AND STORAGE
Harvest throughout the growing season. Onions for storing must be fully mature before lifting. When the onions are mature, the leaves start to turn yellow and flop over. Move the foliage to one side to allow maximum sunlight to penetrate, which will aid the maturing process. At this point lift each bulb slightly with a fork, thus preparing the bulb for lifting which can be done in a dry period two weeks later. Remove all the soil and dry in a sunny place (if left outside bring indoors during wet periods).

PESTS AND DISEASES
The main pest is the onion fly. The maggots eat the bulbs, resulting in yellow drooping leaves. Onion fly usually affects onion seeds rather than sets. Onion eelworm causes swollen and distorted foliage, kills young plants and softens bulbs on older plants. Destroy any affected plants. Onions are also susceptible to neck rot and white rot.

CULTIVATION
SETS
Planting time Early spring; early autumn (overwintering varieties)
Planting distance 10cm (4in)
Planting depth Tips of onions just showing through soil
Distance between rows 25cm (10in)
Harvesting Late summer (most varieties); mid-summer (over-wintering varieties)
SEED
Sowing time Mid-winter (under glass); late summer outside
Sowing distance Sow thinly
Sowing depth 1cm (½in)
Distance between rows 25cm (10in)
Thinning distance 5–10cm (2–4in)
Harvesting Late summer to autumn

VARIETIES
FROM SEED
'Ailsa Craig' An old variety with globe-shaped bulbs and golden skin.
'Hygro F1' A high yielder which stores well. Round-shaped bulb, slim neck and pale-coloured skin.

SETS FOR SPRING PLANTING
'Jet Set' A recent introduction which tastes delicious. Round and smooth skinned. Matures readily.
'Sturon Globe' A large-sized onion with excellent storage qualities.
SETS FOR AUTUMN PLANTING
'Radar' Hardy and early maturing. Mild flavour and a crunchy texture.
'Senshyu' Yellow, flat bulb with a mild flavour.

red onion

brown onion

small brown onions

white onion

SPRING ONIONS (SCALLIONS)

Allium cepa

These slender plants with a white or red shank have a small bulbous base, which can be eaten either raw or cooked. Unlike bulb onions, however, spring onions must be eaten fresh. Sow continuously throughout the growing season and harvest eight weeks after sowing.

Left: *Spring onions produce small bulbs that are little more than a slight swelling at the base of the plant.*

SOIL

Like most onions, spring onions prefer a light soil, but they will grow in most soils that are rich in organic matter. Crop rotation helps prevent infection from pests and diseases. They can also be grown in tubs or window boxes in a peat-free potting mix.

ASPECT

Spring onions grow best in an open sunny site, but can tolerate some shade.

SOWING

Sow every three weeks from early spring to late summer for a continuous crop from spring through to early autumn. To harvest an early spring crop, sow 'White Lisbon Winter Hardy' or any other hardy variety in late summer or early autumn. This crop will overwinter and be ready for picking in early spring. Sow crops thinly in rows 1cm (½in) deep with 10cm (4in) between each row.

AFTERCARE

Water in dry conditions and weed during the growing season. Protect overwintering spring onions with a cloche in cold weather.

Above: *Thin out congested rows of spring onions. Larger thinnings can be used to add interest to summer salads.*

Above: *If the spring onions are difficult to lift, use a small fork in order to avoid breaking the stems.*

HARVESTING AND STORAGE

From sowing to harvesting takes around seven to eight weeks. Use a small hand fork to loosen ground before pulling. Thin out the crop when harvesting, taking out every other plant and leaving the remaining plants to grow on.

PESTS AND DISEASES

Onion fly is the main pest, turning the leaves yellow as the bulb is eaten by the maggots, eventually killing the plants. Onion eelworm is another major pest, killing young plants and severely damaging older plants by softening the bulbs. Destroy affected plants. Diseases such as onion white rot and onion downy mildew can also affect the plant. This is not a severe problem, however, as their lifespan is so short. Move to another growing site if symptoms appear.

CULTIVATION
Sowing time Early spring to early autumn
Sowing distance Thinly, around 1cm (½in)
Sowing depth 1cm (½in)
Distance between rows 10cm (4in)
Thinning distance Sow correctly to avoid thinning, otherwise thin out rows when harvesting
Harvesting 8 weeks after sowing

VARIETIES
'White Lisbon' Excellent variety for successional sowing.
'White Lisbon Winter Hardy' Good for autumn sowing; hardy throughout the winter.

spring onions (scallions)

SHALLOTS

Allium cepa Aggregatum Group

Shallots are very closely related to onions, but they have smaller bulbs with a milder flavour. They usually taste sweeter than onions and the leaves can be used as a substitute for chives in a range of dishes. Shallots will grow clusters of bulbs instead of the single bulb that we are used to with onions. They vary in size and shape. Some varieties are torpedo-shaped, whereas others are rounded, with colours varying from light brown to red.

SOIL

Shallots thrive in a light soil. Plant in ground manured the previous autumn or, if not, add garden compost to the soil before planting. Do not plant in freshly manured soil as this will cause bulb rot.

ASPECT

An open sunny site, but they will tolerate a little shade.

PLANTING

Higher yields are obtained from planting sets rather than by sowing seeds. Seeds will produce a single bulb for harvesting whereas sets will cluster up to produce many bulbs per plant. Planting can begin in early winter in mild areas that have a well-drained soil, but, in general, shallot sets are best planted out in late winter or early spring. Plant sets individually, using a dibber or trowel, in rows 15cm (6in) apart and with 25cm (10in) between the rows. The tip of the set should be just showing above the surface of the soil.

AFTERCARE

After planting look out for any sets that may have been lifted by the frost and replant. Weed throughout the growing season and water the crop during dry spells.

HARVESTING AND STORAGE

Lift the bulbs in mid-summer, when the leaves have turned yellow, and separate the clusters. Leave the shallot bulbs to dry out on a rack of wire netting. They will be ready to store when the leaves have shrivelled. Remove the dead leaves and any dirt on the bulbs. Store the shallots in a cool dry place on trays or in netting bags.

PESTS AND DISEASES

Although they are generally trouble free, shallots can occasionally be attacked by the same pests and diseases as onions.

Left: *This is a healthy young crop of shallots with the bulbs beginning to form. They will soon be ready for harvesting.*

CULTIVATION
Planting time Late winter to early spring
Planting distance 15cm (6in)
Planting depth Tips showing through
Distance between rows 25cm (10in)
Harvesting Mid-summer

Left: *Plant shallots using a dibber (dibble) or a trowel to insert the bulb. Only the tips of the bulbs need to be showing above the surface of the soil.*

Above: *Place harvested shallots on wire racks or trays in order to dry them before putting them into storage.*

Onion fly and onion eelworm attack the leaves and the bulb. Destroy affected crops. Diseases such as neck rot can also be a problem, especially in hot dry summers.

VARIETIES
'Delvad' Stores well and has an excellent flavour.
'Longor' Elegant elongated bulb, with a mild flavour.
'Sante' Large round bulb, high yield.

shallots

LEEKS

Allium porrum

If a range of leek varieties are grown, this traditional winter vegetable can be harvested over a long period of time. The long white shafts have many culinary uses, while the green or blue foliage looks very decorative in the vegetable garden.

SOIL
Grow in a rich fertile soil. Dig thoroughly in autumn, adding well-rotted manure or garden compost. Although leeks prefer moist soil, they perform poorly on waterlogged or compacted soil. Crop rotation discourages diseases such as leek rust.

ASPECT
Require an open sunny position.

SOWING
In early to mid-spring, sow very thinly in rows, 1cm (½in) deep, with 15cm (6in) between the rows. Transplant when the seedlings are 20cm (8in) tall and as thick as a pencil (normally after two to three months). If the soil is dry, water the evening before transplanting to avoid tearing the plants when lifting. Dig out the leeks in batches and transplant out into rows, 30cm (12in) apart, with 15cm (6in) between the

Above: *Earthing up leeks is essential in order to blanch the stems. You can also plant the leeks in trenches and fill these in.*

plants. Use a dibber to make a hole 15cm (6in) deep and drop a single plant into the hole, leaving 5cm (2in) of foliage showing. Do not firm around the base of the plant, but gently water the plant and the soil will settle in around the base.

AFTERCARE
Earth (hill) up the leeks as they grow, moving the soil up around their stems to blanch them. Keep the rows of leeks weed-free and water the plants if dry, especially when they are young.

HARVESTING AND STORAGE
Leeks will be ready to harvest from early autumn to late spring. Lift the leeks with a fork when needed, as they will keep fresh in the soil for many weeks until they are required. Autumn varieties will not survive winter frosts and therefore need to be harvested before mid-winter.

PESTS AND DISEASES
Leek rust can occur in warm dry weather, causing bright orange pustules to form on the leaves. It often disappears when cooler wetter weather arrives in autumn. Destroy plants if they are severely affected.

Leeks can very occasionally be prone to the same pests and diseases as onions. Destroy any affected plants.

Left: *The green-blue architectural foliage of leeks provides a striking decorative effect in the organic vegetable garden.*

Above: *Leeks will stay fresh in the ground for many weeks. Lift when required with a fork as they tend to snap off if pulled.*

CULTIVATION
Sowing time Early to mid-spring
Sowing distance Sow very thinly
Sowing depth 1cm (½in)
Distance between sown rows 15cm (6in)
Transplanting time When seedlings reach 20cm (8in)
Planting depth 15cm (6in)
Distance between planted rows 30cm (12in)
Harvesting Early autumn to late spring

VARIETIES
AUTUMN AND MID-SEASON
'King Richard' Good early cropper.
'The Lyon' Thick white stems, with a mild flavour.

WINTER
'Alvito RZ' Resistant to rust and not prone to bolting.
'Giant Winter' Produces well in extremely cold climates.
'Musselburgh' A reliable and versatile favourite.

leeks

GARLIC

Allium sativum

This aromatic bulb is used to season many cooked dishes. Its strong flavour is more prominent in home-grown crops. Garlic does not produce seed, so it must be grown from bulbs, which are available from garden centres or seed merchants. Choose a variety that suits your soil and climate. Garlic bulbs bought at supermarkets can often fail or produce distorted plants.

SOIL

Garlic grows better in light sandy soils, especially if planting takes place in autumn. It does best in soils manured for the previous crop. Do not plant in freshly manured soil.

ASPECT

Garlic will flourish in an open sunny site.

PLANTING

Plant out in mid- to late autumn if your soil is light and free-draining. Break the bulbs up into individual cloves just before planting. Plant the cloves in rows, using a dibber or trowel, to 5cm (2in) below the soil surface. Leave 7.5–10cm (3–4in) between the cloves and 30cm (12in) between the rows. If your soil is heavy and retains water easily, plant out in early to mid-spring. Starting your individual cloves off in pots under glass or in cold frames three to four weeks before planting will benefit the maturing of the crop.

Above: *Wet springs can rot off newly planted garlic bulbs. This can be overcome by starting off the bulbs under glass.*

Left: *The garlic bulbs form below the surface, unlike those of its close relative, the onion, which mainly form above ground.*

AFTERCARE

Weed throughout the growing season and water in spring during dry periods.

HARVESTING AND STORAGE

The leaves will turn yellow when the bulbs are ready for lifting, usually in mid- to late summer. Remove any soil or long roots before spreading the bulbs out on trays or wire staging to dry out. Remove the leaves as well if you are not intending to plait (braid) them later. Store by threading the bulbs on a string or stiff wire, or by tying or plaiting the leaves together. Hang in a cool, frost-free area such as a garage or shed.

PESTS AND DISEASES

Garlic is generally trouble free, although it may be affected by onion white rot and leek rust.

CULTIVATION

Planting time Mid- to late autumn in light soils, early to mid-spring in heavy soils
Planting distance 7.5–10cm (3–4in)
Planting depth 5cm (2in)
Distance between rows 30cm (12in)
Harvesting Mid- to late summer

VARIETIES

'Long Keeper' Good storage qualities. Often just listed as garlic.
'Printanor' Best planted in early to mid-spring.
'Thermidrome' Suits early planting.

garlic

Above: *Plant bulbs using a dibber (dibble) or trowel 7.5–10cm (3–4in) apart. Use a line of string to keep the rows straight.*

Right: *Store garlic by threading a stiff piece of wire through the dry neck of the bulbs. You can also tie them together with string.*

LEAFY VEGETABLES

SWISS CHARD

Beta vulgaris Cicla Group

Swiss chard is easier to grow than spinach and much less prone to bolting. Swiss chard is also known under the names of chard (rhubarb, red or ruby) and seakale beet. Spinach beet or perpetual spinach is a type of Swiss chard which is categorized within this section.

SOIL
Swiss chard and perpetual spinach require a soil that is fertile and does not dry out easily. Dig in plenty of well-rotted manure or garden compost in the autumn.

ASPECT
Prefer an open site, but will also tolerate light shade.

SOWING
Sow seeds in late spring 10cm (4in) apart in rows 2.5cm (1in) deep. Keep 38cm (15in) between the rows. When the seedlings have germinated, thin them to a distance of 45cm (18in) for Swiss chard and 38cm (15in) for perpetual spinach.

A sowing can be done in late summer to prolong the season. This crop will harvest until the following summer. Provide winter protection throughout the cold months.

AFTERCARE
Water during dry spells and keep the bed weed-free. Mulching with garden compost will help retain moisture in the soil and suppress weed growth. Remove any flower heads if they appear.

Above: *Swiss chard grown in colder areas benefits from protection in the winter months. Cloches or low tunnels are ideal.*

Left: *Many varieties of Swiss chard produce brightly coloured stems that make for a very decorative display in the vegetable plot.*

Below: *Harvest the crop by cutting off the stems when needed. Cut from the outside inwards to allow the inside to regrow.*

CULTIVATION
SWISS CHARD AND PERPETUAL SPINACH
Sowing time Late spring
Sowing distance Sow 10cm (4in) between the seeds
Sowing depth 2.5cm (1in)
Distance between rows 38cm (15in)
Thinning distance To 45cm/18in (Swiss chard); to 38cm/15in (perpetual spinach)
Harvesting Late summer to spring

HARVESTING AND STORAGE
Harvest when the leaves are small; if they are picked when they have matured the flavour of the leaf will be bitter. Always pick around the outside of the plant, leaving the inner area to regrow. To avoid damage, cut with a sharp knife. Both crops do not store well and are best eaten fresh.

PESTS AND DISEASES
Swiss chard and perpetual spinach are generally trouble free. Slugs are the only major enemy that they might encounter. Spacing plants correctly discourages the overcrowding which causes the humid conditions in which slugs as well as diseases such as downy mildew thrive.

VARIETIES
SWISS CHARD
Often simply listed as Swiss chard.
'Bright Lights' Very ornamental containing a mixture of red, orange, cream, pink and yellow stems.
'Charlotte' This has an unusual combination of purple leaves and red stems.
'Fordhook Giant' A very attractive variety with large green leaves and white stems.

Perpetual spinach is normally listed simply as Perpetual Spinach or Leaf Beet.

Swiss chard

red-leaved Swiss chard

KALE

Brassica oleracea Acephala Group

Kale is one of the hardiest vegetables and can withstand wet and poor soil conditions. Coupled with the fact that kale does not have the same problems with pests as cabbages, for example, it is surprising that more people do not grow this delicious winter green. This may be due to the fact that kale has a strong flavour and a bitter taste if it is not cooked properly. Try one of the new cultivars and harvest the young succulent leaves. Many varieties of kale are grown solely for ornamental purposes.

SOIL
Kale thrives on fertile well-drained soil and will tolerate poorer soils that other brassicas, such as cabbages and cauliflowers, will not. Dig the soil in autumn, incorporating some well-rotted manure or garden compost. Kale does not grow well in acidic conditions, so you will need to lime the soil after cultivation.

ASPECT
Grow in an open sunny situation.

SOWING
Begin sowing kale thinly in rows in late spring in the open ground. The rows should be 1cm (½in) deep with 20cm (8in) between the rows. When the seedlings have germinated, thin to a distance of 5cm (2in). Lift and transplant the seedlings when they are 13cm (5in) high and plant them in their final location. Water the seedlings the night

Above: *The foliage of curly kale has a wonderfully textural effect in the organic vegetable garden.*

before lifting in order to make this operation easier. Plant out in rows, with 45–60cm (18–24in) between the plants, depending on the variety grown. Keep a distance of 60cm (24in) between the rows.

AFTERCARE
Weed throughout the growing season and water the kale crop if it is dry, especially in the summer. Mulching with garden compost will help to retain moisture in the soil and also to suppress weed growth.

HARVESTING AND STORAGE
Kale has a long harvesting period, from autumn through to mid-spring. Remove a few leaves from each plant, starting with the crown. This will encourage new succulent side-shoot growth which can be harvested in spring. All growth is best removed with a sharp knife.

PESTS AND DISEASES
Kale is not prone to the worst of the cabbage family pests such as cabbage root fly and club root. However, whitefly, cabbage caterpillar and cabbage aphid can all be troublesome.

Left: *When harvesting kale, select the younger, more succulent leaves. Remove only a few leaves from each plant because this will help the plants to recover and produce more.*

CULTIVATION
Sowing time Late spring
Sowing distance Sow thinly
Sowing depth 1cm (½in)
Distance between sown rows 20cm (8in)
Thinning distance 5cm (2in)
Transplanting time When 13cm (5in) high
Planting distance 45–60cm (18–24in) apart
Distance between planted rows 60cm (24in)
Harvesting Autumn to mid-spring

VARIETIES
'Darkibor F1' Densely curled medium green leaves of uniform habit. Harvest in early winter.
'Nero di Toscano' Extremely dark green leaves which have a blistered appearance. Has a strong peppery taste.

curly kale

CAULIFLOWERS

Brassica oleracea Botrytis Group

The soil requirements and aftercare of cauliflowers are demanding. Failure to provide the right conditions can result in small button-headed plants and low yields. The effort is well rewarded, however, with beautiful white or purple heads (also known as curds) that taste delicious.

SOIL
Cauliflowers need a well-consolidated soil, which is deep, fertile and moisture-retentive, so dig several months before planting, incorporating well-rotted manure or garden compost. Alternatively, plant after a crop of nitrogen-fixing green manure.

ASPECT
Cauliflowers like an open sunny site. It is important to avoid frost pockets if growing winter varieties.

SOWING
Sow the seeds of summer varieties in a cool greenhouse in mid-winter for an early crop. Prick out the seedlings when they are large enough. When they reach 13cm (5in), harden off for a couple of weeks and plant out in cloches in early spring. Plant in rows, 55cm (22in) apart, with 60cm (24in) between the rows. Firm around the plants.

Autumn and winter varieties can be sown outdoors in late spring. Sow thinly in nursery beds before planting in a permanent site. Sow in rows, 1cm (½in) deep, with 20cm (8in) between rows. Thin to 5cm (2in) apart. Transplant seedlings when they are

Above: *Protection from the sun is needed for the developing heads. Snap the outside leaves over the heads.*

Above: *Harvest the firm heads of cauliflower by cutting with a sharp knife just below the first set of leaves.*

13cm (5in) tall and bearing 5 to 6 leaves, watering in well and taking care when lifting them. Plant out between 60–70cm (24–28in) apart, depending on the variety, in rows 70cm (28in) apart. Firm in well.

AFTERCARE
After planting, mulch the crop with garden compost. Water in dry periods and feed occasionally. Cover with netting or wire mesh in order to protect leaves from birds. In winter, tie up or fold the leaves around the head to protect it from rain and frost. Protect from sun in the same way. Use felt or plastic collars around the plants to protect from cabbage root fly.

HARVESTING AND STORAGE
Start harvesting when the heads are small so that not all of the crop is harvested at the same time. When the florets separate or turn brown, they are too mature. Hang upside down in a cool dark shed for up to three weeks; mist the heads now and then.

PESTS AND DISEASES
Susceptible to the same pests and diseases as cabbages.

CULTIVATION
SUMMER CAULIFLOWER
Sowing time Mid-spring (outdoors); mid-winter (under glass)
Sowing distance Sow thinly
Sowing depth 1cm (½in)
Distance between rows 20cm (8in)
Thinning distance 5cm (2in)
Transplanting time Spring (seedlings sown outdoors); early spring (seedlings sown under glass)
Planting distance 55cm (22in)
Distance between planted rows 60cm (24in)
Harvesting Late summer (if sown outdoors); mid-summer (if sown under glass)

AUTUMN CAULIFLOWER
Sowing time Late spring
Sowing distance Sow thinly
Sowing depth 1cm (½in)
Distance between rows 20cm (8in)
Thinning distance 5cm (2in)
Transplanting time Early summer
Planting distance 60cm (24in)
Distance between planted rows 70cm (28in)
Harvesting Autumn

WINTER CAULIFLOWER
Sowing time Late spring
Sowing distance Sow thinly
Sowing depth 1cm (½in)
Distance between rows 20cm (8in)
Thinning distance 5cm (2in)
Transplanting time Summer
Planting distance 70cm (28in)
Distance between planted rows 70cm (28in)
Harvesting Late winter to early spring

VARIETIES
SUMMER
'All the Year Round' A heavy yielder, producing heads all through the summer.
'Idol' This mini cauliflower is ideal for growing in a small garden. Good for successional sowing.

AUTUMN
'Stella F1' Suitable for all soil types and less demanding than other varieties. High-quality heads produced.

'Violet Queen' Purple-headed and maturing from late summer to mid-autumn.

WINTER
'Purple Cape' Bears rich purple heads with an excellent flavour. Harvest in early spring.
'Wainfleet' Good frost resistance.

cauliflower

CABBAGES

Brassica oleracea Capitata Group

Cabbages come in a variety of different shapes, colours and sizes. Due to the range of varieties available, it is now possible to harvest this crop fresh all the year round. They are invaluable in winter when there is a limited range of fresh vegetables available. Cabbages can be cooked or eaten raw in salads or coleslaw.

SOIL

Cabbages thrive in firm, well-consolidated soil that is not freshly manured. Therefore, cultivate the land several months prior to planting, adding well-rotted manure or garden compost. Cabbages do best in a soil with a pH of 6.5–7 – if the soil is too acidic, lime after digging and before planting. The fungal disease clubroot thrives in damp acid soil, so improve any drainage problems. Crop rotation helps to prevent an infection.

ASPECT

Likes an open sunny site and will tolerate exposure.

SOWING OUTDOORS

For all varieties start off by sowing cabbage seeds in a nursery bed. Sow thinly in rows 1cm (½in) deep, with 15cm (6in) between rows. After germination thin out the seedlings in the rows to 8cm (3in) apart to prevent the seedlings becoming weak and

Left: *Cabbages are prone to the fungal disease clubroot. You can reduce the risk of this disease occurring by practising crop rotation.*

spindly. Transplant the young cabbage plants to their permanent position when they are 10cm (4in) tall and have grown 5 or 6 leaves. Water the rows the day before lifting. This will aid lifting and minimize root and stem damage. Apply a general organic fertilizer a week prior to planting for all varieties except spring cabbage. Plant in their final rows, 35cm (14in) apart for spring and summer cabbage and 50cm (20in) for

autumn and winter cabbage. Leave 60cm (24in) between the rows for spring and summer cabbages and 65–70cm (26–28in) for autumn and winter varieties. Plant firmly for all varieties. Water thoroughly after planting.

SOWING UNDER GLASS

To grow an early crop of summer cabbage sow in seed trays, pots or modules in a cool

VARIETIES

SPRING

'Flower of Spring' Large pointed heads that are ready in mid-spring.
'Spring Hero F1' Good-sized heads that are ready in late spring to early summer.
'Wintergreen' Spring greens that are ready from late winter or hearting up in late spring.

SUMMER

'Golden Acre' Has lovely round firm heads. Great for cooking or used raw in coleslaw.
'Minicole F1' A white compact type that stores well.
'Stonehead F1' Shows some resistance to mildew and is not prone to splitting. Also stores well.

AUTUMN

'Cuor di Bue' Light green pointed leaves and with plenty of flavour.
'Hardora F1' A red cabbage which produces a good uniform crop. Excellent storage qualities.

WINTER CABBAGE AND SAVOYS

'Best of All' An early maturing Savoy which can be harvested from early to late autumn.
'Christmas Drumhead' An old blue dwarf variety with flat solid hearts.
'January King' Excellent frost resistance, crisp with a sweet flavour.
'Vertus' A Savoy which can withstand severe frosts.

red cabbage

winter cabbage

loose-leaf cabbage

Left: *Blue varieties of cabbage are unusual, but very striking in the vegetable plot.*

Below: *This healthy crop of cabbages is growing well and will soon be ready for harvesting.*

greenhouse in mid-winter. When the seedlings are large enough prick out into individual pots or modules. Grow on and harden off before planting outside under cloches in early spring. Follow the same spacing as for transplants (see opposite). Small plants can also be bought from a nursery or garden centre, but always buy from a reputable source as introduced plants may contain clubroot.

AFTERCARE
Water young plants, especially transplants, until established. Keep the beds weed free. Mulch beds with garden compost to help retain moisture and suppress weed growth. If your vegetable patch is prone to attracting cabbage root fly, apply a felt or plastic collar around the base of the cabbage to stop the fly laying its eggs.

HARVESTING AND STORAGE
Cut the hearts when they have become hard and dig up the stalks. Spring cabbage stalks can be left and cut on top with a knife in a cross shape. This will produce another four smaller cabbages.

PESTS AND DISEASES
Cabbage root fly is one of the major pests. Place a collar of felt or plastic around the base of the plant to stop the fly laying its eggs near the plants.

Caterpillars, mainly from the small white butterfly, can munch their way through a considerable amount of leafage. Pick them off by hand or erect a cage around the crop to keep out the adult butterflies. If you see small holes in the young leaves of cabbages it is almost certainly flea beetles. Slugs and snails will also cause damage to the leaves.

Protect from pigeons by erecting netting or wire mesh cloches. Cabbages are prone to the soil-borne fungal disease clubroot. The roots of the plant begin to swell and the plants become stunted with all growth severely affected. Destroy any infected plants.

Left: *Protect young cabbage seedlings from cabbage root fly by placing a felt or plastic collar around the base of the plant.*

CULTIVATION
SPRING CABBAGE
Sowing time Late summer
Sowing distance Sow thinly
Sowing depth 1cm (½in)
Distance between sown rows 15cm (6in)
Thinning distance 8cm (3in)
Transplanting time When 10cm (4in) tall
Planting distance 35cm (14in)
Distance between planted rows 60cm (24in)
Harvesting Spring

SUMMER CABBAGE
Sowing time Early to mid-spring
Sowing distance Sow thinly
Sowing depth 1cm (½in)
Distance between sown rows 15cm (6in)
Thinning distance 8cm (3in)
Transplanting time When 10cm (4in) tall
Planting distance 35cm (14in)
Distance between planted rows 60cm (24in)
Harvesting Mid-summer onwards

AUTUMN CABBAGE
Sowing time Late spring
Sowing distance Sow thinly
Sowing depth 1cm (½in)
Distance between sown rows 15cm (6in)
Thinning distance 8cm (3in)
Transplanting time When 10cm (4in) tall
Planting distance 50cm (20in)
Distance between planted rows 65–70cm (26–28in)
Harvesting Autumn

WINTER CABBAGE
Sowing time Late spring
Sowing distance Sow thinly
Sowing depth 1cm (½in)
Distance between sown rows 15cm (6in)
Thinning distance 8cm (3in)
Transplanting time When 10cm (4in) tall
Planting distance 50cm (20in)
Distance between planted rows 65–70cm (26–28in)
Harvesting Winter

BROCCOLI

Brassica oleracea Cymosa Group

Broccoli is also known as purple sprouting broccoli or sprouting broccoli and is closely related to calabrese. The two can be easily confused because calabrese, which has green heads, is often sold in the supermarkets under the name of broccoli. As the common name suggests, most varieties of broccoli have purple heads, but you can also grow varieties with creamy white heads that look rather like small cauliflowers. The harvesting of broccoli fills a period in which there are very few other vegetables maturing.

SOIL

Manure the soil in autumn, as rich soil is required for good growth. Apply a general organic fertilizer before sowing or alternatively sow a nitrogen-fixing green manure as the previous crop. Broccoli requires a pH of 6.5–7. Lime if necessary to bring the pH up to the recommended level.

ASPECT

Broccoli requires an open sunny position free from strong winds.

Above: *Harvest the shoots of broccoli when they have begun to bud up and before they have come into flower.*

SOWING

During spring sow seeds thinly in rows to a depth of 1cm (½in) with 15cm (6in) between the rows. After germination, thin to 5cm (2in) apart within the rows. When the plants reach 13cm (5in) high, lift them and transplant to their final location. Water the young plants the day before transplanting to soften up the soil which will make them easier to move. Plant out in rows 60cm (24in) apart with 75cm (30in) between the rows. Plant deeply (with the first leaves sitting on the soil surface) to discourage cabbage root fly and to help stabilize the plant. Firm in well around the base of the plants, again to help stabilize the transplants and to remove any air pockets.

For an early crop, sow broccoli in seed trays or modules under cover from mid- to late spring. Harden off for two weeks in a cold frame before planting out.

AFTERCARE

Keep well watered during dry periods to allow healthy growth throughout the growing season. Mulching the rows with garden compost will help the soil retain moisture and keep weeds in check. Weed the rows throughout the season. Use crop covers of fleece to protect the plants from

Left: *Purple sprouting broccoli is one of the most colourful and decorative of vegetables for the kitchen garden.*

cabbage root fly in the early stages or protect the plants individually by putting a cabbage root fly mat around each one.

HARVESTING AND STORAGE

Start harvesting in late winter and continue through to mid-spring, depending on the varieties grown. Harvest the shoots before they flower. Cut the shoots when they have begun to bud up and are 15cm (6in) long. Cut the shoots from all around the plant; regular cutting encourages new shoots. Pick off any flowering shoots – if they are left on, the plant will become exhausted and cease to produce new shoots for picking.

PESTS AND DISEASES

Broccoli is prone to the same pests and diseases as cabbages.

BRUSSELS SPROUTS

Brassica oleracea Gemmifera Group

This hardy vegetable is delicious if cooked correctly. Try growing some of the tasty new F1 hybrids, which freeze very well. If a range of varieties is grown, harvesting can begin in late summer and finish in early spring.

SOIL
Dig the ground and incorporate well-rotted manure or garden compost in autumn. Brussels sprouts do not grow well in acidic soil conditions, so add lime if necessary to bring the pH up to 6.5–7.

ASPECT
Brussels sprouts thrive in an open sunny position that is protected from strong winds.

SOWING
Sow outside in a nursery bed from early to mid-spring. Start by sowing the early varieties and successively sow mid-season and late varieties in turn. Sow thinly in rows 1cm (½in) deep with 15cm (6in) between rows. After germination, thin out the seedlings to 8cm (3in) apart. Transplant when the seedlings are 13cm (5in) high, watering the previous evening to make lifting easier. Plant in rows, 75cm (30in) apart, with 75cm (30in) between the rows. Firm well to remove any air pockets. You

Below: *Many gardeners believe that Brussel sprouts are best harvested after the first frost because this improves the flavour.*

can intercrop between the rows at this early stage. For late-summer picking start the sowing off under glass in late winter. Harden off and plant outside when the young plants are 13cm (5in) high. Use cloches to protect the early stages of growth.

AFTERCARE
Use wire-mesh cloches to deter pigeons. Weed throughout the growing season and water in dry periods. Apply a foliar feed during the summer. Stake any plants if needed and, as early autumn approaches, draw up the soil around the stems to steady the plants against wind. Apply felt or plastic collars around the base of the plants to prevent cabbage root fly from laying its eggs.

Left: *As these Brussels sprouts develop, the bottom leaves will turn yellow. Remove these as they do so.*

HARVESTING AND STORAGE
Start harvesting from the bottom of the plant, picking the sprouts when they are still tight, after the first frosts as this improves flavour. Crop only a few from each plant. Every time the crop is harvested work further up the stem. When all the sprouts have been harvested, cut off the top of the plant and cook as a cabbage.

PESTS AND DISEASES
Prone to the same problems as cabbages. The main problem is clubroot, a soil-borne fungal disease. Destroy infected plants. Small white butterfly caterpillar and aphids may also affect the crop. Remove caterpillars by hand and spray aphids with an insecticidal soap.

VARIETIES
'Braveheart F1' One of the sweetest flavoured sprouts. Matures in early winter to early spring.
'Oliver F1' An extremely early variety, cropping from late summer if sown under glass. Produces large sprouts.
'Trafalgar F1' This will provide sweet sprouts in early winter. It has a good root system.

Brussels sprouts

CALABRESE (ITALIAN SPROUTING BROCCOLI)

Brassica oleracea Italica Group

There is often confusion over the difference between broccoli and calabrese. This occurs because the green spearheads of calabrese are misleadingly sold under the name of broccoli in supermarkets. Calabrese normally has green-headed spears, whereas broccoli has purple or white. Calabrese has a taste similar to asparagus and a succulent texture when it is steamed, rather than boiled.

SOIL
Calabrese grows well in a firm rich soil, which has been well manured in the autumn or for a previous crop. They do not mature well in poor soil.

ASPECT
Calabrese thrives best in a sunny location that is sheltered from wind.

SOWING
Calabrese does not transplant well, so sowing directly in rows outside is the best method of growing. Position seeds in groups of two or three in drills 30cm (12in) apart. Rows are best positioned 30cm (12in) apart. After germination, select the strongest seedling and thin out the others.

Above: *Calabrese (Italian sprouting broccoli) does not transplant particularly well and so it is best to sow the seed in situ and then thin the seedlings.*

AFTERCARE
The young growth of calabrese is susceptible to "pecking" by pigeons and other birds. Protect the crop by using netting or other barrier methods. Keep the crop well watered throughout the summer. Apply a mulch of garden compost during the growing season in order to help conserve moisture. Regular weeding will also help to do this. Plants that are grown for harvesting towards the end of the season may require staking to stabilize them from autumn winds.

HARVESTING AND STORAGE
Harvest from late summer to mid-autumn depending on variety. Cut the heads (spears) and side shoots while the flower buds are closed. Once the flowers have opened the heads become woody and unpalatable and the production of new ones will cease. Cut the central flower head first to promote the growth of side shoots. Always spread harvesting of the crop, never completely stripping a plant. Cutting of a plant may continue under favourable conditions for up to six weeks.

Left: *Harvest calabrese from late summer to early autumn. Cutting the central flower head first promotes the growth of side shoots.*

PESTS AND DISEASES
Calabrese is prone to the same pests and diseases as cabbages.

CULTIVATION
Sowing time Successional sowing from mid- to early summer
Sowing distance Sow 30cm (12in) apart in groups of two to three. Thin to strongest plant later
Sowing depth 1cm (½in)
Distance between rows 30cm (12in)
Harvesting Late summer to mid-autumn

VARIETIES
CALABRESE (ITALIAN SPROUTING BROCCOLI)
'Corvet' Matures 60 days after planting out. Good large heads that produce well after cutting.
'Express Corona' Produces a succession of spears after the main head is cut. Quick to mature.
'Green Comet' A good early cropper with large heads. Little spear production after the main head is cut.
'Green Sprouting' Spears are ready for harvesting in mid-summer; good flavour.
'Italian Sprouting' An excellent flavour with a long cropping season.

ROMANESCO (ROMAN BROCCOLI)
'Romanesco' A large headed variety that is yellow-green in colour. A good substitute for cauliflower.

calabrese (Italian sprouting broccoli)

CHINESE CABBAGE

Brassica rapa var. *pekinensis*

Although this vegetable has been grown in Asia since the 5th century, it is relatively new elsewhere, having arrived in Europe in the 20th century. With its tall erect habit and slender leaves, Chinese cabbage could easily be mistaken for cos (romaine) lettuce. It has a mild flavour and can either be cooked, stir-fried or eaten raw as a salad leaf.

SOIL

Chinese cabbage prefers a fertile soil that retains moisture. Dig in plenty of well-rotted manure or garden compost in the autumn as it performs poorly on denuded soils.

ASPECT

Likes an open position and will tolerate a little shade in summer.

SOWING

It is best to sow in situ because they do not transplant well. Sow in rows 1cm (½in) deep with 10cm (4in) between the seeds and 25cm (10in) between the rows. Once large enough, thin out seedlings to 30cm (12in) apart. If starting off inside, sow into modules or small pots to avoid disturbance during transplanting.

AFTERCARE

Water liberally in dry conditions. Mulch with garden compost to help retain moisture and suppress weed growth.

HARVESTING AND STORAGE

Chinese cabbage is quick growing, maturing 7–10 weeks after sowing. Cut the heads off and leave the stump in the ground to sprout new leaves. Chinese cabbage needs to be eaten fresh.

PESTS AND DISEASES

Older varieties can be prone to bolting; there are a number of varieties on the market that are more resistant to this problem. Slugs, snails and cabbage caterpillars can be a problem. Although Chinese cabbage can be prone to other cabbage pests and diseases, they are not a major problem.

Below: *This young crop of Chinese cabbage is flourishing. The variety is 'Green Rocket F1'.*

CULTIVATION
Sowing time Early to mid-summer
Sowing distance 10cm (4in)
Sowing depth 1cm (½in)
Distance between rows 25cm (10in)
Thinning distance 30cm (12in)
Harvesting Late summer to late autumn

Left: *Chinese cabbage grows very quickly and is ready to harvest in just seven to ten weeks after sowing. Remove the heads and leave the stump in the ground to sprout new leaves. If successional sowing is practised, harvesting can take place until late autumn.*

Above: *The yellow flowers of this Chinese cabbage look very striking against the dark green leaves.*

VARIETIES
'Kasumi' Has a loose habit with extremely good resistance to bolting.
'Jade Pagoda' Extremely tall and thin heads.
'Tip Top' Shows resistance to bolting.

Chinese cabbage

CHICORY

Cichorium intybus

Chicory has a bitter taste that you either love or hate. It is split into three main types: witloof (Belgian chicory), sugarloaf and red chicory (radicchio). Witloof is the traditional forcing type that produces tight leafy heads called chicons. These are produced in winter when the roots are lifted and blanched. Sugarloaf looks rather like a cos (romaine) lettuce, with its large outer leaves encompassing the inner leaves, therefore blanching naturally. Red chicory is self-blanching, but can be forced to produce red and white leaves. They are all a welcome addition to the winter salad bowl.

SOIL

Chicory will grow in most fertile soils. Manure or incorporate garden compost the previous autumn.

ASPECT

Thrives in an open sunny position.

SOWING

Start to sow chicory from spring through to mid-summer, depending on the type grown. Sow thinly in rows to a depth of 1cm (½in). Keep a distance of 30cm (12in) between the rows. Thin to a distance of 15–30cm (6–12in), depending on the variety. For later sowing protect the crop with a cloche.

FORCING CHICORY

To blanch chicory, cut off the leaves in late autumn to just above the level of the soil. Cover the stump with 15cm (6in) of a

Above: *Red chicory (radicchio) does not need the same care as Belgian or witloof chicory. This variety is 'Alouette'.*

mixture of compost and grit. The leaves will grow in the darkness under the soil, becoming blanched. Alternatively, lift the chicory roots and plant five in a large pot of free-draining potting mix so the cut tips are just showing. Cut the roots so they fit into the pot. Cover with a pot or a bucket and place inside in a warm dark place. The chicon will be ready to harvest in 2–3 weeks. Cut and re-start the process.

AFTERCARE

Water throughout dry periods and weed during the growing season.

HARVESTING AND STORAGE

Witloof forcing type They will be ready to cut 3–4 weeks after the start of the forcing process. Cut the chicons just above the

Below: *Chicory should be sown in rows from spring to mid-summer. Allow 30cm (12in) between the rows.*

crown, when the tips of the plants start to show through the potting mix. Leave the roots in, water the compost and a smaller secondary crop may be harvested.

Sugar and red chicory – non-forcing type Cut the chicons when they are 15cm (6in) long. The stumps may shoot again.

PESTS AND DISEASES

Generally trouble free, although slugs can be a problem in mild, damp weather. Do not plant too close together to allow for maximum air movement. This reduces hot moist conditions that slugs thrive in.

CULTIVATION

Sowing time Spring to mid-summer
Sowing distance Thinly
Sowing depth 1cm (½in)
Distance between rows 30cm (12in)
Thinning distance 15–30cm (6–12in)
Harvesting Autumn into winter

VARIETIES

WITLOOF
'Brussels Witloof' Good for winter forcing.
'Normanto' No soil layer needed when forcing.

SUGARLOAF
'Crystal head' A modern variety which has improved hardiness.
'Sugarloaf' Sweeter than other varieties. Good drought resistance but will only tolerate mild frosts.

RED CHICORY
'Pallar Rossa' Good taste. Green leaves turn dark red. Needs winter protection.
'Rossa di Treviso' Deep red leaves and is non-hearting. Becomes pink and white when it is blanched.

chicory

LETTUCE

Latuca sativa

There are many different types of lettuce to choose from now – cos (romaine), butterhead, crisphead and loose-leaf. These different types come in various shapes, sizes and colours, and are often used in the ornamental garden. With careful planning, it is possible to crop lettuce nearly all the year round, with the help of a cloche or two.

SOIL

A good quantity of organic matter is needed in the soil, which will help retain moisture. Dig plenty of well-rotted manure or garden compost into the soil in the autumn. Lettuce does not grow well on acidic soil, so lime if necessary after digging.

ASPECT

Lettuce likes an open sunny position, but will welcome partial shade if grown in the heat of the summer.

SOWING

EARLY CROP For early crops start by sowing under glass in trays or modules in late winter to early spring. Plant these under cloches to protect against frost.
MAINCROP Start sowing outside from early spring onwards. Sow in rows 1cm (½in) deep with 30cm (12in) between the rows. Thin to 15–30cm (6–12in) apart, depending on the variety grown. Thinnings can be used as transplants for other rows, although this is not usually successful during the hot summer months due to excessive heat.
LATE CROP Late-summer sowings will mature from autumn and early winter. Provide protection for these crops by covering with cloches in mid-autumn. Selected varieties will overwinter under cloches or can be grown under glass.

AFTERCARE

Planted areas need to be weeded throughout the growing season. Keep the crop well watered. It is better to do this in the morning rather than in the evening. The plants will use up the water during the day and the planted area will not be damp in the evening. This will discourage slugs and cause less fungal disease. If slugs are a problem, protect young plants with plastic bottle cloches until well established.

Above: *Many varieties of lettuce are extremely decorative and can be planted out to enhance decorative borders.*

HARVESTING AND STORAGE

HEARTED LETTUCE This is ready for cutting when the heart is firm. If left long after this, they are likely to bolt.
LOOSE-LEAF Pick leaves as needed or cut the whole plant.

PESTS AND DISEASES

Slugs relish lush green vegetation and lettuce is no exception. If slugs are a severe

Above: *A hearted lettuce is ready for harvesting when the heart (middle) feels firm. If left longer the plant is likely to bolt.*

problem, grow on in modules before planting out, as they are less likely to severely damage established plants. Aphid attacks are common too. Other pest attacks can come from cutworms and root aphids. If the lettuces are planted too close together or are overwatered, fungal diseases such as downy mildew and grey mould may occur. Careful planting and watering can alleviate much of this.

CULTIVATION

Sowing time Late winter (under glass) to early spring onwards
Sowing distance Thinly
Sowing depth 1cm (½in)
Distance between rows 30cm (12in)
Thinning distance 15–30cm (6–12in)
Harvesting Early summer onwards

VARIETIES

COS
'Little Gem' Extremely quick maturing. A compact little plant with a sweet flavour.
'Winter Density' Sweet variety which is excellent for overwintering to crop in spring.

BUTTERHEAD
'Avondefiance' Resistant to root aphid and mildew, and slow to bolt.
'Buttercrunch' Dark green in colour with a compact habit.

CRISPHEAD
'Floreal RZ' A firm heart with bubbled leaves. Resistant to bolting and tipburn as well as mildew and root aphid.
'Roxette RZ' An iceberg with a superior flavour. Fast growing, with a solid heart.

LOOSE-LEAF
'Malibu RZ' A vigorous red-leaved lettuce which is resistant to mildew. Uniform in habit.
'Salad Bowl' Green leaves with serrated edges. Harvest for a long period.

hearted lettuce

iceberg lettuce

loose-leaf lettuce

cut-and-come-again lettuce

SPINACH

Spinacia oleracea

Spinach is a close relative of the beetroot and not the lettuce as might first appear. This crop contains an extremely high iron content, similar to that found in peas. It is a relatively hard crop to grow because it requires a high content of organic matter in the soil and needs copious amounts of water throughout the summer. If the conditions are not ideal, the plants tend to bolt and the crop will be lost. Spinach tastes delicious steamed with fresh crushed garlic or when used in quiches or egg florentine.

SOIL

Incorporate plenty of garden compost or well-rotted manure in the autumn. This will aid moisture retention in the soil during the following summer, which is a must for healthy growth.

ASPECT

Spinach is best grown in light shade in summer, making it a good choice for intercropping. This also reduces the chance of the crop running to seed. Spinach will grow just as well in an open sunny site if the soil remains moist and the area is not too hot.

Above: *This well-maintained vegetable plot includes a thriving crop of spinach. Spinach needs large amounts of water in summer.*

Above: *Spinach is prone to bolting, so choose resistant varieties or site summer crops in light shade to reduce the risk.*

SOWING

Start by sowing in early spring and successional sow until late spring. Sow thinly in rows to a depth of 1cm (½in), with 30cm (12in) between the rows. Apply a general organic fertilizer prior to sowing. When the seedlings are large enough, thin them to 15cm (6in) apart. They will be ready to harvest in early to late summer.

A crop can be sown in late summer or early autumn. Cover with cloches for protection during the winter. This crop can be harvested over winter and spring.

AFTERCARE

Water throughout dry periods. Weed throughout the growing period. Mulch with garden compost to help retain moisture.

HARVESTING AND STORAGE

Start by harvesting the outer leaves when they have reached a reasonable size; it is possible to remove half of the foliage at any one time. Pick more sparingly with winter varieties. Cut and harvest continually to promote new growth.

PESTS AND DISEASES

The main problem is bolting. This is when the plant grows quickly and starts to flower and set seed, making the crop inedible. This condition is encouraged by hot, dry weather. Site the crop carefully before sowing and choose less prone varieties. Spinach is susceptible to downy mildew, but there are plenty of resistant varieties. Spinach blight can also affect the crop. In both cases destroy infected material.

Above: *When harvesting select young fresh outer leaves. Do not remove more than half the foliage or this will weaken the plant.*

CULTIVATION

Sowing time Successional sow from early spring to late spring
Sowing distance Thinly
Sowing depth 1cm (½in)
Thinning distance 15cm (6in)
Distance between rows 30cm (12in)
Harvesting Early to late summer

VARIETIES

'Avanti RZ' An early maturing variety, suitable for greenhouse production or summer sowings outside. Resistant to powdery mildew.
'Giant Winter' Very hardy and ideal as a winter crop.
'Medinia' A good vigorous summer variety which is slow to bolt and resistant to mildew. A good all-rounder.

spinach

SALAD LEAVES

As salad has become more popular in recent years, alternatives to lettuce are becoming more widely grown. Crops such as endive (*Chichorium endivia*), rocket (arugula; *Eruca vesicaria*) and lamb's lettuce (mache; *Valerianella locusta*) are all delicious salad leaves. Rocket is particularly worth growing as it has a rich spicy flavour. Nowadays many different leaves can be included in one salad bowl, therefore it is not unusual to choose all of the above when preparing a salad. Rocket and lamb's lettuce are mainly grown for winter use when other salad crops are scarce, but can also be grown in the summer.

SOIL
Salad leaves thrive in moisture-retentive soil.

ASPECT
All grow best in cool conditions, so partial shade in summer is ideal. Bolting can occur if the plants get too hot. They are ideal for intercropping.

SOWING
Sow rocket and lamb's lettuce in late summer. Rocket can also be sown through to early autumn. Sow thinly in rows 1cm (½in) deep with 30cm (12in) between the rows. Thin the seedlings when large enough to 15cm (6in) apart for rocket and 10cm (4in) apart for lamb's lettuce. Early sowings can take place for both crops in spring. These will be ready to harvest in summer.

Endives can be sown from spring until late summer. Sow thinly in rows 1cm (½in) deep with 38cm (15in) between the rows. Once the seedlings have germinated, thin out to a distance of 30–35cm (12–14in), depending on the variety. Harvest in summer to winter.

AFTERCARE
Cover with cloches in late autumn or early winter. Water liberally in dry weather. Mulching with garden compost will help to conserve soil moisture as well as suppress weed growth.

HARVESTING AND STORAGE
Individual leaves can be cut off as required. Endives will re-sprout from cut stalks. All

Above: *Broad-leaved endives are more tolerant of cold conditions than the curly-leaved varieties.*

salad leaves need to be eaten fresh as they do not store or freeze.

PESTS AND DISEASES
Generally trouble free, although rocket may occasionally be attacked by flea beetles. Slugs and snails may pose a problem for all types of salad leaves.

Right: *Curly-leaved endive can be used in salads or cooked. Unblanched leaves like these are more bitter than blanched ones.*

CULTIVATION
ROCKET AND LAMB'S LETTUCE
Sowing time Spring (early sowing); late summer to early autumn (later sowings)
Sowing distance Thinly
Sowing depth 1cm (½in)
Distance between rows 30cm (12in)
Thinning distance 10–15cm (4–6in)
Harvesting Summer to winter

ENDIVE
Sowing time Spring to late summer
Sowing distance Thinly
Sowing depth 1cm (½in)
Distance between rows 38cm (15in)
Thinning distance 30–35cm (12–14in)
Harvesting Summer to winter

VARIETIES
ENDIVE
'Monaco RZ' A curly-leaved type, with a blanched heart and large green outer leaves.
'Stratego' A broad-leaved type. Compact, slow to bolt and resistant to tip burning.

ROCKET
More commonly sold under one of its common names, rucola or salad rocket, rather than varieties.

LAMB'S LETTUCE
Sometimes sold under the common name of corn salad.
'Verte de Cambrai'
An old French variety with a good flavour.

endives

rocket

lamb's lettuce

ROOT CROPS

BEETROOT (BEETS)

Beta vulgaris

For many of us, the word beetroot conjures up a picture of a small, round, red vegetable pickled in a jar. However, this delicious vegetable comes in a range of colours, such as white, yellow, the commonly grown red and a variety with concentric rings of pink and white. Shapes range from round through cylindrical to tapered, depending on the variety grown. Extremely easy to grow, beetroot can be eaten fresh from early summer to mid-autumn. Pickling excess crops will ensure a supply all year round.

SOIL

Grows in most soil types (except acid soils) and thrives on rich moist soils. Adding organic matter to the soil in autumn or early winter will increase water retention, but is only necessary if none was incorporated the previous year. Never sow or plant in newly manured ground. Cylindrical and tapered varieties keep their shape and mature better in sandy soil.

ASPECT

An open sunny site is preferable for growing beetroot. It thrives in seaside locations

Above: *Harvesting can begin seven weeks after sowing by pulling the smaller beetroot (beets) out. Continue to pull as required.*

due to its tolerance to salt, the wild ancestor of beetroot being native to coastal situations.

SOWING

Sow the seeds in drills 2.5cm (1in) deep with 20cm (8in) between the rows. Sow 8cm (3in) apart. Some thinning may be required as the seedlings begin to develop. Sow from early spring through till early summer, sowing at two-week intervals. Excess cropping and late sowing can be used for pickling. If earlier crops are desired, then these may be sown under cloches.

AFTERCARE

Thin out seedlings if necessary, leaving the healthiest in situ. Keep any thinnings for the compost heap. Keep the crop weed-free, taking care if using a hoe as they are easily damaged. Beetroot needs a moist soil and should be watered every two weeks in dry periods to avoid "hardening" of the crop. Consistency in watering is essential as successive wet and dry conditions will make the roots split. Mulching with compost will help the soil retain moisture.

Left: *Beetroot grows best in light soils. Growing in raised beds allows you to choose the growing medium best suited to the crops.*

CULTIVATION

Sowing time Early spring through to early summer. Successional sow every two weeks
Sowing distance 8cm (3in) and thin out after germination
Sowing depth 2.5cm (1in)
Distance between rows 20cm (8in)
Harvesting Late autumn to early spring

HARVESTING AND STORAGE

The first crop will be ready to pick about six to seven weeks after sowing. Pull as required, twisting the leaf off rather than cutting. Store autumn-harvested beetroot in boxes, covering the crop with moist peat-substitute or sand. These boxes should then be placed in a cool dry place.

PESTS AND DISEASES

Usually trouble free.

VARIETIES

'Barabietola di Chioggia' Rosy pink skin and white flesh with concentric pink circles.
'Carillon' A cylindrical, long red variety with resistance to bolting.
'Detriot Globe' Good uniform shape and flesh free from rings. Large roots are good for exhibiting.
'Egyptian Turnip Rooted' Early and quick-growing.
'Libero' Good resistance to bolting; fast growing with high yields.

purple beetroot

white beetroot

golden beetroot

SWEDES (RUTABAGAS OR YELLOW TURNIPS)

Brassica napus

Swedes are very similar to turnips, but their skin is normally yellow and they have a sweeter, milder flavour. Although this vegetable is grouped within root crops, it is botanically a member of the cabbage family. Crop rotation must therefore be planned carefully, grouping swedes in with cabbages because they suffer from the same pests and diseases.

SOIL

Although they will grow on heavy soils, swedes prefer a light soil that contains plenty of organic matter. Dig in the autumn, incorporating plenty of well-rotted manure or garden compost. Adding organic matter increases the moisture retention of the soil in summer, which is essential for good growth.

ASPECT

Thrive in an open sunny location.

SOWING

In late spring to early summer sow thinly in rows 1cm (½in) deep. Keep the rows 40cm (16in) apart. Once the seedlings are large enough, thin out to 25cm (10in) apart.

AFTERCARE

Swedes must be well watered throughout the summer months, otherwise they will turn woody and split. Mulch rows to retain moisture in dry periods. Keep well weeded throughout.

HARVESTING AND STORAGE

Harvest from autumn into the winter months. Lift when they are large enough to use – you do not need to wait until they are maximum size. The crop can stay in the soil until spring, lifting only when required. Alternatively, lift and cut off the leaves and store in boxes filled with dry sand. Keep in a cool shed or garage.

PESTS AND DISEASES

Prone to the same problems as cabbages. Flea beetles are a frequent pest. To help prevent infestations, prepare the soil well by incorporating plenty of organic matter. Watering in dry periods and mulching will also help. Mildew and clubroot are another problem. Resistant or tolerant cultivars are available.

Above: *Swedes are usually round, but can vary in shape according to the variety and growing conditions.*

CULTIVATION
Sowing time Late spring to early summer
Sowing distance Thinly
Sowing depth 1cm (½in)
Distance between rows 40cm (16in)
Thinning distance 25cm (10in)
Harvesting Autumn onwards

VARIETIES
'Acme Purple Top' Medium-sized roots with a good flavour.
'Joan' Good for early sowings. Has a moderate resistance to clubroot and mildew.
'Marian' A fairly new variety with excellent texture and flavour. Moderately resistant to clubroot and mildew.

swedes

Right: *Swedes can be harvested from autumn onwards. You can leave the crop in the soil until spring, lifting it as required. Cut off the leaves and store in boxes filled with dry sand.*

KOHL RABI

Brassica oleracea Gongylodes Group

This curious vegetable is a member of the cabbage family. It is the swollen stem, found at the base of the plant, that is eaten. Tasting something like a cross between a cabbage and a turnip, kohl rabi can be eaten raw or cooked. Although not widely grown, it has a number of good qualities. It grows very well on shallow soils and performs well in hot dry weather, whereas its culinary rival, the turnip, needs a firm, fertile soil. The green varieties are used for cropping in summer, while the purple types are mainly grown to harvest in autumn and early winter.

Above: *This extremely healthy crop of kohl rabi has been grown in a free-draining soil in an open sunny position.*

Right: *This perfect specimen of kohl rabi has been watered throughout any dry periods to prevent the swollen stem from splitting.*

SOIL
Thrives in light soil conditions, but will grow on heavier soils. Dig the soil in the autumn, incorporating well-rotted manure or garden compost if this has not already been done in the previous autumn.

ASPECT
Grow kohl rabi in an open sunny site.

SOWING
Sow the seeds thinly in rows 1cm (½in) deep. Keep 30cm (12in) between the rows. Start sowing under cloches in late winter and outside in early spring. Successionally sow kohl rabi at three-week intervals until late summer. This will provide a fresh supply of tender globes. Thin out the rows when the seedlings are large enough to 15cm (6in) apart.

AFTERCARE
Weed regularly throughout the growing season, taking great care not to damage the shallow roots if you are using a hoe for weeding. Mulching with garden compost will also help to prevent the germination of any weed seedlings. Watering in dry periods will help to prevent the stems of the kohl rabi from splitting, although they are less likely to split than turnips.

HARVESTING AND STORAGE
Pull kohl rabi from the ground when they are about the size of a tennis ball because they tend to become woody if they are left to grow much bigger. Harvest as and when

CULTIVATION
Sowing time Late winter (under cloches); early spring to late summer (outdoors)
Sowing distance Thinly
Sowing depth 1cm (½in)
Distance between rows 30cm (12in)
Thinning distance 15cm (6in)
Harvesting Summer through to early winter

required because they do not store well and tend to shrivel. Later crops will keep in the ground until winter. Cut back the leaves and shorten the roots before taking them indoors to prepare.

PESTS AND DISEASES
Kohl rabi is prone to the same pests and diseases as cabbages. Flea beetles are the main problem. Symptoms of an attack include small holes in the leaves and stems during summer. To avoid an attack, do not let the plants dry out and encourage quick seedling growth.

VARIETIES
'Azur Star' Purple-blue bulbs with white flesh. A quick-maturing variety.
'F1 Cindy RZ' An early maturing variety which is slow to bolt. Large white bulbs with strong green foliage.
'Green Delicacy' An extremely old variety. Pale green globes with white flesh.
'Green Vienna' Green-skinned with white flesh. Good for early sowings.
'Purple Vienna' Purple-skinned globes with white flesh. Good for late sowings.
'Rowel' Lovely sweet flesh. Tends not to become woody if picked after it becomes the size of a tennis ball.

kohl rabi

TURNIPS

Brassica oleracea Rapifina Group

Turnips are a very easy crop to grow. Like carrots, home-grown turnips are much tastier than shop-bought specimens. Although the root is normally round, cylindrical root shapes are not uncommon in the early varieties. Turnip roots usually have a white skin that is coloured green, purple or yellow at the top. Inside the root, the flesh colour can vary from white to yellow. Group turnips in with cabbages when planning crop rotation as they are closely related and suffer from the same pests and diseases.

SOIL
Turnips thrive in firm, fertile soil that retains moisture. Dig in the autumn and incorporate plenty of well-rotted manure or garden compost to help retain moisture. If the soil is acidic, lime after digging. Practise crop rotation to avoid soil-borne diseases.

ASPECT
Grow best in a sunny position, but can take some degree of shade.

SOWING
For an early crop, start by sowing under cloches in late winter. Sow direct outside from early spring onwards. Sow thinly in rows 1cm (½in) deep, with 25cm (10in) between the rows for early crops. After germination, thin to 15cm (6in) apart. Successional sowing during spring and summer will ensure a steady supply of turnips. For turnips to be harvested in autumn and winter, sow in late summer. Sow to the same depth, but allow for 30cm (12in) between the rows and thin seedlings to 20cm (8in).

Right: *Harvest early and summer varieties as soon as they are the size of golf balls for optimum flavour.*

Below: *Do not allow turnips to turn woody. If lifted when young, the crop will not only taste better but be easy to pull.*

AFTERCARE
Regular watering is required, otherwise they run the risk of bolting. Weed throughout the growing season.

HARVESTING AND STORAGE
Pick turnips harvested in summer when they are the size of a golf ball. Varieties for picking in autumn and winter are harvested when required, or lift and store in trays of moist sand and keep in a shed or garage.

PESTS AND DISEASES
Prone to the same pests and diseases as cabbages, mainly flea beetle. Keep watered and prepare soil well to avoid attack. Violet root rot and clubroot are also a problem. Destroy all diseased material. Practise crop rotation to help avoid clubroot.

Left: *Turnips belong to the cabbage family and can suffer from clubroot. Practise crop rotation in order to prevent infection.*

CULTIVATION

Sowing time Late winter (under cloches); early spring and summer (outside)
Sowing distance Thinly
Sowing depth 1cm (½in)
Distance between rows 25–30cm (10–12in)
Thinning distance 15–20cm (6–8in)
Harvesting Summer to winter

VARIETIES

'Golden Ball' A relatively old variety with excellent storage qualities. Round golden roots with tender flesh.
'Market Cross F1' A quick grower. White roots that have an excellent flavour.
'Snowball' Fast maturing and best eaten small; lovely white skin.
'Veitch Red Globe' Roots are two tone, a red top and white bottom. Quick to mature.

turnips

CARROTS

Daucus carota

If there is a vegetable that tastes incomparably better if it has been grown in your own garden, it must be the carrot. Home-grown carrots have a sweet, juicy flavour compared with the bland, watery taste of those sold in supermarkets. The edible part of the carrot is the root, which is usually orange, although there are also pale yellow and white varieties. Root shapes vary from round to long and tapered. Carrots that are planted within an ornamental area and left in the ground over winter will flower in their second year. The flowers are ideal for attracting beneficial insects into the garden.

SOIL

Although carrots will grow in heavy clay soils, they do best on light sandy soils where the drainage is good and root growth is not impaired. The soil should be free of stones and fresh manure, as both will cause the carrot roots to fork. Do not manure the soil in the season before sowing.

ASPECT

Carrots require an open sunny site.

SOWING

Sow outside from early spring, or under cloches from late winter. Sow thinly in rows 1cm (½in) deep with 15–20cm (6–8in) between the rows. Sow successively until

early summer. If your soil is very heavy, use a crowbar to make holes, fill with a compost-and-grit mix and then sow into these holes. Thin the young seedlings to 5–8cm (2–3in) apart. Try to thin on a still evening to avoid attracting carrot fly. Bury the thinnings in the compost heap or wormery to avoid dispersing the smell.

AFTERCARE

Weed the crop regularly, making sure not to disturb the roots or shoots too much. Mulch the crop to help retain moisture and suppress weed growth. It is important to water during dry periods.

HARVESTING AND STORAGE

Start to harvest from late spring onwards, usually seven to eight weeks after sowing. Lift with a fork, especially when the soil is dry. Maincrop carrots can be left in the ground and harvested when required. In colder areas, cover over with straw until harvesting. Alternatively, carrots can be lifted in mid-autumn. After cleaning the roots and trimming the foliage to 1cm (½in), they can be stored in boxes containing a mixture of dry potting mix and sand. The carrots must not touch each other. These will keep until early spring.

PESTS AND DISEASES

The main pest is carrot root fly which lays its eggs on the plant and can destroy the crop in severe cases. There are several methods to deter the fly from laying eggs. By delaying sowing until early summer, you will miss the first batch of egg laying in late spring. The second batch is in late summer until early

Left: Plant carrots near onions or chives. This helps mask the smell of the carrots to deter its main pest, the carrot root fly.

Left: You can start harvesting carrots from late spring onwards.

autumn. Lift your early summer crop before risk of infestation. Another effective method is to erect a barrier of fleece or fine mesh around the crop. Companion planting can also help. Onions, for example, will mask the smell of carrots. Plant four rows to every row of carrots or plant in a mosaic pattern.

> ### CULTIVATION
> **Sowing time** Early spring (under cloches) and successively to early summer
> **Sowing distance** Very thinly
> **Sowing depth** 1cm (½in)
> **Distance between rows** 15–20cm (6–8in)
> **Thinning distance** 5–8cm (2–3in)
> **Harvesting** Late spring onwards

> ### VARIETIES
> **EARLY**
> **'Amsterdam Forcing'** Small roots that are ideal for freezing.
> **'Nantes 2'** Matures quickly. Has a lovely sweet flavour.
> **'Parabel'** Small and spherical root that is sweet flavoured.
>
> **MAINCROP**
> **'Berlicum'** Produces a uniform crop. The roots have good colour and flavour.
> **'Fly Away F1'** Sweet flavour. Bred for carrot fly resistance.
> **'F1 Magno RZ'** Vigorous grower with good colour. Stores well.

carrots

JERUSALEM ARTICHOKES

Helianthus tuberosus

The edible parts of the Jerusalem artichoke are the knobbly tubers that grow underground, like the potato. You can boil, fry, bake, roast or stew them. Sample a few from the supermarket before splashing out on a row of them for your vegetable garden. Take care when planning your crop as they are a type of sunflower and can easily reach heights of 3m (10ft). It is advisable to select a variety that has been bred to reach a more manageable size of 1.5m (5ft) if you are gardening in a confined space.

Left: *These Jerusalem artichokes are freshly dug. This variety is 'Fuseau'.*

SOIL

Grow in any type of soil provided it is not too acid or has prolonged periods of waterlogging. Dig garden compost or well-rotted manure in autumn. Do not be liberal with this, or too much leafy growth will be produced at the expense of the tubers.

ASPECT

Thrive in full sun, but will also grow well in dappled shade.

PLANTING

If space is limited it is best to plant one of the compact varieties, otherwise plant tubers bought from a supermarket. Plant at any time from early to late spring. Plant out in rows 40cm (16in) apart. Use a trowel

Left: *Jerusalem artichokes can be lifted when the foliage starts to turn brown in the autumn. Make sure that you remove all of the tubers because any left in the ground will grow the following year.*

CULTIVATION

Planting time Early to late spring
Planting distance 40cm (16in)
Planting depth 10–13cm (4–5in)
Distance between rows 90cm (3ft)
Harvesting Autumn onwards

---

or a dibber (dibble) to plant the tuber 10–13cm (4–5in) deep. Rows need to be 90cm (3ft) apart.

AFTERCARE

Earth up the bases of the plants when they are 30cm (12in) high. Water throughout dry periods. Remove flowering heads in the summer months. If the plants are grown on a windy site stake to support tall stems.

HARVESTING AND STORAGE

Lift the tubers when the foliage starts to turn brown in autumn. Cut the stems down before lifting the tubers, taking care to remove all the tubers. Any left in will grow the following year. Lift the tubers throughout autumn and winter when required. If frost is forecast, lift the amount needed and store in a box of moist sand.

PESTS AND DISEASES

Generally trouble free, although they can be attacked by slugs.

Above: *This healthy row of Jerusalem artichokes has been mulched with a layer of farmyard manure.*

VARIETIES

'Dwarf Sunray' Compact habit with ornamental merits. Lovely white skin that does not need peeling.
'Fuseau' Considered the best variety due to the smooth surface of the tuber. This is a compact plant that is suitable for the small garden.

Jerusalem artichokes

PARSNIPS

Pastinaca sativa

Parsnips are a good vegetable for the inexperienced gardener as they require very little work and are easy to grow. It is the underground swollen root that is eaten. The root looks similar to a carrot but is creamy white in colour and slightly longer. Parsnips taste great used in stir-fries, mashed up with carrot or as an accompaniment to fish or roast meats.

SOIL

Do not grow on freshly manured ground, but on ground that has already been manured for the previous crop. Ideally, the soil needs to be dug over during the winter and be stone-free to produce good-quality parsnips. Compost from your heap may be added to improve the soil structure.

ASPECT

Parsnips like an open sunny site, but will tolerate light shade.

SOWING

It is essential to sow fresh seed every year. Sow in late winter through to late spring in drills 1cm (½in) deep and space seeds

Above: *It is advisable to sow fresh parsnip seed every year because even one-year-old seed is unlikely to germinate successfully.*

15cm (6in) apart. Alternatively, sow sparingly and thin out at the seedling stage. Rows are spaced 30cm (12in) apart. Germination can be slow, sometimes taking up to three weeks. This allows for intercropping between rows by sowing radish or lettuce.

AFTERCARE

Thin out rows of seedlings (where necessary) to 15cm (6in) apart. Throw thinnings on to your compost heap as they do not transplant easily. Water the crop during dry periods, never allowing the soil to dry out. Carry out regular weeding, taking care not to damage the crowns of the new plants.

HARVESTING AND STORAGE

Start harvesting when the foliage starts to die down in mid-autumn. The best-tasting parsnips are lifted after the first frosts. Lift only when required; the remainder can be left in the ground through to late winter. A certain number may also be lifted and stored in a box of moist sand to ensure supplies throughout the winter.

PESTS AND DISEASES

Generally trouble free, but parsnip canker can affect the crop. Do not plant in freshly manured ground. Instead, sow later or use canker-resistant varieties. Acidic soil conditions can also cause canker. Carrot fly and celery fly may attack parsnips.

Left: *Parsnips can be left in the ground and harvested as they are required. The best-tasting parsnips are lifted after the first frost.*

Above: *Parsnips are hardy plants and so they are best left in the ground until ready for harvesting. Lift with a fork in order to avoid damaging the root.*

CULTIVATION

Sowing time Late winter to late spring
Sowing distance 15cm (6in) or sow sparingly and thin out at seedling stage
Sowing depth 1cm (½in)
Distance between rows 30cm (12in)
Thinning distance 15–20cm (6–8in)
Harvesting Mid-autumn to late winter

VARIETIES

'Avonresister' Resistance to canker.
'Half Long Guernsey' Heavily tapered roots with a sweet flavour.
'Tender & True' Excellent flavour, good resistance to canker.
'White King' A heavy yielding variety with delicious, well-textured roots.

parsnips

RADISHES

Raphanus sativus

This extremely fast-growing vegetable has a wider crop diversity than is commonly known. Along with the familiar round red radish commonly used in salads, there are also varieties with pink, yellow or white roots. Winter varieties can have roots the size of carrots and other types are grown for their pods. Due to their attractive roots, which sit slightly above the soil, they are often grown among decorative plants in the ornamental garden.

SOIL

Radishes will grow in most soils, but thrive in soil that is rich in organic matter and is moisture retentive. Dig in plenty of garden compost before sowing if the ground was not manured for a previous crop.

ASPECT

Thrive in an open sunny site, but will welcome some dappled shade at the height of summer. This makes radishes ideal for intercropping during this period.

SOWING

Summer crops can be started by sowing outside under cloches in late winter and in early spring. Sow thinly in rows 1cm (½in) deep with 15cm (6in) between the rows. Thin to 2.5cm (1in) apart. Successional sowing will prevent a glut at harvest time.

Above: When harvesting radishes, discard any that have become large or old, as they will be too woody and hot to eat.

Sow in small rows every two weeks. Sow winter varieties in mid-summer. They are larger than the maincrop varieties, so the rows should be spaced 25cm (10in) apart and the crop thinned to 15cm (6in) apart.

AFTERCARE

Keep weed-free throughout the season and water in dry periods.

HARVESTING AND STORAGE

Pick before they get too old and woody. Select the larger roots first and leave the rest of the crop to grow. Winter cultivars can be left in the soil with a layer of straw

Below: For small quantities of radishes, it is best to sow short rows every two weeks to obtain a succession of crops.

CULTIVATION

SUMMER RADISH
Sowing time Late winter (under cloches); early spring onwards (outside)
Sowing distance Thinly
Sowing depth 1cm (½in)
Distance between rows 15cm (6in)
Thinning distance 2.5cm (1in)
Harvesting Late spring onwards

WINTER RADISH
Sowing time Mid-summer
Sowing distance Thinly
Sowing depth 1cm (½in)
Distance between rows 25cm (10in)
Thinning distance 15cm (6in)
Harvesting Autumn onwards

---

over the top for protection. Harvest when required; otherwise lift the radishes and store them in trays of sand until needed.

PESTS AND DISEASES

Radishes are related to cabbages and are prone to the same pests and diseases. Flea beetle and slugs are normally the main problems. If more problematic pests or diseases take hold, destroy plants and grow in an alternative location.

VARIETIES

'Berosa' Grown for winter use. Grows up to 15cm (6in) long. Ideal for slicing.
'Rondeel RZ' A bright red round radish. Good uniformity.
'Sirri RZ' Excellent root colouring with strong foliage. Stores well.
'Sparkler' A spring variety that has a red base to the root with a white tip.

radishes

POTATOES

Solanum tuberosum

This native of South America is one of the easiest vegetables to grow. Potatoes are split up into two main groups: earlies and maincrop. Earlies are harvested in summer, offering the welcome taste of new potatoes, whereas maincrop potatoes are harvested later and can be stored for use during the winter.

SOIL

Potatoes thrive on sandy soil that is slightly acidic, but will grow almost as well on nearly every other type of soil. However, they grow best on a fertile soil that is rich in nitrogen. Plant in soil that has had organic matter added in the autumn; they should never be planted on freshly manured ground.

ASPECT

A warm sheltered site is best. Always avoid frost pockets, which can damage the foliage of early varieties emerging from the soil.

PURCHASING SEED POTATOES

Seed potatoes are not actually seeds, but swollen tubers from the potato plant. They can be purchased from mid-winter to mid-spring. It is important to purchase certified seed potatoes, as this will ensure a healthy virus-free stock.

CHITTING

Before planting outdoors, place seed potatoes with the seeds' eyes (the dormant buds on the surface) facing upward on a 2.5cm (1in) layer of potting mix in trays or egg boxes. They should be left indoors in light warm conditions to encourage the

Above: *It is only the tubers of the potato plant that are edible. All other parts such as the leaves and fruits are poisonous.*

sprouting of small shoots. This is called chitting. In six weeks the shoots will have grown to 2.5cm (1in), the ideal length to plant. Chitting is essential for earlies but not necessary for maincrop potatoes, although this can still prove beneficial in colder years.

PLANTING

Planting is normally carried out in trenches 10–15cm (4–6in) deep with 30–40cm (12–16in) between the tubers. Keep 45cm (18in) between the rows for first earlies and 65–75cm (26–30in) for second earlies and maincrop varieties. Always plant the seed potatoes with their "eyes" facing upwards, taking care not to break off the new growth. An alternative to hoeing out the trenches is to plant the potatoes individually (to the same specifications) using a trowel or potato dibber. Once planted and covered with soil, create a small mound above them.

If you cannot face digging over a vegetable bed, why not try the "no-dig bed system"? Cover the soil with well-rotted manure or compost and simply place the seed potatoes on top, 30–40cm (12–16in) apart. Cover the seed potatoes with a 10cm (4in) layer of old straw. Alternatively, if you are gardening in a confined space, try planting the seed potatoes in pots. This

Above: *Earth up the potatoes in order to increase yields and prevent light reaching the new potatoes. Light will make them turn green and they will be poisonous.*

method can allow people with even the smallest gardens to experience home-grown, pesticide-free new potatoes.

AFTERCARE

PROTECTION FROM FROST

Cover the young growth with straw or fleece if there is any risk of frost.

EARTHING UP

This task is essential if large yields are to be obtained. Earthing up also stops light getting to the new potatoes, which makes them turn green and poisonous. Another

Above: *Before planting out potato tubers, place them in a tray in order to "chit" them. This is essential for early potatoes.*

Above: *When harvesting maincrop potatoes, leave them on the surface for an hour or two to let them dry out and to harden the skins.*

benefit of this is that it makes the soil easy to work for crop rotation. Earth up when the foliage is 20cm (8in) tall. Hoe up the earth around the foliage until only a small amount of leaf is still showing at the top. This process is carried out again just before the foliage between the rows joins up.

WATERING
Potatoes need copious amounts of water throughout their growing period in order to develop plenty of good-sized tubers. It is essential to water heavily in the early stages of development. Watering every 10 days during dry periods is a good guide to follow.

HARVESTING AND STORAGE
EARLIES These are ready to lift when the potato plant is flowering – usually towards the end of early summer or the beginning of mid-summer for first earlies, and late summer for second earlies. Harvest the potatoes using a potato fork (with balls on the end of the tines) or a flat-tined fork to reduce damage to the crop.
MAINCROP These are harvested in early autumn, 10–14 days after the withered brown foliage has been removed and put on the compost heap. Lift the potatoes on a warm dry day and leave on the surface for several hours to dry out. Store only perfect potatoes in a sack or in trays in a cool, dark, frost-free place. Diseased potatoes do not store well and must be used at once.

PESTS AND DISEASES
The potato's worst enemy is blight. This is particularly bad in wet summers where the weather is hot and humid. The first sign of

the disease is brown patches on the leaves. These should be cut off to prevent the spores being washed off into the soil to infect the tubers. Choose resistant varieties if possible. Scab disfigures the tuber by cracking and brown discoloration. Water the crop heavily to help overcome the problem and do not grow on ground that has been recently manured. Potatoes are also damaged by diseases such as violet root rot and blackleg. Slugs, eelworms and cutworms are the worst pests, all of them eating and damaging the tubers.

CULTIVATION
FIRST EARLIES
Planting time Early spring
Planting distance 30–40cm (12–16in)
Planting depth 10–15cm (4–6in)
Distance between rows 45cm (18in)
Harvesting Early summer

SECOND EARLIES AND MAINCROP
Planting time Mid- to late spring
Planting distance 30–40cm (12–16in)
Planting depth 10–15cm (4–6in)
Distance between rows 65–75cm (26–30in)
Harvesting Summer onwards

VARIETIES
FIRST EARLIES
'Accent' Attractive yellow skin and flesh, high yielding.
'Premiere' Resistant to blight and high resistance to common scab.
'Red Duke of York' Superb texture and flavour.
'Swift' Resistant to golden eelworm and tolerant to blackleg.

SECOND EARLIES
'Cosmos' Resistant to blight and common scab.
'Kestrel' Great flavour, ideal for baking. Performs well in drought conditions.
'Marfona' Good for baking, stores well.
'Wilja' Good resistance to disease and drought.

MAINCROP
'Cara' Stores well, good blight resistance.
'Désirée' Distinctive flavour and a superb roaster.
'Milva' Good flavour with resistance to blight.
'Valor' Good overall disease resistance together with high eelworm resistance and high resistance to blight.

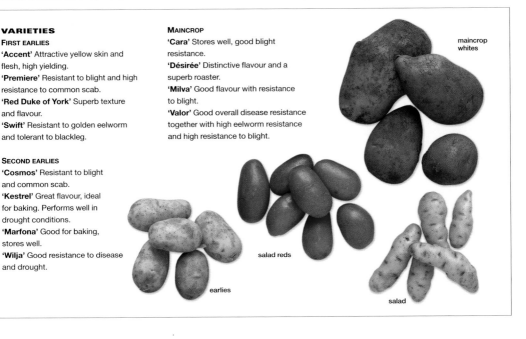

maincrop whites

salad reds

earlies

salad

SALSIFY AND SCORZONERA

Tragopogon porrifolius and *Scorzonera hispanica*

These two unusual root vegetables are underused. Salsify is a biennial that has a similar appearance to a skinny parsnip and has a distinctive flavour that has been likened to that of a cross between asparagus and oysters. Scorzonera is a perennial that has black-skinned roots with white flesh and a delicious flavour.

SOIL
Both root crops prefer a light stone-free soil. They do not like freshly manured ground. Ideally, manure should have been added to the ground for the previous crop. Dig deeply in the autumn to ensure good root development, adding garden compost if the soil is poor.

ASPECT
Salsify and scorzonera thrive in an open sunny site.

SOWING
Sow in mid-spring to ensure a long growing season. This will allow for large root development to take place before harvesting. Sow fresh seed every year, as it does not keep well. Sow thinly in rows 1cm (½) deep, with 25cm (10in) between the rows. After germination thin the seedlings to 15cm (6in).

AFTERCARE
An easy vegetable to look after. Keep weed-free. Do this carefully, as roots can be easily damaged by a hoe. Mulching with garden

Left: *This crop of salsify has just been harvested. The taste of the vegetables is enhanced if they are lifted after the first frosts.*

Above: *This abundant crop of scorzonera has been harvested in a garden trug. Some plants are still remaining.*

compost will help to keep weeds down. It will also help the soil to retain moisture in dry periods.

HARVESTING AND STORAGE
Both salsify and scorzonera can be harvested from autumn onwards. Like many crops, the taste of both vegetables is enhanced after the first frost. As both crops are hardy they can be left in the ground throughout the winter and lifted when needed. If the roots of scorzonera are not large enough to harvest during the first season they can be left in the ground until the following autumn and winter.

PESTS AND DISEASES
Usually trouble free.

Left: *Although salsify produces a mass of untidy foliage, it is worth growing just to taste its unusual flavour.*

CULTIVATION
Sowing time Mid-spring
Sowing distance Thinly
Sowing depth 1cm (⅜in)
Distance between rows 25cm (10in)
Thinning distance 15cm (6in)
Harvesting Autumn and winter

VARIETIES
SALSIFY
'Sandwich Island' An old variety. Very large tapering roots with yellow skin.

SCORZONERA
'Russian Giant' Long black roots. Young leaves can be eaten in salads.

Both crops are often simply listed under salsify (or vegetable oyster) and scorzonera.

salsify

scorzonera

PEAS AND BEANS

RUNNER BEANS

Phaseolus coccineus

These climbing plants are often grown in ornamental gardens for their lovely red flowers and long green pods. They look wonderful growing up decorative supports or arches. New varieties offer flower colours in white or mauve. The production of the pods requires pollination by bees.

SOIL

Runner beans thrive in a deep, rich, moisture-retentive soil, but they will grow in relatively poor soil. Manure the previous autumn.

ASPECT

They like an open, sheltered, sunny position. Do not plant in windy areas as this will make pollination difficult and the support structures for the crop will be prone to blowing over.

SOWING/PLANTING

Runner beans are half hardy and therefore should not be planted or appear above ground until the risk of frost has gone. For an early start, sow the crop under glass in early spring. The beans are best sown individually in pots and then hardened off to be ready to plant out in early summer. Alternatively, sow directly outside in late spring. Before sowing, build a support for the crop. This is traditionally made up of a double row of canes tied at the top. For a more decorative effect, construct a tepee which can be placed in a vegetable garden or ornamental garden. Keep 25cm (10in) between each cane. Plant two seeds 50cm (2in) deep per cane and remove the weaker seedling after

Above: *Many gardeners sow three beans at the base of each pole – "one for the crow, one for the slug and one for the kitchen".*

germination. Dwarf varieties are grown in single rows at 15cm (6in) apart and with 45cm (18in) between the rows. Sow direct or grow on under glass for an early start.

AFTERCARE

Keep the soil moist at all times, mulching with garden compost to help the soil to retain moisture. After harvesting leave the roots to rot down in the soil as the root nodules contain a valuable source of nitrogen. Turn in the roots when digging the soil during the autumn.

HARVESTING AND STORAGE

Pick the pods when they have reached 20–30cm (8–12in) in length and before they have become stringy and hard. It is important to pick regularly or the plants will stop flowering. Most plants will continue to flower until the first frosts. The only successful method of storage is to freeze any surplus beans.

PESTS AND DISEASES

One of the commonest problems with runner beans is their failure to set pods. This is often the case in periods of hot dry weather. Regular watering will help flowering

Above: *A larger crop of beans will be produced if picked regularly. Select young pods and discard any old stringy ones.*

and pod formation. Mulching will help to retain soil moisture. Pest damage from slugs and snails can pose problems when the plants are young. Diseases such as powdery mildew and chocolate spot may occasionally occur.

FRENCH (GREEN) BEANS

Phaseolus vulgaris

French beans are split into two distinct categories: dwarf and climbing. The dwarf varieties are by far the most popular as they do not take up much room. Both types are frost tender and need to be sown or planted out after any risk of frost has gone. Nowadays, there are many good varieties, which offer colourful pods in yellows and purples to liven up the vegetable garden.

SOIL

They thrive in fertile, free-draining soil that has preferably been manured in the previous autumn.

ASPECT

French beans require an open sunny site.

SOWING

French beans can be sown early under glass in pots in late spring, but they are best sown outdoors in early summer in a single or double row 4cm (1½in) deep with 8cm (3in) between the seeds. Place the rows 45cm (18in) apart. Plant outside in early summer when the threat of frost has passed. Treat climbing varieties in the same way as non-dwarf runner beans.

Below: *The pods of French beans are now found in a variety of colours. This purple pod variety is often grown in decorative borders.*

Above: *Leave the pods that you want to treat as haricot (navy) beans until the pods have swollen and turned yellow.*

AFTERCARE

Water regularly when the crop is in flower. Keep the plot weed-free throughout the growing season.

HARVESTING AND STORAGE

Harvest when the seeds are still immature on the plant. Pick regularly to encourage new pods. The beans are best eaten fresh,

Above: *Harvesting can begin seven to eight weeks after sowing. It is best to pick while the seeds are still immature.*

but they can be frozen. French beans can also be dried and stored in airtight jars and named haricot (navy) beans.

PESTS AND DISEASES

Generally trouble free. Blackfly and fungal diseases can cause problems. Slugs and snails are the main problem, especially at the seedling stage.

CULTIVATION
Sowing time Late spring (under glass); early summer (outdoors)
Sowing/planting distance 8cm/3in (dwarf); 25cm/10in (climbing)
Sowing depth 4cm (1½in)
Distance between rows 45cm/18in (dwarf); 90cm/3ft (climbing)
Harvesting Late summer until first frosts

VARIETIES
CLIMBING
'Blue Lake' A heavy-yielding variety that is suitable for freezing. The stringless pods contain small white beans.
'Farba RZ' Pods are round and stringless, growing up to 12cm (5in) long.
'Mantra RZ' A good cropper that produces uniform pods 20cm (8in) long. This variety is resistant to common bean mosaic virus.

DWARF
'Annabel' A compact variety that is good for growing in pots or grow bags. A heavy cropper of thin stringless pods.
'The Prince' An early variety. The dwarf-growing flat pod is often used for exhibiting.

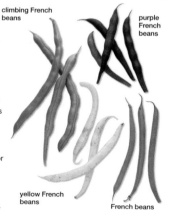

climbing French beans

purple French beans

yellow French beans

French beans

PEAS

Pisum sativum

There is nothing like the taste of freshly picked peas. This is because the moment that a pea is picked its natural sugars start to break down into starch, which affects the flavour. With careful planning and by using a range of varieties, peas can be freshly harvested from late spring until late autumn.

SOIL

Grow in a fertile moisture-retentive soil. Dig to a good depth in autumn and incorporate well-rotted manure or garden compost. Do not grow in soil that might get waterlogged, as this will cause basal rotting to the plants.

ASPECT

Peas thrive in an open sunny site, but will withstand light shade.

SOWING

Varieties are categorized as first earlies, which are smooth-skinned, and second earlies and maincrop, which have wrinkled skins. Sow first earlies outside in mid- to late autumn and overwinter the crop under cloches. For a slightly later crop, sow second earlies in late winter to early spring, starting them off under cloches to protect

Above: *Choose old seed varieties if you wish to harvest the crop at intervals, as many modern varieties mature at the same time.*

Above: *Wire netting can support smaller pea varieties, whereas the more decorative hazel sticks are used for larger ones.*

against frost. Maincrop varieties are sown at regular intervals from early spring to mid-summer without protection. Sow in flat-bottomed trenches, 23cm (9in) wide and 5cm (2in) deep. Sow the seed in a double row, 5cm (2in) apart, or in single rows with 60–90cm (24–36in) between trenches or rows.

AFTERCARE

Immediately after sowing protect the crop from birds by covering with wire netting, twiggy branches or tie black cotton thread over canes. Provide support, using pea sticks or plastic or wire netting, when the crop reaches 8cm (3in) high. For tall varieties place the supports on either side of the growing stems. Water regularly during dry spells, especially when the crop is in flower. Mulch with garden compost to improve soil-moisture retention.

HARVESTING AND STORAGE

Harvest when the pods are plump but not fully grown, starting from the bottom of the plant and working your way up. Keep picking to encourage production. Mangetouts (snow peas) need to be picked before the pods get tough. Fresh peas freeze well in plastic bags or containers. Dry peas by leaving them on the plant until they rattle about in their pods. Shell peas and store in an airtight container.

PESTS AND DISEASES

Peas are prone to a number of pests and diseases. Pigeons and sparrows can devastate young crops. Netting is the best protection. Mildew can also be a problem. Pea and bean weevil can cause checking of plant growth. The crop may be attacked by pea thrips in hot sunny weather. Silvery patches are seen on the pods and leaves, which will affect the yield. Sow early to avoid major attacks. The white-bodied caterpillar of the pea moth feeds on the peas inside the pods. The adults lay their eggs when the peas are in flower. Sow early or late to avoid the moth's flying period.

CULTIVATION

Sowing time Mid- to late autumn (first earlies); late winter to early spring (second earlies); early spring to mid-summer (maincrop)
Trench width 23cm (9in)
Trench depth 5cm (2in)
Sowing distance in trenches Sow a double row 5cm (2in) apart
Distance between trenches or rows 60–90cm (24–36in)
Harvesting Late spring until late autumn depending on variety

VARIETIES
FIRST EARLIES
'Feltham First' A vigorous grower suitable for autumn sowing.
'Meteor' Compact plants which produce heavy yields.

SECOND EARLIES AND MAINCROP
'Alderman' A tall variety with large pods. A high yielder, but needs support.
'Onward' Large peas with a superb flavour. Crops heavily and has good disease resistance.

MANGETOUT
'Carouby de Mausanne' Purple flowers and large pods. Tastes delicious.
'Oregon Sugar Pod' Superb sweet flavour. Fast growing and tall.

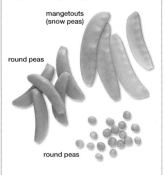

mangetouts (snow peas)

round peas

round peas

BROAD (FAVA) BEANS

Vicia faba

These are the hardiest and earliest of all the beans grown. Like many vegetables, the fresh or frozen produce that can be purchased from a shop does not do its flavour justice. Try growing this crop in your organic vegetable garden to experience the true succulent flavour. Varieties can be selected to grow green, white or red seeds.

SOIL
Grow broad beans in heavy soils that are well manured and have good drainage. Dig and incorporate manure during the autumn.

ASPECT
Broad beans thrive in an open sunny site that is sheltered from strong winds. This is essential if you are growing the crop over the winter.

SOWING
Overwintering varieties are sown in late autumn. Other varieties are sown from late winter to late spring. Sow in double rows in a shallow trench, 23cm (9in) wide and 4cm (1½in) deep with 23cm (9in) between the seeds. Alternatively, the crop can be started off under glass in late winter. Sow individually in pots to be planted out in spring.

AFTERCARE
Keep weeds down throughout the growing season. If there is a dry spell, give plenty of water throughout this period until the pods start to swell. Provide support for taller varieties. Place stakes or canes on either side of the crop, 25cm (10in) apart, and run

Left: To grow a healthy crop of broad beans, choose an open sunny site which is protected from strong winds.

string from stake to stake to support the stems. When the first pods start to form pinch out the top 8cm (3in) of growth. This will reduce the danger of blackfly attack and aid pod formation.

HARVESTING AND STORAGE
Pick the pods when they have become swollen. Do not allow the pods to be too mature because they will become leathery and tough. Continuous harvesting extends the cropping season. Broad beans are best picked and used fresh. Any surplus beans can be frozen or dried.

PESTS AND DISEASES
The most serious problem is blackfly. Removing the growing tips when the pods are starting to mature will help to deter this problem. The only other major problem is

chocolate spot, which can sometimes affect the crop. Avoid autumn sowings if this is a problem and destroy affected material.

broad (fava) beans

Above: *Pinch out the tops of the plants when the first pods have begun to form. This aids pod formation and discourages blackfly.*

Above: *Taller varieties require support. Place canes at regular intervals on each side of the crop, tying string between each pole.*

MARROWS AND SQUASH CROPS

PUMPKINS

Cucurbita maxima

Pumpkins are popular with children because they look so impressive and can be carved out and used as lanterns. The flesh is cooked and makes good soups and pies. They are found in colours such as blue and green as well as the popular yellow-orange. Smaller varieties of pumpkin can be grown which are bred for flavour rather than size.

SOIL
Deep fertile soil that is rich in humus. Before planting dig out a planting pit 45cm (18in) deep and 60cm (24in) square. Fill half the dug-out pit with well-rotted manure or garden compost and fill back in again.

ASPECT
Plant or sow in a sunny position and protect from strong winds.

SOWING
Sowing can begin under glass in late spring at a temperature of 15–18°C (59–64°F). Soak the seeds overnight to speed up germination. Sow the seeds individually in pots. Plant out in early summer in the prepared planting pits after all threat of frost has passed. Plant at distances of 1.8m (6ft) apart. Alternatively, sow directly outside into prepared planting pits 1.8m (6ft) apart in early summer. Keep a distance of 1.8m (6ft) between the rows.

AFTERCARE
To keep the vigorous growth in check train the stems around the plant, pinning them to the ground with wire pegs. For larger

Above: *Pumpkins take up a lot a space, so careful thought is needed when siting them within the confines of a small garden.*

pumpkins, choose one to three good fruits when they are small and remove the rest. Watering needs to take place throughout the growing season. It is advantageous to feed every two weeks during this period. Pinch out the tips of trailing varieties towards the end of the summer. Stop watering and feeding once the fruits are mature.

HARVESTING AND STORAGE
It is best for the fruits to mature on the plant. Harvest the entire crop before the first frosts, leaving a stem on the fruit of about 5cm (2in) in length. Leave them in a sunny location for about a week for the skins to harden. Pumpkins store well. The popular orange-skinned varieties will store for several weeks whereas the blue-skinned type will last for up to three months.

PESTS AND DISEASES
Slugs are a problem, especially when the fruits start to grow. Mice can also cause damage. Destroy the plant if it contracts cucumber mosaic virus.

Left: *Harvest pumpkins when they have reached their mature colour. A good indicator is when the stems begin to split.*

CULTIVATION
Sowing time Early spring (under glass); early summer (outdoors)
Planting time Early summer
Sowing and planting distance 1.8m (6ft)
Sowing depth 4cm (1½in)
Distance between rows 1.8m (6ft)
Harvesting Autumn

Above: *Although pumpkins take time and patience to grow, they are ideal plants with which to encourage young gardeners.*

VARIETIES
'Atlantic Giant' Largest pumpkin of all. Stores very well.
'Jack be Little' Produces small fruits that are only 8cm (3in) across. The orange fruits have an excellent taste when stuffed or baked.
'Tom Fox' Medium-sized orange fruits that are great for making pumpkin pie.

pumpkins

SQUASHES

Cucurbita maxima

Squashes are very closely related to marrows (zucchini) and pumpkins and there is very little difference in their cultivation requirements and culinary preparation. Squashes come in a diverse range of shapes and sizes. The outside flesh colour is also very varied, ranging from almost white to deep orange. They look delightful when used in the ornamental garden, climbing over trellis walkways and arches.

Squashes can be divided into two main groups: summer and winter types. The difference between the two groups lies in their storage qualities. Summer types will keep for two to three weeks, but are best used fresh from the plant, whereas winter types can still be used fresh but will also keep for long periods in storage.

SOIL

Squashes prefer a soil that is rich in organic matter. Dig over the soil in the autumn, incorporating copious amounts of well-rotted manure or garden compost. This not only enriches the soil with nutrients, but also helps to retain moisture in the soil, which is essential for healthy growth. Mulching with garden compost or straw will also help to prevent water evaporating from the soil.

ASPECT

Squashes thrive in an open sunny site that is protected from strong winds. These conditions are vital for successful growth because they are neither hardy nor robust.

Above: *Squashes undoubtedly have a culinary value, but they are often grown simply for their attractive looks. They look extremely ornamental if they are grown over archways or trellis.*

Left: *If you are growing squashes in a restricted space, cut off the trailing stems two leaves above a fruit.*

SOWING

Squashes can be started off by sowing individually in pots under glass in early spring. Sow individually in modules or fibre pots because they do not like their roots to be disturbed. Ideally, the temperature needs to be a constant of 18°C (64°F). Harden off and plant outside in early summer, after the risk of frost has passed. They need a lot of room to grow, so leave 1.8m (6ft) between the plants. If you do not have access to a greenhouse, sow directly outside in rows during early summer at a depth of 4cm (1½in). Keep 1.8m (6ft) between each seed and 1.8m (6ft) between rows. It is common to sow two seeds next to each other, removing the weaker seedling after germination. This ensures a plant at each station.

Above: *Squash fruits will quickly rot if left to mature on the bare soil. Support the fruits with straw to prevent damage.*

AFTERCARE

As the plants grow, train the trailing stems around the plant in a spiral to save space. When training the plants, pin the stems down with wire pegs. Alternatively, the size of the plants can be reduced by cutting off the trailing stems, two leaves above a fruit.

There are numerous varieties of climbing squash available. These can be extremely ornamental, especially when the growth is trained up ornate wire or wooden trellis supports. Keep the crop well watered throughout the growing season and give a high-potash feed every two weeks.

HARVESTING AND STORAGE

Harvest the summer squashes when the skin is tender and they are big enough to eat. Cut off the fruits, leaving 5cm (2in) of stem. Cut winter squashes in the same way

if they are to be used fresh, otherwise leave them on the plant and harvest them just before the first frosts. Leave them in a sunny position for one week to harden the skins before storing.

Summer squashes have a relatively short storage life of up to two to three weeks. They are best used fresh from the plant. Winter squashes will keep up to two months if they are kept in a frost-free area. Store the squashes individually by hanging them in nets or boxing them and surrounding them with straw.

PESTS AND DISEASES

Slugs can cause serious damage to crops because they can eat completely through a stem if they are left unchecked. Cucumber mosaic virus is the most serious of the diseases to which squashes are susceptible. The leaves become mottled

CULTIVATION
Sowing time Early spring (under glass); early summer (outdoors)
Planting out time Early summer
Sowing distance 1.8m (6ft)
Sowing depth 4cm (1½in)
Distance between rows 1.8m (6ft)
Harvesting Late summer to early autumn

and the fruit is distorted. Destroy any infected plants. Powdery mildew can cause problems in dry years. This can largely be ignored because the problem is normally not too serious. Keep the soil moist and plant at the correct distances to prevent overcrowding and allow for the free movement of air between the plants. This will help to prevent infections.

Left: *Squashes, like pumpkins, are ready to harvest when the stems begin to split. Cut them off with a small stem attached.*

VARIETIES

SUMMER

'Custard Squash' White- and yellow-skinned varieties are available.
'Table Ace' A small, acorn-shaped fruit with dark green skin and orange flesh.
'Tender and True' Ball-shaped fruits with mottled green skin. Bush variety.
'Vegetable Spaghetti' An unusual squash. When cooked, the spaghetti-like strands can be scooped out.

WINTER

'Pompeon' Shiny dark green flat globe-shaped fruit. Golden flesh. Semi-bush habit.

'Turks Turban' A good ornamental variety that is also delicious to eat. A trailing variety.
'Vegetable Spaghetti' Fruits are cylindrical in shape. The flesh when boiled breaks up into strands similar to spaghetti. A trailing variety.

squashes

MARROWS AND COURGETTES (ZUCCHINI)

Cucurbita pepo

Marrows and courgettes are mainly grown for their delightful juicy fruits, although the young leaves, male flowers and small fruits are delicious to eat in summer salads.

SOIL

Marrows and courgettes thrive in soil that is rich in organic matter. To ensure optimum growth, dig in plenty of well-rotted manure or garden compost in the autumn. They grow extremely well on compost heaps.

ASPECT

An open sunny position. They are frost tender, so do not plant out until early summer after the risk of frost has subsided.

SOWING/PLANTING

You can start the crop off in late spring under glass by sowing individually into 9cm (3in) pots. Soak the seeds in water

Below: *The male flowers of marrows and courgettes (zucchini) can be eaten raw in salads or cooked.*

overnight because this will speed up the germination process. Grow on the seedlings and harden them off before planting out in early summer. Alternatively, you can sow direct outside in early summer to a depth of 4cm (1½in). Sow two seeds at one time and then remove the weaker one after germination. Covering with cloches will enhance the germination of the seedlings. Within the rows keep a distance of 90cm (3ft) between each plant for bush varieties and 1.2–1.8m (4–6ft) for trailing varieties. Leave the same distances between each of the rows.

AFTERCARE

Water marrows and courgettes regularly throughout the growing season. Trailing varieties will need to be trimmed in order to prevent them from taking over your vegetable plot.

CULTIVATION

Sowing time Late spring (under glass); early summer (outdoors)
Planting out time Early summer
Sowing/planting distance 90cm/3ft (bush varieties); 1.2–1.8m/4–6ft (trailing varieties)
Sowing depth 4cm (1½in)
Distance between rows 90cm/3ft (bush varieties); 1.2–1.8m/4–6ft (trailing varieties)
Harvesting Mid-summer onwards

Left: *When harvesting, use a sharp knife and cut through the stem 2.5cm (1in) away from the fruit.*

HARVESTING AND STORAGE

Courgettes taste delicious when they are young. Harvest them when they are approximately 10cm (4in) long. If left to grow much larger they are classed as a small marrow or they can be left to mature into a fully grown marrow. Harvesting can take place until the first frosts. Courgettes do not store well and are best picked and used fresh. They can be frozen but will lose their firmness. Marrows store well, especially if they are left to mature on the plant. Store in a frost-free place in trays or hanging up in nets.

PESTS AND DISEASES

Cucumber mosaic virus is the most common problem. Destroy affected plants. Slugs love the vegetation. Pick them off by hand or encourage natural predators such as frogs and beetles.

VARIETIES

'All Green Bush' A heavy-yielding variety with mid-green courgettes.
'Jemma F1' An attractive variety with bright yellow courgettes. Has a slightly different flavour to normal green varieties.
'Kojac' Hairless and spineless for easy picking. A high-yielding variety.
'Nero Milan' This has dark-green fruits that are easily picked due to its open habit. A good variety for freezing.

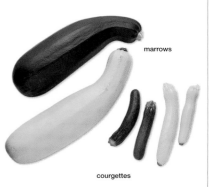

marrows

courgettes

CUCUMBERS

Cucumis sativus

There are two main types of cucumber: greenhouse varieties and outdoor or ridge varieties. Plants for growing under glass are tall climbing ones that bear long, tasty, slender fruits. Outdoor varieties are bushier in habit and produce shorter fruits. Those grown in the open are less prone to pest and disease attacks than when grown under glass. Many of the old outdoor varieties taste inferior compared with the greenhouse types. Choose a new outdoor variety as the taste has improved due to recent breeding.

SOIL

Grow outdoors in a well-drained soil that has been manured the previous autumn. Indoor varieties can be grown in large grow bags, large pots, soil borders or straw bales.

ASPECT

Outdoor cucumbers are a tender crop, so grow in a sheltered sunny location that is protected from strong winds.

SOWING

Start off indoor varieties under glass from late winter onwards at a temperature of 24°C (75°F). Sow individually in pots. Sow two seeds per pot and then remove the weaker seedling. Cucumbers do not like root disturbance, so plant into their final positions with care.

Sow outdoor (ridge) varieties under glass in late spring or directly outside in early summer. If sown outside, cover with a cloche or bell jar to raise the temperature until after germination. Sow or plant outside, leaving 75cm (30in) between the plants, with the same distance between the rows.

Left: *Ridge cucumbers are ideally suited for growing outdoors and can be grown as easily as courgettes (zucchini).*

Above: *As the name suggests, greenhouse varieties need to be grown under glass.*

AFTERCARE

Indoor varieties will need supporting with poles and horizontal wires, tying in the climbing stems as they grow. Pinch out the tips when they reach the top of the supports. Tie in the side stems (laterals) along the horizontal wires. Pinch these out two leaves after the development of the first fruit. Greenhouse varieties taste bitter if fertilized, so remove any male flowers. Give a high potash liquid feed when the fruits start to develop. Keep well watered, taking care to water the soil around the plant, but not the plant itself. Misting the plants and watering the paths will help keep the humidity up. Shade the greenhouse with paint or netting to avoid strong sunlight.

Outdoor (ridge) varieties that are grown on the ground will need to be mulched with straw to keep the fruit clean and to stop them rotting. This also raises the soil temperature, helps retain moisture and suppresses weed growth. Pinch out the tips from the main shoots at 6–7 leaves. Mist plants in dry periods to increase humidity and keep well watered. Outdoor varieties need to be pollinated, so it is essential to leave the male flowers on the plant. Give a high potash feed every two weeks when the fruits start to develop.

HARVESTING AND STORAGE

Cut the cucumbers with a knife from the plant before they reach maximum size as

this encourages new fruits. Keep harvesting the crop until the first frosts. Cucumbers will keep in the refrigerator for about one week, but otherwise they do not store well.

PESTS AND DISEASES

Slugs and snails are a problem. Red spider mite and whitefly attack greenhouse varieties.

CULTIVATION

Sowing time Late winter onwards (under glass); early summer (outdoors)
Planting out time Early summer
Sowing/planting distance 60cm/24in (under glass); 75cm/30in (outdoors)
Sowing depth 2.5cm (1in)
Distance between rows 75cm (30in)
Harvesting Mid-summer onwards

VARIETIES

GREENHOUSE
'Conqueror' An extremely old variety that tolerates lower temperatures than normal. Good-sized fruits.
'F1 Cumlaude RZ' A vigorous variety that produces heavy yields. Can be grown in an unheated greenhouse. An all-female variety.
'F1 Deltastar RZ' Delicious fruits that keep well. An all-female variety.

OUTDOOR (RIDGE)
'Bush Champion F1' Good compact variety. Fruits reach up to 25cm (10in). Resistant to cucumber mosaic virus.
'Marketmore' A high-yielding variety. Resistance is shown to cucumber mosaic virus.
'Stimora MIX F1' Can be used for gherkin pickling if harvested at 5cm (2in) or for slicing grown at 10cm (4in).

ridge cucumber

greenhouse cucumber

SHOOT CROPS

CELERY

Apium graveolens

Growing celery using the traditional trench method can be labour-intensive. The young seedlings are planted out in trenches and earthed up, a process that is called blanching. Earthing up makes the harvested stems white, less stringy and longer. The alternative is to grow self-blanching varieties which are planted closely together to carry out the blanching process. Self-blanching types are not as crisp and tasty as the trench type.

SOIL

There are two methods of soil preparation: the trench method and that for self-blanching varieties. For trench celery, dig out a trench that is 38cm (15in) wide and 30cm (12in) deep. Put an 8cm (3in) layer of rotted manure at the bottom of this and back fill with soil. This should be done in autumn or winter and allowed to settle before planting. Self-blanching celery is planted out in blocks and not rows. Dig over the soil in the autumn incorporating copious amounts of well-rotted manure or garden compost.

ASPECT

All celery varieties require a sunny site.

SOWING

Trench varieties are best started off under glass in module trays in early spring at a

Left: *This form of celery, known as green or American celery, is popular because it does not require blanching.*

Above: *When the stems are 30cm (12in) high a cardboard collar is fitted around the plant to blanch the stems.*

temperature of around 15°C (59°F). Harden off by placing them in cold frames two weeks before planting out in early summer. Plant out in trenched rows 30cm (12in) apart with 60cm (24in) between the rows. Self-blanching celery is started off under glass in the same way. Harden off the plants before planting out in blocks in early summer. Block planting at intervals of 23cm (9in) helps the process of self-blanching.

AFTERCARE

Water thoroughly in dry periods and feed with a liquid feed every two weeks. When trench celery varieties reach 30cm (12in), earth up over part of the stems. Repeat this process at three-week intervals until the soil is up to the lower leaves. An alternative to earthing up is to wrap cardboard around the celery stems when they are 30cm (12in) tall and again three weeks later. For self-blanching celery, place straw around the outside of the block to keep out the light. Green celery varieties do not need straw around the perimeter.

HARVESTING AND STORAGE

Trench celery is ready for harvesting from autumn onwards. Harvest as needed, but remember that the flavour is enhanced by the first frosts. Cover plants in the winter with straw if severe weather is expected. Lift self-blanching celery from autumn by the first frosts. Leave trench varieties in the

ground until required, but, in cold regions, lift and store in a frost-free area where the crop will last for weeks. Celery can be frozen, but may turn soft after defrosting, so use only in cooked dishes.

PESTS AND DISEASES

Slugs, snails, celery fly and carrot fly can all be a problem, as can diseases such as celery heart rot and celery leaf spot. Destroy affected plants. Irregular watering and feeding can make the celery stalks split.

CULTIVATION

TRENCH
Sowing time Early to mid-spring (under glass)
Planting out time Early summer
Planting distance 30cm (12in)
Distance between rows 60cm (24in)
Harvesting Autumn
SELF-BLANCHING
Sowing time Early to mid-spring
Planting out time Early summer
Planting distance in blocks 23cm (9in)
Harvesting Autumn

VARIETIES

TRENCH
'Giant White' Has a good flavour but requires good soil conditions. Stalks are white and tall.
'Solid Pink' An extremely old variety that will stand a number of frosts. Harvest in late autumn to early winter.

SELF-BLANCHING   celery
'Golden Self-Blanching' Yellow dwarf variety with cream stalks which requires little or no earthing up.
'Tall Utah' Long green stalks that need no earthing up. Harvest in early autumn. Inner stalks self-blanch.

CELERIAC

Apium graveolens var. *rapaceum*

This is a delicious winter vegetable that can be cooked or grated into salads. The part of the vegetable that is eaten looks like a root, but it is, in fact, a swollen stem. It tastes similar to celery but is easier to grow. This vegetable needs a long time to mature, so start it off under glass to allow the maximum growing season available.

SOIL
Celeriac thrives in a fertile soil that retains moisture throughout dry periods. To ensure this incorporate plenty of well-rotted manure or garden compost when digging over the soil in the autumn.

ASPECT
An open sunny location but will tolerate a little shade.

SOWING/PLANTING
Start off under glass in late winter to early spring. Sow in modules or individually in pots and keep them at a temperature of 15° C (59°F). Grow on in this environment until late spring when the young plants need to be moved to a cold frame or cold greenhouse to harden off for 10–14 days before planting out. Plant out 30cm (12in) apart in rows in early summer. Keep 30cm (12in) between each row.

AFTERCARE
Keep well watered throughout dry periods. Mulching with garden compost in early

Above: *Earth up the swollen stems in early autumn so that they will remain white before harvesting starts in mid-autumn.*

Left: *Celeriac is not a true root vegetable. It is, in fact, a swollen stem that forms a hard, round, knobbly base.*

Left: *Remove any side shoots that may appear and in mid-summer remove the lower leaves to expose the crown.*

summer will help conserve moisture and suppress weed growth. Remove the side shoots and from mid-summer remove all the lower leaves to expose the crown. Earth up around the stems in early autumn to ensure the swollen stems stay white. Cover the stems with straw in cold areas.

HARVESTING AND STORAGE
Harvesting can begin from mid-autumn onwards. Lift the crop only when it has reached its maximum size. Harvesting can take place right through until early spring. In most cases celeriac can be left in the ground until it is harvested. If the winter weather is too severe, lift the stems, clean them and place in trays with moist sand and store in a frost-free area.

PESTS AND DISEASES
Slugs are more likely to attack young plants than older plants. Celery fly and carrot fly can cause the occasional problem.

CULTIVATION
Sowing time Late winter to spring (under glass)
Planting out time Early summer
Sowing distance 30cm (12in)
Distance between rows 30cm (12in)
Harvesting Mid-autumn onwards

VARIETIES
'Marble Ball' A popular variety with medium-sized globular stems. The swollen stems have a strong flavour. Stores well.
'President RZ' Roots have crisp white flesh. Resistant to hollowness and tolerant of septoria.
'Snow White' A good-flavoured variety with a slightly nutty taste. Produces large white swollen stems.

celeriac

ASPARAGUS

Asparagus officinalis

This perennial crop is a good long-term investment for the garden. After nursing the crop over the first two years in which no harvesting takes place, the crop will last for 20 years. The delicious tender young shoots (spears) are available from mid-spring to early summer. Asparagus is best picked and eaten fresh. The summer foliage is much prized by florists.

Left: *After harvesting the young asparagus shoots, the crop is left to grow to its full height, thus strengthening itself for producing next year's shoots.*

SOIL

Asparagus thrives in well-drained soil. Before planting or sowing, dig the soil in the autumn and incorporate plenty of well-rotted manure or garden compost. Lime the soil if the pH is acidic.

ASPECT

A well-sheltered, sunny spot to ensure optimum growth.

SOWING/PLANTING

Sowing

Soak the seed overnight before sowing to speed up the germination time. In spring, sow in rows 1cm (½in) deep keeping 30cm (12in) between the rows. Thin to 15cm (6in) between the plants and leave to grow on for one year. Lift the crowns in the following spring and transplant to a permanent site.

Planting

Asparagus plants are sold as crowns during the dormant season and are best planted out in early spring. To plant the crowns, dig out a trench 20cm (8in) deep with a ridge of 8cm (3in) running down the middle. Set out the asparagus in the centre of the ridge, placing the crowns 45cm (18in) apart.

Above: *Harvest the crop when the shoots have reached 15cm (6in). Cut the stems 5cm (2in) below the level of the ground.*

Cover the trenches over with soil to a depth of 8–10cm (3–4in). If more than one row is required, leave a space of 90cm (3ft) apart.

AFTERCARE

Keep the beds clean of weeds throughout the year, but do not use a hoe as this can damage the roots and newly emerging spears. An application of mulch can be given to keep the weeds down and retain soil moisture.

Once the foliage has turned yellow in the autumn, cut back to 5cm (2in) above the soil surface. Draw up a small ridge of soil over the plants before the new shoots emerge in the spring.

HARVESTING AND STORAGE

Newly planted crops will produce their first spears during the growing season, but do not cut any of them. Follow the same practice the second year. Harvesting is carried out in the third growing season in mid-spring to early summer when they have reached a height of 15cm (6in). Cut the spears 5cm (2in) below ground level. Stop cutting in early summer and let the remaining spears develop into foliage. This allows the food reserves to be built up for the following year. Asparagus does not store well and is best eaten fresh.

PESTS AND DISEASES

Asparagus beetle can attack the stems and foliage. This pest likes to overwinter in the foliage. Cutting stems back in autumn can help. New succulent spears are prone to damage by slugs. Violet root rot can cause severe problems. The roots are covered in purple mould and the leaves prematurely turn yellow. In bad cases, destroy plants and make a bed in a new site.

CULTIVATION

Sowing
Sowing time Spring
Sowing distance Thinly
Sowing depth 1cm (½in)
Distance between rows 30cm (12in)
Thinning distance 15cm (6in)
Transplanting time Following spring, same distances as for planting
Planting
Planting time Early spring
Planting distance 45cm (18in)
Planting depth 8–10cm (3–4in)
Distance between rows 90cm (3ft)
Harvesting (from the third year) In late spring for six weeks

---

VARIETIES

'Cito' A heavy cropper that produces long spears.
'Connover's Colossal' An old variety. Has delicious flavoured spears.
'Franklim F1' Heavy yields of thick spears. A small crop may be harvested in the second year.

asparagus

GLOBE ARTICHOKES

Cynara cardunculus Scolymus Group

This perennial is unusual in that it is the flower that is eaten and not the leaves or the roots, as with most vegetables. After harvesting, the flower bud is boiled or steamed and the various parts are eaten. Globe artichokes do take up a lot of room, so you might consider adding this ornate crop to a herbaceous border if you do not have space in the vegetable garden.

SOIL
As this crop will be in the same location for several years, you should prepare the soil to a high standard before planting. Dig deeply in the autumn, incorporating plenty of well-rotted manure or garden compost. Globe artichokes do not grow well on heavy clay as good drainage is essential.

ASPECT
An open sunny site in a sheltered location.

PLANTING/SOWING
Plant offsets of globe artichokes in the spring at 75cm (30in) apart with 90cm (3ft) between the rows. Alternatively, sow seeds thinly in spring in rows 2.5cm (1in) deep with 30cm (12in) between the rows. Thin the seedlings to 15cm (6in) apart ready to transplant the following spring. Plant in the permanent site as above.

Below: *It is easy to see why the globe artichoke is used by garden designers who are looking for architectural form.*

AFTERCARE
Water copiously throughout the growing season and feed every two weeks. Stems can be cut down in autumn and soil drawn around the crown of the plant. Protect the crowns in cold areas by covering with straw or bracken. Lift, divide and replant the crop every 3–4 years. Cultivate and incorporate organic matter to the soil during this process.

CULTIVATION
Planting time Spring
Planting distance 75cm (30in)
Distance between rows 90cm (3ft)
Sowing time Spring
Sowing distance Thinly
Sowing depth 2.5cm (1in)
Distance between rows 30cm (12in)
Thinning distance 15cm (6in)
Transplanting time Following spring
Harvesting Summer of second year onwards

Left: *Harvest the flower heads of the globe artichokes just before they open and while they are still green.*

Left: *Cut the stems down in autumn and draw the soil around the crown of the plant. The stems can be put on the compost heap.*

HARVESTING AND STORAGE
Begin harvesting in the second year. Cut the flower heads off just before they open and while they are still green. Leave on a stem of 2.5cm (1in) below the head. The heads are best eaten when they are fresh.

PESTS AND DISEASES
Generally trouble free, although they can be affected by blackfly, which is treated by spraying with insecticidal soap.

VARIETIES
'Camus de Bretagne' Large heads with a good flavour. It can be relatively tender compared to other varieties.
'Green Globe' Produces lovely green flower buds. Very popular variety and widely available.
'Purple Globe' Hardier than its green relative but the flavour is inferior.

globe artichokes

SEAKALE

Crambe maritima

This vegetable can be found growing wild along the British coast. It is a favourite among ornamental gardeners who appreciate its architectural structure. Seakale leaves have to be blanched to make them palatable. The blanched stems are harvested from mid- to late summer. A bed of seakale will crop well for around seven years before you need to discard it and start again.

SOIL

Thrives in soils that are fertile and free draining, especially sandy or gravelly soil. This crop can grow on heavy soils if grit or gravel is incorporated before planting or if it is grown on raised beds. Dig in plenty of well-rotted manure or garden compost in the autumn.

ASPECT

Requires an open sunny site.

SOWING/PLANTING/THONGS

Sowing Seakale can be started off by sowing seed in spring, soaking the seed overnight in order to speed up the germination process. Sow thinly outside in rows, 4cm (1½in) deep with 30cm (12in) between the rows. After germination thin the seedlings to 23cm (9in). Let the seedlings grow on and transplant them to their final destination in the following spring.
Planting Plant out seakale in spring, leaving 45cm (18in) between the plants and the same distance between the rows.

Above: *Seakale is a favourite with gardeners who let it grow naturally and admire its architectural structure.*

Thongs (root cuttings) Take thongs from existing plants in autumn. The cuttings need to be 1cm (½in) thick and 15cm (6in) in length. Tie these in a bundle and insert the roots vertically into well-drained soil. Make sure that the top of the root is uppermost. It needs to be 5cm (2in) below the soil surface. Alternatively, the cuttings can be placed in large pots of well-drained potting mix. By the following spring they will have sprouted. Plant out the rooted cuttings to the same specifications as for planting.

AFTERCARE

The stems of seakale are blanched by covering the plants in late winter or early spring with long pots especially made for the job. No light must reach underneath the pots or the stems will turn green and taste bitter.

HARVESTING AND STORAGE

Plants and thongs are harvested in their second year, plants grown from seed one year later. Harvest when the stems are long enough. Remove the cover when all the shoots have been removed. Plants are normally kept for seven years.

Left: *Seakale can be blanched. This plant has been blanched, but has again been exposed to light.*

CULTIVATION
SOWING
Sowing time Spring
Sowing distance Thinly
Sowing depth 4cm (1½in)
Distance between rows 30cm (12in)
Thinning distance 23cm (9in)
Transplanting time The following spring
Harvesting Summer of second year onwards
PLANTING
Planting time Spring
Planting distance 45cm (18in)
Distance between rows 45cm (18in)
Harvesting Summer of second year onwards
THONGS
Cutting strucks Autumn
Transplanting time Late spring
Planting distance 45cm (18in)
Distance between rows 45cm (18in)
Harvesting Second summer onwards

Alternatively, discard the plants after harvesting, taking root cuttings for the next crop. Seakale does not store well and is best eaten fresh from the plant.

PESTS AND DISEASES

The caterpillars of the cabbage white butterfly can feast on the foliage of seakale. Pick them off by hand if possible. Slugs can also be a nuisance.

VARIETIES
Normally sold under the name of seakale.

seakale

FLORENCE FENNEL

Foeniculum vulgare var. *dulce*

This wonderfully decorative plant is grown for its white bulbous base that tastes of aniseed. It can be eaten raw in salads or braised as a vegetable. Its finely cut bright green foliage is attractive enough to grow as an unusual ornamental plant for the decorative garden. The leaves can also be used as a herb for flavouring dishes.

SOIL

Florence fennel thrives in light well-drained soils. If your soil is too heavy, incorporate grit or gravel before planting or build a raised bed. When digging in the autumn incorporate plenty of well-rotted manure or garden compost. This will increase water retention in the soil.

ASPECT

Requires an open sunny site with shelter from the wind.

SOWING

The best time of year to sow is early to mid-summer as crops sown earlier are likely to bolt. Sow thinly in rows 1cm (½in) deep with 45cm (18in) between the rows. After germination thin the seedlings to 23cm (9in) apart. Alternatively, the seeds can be started off under glass, but, as they do not like transplanting, it is best to sow in situ.

AFTERCARE

Water copiously, especially during dry spells. Earth up the soil around the bulbs, as they begin to swell, to around half of their height. Continue to draw up soil as the bulbs expand. This will blanch the bulbs resulting in a sweeter flavour.

HARVESTING AND STORAGE

Two to three weeks after earthing up check the bulbs. If they have reached the size of a tennis ball they are ready for harvesting. Pull the whole plant up or cut underneath the bulb and leave the root in the soil. This will re-sprout and offer new foliage, which can be used in flower arranging. Fennel does not store well and is best eaten fresh. It will keep for a few days in the refrigerator.

PESTS AND DISEASES

Bolting is the main problem. Do not sow too early or use resistant cultivars such as 'Argo RZ'. Other than that, generally trouble free.

Above: *When the bulbs begin to swell, draw up the soil around them. This will blanch the bulbs and make them taste sweeter.*

Florence fennel

Above: *The secret of growing successfully is to keep the soil moist and weed-free, thus ensuring fast healthy growth.*

Above: *Florence fennel is often planted in flower borders to display its decorative, finely cut foliage.*

RHUBARB

Rheum x hybridum

Although rhubarb is classed as a vegetable, it is mainly used as a fruit. The leaves are extremely poisonous and no part of them should be eaten. Rhubarb looks superb in an ornamental border, being easy to mix in with other perennials and shrubs in the garden.

SOIL

Rhubarb grows well in soil that is rich in organic matter. Before planting incorporate plenty of well-rotted manure or garden compost into the soil when preparing the site. Remove any perennial weeds as they are difficult to eradicate after the crop has been planted.

ASPECT

A sunny location, away from shade.

SOWING/PLANTING

Sowing Rhubarb can be grown from seed, but the uniformity and quality of the plants cannot be guaranteed. Sow the seeds thinly in rows 2.5cm (1in) deep with 30cm (12in) between the rows. After germination thin out the seedlings to 23cm (9in). The crop is ready to transplant to its final destination during the following winter. Plant to the same specifications as described for planting below.

Above: *A bed of healthy rhubarb is an impressive sight. Rhubarb leaves are poisonous and cannot be eaten.*

Above: *Forcing should only be carried out every other year to prevent weakening the plants. This is a wicker rhubarb forcer.*

Above: *Harvest rhubarb sticks by pulling so that they come out of their "socket". Cut off the leaves and put on the compost heap.*

Planting Rhubarb plants can be bought in pots at any good garden centre or nursery. Alternatively, offsets can be divided off established plants during the dormant season. Plant the rhubarb plants that have been bought in pots throughout the spring. Offsets, on the other hand, are planted straight after being split in the winter. Space all the plants 90cm (3ft) apart.

AFTERCARE

Water well during dry periods. Mulch with well-rotted manure or garden compost in the spring and autumn to help retain moisture and suppress weed growth. Plants can be forced into producing shoots early if covered with a bucket or plastic bin in mid-winter. This crop will be ready to pick after six weeks. Do not force the same plants two years running or they will be weakened.

HARVESTING AND STORAGE

The red stems can be harvested from spring to early summer. Pull each stem from the base and it will come away with part of the base. Cut off the leaves and put on to the compost heap. Never strip a plant of all

CULTIVATION
SOWING
Sowing time Spring
Sowing distance Thinly
Sowing depth 2.5cm (1in)
Distance between rows 30cm (12in)
Thinning distance 23cm (9in)
Transplanting time Following winter, plant as below
PLANTING
Planting time Winter (offsets); spring (pots)
Planting distance 90cm (3ft)
Distance between rows 90cm (3ft)
Harvesting From the second year onwards

its stems; it is best to leave at least four stems per plant. This enables the plants to recover and produce new growth, allowing the plant to be harvested the following year. Rhubarb will freeze for up to one year.

PESTS AND DISEASES

Sometimes prone to white blister. Cut off and destroy diseased foliage. Otherwise generally trouble free.

VARIETIES
'Champagne Early' Beautiful red stems that are among the first to be harvested.
'Glaskin's Perpetual' Extremely quick growing and lasts for many years. Produces lovely red stems that can be cut in the first year.
'Victoria' A popular variety with thick stems that are ready in late spring.

rhubarb

FRUITING VEGETABLES

PEPPERS

Capsicum species

Sweet or bell peppers (*Capsicum annuum* Grossum Group) are commonly used in salads and in many cooked dishes. Sweet peppers do not taste hot like their close relatives, cayenne or tabasco peppers (*Capsicum frutescens*) and chilli peppers (*Capsicum annuum* Longum Group). The plants bear fruits that are green when unripe, turning yellow, red and orange. Cayenne or tabasco peppers are exceptionally hot peppers that need to be used with care.

Chilli peppers are a little less hot than cayenne or tabasco peppers, but are still quite fiery (the seeds, which are the hottest part of the fruit, may be removed).

SOIL
Outdoor crops thrive in a well-drained, fertile soil. Greenhouse types need to be planted up in grow bags or large pots in peat-free potting mix.

ASPECT
Peppers require a sunny sheltered spot, otherwise they do well in a greenhouse, conservatory or on a vacant windowsill.

SOWING/PLANTING
Sow seeds in trays, modules or individual pots under glass in spring, at a temperature

of 18–21°C (65–70°F). If grown in trays, prick out the seedlings into small pots as soon as the seed leaves are large enough to handle.

Peppers have short root systems, so it is essential to pot up the plants gradually until they reach their final pot size of around 23cm (9in). Alternatively, pot up the young pepper plants until they are large enough to plant into grow bags or soil beds in mid- to late spring.

Plant outdoor peppers outside after hardening off in early summer. Plant in rows 50cm (20in) apart with the same distance between the rows. Peppers can be grown in a vegetable patch, in an ornamental border or in pots on the patio.

AFTERCARE
Keep the crop well watered, feeding once a week with a liquid organic fertilizer high in

Left: Not all peppers are the evenly shaped fruits to which we are accustomed in supermarkets. These red peppers have reached the final stage of ripening.

potash. Stake and tie the plants as they grow. Good ventilation in the greenhouse is recommended in hot weather.

HARVESTING AND STORAGE
Start to harvest sweet peppers from mid- to late summer. Pick the fruits when they are green, yellow, red, orange or purple. They are best eaten fresh although they will keep for up to two weeks in a refrigerator. Harvest hot or cayenne peppers when they are fully ripe and coloured. Use fresh or store in airtight jars after drying.

PESTS AND DISEASES
Grown under glass they suffer problems such as aphids, red spider mite and whitefly. Damp down the floor and mist the plants to increase humidity and deter red spider mite. Outdoors they may be attacked by aphids.

Above: Chilli peppers, like sweet peppers, are green when they are unripe, turning yellow and then red when they are ripe.

VARIETIES
SWEET PEPPERS
'F1 Mandy RZ' Produces large sweet tasting green fruits that turn red when mature. Resistant to mosaic virus.
'Red Skin' An F1 hybrid that produces uniform compact plants suitable for container growing. It has early maturing fruits.

CAYENNE AND CHILLI PEPPERS (HOT PEPPERS)
'Cayenne Large Red' Long, pointed, hot fruits that are produced in abundance.
'Habenero' An extremely hot chilli pepper. The green wrinkled fruits turn light orange when mature.

sweet peppers

chilli peppers

TOMATOES

Lycopersicon esculentum

Tomatoes are probably the most widely used vegetable for cooking. It is worth growing a few, either in the garden or in the conservatory (sun room) or greenhouse, so that you can experience the sweet juicy flavour offered by home-grown produce. Outdoor varieties look striking dotted among ornamental plants in borders or potagers. However, take care when siting tomato plants because they are closely related to the potato and suffer from several of the same pests and diseases. Include tomatoes on the same crop-rotation programme as potatoes or use grow bags to prevent the spread of soil-borne pests and diseases.

SOIL

Outdoor tomatoes like humus-rich soil. Dig over in winter, incorporating garden compost into the soil. Plant indoor varieties in grow bags or pots. If planted in a soil border in a greenhouse, change the soil every year to stop transference of diseases. Add garden compost to improve the soil structure.

ASPECT

Outdoor tomato varieties are tender, so choose a warm sheltered spot that receives plenty of sun.

SOWING/PLANTING

INDOORS These varieties can be started off under glass in temperatures of 18°C (65°F) in early to mid-spring. Sow seed in the same way as for outdoor varieties. Plant up into grow bags, pots or soil borders in mid- to late spring. Plants grown in borders need to be spaced 45cm (18in) apart.

OUTDOORS These varieties are best sown under glass in gentle heat or an unheated greenhouse in mid-spring. Sow thinly in seed trays if a large number of plants are required or sow individually in pots if only a few plants are needed. Seed sown in trays will need to be pricked out and transplanted into individual pots. Grow on and harden off, ready to plant outside in early summer. Plants need to be planted 45cm (18in) apart for cordon varieties and 60cm (24in) for bush varieties. Keep 75cm (30in) between the rows for both types. Alternatively, tomatoes can be planted into larger pots or grow bags before being placed outside. Harden off for 10 days before moving outside in early summer.

Above: *Tomatoes can be grown indoors or outside. Using grow bags in a greenhouse prevents the spread of soil-borne diseases.*

AFTERCARE

The tomato crop needs to be well watered. Feed every two weeks with a high-potash feed when the fruit begins to swell. If the crop is irregularly watered, causing wet and dry periods, this can cause blossom end rot. Support the crop using canes or suspended strings within the greenhouse and tie in the stems as they grow. Pinch out the top of the shoots when they reach the end of their supports. Side shoots need to be removed from cordon types.

Above: *Spiral supports are ideal for supporting cordon tomatoes because it saves you from having to tie them in.*

Left: *Plant outdoor tomato crops in a sunny sheltered spot. This will not only aid plant growth, but it is essential for fruit ripening.*

HARVESTING AND STORAGE

Harvest as they ripen and are fully coloured. A mature fruit is normally deep red in colour. Twist the fruit off the plant to avoid tearing the stem.

Tomatoes are best eaten straight from the plant. If you have a glut at the end of the season they can be frozen. Only use frozen fruits in cooked dishes as they will lose their firmness. At the end of the season there may be many green tomatoes left on the plants. Sever the plants at the base and hang upside down in a greenhouse or frost-free shed until the tomatoes ripen or put in trays into a drawer to ripen.

PESTS AND DISEASES

Tomatoes are prone to a number of pests and diseases. Aphids, potato cyst eelworm, whitefly and red spider mite are the main pests to which they are susceptible. Tomato blight, grey mould, potato mosaic virus, greenback, tomato leaf mould and scald are the diseases most likely to cause problems. Many of the problems listed here can be solved by undertaking good horticultural practices such as removing dead, decaying and diseased growth from the plants every day. Correct watering and good ventilation will also help to improve the health of the crop.

Above: *Do not throw away the remaining plants at the end of the season. Collect any that are left and hang them upside down under cover to ripen.*

Above: *Remove the side shoots from cordon tomatoes when they are small. Pinch or cut them out with a sharp knife.*

Above: *There is nothing better than to taste the warm sweet flavour of tomatoes harvested from home-grown plants.*

CULTIVATION

INDOOR VARIETIES
Sowing time Early to mid-spring
Planting time Mid- to late spring
Planting/sowing distance 45cm (18in)
Harvesting Summer onwards
OUTDOOR VARIETIES
Sowing time Mid-spring
(under glass)
Planting out time Early summer
Planting distance 45cm/18in (cordon);
60cm/24in (bush)
Distance between rows 75cm (30in)
Harvesting Late summer onwards

VARIETIES

GREENHOUSE
'Big Boy F1' Tall plant with large fruits that are good for stuffing and slicing. Nice bright red fruits.
'F1 Aromata RZ' Extremely productive variety with fruits averaging 100g (4oz). Resistance shown to tomato mosaic virus.
'Shirley F1' Popular variety that produces heavy yields. Resistant to fusarium, cladosporium and tomato mosaic virus.
'Super Sweet 100 F1' A tall and strong-growing variety, bearing many small red fruits which are rich in vitamin C.

OUTDOOR
'Gardeners Delight' Produces small cherry red tomatoes that have a superb sweet flavour. Can be grown under glass or outside.
'Red Alert' A high yielding outdoor variety with small delicious tasting fruits.
'Totem F1' Has a good compact habit. Ideal for pots and window boxes.
'Tumbler' A trailing variety that can be used in hanging baskets and containers. Has lovely, small, red fruits.

tomatoes "on the vine"

"beefsteak" tomatoes

standard-size tomatoes

cherry tomatoes

AUBERGINES (EGGPLANT)

Solanum melongena

Not so very long ago, aubergines were a rare sight on the shelves of our supermarkets and shops. Nowadays, they are more widely available and frequently grown by amateur gardeners in the garden or greenhouse. However, aubergines are tender and in temperate climates are best grown under glass rather than outside where they will struggle to thrive in anything but a hot sunny season. The large, conspicuous, shining fruits range in colour from purple through to white. They taste delicious when they are cooked, stuffed with meat, rice or vegetables, or when used to make ratatouille or moussaka.

SOIL

Grow under glass in grow bags or pots, using a peat-free potting mix. Plants grown outside require a fertile, well-drained soil and should have a general fertilizer applied before planting.

ASPECT

Aubergines thrive in a warm sunny spot that is sheltered from the wind. These conditions are ideally found in a greenhouse, cold frame or in barn cloches.

SOWING

Best conditions for growth are provided under glass. Soak the seeds overnight to

Above: *The aubergine is a tropical plant. The most commonly grown varieties produce magnificent purple fruits.*

improve the germination rate and then sow into individual pots in spring. Ideally the temperature within the greenhouse will be 21–25°C (70–77°F). Once the plants are large enough they can be planted into bigger pots or grow bags. Aubergines can be hardened off and planted outside if the temperature does not drop below 15°C (59°F). Plant to a distance of 50cm (20in) between plants in a row with the same distance between the rows.

AFTERCARE

Canes and string may be needed to support the plants once they have reached 45–60cm (18–24in). Pinch out the tips of the plants when they reach 38cm (15in) in height in order to encourage fruit formation. Water well throughout the growing season and feed once every two weeks with a high-potash liquid feed.

Left: *Aubergines can be planted up under glass in window boxes or tubs and then moved outside in early summer when the weather is warmer.*

CULTIVATION
Sowing time Spring (under glass)
Planting time Mid-spring (under glass); early summer (outside)
Planting distance 50cm (20in)
Distance between rows 50cm (20in)
Harvesting Mid-summer onwards

HARVESTING AND STORAGE

Cut each aubergine fruit from the plant when it is large enough – the flavour quickly deteriorates if they are allowed to become overripe. Harvest under glass from mid-summer and autumn for outside varieties. Aubergines are best used fresh from the garden although they can keep for up to two weeks once picked.

PESTS AND DISEASES

The usual greenhouse pests affect this crop if grown under glass. Aphids, red spider mite and whitefly are the main pests. Damping the floor down and misting the leaves will increase humidity, which will in turn discourage red spider mite.

VARIETIES
'Black Beauty F1' Produces dark violet coloured fruit that are oval to globe shaped. A very vigorous grower.
'Black Enorma' The largest fruit of all the varieties – up to 675g (1½lb).
'Easter Egg' A novelty fruit which is the colour and size of a large hen's egg. Taste is inferior to the traditional purple varieties.
'Long Purple' An old variety that has deep violet fruits that taste delicious. Not a heavy-yielding type.
'Money Maker' A popular new variety that produces good-sized purple fruits. Crops early.

aubergines (eggplant)

SWEETCORN (CORN)

Zea mays

This giant ornamental crop can reach a height of 1.5m (5ft) and needs a lot of room if it is to be grown in the vegetable garden. Sweetcorn is frost tender and is therefore best started off in the greenhouse and planted out in early summer in order to allow it the maximum growing season.

SOIL

Sweetcorn thrives on a free-draining soil that contains large amounts of organic matter. Dig the ground in the autumn and incorporate plenty of well-rotted manure or garden compost.

ASPECT

Requires a warm sunny location that is sheltered from strong winds.

SOWING

For an early crop, sow seeds under glass in mid-spring. For maximum germination the temperature should be around 13–15°C (55–59°F). Sow individually in pots, grow on and harden off before planting outside in early summer. Seed sown directly outside needs to be sown in late spring through to early summer after the danger of frost has passed. Crop protection is needed in the form of a cloche or cut-up plastic bottle.

> **CULTIVATION**
> **Sowing time** Mid-spring (under glass)
> **Planting out time** Early summer
> **Sowing time** Late spring to early summer (outside)
> **Sowing/planting distance** 30cm (12in)
> **Sowing depth** 2.5cm (1in)
> **Distance between rows** 30cm (12in)
> **Harvesting** Autumn

Sow in blocks, sowing two seeds 2.5cm (1in) deep every 30cm (12in) with 30cm (12in) between the rows. Remove the weaker seedlings after germination. Planting in blocks will ensure efficient wind pollination for the female flowers.

AFTERCARE

If cloche protection has been used to help get the crop off to a good start, remove the cloches when the leaves begin to touch the sides. Keep weeds down around the crop, but do not hoe as it is a shallow rooter. Water well throughout the growing season, especially during dry weather. Add liquid feed every two weeks when the cobs begin to swell.

HARVESTING AND STORAGE

The cobs are ready for harvesting when the tassels on the cobs turn brown. Test the cobs for ripeness. Pull back the sheath hiding the cobs, and squeeze one of the seeds. It is ripe if the liquid that oozes out is milky in colour. If the liquid is clear it is unripe. These are best eaten fresh because once they are cut the sugars change to starch. They will also keep well in the freezer.

PESTS AND DISEASES

Can be troubled by smut in hot dry weather. Large galls appear on the cobs which should be removed and destroyed. Destroy all plants after harvesting. Frit fly maggots can distort the growth of the crop at seedling stage.

Left: *The dying tassel of the female flower hangs from the developing cob. This indicates that it is ready for harvesting.*

Above: *To produce an early crop, start off the sweetcorn in a greenhouse and grow on before planting out in blocks.*

VARIETIES

'**Golden Sweet F1**' A sweet-tasting variety with bright yellow cobs. It has a high resistance to rust.
'**Kelvedon Glory F1**' An extremely heavy cropper with a good flavour.
'**Minisweet**' Produces mini cobs which are harvested at 10cm (4in) long.

mature sweetcorn

immature sweetcorn

DIRECTORY OF HERBS

Herbs have been an important part of human culture for thousands of years. Before the advent of modern medicine they were widely used as a cure for many ailments and some are still used for medicinal purposes to this day. However, the majority of people grow herbs for culinary purposes, either as a small collection of favourite herbs in pots or in a herb garden. Every garden has some space for herbs and many are highly decorative or have great value as companion plants. Whichever way you grow them, herbs are an invaluable addition to both the garden and kitchen.

CHIVES

Allium schoenoprasum

Chives are bulbous herbaceous perennials which can grow to a height of 70cm (28in) or more. Smooth, slim, hollow, green leaves are produced in thick tufts. Small white bulbs appear in clumps on the base of the plant below the surface of the soil. Rose-purple or mauve flowers are carried on leafless stalks, making this an attractive herb for the ornamental garden. Garlic chives (*A. tuberosum*) are slightly smaller, growing to 50cm (20in), and their main storage tissue is a rhizome rather than a bulb. The leaves are similar to chives but are flat instead of hollow and the flowers are white. They are one of the kitchen herbs that few gardeners would want to be without.

SOIL AND ASPECT

Chives need a well-drained, fertile soil with a pH of 6–7. They are equally at home in full sun or partial shade, although shade can produce stragglier plants and fewer flowers.

Nitrogen is important and a regular application of composted manure is also recommended.

PROPAGATION

Chives can be grown as an annual or a perennial. Space plants 10cm (4in) apart in rows 30cm (12in) apart. They grow better if cut down to 10cm (4in) in summer. Chives are readily propagated from seed which can be sown under glass in early spring and transplanted or sown directly outdoors. Germination takes 10–14 days. Several cuttings can be obtained each year but the number may be limited by rust disease as the season progresses.

HARVESTING AND STORAGE

The leaves are cut as needed. Although best used fresh, they can be frozen or dried. *A. tuberosum* is sometimes blanched to soften the leaves before eating.

CULINARY USES

The fresh and dried leaves can be used in a variety of dishes. The bulbs can be pickled and the flowers can be used fresh or dried.

CULTIVATION
Sowing time Early spring (under glass); spring (outside)
Planting out time Spring
Thinning and planting distance 10cm (4in)
Distance between rows 30cm (12in)
Harvesting Any time the plant is in growth
Storage Frozen or dried

Above: *The pretty flowers of chives make a tasty and colourful addition to summer salads as well as to the herb garden.*

DILL

Anethum graveolens

This annual, with its round, erect stem, grows 30–60cm (12–24in) tall and has finely divided, thread-like, blue-green leaves. The flowers are yellow and, although the fruit is commonly called a "seed", it is actually a dry half-fruit. This herb exists as two general types: the familiar garden dill (*A. graveolens*), which is known as American or European dill, and Indian or Japanese dill (*A. sowa*). European dill is the most common type and is grown in temperate and subtropical countries around the world. There are a number of different varieties of *A. graveolens*, each with their own fragrance or growth properties.

SOIL AND ASPECT

Dill is adaptable to many soils, but a slightly acidic soil (with a pH of 5.6–6.5) and good drainage is preferred. Germination can be poor in drought-prone, sandy soils or on clays where surface capping is a problem. Position dill in full sun.

Dill can be grown outdoors or in a greenhouse. It can be invasive if it is allowed to go to seed.

PROPAGATION

Sow seed in spring to early summer in shallow drills 3–5mm (⅛–¼in) deep. Germination takes approximately 7–14 days; successional sowing can provide a season-long supply. Thin to 23cm (9in).

HARVESTING AND STORAGE

Harvest the dill leaves or cut back the entire plant once it reaches approximately 30cm (12in) in height. Harvest the seed when it begins to turn brown.

CULINARY USES

Fresh dill leaves are used in a wide range of dishes such as soups and salads. The seed can be used in the preparation of pickles and condiments. The immature or mature seed-heads are also used whole in pickles.

Right: *The tall stems and graceful feathery leaves of dill make this herb a decorative addition to the kitchen garden.*

CULTIVATION
Sowing time Spring to early summer
Sowing depth 3–5mm (⅛–¼in)
Thinning and planting distance 23cm (9in)
Harvesting As required (leaves); when it begins to turn brown (seed)
Storage Dried (leaves and seed)

ANGELICA

Angelica archangelica

Angelica can be grown as an aromatic biennial or a short-lived perennial (for about four years). It grows to 1.5–2.4m (5–8ft) tall. It has upright, ridged, hollow stems and large bright green leaves. The small, white or greenish flowers are borne in summer.

SOIL AND ASPECT
Prefers moist, fertile soil in partial shade and will grow in a wide range of pH from 4.5–7.3.

PROPAGATION
Propagate by seed or root division. Seeds germinate in 21–28 days. The viability of seed decreases quickly so fresh seed is best. It can be sown directly outdoors in the summer or started indoors and planted out later. Space plants 30cm (12in) apart in a row with 60–90cm (24–36in) between rows. Angelica may live up three years before flowering.

> **CULTIVATION**
> **Sowing time** Late summer
> **Sowing depth** 1cm (½in)
> **Thinning and planting distance** 30cm (12in)
> **Distance between rows** 60–90cm (24–36in)
> **Harvesting** Until flowering (leaves); while young (stems); when ripe (seed); early autumn (roots)
> **Storage** Dried (leaves); crystallized (stems); dried (seed)

HARVESTING AND STORAGE
Pick angelica leaves before flowering takes place, and use fresh or dried. Cut the stems while young for crystallizing and storage. The seeds should be picked when ripe and dried. Harvest the roots in early autumn and dry them at 38–60°C (100–140°F).

CULINARY USES
Stems can be steamed and eaten like a vegetable or candied. Dried leaves can be made into a tea and fresh leaves added to salads, soups or stews.

Above: *Although less commonly used than it once was, angelica still makes a striking plant in the herb garden. It can also be a feature in the ornamental garden.*

CHERVIL

Anthriscus cerefolium

This tall, hardy biennial plant is often best grown as an annual. Chervil reaches a height of 30–60cm (12–24in). It has large white flower heads. The delicately cut leaves make it a valuable addition to the ornamental garden as well as the herb and kitchen garden. Although it is more often grown as an ornamental plant, many people use the seed to make herb teas and crystallize the young stems. The leaves can also be used to flavour fish dishes and fruit desserts.

SOIL AND ASPECT
Chervil should be grown in a well-drained, fertile soil with a good organic content and a pH of 6–7. The plants do best in full sun or partial shade. Growing chervil in an open, hot, sunny site may result in the plants going to seed quickly if not kept well watered.

PROPAGATION
Chervil seed should be sown in a sunny position in the spring and then again in

> **CULTIVATION**
> **Sowing time** Spring to early summer
> **Sowing depth** 1cm (½in)
> **Thinning and planting distance** 20cm (8in)
> **Harvesting** Late spring onwards
> **Storage** Dried

early summer. Sow the seed in drills 1cm (½in) deep. A successional sowing every three to four weeks will extend the life of this crop. The seedlings should be thinned or transplanted to 20cm (8in) apart.

HARVESTING AND STORAGE
If you wish to use fresh chervil, pick the tips of the stems once a month. If the leaves are to be used dry, then harvest the leaves just before the blossoms open and dry them on trays in a warm room or cool oven.

CULINARY USES
Chervil leaves are used as a condiment and in salads and have a flavour reminiscent of both aniseed and parsley. Chervil combines well with parsley and chives.

Above: *The delicately cut leaves of chervil make it ideal for both the kitchen and ornamental garden.*

HORSERADISH

Armoracia rusticana

This rather large plant has leaves that are reminiscent of a dock (*Rumex*) and is used as a herb and a vegetable. The plant has a strong taste and is consequently used only in relatively small quantities. Horseradish is easy to grow and the main problem may be preventing it from spreading too much.

SOIL AND ASPECT

Thrives in any light rich soil, although it will prosper in most soils, particularly those that have been well prepared. If you intend to lift plants completely that are growing on lighter soils then you must remove all the roots to prevent dense regeneration of deep-rooted horseradish plants all over the vegetable garden. Contain plants by planting in a plastic bucket with lots of small holes punched in the bottom. Horseradish is usually best given its own growing area and is not recommended for growing among rows of other crops.

PROPAGATION

Mature horseradish plants are divided and clumps or root sections are planted out in the autumn or spring. You will probably find that one plant is enough but if more are needed they should be planted 30cm (12in) apart.

HARVESTING AND STORAGE

Horseradish is best harvested as it is needed throughout the growing season. For winter use, the roots can be lifted and stored in trays of moist sand for up to two months. The leaves are best harvested when young.

CULINARY USES

The roots are the principal harvest from this plant. They can be simply peeled and grated for use in salads or mixed with other ingredients to make a sauce. Horseradish greens can also be diced and used in various dishes.

Right: *Horseradish is a large and vigorous plant that needs careful placing in the garden if it is not to take over.*

> **CULTIVATION**
> **Planting time** Autumn or spring
> **Planting distance** 30cm (12in)
> **Harvesting** As required (roots); while young (leaves)
> **Storage** In trays of sand (roots)

FRENCH TARRAGON

Artemisia dracunculus 'Sativa'

This is a half-hardy perennial plant that grows up to 60cm (24in) tall. Tarragon will need winter protection in colder areas or annual replacement. The closely related Russian tarragon (*A. dracunculus dracunculoides*) has a more bitter taste, but is considerably hardier and often grown as a substitute for French tarragon in colder areas. The taste of Russian tarragon improves with age.

SOIL AND ASPECT

Tarragon grows in any well-cultivated soil. The less hardy French tarragon may be best "plunged" into the ground for the summer growing season and lifted before the winter cold sets in. Divide frequently (every two to three years) or the plant will become root-bound. You should overwinter some plants indoors even in mild areas.

PROPAGATION

French tarragon cannot be grown from seed and so plants will need to be purchased.

Once established, clumps can be divided in order to increase stock. The hardier Russian tarragon can be grown successfully from seed and can be raised in pans or shallow drills outside. Both types should be planted out in spring at a distance of 30cm (12in).

HARVESTING AND STORAGE

Harvest tarragon in early summer for steeping in vinegar. For drying, harvest in mid-summer. Harvest fresh tarragon by picking off leaves or tips of branches with multiple leaves.

CULINARY USES

The leaves are widely used for flavouring and seasoning and it is an essential ingredient in French cooking. The French sometimes refer to it as *herbe au dragon*, due to its reputed ability to cure snake bites. It is often used in various sauces, such as tartare and white sauce, and for making herb vinegar.

> **CULTIVATION**
> **Sowing and planting time** Spring
> **Sowing depth** 1cm (½in)
> **Thinning and planting distance** 30cm (12in)
> **Harvesting** Early summer (fresh); mid-summer (for drying)
> **Storage** Dried or frozen

Above: *Tarragon is an excellent plant for herb gardens, but it must be protected in winter in cool areas.*

BORAGE

Borago officinalis

Borage is an annual that grows to 45–60cm (18–24in) high. The fresh leaves and the sky-blue flowers have a spicy, cucumber-like taste and an onion-like smell. The plant attracts bees and is also a useful companion plant for tomatoes. It is very attractive and worth including in both the ornamental and herb garden.

SOIL AND ASPECT

Borage thrives in average and poor dry soils (pH between 5–8). The plants usually do best in full sun, although they will grow in partial shade. To encourage leaf growth, supply rich moist soil, but if flowers are the object, restrict the use of organic fertilizer and make sure that the plants get plenty of sun. Borage is difficult to transplant once it is actively growing because of its tap root. Transplantation should therefore be done at the seedling stage. Ideal for container culture, borage can be planted in a large tub with smaller herbs around the edge.

PROPAGATION

Sow the seeds 1cm (½in) deep in the spring to early summer. The seeds will germinate in about 7–14 days. Thin or transplant the seedlings so that they are approximately 30cm (12in) apart.

HARVESTING AND STORAGE

The fresh leaves of borage are best, but they can also be dried. Harvest leaves for drying as the plant begins to flower. Dry the leaves quickly, ensuring good air circulation and with no overlapping of leaves. The flowers can be frozen in ice cubes for summer drinks.

CULINARY USES

Borage is primarily used in herb teas but the young leaves or peeled stems can also be chopped and used in salads or boiled as a pot-herb. The flowers make a colourful addition to salads and summer drinks and can also be candied.

Right: *Borage flowers can be used dried in potpourri, but leave on some of the flowers so that you can collect the seed.*

> **CULTIVATION**
> **Sowing time** Spring to early summer
> **Sowing depth** 1cm (½in)
> **Thinning and planting distance** 30cm (12in)
> **Harvesting** Any time (flowers); when young (leaves)
> **Storage** Frozen in ice cubes or crystallized (flowers); dried (leaves)

CARAWAY

Carum carvi

Caraway has aromatic, feathery, finely cut leaves and a thick, tapering root. During the second year, tiny white or pink flowers and reddish brown, crescent-shaped fruits develop. Caraway plants generally grow 75–150cm (30–60in) high when they are in flower. This biennial herb has a variety of uses but is mostly grown for its small aromatic fruit. The leaves can also be used.

SOIL AND ASPECT

Caraway should be grown in full sun in fertile, well-drained soil with a pH of 7.5. It will tolerate most soil types but seed germination can be poor on clay if the soil surface is prone to capping. Caraway needs a position that it can occupy for two seasons, as it will not produce seed until the second. A dressing of garden compost or well-rotted manure should be applied in the first year before planting with an additional mulching in the second year. It will tolerate light frost.

PROPAGATION

Sow seed 1cm (½in) deep in late spring to late summer in rows 40–50cm (16–20in) apart. Germination takes about 10–14 days. Thin to 15cm (6in) between plants. To grow caraway as a root crop, thin to 20cm (8in) apart. Caraway will easily self-seed around the herb garden if a few of the flower heads are left.

HARVESTING AND STORAGE

Harvest the seeds when they are ripe and before the first seeds fall. Harvest the roots in the autumn of the second year. Harvest the leaves when young. The seed can be dried and then stored.

CULINARY USES

Caraway seeds can be used in a number of different dishes, while the shoots and leaves can be added to vegetable dishes and salads. The roots, which are like a small, thin parsnip, are sometimes eaten as a vegetable.

Right: *Caraway produces pretty white or pink flowers before seeding and dying in the second year.*

> **CULTIVATION**
> **Sowing time** Late spring to late summer
> **Sowing depth** 1cm (½in)
> **Thinning and planting distance** 15cm/6in (leaf crop); 20cm/8in (root crop)
> **Distance between rows** 40–50cm (16–20in)
> **Harvesting** While young (leaves); when ripe (seed); autumn of second year (roots)
> **Storage** Dried (seeds)

CORIANDER (CILANTRO)

Coriandrum sativum

This hardy annual, which is a member of the parsley family, grows to 60–90cm (24–36in) in height and occasionally survives into a second year. Its erect slender stems are branching and bright green. The small pink, pale blue or white flowers are borne in compound umbels. The seeds are used as a condiment and as a component of beverages.

SOIL AND ASPECT

Coriander grows on most soils, but it does demand a sunny situation. If the plant is to be raised for its leaves, then a rich, free-draining soil with good organic content is recommended. For seed, the soil can be less nitrogen-rich and must be in full sun.

PROPAGATION

Coriander is best sown fresh each season, but it will self-sow in a favourable situation. Plants can also be raised from seed in a greenhouse during the colder winter months for a year-round supply of leaves. Alternatively, the seed is sown outside in autumn or spring in shallow 1cm (½in) drills. Germination can be slow, but once the plants emerge they should be thinned to about 15cm (6in). Plants that are grown for their leaves will benefit from successional sowings every three to four weeks throughout the summer.

HARVESTING AND STORAGE

Coriander seed is usually ready for harvesting just as the seeds are ripe and before they drop. The leaves are gathered when young throughout the summer. The seeds can be stored if they are dried and the leaves can be dried or frozen.

CULINARY USES

The dried powdered seeds are used as a flavouring in dishes such as curries. The aromatic leaves can be used dried or fresh.

Right: *The young succulent leaves of coriander are ideal for both cooking and summer salads.*

CULTIVATION
Sowing time Autumn or spring
Sowing depth 1cm (½in)
Thinning and planting distance 15cm (6in)
Harvesting When ripe (seed); while young (leaves)
Storage Dried (seed); dried or frozen (leaves)

FENNEL

Foeniculum vulgare

Fennel is widely used as a culinary herb. It is a biennial or perennial plant that will grow as an annual if it is not protected. Fennel reaches 1–1.5m (3–5ft) in height. The roots, stalks and leaves are all edible, with the spice coming from the dried seeds. The tiny yellow flowers and finely cut leaves, which can be bronze in some varieties, make it a highly decorative plant for the ornamental garden.

SOIL AND ASPECT

Thrives in a sunny position and a well-drained, rich soil though it will do quite well in poorer conditions. Applying a mulch of well-rotted compost will favour the development of the leafy growth, whereas a poorer site will encourage flowering. Fennel resembles dill, with which it can cross-pollinate, so keep these two apart.

PROPAGATION

Fennel can be grown from seed that is station sown in the spring at intervals of

CULTIVATION
Sowing time Spring
Sowing depth 1cm (½in)
Thinning and planting distance 45cm (18in)
Harvesting Before seeds ripen (flower heads); while young (leaves); when ripe (seeds)
Storage Dried (seed); frozen (leaves)

45cm (18in) in 1cm (½in) drills, although one or two plants are usually sufficient. Can become invasive if allowed to self-seed.

HARVESTING AND STORAGE

The flower heads are collected before the seeds ripen and the seeds are threshed or bashed out when completely dried. The leaves are collected fresh when young and used as needed. They can also be frozen for use during the winter.

CULINARY USES

Fennel leaves are used in salads and sauces and the seeds can be used in sausages and cakes.

Above: *All parts of the fennel plant are edible, making this both a useful and handsome garden plant.*

HYSSOP

Hyssopus officinalis

Hyssop is a shrubby perennial that grows up to 1.2m (4ft) high. It is used as a pot herb and as an ornamental addition to the edible landscape or potager garden. It is particularly useful for creating low hedges in parterres and knot gardens.

CULTIVATION
Sowing time Spring
Sowing depth 1cm (½in)
Thinning and planting distance 30cm (12in)
Planting and transplanting time Spring
Harvesting Any time
Storage Dried

SOIL AND ASPECT

Hyssop thrives in a sunny position in free-draining soil. Wet soils will considerably reduce the life of the plant. A light mulching of rotted garden compost and dried blood in spring will promote good leafy growth. The plant will benefit from regular trimming, which will also provide the new leafy growth that is most suited to culinary use.

PROPAGATION

Despite being a shrubby perennial, hyssop is not particularly long lived, especially on heavier, wet soils, and may need replacing every three to four years. It can easily be raised from seed, either sown in a seedbed and transplanted or sown directly where it is needed. Sow seed in spring in 1cm (½in) drills, thinning to about 30cm (12in). Purchased plants and those raised from cuttings taken in early summer are also planted out at the same distance in spring.

HARVESTING AND STORAGE

Hyssop leaves can be harvested as required and may be dried for later use.

CULINARY USES

Hyssop is used to flavour various liqueurs, including Chartreuse. The leaves, which have a rather bitter taste, are used sparingly to counter fatty dishes.

Above: *The shrubby nature of hyssop makes it ideal for use as a low hedge in a potager.*

BAY

Laurus nobilis

A hardy evergreen tree or shrub that grows widely in the Mediterranean region. In warm areas bay can grow as tall as 18m (60ft). Inconspicuous white flowers appear in clusters in late spring. Bay can be grown in cooler locations but it must be sited in a sheltered spot and may only make a relatively small tree. Alternatively, bay trees make good pot specimens for a patio and can be overwintered in a cool greenhouse or conservatory (sun room). The leaves are best used when they are fresh or within a few days of picking.

CULTIVATION
Planting time Spring
Planting distance 1.2m (4ft) or more
Harvesting Any time
Storage Dried

SOIL AND ASPECT

Bay trees appreciate a moist, rich but free-draining soil, although they are surprisingly tolerant of poor conditions, especially if sited in a hot sunny position.

PROPAGATION

Take semi-ripe cuttings from the current season's shoots in mid- to late summer.

Purchased plants and those raised from cuttings can be planted out in spring at a distance of 1.2m (4ft) or more.

HARVESTING AND STORAGE

Bay leaves can be harvested at any time; the mature leaves have the best flavour. The leaves can also be dried and stored in an air-tight container.

CULINARY USES

Bay is a very popular culinary herb, with one or two leaves at a time being included in a large number of dishes. The leaves are widely used in bouquets garnis or added to soups, sauces or stews. Bay leaf is often included as a pickling spice. It is settling to the stomach and has a tonic effect, stimulating the appetite and the secretion of digestive juices.

Above: *Bay makes a highly decorative specimen shrub for cool conservatories or a warm place outside.*

LOVAGE

Levisticum officinale

Lovage is a hardy perennial with ribbed stalks similar to celery and hollow stems that divide into branches near the top. Yellow flowers, about 3cm (1¼in) across, are borne in summer. The leaves have a strong taste, whereas the roots have a nutty flavour. Lovage is very robust and can grow as tall as 2m (6½ft) and spread to form a clump several yards wide.

SOIL AND ASPECT

Lovage prefers a well-drained soil rich in organic matter with a pH of 6–7.5. It can tolerate heavy clay soil, but grows best in a more loamy soil.

PROPAGATION

Lovage is easily propagated in autumn by seed, which can be slow to germinate (about 10–28 days), or by root division. Plant seed in rows in autumn at a depth of 1cm (½in) and thin to 60cm (24in). However, as it is such a vigorous plant, you may only want one plant. If more are required, then plant them 60cm (24in) apart in spring. Lovage is hardy but mulching assists winter survival.

HARVESTING AND STORAGE

Leaves are usually harvested twice a season starting in the second year, although large specimens will support a limited harvest continually through the season. The stems are cut in spring and the roots are dug in the autumn of the third year and can be used fresh or dried. Seeds can be harvested in late autumn or when ripe and dried for use.

CULINARY USES

Use the fresh leaves in salads, soups, stews, stir-fries and potato dishes and the seeds whole or ground in cakes, biscuits, sauces, pickles or salad dressings or with meats. Use the dried root as a condiment and cook the grated fresh root as a vegetable. The fresh root can also be used raw in salads, in herbal teas or preserved in honey.

Right: *Lovage is a splendid architectural plant, but it must be prevented from spreading too much.*

> **CULTIVATION**
> **Sowing time** Autumn
> **Sowing depth** 1cm (½in)
> **Planting time** Spring
> **Thinning and planting distance** 60cm (24in)
> **Harvesting** Any time (leaves); when ripe (seed); from autumn of third year (roots); spring (stems)
> **Storage** Dried (leaves and seed)

LEMON BALM

Melissa officinalis

This herbaceous perennial has lemon-scented leaves and clusters of small, white or yellowish, tubular flowers. It grows to a height of 1.5m (5ft) and can be invasive if not regularly cut back to prevent self-seeding. The foliage is a welcome addition to the herb garden and is best sited near to a path so that the fragrance is released when brushed against. Bees are attracted by the scent.

SOIL AND ASPECT

The ideal soil for lemon balm is moist but well drained and with a pH of 4.5–7.5. It will grow in sun or partial shade but should not be planted in very dry conditions.

Apply a good dressing of composted manure and a fertilizer such as fish, blood and bone annually to encourage good leafy growth. It is an attractive plant for the first part of the year but can become straggly. It is best cut back to stimulate new, fresh and attractive growth. Cutting back also prevents self-seeding around the garden.

PROPAGATION

Propagate from seeds, root divisions or stem cuttings. The seeds can be planted directly outside in 1cm (½in) drills in the spring or started off in a greenhouse in late winter. The plants should be thinned to 30–45cm (12–18in) apart.

HARVESTING AND STORAGE

Plants should be cut as flowering begins by cutting off the top growth, leaving a 5cm (2in) stubble for regrowth. Lemon balm can be susceptible to frost and so mulching is recommended if hard frost is likely. The leaves can be dried and then stored for later use.

CULINARY USES

The fresh leaves give a lovely lemon flavour to salads, vegetable dishes, chicken dishes, poultry stuffing and drinks. The dried leaves can be used to make herbal tea and are also added to potpourri and herb pillows.

Right: *Lemon balm is beautifully scented but like all members of the mint family can spread rapidly.*

> **CULTIVATION**
> **Sowing time** Winter (indoors); spring (outside)
> **Sowing depth** 1cm (½in)
> **Thinning and planting distance** 30–45cm (12–18in)
> **Harvesting** When the leaves are still fresh-looking
> **Storage** Dried

MINT

Mentha

Mint is an aromatic herb, with square, erect stems and flowers in the leaf axils. It is an invasive perennial or annual. Most mints grow to about 30–90cm (12–36in) in height. Spearmint (*M. spicata*) leaves are green, slightly crinkled and almost hairless with a very pungent lemony mint aroma and bitter taste. Peppermint (*M. × piperita*) has flat, smooth, shiny, pointed green leaves and reddish-lilac to purple flowers. Peppermint and spearmint spread rapidly by stolons and rhizomes and can become a weed problem.

SOIL AND ASPECT

A well-drained, fertile soil with a pH of 5–7 in full sun is preferred, although mints will prosper in a wide range of soil types in sun or partial shade. Mint can become invasive and it is a good idea to plant it in a below-ground container in most garden situations. Plants can suffer from mildew and rusts and a wilt disease caused by the soil fungus verticillium. Despite this, they have a tendency to spread rampantly through borders if left unchecked. Where mint is regularly cut back, apply a nitrogen- rich fertilizer such as dried blood or pelleted poultry manure and top-dress with well-rotted compost.

PROPAGATION

Mints are usually propagated from cuttings of stems, stolons and root divisions. Plant out propagated or purchased plants in spring, 30cm (12in) apart.

HARVESTING AND STORAGE

Mint can be harvested twice a season, leaving a stubble of at least 10cm (4in), although it is more usually collected as needed, picking the leaves when they are young and fresh. Cutting back stimulates new growth that is perfect for picking. The leaves can be dried or frozen.

CULINARY USES

Mint leaves are added to beverages, jellies, soups, stews, sauces, vinegar and used to flavour meats such as lamb.

CULTIVATION
Planting time Spring
Planting distance 30cm (12in)
Harvesting While leaves are young
Storage Dried or frozen

Above: *Mint is a must for the herb garden but take care not to let it spread unchecked in open ground.*

BERGAMOT

Monarda didyma

Bergamot is not widely used as a culinary herb today, but its whorled flower heads make it worthy of inclusion in the herb garden. There are various colours to choose from, including bright red. The leaves release an aromatic fragrance when they are brushed against which makes weeding among these herbs an absolute pleasure.

SOIL AND ASPECT

Bergamot thrives in a rich, moist soil. Soils with a tendency to dry out will quickly kill the plant unless watered. The plants are best replanted in a fresh patch every three years or so and clumps benefit from a light mulching of well-rotted garden compost after a dressing of fish, blood and bone or similar general-purpose organic fertilizer. *M. didyma* can spread by means of flat stems near the surface, resulting in it needing to be divided and re-situated every two to three years or so. It is also prone to mildew. Other species are much less prone to mildew (and also grow and flower much better) in a moist soil, or at least in a place where they do not get too dry in summer.

PROPAGATION

Bergamot can be raised by division, cuttings or by seed in spring. The seed can be sown in spring in rows at a depth of 1cm (½in), but plants tend to look better in drifts or clumps. In either case the plants should be spaced about 45cm (18in) apart.

HARVESTING AND STORAGE

The leaves should be harvested when they are still young. The flowers can also be picked as they are just opening and both can be dried and then stored.

CULINARY USES

The leaves of bergamot dry well and can be used to make a herbal tea. This is not the same as the bergamot in Earl Grey, which is a tropical citrus. Both the leaves and flowers can be used.

Right: *Garden bergamot is most commonly grown for its looks, rather than for using in the kitchen.*

CULTIVATION
Sowing time Spring
Sowing depth 1cm (½in)
Planting time Spring
Thinning and planting distance 45cm (18in)
Harvesting While young (leaves); as they are opening (flowers)
Storage Dried

SWEET CICELY

Myrrhis odorata

Sweet cicely, an early-summer-flowering perennial, is something of a rarity these days and usually only grown by devotees. It is reminiscent of cow parsley and the seed-heads produced later in the summer are quite attractive in their own right. The leaves are a pretty mottled green, and are large and fairly deeply cut. It grows to a height of 60–90cm (24–36in) and can become invasive when it likes the conditions. Sweet cicely is a good choice for including in a wild garden.

SOIL AND ASPECT

Sweet cicely likes a moist humus-rich soil and, unusually for a herb, will thrive in shade. It is perfectly at home at the base of a hedgerow and provides a pretty effect in late spring and early summer. Like many of its close relatives, the individual plants are short lived, but it self-seeds prolifically and must be prevented from becoming a weed in a herb garden.

PROPAGATION

Sweet cicely can be slow to germinate and difficult to transplant, so it is best sown in situ using freshly ripened seed. Sow seed in autumn in drills 1cm (½in) deep. The seedlings should be thinned to 60cm (24in). Plants should have their seed removed before it gets the chance to self-seed.

HARVESTING AND STORAGE

The leaves of sweet cicely are harvested from spring to early summer, and can be dried. The seeds taste of aniseed only when they are still greenish, so collect them when they are still unripe. The seeds have no taste if they are completely black.

CULINARY USES

Sweet cicely has a mild aniseed flavour that can be used to counter the acidity of sharp-tasting fruit. It was used as a sweetening agent for stewed soft fruits and rhubarb. The leaves make an attractive garnish.

Right: *Sweet cicely is something of a rarity in that it is ideally suited for both herb and wild gardens. It can be used in potpourri.*

CULTIVATION
Sowing time Autumn
Sowing depth 1cm (½in)
Thinning and planting distance 60cm (24in)
Harvesting Spring to early summer (leaves); unripe, when green (seed)
Storage Dried (leaves and seed)

BASIL

Ocimum

The height, leaf colour, flower colour, and growth habit of basil can vary a great deal depending on the variety. Sweet basil (*Ocimum basilicum*) has smooth, bright green leaves and small, white flowers. It can grow 60–90cm (24–36in) high and has an erect and branched habit. Cinnamon basil (*O. basilicum* 'Cinnamon') has a similar habit but is smaller, growing only 30–40cm (12–16in) tall. This type has smaller, purplish leaves, pink flower spikes and an anise-cinnamon-like odour. Lemon basil (*O. × citriodorum*) has a growth habit resembling cinnamon basil but has smooth, bright green leaves and small white flowers. Purple basil (*O. basilicum* var. *purpurascens*) is noted for its strongly scented purple leaves.

SOIL AND ASPECT

Basil requires a minimum temperature of 10–15°C (50–59°F) and pH of 5–8 in order to thrive. The growing area should be in full sun with light, fertile, well-drained soil. The application of garden compost or well-rotted manure can aid growth. Avoid applying too much nitrogen, as this will decrease the essential oils in the growing tissue, resulting in weak-flavoured leaf and stem tissue. Keep well watered. Basil is a good companion plant for tomatoes.

PROPAGATION

For an early supply, sow seeds in plug trays in a greenhouse and transplant outside in warm weather. Seed can be sown outdoors in 1cm (½in) drills in the late spring, provided that the soil is kept moist. Thin or plant out at 20–23cm (8–9in) intervals.

HARVESTING AND STORAGE

Pick frequently to avoid the development of woody stems. Regular picking is advised as the leaves become bitter if the plant is allowed to flower. Take care when harvesting as the leaves bruise easily.

CULINARY USES

The fresh or dried leaves are used in tomato dishes, pasta sauces, vegetables and soups. Basil is useful in Mediterranean dishes and is always best used fresh.

Above: *Basil combines well with tomatoes both as a companion plant in the garden and as an ingredient in cooking.*

CULTIVATION
Sowing time Late spring
Sowing depth 1cm (½in)
Thinning and planting distance 20–22cm (8–9in)
Harvesting Any time
Storage Dried or frozen

SWEET MARJORAM AND OREGANO

Origanum majorana, O. vulgare

Sweet marjoram grows to a height of 30cm (12in) and makes a good companion plant for aubergines, pumpkins and courgettes. Oregano can grow to a height of 60cm (24in) and is generally hardier than marjoram. It is a sprawling herb and, unlike sweet marjoram, is not suited for growing indoors. Oregano makes a good companion plant for cauliflower, but should not be planted with broccoli or cabbage. Many plants are classified as oregano and their flavour depends on where they are cultivated. In general, the hotter the sun, the stronger the flavour.

SOIL AND ASPECT

Sweet marjoram and oregano thrive in full sun and prefer a light, fairly rich, well-drained, slightly alkaline soil, with a pH of 7–8. Poorer soils result in a more pungent taste and can stimulate early flowering. As it is not entirely hardy, pot up sweet marjoram in autumn and overwinter indoors or sow seed each year.

PROPAGATION

Sweet marjoram is easily grown from seed sown in spring in 1cm (½in) drills or by cuttings taken in summer. Thin or plant out at 30cm (12in) intervals. In cooler areas, marjoram can be overwintered indoors in pots. Oregano can be grown from seed sown similarly to that of marjoram or by taking stem cuttings or root divisions. The seed can be slow to germinate and the resulting plants may not be true to the parent plant, or may even be flavourless, making vegetative propagation the preferred option.

HARVESTING AND STORAGE

Harvest and dry the leaves before flowering occurs. Dry by tying the stems together and hanging in a warm, dry, well-ventilated place. Both herbs can also be frozen.

CULINARY USES

These flavourful herbs are used in many dishes, especially in Italian recipes.

CULTIVATION
Sowing time Spring
Sowing depth 1cm (½in)
Dividing time Spring
Thinning and planting distance 30cm (12in)
Harvesting While young
Storage Dried or frozen

Above: *Marjoram is a good companion plant for pumpkins, courgettes and aubergines as well as a culinary herb.*

PARSLEY

Petroselinum crispum

Although it is a biennial plant, parsley, which grows up to 45cm (18in), can only be cropped in the first year and is usually grown as an annual. In its first year, it develops plenty of leaves, on fairly long stems that come from the crown of the plant. In the second year, the plant produces only a couple of leaves and a long bloom stalk that will self-sow if you allow it. Parsley is one of the most popular and versatile culinary herbs and can be grown indoors or outdoors. It makes an excellent subject for a container or as an edging to paths. There are two forms: curly-leaved parsley (*P. crispum*) and French or flat-leaved parsley (*P. crispum neapolitanum*).

SOIL AND ASPECT

Parsley does best in a sunny spot, but will also prosper in light shade. It should be grown in a moist fertile soil and benefits from the addition of well-rotted garden compost or manure and a nitrogen-rich fertilizer such as dried blood or pelleted chicken manure. Keep well watered in long hot, dry spells.

PROPAGATION

The seeds should be soaked in water and then sown either under cover or outside in 1cm (½in) drills. Thin or plant out at 20–25cm (8–10in) intervals. A spring sowing will provide leaves through summer while a second sowing in late summer will provide winter leaves. These will need protection with a cloche.

HARVEST

Young leaves should be snipped just above ground level as needed. The harvested leaves can be dried or frozen for later use.

CULINARY USES

The leaves and stem are used to flavour and garnish a wide variety of dishes. Curly-leaved forms have a subtle flavour whereas the flat-leaved types have a stronger taste.

CULTIVATION
Sowing time Spring or late summer
Sowing depth 1cm (½in)
Thinning and planting distance 20–25cm (8–10in)
Harvesting Any time
Storage Dried or frozen

Right: *Parsley is one of the most popular and versatile herbs for use in the kitchen. It also looks decorative in the herb garden.*

ROSEMARY

Rosmarinus officinalis

This greatly valued herb, which is native to southern Europe, grows up to 1.2m (4ft) tall. As well as a being a useful culinary herb, rosemary is also a beautiful, drought-resistant plant that can be used in landscaping. It has attractive blue flowers that are a good source of nectar for bees. There are two basic types: the trailing or prostrate type and a bush type that will, in time, become large enough to be considered a shrub. Prostrate rosemary makes an excellent groundcover plant.

SOIL AND ASPECT

Rosemary thrives in a well-drained soil in a sunny position. It is slightly tender and will suffer if it is planted in a wet soil during the cold winter months. It is an excellent plant for use in coastal areas. Rosemary is a plant that actually thrives on neglect and will die if you fertilize or water it too much or plant it in very rich soil.

PROPAGATION

Rosemary is best bought as an established plant or raised from cuttings. Plant out in the eventual position in spring to late summer. One plant is usually enough for most culinary requirements, but, if you do want to grow more than this, space the plants 75cm (30in) apart.

HARVESTING AND STORAGE

Harvest the young, tender stems and leaves, taking off no more than one-third of the plant at one time. For drying, harvest just before the plant flowers. After drying, the leaves can be stored for later use.

CULINARY USES

Rosemary leaves can be used for making tea, in sauces or for flavouring many meat (especially lamb) and vegetable dishes. It may also be used in herb breads and is excellent for including in potpourri. It can be used either fresh or dried.

Right: *Rosemary, which is native to southern Europe, will thrive in coastal areas or in a dry sunny spot.*

> **CULTIVATION**
> **Planting time** Spring to late summer
> **Planting distance** 75cm (30in)
> **Harvesting** Any time
> **Storage** Dried

SAGE

Salvia officinalis

Sage is a long-lived, hardy, shrubby perennial with grey, felted leaves. It can reach 80cm (32in) in height. It has a distinctive flavour that combines well with a variety of meats and vegetables. Sage is an excellent decorative specimen for use in the ornamental and kitchen garden. There are coloured-leaved forms, including deep purple and bright yellow, as well as the culinary grey-leaved form. The spikes of blue-purple flowers appear in late spring and will attract bees.

SOIL AND ASPECT

Sage is very easy to grow in the right conditions. It prefers full sun and a reasonably fertile, well-drained soil that does not get too dry. The main problem with sage is to keep it under control. Pinch small plants to make them branch, then let them grow to harvesting size and avoid letting the stems get so tall that they lie down or you will end up with a twisted, woody tangle in a couple of years.

PROPAGATION

Sage is best grown from cuttings taken in early to mid-summer or purchased as young plants. They can also be raised from seed. Seeds require 20 days at 20°C (68°F) for germination to take place and are best raised under cover. Sow seed in trays or shallow pans or under cloches in spring in 1cm (½in) deep drills. Plants should be thinned out, transplanted or planted 60cm (24in) apart in their required position.

HARVESTING AND STORAGE

Sage is best harvested when it is just starting to flower and used either fresh or dried. Harvest after the dew dries in the morning, cutting the stems so that there are one or two leaves remaining at the bottom. Air-drying sage will result in a leathery rather than a crisp product that should be stored in airtight jars. Chop or rub the leaves into a powder when you need to use them.

CULINARY USES

The leaves are used to flavour soups, stews, stuffings, sausages and roast meats as well as to make tea. The coloured leaf forms taste the same as the grey-leaved form.

> **CULTIVATION**
> **Sowing time** Spring
> **Sowing depth** 1cm (½in)
> **Cuttings** Taken early to mid-summer
> **Thinning and planting distance** 60cm (24in)
> **Harvesting** Any time
> **Storage** Dried

Above: *The pungent leaves of sage are ready for harvesting when the handsome flowers appear.*

SAVORY

Satureja

Summer savory (*S. hortensis*) is an annual that grows to about 45cm (18in). It has a less tidy appearance than winter savory (*S. montana*). Winter savory is a perennial that also grows to about 45cm (18in) high, but is much hardier in cultivation. It can be treated in the same way as common thyme, which it closely resembles, although it is slightly more compact, with darker leaves and white flowers. Like thyme, winter savory makes a good edging plant and will benefit from a light pruning in spring to keep it compact. Both winter and summer savory can be grown in containers and are occasionally raised as rock garden plants.

SOIL AND ASPECT

Both types of savory are Mediterranean herbs that need a warm sunny site with free-draining soil. In colder areas winter savory may need some form of winter protection.

PROPAGATION

Summer savory is an annual that needs reasonably warm, damp conditions for germination, but only a little water thereafter. Both types of savory grow well from seed that should not be sown too deeply. They are best station sown at 30cm (12in) intervals in mid-spring in 1cm (½in) drills. Thin to 30cm (12in).

HARVESTING AND STORAGE

You can gather the young stem tips early in the season but when the plant begins to flower, harvest the entire plant and then dry. The dried leaves can be stored for later use.

CULINARY USES

Although these are among the oldest of herbs, they are not widely grown or used today. Summer savory is sometimes called the bean herb because it goes so well with green beans and is used in a range of bean dishes. Both types of savory have a spicy, peppery flavour and are used to flavour fresh garden beans, vinegar, soups, stuffings and rice.

> **CULTIVATION**
> **Sowing time** Mid-spring
> **Sowing-depth** 1cm (½in)
> **Thinning distance** 30cm (12in)
> **Harvesting** Before flowering (stem tips); on flowering (whole plant)
> **Storage** Dried

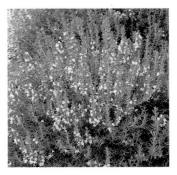

Above: *Savory thrives in warm sunny conditions and provides a spicy addition to many dishes.*

THYME

Thymus vulgaris

Thyme is a perennial plant that reaches 30–45cm (12–18in) in height. It can be grown indoors or outdoors and in sun or partial shade. There is a very wide range of thymes that can be grown in the herb garden. Most are similar in terms of their culinary value, although the broad-leaved forms have a slightly stronger flavour. The wide range of colours available makes them excellent subjects for ornamental gardens and edible landscaping.

SOIL AND ASPECT

Thyme likes a sunny situation and a well-drained soil. It is not particular about the soil type and will even grow in poor "gravelly" soils. Thymes are excellent plants for edging borders and can be grown in containers and between the cracks in the paving in patios. They are durable and will even withstand being walked on. They can get straggly after a few years, although a light trimming will help maintain a good habit.

PROPAGATION

Thyme can be grown from seed in spring, although this does not allow for the propagation of particular forms or varieties. Seeds require 25 days at about 16°C (61°F) for germination and are best raised under cover and transplanted out later. Plants can also be raised vegetatively from cuttings or layers taken in early to mid-summer. Plants should be spaced at 30cm (12in) intervals.

HARVESTING AND STORAGE

Nip off leafy stem ends and flowers as and when they are needed when the plants are at the full-flowering stage. These can be used fresh or dried by hanging a bunch in a warm place. They can also be frozen.

CULINARY USES

The leaves can be used with meats, soups, sauces and egg dishes. Thyme improves digestion, destroys intestinal parasites and is a good antiseptic and tonic. Its leaves can be used as a condiment and a tea.

> **CULTIVATION**
> **Sowing time** Spring
> **Cuttings or layers** Early to mid-summer
> **Thinning and planting distance** 30cm (12in)
> **Harvesting** Any time
> **Storage** Dried or frozen

Right: *Despite the wide range of cultivated thymes that are available, most have similar uses in the kitchen.*

DIRECTORY OF FRUIT

Every garden has space for fruit. Even trees such as apples are available in compact varieties suitable for pots. Fruit trees can be trained into decorative shapes and also provide screens and boundaries. Larger gardens, however, may benefit from the cool tranquillity of an orchard of fruiting trees. Many people are reluctant to grow fruit because they are put off by what they see as the complex art of pruning. Fruit trees and bushes take two or more years before they start cropping and so give new gardeners time to learn their habits and master the intricacies of their culture.

COBNUTS AND FILBERTS

Corylus avellana and *C. maxima*

Both of these nuts are derived from two European species of corylus. The cobnuts are *Corylus avellana*; the filberts are *C. maxima*. The origin of cultivars is confusing and so both are often grouped together. Cobnuts and filberts are largely self-sterile, and are pollinated by compatible varieties grown nearby. There are numerous selections of cobnuts and filberts, many of which are the product of crossbreeding between the two.

OBTAINING PLANTS

Because of the need for cross-pollination, varieties do not come true from seed, and bushes are propagated by layering the "wands" (self-coppicing suckers that grow from the base) or by grafts.

SOIL AND PREFERRED ASPECT

Both cobnuts and filberts will grow on almost any soil that is well drained, but grow best on a loamy soil with a pH of 7.5–8. They tolerate shade, although a sunny position will generally yield a heavier crop. They need a relatively sheltered position as the flowers that appear in mid- to late winter can be susceptible to wind damage.

CULTIVATION

The bushes are generally planted 4.5–5m (15–16ft) apart, although this can be closer and a number of varieties can be grown in one area. The useful life of each bush is long, with bushes well over 100 years old still able to crop well. Fine sunny days with a light breeze at pollination time favour a good crop. Both cobnuts and filberts benefit from a good mulching in autumn. Keep the ground clean by hoeing regularly in the summer.

PRUNING

Both cobnuts and filberts are best grown as bushes or small trees with a 1m (3ft) tall stem and six or seven main branches. Each branch or wand is pruned to a height of about 2m (6½ft) to allow the maximum amount of light to reach all parts of the bush (essential for nut production) and keep the crop within picking reach. Prune from early winter to mid-spring, preferably to coincide with flowering and thereby aid pollination.

HARVESTING AND STORAGE

Cobnuts and filberts are best enjoyed fresh. Shake from the branches from around early to mid-autumn, repeating this at intervals.

PESTS AND DISEASES

Though relatively trouble free, one important pest is the nut weevil (*Balaninus nucum*). Weevil-infested nuts can be separated by placing them in cold storage for a few days, which induces the weevil grub to emerge. Squirrels and other nut-loving mammals can also be a problem.

Above: *Cobnuts and filberts are easy to grow on most soils but sunny positions ensure the best crops.*

VARIETIES

COBNUTS

'Kentish Cob' A moderately vigorous, upright grower with large nuts of good flavour. Better pollination is achieved when two different varieties are planted.
'Pearson's Prolific' A compact variety with small to medium nuts of good flavour. Best pollination is achieved when two different varieties are planted.
'Purpurea' Red catkins and purple leaves and small nuts of good flavour.

FILBERTS

'Barcelona' A popular variety needing moist soil and shade in hot climates. Pollinated by any filbert except 'Ennis'.
'Butler' Needs moist soil and shade in hot climates. Pollinate by any other filbert. A pollinator for 'Barcelona' and 'Ennis' with a crop of large nuts.
'Duchilly' A fine-flavoured, long nut. Needs moist soil and afternoon shade. Pollinate by any other filbert.
'Ennis' The largest nut and the heaviest crops in early autumn. Needs good soil moisture and afternoon shade. Pollinate by 'Daviana' or 'Butler'.

cobnuts

PRUNING AN ESTABLISHED COBNUT TREE

Late summer *Established trees should be pruned in late summer. Strong lateral growths are broken off by hand to about six to eight leaves from the base and left to hang.*

Late winter *Cut back all the broken growths to three or four buds. Never prune back laterals carrying female flowers but remove crowded growths and suckers.*

MELONS

Cucumis melo

Melons are popular with gardeners who have plenty of space to accommodate their spreading vines. They must be grown in a greenhouse or cold frame in cooler climates. Cantaloupes (muskmelons) do not tolerate cool temperatures or transplant very well, so wait until the soil is warm before planting seeds. Of the different types of melon available, cantaloupes are reputed to have the sweetest flavour, whereas honeydew melons store especially well.

OBTAINING PLANTS

Melons are grown annually from seed, which is sown from early to mid-spring, under glass in cooler areas. The seeds are sown about 1cm (½in) deep in pairs in a 7cm (2¾in) pot and the weaker one is thinned if both germinate. They can be potted on if outdoor conditions delay planting out. Greenhouse melons should be planted into their final position as soon as possible.

SOIL AND PREFERRED ASPECT

Melons can be grown outside in sheltered locations, but do better under cover in cooler areas. Melons require a fertile, well-drained soil that is not too rich and has a pH of 6.5–7. This should be cleared about three to four weeks before planting and the planting pit prepared. Each pit should measure 30 x 30 x 30cm (12 x 12 x 12in).

Above: *Melon vines are vigorous growers that must be restricted in order to ensure good-sized fruit.*

Place a good spade-full of well-rotted manure in the base before backfilling. Water the pit well and cover with plastic to warm up the soil in readiness for planting.

CULTIVATION

Seedlings are best planted out when they have developed four leaves and all danger of frost has passed. They should be planted with about 2–3cm (¾–1¼in) of the pot soil above ground level as a precaution against soft collar rot. Do not firm the soil but water each plant, keeping water off the stem. Plant the melons at 1–1.2m (3–4ft) intervals and place cloches and light shading over them for 7–10 days until they are established.

Melons should be stopped at the fourth or fifth leaf to encourage the production of side shoots. The four strongest side shoots should be kept and the rest removed after two to three weeks. Plants growing in cold frames should be trained into an "X"-shape.

Cantaloupes can also be grown on a trellis, but the fruit must be supported with a sling. Control the vigorous vines by pinching out the growing terminals once the melon crop has set. After this, pinch out all other lateral growths and flowers as they appear. Thinning may be necessary, particularly in areas with a shorter growing season. Bees are necessary for pollination and plants growing under cover may need pollinating by hand. One male flower should be sufficient for about four female flowers. Female flowers are easily recognized by the small embryonic fruit immediately behind them. Regular feeding and watering will aid the development of the crop. A good compost tea is especially useful for this.

HARVESTING AND STORAGE

The fruits are mature when there is a characteristic melon scent and circular cracking appears near to the stalk. When lifted they should part easily from the stalk. Melons do not store for more than a few days and are best eaten straightaway.

PESTS AND DISEASES

Melons are prey to relatively few diseases but a couple can be serious. Powdery mildew can be a problem as can soft collar rot if the stems are allowed to get wet. Verticillium wilt is a serious threat and affected plants should be removed. Many newer hybrid varieties are resistant to major diseases. Pests are generally less troublesome, red spider mite being the only potentially serious one in greenhouses and warmer areas.

Above: *Melons can be trained to grow as greenhouse climbers, provided that the fruit is supported in a sling.*

VARIETIES

'Hero of Lockinge' Large fruits of a good flavour with a golden, fine-textured flesh. Good for forcing in cold frames.
'Ogen' Small fruits with a good flavour are borne on this early cropping variety. A good plant for cooler areas.
'Superlative' Large, almost round, green fruits with scarlet flesh. A good variety for greenhouses or cloche culture.
'Sweetheart' Medium-sized fruits with firm salmon-pink flesh. A hybrid variety suitable for colder areas.

cantaloupes (muskmelons)

water melons

QUINCE

Cydonia oblonga

The true quince is a low, deciduous, thornless tree with a crooked growth habit. It will reach a height and spread of about 3.5m (12ft), and can even grow to 5m (16ft) or more on a fertile soil. Quinces need little attention once established, and begin to yield apple- or pear-shaped fruits after four or five years. Fruit grown in cooler areas is too acidic to be eaten fresh (although it can be used to make jellies and preserves). It may be sweeter if grown in warmer regions.

OBTAINING PLANTS

Quince is a difficult tree to raise and maintain in the first year and it is best to buy a specimen that has already been raised and shaped for a couple of years in a specialist nursery. It has a crooked shape at first and it is advisable to support the tree for the first few years following planting until it is fully established and has the strength needed to support the crown. Plant bare-rooted trees in the winter dormant season and container-grown stock at any time, provided that it is kept properly watered.

SOIL AND PREFERRED ASPECT

Quinces will succeed in most soils but grow best in a deep, light, fertile and moisture-retentive soil. They do well near water but are equally at home in an open sunny site in warmer areas. They are hardy in most areas but warmth is required to ripen the fruit.

CULTIVATION

In cooler locations quinces need some protection, the ideal position being a sunny corner where two walls meet, with the tree trained as a fan. Prepare the ground well

Above: *Quince is an unusual fruit tree in that it is quite easily grown in a warm part of the garden.*

prior to planting by digging over the whole area, removing all perennial weeds and applying a base dressing of compound fertilizer such as hoof and horn. Drive in the supporting stake first, before the tree is planted and tied on to it. Space bush trees about 3.5m (12ft) apart and standard trees about 6m (20ft) apart. Apply a dressing of general-purpose fertilizer such as fish, blood and bone in late winter and mulch with a generous layer of well-rotted manure or compost. Keep the area around the tree base free of weeds for a diameter of about 1m (3ft) throughout the growing season.

PRUNING

The aim of any pruning is to achieve a goblet-shaped tree with an open (but not barren) centre. Cut back the previous season's growth by about half in winter for the first three or four years, making the cut to an outward-facing bud. Cut back side shoots to two or three buds if competing with the leader or crowding the centre, but leave all others. After four years, little pruning is required except to tidy up the plant or remove dead, diseased or badly placed branches. Remove any suckers or branches growing from the main stem below the crown.

HARVESTING AND STORAGE

Leave the fruits on the tree for as long as possible so that they can develop their full flavour, but remove before any heavy frosts. The fruits usually ripen in mid- to late autumn.

Left: *Growing a quince against a warm, sunny wall will help the fruit to develop its full flavour.*

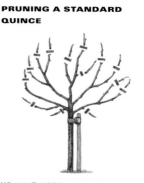
Store like apples for about a month before use, keeping them separate from other fruits because they are strongly aromatic.

PESTS AND DISEASES

Quince suffers generally from the same pests as apples. Likely diseases include leaf blight and brown rot of the fruit.

PRUNING A STANDARD QUINCE

Winter *Establish a strong branch framework immediately after planting. Each winter after this, cut back the leaders of the main branches by about one-third of the previous summer's growth. Make all of the cuts above an outward-facing bud and remove any weak or badly placed branches.*

FIGS

Ficus carica

Figs are deciduous trees from the Mediterranean areas of Europe and the Middle East. They grow mainly in warmer regions but can be grown in cooler temperate areas. Figs grown in temperate areas set fruit without needing to be fertilized, so only one plant need be grown.

OBTAINING PLANTS

Figs are usually bought from a specialist nursery, although they can be raised quite easily from cuttings taken in summer.

SOIL AND PREFERRED ASPECT

Figs are tolerant of a wide range of well-drained soils, and need full sun. Excavate a pit and place paving slabs around the sides, letting them protrude about 2–3cm (¾–1¼in) above the soil. This restricts the fig's root run and ensures good cropping. Tightly pack bricks or other inert rubble into the bottom. Wall-trained figs need a box of about 2 by 0.6m (6½ by 2ft), whereas freestanding trees need a box that is 1 by 1m (3 by 3ft). Both boxes should be 50–60cm (20–30in) deep. Figs in cooler regions need the protection of a sunny wall and are best grown as a fan.

CULTIVATION

Feed figs in spring using a compound fertilizer such as fish, blood and bone. Apply

Above: *Young embryo figs that form in the first year will only fully ripen in the following season.*

a light mulch of well-rotted manure or compost. Root-restricted figs need regular feeding throughout the growing season with compost tea or worm liquid. Water root-restricted figs, as they can quickly become stressed after even a short period of hot or dry weather. Protect outdoor trees in winter in cooler areas by thatching them with bracken or draping with horticultural fleece. Figs grown in a greenhouse are treated in a similar way to outdoor fans.

PRUNING

The pruning of figs in cooler temperate areas differs to that of warmer climates. In cool regions, the fig bears two crops per

year but only one ripens. The fruit that is harvested forms at the top of the previous season's growth and extends back about 15–30cm (6–12in). These are carried over the winter as embryo fruits and ripen the following year. Any figs that form on the current season's growth will not ripen before the autumn and should be removed.

Fan-trained figs are formed in the same manner as for a peach or sour cherry. Established fans should have about half of their developing shoots tipped back in mid-summer. In mid-winter, half of these shoots that carry fruit are pruned back to 2.5cm (1in) to encourage new growth next year. The remaining pruning involves maintaining an open framework.

Where conditions allow for the growth of freestanding trees, these require little pruning save to maintain an open framework and health and vigour.

HARVESTING AND STORAGE

Ripe figs are soft to the touch and hang downwards. Slight splitting of the skin and drops of nectar dripping from the eye are also signs that they are ripe. Figs are best eaten fresh.

PESTS AND DISEASES

Figs are generally trouble free although older specimens can become infested with coral spot fungus. Figs grown under glass can suffer from pests such as red spider mite, scale and mealy bugs.

PRUNING AN ESTABLISHED FAN-TRAINED FIG TREE

Mid-summer *Pinch out the growing tips of about half of the young shoots that are carried on the main framework branches. You should do this towards the end of mid-summer. As the shoots develop, tie them to the wires.*

Late autumn *Prune back half the shoots that carried fruits to about 2.5cm (1in) to encourage new growth from the base. Tie in the other shoots, parallel with the wall, about 23–30cm (9–12in) apart, removing any surplus ones.*

STRAWBERRIES

Fragaria × ananassa

Strawberries are a popular fruit and also dependable for home production. The management of this crop is easier than that of tree fruits and even a small garden patch can yield a good crop of this delicious summer fruit.

OBTAINING PLANTS

While some strawberry varieties can be raised from seed, it is more common to buy plants. To be sure that your plants are true-to-type, vigorous and virus-free, purchase them from a reputable nursery. Always try to get registered virus-free plants as these can yield 50–75 per cent more fruit than ordinary stock plants. It is generally not advisable to transplant strawberries out of an old bed because diseases may be introduced.

SOIL AND PREFERRED ASPECT

Strawberries thrive on sandy loam soil, but will produce adequately on heavier soils provided they are well drained. A sloping site ensures good surface water drainage. The ideal soil pH is slightly acidic at between 6.0 and 6.5. The soil should contain adequate organic matter. Garden compost or manure is best dug in at the beginning of the season before planting. Alternatively, a green manure can be grown and dug in. When preparing strawberry plants for planting, never allow them to dry out. Cover the roots with moist peat moss or cloth, and keep the plants shaded at all times. Strawberries begin blooming in spring and can be subject to frost injury, so select a site that has good air movement. Avoid low-lying frost pockets and remember

Above: *Strawberries are so named because straw is placed under the ripening berries to keep them clean.*

that slopes facing the sun warm up faster in spring and stimulate earlier flowering, but can actually increase the danger of frost injury. In very frost-prone areas, a less sunny slope that delays blooming until after the seasonal danger of frost has passed can be to your advantage.

CULTIVATION

The goal during the first summer of growth after the spring planting is to establish healthy plants as early in the season as possible. In early summer, the parent plant sends out runners once it is established. Frequent, shallow cultivation between the rows, hand pulling of weeds and mulching with 5cm (2in) of hay, straw, or coarse sawdust two or three weeks after planting will greatly reduce the number of weeds.

Apply a fertilizer that is rich in potassium in late summer at the time flower buds are initiated for the next spring's fruit as this will help harden the plants for the coming winter.

Protect the crowns of plants during very cold periods in winter. Do not apply mulch too early in autumn as it can increase crown

rot and prevent the plants from completely going dormant, making them more subject to winter injury. Suitable mulches include newspapers, coarse sawdust, straw, hay or any loose mulch that does not compact.

Strawberry fruit is 90 per cent water and any moisture-stress during development will reduce yield. Always ensure that the crop is well watered while cropping.

HARVESTING AND STORAGE

Harvest when the berries are fully ripe. White areas indicate immaturity. Allowing the berry to reach full colour on the plant increases the sugar content and the size of the berry. Pick the berries with the stem and cap attached to allow the fruit to keep for a longer period. Berries that have their caps removed or are injured quickly go off.

The first harvest can occur about 30 days after the first bloom. Check every other day for ripe fruit. Place in shallow containers to minimize injury and chill promptly.

PESTS AND DISEASES

To avoid diseases, do not plant where tomatoes, potatoes, peppers or aubergines (eggplant) have been grown, or back into a site where strawberries have been grown in the last two years. Protect the fruit from birds with netting.

VARIETIES

'Baron Solemacher' Main cropper with a superb flavour and will tolerate a little shade. Tiny dark red fruits.
'Cambridge Favourite' Produces large red fruits that are mild in flavour. A good heavy cropper.
'Royal Sovereign' An early variety that has a superb flavour. Susceptible to pests and diseases.
'Trellisa' Really good-flavoured medium-sized fruit. Good variety for strawberry barrels.

strawberries

Above: *The developing fruit trusses can be protected from muddy splashes or soil borne rots with a mulch of straw.*

Above: *Removing the leaves and straw mulch after fruiting will prevent the build-up and spread of diseases.*

WALNUTS

Juglans regia

The common, or English, walnut is, in fact, native to southern Europe and Asia. The related eastern black walnut is commonly grown in the eastern and central USA and is hardier and larger. It also yields a high-quality wood, although the fruit is not as good as the common walnut. Both become relatively large trees and are therefore best grown in larger gardens. Walnuts are best grown from a known variety that will yield good-quality nuts. The variety chosen will depend entirely upon personal taste, although most will not begin cropping for 5 to 10 years.

OBTAINING PLANTS

Walnuts are almost always bought in from specialist fruit nurseries and, although they can be grown from seed, it is better to raise a variety if good-quality nuts are needed. The trees are planted in the same manner as all other fruit trees and can be purchased as bare-rooted stock or container-grown trees. Bare-rooted is generally the best option for the long-term health of the plant and these should be planted in the dormant winter season.

For fruiting purposes, you should try to get a three- or four-year-old grafted standard or half-standard tree of a known variety. If you wish to plant more than one tree, allow a space of at least 14m (50ft) between them.

Above: *The familiar walnuts are enclosed in a thick husk, which must be removed immediately after harvesting.*

SOIL AND PREFERRED ASPECT

Walnuts grow best in a deep, fertile and well-drained soil. The ideal soil is a deep heavy loam over limestone, with a pH of 7.5–8. Soils that are less alkaline than this will need a dressing of lime at least two months prior to planting. Thoroughly cultivate the ground at the same time, removing all perennial weeds and adding well-rotted compost and a base dressing of fertilizer such as hoof and horn. Choose an open position with shelter from spring frosts to protect young growth and flowers early in the season as temperatures that dip just below freezing may kill the female (nut-generating) flowers.

CULTIVATION

Walnuts are usually grown as standard trees with a strong central leader and can ultimately reach 20m (66ft) or more. The trees can be slow to crop initially, taking five to ten years before they begin cropping.

VARIETIES

'Bijou' This rather tall tree yields large nuts with a good flavour, rough skins and thin shells. The nuts ripen in mid- to late autumn. The nuts tend to lose flavour in storage.

'Cornet du Perogord' The nuts of this variety have a good flavour and are medium to large with a hard shell. The tree is late flowering although the nuts ripen in mid- to late autumn.

'Franquette' The large oval nuts of this tree have a good sweet flavour and moderately thick shells. The tree is late flowering although the nuts ripen in mid- to late autumn. The tree is vigorous and spreading.

'Mayette' The large, round, tapering nuts of this variety have a delicate flavour that is reminiscent of hazelnuts. It is a vigorous, spreading tree and is late flowering with nuts that ripen in late autumn.

walnuts

Despite this they are relatively trouble free and make a fine specimen tree where space allows them to develop fully.

PRUNING

Once the crown of the tree has formed, very little pruning is needed, save to cut out dead, diseased or badly positioned branches. Walnuts can suffer from extensive rot if they are pruned excessively. Any pruning is best done in late summer.

HARVESTING AND STORAGE

Walnuts should be picked up off the ground as soon as they have fallen, and de-husked as soon as possible. They should be scrubbed to remove all the fibres and spread out in a warm place to dry. Walnuts can be stored with alternate layers of equal parts of sawdust and salt for up to six months in a cool, dry, frost-free place.

PESTS AND DISEASES

Walnuts rarely suffer from serious pests and diseases, although honey fungus can cause serious damage and rapid death.

PRUNING AN ESTABLISHED WALNUT STANDARD

Walnuts naturally form quite large trees that do not respond well to excessive pruning. Early formative pruning can be useful and should be limited to removing the lower lateral branches and encouraging a good-shaped head (crown) above a straight stem. Walnuts require little pruning once the head has been formed. Summer is the best time to remove any congestion caused by excessive side growths but this should only be carried out if and when it is required.

APPLES

Malus domestica

There are currently numerous projects being undertaken worldwide to assess which varieties are best for organic garden culture. With such a wide choice of apples, this is a complex undertaking and the best advice is to grow a variety that is suited to your climate and taste. You may wish to consider those that are immune or quite resistant to apple scab. Others seem to be resistant to fireblight. If you choose a non-disease-resistant apple, you will have a very wide range of choice, but you will need to put more effort into controlling pests and diseases.

OBTAINING PLANTS

Propagation of apple trees is usually carried out by grafting a known variety on to a rootstock. This allows the grower to get the particular type of fruit that they want and the rootstock may confer other advantages such as disease resistance or dwarfing of the tree. It is possible to raise trees from seed but the results can be variable at best and at worst disappointing. This does not mean that a chance seedling would not produce a fine-tasting apple but most gardeners opt for the known variety and purchase stock for their gardens.

SOIL AND PREFERRED ASPECT

Apples are hardy in any open, sunny site, provided that it is not too exposed to strong winds. Apples tolerate a broad range of soils but thrive in a clay loam. They prefer a

Above: *Apples, restricted for growing in rows by hard pruning, will still yield large amounts of fruit.*

ROOTSTOCKS

The rootstock on an apple tree affects the size and rate of growth of the tree.

M27 An extreme dwarfing stock (bush, dwarf pyramid, cordon)
M9 Dwarfing stock (bush, dwarf pyramid, cordon)
M26 Semi-dwarfing stock (bush, dwarf pyramid, cordon)
MM106 Semi-dwarfing stock (bush, spindle bush, cordon, fan, espalier)
M7 Semi-dwarfing stock (bush, spindle bush, cordon, fan, espalier)
M4 Semi-vigorous stock (bush, spindle bush)
MM4 Vigorous stock (standard)
M2 Vigorous stock (standard)
MM111 Vigorous stock (half-standard, standard, large bush, large fans, large espaliers)
M25 Vigorous stock (standard)
MM109 Vigorous stock (standard)
M1 Vigorous stock (standard)

PRUNING APPLES

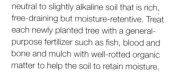

Spur pruning an apple bush tree
After planting, cut back the leader to about 75cm (30in) above the ground. Leave any side shoots that appear just below this cut and remove any others lower down. The following year, reduce all new growth by about half. This will form the basic framework. Subsequent pruning is restricted to reducing the length of new growth by about a third and removing overcrowded growth.

Planting and pruning an apple cordon *These are planted as feather maidens at 45° to the wirework. All side shoots are cut back to three buds on planting. Subsequent summer pruning (far right) consists of cutting back any new side shoots to three leaves and new growth on existing side shoots to one leaf. Winter pruning (right) consists of thinning out any of the older spurs if they have become congested.*

neutral to slightly alkaline soil that is rich, free-draining but moisture-retentive. Treat each newly planted tree with a general-purpose fertilizer such as fish, blood and bone and mulch with well-rotted organic matter to help the soil to retain moisture.

CULTIVATION

Apply mulch at regular intervals as the old mulch gradually breaks down. Keep the trees well watered in dry climates. Every spring, feed each tree with a general-purpose fertilizer. Some varieties only bear well every second year, with light crops every other year. Prevent this by thinning excess fruit in good years to give the tree strength for the following year. A light fall of apples is natural due to poor pollination. Excess fruit drop could be a sign of boron or magnesium deficiency or insufficient moisture.

PRUNING

Flower buds and fruit develop on the tips of the branches or on short two-year-old spurs along the branches. Train apples early in their life to the desired framework. As

HARVESTING AND STORAGE

Harvest the fruit when fully matured and well coloured, according to the variety that you are growing.

PESTS AND DISEASES

If you are putting in trees for the first time, consider planting disease-resistant cultivars. Many new varieties will go a long way towards solving disease problems before they start.

Common diseases include apple scab, which shows as rough spots on fruits and leaves. Powdery mildew appears as a whitish powder on foliage. Both these diseases can be avoided by planting resistant cultivars or using sulphur spray in spring and summer. Fireblight is another problem, causing withering of branch tips, then entire branches, and sometimes, whole trees. Plant resistant cultivars and prune out infected wood. Codling moths create large tunnels to the core of the apples. Wrap tree trunks in corrugated cardboard to trap larvae that have left the fruits and are looking for a place to pupate. You can also use sticky pheromone traps to attract male codling moths.

To avoid some of these diseases, follow commonsense techniques. Prune trees for good air circulation, which lessens fungal problems, and clean up fallen apples.

trees mature, pruning mainly involves removing crowded branches. Annual pruning encourages new growth shoots and continual fruiting spur development. Large vegetative growth may indicate too heavy pruning. A large crop of small fruit indicates too little pruning.

POLLINATION USING CRAB APPLES

All apple varieties, whether they are cooking apples or dessert types, need pollination with another apple variety. This involves planting two trees near to each other. A good way to make sure that most varieties will be pollinated is to use a crab apple with a long flowering period. There are many of these and two of the best varieties for this purpose are listed below. Alternatively, you can purchase trees that have two (or more) varieties grafted on to the one rootstock.

Malus 'John Downie' has a long flowering period and thus pollinates most other apples. It is good for wildlife and very attractive, bearing bright red fruit.

Malus x *zumi* var. *calocarpa* 'Golden Hornet' is a spreading tree which has dark green leaves, white flowers and abundant golden-yellow apples. It is an excellent pollinator.

PEARS

Pyrus communis

Pears are among the easiest of the tree fruits to produce organically because their fertility requirements are not high. They are adapted to a wide range of climates and soils and pest problems are less than for other tree fruits. There are many varieties of pear. Asian and European pears can pollinate each other, but Asian pears often finish blooming by the time Europeans get started. For cross-pollination between pear species, avoid teaming early bloomers among the Asians, such as 'Seuri' and 'Yali', with late bloomers among the Europeans, such as 'Comice' and 'Ubileen.'

OBTAINING PLANTS

Pears can be grown from seed, but you cannot guarantee the quality of the resulting fruit. It is better to purchase known stock from a recognized nursery.

SOIL AND PREFERRED ASPECT

Pears are hardy in any open, sunny site, provided that it is not too exposed to strong winds. They can grow in most soils, but a moderately rich, well-draining soil that is neutral or slightly alkaline is usually best. Very rich soils will stimulate rapid leafy growth that can be disease susceptible and

ROOTSTOCKS

As with apples, the rootstock on which a pear tree grows affects the size and rate of growth of the tree.

Quince C Moderately dwarfing stock (bush, cordon, dwarf pyramid, espalier or fan)
Quince A Semi-vigorous stock (bush, cordon, dwarf pyramid, espalier or fan)
Pear Vigorous stock (standard, half-standard)

Right: *Most pears are ready for picking by the autumn, but they must be fully ripened off the tree.*

there is therefore no need to add lots of organic matter unless the soil is very poor or excessively free draining.

CULTIVATION

European pears Pears, like most other fruit trees, are grown by grafting the variety on to a rootstock. Seedlings of European pears (often from Bartlett pears) are usually used for rootstocks. Plant standard-sized trees about 5–8m (16–26ft) apart and dwarf trees about 3–4.5m (10–15ft) apart. Some varieties of pear always need cross-pollination, while others are reliably self-fertile.

Asian pears These are slightly less cold hardy than European types and may suffer tissue damage at temperatures below -20°C (-4°F). Most Asian pears also bloom slightly earlier than their European counterparts and may lose some blooms or buds to freezing in areas that are prone to late frosts. Growing Asian pears is similar to growing European types, but not identical. Asian pears tend to set too heavy a fruit crop, which requires hand thinning of young fruits soon after bloom to ensure a good crop. If heavy-bearing Asian pear varieties are not properly thinned, then the fruit size and quality will suffer.

PRUNING PEARS

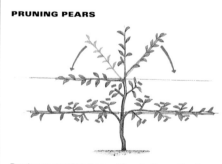

Pruning an espaliered pear *After planting, cut back to two buds above the bottom wire. In the first summer, tie the central growth to a vertical cane and the next two shoots to canes at 45°. Cut back all other shoots to two leaves. In autumn, lower the two side shoots to the horizontal and tie the cane to the bottom wire. In winter, cut back the leader to two buds above the second wire and repeat the above until the espalier covers all the wires. When established, cut back all new shoots to three leaves each summer.*

Pruning a dwarf pyramid pear *After planting, cut back the leader by about a third. Cut back the side shoots to about 15cm (6in). In the first summer, cut back the new growth on the main side shoots to about five leaves and on the secondary shoots to three leaves. Thereafter, cut back new growth on the main stems to five leaves and reduce other new growth to one leaf. During the winter, thin out any congested spurs.*

PRUNING

Pruning pears is generally similar to that of apple trees and involves cutting off unnecessary branches so that light can reach all parts of the tree. Pear trees are also best kept quite low to make it easier to pick the fruit.

HARVESTING AND STORAGE

Bartlett pears ripen in summer, but most other varieties ripen later, usually in early autumn. European pears ripen to perfection only when they are removed from the tree and so are picked while they are still green and hard. The fruit will ripen in a cool place where the temperature does not exceed 24°C (75°F). Asian pears, however, will ripen on the tree and do not have to be picked and then cured like European pears. Pick them once they colour up, when they should be sweet.

PESTS AND DISEASES

Pears have most of the same pest and disease problems as apples, but usually to a considerably lesser degree. One problem that can cause serious damage is fireblight. Fireblight is greatly favoured by young, succulent tissues and it is better to try and limit the rate of growth to avoid this. Never try to compensate for rapid growth rates by pruning, as this will only stimulate the production of more susceptible soft tissue growth. Using less compost than for

apples, never using manure, not applying large amounts of fertilizer and avoiding growing clovers and other legumes around the tree will ultimately yield better results.

Choosing fireblight-resistant pear cultivars is also a good start, but cultural controls are the best way to limit the spread of this disease. As a group, it is probably accurate to say that Asian pears are slightly more resistant to fireblight than European types. Once fireblight infection has occurred, there is no spray or other treatment (beyond quickly cutting out newly infected limbs) that will minimize damage. If cutting during the growing season, all blighted twigs, branches and cankers should be removed at least 10cm (4in) below the last point of visible infection, and burned. After each cut, the secateurs (hand pruners) should be sterilized in a disinfectant solution. During winter, when temperatures render the bacteria inactive, pruning out of fireblight-infected wood can proceed without sterilization.

The codling moth is probably the most important direct pest of the fruit. Capsid bugs and other "true" bugs will also feed on pears. Early feeding damage may result in a puckering or dimpling. Mid- and late-season feeding often leads to the development of so-called "stone cells" beneath the feeding site. The best way to deal with insect pests is to encourage natural predators such as lacewings around your pear tree.

Above: Pear trees can be trained into a variety of decorative shapes such as this elegant cone.

VARIETIES

EUROPEAN PEARS

'Bartlett' Ripens mid-season but stores poorly. Blooms early and so needs an early companion variety for pollination. Fruit tolerates intense sun better than average.

'Beth' An excellent, English-bred, self-fertile dessert pear that fruits in mid-autumn. A high-yielding and regular cropper, with white flesh that has a melting texture and excellent flavour. Will commence fruiting from early in its life.

'Comice' Juicy, yellow fruit with good flesh that ripens in mid-autumn, but will keep till mid-winter. Resists fireblight. Best in mild winters. Blooms very late, so not a reliable pollinator for early-blooming varieties.

'Conference' The large, yellow fruit is juicy and sweet, ripening in mid-autumn and keeping till mid-winter. Blooms early and will cross-pollinate with most Asian pears.

'Ubileen' An early ripener (but not bloomer), usually picked in mid-summer and ripening in late summer. The large fruit is yellow with a red blush and a buttery texture. This variety is quite disease resistant.

ASIAN PEARS

'Chojura' A late-blooming variety that has russeted fruit, with slightly astringent skin, which ripens in early autumn and keeps well.

'Seuri' This productive, fireblight-resistant and cold-hardy variety has very large orange fruit that ripens in mid-autumn and does not keep well. This variety blooms very early and is best planted with another early bloomer such as 'Yali'. It will not reliably pollinate any European pear.

'Shinsui' This variety forms a vigorous, upright tree with russeted fruit that is small, juicy and sweet.

'Yali' A hardy variety with deep red autumn foliage. The fruit is classically pear-shaped, yellow and ripens in mid-autumn. This early-blooming variety is a reliable pollinator only for 'Seuri' and other early-blooming varieties (not Europeans) and needs a fairly long cold season.

pears

APRICOTS

Prunus armeniaca

Apricots originally come from warm climates so will need a sunny sheltered spot in cooler regions. In temperate climates, they are best grown as fans against a sunny wall or in a greenhouse, although they can be grown as dwarf pyramid trees in warmer areas.

Left: *Apricots make fine specimens when trained as fans. Canes and wires help to maintain the shape.*

OBTAINING PLANTS

Apricots are propagated by budding them on to rootstocks. Most apricot plants are obtained as bought plants from specialist nurseries. Trees are usually planted during the dormant winter period. Only plant freestanding bush trees in warmer areas where the early flowers will not be damaged by early spring frosts.

SOIL AND PREFERRED ASPECT

Apricots require a moisture-retentive, friable and well-drained soil, rarely prospering in a stiff clay or heavy loam, and a sunny, sheltered site. A pH of 6–6.5 is desirable.

CULTIVATION

Water regularly in the first season and subsequently in dry spells as mature trees may wilt badly. Saturate greenhouse soils in late winter and mulch with well-rotted organic material. Protect the blossom of outdoor specimens from frost by draping horticultural fleece over the trees at night and removing it by day to allow pollinating insects to work. It may be necessary to assist pollination in cooler areas and under glass by hand.

If the fruit set is heavy, then the crop may need thinning. This is done first at "pea-size" to one fruitlet per cluster, then again after stoning, and when the natural drop is over. Test for stoning by pressing a pin into a few fruitlets. The final spacing of fruit should be about 8–15cm (3¼–6in) apart.

Plants up to fruiting age should be fed in early spring with a general-purpose fertilizer such as fish, blood and bone to encourage growth. Once they reach fruiting age, mulch annually with well-rotted farmyard manure.

PRUNING

Fruit forms on both young wood and old spurs and so it is best to maintain a proportion of each. Shorten the leaders annually by one-third and tie in one healthy shoot per 25cm (10in) of main branch, remove ill-placed and upright growing shoots. Pinch back the rest to four leaves from early summer onwards. Prune fan-trained specimens every year.

ROOTSTOCK
The rootstock will affect the size and rate of growth of the tree.
St Julien A Semi-vigorous stock (bush, fan)
Brompton A Vigorous stock (bush)

HARVESTING AND STORAGE

Leave to ripen on the tree to develop their flavour. The fruit is ripe when it comes away easily by lifting it with a twisting motion.

PESTS AND DISEASES

The main diseases are silver leaf, bacterial canker and brown rot diseases. Aphids, wasps and flies are the main pests.

PRUNING AN ESTABLISHED APRICOT FAN

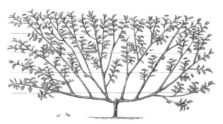

Once the fan has been established, the object of subsequent pruning is to maintain the shape. Cut out any shoots that are pointing in the wrong direction, especially those that point towards or away from the wall. Thin new shoots, leaving one every 15cm (6in). Prune the remaining shoots to five leaves in the spring and then again, after fruiting, back to three leaves.

VARIETIES

'Alfred' Produces fruit of a good flavour that is orange with a pink flush. Fruit ripens in mid- to late summer. A vigorous tree that flowers early and tends to crop biennially.

'Breda' This variety has fruit that is medium to large and orange with a dark red flush. It ripens against a wall in late summer or early autumn in the open. Heavy cropping, but tends to be short-lived.

'Moorpark' An extremely popular variety that has large fruit of a rich sweet flavour. It is a regular cropper that ripens in late summer. A moderately vigorous plant that is prone to dieback.

apricots

PLUMS

Prunus domestica and *P. salicina*

Plums are divided into two categories: the European plum, *Prunus domestica*, and the Japanese plum, *P. salicina*. European plums are usually self-fertile, but cross-pollination will ensure a better crop. Japanese plums are mostly self-infertile. There are many suitable cultivars but the most popular are the ones that provide fruit until late in the growing season.

OBTAINING PLANTS

Plums are almost always obtained as bought plants from specialist nurseries. There is no truly satisfactory dwarfing rootstock for plums, although trees are sometimes grown on rootstocks described as "semi-dwarf". Even these would be too large for a small garden, as a bush-type tree requires a spacing of 4–5m (13–16ft).

SOIL AND PREFERRED ASPECT

Plums need a well-drained soil, with plenty of organic material to hold moisture in the growing season, and a pH of 6.0– 6.5. An acid soil can be limed, but do not plant in an alkaline soil. Trees in thin soils over chalk often suffer from lime-induced iron deficiency. Grow fan-trained plums against a sunny wall.

Above: *While this cluster of plums growing against a sunny wall looks very appetizing, it could have been thinned earlier to ensure larger fruit.*

CULTIVATION

Plant plums between late autumn and early spring. Stake and mulch with well-rotted manure. An established plum needs plenty of nitrogen but, until good crops are being carried, it is usually sufficient to mulch with rotted manure or compost in spring. When crops are being borne, supplement the yearly mulch with a dressing of pelleted chicken manure.

PRUNING

Plums are not very amenable to training, and are seldom satisfactory as cordons or espaliers. They may, however, be grown as

fans for wall-training or with the support of posts and horizontal wires. Root-pruning will probably be necessary every five years to restrain growth and maintain fruiting.

Plums may also be grown as semi-dwarf pyramids on a St Julien A rootstock. Such a tree requires a spacing of 3.5m (12ft).

HARVESTING AND STORAGE

Leave on the tree until ripe, then handle carefully. Pick when a bloom appears on the skin for cooking or preserves.

PESTS AND DISEASES

The main problems are aphids, red spider mite, plum sawfly, wasps and birds as well as rust, silver leaf and bacterial canker.

ROOTSTOCK

The rootstock chosen for a plum tree affects the size and rate of growth.

Pixy Dwarfing stock (bush, pyramid)
Damas C Moderately vigorous stock
St Julien A Semi-vigorous stock (bush, fan, pyramid)
Brompton A Vigorous stock (half-standard, standard)
Myrobalan B Vigorous stock (half-standard, standard)

PRUNING AN ESTABLISHED PLUM FAN

Pruning a plum fan in spring and summer
The main aim when pruning a plum fan is to maintain the fan shape. In spring (above left), cut out any new side shoots that are pointing to or away from the wall. If necessary, reduce the number of new shoots to about one every 15cm (6in). In summer (below left), cut back all new shoots to about six leaves, leaving any that are needed to fill in gaps in the framework. In autumn, after cropping, further cut back the shoots to three leaves.

VARIETIES

'Czar' A reliable bearer of juicy, blue-black fruit with yellow-green flesh in late summer. A fairly compact tree, hardy and usually frost-resistant. Succeeds in shade and fully self-fertile.
'Merryweather' A self-fertile damson, with large, blue-black fruit. Fruits well into the autumn.
'Victoria' Pale red, oval fruits with a greeny-yellow flesh. It can be a heavy cropper on a reasonably frost-free site and is fully self-fertile, bearing fruit in late summer to early autumn.

red plums   yellow plums

PEACHES AND NECTARINES

Prunus persica and *P. persica nectarina*

Peaches and nectarines are identical in all their cultivation requirements, although peaches are slightly hardier and more reliable in cooler areas. They both originate in warm climates and so need a sunny, sheltered spot. For this reason, they are best grown as fans against a sunny wall or in a greenhouse.

Both peaches and nectarines are self-fertile, so only one plant need be grown` if space is limited. They do not fruit until their fourth year of growing but will live for about 30 years once established.

OBTAINING PLANTS

Both peaches and nectarines are grown from stock bought from specialist nurseries. They are are normally planted during their dormant phase in winter. They are not particularly vigorous and dwarfing rootstocks are not essential. If you intend growing peaches or nectarines as a fan, use a plant that is grafted on to St Julien A or Brompton rootstock. If a very small bush is required for container growing, use a plant on Pixy rootstock.

SOIL AND PREFERRED ASPECT

Peaches and nectarines require very fertile, deep, well-drained loam, with a pH of 6.5–7.0. Full sun is essential if the bushes are to prosper. Only plant freestanding bush trees in warmer areas where early flowers will not be damaged by early spring frosts. If these are a problem grow as a fan against a sunny wall for protection.

Above: *Peaches, grown as fans, are both a decorative and productive way to cover a sunny wall.*

ROOTSTOCKS

The rootstock will affect the size and rate of growth of the tree.

Pixy Dwarfing stock (small bush)
St Julien A Semi-vigorous stock (bush, fan)
Brompton A Vigorous stock (bush)

CULTIVATION

Plants that have not reached fruiting age should be fed in early spring with a general-purpose fertilizer such as fish, blood and bone to encourage growth. Once they reach fruiting age, mulch annually with well-rotted farmyard manure. Protect the flowers from frost in the early part of the year with a horticultural fleece drape, ensuring that this is removed during the day to allow access for pollinating insects (smaller plants can be hand pollinated using a small sable brush). Never allow plants to become drought stressed once fruit has set, particularly when plants are growing against a sunny wall.

PRUNING

Like other stone fruit, never prune in the winter due to the risk of infection from silver leaf and bacterial canker. Prune freestanding trees in early spring by removing dead or diseased wood, crossing branches that can cause damage by rubbing and overcrowded branches. Prune fan-trained bushes every year. They are pruned by a renewal method in a similar way to that used for fan-trained cherries.

HARVESTING AND STORAGE

Allow to ripen fully before harvesting. The fruit is ripe when it comes away from the tree easily. Store for a few days once picked. Preserve for later use as freezing destroys much of the fruit's texture.

PESTS AND DISEASES

Both peaches and nectarines are prone to the same ailments. Common diseases include peach leaf curl, silver leaf, bacterial canker and mildew. Pests are only an occasional problem, the most serious ones being aphids and red spider mites. Scale insects can be a problem in the greenhouse.

PRUNING AN ESTABLISHED PEACH BUSH TREE

Not a great deal of pruning is required for a peach bush tree. In spring, cut back some of the older barren wood as far as a replacement new shoot. Also remove any awkwardly placed branches and keep the bush open and airy. Avoid making large cuts, as this is likely to allow canker to infect the tree.

VARIETIES

PEACHES

'Amsden June' Produces fruit with a good flavour. Ripens in mid-summer. Grow under glass or in the open.
'Peregrine' Large, round, crimson fruit with an excellent flavour. Crops well, ripening in late summer. Is suitable for growing in the open in warmer areas.

NECTARINES

'Early Rivers' Large yellow fruits with a rich flavour. Ripens in mid-summer.
'Lord Napier' Large yellow-orange fruits with a rich flavour. Ripens in late summer.

nectarines

peaches

CHERRIES

Prunus species

There are two main groups of cherry that are cultivated for their fruit: the sweet or dessert cherry (*Prunus avium*) and the acid or sour cherry (*Prunus cerasus*). The sweet is the type eaten as a raw dessert fruit, whereas the acid is usually cooked.

OBTAINING PLANTS

Named varieties are propagated on to rootstocks by budding in mid- or late summer or by grafting in early spring. There is currently no dwarfing rootstock available and a mature sweet cherry tree may grow up to 10m (33ft) in height. Bush Morello (acid) trees, on the other hand, rarely reach a height of 5m (16ft). Many varieties can be grown as fan-trained specimens.

SOIL AND PREFERRED ASPECT

Grow in a deep, very fertile, well-drained loam with a pH of 6.0–7.0. Sweet cherries need full sun, but acid cherries prefer light shade and can be trained as fans against a wall receiving little sun.

CULTIVATION

Plant at any time from mid-autumn to early spring. Mulch trees annually with manure or compost and feed fan-trained specimens regularly with a liquid feed.

Above: Few fruits can rival fresh juicy cherries that have been ripened to perfection on the bush.

PRUNING

Standard and bush trees need little pruning. Maintain an open, balanced habit and remove dead, crossing and rubbing branches. Sour cherries fruit on shoots formed the previous season. For fan training, after the basic fan of branches has been built up, annually replaced side growths are tied in parallel to the permanent branches. The replacement shoots are selected during late spring through to late summer.

HARVESTING AND STORAGE

Leave to ripen on the tree for as long as possible. Sweet cherries are best eaten at once but acid cherries can be stored for a few days. Freeze or preserve to store for longer.

SWEET CHERRY POLLINATION GROUPS

Cherries fruit best if grown near to another variety from the same group that flowers at the same time. This is not necessary for self-pollinating varieties such as 'Morello' or 'Stella'. Flowering period: (e) early; (m) mid-season; (l) late.

Group 1 'Early Rivers' (e), 'Bedford Prolific' (e), 'Knight's Early Black' (e), 'Roundel Heart' (m)
Group 2 'Bigarreau de Schrecken' (e), 'Waterloo' (e), 'Merton Favourite' (e), 'Frogmore Early' (m), 'Merton Bigarreau' (m), 'Merton Bounty' (m)
Group 3 'Bigarreau Napoleon' (m), 'Emperor Francis' (m)
Group 4 'Merton Premier' (m), 'Amber Heart' (m)
Group 5 'Merton Heart' (e), 'Governor Wood' (m)
Group 6 'Bradbourne Black' (l), 'Geante de Hedelfingen' (l)
Universal Donors 'Noir de Guben' (e); 'Merton Glory' (m), 'Bigarreau Gaucher' (l)

PESTS AND DISEASES

Bacterial canker and silver leaf, both of which are spread by pruning. The main pests are birds, blackfly (aphids) and winter moths.

PRUNING ESTABLISHED CHERRY TREES

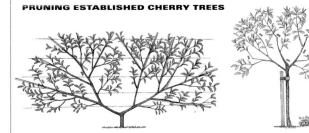

Sour cherry fan *Once established, there are two purposes to pruning a cherry fan: to keep the fan shape and to ensure that there is a constant supply of new wood. To keep the shape completely, remove any shoots that are pointing in the wrong direction. For renewal, cut back in summer all shoots that have fruited, preferably as far back as the next new shoot. Tie these new shoots to the cane and wire framework.*

Sour cherry bush or tree *Once established, bush and full-sized sour cherry trees need little pruning other than to remove a third of the old fruiting wood, cutting back to a new growth. You should also remove any branches that are crossing.*

VARIETIES
DESSERT
'Bradbourne Black' A large, rich, dark crimson cherry that ripens in mid-summer and is a heavy cropper.
'Kentish Red' A bush of medium vigour that ripens in mid- to late summer. Good on a non-sunny wall. Fruits have a good resistance to bacterial canker.
'Stella' A vigorous variety with large, dark red fruits. A heavy-yielding variety that is also self-compatible.

ACID
'Morello' Juicy fruit with a bitter-sweet flavour when ripe. Crops regularly and is moderately vigorous, ripening in summer to early autumn.

cherries

BLACKCURRANTS

Ribes nigrum

Blackcurrants need a lot of space but are worth growing, as they are extremely high in vitamin C. Aside from this they are one of the true pleasures of summer and more than compensate for their space demands. They also have the advantage of being self-fertile, which means that you only need to grow one bush in order to get a good crop.

OBTAINING PLANTS

Blackcurrants can be propagated quite easily from hardwood cuttings during the dormant season. Choose healthy, blemish-free branches from the previous season's growth that are about 15–20cm (6–8in) long and about the thickness of a pencil. These will make good plants in about three years. More usually, however, plants are bought in.

SOIL AND PREFERRED ASPECT

Blackcurrants are heavy feeders that need a deep, fertile and well-drained soil. It is well worth while taking the time to prepare the soil properly prior to planting. The ideal soil pH is 6.5 and the site should be sheltered and sunny. Blackcurrants will tolerate light shade but the amount of fruit produced will be less.

CULTIVATION

Bare-rooted stock is planted in late autumn or early winter, whereas container-grown stock can be planted out at any time of the year. Plants should be spaced 1.8m (6ft) apart with 2m (6½ft) between rows.

Above: *Blackcurrants should be picked as whole trusses complete with the stalks to prevent damage.*

Blackcurrants grow as stooled bushes, which means that they send up new shoots from below ground level. When planting, set the plant 5cm (2in) lower in the ground than it was when grown in the nursery or pot, as this will encourage the formation of new shoots. Ensure that you cut back all the shoots to ground level after planting.

Blackcurrants have a high nitrogen requirement and need feeding with about 100g (4oz) fish, blood and bone or a similar organic compound fertilizer in spring. They benefit from a mulch of well-rotted manure or garden compost and, if growth seems poor, give a further feed in early summer.

PRUNING

Blackcurrants are always grown as freestanding bushes, so no support or training is needed. They produce fruit on wood made the previous year which means

that in the first year, little or no pruning will be needed, save removing dead, diseased or damaged branches. The second and subsequent years' pruning involves cutting the fruited wood back to ground level to encourage further strong growth. This is done in late summer after fruiting and, as the bushes get older, you may find that fewer shoots are produced from below ground level. If this happens, prune out all the old wood as low as possible just above a young shoot.

It is best to work on a three-year cycle, in the third year cutting out the first year's wood, in the fourth year cutting out the second year's growth, etc. This keeps the bush with a set of branches that will fruit and a set that will fruit the following year.

HARVESTING AND STORAGE

Pick the fruits as clumps when they are ripe. Some gardeners prefer to cut out the whole branch for convenience because this also prunes the bush at the same time. Blackcurrants are practically impossible to store fresh and are best eaten straightaway. They can be frozen or preserved as jelly.

PESTS AND DISEASES

Commonly encountered diseases include mildew, botrytis, leaf spot and reversion disease. The more commonly encountered pests are aphids, sawfly, big bud mite and birds. Provide netting in order to protect against marauding birds.

PRUNING A BLACKCURRANT BUSH

After planting, cut blackcurrant bushes back to a single bud above the ground. The following winter, remove any weak or misplaced growth. Subsequent pruning should take place after fruiting and consists of cutting out up to a third of two-year-old or older wood in order to stimulate new growth. Also remove any weak or misplaced stems.

RED AND WHITE CURRANTS

Ribes rubrum

Red and white currants are relatively easy to grow, even tolerating a little light shade. They can be grown as a bush or trained on walls. Currants fruit on wood that is one year old or off spurs on very old wood. The limited range of varieties belies their versatility as a culinary fruit.

OBTAINING PLANTS

Currants are usually bought in or raised from hardwood cuttings taken during the dormant period.

SOIL AND PREFERRED ASPECT

Grow in a deep, fertile and well-drained soil that has had well-rotted garden compost or manure worked in. The pH of the soil should be kept at about 6.5 to maintain healthy growth. The site should be sheltered and sunny to ensure the best cropping. Currants flower in early spring, so may need some form of protection against frost.

CULTIVATION

Plant bare-rooted stock in autumn or early winter and plants raised in containers at any time. Allow 1.8m (6ft) between plants and 2m (6½ft) between rows. When planting, set the plant at the same level as it was in the nursery or pot. Single cordons should be planted so that the arms are 30cm (12in) apart, double cordons 60cm (24in) apart and triple cordons 90cm (36in) apart.

All varieties of currant are self-fertile, making them ideal for even the smallest of

Above: *Red currants should only be picked when the fruit is fully ripe and has turned completely red.*

Above: *Red and white currants, grown here as cordons, are tied to vertical canes that are attached to lateral wires.*

gardens. They require a lot of potassium to flourish and will need feeding each spring. A browning on the leaf margins indicates a potassium deficiency, best countered with a liquid foliar feed of seaweed extract.

PRUNING

Freestanding bushes need training to produce a strong cup-shaped bush. Prune the bush in the summer, immediately after harvesting. Reduce the side shoots to five leaves and when the main stems have reached the desired height, treat these in the same way.

Train cordon-grown currants upwards rather than at an angle by pruning the main arms in winter. Cut back the leading shoot, leaving two-thirds of the last season's growth. The following summer, prune after harvesting by cutting any side shoots back to 7cm (2¾in) and any secondary shoots back to 2.5cm (1in).

Pruning a red or white currant cordon *On planting, cut back the leader by half of its new growth and the side shoots to one bud. Thereafter, cut back the side shoots every summer to five leaves and, in winter, further reduce these to one bud.*

Pruning a red or white currant bush *After planting, cut back each shoot by about half. Subsequent pruning involves ensuring that the plant becomes an open bush. Cut back all new growth on the main shoots and reduce the new growth on all side shoots to one bud.*

VARIETIES
RED CURRANT
'Red Lake'
Long trusses of large red berries in mid-summer. An excellent cropping variety.

red currants

WHITE CURRANT
'White Versailles'
A large currant in mid-summer. Excellent variety for making jams.

white currants

HARVESTING AND STORAGE

Pick the sprigs of fruit whole when ripe. Eat straightaway, preserve as jelly or freeze.

PESTS AND DISEASES

Currants are generally trouble free if grown in good soil and well fed. Common diseases include mildew and leaf spot, while pests include aphids, sawfly and birds.

GOOSEBERRIES

Ribes uva-crispum

Gooseberries are one of the earliest soft fruits of the year. The traditional method of growing was as a bush but modern techniques include single, double and triple cordons. Cordons can take up as little as 15cm (6in) of growing space. All varieties are self-fertile, so only one plant can be grown if space is at a premium.

OBTAINING PLANTS

Gooseberry plants should be bought from a reputable organic supplier.

SOIL AND PREFERRED ASPECT

Gooseberries do best in a soil with a pH of 6.5 in a sunny, sheltered site. Fork over a wide area to break up the soil and remove weeds before digging the planting hole. Add garden compost or rotted manure to the soil at the base of the pit, along with about 50g (1¾oz) of fish, blood and bone or a similar general-purpose organic fertilizer.

CULTIVATION

Plant bare-rooted stock in autumn or early winter and container-grown plants at any time. Gooseberries are grown on a "leg" or stem so cut back all the side shoots before planting. Spread out the roots of bare-rooted bushes in the hole and cover with well-conditioned soil. Firm the soil around the roots. With container-grown bushes, keep the surface of the rootball level with the surrounding soil. Apply two handfuls of bonemeal to the soil when filling in and mulch with a well-rotted manure or compost. Plant bushes 1.2–1.8m (4–6ft) apart in rows, depending on the vigour of the variety. Allow a spacing of around 2m (6½ft) between each row. Plant single cordons

Above: *Start picking gooseberries before the first berries are fully ripe in order to give the remainder an opportunity to ripen.*

30cm (12in) apart, double cordons 60cm (24in) apart and triple cordons 90cm (36in) apart, allowing 1.2m (4ft) between rows.

Keep well watered until established, and cover the soil around them with a 5–7.5cm (2–3in) thick mulch of compost or bark.

Freestanding bushes need no support. Cordons require wires, either attached to the fence or to posts. Gooseberries need high levels of potassium and feeding with a general-purpose fertilizer in spring as well as mulching with well-rotted manure or compost. If growth is poor, feed again in early summer. Browning of the leaves indicates a potash deficiency; apply a liquid foliar feed of seaweed extract. Cover the fruits with fleece to protect against frost.

PRUNING

Prune freestanding bushes after harvesting by reducing side shoots to five leaves. Treat the main stems in the same way when they reach their required height and cut out any damaged, dead or overcrowded stems. Prune cordons after harvesting by cutting any side shoots to 7cm (2¾in) and any secondary shoots to 2.5cm (1in).

HARVESTING AND STORAGE

Start picking heavy crops before they are fully ripe to allow remaining berries to ripen. Use the unripe berries in cooking. Eat straightaway, freeze or preserve.

PESTS AND DISEASES

Mildew and leaf spot are common. Pests are usually limited to aphids, sawfly and birds. Protect against birds with netting.

Left: *Gooseberries make excellent cordons. Train them up canes that are supported by lateral wires.*

PRUNING A GOOSEBERRY

The basic aim when pruning gooseberries is to create an open framework. Establish a framework, first of all, by removing the basal shoots and cutting back the main shoots by about half in their first and second years. After this, cut back the new growth on the leaders in winter by about half and reduce the side shoots from these to two buds. Remove any damaged wood and any branches that cross or rub. Remove suckers and basal growth. In summer, prune the side shoots back to five leaves, but leave the main stems uncut.

VARIETIES

'Careless' Large green-skinned fruits ripening to white in summer. A reliable and heavy-yielding variety.

'Keepsake' Excellent flavoured fruits that are green-white in colour, transparent and slightly hairy. Can be picked early for cooking.

'Lancashire Lad' This bush produces large, dark red, oblong, hairy fruits that are extremely juicy. It has some resistance to mildew.

'Leveller' A fertile soil is required to ensure heavy cropping. This variety produces large, oval, yellow-green fruits with a slightly hairy skin and an excellent flavour.

gooseberries

RASPBERRIES

Rubus idaeus

Raspberries are unique because their roots and crowns are perennial, while their stems or canes are biennial. During the first growing season, the shoots of summer-bearing raspberries are strictly vegetative (non-fruiting). The following year, these canes flower, produce fruit, and then die. Autumn-bearing raspberries, on the other hand, produce fruit in the autumn at the tips of the current season's growth.

OBTAINING PLANTS

Raspberry bushes are almost always bought plants, although it is possible to raise them from seed. Existing bushes can be divided in winter and are usually available in late winter as bare-rooted plants in bundles.

SOIL AND PREFERRED ASPECT

Raspberries require an open sunny site, although they tolerate slight shade, and prefer a deep, well-drained but moisture-retentive soil with a pH of around 6.0. They suffer iron deficiency above a pH of 7.0.

CULTIVATION

Raspberries, whether bare-rooted or container-grown, should be planted out in late autumn or early winter. Plant them a little deeper than they were in the pot or nursery and space 45cm (18in) apart with 1.8m (6ft) between rows. Cut the canes to 15cm (6in) above ground and water thoroughly after planting. Winter-planted specimens will commence growth in the spring and produce tall canes. Raspberries need little or no feeding once they have been planted. Mulch, applied in the spring, will usually supply their nutrient needs.

Above: Wires fixed to a sturdy wooden framework support this flourishing double row of raspberries.

PRUNING

AUTUMN-BEARING RASPBERRIES

In early spring, prune back all canes to ground level and maintain the plants in a 30–60cm (12–24in) wide "hedgerow". No summer pruning is necessary.

SUMMER-BEARING RASPBERRIES

In early or mid-spring, remove all weak, diseased and damaged canes at ground level. Leave the most vigorous canes, those about 1cm (½in) in diameter when measured 90cm (3ft) from the ground. Space the remaining canes about 15cm (6in) apart and cut back the tips to live tissue if any have died back in winter. Maintain plants in a 30–60cm (12–24in) wide "hedgerow" and remove old fruiting canes at the soil surface after the last harvest of the summer, as this encourages the growth of new shoots the following year.

VARIETIES

EARLY AND MID-SEASON VARIETIES
'Glen Clova' Small- to medium-sized fruits that have a mild flavour. It is a heavy cropper with strong growth.
'Malling Jewel' Sweet-tasting, medium to large, red fruits.
'Malling Promise' Full-flavoured large red berries. A heavy yielding variety that is a vigorous grower.

AUTUMN FRUITING VARIETIES
'Fallgold' Produces yellow sweet-tasting fruits on vigorous canes. Ripens in early autumn.
'Heritage' Mild-flavoured round red berries. A prolific producer that requires a sunny location.
'Zeva' Dark red fruits that are prone to crumbling. A less vigorous variety that ripens in early autumn.

raspberries

HARVESTING AND STORAGE

Raspberries should be picked early in the morning before it gets too hot. They can be eaten fresh, preserved or frozen.

PESTS AND DISEASES

The main diseases that commonly affect raspberries are botrytis (fruit rot), mildew, late leaf rust (*Puccianiastrum americanum*) and *Phytophthora* (root rot) on wet sites. They may be affected by a number of pests including aphids, raspberry beetle, two-spotted spider mite, Japanese beetle, tarnished plant bug, cane borers and clipper beetle. Netting may also be needed as protection against bird damage.

GROWING RASPBERRIES ON POSTS AND WIRES

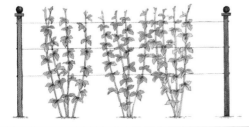

It is essential that raspberries have a strong supporting system of posts and wires. The plants are set at 45cm (18in) intervals. Each year, new raspberry canes are thrown up. When fruiting has finished on the old canes, these are cut out and the new canes are tied to the wires in their place. This sequence is followed every year. Raspberry plants put out suckers which can become established in the gangways between the rows. These should be dug up as soon as they appear.

BLACKBERRIES

Rubus fruticosus

Wild blackberries are gathered in late summer and early autumn in many areas. Growing blackberries offers the promise of high-quality fruit as well as ease of harvesting. The fruit of home-cultivated blackberries is usually much larger and often sweeter. Thornless varieties will make picking much easier.

OBTAINING PLANTS

Blackberries are usually propagated in late winter or early spring by planting root cuttings from healthy plants. Root cuttings should be 10–15cm (4–6in) long and about 1cm (½in) thick. Plant these cuttings 60cm (24in) apart in rows spaced 3m (10ft) apart for a "hedgerow". The root cuttings are best placed about 2–5cm (¾–2in) deep. Prepare the soil first by adding plenty of well-rotted compost and a generous base dressing of general-purpose fertilizer such as fish, blood and bone. Add more fertilizer about one month after planting and again in early to mid-summer.

SOIL AND PREFERRED ASPECT

Blackberries are hardy in any open, sunny site, provided that it is not too exposed to strong winds. They grow on a wide range of soil types. A soil pH of 6.0–6.5 is best, but blackberries will grow in soils ranging from a pH 4.5–7.5. A deep, fine, sandy loam is ideal, but blackberries grow well in heavier soils if they are well drained.

Above: *Blackberries often fruit over a long season, starting in late summer and lasting until late autumn.*

CULTIVATION

Canes from erect blackberries will be semi-erect or almost trailing in the first growing season. They should be kept in the row area since they will produce fruit the next year.

PRUNING

Blackberry canes are biennial. Vegetative canes develop the first year, bear fruit the second year, and die after fruiting. New canes produced in the second and later years will be erect and should be cut to a height of 1–1.2m (3–4ft) in mid-summer to encourage lateral branching. Prune hedgerows to a width of about 1–1.2m (3–4ft).

HARVESTING AND STORAGE

Blackberries need to be harvested when fully ripe, as they will not ripen after harvesting. Harvested fruit should not be allowed to sit in the sun and needs to be chilled as soon after harvesting as possible. Most blackberry varieties do not freeze particularly well and are best eaten fresh. Alternatively, they can be made into jelly or stewed before freezing.

PESTS AND DISEASES

While most blackberries are trouble free, spur blight, mildew, botrytis and cane spot are occasional disease problems. Pests are also mercifully few but can include wasps, aphids and raspberry beetle. Birds also love this summer treat and the plants may need protection with netting during their fruiting period.

VARIETIES

'Himalayan Giant' Sharp-flavoured blackberry that is a heavy cropper. Vigorous growth in stems and strong thorns.

'Oregon Thornless' A cut-leaved, thorn-free form of the blackberry. Berries are small, mild and sweet, ripening in early autumn.

'Smoothstem' Large shiny fruits that are rather sharp in taste. Enjoys a sunny location.

 blackberries

METHODS OF TRAINING BLACKBERRIES

Alternate bay *One way in which you can train blackberries is to tie all the new growth to one side of the wirework. After fruiting, remove the previous year's growth from the other side and then use this for the next year's new growth. Repeat each year.*

Rope training *A second way to train blackberries is to temporarily tie in all new growth vertically to the wirework and along the top wire. The current fruiting canes are tied in groups horizontally. These are removed after fruiting and the new growth tied into their place.*

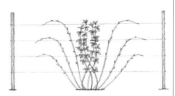

Fan training *The new canes are temporarily tied vertically and along the top wire, while the fruiting canes are tied in singly along the wires. Any excess canes are removed. After fruiting, these canes are taken out and the new growth tied into their place.*

BLUEBERRIES

Vaccinium corymbosum and *V. ashei*

Blueberries are divided into two main groups: lowland blueberries (*Vaccinium ashei*), which include the whinberries or bilberries, and the better known blueberries (*V. corymbosum*). Despite some differences between the plants, the berries are essentially the same. Highland blueberries are self-pollinating, but set more fruit if they are grown with other varieties. Bilberries need another variety for successful pollination so at least two bushes of different varieties will have to be grown. The varieties listed in the panel are derived from *V. corymbosum* and will set fruit with their own pollen. For maximum crops at least two varieties should be planted together.

OBTAINING PLANTS

Blueberries can either be propagated from cuttings taken in spring or purchased as plants in containers or as bare-rooted plants. Take 10–15cm (4–6in) softwood cuttings in late spring from the tips of the current season's growth. Alternatively, hardwood cuttings are taken during the dormant season after sufficient chilling has occurred, usually in mid- to late winter.

SOIL AND PREFERRED ASPECT

Blueberries are hardy in any open, sunny site, provided that it is not too exposed to strong winds. They need a very acidic soil, with a pH of 5.0–5.5. The soil should be consistently moist but never waterlogged. It should not be too rich in nutrients prior to planting.

CULTIVATION

Before planting, cut plants back to a height of 15–30cm (6–12in) or remove at least 50 per cent of the top, including all flower buds. Do not allow newly set plants to flower and fruit the first year.

Set the plants at the same depth they grew in the nursery or 1cm (½in) deeper and mulch with a well-rotted manure or compost.

Blueberries are grown as freestanding bushes, so no support or training is needed. They are not heavy feeders, but an annual application of about 100g (4oz) of fish, blood and bone and an annual mulch in late winter will ensure good growth. Blueberries require from 2.5–5cm (1–2in) of

Above: *Pick blueberries when they are ripe – approximately ten days after they turn blue – and use immediately.*

water per week. Newly established plants have the most critical water needs and can be damaged by either over- or under-watering. Short periods (one to three weeks) without rain can stress blueberry plants severely. Irrigation during dry periods is required for them to establish properly.

Bilberries require cross-pollination between different varieties for good fruit set and two or more varieties should be planted close by each other. Highland blueberries are self-fertile, but planting with other

PRUNING AN ESTABLISHED BLUEBERRY BUSH

Blueberries fruit on older wood, so no pruning is needed for several years. Thereafter, cut out any weak or misplaced shoots as well as the old wood that has ceased fruiting in order to stimulate new growth.

varieties may increase fruit set and size. Insects, especially wild bees and honeybees, are necessary to pollinate blueberries. For this reason, efforts to attract these insects into your garden will be rewarded by a good fruit set.

PRUNING

In the first few years after planting blueberries, remove the tips of the branches in autumn. As the bush gets larger, cut out any old, weak or damaged growth and ensure a free air supply by allowing about 15cm (6in) between each branch.

Prune bilberries immediately after harvesting because this permits shoot regrowth and flower bud formation before plants become dormant.

HARVESTING AND STORAGE

Blueberries should be picked when they are ripe, approximately ten days after they have turned blue. They are best used immediately as they do not store well, but can be stewed and then frozen.

PESTS AND DISEASES

Bilberries are generally more resistant to both pests and diseases than Highland blueberries. Where diseases do occur they are mainly limited to mildew and botrytis, while pests are usually restricted to an occasional outbreak of aphids. Birds are a more common problem and the bushes may need netting to protect against them.

CRANBERRIES

Vaccinium macrocarpon, V. trilobum and *V. vitis-idaea*

True cranberries (*V. macrocarpon*) grow in low-lying bogs. Many cranberry varieties exist, most of which are wild selections and not the product of breeding programmes. They are generally only available in the USA and are mostly grown as a commercial crop. The easiest of the three to grow is the highbush cranberry (*V. trilobum*), a deciduous shrub that grows up to 3m (10ft) high. Highbush cranberries require no special soil conditions and tend to be grown from the species and not varieties. Lingonberries (*V. vitis-idaea*) are relatives of cranberries that are grown in many Scandinavian countries and can only be cultivated in cooler locations. There are only a few lingonberry varieties available.

Above: *Cranberries should be harvested fresh from the plant once they redden but are still firm.*

OBTAINING PLANTS

Cranberries and lingonberries are propagated from cuttings and are available from a few specialist growers. The highbush cranberry can be propagated by hardwood and softwood cuttings, layering, crown division and by seed.

SOIL AND PREFERRED ASPECT

Cranberries grown in open soil will need a certain amount of soil modification. They need an acidic soil, ideally with a pH of 4–5, and should be grown in full sun. If your soil is sandy remove topsoil to a depth of 20cm (8in) and add a heavy-duty plastic liner. Pierce the liner and add about one-tenth of the volume of the excavated soil with well-rotted, but acidic, compost. Mix in about 50g (1¾oz) of bonemeal, rock

phosphate and dried blood per square metre (yard). Wet the planting mix thoroughly before planting.

If your soil is clay or silty, dig out an area 20cm (8in) deep and add the compost without a plastic liner, adding fertilizer and watering as above.

The highbush cranberry is tolerant of a wide variety of soil types, but it will do best where the soil is consistently moist and well-drained.

CULTIVATION

Cranberries can be planted in mid- to late autumn or in mid- to late spring. Highbush cranberries are best planted in late autumn

or early spring. The growing mix needs to be moist to the touch, but does not need to be saturated. Apply a general-purpose fertilizer such as fish, blood and bone in the early summer of each year.

Weed the cranberry bed regularly during the summer. Mulch the plants with pine needles or leaves in late autumn in order to protect against the drying effects of winter winds.

PRUNING

Once the cranberry bed is established, pruning is restricted to the removal of excess runner growth and older uprights as needed. Lingonberries rarely need pruning.

Pruning of a highbush cranberry should also be kept to a minimum and light renewal pruning should be all that is needed.

HARVESTING AND STORAGE

Harvest berries of all types by hand when red. Pick before a hard frost or protect them with covers.

PESTS AND DISEASES

Cranberries and lingonberries have few insect predators or diseases in domestic settings. Highbush cranberries will occasionally suffer with bacterial leaf spot, powdery mildew, shoot blight, plant bugs or thrips.

VARIETIES

CRANBERRIES
'Early Black' This early-season selection has small deep red berries.
'Howes' This is a late-season selection which has small red berries.
'Stevens' This selection is a mid-season cropper with large red berries.

LINGONBERRIES
'Regal' Developed from seed collected in Finland, 'Regal', like 'Sussi', was selected for its superior fruit size.
'Sussi' (patented – Balsgård, Sweden) was the first lingonberry to be selected and named for its exceptionally good crops of larger-than-average fruit.

cranberries

CUTTING BACK CRANBERRIES

Cranberries have no specific pruning requirements and any pruning should be restricted to the removal of excess runners and older uprights as and when it is needed. Use a pair of sharp shears to cut off any semi-erect or wispy stems in early spring and top-dress with 50g (1oz) fish, blood and bone per square metre (yard) in order to encourage new growth.

GRAPES

Vitis vinifera

In high and low latitudes, where hot summers cannot be guaranteed, grapes are usually grown in a greenhouse. Modern breeding practices have yielded a few varieties that can be grown outdoors in these regions but these are really only suitable for wine-making.

OBTAINING PLANTS

Vines can be propagated from cuttings, commonly referred to as "vine eyes". These cuttings should be 30cm (12in) long and inserted to half their length in good soil in late autumn to early winter. Plant out rooted cuttings in autumn or early winter of the following season. Prune the young plant to within 30cm (12in) from its base. Mulch with well-rotted manure or compost.

SOIL AND PREFERRED ASPECT

Despite being hardy, in cooler places vines can only be grown in a sheltered position that remains warm and sunny while the fruit is ripening. They thrive on a poor soil as long as it contains plenty of organic matter. The pH of the soil should be around 6.5–7.0. Soils should be free draining but not prone to drought, especially in the fruiting season.

Above: Grape vines, grown over an arch or pergola, provide an ideal decorative feature for the small garden.

CULTIVATION

Grow out of doors in favourable areas, preferably given the protection of a warm wall. Mulch annually in spring with well-rotted manure or compost and, if growth seems poor, feed with fish, blood and bone.

PRUNING

Plants grown outdoors can be grown as cordons, espaliers, fans or bushes. The bush method is the simplest, although the straggly habit of the bush form makes it a nuisance in the garden and trailing on the ground may spoil the berries. The cordon consists of a rod trained to a wire framework about 1.2m (4ft) high. The laterals from the rod are cut back each winter to one bud. Espaliers are grown by developing pairs of branches 30cm (12in) apart from the main stem.

HARVESTING AND STORAGE

The fruit is ready for picking when the stems turn brown. Cut the stem on either side of the bunch to leave a small "T"-shaped handle.

PESTS AND DISEASES

There are a multitude of pests and diseases that can affect grape vines. The main diseases in domestic settings are botrytis and mildew. Pests are few, but include red spider mites, wasps and birds. Use netting to protect against bird damage.

PRUNING ESTABLISHED GRAPES

Established double guyot, winter pruning *Each year remove the horizontal branches that carry fruiting stems, leaving three vertical central shoots. Pull two of these down on each side of the central shoot, so they are horizontal, and tie in place on the wire. The third shoot should be cut back to leave three strong buds which will form the three verticals for the following year. Mulch the plants with a generous layer of well-rotted compost.*

Established double guyot, summer pruning *Train the new shoots from these buds vertically, removing any side shoots that develop on them to one leaf. Allow the vertical fruiting shoots to grow on the horizontal branches, removing any side shoots that appear. Cut back above the top wire to three leaves. After fruiting, remove the horizontal branches and train the remaining three central shoots as described above.*

CALENDAR OF CARE

WINTER

THE ORNAMENTAL GARDEN

EARLY WINTER
- Continue cultivating the soil, if not already done, when the ground is not wet.
- Continue planting and transplanting on mild days.
- Press plants that have been lifted by frost back into the ground.
- Plant herbaceous perennials for next year.
- Last chance to plant roses.
- Move greenhouse plants to the house as they come into flower.
- Start pruning deciduous shrubs and trees during spells of fine, frost-free weather.

MID-WINTER
- Finish digging and trenching and fork over borders.
- Order seeds for coming season.
- Protect autumn sown annuals from frost.
- Prepare ground that is to be planted out with bedding plants with manure.
- Tidy up climbing plants and remove any dead wood.
- Firm down herbaceous plants that have been lifted by the frost and protect the new shoots of young tender plants.
- Plant evergreen and deciduous shrubs.
- Trim deciduous hedges and shrubs to start bringing them into shape.
- Take hardwood cuttings and layers of deciduous shrubs.
- Sow annuals in gentle heat.
- Take cuttings of tender shrubs and start under gentle heat.

LATE WINTER
- Tidy up unused ground and apply a top-dressing of manure or leaf mould.
- Protect bulbs from mice, snails and birds.
- Prune roses planted this month.
- Start to train and trim climbers.
- Divide herbaceous plants.
- Sow annuals in gentle heat.
- Transplant autumn sown annuals.
- Plant edgings such as box (*Buxus*) hedging, pinks (*Dianthus*) or thrift (*Armeria*).

THE WILDLIFE GARDEN

EARLY WINTER
- Try to maintain a fresh supply of clean unfrozen water for wildlife.
- To keep some open water on ponds, put in a floating ball or anchored block of polystyrene, preferably painted black, to absorb the warmth of the sun.
- Leave tidying the garden until late winter to shelter overwintering insects.
- Leave log and leaf piles completely undisturbed until spring.
- Feed resident birds with high energy supplements such as fat balls.
- Order seed now for early sowings of perennials and annuals.

MID-WINTER
- Put plenty of food in the garden for resident birds.
- Hang nesting boxes ready for breeding birds.
- Build dry-stone walls with gaps to provide shelter for reptiles and amphibians.
- Look out for wildlife tracks in snow and position cat deterrents at entry points.
- Provide food for non-hibernating mammals if present.
- Keep a record of wildlife to help you target future feeding and habitat creation.

LATE WINTER
- Continue feeding resident birds.
- Put up a range of different nesting boxes and make each box as inconspicuous as possible. Reposition any nesting boxes that were unused last year.
- Stretch wires or heavy-duty cord at least 10cm (4in) proud of walls and fences and train climbing plants to form a screen with a gap behind it for nesting birds.
- Trim one side of hedges to encourage dense new growth as nesting cover, but leave some flowering stems on spring-blossoming species such as hawthorn (*Crataegus*) for nectar.
- Protect bulbs from mice, snails and birds.

SPRING

EARLY SPRING
- Feed lawns where the grass is thin and seed areas where the grass has been completely worn away.
- Prepare borders ready for biennials and perennials next month.
- Remove leaves and other debris from borders and fork over.
- Tidy up spring bedding plants.
- Sow hardy annuals when the weather is dry and mild.
- Start pruning roses.
- Trim box edging and damaged evergreens.
- Prick out annuals started last month.
- Start to harden off early seedlings ready for bedding out.
- Look for pests and diseases and deal with them as they occur.

MID-SPRING
- Hoe off weeds.
- Watch for signs of frost and protect young shoots.
- Watch out for pests and diseases.
- Give the lawn its first cut and tidy its edges.
- Stake and tie any plants that need it.
- Sow hardy annuals.
- Propagate hardy perennials, including water plants.
- Finish winter pruning and prune late winter/early spring flowering shrubs before they commence growth.
- Continue hardening off summer bedding and pinch out the tops.
- Trim and tidy up all climbers before they start into growth.
- Sow half-hardy annuals and take cuttings.
- Give box hedges their first clipping.

LATE SPRING
- Hoe off weeds.
- Finish off digging and rotavating to prepare the beds for planting.
- Water newly planted plants in dry weather.
- Keep an eye open for pests and diseases.
- Tidy bulb beds after the foliage has died down.
- Tie in sweet peas (*Lathyrus odoratus*) and check the support of other climbers.
- Finish sowing hardy annuals and plant out those raised under glass. Thin outdoor sowings and transplant where necessary.
- Plant half-hardy bedding plants when the danger of frost is over.
- Divide spring-flowering plants, like primroses (*Primula vulgaris*), for next season.
- Shrubs should have old wood removed and thinned out.
- Continue taking cuttings.

EARLY SPRING
- Put plenty of food in the garden for resident birds.
- Create a wildlife pond ready to plant up next month.
- Supplement the diet of resident early nesting birds with mealworms and waxworms.
- Emerging hedgehogs will benefit from a feed of cat food near their nesting sites.
- Hang nesting boxes for solitary bees.

MID-SPRING
- Plant new garden ponds and replace dead plants in established ponds.
- Sow seeds of hardy annuals in a sunny spot to attract insects during the summer until late autumn. Mix them up with salad crops to act as helpful companion plants.
- Install a "cage" of large-gauge chicken wire around nesting sites to allow nesting birds in but keep out magpies, grey squirrels and other nest-robbing species.
- Keep one or two nest boxes sealed so as to prevent the entry of resident birds until migrant bird species arrive.
- Continue feeding garden birds.
- Continue feeding hedgehogs until natural prey increases in numbers.
- Propagate hardy perennials, not forgetting water plants.

LATE SPRING
- Plant pot-grown seedlings of spring-flowering wild flowers in an area of lawn where you can leave the grass uncut until mid-summer.
- Sow the seeds of wild flowers thinly on the surface of gritty potting mix.
- Divide spring-flowering plants, such as primroses (*Primula vulgaris*) and cowslips (*P. veris*), for next season.
- Continue feeding garden birds.
- Put up bat boxes to encourage bats to roost in the summer.

SUMMER

EARLY SUMMER
• Mulch round plants and shrubs that need to be kept moist.
• Keep an eye out for pests, and keep weeds under control.
• Cut down and tidy perennials as they finish flowering.
• Feed roses and sweet peas (*Lathyrus odoratus*) with manure or compost tea.
• Sow biennials and perennials.
• Plant out plants raised under glass, dividing and planting out those that have finished flowering in other areas.
• Thin out seedlings and stake carnations (*Dianthus*), dahlias and sweet peas.
• Sow hardy annuals for autumn planting.
• Spray the foliage of new trees with water in hot or dry weather.
• Tidy up rhododendrons and other plants by removing seedheads, unless leaving them for decoration and food for the birds.

MID-SUMMER
• Continue to hoe weeds and water newly planted specimens.
• Stake and tie plants.
• Layer or take cuttings from carnations.
• Pinch out the tops of chrysanthemums to prevent straggly plants.
• Water and feed sweet peas with a compost or manure tea.
• Sow perennial and biennial seeds for next year.
• Continue taking cuttings.
• Sow seeds for overwintering in the greenhouse.
• Pot plants that need repotting.
• Cut away dead and unwanted foliage on vigorous shrubs.
• Trim deciduous hedges.
• Propagate shrubs by cuttings or layering.

LATE SUMMER
• Continue watering, mulching and hoeing.
• Remove all dead flowers, stalks and leaves.
• Train and tie clematis, honeysuckle (*Lonicera*) and wisteria.
• Trim plants such as lavender and penstemons after flowering.
• Water and feed sweet peas with a compost or manure tea.
• Take cuttings of old-fashioned roses.
• Thin perennial seedlings.
• Divide and replant spring-flowering perennials.
• Take cuttings of fuchsias, pelargoniums, heliotrope, hydrangeas and all half-hardy plants.
• Remove dead flowers and stalks from summer-flowering shrubs, unless they are berry producing.

AUTUMN

EARLY AUTUMN
• Hoe off any late weeds.
• Start tidying up for winter, but leave seedheads for birds.
• Put unwanted debris on the compost heap.
• Collect seeds and label for sowing next year.
• Start digging, manuring and rotavating heavy soils.
• Repair patches on lawns.
• Start collecting fallen leaves to make leaf mould.
• Tie and stake dahlias and tall shrubs.
• Cut back and support climbing plants.
• Sow spring-flowering seeds, starting with hardy annuals.
• Plant spring bulbs.
• Plant or transplant evergreen shrubs, conifers and herbaceous plants.

MID-AUTUMN
• Collect fallen leaves to make leaf mould.
• Prepare areas for planting.
• Repair and lay new lawns, repair paths and walkways.
• Make final plantings of bulbs.
• Collect seeds of late-flowering plants.
• Lift and store half-hardy bulbs, corms and tubers.
• Lift, divide and replant herbaceous plants.
• Sow early sweet peas (*Lathyrus odoratus*).
• Start planting out spring bedding.
• If moving deciduous shrubs, do so to encourage new root growth.
• Take cuttings until the cold weather sets in.

LATE AUTUMN
• Continue digging heavy and medium soils, leaving the light soils for spring.
• Spread surplus manure around flowerbeds if leaf mould is not available.
• Fork over herbaceous borders, leaving dead foliage until spring.
• Take cuttings of plants that may need replacing.
• Make final plantings of spring bedding.
• Take rose prunings from choice plants and push into the ground in a sheltered position where they may strike and give you more plants.
• Put bulbs for forcing under glass in pots.
• Plant flowering shrubs and trees for next season.

EARLY SUMMER
• Plant tobacco plants (*Nicotiana*) to guarantee interesting night-flying moths and the bats that feed on them.
• Check fruit nets each day to ensure no birds are trapped inside.
• Choose bedding plants with simple flowers and keep a note of which the bees and butterflies prefer.
• Leave seedheads on spring-flowering shrubs such as rhododendrons as food for birds.
• Continue feeding garden birds, with seed and waxworms or mealworms, especially if there is a dry spell.

MID-SUMMER
• Watch for night-flying moths on tobacco plants, late flowers on the honeysuckle, and tall yellow evening primroses.
• Continue to check fruit nets each day for birds.
• Take special care when turning compost heaps as grass snakes may be nesting and hedgehogs often sleep in them.
• Make log piles for wood feeding insects such as stag beetles.
• Lightly trim deciduous hedges if birds have finished nesting to encourage dense cover in the winter.
• Continue feeding garden birds, especially if there is a dry spell.

LATE SUMMER
• Plant early spring bulbs now for nectar next year, especially for overwintering insects.
• Lightly trim nectar-rich plants such as lavender (*Lavandula*) and nepeta after flowering to encourage new growth.
• Dead-head herbaceous plants to encourage fresh flowers that give an extra boost to pollinators in the early autumn.
• Leave seedheads and berries on summer-flowering shrubs for birds.
• Continue feeding garden birds.

EARLY AUTUMN
• Let one or two old vegetables flower, such as leeks, carrots and almost any member of the cabbage family, to boost nectar supplies for autumn insects.
• Look now to see if there is a shortage of nectar and redesign flower borders accordingly. Remember to select single-flowered plants where possible.
• Build new log piles, rock piles and brush piles ready for overwintering insects, reptiles, amphibians and mammals.
• Place nest boxes outside for overwintering mammals such as hedgehogs.
• Continue planting spring bulbs for early nectar next year.
• Plant evergreens to provide dense winter cover for birds and mammals.
• Continue feeding garden birds.

MID-AUTUMN
• Start a new compost heap.
• Let hedge prunings, raspberry canes and other woody waste accumulate and leave them to become a hibernation heap for hedgehogs.
• Weed among and divide most pond plants before they die back. This removes excess nutrients from the pond and minimizes next summer's algal blooms.
• Pile weeds and thinnings from ponds at the side until the following day to give trapped pond dwellers time to escape.
• Place nest boxes outside for overwintering mammals such as hedgehogs.
• Continue planting spring bulbs for early nectar next year.
• Begin putting out high energy supplements such as fat balls for birds.

LATE AUTUMN
• Plant hedgerows using native shrubs and trees.
• Plant late-flowering nectar plants like English ivy (*Hedera helix*) against a boundary that catches autumn sun.
• Put in late bulbs at least 7.5cm (3in) deep and bury chicken wire just below the surface to avoid them being eaten by squirrels.
• Feed resident birds with high energy supplements such as fat balls.

WINTER

THE KITCHEN GARDEN

VEGETABLES

EARLY WINTER
- Hoe between crops on fine days.
- Examine stored onions and potatoes for any sign of disease and discard second-class seed. Any potatoes that are sprouting should be placed apart in dry trays.
- Protect more tender plants with leaves or cloches.
- Begin forcing rhubarb and seakale under a light-proof cover.
- Order seed catalogues and plan the new season's crops.

MID-WINTER
- Tidy up and put vegetable waste on the compost heap.
- Hoe between growing crops when dry.
- Sow broad (fava) beans and peas in warm sheltered positions.
- Sow early vegetables under glass or cloches.
- Start potatoes in a frost-free shed.
- Plant rhubarb in well-manured beds.

LATE WINTER
- Hoe weeds when the weather allows.
- Clear old beds ready for new season.
- Cut pea and bean sticks.
- Sow early vegetables under glass or cloches.
- Plant artichokes, garlic, shallots, lettuce (winter), potatoes (early), rhubarb and seakale.
- Plants overwintering under cloches should be hardened off and only protected when the weather is frosty.

FRUIT

EARLY WINTER
- Finish pruning fruit trees and bushes on frost-free days. Large standard trees will need pruning every second or third year.
- Firm newly planted trees where the frost has been at work.
- Do not plant any more trees until the spring; just prepare the ground.
- Currants and gooseberries should be pruned if not already done.
- Prune outdoor vines.
- Remove unwanted suckers from raspberry stools but do not prune until early spring.

MID-WINTER
- Start pruning hardier trees such as apples. Do not prune apricots, cherries, figs, nectarines and peaches.
- Prepare grafting material.
- Plant container-grown trees and cover soil with well-rotted manure.

LATE WINTER
- Prune damsons, pears, plums and quince.
- Spread manure around fruit trees and dig it in.
- Prepare new strawberry beds.
- Fertilize by hand the blossom of fruit trees grown under glass.

HERBS

EARLY WINTER
- Prepare ground for planting when conditions allow.
- Protect tender herbs under cloches.
- Continue to remove dead stems from herbaceous types.

MID-WINTER
- Prepare ground ready for planting.
- Force early growth under cloches.
- Make early sowings under glass.

LATE WINTER
- Remove dead stems from herbaceous types.
- Continue forcing under cloches.
- Continue sowing under glass.

SPRING

EARLY SPRING
- Hoe weeds when the weather allows.
- Prepare seedbeds.
- Protect early crops from birds.
- Begin sowing in sheltered places in the open.
- Sow early vegetables under glass or cloches.
- Plant out early crops raised under glass and early potatoes.
- Plant early broad (fava) beans out in the garden under glass.

MID-SPRING
- Hoe weeds regularly.
- Prepare beds for planting out.
- Feed cabbages with high-nitrogen fertilizer such as chicken manure.
- Potatoes need the soil drawn over their leaves to protect them from frost.
- Begin sowing remaining summer crops outdoors.
- Continue sowing more tender crops under glass.

LATE SPRING
- Hoe weeds regularly.
- Cut asparagus when shoots reach 15cm (6in).
- Maintain the succession of seed sowing to give salad throughout the summer season.
- Continue planting out summer crops.
- Sow late crops such as broccoli and plant out winter crops previously sown under cover.
- Last chance to plant late potatoes.
- Plant out cucumbers, pumpkins and melons in beds previously used for protected early crops.

EARLY SPRING
- Protect blossom with fleece on cold nights.
- Last chance to plant container-grown fruit bushes.
- Graft apples, cherries, pears and plums that were prepared in mid-winter.
- Finish pruning fruit trees and bushes.

MID-SPRING
- Continue protecting blossom.
- Wall trees will need moisture from now on.
- Watch for pests and diseases.
- Grapes will require thinning in order to swell their size.

LATE SPRING
- All fruit will benefit from a mulch.
- Apricots, peaches and Morello cherries should have fruiting spurs shortened back to three to four leaves.
- Limit raspberry suckers to around four to six to each stool.
- Put straw around strawberries to protect the fruits from the ground.

EARLY SPRING
- Continue sowing under glass.
- Plant out hardy herbs once hardened off.
- Prune shrubby types.
- Lift and divide herbaceous types until late spring.

MID-SPRING
- Continue sowing under glass.
- Continue planting out.
- Take basal cuttings.

LATE SPRING
- Sow herbs like parsley (*Petroselinum crispum*) and chervil (*Anthriscus cerefolium*) for winter use.
- Continue sowing under glass and planting out.

SUMMER

EARLY SUMMER
• Hoe weeds regularly throughout summer.
• Water all salad crops regularly.
• Feed heavy feeders like cauliflowers with liquid manure or compost tea.
• Keep picking peas to stimulate flowering.
• Harvest early potatoes and replace with winter turnips or late celery.
• Support runner beans.
• Sow the last of the outdoor salad crops and continue sowing seed of late or winter crops.
• Thin out seedlings.
• Plant late-season crops raised under cover.

MID-SUMMER
• Water all salad crops regularly.
• Remove debris, following harvest, to the compost heap until late summer.
• Potatoes and other crops may need earthing-up.
• Pinch out and stop tomatoes and marrows.
• Maintain the succession of seed sowing for late or winter crops.
• Thin out the beetroot crop so that the roots can form properly.
• Plant late-season crops raised under cover.

LATE SUMMER
• Water all crops regularly.
• Remove debris, following harvest, to the compost heap.
• Harvest seed from French (green) beans and onions.
• Garlic and onions can be harvested this month and then ripened.
• Potatoes for next year's seed should be dug up and dried in the sun.
• Maintain the succession of seed sowing for late or winter crops.

EARLY SUMMER
• Continue mulching trees and bushes to conserve moisture.
• Cut back untidy vigorous growth.
• Over-laden trees may need support. Aphids will appear, so take appropriate action.
• Throw nets over fruiting trees and shrubs to prevent the birds getting the fruit first.
• Peaches and apricots may need some thinning.
• Strawberries should have regular watering.

MID-SUMMER
• Thin trees and remove unnecessary growth.
• Hoe round the roots of fruit trees and water them.
• Fruit trees may be budded when the weather is moist.
• Espalier and dwarf fruit trees will need training and protection from birds.
• Strawberries and loganberries should be layered and clipped to the soil to secure their position.

LATE SUMMER
• Protect fruit on walls from wasps and birds as it ripens.
• Pruning can be started and trees budded.
• Apples, pears and plums may need the fruit thinning out if the crop is heavy.
• Cut down the old canes of loganberries and raspberries after harvesting.
• Cut off unwanted runners from strawberries and remove the old straw from round the crowns.

EARLY SUMMER
• Continue sowing under glass.
• Continue planting out until late summer.
• Harvest herbs for storing before they flower.
• Plant out tender herbs.
• Dead-head unless seed is required until late summer.
• Cut back herbaceous types to stimulate growth until late summer.

MID-SUMMER
• Cut mint (*Mentha*) and other sweet herbs for drying.
• Pull out parsley (*Petroselinum crispum*) unless it is being kept for seed.
• Propagate sage (*Salvia*) or savory (*Satureja*) from cuttings or division.

LATE SUMMER
• Harvest herbs as required.

AUTUMN

EARLY AUTUMN
• Hoe weeds regularly throughout autumn.
• Water all crops regularly.
• Harvest onions and bend down the necks of the remainder to prevent seeding.
• Continue to lift potatoes.
• Expose the fruit of outdoor tomatoes to the sun by removing the covering leaves.
• Maintain the succession of seed sowing for late or winter crops.
• Plant late season crops raised under cover.

MID-AUTUMN
• After beans and peas have been harvested, turn the soil over and leave it fallow over the winter.
• Lift root vegetables when their tops fade.
• Cut down asparagus foliage when mature.
• Onions and turnip beds should be thinned.
• Clear the last of the potatoes and store them.
• Earth up celery and leeks.
• Plant out late-season crops and protect tender types such as cauliflower.

LATE AUTUMN
• Get the soil ready for spring sowing.
• Protect crowns of tender crops with a mulch of leaves.
• Lift the last of the beetroot and carrots.
• Earth up celery and leeks if not already done.
• Spinach will continue to crop as it is thinned.
• Dry off the late potatoes for seed stock next year.
• Continue to plant out late-season crops and protect tender types such as cauliflower.

EARLY AUTUMN
• Wall fruit that has ripened will need protecting.
• Fruit trees may be budded and light pruning continued.
• Early varieties of apples and pears that do not keep well should be gathered.
• Prune currants and gooseberries to keep them in shape. Raspberry canes that have fruited should be removed to make room for the new growth.
• Strawberries should have unwanted runners removed to give space to the main plants.

MID-AUTUMN
• Look though the nursery catalogues and order fruit stock, then prepare the ground and remove stock to be replaced.
• Move any trees or bushes that are in the wrong place.
• Apples and pears can now be gathered.
• Apricots, cherries, currants and gooseberries should be pruned and the cuttings burnt.
• Loganberries and raspberries should be planted now.

LATE AUTUMN
• This is the time to plant fruit trees in well-prepared ground.
• Begin winter pruning of fruit trees.
• Plant currants and gooseberries.
• Figs will need thinning.
• Spread manure between rows of new strawberry plants.

EARLY AUTUMN
• Harvest seed as it ripens.
• Harvest leaves and stems as required.
• Cut back herbaceous types to stimulate new growth.

MID-AUTUMN
• Harvest seed as it ripens.
• Tidy away dead material.
• Protect tender herbs.
• Plant shrubby and herbaceous types until late autumn.
• Move tender container herbs under some protection.
• Divide herbaceous herbs until late autumn.

LATE AUTUMN
• Prepare ground for planting when conditions allow.

THE ORGANIC KITCHEN

The organic cook has a vast array of ingredients available, from fresh fruit and vegetables to fine-quality meat and store-cupboard staples. Take the same care with preparation as you do with selection and storage and you will be rewarded with delicious dishes. Exploring the range of fresh and store-cupboard items is a rewarding experience. If you buy fresh produce direct from the grower, ask the names of varieties so you can seek out your favourites. The section that follows is not intended to be an exhaustive guide to every organic item, but it does introduce some of the best buys from organic growers and producers around the world.

WHAT IS ORGANIC COOKING?

Organic food is the fastest growing sector of the entire food industry. Step into any supermarket and you will see an impressive array of organic produce, not tucked away at the end of an aisle, but proudly and prominently displayed. This is often the first point of contact for shoppers unfamiliar with organic food, but having experienced the superior flavours and learned of the undeniable health benefits, many people go on to investigate box schemes, farmers' markets featuring organic produce and small, local organic suppliers.

Interest in organic food and farming is at an all-time high. This is partly due to the fact that people are better informed about nutrition, more concerned about the environment and more cautious about the short- and long-term effects of diet on health than at any time in the past, but there are also more fundamental reasons, such as flavour. To put it simply, we appreciate good food. This generation is more widely travelled than any previous one, and is discovering

Below: Organic sheep and lambs graze on unsprayed grass, free from pesticides.

exotic cuisines and exciting new tastes from all over the world. People eat out more, and are more adventurous when cooking at home. As palates become increasingly sophisticated, we demand more from the ingredients that make up our meals, so it is hardly surprising that we increasingly favour organic food.

WHAT IS ORGANIC FOOD?
Organic farming is the cultivation of crops and rearing of livestock with natural soil fertility at the heart of the system. Organic farmers believe that by working hard to maintain and encourage good soil structure on their land, the crops and livestock grown and bred there will flourish. They work with nature, rather than trying to bend nature to their purpose, so produce is grown without the routine use of pesticides or artificial fertilizers, and animals are reared without being treated with growth promoters or unnecessarily dosed with antibiotics.

If this sounds like a return to the way things used to be, it is, but only to a point. Modern organic farming is highly scientific and makes considerable use of

Above: Organic pumpkins and squash are grown free from artificial fertilizers.

technology. Research into more efficient organic farming methods is ongoing. For food to be labelled organic, it must have been produced according to strict guidelines, which are rigidly regulated.

Soil fertility is promoted by crop rotation, composting and planting crops that supply specific nutrients. Farmers encourage predator insects such as ladybirds (ladybugs) to visit by planting their favourite flowers. They may also sometimes introduce other predators to control pests biologically. When coupled with preventative methods, such as growing in polytunnels, where insects can be kept out, the need to use agrochemical pesticides is avoided.

AGROCHEMICAL FARMING
The cultivation of crops and rearing of livestock using agrochemicals was first promoted on a large scale in the 1950s, in response to widespread food shortages during and immediately after World War II. This was a period of modernism, with technologies of all kinds being optimistically embraced. Agrochemicals held the promise of maximizing food production, so they were universally adopted. They achieved

Right: Organic cattle are less susceptible to disease because they are always free-range and have access to the outdoors.

their immediate objectives, but at a cost to the environment that is only now beginning to be fully appreciated.

Yields from organic and agrochemical farms are now almost identical, and organic yields continue to grow as a result of continued research into intensive organic agriculture. Organic farmers also benefit from access to much wider seed banks than those customarily used by agrochemical farmers, so can select the best varieties of crops for their climate and terrain.

Organic farming now utilizes some of the same non-invasive technology as agrochemical farming. Satellites, for example, are used to predict weather patterns or map insect migrations.

THE COST OF GOING ORGANIC
If yields are improving and organic food production is becoming steadily more efficient, why does organic food tend to cost more than agrochemical food? The answer lies in outdated government subsidy schemes, which are based on the aspirations and knowledge of post-World War II policymakers. Agrochemical farmers receive a much higher amount of taxpayers' money than organic farmers. Historically, this was because farmers were encouraged to experiment with chemicals to increase yields. Thinking has changed radically since those days, but subsidizing policy has not altered for the last fifty years.

Farmers are actively encouraged to spray their fields with chemical pesticides and fertilizers. When these chemicals run off farms and pollute the water table, huge sums of money must be spent internationally in clean-up operations. It is not the chemical companies or the farmers who pay for this pollution management; it is the taxpayer.

Consumers pay for agrochemical products three times. First at the checkout, then – about half the price of the item again – through taxes as a subsidy to agrochemical farmers, and

finally through further taxes to clean up the water table. This economic breakdown does not include any costs incurred to industry through the ill health of agrochemical farm workers who have been exposed to toxins.

Organic food will continue to be marginally more expensive than agrochemical food until government policies change. However, the difference in food quality that organic food offers more than justifies this price premium. An organic apple contains more vitamins, minerals and phytonutrients than a non-organic apple. It also contains about 25 per cent less water. It is likely to be a more interesting variety, will almost certainly taste better and will have a

more enjoyable texture. Most importantly, it will not be coated in an untested cocktail of up to twenty artificial chemicals and waxes.

ORGANIC LIVESTOCK
Animal welfare is a fundamental principle of organic livestock, poultry and dairy farming. Organic animals are always free range. Because they have access to the outdoors and are not intensively reared in enclosed spaces, they are less susceptible to disease and, although farmers will take appropriate action if an animal becomes unwell, there is no need for the routine administration of antibiotics that is standard preventative practice on agrochemical farms.

Above: These dairy cows are being reared organically, free from hormones that increase milk production or encourage growth.

Organic farmers will often use such complementary medicines as homeopathic treatments to cure a sick animal and inject antibiotics only as a last resort when other treatments have failed.

Organic farmers are not allowed to use hormones to encourage animal growth or increase milk production. In countries where growth hormones such as BST (bovine somatotropin) are administered, dairy cows often suffer intense pain from unnaturally swollen udders. Their milk – and dairy products produced from it – contains the same hormones, increasing the consumer's risk of multi-generational cancers and hormone disruption disorders.

FISH
Organic fish, whether wild or farmed, should come from sustainable fisheries and farms, and be caught using fishing practices that protect the environment.
Wild fish Logic dictates that all wild fish are organic, since they swim and eat where they will. However, pollution, insensitive fishing methods and proximity

to major shipping lanes all have a detrimental effect on wild fish stocks, and there is no standard for organics in wild fish. The Marine Stewardship Council is an international organization offering an accreditation scheme for sustainable wild fisheries.

Farmed fish The conditions under which fish are farmed vary widely. For farmed fish to be labelled organic, they must be reared responsibly. This means giving them adequate room to move, letting them grow and develop naturally and giving them organic feed. This is not the case on many agrochemical fish farms, where fish populations can be so high and intensive that infestation and disease are commonplace and chemical pesticides must be used liberally to control them. Pesticides, waste fish food and sewage from agrochemical fish farms frequently pollute our rivers and waterways, and it is not just these substances that escape. Fish get under the wire, too, and in many European rivers, four out of every five salmon caught originated on an agrochemical farm.

Farmed fish are bred to mature later and be less aggressive than their wild counterparts in order to produce a greater yield and be easier to manage.

The damage from wild and farmed salmon interbreeding is immense, with natural fish stocks at ever increasing risk. Intensive fish farms are beginning to address these problems in many areas of the world, but to be sure that your farmed fish is produced responsibly, make sure it carries the mark of an organic certification body that you trust.

HEMP
This is a wonder crop that puts more nutrients back into the soil than it needs to grow. It is therefore ideal for farmers who are converting their land to organic methods. The conversion period required for organic certification can be a difficult time financially for farmers. While the land is renewing itself, farmers may not sell their produce as organic even though they are not using agrochemicals. Hemp can usefully bridge the gap by providing a saleable crop while improving soil fertility.

The applications of hemp are extraordinary. The ropes and sails used on the ships that first charted our seas were made of hemp. So was the first pair of Levi's jeans. Hemp also made the paper on which the original American Constitution was written. Hemp is the most versatile organic crop we have. You

Below: Organic fish are farmed with care for the environment.

Above: *Organic fruit contains more vitamins, minerals and phytonutrients than non-organic fruit. It also tastes better.*

can make cosmetics from its oil, power cars with it, and even use it for making plastics. In fact, hemp can do anything that a hydrocarbon can do. In these times of dwindling fossil fuel reserves, hemp is potentially a major part of the solution because it actually reduces greenhouse gases plus it manufactures oxygen when it grows, and can easily be processed into a powerful fuel source to rival oil.

Hemp seed is the only complete vegetable protein known, with a nutritional make-up that is even more balanced than soya. Sixty-five per cent of the protein in hemp is in globular edestin form, which is the most easily digestible form of protein. The oil content of hemp seeds typically consists of 60 per cent Omega-6; 20 per cent Omega-3 and 10 per cent Omega essential fatty acids (EFAs). This is seen as the most suitable ratio of dietary fat for long-term human consumption. Hemp seed oil also contains GLA, which is the active constituent of evening primrose oil. This makes the oil ideal for the treatment of PMS, eczema, joint conditions and even some cancers.

Left: *Hemp products include such beauty products as soaps, moisturizers and loofah-like scrubs.*

NOT EVERYTHING ORGANIC IS FOOD!

Non-organic cotton and tobacco are two pesticide-dependent crops grown widely in the Americas and in developing countries. Dangers to the consumer from agrochemicals used in the cultivation of non-food crops are minimal, but when the soil's natural fertility is undermined by artificial fertilizers, farmers become reliant on agrochemicals. Concerns are high for farm workers in developing countries exposed to pesticides deemed too strong for use on food crops. Where protective clothing is absent, they have a higher than average incidence of cancers and respiratory conditions. There is also a high rate of early mortality among the farmers themselves.

Organic cotton and tobacco are available. The Scandinavian Oeko-Tex mark is an assurance that fabrics are organic or sustainable. The American Spirit tobacco company manufactures organic cigarettes.

Seeds and garden flowers are two more areas of environmental concern. Because it is vital that no weed seeds contaminate the product, agrochemical seed producers spray their crops liberally with herbicides.

Cut flowers are not regulated as stringently as food crops, so farm workers and the environment can lose out. Buying organically grown flowers benefits both the people who grew them and the planet.

Organically grown hyacinths

WHY GO ORGANIC?

There are dozens – many would say hundreds – of excellent reasons for choosing the organic option. Apart from benefits to the individual in terms of health, avoidance of chemicals and the sheer enjoyment of eating food that is full of flavour, there are environmental issues to consider, as well as moral questions such as animal welfare, the health of farm workers and fair trade.

IMPROVED HEALTH

All organic food is better for you than the non-organic equivalent. Fresh organic produce contains more vitamins, minerals, enzymes and other micro-nutrients than intensively farmed produce. It also tastes better. Organic fruit and vegetables are full of juice and

Below: *Organic cauliflower, cabbage, broccoli and Brussels sprouts are high in glucosinolates, which help prevent cancer.*

flavour, and there are many different varieties to try. Organic meat, poultry and dairy produce are of excellent quality and usually lower in saturated fat.
Vitamins and minerals The reason why fresh organic produce contains more vitamins and minerals than the agrochemical equivalent is largely due to the method of cultivation. Unlike agrochemical fruit and vegetables, which are sprayed with artificial fertilizers that force the plants to grow quickly, even in inferior soil, organic fruit and vegetables are allowed to grow and ripen more naturally in richer soil, obtaining the maximum variety of micronutrients.

These micronutrients are also more concentrated in organic fruit and vegetables, because they contain much less water than agrochemical produce.
Phytonutrients Organic produce is rich in naturally occurring chemical compounds known as phytonutrients. These are

found in fresh fruit and vegetables and help to fight disease and promote good health. More research is needed to pinpoint the precise benefits of all these compounds, but much is already known. Glucosinolates in cabbage, broccoli, cauliflower and Brussels sprouts help to prevent cancer. Flavonoids are powerful antioxidants. The strongest flavonoids are found in onions and garlic. Eating onions and garlic regularly significantly reduces the risk of heart disease and the spread of cancer.

While all fresh produce contains phytonutrients, organic produce contains more than its non-organic equivalent. This is because all plants produce phyto-nutrients as part of their natural defence against pests. If a plant is protected from pests by agrochemicals, there is no need for it to produce phytochemicals in the same quantity. Also, studies have found that when plants take up high levels of

Above: *Just some of the fruits available organically: apples, grapes, pineapple, oranges, kiwi fruit and passion fruit.*

nitrogen from the soil, they produce fewer and less diverse phytonutrients. Agrochemical crops are liberally sprayed with nitrogen fertilizers to make them grow quicker, whereas organic crops are grown in more balanced and less nitrogen-rich soil.

Fats Hydrogenated fats are oils that have had hydrogen added to them so that they become solid or semi-solid at room temperature. They are widely used in the food industry despite the fact that nutritionists universally agree that they are a major cofactor in heart disease, cancer, diabetes and obesity. The surest way to remove hydrogenated fats from your diet is to go organic. Organic food regulations throughout the world prohibit the use of hydrogenated fats.

Eating too much saturated fat is a contributing factor in cardiovascular diseases such as heart attacks and stroke. Saturated fat is present in organic beef as well as in intensively reared beef, but the percentage is likely to be lower. Saturated fat is also easier to remove from organic

beef. In intensively reared cattle saturated fat is more evenly distributed, so is harder to cut away when you are preparing the meat for cooking. Since it clogs up your arteries, the more saturated fat you can remove from your food the better.

Meat, poultry, eggs and milk from grass-fed animals also contain more conjugated linoleic acid or CLA. This substance helps those who consume it to maintain a healthy weight, and studies have shown that it reduces the risk of heart disease and may help to prevent cancer. So although organic meat contains saturated fat, it also contains CLA to balance it.

The balanced diet

A wholesome, organic diet provides balanced nutrition, including a healthy range of vitamins, minerals and phytonutrients. This is an important consideration in a world where many people opt for convenience foods that are

often high in fat and sugar and offer little in terms of nutrition. The body craves the nutrients it lacks, and this can drive people to overeat, yet remain malnourished. There is a direct correlation between over-consumption malnutrition trends in industrialized nations and eating non-organic food. Obesity epidemics have occurred in countries that rely on agrochemicals to grow and process their foods.

Improved immunity There is evidence to suggest that people who eat organic food build up a stronger immunity to disease than those who consistently eat food that is laden with chemicals. Eating over-processed, non-organic junk food puts a strain on immune systems already compromised by living in a polluted world, by forcing the liver and kidneys to work harder to remove the toxins they frequently contain.

A New Zealand report into the possible benefits of an organic diet suggested that people who follow an organic diet benefit from a very marked decline in influenza and experienced far fewer colds and catarrhal problems than other members of the population. Further reported benefits included clear, healthy skin, improved dental health and excellent general health.

Below: *Organic eggs are high in linoleic acid, which helps maintain a healthy weight.*

Above: Eating an organic diet before conception and during pregnancy will help rid the body of toxins.

Increased fertility Studies appear to support a link between organic diets and increased fertility in men. The World Health Organization estimates that the average sperm count for male adults is about 66 million/ml. Two recent studies recorded that men who eat organic food have between 99 and 127 million sperm/ml. More research is needed to confirm these findings. However, the fact that a balanced organic diet is more nutritionally sound and contains fewer chemicals or artificial hormones than a non-organic diet, is bound to offer the best option for men – and women – wanting to support their sexual health and improve their chances of conceiving.

AVOIDING THE CHEMICAL COCKTAIL

The average adult living in one of the industrialized nations has between 300 and 500 agrochemical pesticides in his or her body at any one time. Each of these toxic chemicals is stored in body fat, and each is toxic enough to kill insects. In combination, they are certainly more poisonous. Pesticides can remain stored in body fat for many years. No long-term studies have truly evaluated the damage to our health that these chemicals pose, but there is evidence to suggest that they exacerbate chronic conditions and seriously undermine health.

Children are particularly susceptible to agrochemical toxins. They have a higher intake of food than adults in relation to their body weight, and their bodies are less efficient at eliminating toxins. Breast milk from mothers whose diets are not organic generally contains concentrations of pesticides. These have been shown to adversely affect brain development in babies. Ideally, a woman planning to conceive a child should adopt an organic diet at least one year before falling pregnant. This gives her body time to detoxify, helping to create a healthier environment for the foetus to grow in and then purer breast milk for the baby once it has been born.

Artificial additives Every year, the average American eats more than two kilograms of chemical food additives. Seven thousand artificial additives are permitted to be used in conventional food. Only seven of these – the most innocuous – are allowed to be used in processed organic food. Artificial additives are used by manufacturers to improve the shelf life, flavour, colour, sweetness and saltiness of non-organic

Below: Organic fruit and vegetables, on sale at a local farmers' market, are fresh and full of goodness.

processed foods. Flavour enhancers may be added to disguise inferior quality ingredients. Although some artificial additives are absolutely harmless, many undermine our health. Generally they are used in combination, unleashing an unresearched toxic combination upon the consumer, which may well have implications in terms of cancer, asthma, liver disease and osteoporosis.

When food deteriorates naturally, you can see at a glance when it is past its best. Preservatives may artificially prolong a food's shelf life, but they do not prolong the life of all the nutrients within the product. When preservatives are banned, as in processed organic food, you can be sure that as long as the food is fresh, it is full of goodness.

Antibiotics and hormones Intensively reared livestock are routinely fed and injected with antibiotics to keep them healthy. These substances pass into their meat. People who eat this meat develop reduced immunity through over-exposure to antibiotics. On the other hand, bacteria that become over-exposed to antibiotics become increasingly resistant to them. The British Medical Association has stated that: "The risk to human health of antibiotic resistance...is one of the major health threats that could be faced in the 21st century."

Hormones and endocrine disrupting chemicals (EDCs) also pose a threat to health. Five out of the twelve most commonly used pesticides in the world are known to be EDCs. This means that they are known to affect the delicate balance of human hormones. Some women in Hawaii have extremely high rates of breast cancer. Hawaii also has a high rate of zeno-oestrogens from pesticides in its groundwater. A Danish scientific study, which tracked more than seven hundred Hawaiian women over twenty years, concluded that there is a probable link between the pesticides in the water and breast cancers.

There is also evidence that growth hormones from intensively farmed meat can lead to a wide variety of human endocrine disorders, from obesity to multi-generational cancers.

Above: Heirloom and rare varieties of potatoes are appearing at markets as organic farmers seek out new crops.

FOOD SAFETY

All organic animals that are naturally vegetarian are fed only vegetarian food. This was a huge benefit during the UK's BSE (Bovine Spongiform Encephalopathy) crisis. BSE was caused and spread because cows were fed contaminated food, which was itself animal in origin. All organic farms in the UK are completely BSE-free because organic cows are always fed food that is 100 per cent vegetarian.

Organic meat and dairy produce is free from genetically modified organisms or GMOs because all food for organic animals must be GMO-free by law. The diet of organic animals is also solvent free. This may seem obvious until it is considered that non-organic animals regularly eat food contaminated with solvents. Non-organic cooking oil is usually produced by soaking oil-rich vegetable matter in solvents. The oil is then extracted from the liquid, and the remaining solid matter is used for animal feed. Solvent-extracted animal feed is banned from organic farms.

NATURAL FLAVOURS

During the year 2000, 43 per cent of consumers who bought organic food in Britain declared that they did so because they thought it tasted better than non-organic food. Tastes vary from person to person, but there are sound reasons why organic food tastes better.

Most agrochemical crops are grown from seeds bred to produce a high yield. Organic fresh produce, however, comes from seeds bred primarily for flavour. Many organic farmers take pride in growing heirloom crops. These crops were once highly prized but have been overlooked in recent years because they were less commercially profitable than modern varieties. Organic growers in industrialized nations regularly produce about a hundred different kinds of potato. This is considerably fewer than the thousand or more varieties on sale at the farmer's market in the town of Cuzco in Peru, but at least five times more than the twenty or so varieties of agrochemically grown potatoes on sale in the USA or UK.

The slower growth rates of organic crops allow more time for flavour to develop naturally. Phytonutrients often help to flavour the fresh produce in which they occur so, as well as being good for health, high levels of certain

Above: *Flowers planted among vegetables encourage the predator insects that control pests in an environmentally friendly fashion.*

phytonutrients boost the taste factor. Sugar levels are often slightly higher in organic fresh produce than in non-organic varieties; this is particularly obvious in carrots and apples. Organic fruit is more likely to be allowed to ripen naturally on the tree, granting more time for flavours and sweetness to develop.

The lower percentage of water in organic fresh produce concentrates the nutrients and intensifies the flavour. If you were to evaporate all the water from an agrochemical carrot and an organic carrot of equal weight, the remaining dry matter from the organic carrot would be some 26 per cent heavier.

Food animals raised organically also benefit from growing more slowly than their agrochemical equivalents, and their meat becomes more flavoursome during the lengthy process. Another reason why meat from organic farms tastes better is because flavour is an important factor in selecting which type of animal to raise, and farmers are increasingly choosing the

Right: *Fresh produce grown in an organic vegetable garden is an excellent option for the health-conscious consumer.*

traditional heritage breeds that are noted for the tastiness of their meat above yield.

Organic prepared foods are allowed to contain very few of the chemical flavourings and flavour enhancers found in non-organic foods. Monosodium glutamate, for instance, is outlawed in organic food. This substance, commonly known as MSG, has been linked to nausea, dizziness and even asthma attacks. Organic foods taste so good that they do not need flavour enhancers.

Although much organic produce is currently grown a long way from the point of sale, it is best to buy it fresh from local producers. Not only will it have the finest flavour and highest concentration of nutrients, it will not contribute to pollution by having to be transported long distances. The range of fruit and vegetables may not be as great as that on offer in supermarkets, but the pleasure of enjoying seasonal treats such as strawberries in summer is more than adequate compensation.

ANIMAL WELFARE

Organic farm animals and poultry are treated with respect, without recourse to artificial hormones, antibiotics or routine drug therapies. Inhumane practices such as battery farming are banned. Dairy cows raised organically

have, on average, 50 per cent more room in their barns than non-organic cows, and unlike the latter, they are always provided with bedding. They also enjoy much more time out of doors. The same holds true for organic poultry.

WILDLIFE AND THE ENVIRONMENT

Our environment is under immense threat. Over the last 30 years, intensive farming in many countries has led to dramatic erosion of the soil. Bird populations have declined by up to 70 per cent, and some species of butterflies, frogs, grass snakes and wild mammals have been brought near extinction. Wild flowers and shrubs that once flourished in the fields are now seldom seen. Intensive farmers grub up ancient hedgerows that surround their fields to allow access for their giant machinery.

Organic farmers actively promote biodiversity by cherishing hedges, not just for their natural beauty, but for the practical support they offer. They play a vital role in supplying a habitat for the birds and insects that an organic farm needs in order to function. Wild flowers at the edge of a field attract butterflies and useful predators to the crop, so organic farmers always keep a strip of wild land around a field. Intensive farmers destroy resources such as these, either mechanically or by using

Above: *A willow fence forms a natural field boundary and encourages butterflies.*

pesticides. Many chemical pesticides are directly related to nerve gases. They are designed to kill. Those pests that survive being drenched with pesticides may develop immunity. Stronger pesticides must be developed and this leads to an ever-increasing cycle.

Although agrochemical farmers use pesticides to target specific pests, they are toxic to many creatures. Small mammals and birds are often killed or weakened by agricultural pesticides. Equally damaging are agrochemical seeds that have been treated with organochlorides in an attempt to prevent them being eaten. These highly poisonous chemicals, which last for years in the environment, kill numerous birds and animals every year.

Chemicals sprayed on crops eventually either penetrate the plants or trickle down into the soil, polluting the land and draining into the water table. The poisons then flow into streams and rivers, polluting the ecosystem. Agrochemical fertilizers are just as damaging to the ecosystem as pesticides. Nitrate-based fertilizers also seep out of the fields into the water system. In rivers and lakes, they stimulate the growth of algae. Excessive algae throws the whole ecosystem out of balance, poisoning waterways.

FARM WORKERS' HEALTH AND FAIR TRADE

On agrochemical farms, especially those in such developing countries as India, workers are often at direct risk from pesticide pollution. Protective clothing and machinery is expensive, whereas pesticide chemicals are relatively cheap. The result is that many farm workers are forced to apply these poisons to crops while unprotected. It is not only the farm workers themselves who are at risk – pesticides also endanger the general population.

Many farm workers in developing nations are exposed to horrifying amounts of poisons every day from childhood onwards. Pesticide exposure can lead to multi-generational diseases and cancers. The children of farm workers are more likely to have genetic defects that continue to successive generations. The workers often receive only subsistence wages for working long and back-breakingly hard days. In some countries, the average age of death for farm workers is around fifty.

Going organic avoids supporting these types of injustices. Using spending power sensitively is a direct way of working towards a fairer trading world. Many organic products are fairly traded, which means that a buyer will offer a reasonable price for crops. The majority

of trading between the developed and the developing world does not currently follow this principle. A cash-poor farmer may be forced to sell his crop for less than its worth because he does not have the bargaining power of a multinational company. For assurance that an organic product is fairly traded, look out for the Fairtrade seal and consult your supplier or shopkeeper.

PACKAGING

While packaging provides a valuable method of food preservation without the use of additives, unnecessary packaging is wasteful and environmentally insensitive. Many smaller organic companies are beginning to use recycled and recyclable containers for their products, but too many organic foods are still wrapped in the same plastics and bleached non-recycled papers as non-organic products.

Lobbying these organic companies to change their practices can help, but it is equally vital that organic consumers make every effort to recycle their waste. Glass, aluminium and paper are all candidates for recycling. Paper and plastic bags can be reused, and a compost bin is valuable for disposing of waste organic matter.

Below: *Recycling organic waste matter in compost bins is good for the environment and enriches the soil of any garden.*

FRESH PRODUCE

Good fruit and vegetables are at the heart of organic cuisine. The main point of agreement between health experts and nutritionists throughout the world is that we need to eat more fruit and vegetables. The United Nations World Health Organization has stated that if you eat five portions of fresh produce every day, you halve your chances of getting cancer.

If you can't afford to buy organic produce every day, it is better for you to supplement your diet with non-organic alternatives than to cut back on fruit and vegetables. Organic fresh produce is, however, nutritionally richer, tastier and more diverse. As well as the usual varieties on sale, you will find rare heirloom types of fruit and vegetables.

There is a huge global market for both organic and agrochemical produce,

Below: Stock up on fresh organic vegetables at local farmers' markets.

and imported fruit and vegetables often travel thousands of miles before they reach our shores. Because demand for organic produce is growing at such a high rate in industrialized countries, many organic fruit and vegetables are likely to have been transported long distances.

LOCAL PRODUCE

If you can get it, it is better to buy locally grown produce. There are two main reasons why this is superior to imported organic fruit and vegetables: nutrition and the need to avoid increasing pollution.

Locally grown food is more nutritious than food that has been flown in from another country. Fruit and vegetables for export are often picked before they are fully ripe and kept chilled to avoid spoilage. This means that they fail to develop the complex flavours and nutritional compounds available in produce that has been allowed to ripen naturally and has been freshly picked

Above: Growing your own organic herbs will add taste and nutrition to your cooking.

and transported no further than to the nearest farmers' market. Also, organic standards vary in different countries. Some are not as stringent as others in terms of conversion periods from agrochemical to organic farming, or in nurturing natural soil fertility.

The other major advantage of buying locally grown organic produce is to avoid contributing to pollution. Long-distance transportation of food, whether it be organic or agrochemical, currently uses enormous quantities of petrochemicals, to fuel aeroplanes, ships or road vehicles. Burning fossil fuels is the antithesis of the organic ideal. Major ecological advances, such as fuel cell technology, are in the pipeline for green transportation. However, as long as petrochemicals power organic food imports, it is preferable to buy locally grown organic produce where possible.

That said, buying imported organic fruit is sometimes the only option. Citrus trees do not grow outdoors in cool climates, and date palms prefer arid climates to wet ones. Supplementing locally grown organic produce in season with the occasional imported organic treat is probably a good balance for most organic connoisseurs.

GROWING AND BUYING

The best way to take advantage of the hundreds of different varieties of organic fruit and vegetables is to grow your own. Whether you have a couple of tubs on the patio, a vegetable plot or an impressive garden, preparing the soil,

Above: *Freshly dug organic potatoes have a flavour all of their own.*

nurturing the plants and then reaping the harvest is richly rewarding. The pleasures of gardening aside, the fresher the produce, the tastier and more nutritious it will be.

If you don't have green fingers, the best way to ensure that vegetables and fruit are fresh is to buy them from a local farmers' market or through a box scheme. Such schemes are operated by small individual growers or co-operatives. Customers opt for regular deliveries, either specifying which seasonal vegetables and fruit they would like to receive, or paying a fixed amount each week and leaving the selection of produce to the grower. The arrival of the box is then a delightful surprise, and often there will be extra treats, such as a few fresh herbs, a small box of berries or a head of the new season's garlic.

BUYING DIRECT
One key benefit of buying fruit and vegetables direct from the grower is to maintain a valid connection with our food. Purchasing vegetables from the man who grew them allows information about the produce to be exchanged. Stories about an individual crop can be passed on and cooking tips and recipes shared. A farmer might also welcome feedback on a new variety that he is experimenting with, and customers can let him know which fruit or vegetables they have particularly enjoyed.

Children who have watched carrots being lifted or have sifted through sacks of potatoes with soil still clinging to

them, will soon make the connection between their food and the place it comes from, and will be much more likely to enjoy their organic greens.

Farmers get a much better deal selling their organic food directly. Not only do they obtain about double the price at a farmers' market than they would if they sold to the supermarket, but they enjoy the contact with the townsfolk who tuck into their produce. Never before has the connection between urban and rural societies been so weak. Farmers' markets and box schemes help to bridge the gap.

SUPERMARKETS
It is possible, of course, to shop at the supermarket. While it is heartening that supermarkets are providing greater access to organic fresh produce than before, it is useful to be aware of a couple of negative aspects. Supermarkets generally spray non-organic produce with pesticides after it has left the field to ensure that stores remain free of insects. And, to avoid contamination of organic produce, they have to protect it in plastic packaging. This does not alter the organic status of the produce but the packaging does contribute to the environmental pollution that organic farming techniques aim to minimize. With increased public pressure, larger supermarket chains are likely to address this issue.

Another point to consider is that of food miles. Supermarkets tend to pool their products at central depots. This makes for easier distribution, but can be very wasteful of fuel and energy. An organic potato grown near Town A might well be driven to a central washing plant hundreds of miles away, near Town B. It may then be driven to the central supermarket distribution depot a similar distance away in Town C, only to be transported back to Town A for sale in the supermarket there.

Right: *Some packaging, such as this mug and spoon made out of recycled paper, is not harmful to the environment.*

CONVENIENCE FOODS
Enthusiastic organic cooks would doubtless prefer always to buy and cook fresh ingredients, but there are occasions when it is useful to have ready-made meals and frozen foods to hand. The wide range of organic convenience foods extends to pasta sauces, soups, TV dinners and freshly prepared sandwiches.

Organic convenience products are unlikely to be as tasty or nutritionally balanced as organic foods prepared at home, but they are better for you than the non-organic alternative. They contain only a small number of artificial additives and are prohibited from containing hydrogenated fats. Such foods may not be irradiated and are not allowed to contain genetically modified ingredients.

Many non-organic processed foods contain excessive levels of refined white sugar and salt, both of which should be avoided. The quick energy rush provided by white sugar is followed always by energy depletion. Complex natural unrefined sweeteners, such as organic fruit syrups, produce a far more balanced response from the body. Too much salt raises blood pressure, increasing the risk of heart disease and strokes. The majority of organic prepared foods offer a safe level of salt, but it is important to check the salt and sugar content on the label of all convenience products.

The good news is that some convenience foods, such as frozen organic fruit and vegetables, can be more nutritious than the fresh non-organic equivalent. This is because produce is frozen within hours of being picked, whereas fresh non-organic produce may have been picked many days before.

STORING FRESH FRUIT AND VEGETABLES

It is very important to store organic produce carefully because it will not keep as long as non-organic examples.

Store ripe fruit in a cool place, away from direct sunlight. Green bananas will ripen within a couple of days if they are stored in a plastic bag with an over-ripe banana. Soft fruits such as tomatoes, kiwi fruits and avocados can be placed on a sunny window sill to help them ripen. This also brings out the flavour and encourages their natural juices to flow.

Most fresh vegetables are best stored in the refrigerator. Salad crops, including lettuces, rocket (arugula) and spinach, should be eaten within a few days of purchase. Root vegetables should be left unwashed, as the soil or mud coating helps to keep them fresh. Moisture is retained within the root or tuber, so unwashed carrots, turnips and potatoes keep for much longer than the shiny, scrubbed vegetables that look so pretty but perish so much quicker.

Right: *Making flavourful juices from fresh fruit and vegetables is easy and delicious, as in this power booster mix of apple, carrot and beetroot (at back). Blend cucumber, tomatoes, garlic and lemon juice for an energizing summer drink (at front).*

COOKING ORGANIC FRUIT AND VEGETABLES

Cooking fruit reduces valuable vitamins and minerals, so, if you can, eat it raw. Over-cooking vegetables depletes their nutritional value, destroys their texture, impairs their flavour and spoils their natural colour. It is always advisable to steam vegetables rather than boil them. Boiling vegetables destroys up to half their nutrients, although this figure can be reduced if the vegetables are cooked whole and sliced afterwards. Better still, serve vegetables raw. They will contain many more enzymes than if cooked. Enzymes help us to digest the micronutrients in fresh produce, so, apart from potatoes, aim to cook for as short a time as possible.

JUICING

If you need to use up a stock of fruit or vegetables quickly, simply juice them. This is the most direct way of accessing the nutrients. Any vegetables can be mixed together satisfactorily, but apples are the only fruit that work well with vegetables. By the same token, any combination of fruit can be juiced, but if you want to add a vegetable, make it a carrot. Following these rules ensures that juices do not curdle and are refreshing, delicious and nutritious.

PRESERVING

For added variety during the winter months, you can preserve organic fruit. Marmalades and jams are easy to make. Drying slices of fruit, such as apples, by baking them overnight in the oven on a very low heat maintains much of the nutritional value while concentrating the taste. It is important to use organic fruit when preserving, as the peel is included. All kinds of organic dried fruit can be bought, from apricots to bananas and mangoes. Non-organic dried fruits are generally treated with sulphur, fungicides and mineral oils, whereas organic varieties are preserved naturally.

Left: *Pickling is a great way to preserve extra stocks of all sorts of vegetables, including garlic, small onions and shallots.*

ALLIUMS

This family of plants includes onions, leeks, chives and garlic, all of which owe their characteristic odour and flavour to a compound called allicin. Organic alliums contain more allicin than their non-organic counterparts, so have stronger flavours and more health benefits. Organic onions are sweeter, and organic garlic is more pungent. Unfortunately, allicin is also the constituent in alliums that makes us cry, so organic onions should be chopped at arm's length – or by someone else!

Alliums help to lower cholesterol. They also have antibacterial qualities and can help to relieve asthma, bronchitis and other sinus and chest ailments. The cycloallin they contain is an anticoagulant, which thins the blood and helps to protect the heart. Alliums also have anti-fungal properties; the juice can be rubbed on to the skin to relieve fungal infections. Garlic is the most powerful healer of the alliums and has been praised for its medicinal powers for hundreds of years, but all members of the family contain some allicin, so they all have beneficial qualities.

All alliums should be stored in a cool place. It is important to keep them dry or they will begin to sprout. Organic alliums keep just as well as non-organic ones. The wide variety of onions can be enjoyed raw or cooked and, with garlic, add flavour to many savoury dishes.

Above: A bunch of baby leeks is a bonus in the autumn organic vegetable box.

ONIONS

These are indispensable in the organic kitchen and form the basis of innumerable savoury dishes, including salads, stews, soups and gravies. There are many varieties, including big Spanish onions and small, sweet red onions. Add onions on the side when making a classic organic cooked breakfast. Not only do they taste delicious with bacon and sausages, but they have been shown to cut cholesterol radically.

GARLIC

Although it is the most powerful healer of the allium family, this is not garlic's only attribute. It also has a superb flavour. Both hard- and soft-neck varieties are on sale in the organic market, and there is a wealth of taste and colour to explore. Hard-neck garlic, like Pink Music, has a central woody stem surrounded by five to ten easy-to-peel cloves. It has a richer, more rounded flavour than soft-neck garlic, which is the type you often find twisted together, French fashion, to form plaits or braids. Soft-neck garlic, such as Mother of Pearl, has a spicy flavour. Each bulb contains a seemingly endless amount of increasingly smaller cloves.

Below: Red onions have been shown to cut cholesterol radically.

Above: Bulb spring onions (scallions) are at their most nutritious when they are raw.

This type of garlic can be stored for up to a year, unlike hard-neck garlic, which must be used within six months. Fresh organic garlic is available but it is at its best when dried and cured. When the thin skin is papery dry, the cloves are mature and will burst with flavour. Look for a firm head when buying garlic.

Above: Garlic

LEEKS

A bunch of sweet, young leeks is a bonus in the autumn organic vegetable box. They are good enough to eat raw, but also taste great when lightly steamed or sautéed with garlic.

SPRING ONIONS (SCALLIONS) AND CHIVES

These vegetables taste delicious, especially when raw, when they are at their most nutritious. Organic growers often sell bunches of thin, young spring onions which make delicious snacks.

TUBERS

Whether you are shopping for potatoes, yacons or Jerusalem artichokes, you'll be spoilt for choice, since there are many more varieties of organic tubers available than the few agrochemical types.

POTATOES

A farmers' market or box scheme will provide opportunities to sample unusual types of organic potatoes. There are huge variations in the size and flavour of potatoes, and colours include yellow, red, pink, purple and black. There are two textures: waxy and floury. Common waxy varieties include new potatoes, Pink Fir Apple and Charlotte. Maris Piper and Estima are floury. Yukon Gold and Alaskan Sweetheart are also good.

All potatoes are a good source of vitamin C and the B group vitamins. Organic potatoes are helpful in supporting the body's natural resistance and keeping energy levels steady. Their peel can safely be eaten, boosting fibre levels, nutrition and flavour.

Waxy potatoes are ideal for frying and steaming, while floury potatoes are better for mashing or creaming. Use floury potatoes in leek and potato soup or for chips (French fries) that are soft in the middle, and waxy new potatoes as a springtime accompaniment for lamb chops. Potatoes should be stored in a dark, cool place that is perfectly dry.

JERUSALEM ARTICHOKES

Widely available in the autumn months, these delicious vegetables have an unusual, slightly bitter yet buttery flavour, and are excellent served alone or incorporated into dishes. Their bitterness is due to the presence of a compound called *cynarine*. This is a powerful liver stimulant, so eating Jerusalem artichokes will support liver

Above: Jerusalem artichokes help detoxify the body.

action, helping to detoxify the body. Organic Jerusalem artichokes also help to alleviate rheumatism and arthritis. Try Jerusalem artichokes lightly steamed with fish, or mashed with potatoes and swedes (rutabagas).

SWEET POTATOES

When cooked, sweet potatoes become sticky and soft with a gorgeous, smooth taste. Organic varieties are particularly sweet and are an excellent source of vitamins, including vitamins C, E and betacarotene, which helps to prevent cancer. They encourage eye and skin health, too. Because organic sweet potatoes are free of fungicides, they can be scrubbed and cooked whole for a wonderfully caramelized alternative to the ubiquitous baked potato. They are also good when steamed and mashed in the same way as regular potatoes.

YACON TUBERS

Almost all yacon tubers are organic. A staple food of the people of the Andes, they can be savoured cooked or raw. They are a good source of complex carbohydrates, with lots of vitamins and minerals. Their crunchy flesh is sweet and juicy like that of a water chestnut or jicama. Try them sliced or grated in leaf or rice salads. When steamed or roasted, the yacon becomes even sweeter. Yacons are not widely available, but can be found through box schemes and at farmers' markets. Store them in the salad drawer of the refrigerator.

Above: Sweet potatoes are a good source of vitamins, including vitamins C, E and betacarotene.

Below: Organic farmers produce many varieties of white and red potatoes.

ROOTS

The roots are a plant's powerhouse, and root vegetables provide us with a delicious way of tapping into this energy store. Organic root vegetables are often more knobbly and curly than agrochemically grown root vegetables. They deliver more nutrition and flavour than their more uniform counterparts, as well as being more individual in appearance.

All root vegetables should be stored unwashed. As with tubers, a layer of soil helps to seal moisture and nutrients into the roots.

Below: Swedes (rutabaga) contain vitamins A and C.

CARROTS
Organically grown carrots are extremely high in betacarotenes, giving them a rich orange colour. Celebrate this with a sweet Middle Eastern salad. Grate four small carrots and mix with the juice of one orange, a few sesame seeds and 5ml/ 1 tsp honey. Alternatively, simply steam lightly or add to stews and stir-fries.

Below: Turnips are credited with soothing aching joints.

PARSNIPS
Organic parsnips are fragrant and intense. When roasted, they caramelize more successfully than non-organic ones because they are sweeter. Their flavour concentrates and the texture becomes chewy, with a crunch at the tip.

SWEDES (RUTABAGA) AND TURNIPS
There is nothing more comforting on a cold winter night than mashed swede with a little butter and seasoning. Organic turnips have a subtle flavour, underpinned with a bitter edge that people love or hate. They are delicious lightly steamed and served as a side dish for fish. Turnips deliver calcium and potassium and are credited with soothing aching joints.

BEETROOT (BEETS)
Organic beetroot comes in an amazing variety of types. From yellow mangels to the Italian bull's-eye beet, these are the most colourful root vegetables. Young beetroot tastes very good when it is raw and grated. Alternatively, roast them with a medley of other root vegetables.

Left: Radishes are a good source of anti-cancer phytochemicals.

RADISHES
When grown organically, radishes are very hot and spicy. They also have more concentrated amounts of anti-cancer phytochemicals. Traditionally, radishes are eaten to stimulate the gall bladder to manufacture digestive juices. The many varieties range from Japanese daikon to the classic red cherry belle. As with all root vegetables, any sign of springiness indicates that a radish is not fresh. Radishes are delicious sliced raw in salads, especially with watercress or rocket (arugula), and are also good in stir-fries.

MAKING A BASIC VEGETABLE STOCK
Homemade stock is a healthier option than the store-bought version and is easy to make. It can be stored in the refrigerator for up to four days. Alternatively, prepare it in large quantities and freeze.

INGREDIENTS
15ml/1 tbsp olive oil
1 potato, chopped
1 carrot, chopped
1 onion, chopped
1 celery stalk, chopped
2 garlic cloves, peeled
1 sprig thyme
1 bay leaf
a few stalks of parsley
600ml/1 pint/2½ cups water
salt and freshly ground pepper

1 Heat the oil in a large pan. Add the vegetables and cook, covered, for 10 minutes, or until softened, stirring occasionally. Stir in the garlic and herbs.

2 Pour the water into the pan, bring to the boil, and simmer, partially covered, for 40 minutes. Strain, season with salt and pepper, and use as required.

PUMPKINS AND SQUASHES

Organic farmers grow many more varieties of pumpkins and squashes than agrochemical farmers. Summer squashes include the thin-skinned courgettes (zucchini) and patty pans, while winter brings the heavyweights, such as pumpkins and acorn squashes, with their glowing colours, thick skins and superb keeping properties. The natural sweetness of these vegetables makes them a favourite with small children. To cook, simply cut open, scoop out the seeds, slice into cubes and steam or roast until soft.

COURGETTES (ZUCCHINI) AND MARROWS (LARGE ZUCCHINI)

Organic courgettes range in colour from pale yellow to deep green. They can easily be grown in a garden or on a balcony, and are readily available in stores and farmers' markets. Slice them into salads, or fry with onions, garlic, coriander and paprika for a quick side dish. Marrows are best baked. Try stuffing them with brown rice, almonds, onions and cheese.

Summer squash are effective diuretics and their potassium content helps to relieve high blood pressure.

Right: Organic marrows (large zucchini) have a pleasant mild flavour.

Right: Courgettes (zucchini) relieve high blood pressure.

PUMPKINS

Classic round orange pumpkins are full of betacarotene. This has been proven scientifically to help prevent cancer, particularly lung cancer. Pumpkin seeds can be washed, seasoned and roasted for a delicious snack that is rich in protein, minerals and B vitamins. Shell them after roasting to enjoy their nutty flavour, and reap the benefits of their protective action on the human reproductive system.

Above: Pumpkins are full of betacarotene, which has been scientifically proven to help prevent cancer.

ROASTING SQUASH

Cooking squash this way brings out its flavour and retains the goodness.

1 Preheat the oven to 200°C/400°F/Gas 6. Cut the squash in half, scoop out the seeds and place it cut side down on an oiled baking sheet.

2 Bake for 30 minutes, or until the flesh is soft. Serve in the skin, or remove the flesh and mash with butter and seasoning.

GREENS

Green-leaf vegetables, such as cabbages, broccoli, chard, Brussels sprouts and cauliflower, are among the best sources of phytochemicals when organic. They help to defend the body against cancer, and should be eaten every day if possible. Leaf vegetables are a rich source of vitamins and minerals, too, including vitamin C, calcium, iron and betacarotene.

Agrochemical green-leaf vegetables are heavily sprayed with the strongest fungicides, insecticides and herbicides. Some include a compound, lindane, which is banned in the USA but still used in other countries. Organic vegetables are not sprayed in this way. They are nutritionally richer, with a more complex phytochemical profile and a more complex flavour. Lightly steamed or freshly stir-fried they are full of colour, crunch and vitality.

Below: Organic cabbages are among the best sources of phytochemicals.

CAULIFLOWERS

When grown organically, cauliflowers are often quite small, around the size of tennis balls. Try to find vegetables that still have their outer leaves. The leaves should be green rather than yellow to indicate freshness, and they are a usable part of the cauliflower. Remove them from the cauliflower head and steam for a few minutes.

Above: Organic cauliflowers are often quite small, which was how they looked when they were first cultivated.

Below: Spinach is high in folic

SWISS CHARD AND SPINACH

Vegetarians and vegans are advised to eat chard and spinach regularly. Swiss chard is a rich, deep green with bright red or creamy white veins, and is almost exclusively found organically grown. Rich in iron, calcium, vitamins A and C and carotenes, Swiss chard is excellent for menstruating women and also as a treatment for anaemia.

Organic spinach is available as small baby salad leaves or fully-grown. A superb source of chlorophyll and folic acid, it is an excellent food for preconception and pregnancy.

To prepare, cut chard leaves away from their stems. Steam the stems for two to three minutes, adding the leaves at the end for only a few seconds. Likewise, steam spinach for about 20 to 30 seconds as the delicate leaves wilt almost immediately. Alternatively, lightly fry the leaves in organic olive oil or butter for a few moments, or simply eat them raw in a salad.

CABBAGES

These versatile vegetables come in a variety of organic types, from wrinkly January kings to smooth purple red cabbages. Some have tight, compact heads; while others are loose-leaved. Thinly sliced cabbage makes a very good salad or slaw. Stir-frying cabbage leaves brings out their natural sweetness.

SALAD VEGETABLES

Fresh vegetables are at the heart of organic cuisine, and the most nutritious way to eat them is in salads. Most vegetables, with the exception of potatoes, can be used raw in salads, but some are particularly well suited to this treatment.

LETTUCES

Along with other salad leaves, lettuces are the classic basis of a salad, and organic ones are extremely tasty and nutritious. All lettuces contain tiny quantities of opiates, which give the vegetable relaxing qualities that help to relieve stress and relax the lungs. It is these compounds that contribute the characteristic, slightly bitter taste. Organic lettuces contain more phytochemical compounds than agrochemical examples. Nutritionally, lettuce is best eaten raw, but it can also be braised or steamed.

SALAD LEAVES

Pak choi (bok choy), Chinese mustard greens, mizuna and tatsoi are just some of the salad leaves grown organically. Try raising your own lettuces and salad leaves from seed. They are easy to grow all year round on a window sill,

Left: Organic pak choi is free from harmful chemical pesticides and fertilizers.

or outside in spring and autumn. When buying prepared salads, it is absolutely-essential to choose organic. Non-organic prepared salads are washed in chlorine to prevent the leaves from going brown. This is why a home-prepared salad composed of similar ingredients will not last as long. Organic prepared salads and ready-cut vegetables are simply preserved by oxygen exclusion and modern refrigeration methods.

Below: Lettuces are easy to grow all year round on a window sill or outside in the spring and autumn.

CUCUMBERS

Organically grown cucumbers are full of flavour and there are lots of different kinds. The tiny lemon cucumber looks rather like its namesake. Yellow in colour, it is so short and plump that it is almost round. These cucumbers have an extraordinary ability to absorb radiation, an attribute that was underlined during experiments with organic lemon cucumbers at the Los Alamos nuclear research centre in the United States. Lemon cucumbers are just one of the many traditional and heirloom varieties of cucumbers that are grown organically alongside the more familiar long, green cucumbers. With their refreshing, mild flavour cucumbers are perfect in salads.

Below: Traditional cucumbers are available in organic varieties.

Above: *Watercress helps to relieve the symptoms of lung cancer and skin complaints.*

Above: *Avocados contain essential fatty acids.*

WATERCRESS AND CELERY
Unless they are organic, watercress and celery are generally both treated heavily with pesticides and fertilizers. Because it has a high water content, agrochemical watercress can be particularly toxic and could well be laced with nitrates.

Organic watercress may be smaller but the flavour is sharper and more concentrated. The pungent taste is due to an antibacterial phytonutrient, so watercress works well against bacterial disorders such as food poisoning. It is also believed to protect against – and relieve the symptoms of – lung cancer and skin complaints. It can be used in smaller quantities than agrochemical watercress because of its intensity. Try it in salads, or make it into a peppery soup with onions, cream and nutmeg.

Celery helps to flush out excess fluid from the body and is a useful remedy for constipation. It is great in a mixed vegetable juice or stock. When finely sliced, fresh celery adds crunch to a Waldorf salad. Celery is also delicious braised and will add flavour to a stuffing for roast chicken.

AVOCADOS
These are possibly the most indulgent of vegetables. Many dieters are deterred from eating these delicious vegetables because of their relatively high calorie content, but they are packed with the right sorts of fats, essential fatty acids. Non-organic avocados are often picked while they are still bullet hard and ripened artificially, whereas organic avocados ripen naturally over a longer period. The result is creamy flesh that relieves PMS, is great for the skin and helps prevent cancer. Slice or cube avocado for salads, or mash with lemon juice and chilli for an instant guacamole dip. You can even use the empty avocado skins to moisturize your skin.

PREPARING FENNEL

With a sharp knife, cut the fennel bulb in half lengthwise, then either cut into quarters or slice thinly.

FENNEL
The aromatic fennel bulb has a very similar texture to celery and is topped with edible feathery fronds. Organic fennel is smaller and tastier than non-organic fennel, with essential oils that help combat digestive complaints such as flatulence. Its distinctive aniseed flavour is most potent when eaten raw in salads. This tasty vegetable can also be braised, when it acquires a delicious sweetness. Fennel is at its best when it is fresh and should be eaten as soon as possible after purchase.

Below: *Fennel contains essential oils that can help combat digestive disorders.*

VEGETABLE FRUITS

Tomatoes, aubergines (eggplant), (bell) peppers and chillies are treated as vegetables in cooking but classified botanically as fruit.

TOMATOES

There is simply no comparison between the flavour of a freshly picked organic tomato that has been allowed to ripen naturally and the taste of an artificially ripened tomato. Organic growers select the sweetest, tastiest varieties, and whether you buy tiny cherry tomatoes or big beefsteaks, you won't be disappointed.

In terms of nutrition, tomatoes contain a beneficial carotenoid called lycopene. This important micro-nutrient helps to protect the body from cancer, especially cancers of the gastrointestinal tract, breast, cervix and prostate. Lycopene is present in the fresh fruit and is released from the skin when fresh tomatoes are cooked. This means that levels of lycopene are even higher in canned or processed products, such as tomato purée (paste), canned tomatoes, ketchup and pasteurized tomato juice, than they are in fresh tomatoes. However, fresh tomatoes are

Left: Chadwick tomatoes are sweet and juicy.

higher in vitamin C, which is destroyed in cooking. It is absolutely essential to buy organic tomato products since almost all non-organic prepared tomato products contain GMO tomatoes.

CHILLIES

Fresh chillies come in a wide variety of shapes, sizes and colours, with flavours ranging from mild and fruity to intensely fiery. Organic growers like to experiment with the rarer varieties, so you may find unusual types at a farmers' market. More than 200 different types of chilli are available and they now form an integral part of very many cuisines, including Indian, Thai, Mexican, South American and African.

Right: Serrano chillies contain capsaicin, a phytochemical that is essential for heart health.

Above: Naturally ripened organic tomatoes contain a beneficial carotenoid called lycopene, which helps protect the body from cancer.

CHILLI BOOST

For an instant uplift, sprinkle some organic crushed chilli on your food. The chilli will stimulate the release of endorphins, which are the body's "feel-good" chemicals.

Handle chilli peppers with care, as they can irritate the skin and eyes. Wear gloves when preparing chillies.

Chillies are the concentrated relations of sweet peppers, and there are wonderful stories concerning their heart-strengthening abilities. They also have antibacterial properties and help respiration and chest complaints.

Like peppers, chillies contain *capsaicin*. In chillies, however, it is concentrated, and accounts for their heat. Handle them with care, as the *capsaicin* can damage sensitive skin, especially around the lips and eyes. The hottest part of a chilli is the white membrane that connects the seeds to the flesh. Removing this membrane and the seeds removes most of the heat. The heat can also be moderated and the sweetness released if chillies are roasted or grilled (broiled) until charred, and then peeled in the same way as peppers. Chillies prepared in this way freeze well.

Left: Organic aubergines (eggplants) are meaty and delicious.

AUBERGINES (EGGPLANTS)

Organic aubergines are both meaty and delicious. They come in a range of beautiful varieties, from the dappled pink Listada de Gandia to the creamy White Sword. The phytochemical that gives aubergines their bitter flavour helps to prevent and cure the common cold. If you prefer a less bitter taste, slice each vegetable and sprinkle it with salt. Leave for about an hour and the salt will leach out the bitterness, then rinse thoroughly and pat dry before cooking. This also prevents the absorption of excessive oil when frying.

A great way to release the sweetness of aubergines is to bake them. Simply put them, on a baking sheet, in an oven preheated to 180°C/350°F/Gas 4. Cook for about 30 minutes or until tender, then peel the skin from the flesh, chop them and serve drizzled with olive oil, tahini and lemon juice. This popular dish is known as baba ganoush. Aubergines are also delicious roasted, griddled and puréed into garlic-laden dips.

PEPPERS (BELL PEPPERS)

Agrochemical peppers are often grown hydroponically, which is why they tend to taste inferior to organic ones. Organic peppers are full of vitamin C as well as containing the phytochemical capsaicin that is great for heart health. Green peppers are fully developed but less ripe than other examples, which can make them hard to digest. They have refreshing juicy flesh with a crisp texture. In addition to being more mature, orange, red and purple peppers have sweeter flesh and are more digestible than less ripe green peppers. Roasting or chargrilling peppers enhances their sweetness. Peppers are also delicious when they are served stuffed, sliced into salads or steamed.

Below: Sweet (bell) peppers are members of the capsicum family. The very best organic peppers are firm and glossy with unblemished skins.

PEELING (BELL) PEPPERS

1 Roast the peppers under a hot grill (broiler) for 12–15 minutes, turning regularly, until the skin chars.

2 Alternatively, place on a baking sheet and roast in an oven preheated to 200°C/400°F/Gas 6 for 20–30 minutes, until the skin blackens and blisters.

3 Put the peppers in a plastic bag and leave until cool. The steam will encourage the skin to come away from the flesh easily.

4 Peel away the skin, then slice in half. Remove the core and scrape out any remaining seeds. Slice or chop according to your recipe.

MUSHROOMS

Non-organic mushrooms are subjected to vast amounts of chemicals, on the crop itself and to sterilize the straw on which they grow. Fungicides and insecticides are sprayed over them and their growing sheds are regularly bleached. Organic mushrooms have no such hazards. They are also much tastier than most non-organic varieties, whether simply sliced raw in a salad or fried with tamari or soy sauce.

Most organic mushrooms do not contain a wealth of nutrients, but are a useful source of B vitamins, potassium, iron and niacin. Organic shiitake mushrooms, however, are fantastic for the immune system, and have been prized for centuries in Japan for their medicinal properties. They are also a good source of phytochemicals and other nutrients. Dried shiitake mushrooms are readily available in organic stores.

Button (white), cap and flat mushrooms are the most common cultivated variety of mushrooms. They are all one type of mushroom in various stages of maturity, from small button mushrooms, through cap mushrooms to the largest, strongest-flavoured flat mushrooms. Flat mushrooms are good grilled (broiled) or baked on their own or with stuffing.

Left: Fresh and dried shiitake mushrooms are fantastic for the immune system.

Chestnut (cremini) mushrooms look similar to button mushrooms but have brown caps and a nutty flavour. Field (portabello) mushrooms are wild and have intense, rich flavour which makes them ideal for grilling and stuffing.
Chanterelles are a pretty yellow colour, with a funnel-shape and a fragrant but delicate flavour. Available dried as well as fresh, they are delicious sautéed, baked or added to sauces.

Store fresh organic mushrooms in paper bags in the refrigerator, and use within a few days of purchase. When you are ready to eat them, wipe the mushrooms gently with damp kitchen paper and trim the stems. Wild mushrooms often harbour grit and dirt and may need to be rinsed briefly under cold running water but they must be dried thoroughly. Never soak fresh mushrooms or they will become soggy.

PREPARING DRIED SHIITAKE MUSHROOMS

Dried shiitake mushrooms are a useful store-cupboard stand-by. Before they can be used in cooking, however, they must be rehydrated.

1 Quickly wash off any dirt under cold running water, then soak dried shiitake mushrooms in tepid water for about 2–3 hours, or overnight. If you are short of time, soak for at least 45 minutes before cooking.

2 Remove the shiitake from the soaking water, and gently squeeze out any excess water. With your fingers or a knife, trim off the stem and then slice or chop the caps to use in cooking. Add the stems to soups or stock. Don't discard the soaking liquid; rather drain it through muslin (cheesecloth), then use it in soups or stews or for simmering vegetables.

Left: This mixed selection of organic mushrooms is a useful source of B vitamins, iron, potassium and niacin.

PEAS, BEANS AND CORN

These popular organic vegetables can be bought frozen as well as fresh so you can enjoy them all year round. They are frozen within hours of being picked and so are still high in nutritional value.

Left: Organic corn cobs have sweet kernels.

PEAS AND BEANS
Organic farmers often rely on legume crops to keep their fields fertile, so there is usually an abundant and varied supply of peas and beans, from sweet mangetouts (snow peas) to meaty broad (fava) beans. Early summer brings the first garden peas, so sweet and tender that you can eat them raw, straight from the pod. This season is short, but other delights lie ahead. Crisp French (green) beans, sugar snaps and runner beans soon appear on organic market stalls.

Shelled peas are best eaten lightly steamed or added to sauces and stews in the last few minutes of cooking. Mangetouts and beans can be sliced raw into salads, stir-fried or lightly steamed as a side dish. Store fresh peas and beans in the salad compartment of the refrigerator and use them within a week to ensure the best taste.

CORN
Organic corn cobs are often smaller and paler than the agrochemical equivalent, but the kernels are beautifully tender and sweet. Corn cobs are best eaten soon after picking, before their natural sugars start to convert into starch, the kernels begin to toughen and their flavour fades. Remove the green outer leaves and cook whole or slice off the kernels with a sharp knife. Baby corn can be eaten raw, and are also good in stir-fries. One delicious way to serve corn on the cob is to fry it whole in hot olive oil for just a few minutes. The heat will be just enough to release the natural sweetness and caramelize the exterior.

Left: Organic mangetouts and sugar snap peas have a fresh flavour.

EDA-MAME
These are fresh soya beans. They are widely available in Japan and in many parts of the USA. Eda-mame deliver a complete balance of protein and phytochemicals that are good for maintaining healthy hormone levels.

PREPARING EDA-MAME

This is a good way to appreciate young soya beans in the pod.

1 Separate the pods from the stalks, if they are still attached, and trim off the stem end. Sprinkle the pods generously with salt and rub the salt into the bean pods with your hands. Leave for 15 minutes.

2 Boil plenty of water in a large pan, then add the beans and boil over a high heat for 7–10 minutes, or until the beans are tender but still crunchy. Drain immediately and refresh briefly under running water.

3 Serve hot or cold in a basket or a bowl with drinks. To eat, squeeze the pods with your teeth to push out the beans into your mouth.

SEA VEGETABLES

Also known as seaweeds, these amazing vegetables, with unusual, tangy flavours and exotic colours, provide our strongest natural source of minerals and trace elements. Nori, wakame and hijiki are the richest sources of minerals. Nori is also the best source of protein.

Although Japan and China are the countries best known for their use of sea vegetables, seaweeds have been collected all over the world for centuries.

One interesting property of seaweeds is their ability to detoxify the body thanks to the alginic acid they contain. When we ingest this substance, it binds with heavy metals in our intestines and allows them to be released, cleansing the body. Nori, laver, dulse, kombu, wakame and arame are all types of seaweeds with these detoxifying properties.

Fresh seaweed requires little preparation. Having been gathered in clean and unpolluted water, it needs to be rinsed in fresh water before being dried in the sun or in an oven on a very low heat. It can also be chopped and frozen.

Most seaweeds are only available dried. Once reconstituted they can be used as substitutes for fresh green vegetables, toasted and crumbled over soups, salads or stir-fries, or used in sushi. Unopened packets of dried sea vegetables keep well for several months if stored in a cool place. Canned organic seaweeds often taste stronger than the dried versions.

NORI

The traditional sushi wrap, nori is one sea vegetable that does not require soaking. It comes in purple-black sheets which, when toasted for use as a garnish, turn translucent green.

Above: Dried and cut wakame can be used in stews and salads.

Below: Toasted nori sheets add crunch when used as a garnish.

TOASTING NORI
This brings out the flavour and makes nori crispy. Take care not to scorch the nori sheets – or your fingers.

I Hold a sheet of nori with a pair of tongs about 5cm/2in above a gas burner for about I minute, moving it around so it toasts evenly and turns bright green and crisp.

2 Leave the nori to cool for a few moments. Crumble between your fingers and sprinkle over soups, salads or stir-fries, or use in sushi.

WAKAME
A dark-coloured seaweed with a delicate flavour, wakame adds body to stews and can also be used in salads. A small strip, cooked with beans and pulses, will help to soften them. Prepare it in the same way as arame.

KOMBU
A strongly flavoured seaweed with flat fronds, kombu, or kelp as it is also known, is used in slowly cooked dishes. It is an essential ingredient in the Japanese stock, dashi.

PREPARING DRIED HIJIKI

Soaking and cooking times vary depending on how the hijiki is to be used.

1 Rinse the hijiki in a strainer under cold, running water, then place in a bowl and cover with tepid water. Leave to soak for 15 minutes – it will expand to several times its dried volume. Drain and place in a pan.

2 Add fresh water to cover the hijiki and bring to the boil. Simmer for about 20 minutes until tender.

Above: Hijiki requires longer cooking than most sea vegetables.

Below: Laver is high in minerals and vitamins.

ARAME

Mild-tasting arame is a good sea vegetable to try if you haven't tasted these vegetables before. It must be soaked in warm water for 20 minutes before using in salads or stir-fries, but can be added straight from the packet to slow-cooked noodle dishes and soups.

HIJIKI

This twiggy, black sea vegetable looks similar to arame but is thicker and has a stronger flavour. It requires longer cooking than most sea vegetables.

LAVER

Commonly found around the shores of Britain, laver is used in regional dishes such as Welsh laverbread, where it is combined with oatmeal. It can be added to sauces and stuffings.

DULSE

A purple-red sea vegetable, dulse has a chewy texture and spicy flavour when cooked. It can be added to salads. In Wales, Ireland, North America and Canada, dulse is gathered in summer and sold in health food stores and fish markets. It is great in noodle dishes and soups or toasted and crumbled for a nourishing garnish.

Right: Dulse has a spicy flavour.

AGAR-AGAR

A setting agent, derived from a type of seaweed called "rock flower vegetable" in China, agar-agar is an ideal vegetarian alternative to gelatine. Available in strips or as powder, it can be used to make excellent sweet or savoury jellies.

HERBS AND EDIBLE FLOWERS

Fresh and dried herbs have been prized by cooks for centuries for their ability to enhance the flavour of any ingredient they accompany and enliven even the simplest meal. It is a bonus that many herbs have remarkable healing qualities.

Typically, organic herbs have stronger flavours than non-organic ones because they have a higher concentration of phytochemicals. These active components are the main source of a herbal plant's flavour and health-promoting properties. Non-organic herbs all have the medicinal and taste benefits of organic herbs, but often contain much smaller amounts of the essential oils vital for these purposes. Since it is rare for cooks to wash fresh herbs thoroughly before use, pesticide residues on non-organic herbs can be inadvertently included in a meal. Dried non-organic herbs carry the same risk.

Another big plus when buying herbs from organic growers is the sheer variety and number of plants on offer, including unusual and heirloom varieties such as apple mint, purple basil and Chinese chives. By shopping from organic growers direct, or sourcing organic seeds, the organic cook has access to a much broader selection of flavours.

GROWING HERBS

It is essential to use fresh herbs before they start to wilt, and the best way to guarantee freshness is to grow your own herbs in pots or in a window box. Good herbs that grow all year round are parsley, thyme, chives, marjoram, winter savory, sorrel and tarragon. These perennials are quite difficult to grow from seed, so they are best bought as young plants.

Annual herbs such as mint or basil can be grown from seeds sown from late March onwards. They should be sown in seed compost in shallow trays and transferred to bigger containers after about a month. Herbs should always be grown outside, and stone or terracotta pots are best. Traditional herb pots not only look attractive, with their little pockets on the sides, but also work well. All herbs need to be kept under cover on the very coldest nights of winter, but can otherwise stay outside on a window sill or balcony, or in the garden.

Right: Basil is said to have a calming effect on the stomach, easing constipation, sickness and cramps, and aiding digestion.

MAKING BOUQUET GARNI
Tie herbs in a bundle, or bouquet garni, when you want the flavour but not the herbs themselves in a dish.

1 With a long piece of string, tie together a few parsley stalks, a sprig of thyme and a bay leaf, or your own choice of herbs. Add a piece of celery stick to flavour poultry dishes, a spring of rosemary for lamb, or a piece of fennel or leek for fish dishes.

2 Dried or chopped herbs can be bundled together in a small muslin (cheesecloth) bag. Break or tear the herbs into small pieces and place in the centre of a 10–13cm/4–5in square of clean muslin. Bring the edges of the muslin up over the herbs and tie firmly into a bag with a length of string. Make muslin bundles in batches so that they are readily at hand for cooking.

3 Tie one end of the string to the pan handle or leave it hanging over the edge of the casserole to make it easy to remove and discard the herbs before serving the dish.

CULINARY COMBINATIONS

The reason why particular herbs are traditionally added to certain dishes has something to do with complementary flavours, but there are other practical considerations, too. The classic combination of fried lamb's liver with sage not only tastes superb, but the sage helps the body to digest the meat. Organic rosemary contains powerful essential oils that stimulate the digestive system to make extra bile. This makes it the perfect partner for lamb and chicken dishes. Bay leaves added to bolognese sauce aid the digestion of a pasta meal, and the mint tea that customarily concludes the meal in many countries helps to counter indigestion. It also sweetens the breath and because it is a mild stimulant, the diner is less likely to fall asleep on a full stomach.

PREPARING LEAFY HERBS

Organic herbs do not need to be washed, but different herbs should be prepared in different ways. Such woody-stemmed herbs as sage and thyme need their leaves removed from the stems before adding to dishes. Large leaves can be picked off with the fingers. For small leaves, hold a sprig of herb at the tip and strip off the leaves with a fork.

Leafy herbs, including parsley, can simply be chopped once any coarse stalks have been removed. Cutting herbs with a knife or scissors damages the essential oils from the plant, making them taste more bitter. Try tearing the delicate leaves and stems to encourage a sweeter flavour.

Lightly crushing, or bruising, whole leaves or sprigs of herbs with a mortar and pestle helps to release their flavour into dishes that are cooked quickly.

Use herbs as soon as possible after picking. If you must store them briefly, do so in the refrigerator, wrapped in foil or paper, or chop and freeze them.

HERB OILS

Flavoured oils are delicious for cooking chicken and fish or drizzling over roasted vegetables. Strongly flavoured herbs such as thyme, bay, basil, rosemary, marjoram and tarragon are best suited to flavouring oils. Push several sprigs into a clean, empty bottle. Fill with light olive or sunflower oil and store in a cool place for two weeks. Then strain through muslin into clean bottles. Herb oils will keep for three to six months.

EDIBLE FLOWERS

Whole flowers or individual petals can enhance savoury and sweet dishes with their delicate flavours. The visual appeal of adding whole flowers or individual petals to a recipe is immediate and wonderful. Flowers from plants with other culinary uses usually taste like a milder version of that plant.

Cooking with organic flowers rather than non-organic flowers is hugely preferably because they are more likely to be strongly scented and, therefore, strongly flavoured. They are available in a fantastic range of species. Cut deep pink carnation petals from the bitter base of each flower and soak in white wine for half an hour.

Left: Chives and bay leaves add flavour to any organic meal.

Above: Rosemary and sage

DRYING HERBS

Woody-stemmed herbs, including rosemary, thyme, oregano and sage, can be dried for use in winter dishes when fresh herbs may not be available.

Pick herbs before they flower, preferably on a sunny morning after the dew has dried. Tie them in bunches and place each bunch inside a roomy paper bag that you have perforated in several places. Tie the bag closed and hang it in a warm place, with the leaves dangling down. The paper cover helps to prevent the leaves from fading and the bag catches any that drop.

The leaves should be dry and crisp after a week. Leave the herbs in bundles or strip the leaves from the stems and store in airtight jars.

Pour the mixture over a fruit salad. Raw sunflower petals add vibrancy to stir-fries. Deep blue cornflowers and bright orange calendula petals transform a green salad, and nasturtiums add peppery bite. Passion flowers, fuchsias, pansies and violas are a dramatic garnish for cakes. Violet and rose petals are traditionally used throughout Europe candied as cake decorations. Lavender and rose waters are made by steeping the flowers in hot water until it cools, then straining the mixture. In Eastern Europe and the Middle East, dried rose petals and rose water are mixed into such dishes as couscous and tagines.

APPLES AND PEARS

Few sights are more pleasing than an orchard of mature organic apple and pear trees in summer. Fallen white and pink blossoms litter the grass like confetti, and birds and bees dart between the branches overhead. The fruits are beginning to form. Soon they will start to swell and ripen, the fragrance redolent of times in childhood spent climbing trees and scraping knees. Later, in autumn, the ants and other insects on the ground might be lucky with a windfall. But we will be luckier still. The fruit grown in an organic orchard are delicious, self-packaged parcels of vitamins, minerals and phytochemicals.

Agrochemical pears and apples are grown in startlingly different circumstances from the organic ideal described above. Single species trees grow in regimented rows, over-laden with fruit that is systematically sprayed with toxic

Above: Selection of organic apples including Granny Smith, Red Spartan, Bramley and Chive.

fungicides, herbicides, insecticides and growth-regulating hormones. The insecticides are often organophosphate-based products, similar to nerve gases. Before going on sale, the fruit may be treated with preservatives. This process lengthens its shelf life but does nothing to preserve the natural nutrients within the product. Because the fruit is picked before it is ripe, its nutritional value is further undermined. If you buy non-organic apples and pears, peel them to remove the chemical covering. The paradox is that the skin is the most nutritious part of the fruit.

Above: Spartan, and other, apples can cleanse and purify the blood.

MAKING APPLE PURÉE

1 Peel, core and thickly slice the apples. Drop the apple pieces immediately into a bowl of cold water to which a few drops of lemon juice or cider vinegar have been added to prevent discoloration.

2 Barely cover the base of a pan with cold water. Add the apple pieces and cook gently, with the lid on, until soft. Add honey to taste towards the end, if you like.

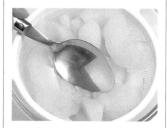

3 If you are using firm eating apples, which will not disintegrate to a purée, cook until very tender, then rub through a coarse strainer with a spoon for a smooth purée.

DRYING APPLES AT HOME

The drying process boosts levels of vitamin C in apples.

1 Peel the apples, remove the cores and slice the fruit into rings. Soak in salted water for a few minutes to prevent discoloration.

2 Thread the apple rings on to a length of string. Hang them from the ceiling or suspend across the room until they are completely dry.

3 Alternatively, arrange the rings in a single layer on a wire rack on a baking sheet, making sure that they are not touching. Place in an oven set to 70°C/150°F/Gas Low for several hours until dried.

APPLES

Rich in pectin and potassium, apples are a good general tonic for the immune system. While an agrochemical apple might look fresh, it could have lost many of its most valuable active vitamins and compounds.

Organic apples can be found in a wealth of varieties, from classic heirloom fruits to modern hybrids. Some varieties, including Bramley's Seedling, are particularly good for cooking and make wonderful pies and crumbles or crisps. The latter are particularly tasty – and even more nutritious – when oats, ground almonds and cinnamon are mixed into the topping. Eating apples, such as Cox's Orange Pippin and Spartan, are often favoured for cooking, too. Their slices stay whole when baked. Classic apples still grown organically include deep red American Salome and the Flower of Kent, an old English variety, which legend has it was the apple that landed on Sir Isaac Newton's head convincing him of the force of gravity. Modern apples range from the sweet and juicy Japanese Shizuka to the multipurpose Australian King Cole. Look out for unusual varieties like these at farmers' markets.

Above: *Conference pears are good at lowering cholesterol as well as easing constipation.*

Below: *Red Williams pears are high in soluble fibre.*

PEARS

Most pears are all-purpose – they can be eaten fresh or cooked. Popular varieties include Conference, Williams, Comice, Bartlett and Anjou. It is good to buy pears slightly under-ripe, as they will ripen over a few days on a sunny window sill. Conference pears, by contrast, should have a little "give" when you buy them. Like organic apples, pears are a good source of soluble fibre and great at lowering cholesterol as well as easing constipation.

EATING AND STORING

When eaten fresh, organic apples and pears should be cut immediately before serving to limit oxidization. Some varieties of apples do not go brown as quickly as others when exposed to air, especially Ginger Gold. Apples and pears can also be eaten cooked or dried. Both fruits juice well, and the juice can be frozen for a few months without losing its nutrient content and flavour. Store apples and pears in a cool, dark place and do not let them touch each other. Check them frequently, especially the pears, as they tend to spoil more quickly than agrochemical fruit.

SUMMER FRUITS

The delicate juicy sweetness of organic summer fruits is one of the greatest joys of the summer months. Like all fruit, these are generally best when home-grown and in season.

CHERRIES AND PLUMS

From the palest of yellow varieties to the dark-red morellos, cherries are the prettiest of fruits. Plums are just as varied, from tiny greengages to regal Victorias. Agrochemical plums and cherries are treated with differing levels of respect by the farmers who grow them, from widespread use of agrochemicals

Above: Cherries are high in phytochemicals.

in some countries to near abstinence in the UK's cherry industry. Unless you can be certain that no agrochemicals have been used, it is safer to choose organic plums and cherries to eat unpeeled. Both plums and cherries are a good source of phytochemicals and may help to prevent cancer and relieve rheumatism and arthritis. Plums contain malic acid and betacarotene, so they can provide protection against heart disease and circulatory disorders. Plums also relieve fluid retention and are good for digestion. Plums can be sweet and juicy or slightly tart; the latter are best cooked in pies and cakes or made into a jam. Sweet plums can be eaten as they are but are also good in fruit salads and fruit pies. There are also two types of cherries: sweet and sour. Some, such as the popular Bing, are best eaten raw, while others, such as Morello, are best cooked.

Above: Elegant Lady peaches

Above: Organic plums contain malic acid and betacarotene, which protect against heart disease.

Below: Victoria plums may help relieve rheumatism and arthritis.

PEACHES, NECTARINES AND APRICOTS

Organic peaches, nectarines and apricots tend to be smaller and more intensely coloured than non-organic fruit, and are much sweeter and tastier. They help to regulate the system and ease constipation. Ripe peaches and apricots should be stored in the refrigerator but brought to room temperature before eating.

STONING A PEACH

1 Slice through the seam line all around the peach.

2 Twist the two halves in opposite directions to separate them.

3 Lever out the stone with a knife.

BERRIES AND CURRANTS

Among the most popular of all fruits are berries and currants, with their glowing colours and sweet, scented juices. Strawberries, raspberries, currants of all colours, cranberries, blackberries and blueberries are just some of the delights that are sold throughout the summer. These are strictly seasonal crops. Buy them out of season and they will be inferior in terms of taste, texture and nutrition and they will almost certainly have been brought great distances by air.

Berries are delicate fruit. Washing them can spoil their texture and flavour. This is just one of the reasons why it is best to buy organic. It is perfectly safe to pop an organic berry into your mouth, whereas the agrochemical fruit will have been heavily sprayed with herbicides, fungicides, insecticides and slug deterrents. Organic berries are smaller and sweeter than non-organic ones.

STRAWBERRIES

From organic growers, strawberries are naturally sweet and delicious. Their flavour is concentrated in smaller, less watery fruit. As with all berries and grapes, they are high in vitamin C. Strawberries are also rich in soluble fibre and beta-carotene and contain phytochemicals that help to ease arthritis.

Below: Organic strawberries are naturally firm and delicious.

Above: Organic blueberries are strong cancer-preventing berries.

Above: Cranberries are a good source of vitamins A and C and potassium.

BLACKBERRIES

These high-fibre berries contain a wealth of minerals including iron, magnesium and calcium. They are rich in the bioflavonoids, which act as antioxidants, inhibiting the growth of cancer cells and protecting against cell damage by carcinogens.

RASPBERRIES

These soft and fragrant berries are effective in removing toxins from the body. To make an uncooked purée or coulis, process some raspberries in a food processor or blender until smooth. Sweeten with maple syrup to taste and add a splash of lemon juice to bring out the flavour. For a smooth purée press through a nylon strainer. Store raspberries in the refrigerator for up to two days.

Right: Raspberries are high in vitamin C.

BLUEBERRIES

These are exciting considerable interest in terms of cancer research, being rich in anthocyanidins, the phytochemicals that give them their blue colour. The consensus is that they can help prevent cancer.

CRANBERRIES

An excellent source of vitamin C, cranberries also provide potassium and vitamin A. Cranberry juice is effective in treating such infections of the urinary tract as cystitis.

REDCURRANTS

These pretty, delicate berries are rich in antioxidants, carotene and vitamins A and C.

Below: Redcurrants

Below: Blackberries

GRAPES, MELONS AND FIGS

Some of the first fruits ever cultivated, grapes, melons and figs are now available in an enormous range of shapes, colours and sizes. They are excellent sources of essential nutrients.

Right: Delicious raw, organic figs can also be poached or baked.

Below: Grapes are high in vitamin C and carbohydrates.

GRAPES

There are hundreds of different kinds of organic grapes available, from the largest black sweet varieties through to tiny seedless white ones. Wine grapes are often incredibly fragrant and remarkably differing in taste, texture, size, consistency and acidity. Semillon grapes are a classic variety from South West France, now grown from Australia to California. They have a delightful honey-like taste. Sauvignon grapes have herbal and melon flavours, with a citrus fruit edge. Friulian grapes are floral and crisply acidic, whereas Marsanne grapes are relatively low in acidity with a smooth nutty tone to their flavour.

Organic grapes are naturally high in antioxidants. They provide the perfect pick-up for convalescents, being a good source of carbohydrates and vitamin C. Grapes are easy to eat and taste delicious. Eat them at any time except after a big meal, as they tend to ferment and upset the stomach if it is full. They are best eaten straight off the bunch, or chopped into fruit salads, and taste excellent in fresh green salads.

FIGS

The wonderful squashy texture of organic figs's flesh is the perfect foil for their crispy seeds, and the delicate fruit has a fantastically sweet and toffee-like flavour. Figs can be eaten raw but are also delicious poached or baked. These fruits are a great cure for constipation and, since they are high in iron, figs can help protect the body against anaemia.

MELONS

There are two kinds of melons – musk melons and watermelons. Musk melons include the honeydew and Israeli HaOgen varieties. Their flesh is typically sweet and peach coloured. Watermelons include the classic pink-fleshed and deep-green-skinned varieties as well as rare paler versions such as the Early Moonbeam with its yellow flesh and striped green skin.

Agrochemically grown melons are sprayed with particularly noxious chemicals, including lindane and paraquat. The danger of ingesting these chemicals through a melon's skin is low, as only the inside flesh is eaten. However, if a melon plant is sprayed with pesticides and then watered, it is possible that some of the agrochemical will be diluted in the water. Melons are storehouses of the water used to irrigate them. Organic melons are refreshing and cleansing, easing fluid retention and urinary problems. Try serving them cubed on sticks or simply serve a crescent in its skin, decorated with small summer fruits. Melons are also delicious in sweet and savoury salads.

Left: Organic watermelons are filled with the unpolluted water used to irrigate them.

CITRUS FRUITS

Native to every warm to tropical country, citrus fruits are the most ubiquitous of tropical fruits and are enjoyed throughout the globe, from northern Europe to the southern tip of Chile. Oranges, grapefruit, lemons, limes, pomelos, tangerines, satsumas, kumquats and mandarins are all grown organically and should be strongly favoured over cheaper agrochemical alternatives.

Agrochemical citrus fruits are heavily treated with a huge range of powerful agrochemical toxins. Over one hundred different agrochemicals are permitted for use on citrus orchards in the USA, with a potentially higher and more dangerous toxic cocktail applied to citrus crops in the developing world. Organic citrus fruits are not dyed, whereas many agrochemically grown ones are injected with artificial colourings.

All of the members of the organic citrus family benefit from being grown as nature intended. Vitamin and mineral levels are boosted and the fruits are packed with bioflavonoids. The benefits of wax-free citrus peel are obvious to jam makers, with organic marmalade being the best choice by far. All citrus fruits are great for preventing or treating colds and sore throats and generally raising immunity.

LEMONS

Smaller and more irregularly shaped than agrochemical lemons, organic lemons are juicy and tart. Although all citrus fruits contain citric acid, lemons have an amazing property that means they work as an alkaline food. When the human body digests lemon juice, a by-product is potassium carbonate. This salt actually neutralizes the digestive system, creating a beneficial balance.

In the kitchen, lemons have limitless uses. From soups to sorbets, there is scarcely a dish that does not benefit from a squeeze of lemon juice or a sprinkling of grated rind. When lemon juice is squirted over cooked meats, fish and vegetables, the lemon juice caramelizes to crisp the main ingredient.

Organic lemons are not dyed and they are sometimes greener than agrochemical ones. Ripe lemons will yield to the touch when you squeeze them lightly. Rolling a lemon firmly over a work surface or in the palms of your hands will help you extract the maximum amount of juice.

Unwaxed, organic lemon rind adds an understated warmth to the dish and contributes bacteria-fighting limonine oils. The juice itself is packed with vitamin C and numerous phytochemicals, supporting the development of general health, and will help the body to build a strong immune system.

Below: Organic oranges

ORANGES AND GRAPEFRUIT

Organic citrus fruits have more vitality – grapefruits are tarter and oranges are rounder in flavour. Like many other agrochemical citrus crops, non-organic oranges and grapefruit are routinely coated with anti-fungal waxes that would contaminate any dishes prepared with citrus rind or peel. If the skin of the fruit is matt, not shiny, this is evidence that it has not been waxed. Both fruits are high in vitamin C and grapefruits offer valuable support for gum health. Try squeezing grapefruit juice into a fruit cocktail to add zest, or simply halve the fruit and eat it with a spoon.

Below: Unwaxed organic lemons

LIMES

Once considered an exotic fruit, limes are now a part of every modern cook's kitchen. The juice has a sharper flavour than that of lemons, so use less juice if you substitute limes for lemons in a recipe. Limes are an essential part of organic holistic cancer treatment.

Left: Organic limes

TROPICAL FRUITS

Organic kiwi fruits, pineapples, papaya and mangoes are abundant sources of vitamin C. All of these fruits tend to be smaller than their non-organic equivalents, with denser and sweeter flesh. They also have higher levels of micronutrients, which result in rounded, more intense flavours.

Most tropical fruits are naturally high in sugar, so they should be picked and eaten as soon as they are ripe. As they are often transported vast distances, this creates a temptation for agrochemical growers to pick under-ripe fruit for shipment. Organic farmers, however, allow fruit to ripen naturally for longer, which improves the nutritional content and flavour. When fully ripe, organic mangoes, kiwi fruit and papayas all feel slightly soft when squeezed. Organic tropical fruit should be eaten as soon as it is ripe, because it has a relatively short shelf life.

Left: Kiwi fruit contain as much fibre as pears.

KIWI FRUITS
Packed with potassium, organic kiwi fruits can alleviate depression and fatigue and help control high blood pressure. Kiwis contain similar amounts of vitamin C to lemons, and about the same amount of fibre as pears. Organic kiwi fruits are smaller and furrier than non-organic ones, with darker and less watery flesh.

PAPAYAS
The enzyme papain contained in organic papayas cleanses the digestive tract and aids general immunity and health. Papaya seeds are crunchy and spicy. Try eating them sprinkled on savoury green salads to add bite.

MANGOES
Organic mangoes are rich in vitamin C and carotene and are also reputed to cleanse the blood. To make an exotic tropical fruit salad, cube mangoes, papayas, kiwi fruits and pineapple and drizzle them with some freshly squeezed orange juice and a little maple syrup.

Papayas (above) and mangoes (below) are rich in vitamin C and carotene.

PREPARING A MANGO

1 Place the mango narrow side down on a chopping board. Cut off a thick lengthways slice, keeping the knife as close to the stone as possible. Turn the mango round and repeat on the other side. Cut off the flesh adhering to the stone and scoop the flesh from the mango slices.

2 To make a "hedgehog", prepare the mango as above and then score the flesh on each thick slice with criss-cross lines at 1cm/½in intervals, taking care not to cut through the skin.

3 Carefully turn the mango halves inside out and serve.

Left: Bananas are high in dietary fibre and a major source of potassium, which can relieve high blood pressure.

Below: Pineapples have an enzyme called bromelain, which is good for the digestive system.

BANANAS

Like kiwi fruits, organic bananas are a major source of potassium. They are also very good for the digestion. It is well known that eating ripe bananas eases constipation, but they are also good for curing diarrhoea. Agrochemical bananas can contain pesticides, so choose organic fruit when feeding children.

PINEAPPLES

Organic pineapples are prized for their high enzyme content. One of these, bromelain, acts as a deep cleanser for the digestive system, improving the uptake of all nutritional compounds. They are also fantastic for the complexion, especially when applied topically.

DATES

Organic dates are a rich source of dietary fibre, potassium and folic acid. Their extremely sweet taste makes dates wonderful to bake with. Add them chopped to fruit cakes and steamed puddings, or eat them whole. They can be given to children instead of sweets (candies), and are a useful food for people needing extra energy, including sportsmen and women, pregnant women and the elderly. Non-organic dates are often soaked in syrups and oils, but you will find that organic dates are naturally sweet.

Left: Organic dates are naturally sweet and high in energy.

DRIED FRUIT

When dried, many of the nutrients in a fruit are concentrated, as are the natural sugars, but, unfortunately, so are pesticide residues. Non-organic dried figs, for instance, not only contain more pesticides weight for weight than fresh figs, but they also contain added fungicides. Organic dried fruit is clearly a better option.

Dried apricots are particularly useful, not only for eating in the hand, but also for baking or in jam. They are a rich source of carotenes and, when eaten in quantity, contain useful quantities of vitamin C. As such they are the staple and only protection from scurvy available to many people in remote mountain communities, such as the Himalayan area of Ladakh. Organic dried apricots have also been credited with helping to reduce high blood pressure, protecting against cancer and supporting clear, naturally beautiful skin.

MEAT, POULTRY AND GAME

Meat and poultry that has been farmed organically is the prime choice for cooks whose criteria are good quality, fine taste and texture, and whose concerns include basic levels of animal welfare. Intensively produced meat is almost always bland, watery, fatty and laced with unnatural hormones, antibiotics and drugs. Welfare conditions for the animals that provide non-organic meat are often horrific, from their rearing to slaughter. Although there are some excellent small non-organic meat farms, and free-range meat is better than meat from intensively reared animals and birds, choosing organic meat and poultry is the only option that fully addresses the issues.

Organic meat labelled as such by a recognized certifying body is also the only option if you want to avoid genetically modified organisms, because about 99 per cent of all non-organic meat is produced from animals whose feed contains some GMOs.

Above: Animals raised on organic farms enjoy a healthy, stress-free lifestyle.

FARMING METHODS

Non-organic, intensively farmed animals and birds are taken away from their mothers within a few days of birth and reared in huge herds and flocks. Most of their lives are spent indoors, and they are fed unnatural dried food pellets laced with growth hormones. Antibiotics are used routinely as a safeguard against the diseases and parasites that flourish in the cramped and stressful conditions in which they are kept. Animals and birds are brought to maturity as quickly as possible, by feeding them growth hormones, which speed up the process.

When intensively farmed livestock are ready for slaughter, they generally travel long distances in cramped lorries to the abattoir. In 2001, the European Union exported about 875,000 tonnes of live cows and beef to the rest of the world. At the same time, about 170,000 tonnes of live cows and beef were imported into Europe from Argentina, Botswana, Poland and Brazil. The growth of intensive meat farms has eradicated small local abattoirs, with huge centralized slaughterhouses replacing them for the processors' convenience.

Animal welfare is at the heart of organic animal husbandry. Animals are allowed to feed more freely and grow naturally, resulting in meat and poultry that tastes very much better.

The absolute freedom of game's wild existence means that it cannot be classified as organic. However, truly wild game from unpolluted countryside areas is an excellent choice for anyone who supports animal welfare and freedom. Farmed game that is organically certified is delicious and sustainable.

Biodynamic farming really comes into its own for meat products. Biodynamic animals live extremely comfortable lives, from birth to the abattoir. Many different kinds of heirloom and rare breed animals are free to mingle under cover or outdoors, in scenes reminiscent of an old-fashioned dream of how an animal farm should be. In the UK, regional species of pig such as the Tamworth porker are reared biodynamically, whereas this breed is almost unheard of on commercial intensive meat farms. While organic farm animals, which are unwell, may be treated with chemical medicines if homeopathy and other

complementary treatments do not work, biodynamic animals must be entirely chemical free. Meat is always hung after slaughter, which helps the flavour to develop. While this process occurs with all quality organic and non-organic meats, biodynamic meat is guaranteed to benefit from this traditional treatment.

BUYING ORGANIC MEAT

Everybody who wants to eat delicious organic meat and poultry is encouraged to experiment with different stores or direct buying schemes. It is convenient to be able to obtain organic meat from the supermarket, but it is worth considering what is on offer at specialist fine organic suppliers and farmers' markets as well as local box schemes.

All organic meat tastes good because the animals are free range and feed on grass. The best organic meat tastes even better, however, because the carcasses are hung in the traditional manner after slaughter. Buying from a local supplier or taking delivery of organic meat from a box scheme will also provide you with cooking tips as part of the service. Another important advantage of buying meat either direct or from a specialist outlet is that the purchaser can often order an old-fashioned cut or ask for meat to be prepared in a particular way.

Organic halal and kosher meat is available in some larger Islamic and Jewish communities through mail order and box schemes. Check local Islamic or Jewish journals or search the Internet for details of a scheme near you.

Biodynamic and organic meats may be more expensive than intensively farmed meat, but this is not necessarily a bad thing. Reducing the quantity of meat we consume is recommended by doctors and nutritionists. When meat becomes an occasional treat, the cost is not so relevant, especially when the quality is first rate. Occasional meat eating is much more in line with man's original diet than daily hamburgers. Enjoyed weekly or fortnightly, organic meat will regain its special place in our diet.

BEEF AND VEAL

Organic beef contains a much better balance of good and bad cholesterol than meat from intensively reared cows. This is because the animals' diet includes a high content of grass, whereas many intensively reared cattle are fed dry food almost exclusively. Some good quality non-organic beef cattle benefit from a free-range, grass-fed existence,

but buying organic beef ensures this happens.

For a classic roast beef, use either sirloin or fore rib. Back rib and topside (pot roast) are both excellent slow roasted. When grilling (broiling) or frying steaks, use sirloin, rib eye, rump or fillet steaks. Neck or clod has an open, slightly sticky texture, and is good for stews, whereas shin (shank), chuck steak and top rump are best for casseroles where whole slices are needed. Pot roast silverside or brisket cuts, as these need to be cooked slowly over a long period. Flank and thin flank are good for making mince (ground beef) for bolognese sauces and cottage pies. Minced (ground) clod and shin are great for hamburgers and steak tartare because they are virtually fat free. Shin makes a good filling for slow-cooked pies.

If you buy veal make sure that it is organic. It will not be as pale as intensively farmed veal but you will have the satisfaction of knowing that it has come from a calf that has been reared with its mother, rather than being removed when only a few days old, which causes both animals great distress. Veal steaks are best simply pan-fried to seal in their flavour.

Above: Organic lamb is especially tender and full of flavour.

MUTTON AND LAMB

Most good supermarkets offer organic lamb, but usually only as chops and mince (ground lamb). Organic lamb is tender and full of flavour. The fat is clearly visible and can be removed easily. Organic mutton can be harder to find but many organic butchers stock it. It is invaluable for many authentic dishes, especially stews with an Arabic flavour. Minced mutton or lamb, which comes from shoulder, belly or leg meat, can be used instead of minced beef.

For a classic roast mutton or roast lamb, use leg, shoulder, saddle or rack. If you like your lamb pink, choose saddle or rack of lamb. Grill (broil) or fry leg steaks, loin or chump chops or cutlets. The rarer the meat, the more tender and flavoursome it will be. Lamb and mutton can both be fatty, but the meat can easily be trimmed. Make kebabs from neck fillet (US shoulder or breast) and butterflied or cubed leg. Casserole middle neck or shoulder meat for classic dishes such as navarin of lamb.

Above: Organic beef rib is a healthier choice.

Right: Organic pork loin is a popular cut for roasting.

PORK

There are lots of delicious organic pork products available, including traditional home-made sausages, honey roasted hams, gammon and bacon. Most organic and non-organic bacon is cured with saltpetre. Although this helps to preserve the pinkish colour of the meat, there are some concerns about whether this traditional process is entirely healthy. A few specialist organic and biodynamic pork farms now offer fine-quality pork products that do not contain this ingredient. The meat they sell is darker, with a brown rather than red tinge, but it tastes just as delicious. High-quality organic pork sausages are widely available in supermarkets and delicatessens, but as with all organic meat products, traditional organic farmers' markets and delivery services offer an even more extensive range. Look out for pork sausages with apple, sage or forest fruits, as well as preserved salamis and saucissons.

Pork is a tender meat, which is suitable for all forms of cooking. Leg is a popular cut for roasting, as is blade, which can be roasted on the bone or boned and stuffed. For a truly succulent roast, try spare rib. Perhaps the most popular cut for roasting is loin, which provides the best crackling. To achieve this, score the fat deeply, rub in salt and roast the joint dry. When grilling (broiling) pork chops or steaks, it is essential to watch them carefully. They must be cooked through, as underdone pork can cause infection, but they should not be allowed to dry out.

Pork fillet (tenderloin) and schnitzel steaks are the best choice for frying. For braising, choose pork chops, steaks, spare ribs, blade, loin or belly meat. Hand and spring meat is a large cut which can be cubed and cooked in tender pork casseroles and stews.

Above: Organic chilli and pepper salami (left) and hot salami are all available from specialist organic butchers and organic stores.

POULTRY

Organic poultry tends to be less fatty than intensively reared equivalents because the birds have more freedom to exercise and are not fed growth hormones. Because it is less fatty the meat benefits from being cooked slowly.

Organic chicken, duck, goose and turkey are easy to obtain, but goose and turkey tend to be more seasonal, their availability linked to festivals such as Christmas, Easter and Thanksgiving. As well as whole birds, poultry portions and breast fillets are available. They may be on the bone or boneless. Buying whole birds and cutting them up is not difficult, however, and provides the perfect opportunity for making homemade stock.

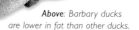

Above: Barbary ducks are lower in fat than other ducks.

Duck and goose These are fatty birds with dark meat that has plenty of flavour. The fat helps to keep the meat moist during cooking. Goose is nearly always roasted, though the legs may be added to casseroles. Ducks are generally roasted whole or cut up for frying or casseroling.

American Long Island and British Aylesbury ducks have paler, tender meat with a significant proportion of fat and a rich flavour. Barbary and Nantes ducks have slightly less fat. The barbary, a big bird, provides a good proportion of firm breast meat. The Nantes is smaller, more tender and with a delicate flavour.

Unlike other domesticated poultry, geese have defied all attempts to rear them intensively. They are not prolific layers and are one of the few remaining sources of seasonal food. Goose fat is used in traditional cooking across central and Eastern Europe and in Scandinavia.

Chicken and turkey Organic birds are raised in humane conditions, fed on a natural and (usually) traditional-style diet. They do not have lurid-coloured skin. The skeleton of an organic bird is bigger and stronger, and the legs are longer. When cooked, the flesh is less uniform in colour and texture; the breast meat is paler and the leg darker. Standards and conditions relating to the scheme or terms by which the birds are classified as organic are usually outlined on the packaging.

As well as whole birds, chicken and turkey are available in a wide choice of portions. Look for birds with a clear, soft skin, with no bruises or blemishes. The tougher the skin, the older the bird.

Organic chicken and turkey need to be cooked slower and longer than non-organic poultry to get the best flavour and texture. When roasting, try stuffing the cavity with grains and herbs, or with fresh fruit and spices, for an aromatic dish. Rub the skin with sea salt and different vinegars for added crispiness and zest. Stock made from the carcase of an organic bird will be incomparably richer in flavour and colour and will set to a firmer jelly.

GAME

Some game is farmed organically, including rabbit and venison. In a few parts of the world, other types of game, such as elk and wild boar are seasonally available, either from rural farmers' markets, or specialist suppliers. Animals and birds that are truly wild cannot be classified as organic, as their habitat and diet is not controlled or able to be inspected by an organic certifier. Wild game from areas with low agrochemically managed farmlands is unlikely to be contaminated with chemical pollutants.

Venison The term venison is used not only for meat from deer but also from elk, moose, reindeer, caribou and antelope. Deer are now farmed organically, but the demand for most farmed game animals is still too slow to stimulate a market.

Venison is a dark, close-textured meat with very little fat; what there is should be firm and white. If it is in good condition and a prime cut, such as

Above: Organic turkeys are free to exercise and are not fed growth hormones.

haunch, loin, fillet or best end, it will be juicy and tender and is best served rare. Other cuts, such as shoulder, neck and shin, are often marinated and benefit from long and gentle cooking to bring out the flavour of the meat.

Rabbit Fresh rabbit is a delicate well-flavoured meat, pale and mild in colour. It is high in protein, low in cholesterol and particularly low in fat. Organically farmed rabbit may be bought all the year round. It can be grilled (broiled), fried, roasted or stewed. Baste it well so that the meat does not dry out.

Wild boar The meat of wild boar has a strong taste. It is dark in colour and, as there is little fat, it can be dry and tough, although the flavour is excellent. For this reason wild boar is usually marinated. It should be cooked in the same way as pork.

Game birds Fresh game birds are only available during the hunting season, which varies from bird to bird and from country to country. In some countries frozen game is stocked all through the year. Simple

cooking methods are often the best for game birds: plain roasting for tender birds and simple casserole cooking for tougher birds. Organic butchers and direct suppliers will be able to provide useful cooking advice.

Pheasants are the most plentiful game birds and are often sold in a brace: a pair of birds that includes a male and a female. The hen is smaller and more tender than the cock. Organic partridge, grouse and quail are also available. Scottish grouse has a wonderful, rich flavour from feeding on the highland heather of Scotland, where it is native.

There are two types of partridge, the French or red-legged partridge, and the English, or grey-legged partridge. The red-legged bird is bigger but the flavour of the grey bird is often preferred.

Below: Wild boar has a strong taste and little fat.

FISH AND SHELLFISH

Organic fish is a delicious source of protein and can be prepared and cooked very easily. Fresh fish is versatile and great for your health. Omega-3 essential fatty acids found naturally in oily fish help to lower cholesterol levels, protecting the heart and circulation system. Eating fish also reduces the risk of developing high blood pressure during pregnancy, and can help to prevent premature births. However, environmentally aware cooks need to shop with care.

Many fish are either caught using deeply environmentally insensitive methods or raised in unsustainable farms. Organic cooks should buy organically farmed fish or wild fish from sustainable farms and fisheries. If you have doubts about the source or sustainability of fish

Below: Organic fish is farmed using environmentally sensitive methods.

that you want to buy, write to or e-mail the head office of the retailer or processor to find out more. Every time an organization receives a letter of interest from a consumer, it is more likely to improve the sustainability of its practices. For information on the Internet, visit the web sites of organic certification bodies. You can ask good fishmongers or restaurateurs about the seafood they prepare, or contact a specialist organization such as the Marine Stewardship Council.

FARMED FISH

Organic fish farms are clean and humane. Chemicals are not permitted to be used routinely, although they may occasionally be administered if infection occurs. Many intensive fish farms need to douse their fish regularly in chemicals simply

Above: Pale, organically farmed salmon

because they are so intensive. The more fish are crammed into a body of water, the easier diseases such as furunculosis and parasites like fish lice can spread. Organic fish farmers keep numbers lower and the result is a radical reduction in disease and pestilence. There are some non-organic fish farms that do maintain healthier numbers, but buying organically farmed fish is the best way of being sure that the fish have been managed well.

Despite the many advantages, organic fish farming poses great challenges to pioneering organic aquaculture experts. To be certified as organic, fish must be fed fishmeal that is half a by-product of fish for human consumption, and half from sustainable sources. The trouble is, most fish by-products are from white fish such as cod. Farmed fish including salmon do not easily digest this sort of fishmeal, so there can be a lot of wasted food which then pollutes surrounding waters. Also, fishmeal from white fish has relatively low levels of fatty acids, so organically farmed fish can have relatively low levels of Omega-3 oils unless they are very carefully managed by an expert organic fish farmer. On the plus side, organically farmed fish are not permitted to be fed any genetically modified foods, so buying organic fish is the only way you can be certain that your farmed fish dinner is GM free.

Although good-quality non-organic salmon usually has relatively low levels of chemical residues, organically farmed salmon has even less. Organically farmed

Right: Seawater fish farms produce excellent sea trout.

fish are generally top class in terms of taste and texture, whereas intensively farmed fish are often bland and fatty. Organically farmed fish also have paler flesh. The stronger colour of non-organic farmed salmon is due to a diet based on fishmeal with added carotenoids. Although these are the same as the beneficial compounds found in carrots, organic cooks will prefer the more natural paler colour of organically farmed salmon.

Salmon, trout and carp taste wonderful grilled (broiled), steamed or fried in olive oil, especially when they are served with a generous squeeze of fresh lemon juice. Smoked in the traditional way, organically farmed fish have incomparable flavour, so different from the bland non-organic product, which is prepared using artificial wood smoke flavouring.

Below: MSC-certified halibut harvested by methods that protect the seabed.

SEAWATER FISH FARMS

Organic seawater fish farms are beginning to rear many more breeds of fish. These include organic sea trout, bass, cod, halibut and bream. Humane and causing the minimum impact on the marine environment, organic sea fish farming is still in its infancy. As wild fish stocks come under increasing threat, this area of organic farming is set to grow.

There are currently only a few experimental organic prawn and shrimp farms, but this sector is certain to increase exponentially. Non-organic farmed prawns and shrimp farms tend to be the antithesis of the organic ideal, and have devastated large areas of the tropical world from the Indian Ocean to the mangroves of Honduras. Abusing the rights of local farmers who rear the crop, the prawn and shrimp industry often replaces rural diverse communities with a single polluting monoculture. To avoid adding to this type of situation, do not buy farmed prawns or shrimps unless they are certified as organic.

Such shellfish as cockles, mussels, scallops and oysters are sometimes farmed in enclosures around coastal seawaters. They feed on naturally occurring plankton and are a healthy source of food whose production has a low impact on the environment. Mussels and oysters are also a good source of betaine, a substance that helps to protect against heart attacks. These shellfish are easy to prepare and make nutritious, high protein meals. Oysters should simply be prised open with a knife and eaten whole, with a squirt of lemon. Clean mussels by scrubbing them in fresh water and pulling off any fibrous "beards" that sprout between the two halves of the shell. Discard any mussels which are open or fail to snap shut when tapped with a knife.

Left: Organic mussels and other shellfish are increasingly farmed in enclosures around coastal seawaters.

There is no organic standard for wild fish. However, the MSC – Marine Stewardship Council – is a certifying body that is beginning to address the issue. It is a leading voice in the sustainable fishing debate, and offers practical guidance to consumers, fishermen and governments alike.

When certifying a fishery, the MSC looks at three areas of activity. First, the state of the fish stocks in the locality is assessed to determine whether fishing is being carried out sustainably. The fishery's effect on the marine ecosystem is also looked at. One major problem of modern fishing methods is catching fish other than the target species – the "by-catch". The MSC standard is only awarded if levels of by-catch for the fishery are acceptable. Finally, management systems are examined to satisfy the MSC that good practice is being maintained.

Fishermen often work under an umbrella organization, which may be a government body, that regulates the area of the sea they harvest. If good management is in place, their practices can be co-ordinated to ensure sustainable fishing.

BUYING MSC-CERTIFIED FISH
A secondary certification scheme traces all fish certified to the MSC standard from the fishery to the retailer, so consumers can buy wild fish with confidence if it carries the MSC logo. You will find the logo on fresh and frozen fish, convenience products and on menus where restaurants support the scheme.

MSC-certified fish is sold through independent fishmongers, farmers' markets, supermarkets and delicatessens in the UK and Europe, USA and Australia. Fish caught at MSC-certified fisheries are also sold in Canada, New Zealand and South East Asian countries. However, not all these countries use the logo.

WILD FISH
The last major wild food resource, the sea, is under intense threat from over-fishing. Worldwide, sea fish are now so over-exploited that many once abundant stocks are now under threat of extinction. Catching wild fish has become a serious technological pursuit. Wild sea fish are hunted with the aid of radar, planes and submarines and caught with lines or trawler nets, trapping the targeted catch and also other fish, mammals and birds. These wholesale raids do not discriminate between adults and young fish.

Wild fish are increasingly subjected to chemical, biological and hormonal attack from such polluted fresh waters as rivers and lakes. Some intensive fish farms release their waste water, with its cargo of chemicals and germs, into nearby rivers and seas. Fish from these farms often escape and interbreed with wild stocks to produce hybrid mutations. Pesticides and fertilizers from agrochemical crops also flow into rivers and lakes through groundwater. The fertilizers promote algae growth, ruining the delicate balance of water ecosystems, while pesticides simply poison the inhabitants.

Wild salmon spend almost all of their lives in the sea, only returning to fresh water when it is time to spawn. They have incredible homing instincts.

Above: *Wild salmon live in the sea, returning to fresh water only when it is time to spawn.*

A salmon that has swum hundreds of kilometres away from its birthplace will return to the very creek where its life began. If the water it has to pass through has been contaminated by fish farm, agrochemical farm or factory pollution, this ancient cycle is irrevocably disturbed.

TYPES OF WILD SEA FISH
Wild sea fish fall into two groups: those that live at the bottom of the sea, and those that live in the middle waters or near the surface. Surface fish include common varieties such as sardines, mackerel, anchovies, pilchards, Atlantic herring and swordfish. Fishermen utilize many methods to catch these fish, including traps, lines and drag nets. In Japan, fishermen sometimes lure squid using mechanical jiggers with bright lights. The squid attach themselves to the machinery, so they can be hauled on to the boats easily. Knowledgeable fishermen easily target surface species, ensuring a good percentage of the catch is the target fish. Despite this, many of these species are now fully or over fished.

Fish species from the middle waters include tuna, salmon and herring. These fish are almost always caught with nets.

Tuna are a similar size to dolphins and often associate with them. In the past, this frequently meant that when tuna were caught, so were dolphins. The public outcry that ensued when this became common knowledge has diminished this practice. All tuna sold in the USA and Canada now has to be dolphin friendly, and most other industrialized nations offer dolphin-friendly tuna.

Catching tuna without catching dolphins is very tricky however. One technique that has replaced dolphin-associated tuna fishing is to use floating aggregate devices, or FADs. These float in the sea and attract the tuna because of the cover they provide. Fishermen then net all of the fish below the FAD, including juvenile tuna and other by-catch species. Although dolphin-friendly tuna does save dolphins, it is often at the expense of other species with a less popular public image.

Probably the best way to catch tuna in terms of the ecosystem is with so-called "long lines". These fishing lines with multiple hooks are dragged behind boats and target tuna extremely efficiently. Some successful long-line tuna fisheries use this method, including one in the Maldives that supplies retailers and restaurants around the world.

Below: Wild cockles can be picked by hand.

Fish that live on the bottom of the sea are generally trawled with big nets. Cod, carp, hake, haddock, hoki and Alaskan pollock all live near the seabed, as do flat fish including plaice, halibut and sole. Cephalopods such as squid and octopus are often also trapped in the nets, but offer a valuable source of under-exploited seafood. Trawling the seabed can be extremely destructive, disturbing ancient ecosystems. The Marine Stewardship Council has approved one fishery that trawls responsibly, and more fisheries that use other sustainable harvesting methods for species at the bottom of the sea. Fisheries awarded MSC certification are sustainable, so you can be sure that buying these products will not contribute to bad fishing practices.

SHELLFISH

Lobsters and crabs also live at the bottom of the sea but they are only harvested in coastal waters. They are usually collected in pots, either using bait or trapdoors. Scallops and oysters, which also live in coastal waters, are traditionally trawled. Today, they are often harvested by divers. This method protects the delicate ecosystems found at the bottom of the sea, while providing top quality seafood for the caring cook. Other shellfish such as wild cockles and mussels are more easily harvested. They can be picked by hand from the bottom of shallower waters. However, most commercially available shellfish are currently farmed.

Intensively farmed prawns and shrimps are bad news for organic consumers. Try to buy wild shellfish. Those from Iceland are particularly acceptable as an alternative to organically farmed prawns and shrimps. Iceland is heavily reliant on its fishing industry, so it has become a benchmark country for sustainable fishing techniques. Most prawns from Iceland are caught by trawling with nets with bigger holes than other fishing nations. The holes allow young prawns to escape, so they can grow and breed.

MOULES MARINIÈRE

1 Chop 1 onion and 2 shallots. Put in a large pan with 25g/1oz/2 tbsp butter and cook over low heat until softened and translucent.

2 Add 300ml/½ pint/1¼ cups white wine, a bay leaf and a sprig of fresh thyme. Bring to the boil. Add 2kg/4½lb cleaned mussels, cover the pan tightly and steam over a high heat for 2 minutes. Shake the pan vigorously and steam for 2 minutes more. Shake again and steam until all the mussels have opened. Discard any closed shells.

3 Stir in 30ml/2 tbsp chopped fresh parsley and serve at once.

DAIRY FOODS AND EGGS

Opting for organic products means obtaining the maximum nutrition from whatever dairy foods you consume, without supporting the negative aspects associated with intensive farming methods. Dairy foods are excellent sources of protein and calcium.

On an organic dairy farm, cows have regular access to open fields. Their diet is made up almost exclusively of organic grasses and grains and they are never routinely treated with the hormones that are used on non-organic farms in some countries to boost milk production. Nor are they dosed with antibiotics except as a last resort. If you prefer not to eat any dairy foods, there are some excellent organic alternatives.

MILK

Organic milk is the only kind of milk that is guaranteed to be free of genetically modified ingredients, as many non-organic cows eat GM feed. It is available with varying amounts of cream, from skimmed to full fat. Full fat (whole) milk generally only contains about 2 percent fat, so all milk is a low fat food. Most milk is pasteurized, homogenized or sterilized, but it can also be found raw. Pasteurization is a heating process that helps to control bacteria levels in the milk. Homogenization distributes

Right: Goat's, cow's, sheep's and soya milk

the fat content throughout the milk, so there is no need to shake it to mix in the cream. Sterilization extends the shelf life of sealed cartons of milk, so that they do not need to be refrigerated. All these processes are permitted under organic certification laws because they are mechanical processes that do not involve the use of chemicals.

Cow's milk is not the only organic option. Goat's milk has a distinctive, musky flavour, which many people love. It is much easier to digest than cow's milk, so individuals who cannot tolerate cow's milk often find they can drink goat's milk without suffering adverse reactions. Organic sheep's milk is sometimes on sale at the larger farmer's markets or in delicatessens. It doesn't taste as pungent as goat's milk, but contains more of the lactose that can cause dairy intolerance.

YOGURTS, CREAMS AND DAIRY DESSERTS

Live yogurt is a natural probiotic. This means it boosts the amount of beneficial bacteria in the intestines of those who eat it. This, in turn, aids the absorption of nutrients, such as calcium, as well as offering some protection from various disorders, including tooth decay and

heart disease. An even better way of improving the levels of good bacteria in your gut is to eat prebiotic foods such as onions, leeks, wheat, oats, bananas and Jerusalem artichokes.

Many of the world's largest non-organic dairy corporations now also offer organic yogurts, creams and dairy desserts. While this ensures improved availability of organic dairy products, the quality is variable. Organic dairy products all have the benefits of humane and environmentally sustainable production, but mass-produced yogurts and dairy desserts are often watery, high in sugar and low in flavour. Whether they are runny or thick, organic creams should always be mouthwateringly rich. The organic connoisseur will choose organic yogurts, desserts and creams from smaller enterprises or companies who are primarily organic.

BUTTER

Organic butter has a much richer taste than non-organic alternatives. Both types, however, are equally high in saturated fats, which can raise cholesterol levels in the body and contribute to heart disease. Consider organic butter a luxurious, delicious and slightly decadent treat, great for the occasional indulgence, as when making the perfect fried egg, but something to be limited. That said, organic butter is far better for your health than many non-organic margarines and spreads. These will often contain hydrogenated or trans fats, which may be far more damaging to the heart than butter.

Right: Organic butter

CHEESES

Organic cheeses are made from organic milk, so they offer all the environmental, humanitarian and healthy eating benefits of other organic dairy products. They come in scores of different varieties, from hard types such as Cheddar, Cheshire, Double Gloucester and Lancashire, through blues like Stilton and Gorgonzola, to soft and creamy Camembert and cottage cheese. Lots of artisan cheesemakers now use organic ingredients. Buying organic cheese is a must if you want to avoid eating genetically modified rennet.

SOYA MILK AND OTHER SUBSTITUTES

Soya beans have been transformed into nutritious "milks" and dairy alternative foods for thousands of years. There are dozens of versions on the market, including the fresh product, which looks like cow's milk but is slightly thicker and has a nutty taste. More readily available is long-life soya milk, which comes in cartons and does not need to be refrigerated until it is opened. Sweetened versions can also be found, and it is possible to buy soya milk that has been fortified with extra vitamins as well as calcium.

Soya milk is low in calories and contains no cholesterol. Easy to digest, it is a valuable food, particularly for those who cannot tolerate cow's milk. Children who suffer from asthma and eczema often get relief when they switch from cow's milk to a non-dairy alternative such as soya milk.

Soya cream is much thicker and richer than soya milk because it is made with a higher proportion of beans. Soya beans are not the only ingredient that can be made into nutritious liquid. Other beans can be used in a similar way, as can some nuts and grains. Rice milk is thin and has a delicate taste. Tiger nut milk has a similar consistency and a sweet taste. Oat milk is pleasantly mild, while pale yellow pea milk is quite creamy. Non-dairy milks can be bought from health food shops or made at home. Try them on muesli or other organic cereals or in creamy soups. When using in tea, put non-dairy milk in first and stir the tea thoroughly to prevent curdling. The high acidity in coffee means that curdling is almost inevitable, so try to avoid using non-dairy milks here.

Above: Organic Stilton and Brie are widely available.

EGGS

Organic free-range eggs come from hens that have ample access to land free from chemical fertilizers and pesticides. The birds are not routinely debeaked to stop them retaliating when hemmed in by other hens, nor are they given growth promoters. Antibiotics are administered only when unavoidable. It is important to look for labels on eggs that attest to organic certification. Although the term "free range" suggests that hens spend their days out of doors, non-organic free-range birds often have limited access to the open air. Organic eggs are the only eggs that can be guaranteed to be free from yolk colourants.

Look out for other types of eggs at farmers' markets. Duck eggs are a pretty shade of blue, goose eggs are big enough for two and quail's eggs are small and speckled. All can be boiled, fried, scrambled or used in cakes, in the same way as hen's eggs. When soft-boiled, organic eggs are far less likely to contain the salmonella that is often found in eggs from intensive chicken barns. Soft-boiled or lightly poached eggs have the advantage of containing fewer Cholesterol Oxidation Products (COPS), which means they can be beneficial to blood cholesterol levels.

Below: When farmed organically, quail and duck eggs are guaranteed free from yolk colourants.

BEANS AND PULSES

These staples are a fantastic resource for any organic cook and provide vital protein for vegetarians and vegans. Organic red and white kidney beans, aduki beans, haricot beans, flageolet or cannellini beans, soya beans, mung beans, black-eyed beans (peas) and chickpeas are all available. A good source of B vitamins and many minerals, including iron, selenium and zinc, organic beans are far better for you than the agrochemical equivalents, which are often grown in developing countries where pesticide use is extremely heavy.

Soya beans are particularly good for women, as they are rich in the phytoestrogens that help to prevent osteoporosis and breast cancer, plus folic acid for preconceptual care. Chickpeas are especially high in calcium.

Left: Aduki beans have a nutty flavour.

Left: Chickpeas have a delicious hearty taste and creamy texture.

COOKING BEANS AND PULSES

Most beans and pulses, with the exception of lentils, must be soaked overnight before being cooked. Lentils can be cooked straight from the sieve after rinsing, but will also benefit from being soaked for an hour or more. Soaking makes beans and pulses easier to digest. So does cooking them with a small piece of kombu seaweed. Cooking with salt toughens beans, so only season them once they have been cooked.

Kidney beans, whether organic or not, must be cooked thoroughly to ensure any natural toxins they contain are neutralized. Boil the beans vigorously for about 15 minutes, then change the water and simmer for about 1¾ hours until they are tender.

Cooked beans and pulses taste great in soups, salad, stews and meat-free pâtés, as well as classic Indian dishes such as dhal. A quick dhal soup can be made by boiling equal amounts of red lentils and yellow split

Above: Haricot, red kidney, flageolet and pinto beans

SPROUTING BEANS, SEEDS, GRAINS AND PULSES

When beans, pulses, seeds and grains germinate, their nutritional levels rise dramatically. B vitamins increase by almost 30 per cent and vitamin C by up to 60 per cent. Organic sprouts are easy to grow yourself.

1 Wash 45ml/3 tbsp beans, pulses, seeds or grains thoroughly in water, then place in a large jar. Fill the jar with lukewarm water, cover with a piece of muslin and hold in place with an elastic band. Leave in a warm place to stand overnight.

2 Drain thoroughly the next morning and refill the jar with water. Shake gently, then drain again. Leave the jar on its side in a warm place, away from direct sunlight. In the evening rinse again, draining well.

3 Continue to rinse and drain twice daily until small roots and shoots have emerged. Most sprouts will be ready within a week. Sprinkle on salads, chop into spreads or add to stir-fries or curries.

Below: White and black soya beans form the basis for quick high-protein meals.

peas, then stirring in onion and a chopped tomato, which has been fried with curry spices. For a delicately flavoured salad, mix cooked flageolet beans with arugula (rocket) leaves and add a drizzle of walnut oil.

Beans and pulses should be stored in a cool, dry place. Keep packets tightly closed or decant into sealed tubs. Beans and pulses can be kept for years and still be capable of germinating, but the fresher they are the better, so buy them in small quantities and use quickly.

SOYA BEAN PRODUCTS

Highly nutritious soya bean products including tofu and tempeh are ideal for keeping in the refrigerator or freezer to form the basis for quick, high-protein meals. It is vital to ensure that all the soya products you buy are organic. Many non-organic soya products have been made from genetically modified beans, bred for resistance to extremely strong pesticides and herbicides. GM soya beans are able to grow in soil that has been drenched in these harsh chemicals, whereas beans that have not been genetically modified are destroyed by the toxicity. There is no benefit to the consumer in eating GM soya beans; the only advantage is to the farmer who is able to use stronger and stronger chemicals.

Tofu Also known as bean curd, tofu is derived from soya milk, which is curdled using a natural coagulant. The curds are drained and pressed to make tofu, in a process similar to that used when making soft cheese. Firm tofu can be sliced and fried. It is a popular ingredient in stir-fries, especially when it has been marinated in soy sauce to strengthen its somewhat bland flavour. For soups, sauces and creamy desserts, choose silken tofu, which is smooth and light. Smoked, marinated and deep-fried tofu are all available in health-food stores and Oriental stores. Organic tofu can also be bought in long-life cartons.

TVP Many vegetarians rely on soya bean products for their protein, especially in the form of Textured Vegetable Protein or TVP. This highly processed ingredient is widely used in organic processed foods and is also available dried. It can be useful to keep some in the cupboard for making vegetarian burgers or lasagne, but

COOKING TIMES FOR PRE-SOAKED BEANS AND PULSES

The table below provides a rough guide only, as cooking times may alter according to how long the items have been stored, and the quantity cooked. In most cases, the volume of water should be three times that of the chosen ingredient, except in the case of butter beans, where double the amount of water will be sufficient. Ingredients that need very long cooking times, such as chickpeas, marrowfat peas and soya beans, may need up to four times the amount of water.

Beans	Time (minutes)
Aduki beans	45–60
Black-eyed beans (peas)	60
Butter (lima) beans	60
Chickpeas	180
Dried green (field) beans	45
Flageolet (small cannellini) beans	50
Haricot (navy) beans	60
Kidney beans	120
Lentils – brown	45
Lentils – green	30
Lentils – red	20–30
Mung beans	60
Peas – marrowfat	120
Peas – split	45
Soya beans	200

TVP is low on taste, lacking in texture and offers limited nutrition. Fresh soya bean products such as tofu and tempeh are superior in every way.

Tempeh This Indonesian food is made by fermenting cooked soya beans with a cultured starter. It has a meatier, nuttier flavour than tofu, and the firmer texture means it can be used in pies. Slices of tempeh taste delicious fried in sunflower oil and tamari or soy sauce and served with pitta bread.

Left: Tempeh freezes well, so conveniently keeps for long periods.

GRAINS

Getting to grips with organic grains is not difficult. There is a wide selection available, from wheat in all its various forms to lesser known grains such as the highly nutritious quinoa.

RICE

Organic brown rice is one of the ultimate grains, in terms of taste, nutrition and healing potential. It is very easily digestible, gently soothing the intestinal tract. It is simultaneously comforting and satisfying to eat, particularly when served with crisp and fresh stir-fried organic vegetables.

Above: Brown rice is high in complex carbohydrates, with protein, fibre and B vitamins. It is one of the ultimate grains.

Although organic white rice is a convenient ingredient and has a much shorter cooking time, it is less nutritious, since most of the minerals and vitamins are lost when the bran and germ of the grain is removed in the milling process.

BULGUR WHEAT

This pale, sand-coloured grain, made from dried and crushed cooked wheat berries, is nutty in flavour and comes in varying degrees of coarseness. When cooked, by soaking in double its volume of boiling water for 15–20 minutes, bulgur wheat is similar in appearance to couscous but is heavier, and has more flavour. Bulgur is usually served cold.

Combined with flat-leaf parsley, mint, tomatoes, cucumber, onion and a lemon and oil dressing, it forms the basis of the Middle Eastern salad, tabbouleh.

Above: Bulgur wheat

MILLET

Another under-used but essential grain, organic millet contains all the essential amino acids. It is the only alkaline grain, making it easily digestible. It is also a rich source of silicon, the substance that helps to build collagen for keeping skin, eyes, nails and arteries healthy, vibrant and flexible. Widely eaten in many parts of Africa, the small ground grain is cream in colour, with a pleasant, neutral taste.

Above: Millet

QUINOA

Until recently this tiny round grain was little known outside its native Bolivia, but quinoa (pronounced "keen-wah") is becoming increasingly popular, partly because it tastes delicious, but also because it is a very good source of protein, fibre and B group vitamins. Like brown rice, quinoa tastes faintly nutty. Quinoa is useful for making stuffings, pilaffs and cereals.

Above: Quinoa

COOKING QUINOA

Quinoa is a quick and easy side dish to prepare at home. When cooked, the tiny bead-shaped grains have a mild, slightly bitter taste and firm texture. It contains all eight essential amino acids and is a rich source of vital nutrients. Quinoa is cooked like rice, but the grains quadruple in size, becoming translucent with an unusual white outer ring.

1 Always wash quinoa before cooking to remove the fine, soapy, white powder that coats the grains.

2 Boil in a pan of water for about 20 minutes until the khaki-coloured round grains turn into pretty translucent white spirals. Serve with curries, stir-fries or casseroles as an alternative to boiled rice.

COOKING TIMES FOR GRAINS

The table below provides a rough guide only, as cooking times may alter according to how long the items have been stored, and the quantity cooked. In most cases, the volume of water should be three times that of the chosen ingredient, except in the case of rolled oats, quinoa and white rice, where double the amount of water will be sufficient. Ingredients that need very long cooking times, such as polenta, may need up to four times the amount of water.

Grains	Time (minutes)
Amaranth	20–25
Barley	80–90
Buckwheat	20
Millet	30
Oats – groats	120
Oats – rolled	10
Polenta – milled corn	25
Quinoa	15
Rice – brown	40–60
Rice – white	15–20
Wheat – whole	90
Wheat – cracked	25
Wild rice	60

OATS

Organic oats are extraordinarily high in soluble fibre and are a fundamental food for heart health. A bowl of porridge or oat-rich muesli (granola) is a great foundation for the day, giving greater stores of energy than high-sugar, non-organic breakfast cereals. Organic oat-based muesli is readily available, but it is also easy to make at home. Simply add chopped organic hazelnuts, linseed (flax), sunflower and pumpkin seeds to an oat base, then sweeten the mixture by stirring in chopped dried fruit. Store the muesli in an airtight container in a dry cupboard, and the muesli will last as long as the nuts – about three months.

Organic breakfast cereals not only retain their micro-nutrients but also tend to contain less refined sugar and salt than non-organic varieties, supporting healthier energy levels and moderating moods throughout the day. For a special treat, make a classic Bircher muesli by soaking equal quantities of oats and milk or dairy-free milk overnight. Stir in an equal quantity of yogurt and honey the next morning, with a freshly grated apple and one other chopped fresh fruit.

Oats are also widely used in baking and are delicious in flapjacks, added to the topping for a fruit crumble or crisp, or sprinkled on homemade breads.

WHEAT BERRIES

These are whole wheat grains with the husks removed. They are packed with concentrated goodness and have a sweet, nutty flavour and chewy texture. Wheat berries are delicious when added to salads. They can be used to add texture to breads and stews, or combined with rice or other grains. They must be soaked overnight, then cooked in boiling water until they are tender. When germinated, the berries sprout into wheatgrass, a powerful cleanser and detoxifier.

COUSCOUS

Although this looks like a grain, couscous is a form of pasta made by steaming and drying cracked durum wheat. When cooked, couscous is light and fluffy in texture. It is a mainstay of Middle Eastern cooking, its fairly bland flavour provides a good foil for spicy dishes. Couscous also tastes great flavoured with ginger or galangal and rose water and served as a traditional accompaniment to a Moroccan tagine.

Left: Couscous

COMBINING GRAINS AND PULSES

To maximize the amount of protein available from non-animal sources, mix grains and proteins. This is good advice for anyone seeking to eat a well-balanced diet, but it is essential advice for vegans. Divide foods into three groups: grains; beans and pulses; and seeds and nuts. In any meal, choose a combination of two of these groups. Cooks do this quite naturally a lot of the time. Baked beans on toast is one classic dish; while rice and dhal forms another traditional combination.

WHEAT BERRIES

When cooked, wheat berries make a delicious addition to salads, and they can also be used to add texture to breads and stews.

1 Place the wheat berries in a bowl and cover with cold water. Soak overnight, rinse thoroughly and drain.

2 Place the berries in a large pan and fill with cold water. Bring to the boil, then cover and simmer for 1–2 hours until the wheat berries are tender. Check regularly and replenish the water when necessary.

FLOUR AND PASTA

Organic food companies produce many different kinds of milled grains, more so than non-organic flour companies. In addition to wheat flour, there are flours made from buckwheat, rice, rye and maize, as well as quinoa and spelt. Organic pastas are also common and come in every shape and colour, from spaghetti to spirals. Japanese pastas such as udon and soba, are also readily available in organic form.

These products have an important part to play in the organic kitchen, particularly for people who wish to

Right: Udon noodles are high in complex carbohydrates and will provide energy over a long period.

Below: Spelt flour and grain

it retains all its valuable nutrients, but white flour is often better in baking. Most pasta and noodles are made of plain durum wheat or wholemeal flour. High in complex carbohydrates, pasta and noodles provide energy over a long period. Wholewheat versions are richer in vitamins, minerals and fibre, and often have a preferable texture. There is a wide choice of organic wheat noodles including Japanese udon noodles, thin, white somen noodles, egg noodles and ramen.

eliminate wheat and other high-gluten grains, such as rye, barley and oats, from their diet because they are allergic to gluten. Consult a qualified nutritionist if you have this allergy.

Many of us rely too heavily on wheat for carbohydrates – eating wheat-based cereals for breakfast, sandwiches for lunch, biscuits or cakes for tea and pasta for supper. Rather than cutting out wheat entirely, assess your average daily intake and make sure that you eat a good spread of different organic grains.

WHEAT FLOURS

Depending on the degree of processing, wheat flour may be either wholemeal (whole-wheat) or white. Stoneground wholemeal flour is the best for you since

NON-WHEAT FLOURS

Spelt is one of the most ancient grains and is rich in vitamins and minerals. It is the ancestor to modern wheat, but many people with gluten intolerance are able to digest spelt flour. Flours that do not contain gluten, such as rice, soya, buckwheat, quinoa and millet flours, have different cooking properties. Buckwheat is used to make blinis in Russia, soba noodles in Japan and pasta in Italy. Buckwheat pancakes are popular in parts of the USA and France. Rice flour is used in sticky Asian cakes and sweets, and to thicken sauces. Opaque-white rice noodles are popular in many South-east Asian countries.

Above: From back to front, hemp spaghetti, gluten-free corn spaghetti and spiralina tagliatelle

BREAD AND BAKED GOODS

All organic breads are better for you than the non-organic equivalent because the grains contain more nutrients and fewer agrochemical toxins. Unless bread is organic, it is likely to have had chemical flour improvers, flour extenders and preservatives added, as well as conditioners and flavourings, and invariably contains excess salt.

Some organic loaves are better than others, however, and it is important to seek out a good supplier whose loaves freeze well, so that you can stock up if necessary. A good organic loaf will have been made in the traditional manner, with enough yeast to ensure an even, close texture, and will taste delicious.

FACTORY-MADE BREADS

Alongside some excellent organic factory-made breads, there are some inferior loaves. Factory-made organic bread is sometimes made by the flash-baking method. This uses excessive amounts of yeast to make the dough rise rapidly. These breads have a spongy texture, mediocre flavour and are not as nutritional as organic loaves made by hand in the traditional way and allowed to rise slowly. The flash-baking method is cheaper for the manufacturer, but bread made this way is contributing to the current yeast intolerance boom.

Below: Organic white baguette, wheatfree loaf and naturally leavened campagne (at back).

BAKING BREAD

If you want to be absolutely certain of the quality of your organic loaf, bake your own. This is much easier than many people appreciate. Bread can be made by hand and baked in the oven or with the aid of an electric bread-maker, which mixes, kneads, rises and bakes the bread in one easy hands-free operation.

Wheat is the easiest type of flour to use for conventional yeast-based breads, as it contains plenty of gluten, the sticky substance that keeps dough stretchy and helps it to rise. Use wholemeal (wholewheat) flour for preference for its fibre content. Quality flours also provide protein and vitamins, especially the B vitamins, and useful amounts of zinc and magnesium, which help to harmonize moods, improve the condition of the skin and promote healing.

Below: Carrot and raisin cake, gluten-free almond cakes and choc chip hazelnut cookies.

Making bread with other flours is more of a challenge, as the gluten content of different grains varies considerably. Rice flour, buckwheat flour, corn meal and oatmeal, which contain little or no gluten, must either be mixed with wheat flour in a yeast loaf, leavened with bicarbonate of soda (baking soda) or used to make flat breads such as rice cakes.

CAKES AND BISCUITS

Commercially baked organic biscuits (cookies) and cakes are almost always superior to non-organic ones because they contain more vitamins and fewer additives. However, some organic sweet products still include too much refined sugar, both in terms of health and taste. To ensure the biscuits and cakes you buy are the best on the shelf, check the ingredients. Better still, bake your own. Experiment with the different organic flours on offer, add sweetness by using chopped dried fruit or flavour with grated orange rind, organic cocoa powder or a pinch of cinnamon or mixed spice.

THE ORGANIC STORE CUPBOARD

A well stocked store cupboard is a valuable asset for any cook, but it is absolutely essential for the organic cook, who may not be able to obtain every ingredient at the last minute by simply popping down to the local store.

It is worth spending a bit of time sourcing organic food. There is already a lot of it out there, and with more and more products becoming available all the time, switching to organic ingredients is relatively easy. You don't have to do it all at once; simply replace non-organic oils, vinegars, jams, nuts, seasonings and other items in your store cupboard with organic alternatives when they run out. A good organic stockist with a rapid turnover is a good place to start, and the Internet can be handy, too.

SUGARS AND HONEYS

Organic sugars are beneficial because they do not cause the pollution to developing countries that agrochemically grown versions often do. Refined and unrefined organic versions of all standard sugars except refined white are readily available, from demerara (raw) to soft brown. Unrefined organic sugars have far fewer vitamins and nutrients stripped out of them during processing than

Below: Molasses is a great source of iron.

Above: Rapadura is an excellent organic alternative to refined sugar.

refined sugars, and for this reason they have a slightly better flavour, too. That said, organic sugar still has a high empty calorie value, so it should always be used sparingly for a healthy balanced diet.

Rapadura This exciting alternative to refined sugar is only available in organic form. Similar in colour and texture to soft brown sugar, it has a much more interesting flavour and nutrient profile because it is made by simply sun-drying organic sugar cane juice, so all the beneficial vitamins and minerals of this natural product are retained. Rapadura is suitable for any style of cooking that calls for sugar, including jam-making and meringues. It is also known as jaggery, the Hindi name for this product.

Molasses Another excellent natural sweetener derived from sugar cane is molasses. Organic molasses has all the minerals in sugar cane in concentrated form, and is a great source of iron. The most nutritionally valuable type is thick and very dark blackstrap molasses. The powerful taste of molasses makes it a good choice for treacly biscuits, cakes, puddings and sauces.

Honey The most popular alternative to refined sugar is honey. Organic honey must come from unpolluted areas if it is to retain its purity. Most non-organic honey comes from bees fed on liquid sugar rather than collecting pollen. It is inferior to the organic version, both in its blandness and its lack of nutrition.

There are some wonderful organic honeys, each reflecting the flavours of the flowering plants visited by the bees. From Australian manuka honey to Zimbabwean forest honey, the choices range from powerful dark solid honeys to delicate golden liquid honeys. It is worth tasting a selection to discover your personal favourite, and familiarizing yourself with each variety so you can select the ideal match when cooking. Try using honey instead of syrup or sugar in cakes, or giving a hint of sweetness to salad dressings and hot sauces.

Honey has long been highly valued for its medicinal and healing properties. Mixed with lemon juice and hot water, it has antiseptic properties and can relieve sore throats. It is also thought to be helpful in treating diarrhoea and asthma.

Left: Organic farmers' markets are a good place to seek out unusual and homemade organic jams, marmalades, honeys, pickles and preserves.

Above: Fruit syrups are natural sweeteners, which can be used in place of sugar.

OTHER NATURAL SWEETENERS

There are lots of other sweetening options for the organic cook to explore including organic maple syrup, maple sugar and a wide range of fruit products.
Maple Syrup and Sugar Made by tapping the sap of the maple tree, organic maple syrup and sugar are not over-processed, so retain their richness. Drizzled over hot pancakes, maple, with its buttery tones, is the ultimate syrup. A small amount, added to a savoury batter, tantalizes the palate. Maple syrup is sweeter than sugar so less is required in cooking.
Fruit Syrups and Pastes Concentrated organic fruit syrups also make great sweeteners, whether you choose the liquid form or the solid paste. They contain none of the pesticides found in agrochemical versions and no added sugar or preservatives. They are just as popular with children as with adults. Concentrates are made from many types of organic fruit, including apples, pears, grapes, dates, peaches, blackcurrants and oranges. Apple and date versions add most sweetness, so can be used more sparingly than some other types. Their flavours are also not particularly dominant, so they will not overwhelm other ingredients. Pastes can also be used in cooking, but will need to be dissolved in water first. On their own, fruit pastes taste delicious when spread on bread. Most organic outlets sell concentrated fruit syrups and pastes. They can be stored in a refrigerator for 2–3 months.

Puréed dried fruits such as prunes, figs, dates and apricots can also be used to sweeten pies, crumbles and cakes. To make spiced apricot purée, place some apricots in a pan with enough water to cover, add a cinnamon stick, two cloves and a little freshly grated nutmeg, and simmer for 20 minutes until the apricots are plump. Leave to cool then purée in a food processor until smooth. Add more water if the mixture seems a little thick.

Above: Organic chocolate comes in dark, white and milk varieties.

COCOA AND CHOCOLATE

Agrochemical cocoa is the most heavily sprayed food crop, and is often unfairly traded, too. By buying organic cocoa and chocolate products you ensure that you are not supporting agrochemical pollution in developing countries.

Organic chocolate products are usually higher in cocoa and lower in sugar than the non-organic equivalent, and are free from hydrogenated fats, emulsifiers and other chemical additives. Organic cocoa is naturally high in tannins and antioxidant flavonoids, plus B vitamins and iron. This means that eating organic chocolate in moderation can do you good, as it is thought to offer some protection against heart attacks.

The darker the chocolate, the higher the percentage of cocoa solids and the more intense the taste. Chocolate with 70 per cent cocoa solids has a proportionally higher nutritional content.

Organic chocolate comes in a wide array of products, from specialist hand-made pralines to slabs of dark (bittersweet), milk and white and flavoured chocolates. They all keep well and can be stored in the refrigerator, so there is no need to eat all the chocolate at once.

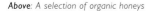

Above: A selection of organic honeys

NUTS AND SEEDS

Organic nuts and seeds are little powerhouses that would grow into new plants or mighty trees if sown and allowed to germinate. This makes them an incredibly rich source of nutrients. High in plant oils and protein, they also yield B complex vitamins, potassium, magnesium, calcium, phosphorus and iron. The fat they contain is largely monounsaturated or polyunsaturated (only coconuts and brazil nuts contain saturated fat) and they are the richest vegetable source of vitamin E, which has been credited with reducing the risk of heart disease, strokes and certain cancers.

Many people equate a healthy diet with a low fat diet, but this is not true. It is important that we eat a balanced diet, including proteins, carbohydrates and fats. While saturated and hydrogenated fats are undesirable, unrefined polyunsaturated fats are essential. They provide energy and help to prevent heart disease, eczema, ulcers and arthritis when eaten as part of a healthy diet and combined with a balanced lifestyle. The best way of obtaining polyunsaturated fats is to eat nuts and seeds, since these also provide the antioxidants necessary to optimise the value of these fats.

Seeds are very good for you for many other reasons, too. Sunflower seeds are rich in many minerals, including zinc, which aids skin regeneration and helps to heal cuts and minor abrasions. The

Walnuts (above) and hazelnuts (below) are a good source of protein.

seeds also contain B vitamins and will ease fatigue, irritability and depression. Flax (linseed) seeds are gentle healers for the intestinal tract. Sesame seeds are a good source of protein, zinc and iron, so are good for sexual health. Pumpkin seeds have similar nutrients, plus calcium and B vitamins.

COOKING WITH ORGANIC NUTS AND SEEDS

Health reasons aside, organic nuts and seeds taste great. You can add chopped nuts and seeds to salads, savoury roasts, breads and cakes. Roasting nuts and seeds in a dry, non-stick frying pan for

Above: Peanuts

Right: Organic chestnuts are sweet and starchy.

Above: Pumpkin seeds make a perfect organic snack food.

NUT NOTES

The perfect snack food, nuts provide plenty of nutrients, too.

• Brazil nuts are a good source of protein, with lots of vitamin B1 and magnesium to aid concentration and support the nervous system.

• Walnuts contain as much protein as eggs, plus potassium, zinc and iron.

• Pecan nuts, walnuts and hemp seeds are a source of linoleic acid, which has anti-inflammatory properties. Smokers who have kicked the habit find it soothes lungs irritated by the free radicals in cigarette smoke. These nuts and seeds are also a first line of defence against other forms of cancer, because of their high vitamin E content, plus the fact that they are the only known sources of an antioxidant group called avenanthramides. People who eat walnuts or pecans five times a week have been discovered to lower their risk of developing coronary heart disease by 35 per cent.

• Pine nuts are the richest source of protein of any nut, with a deliciously buttery flavour that makes them great in salads.

• Peanuts are a good source of both iron and protein.

• Hazelnuts have a sweet flavour but are relatively low in calories.

• Chestnuts are sweet and starchy, and help to bind other ingredients, in nut roasts or stuffings, for instance.

a few minutes greatly improves the flavour. Watch them carefully and toss frequently so that they don't scorch.

Store-bought non-organic nut butters, including peanut butter, often contain unwanted hydrogenated oil and can be loaded with sugar, so buy organic nut or seed butters. Alternatively, make your own by processing your favourite nuts and seeds through a masticating juicer or in a food processor or blender.

Tahini, made by grinding sesame seeds, is especially good. Stir tahini or nut butter into a stir-fry for an instant sauce. When used in this way, nut and seed butters become favourite seasonings. When spread on toast, they make nutritious and very tasty toppings.

OILS

Cold pressed organic oils retain almost all the health and taste benefits of the raw nuts and seeds from which they are made. This is not the case with most agrochemical oils, which are extracted at high temperatures. In the process the natural antioxidants, minerals and other vitamins in the oil are destroyed. Non-organic oil is then further processed with solvents to lessen the colour and tone down the taste of the final product. Cold-pressed organic oils are prized for these very characteristics.

Olive oil is a firm favourite. In terms of colour and taste, it is a wonderful addition to any meal. It is a versatile food that can be eaten alone on bread instead of butter, added to salads or used for cooking, and is the perfect partner for organic food. It is the most digestible oil, and is universally acknowledged as being highly effective in preventing heart disease and treating liver disorders.

Many nut oils make delicious salad dressings when whisked with lemon juice or vinegar. Organic sunflower and safflower oils are rich in polyunsaturates that are great for heart health. Use them in dishes that require a lighter taste than olive oil, such as in oriental cooking and cake baking.

STORING NUTS, SEEDS AND OILS

Buy nuts in the shell, if possible, and eat them as soon as possible after shelling. If you must store them, put them in airtight bags and keep them in a cool place or the refrigerator. Store seeds in the same way. Buy cold pressed organic oils in small quantities, so that they can be used quickly, and store in a cool place. Never allow them to be exposed to heat during storage. Do not store nuts, seeds or oils for more than a few months, or the oil they contain may become rancid.

Below: Black and white sesame seeds

Above: Cold-pressed organic sunflower and safflower oils

SEASONINGS

If you are new to organic cooking, you may find you need to rethink your approach to seasonings of all kinds. Organic ingredients taste so good that to mask their flavours would be a sin. Use spices, condiments and strong flavourings such as vinegar with care, choosing always the organic option.

SPICES

Over sixty different kinds of spices are regularly used in cooking around the world. About twenty of these are easily available organically grown. Try to find organic spices where you can, because non-organic ones have often been heavily sprayed with pesticides. Most of these plants are grown in developing countries where non-organic farming practices can undermine farmers' health and the environment. Until recently dried spices with organic certification were quite difficult to track down. Now they are much more readily available, in good organic stores, direct from the packers or through mail order companies.

Spices are almost always used dried when their flavours are condensed. However, fresh versions of chillies and ginger are also popular. Organic dried chillies are a useful store-cupboard ingredient. They come whole, powdered or in flakes and tend to be hotter than fresh chillies. Especially valuable chillies include fruity, mild anchos, chipotles and hot habaneros.

Below: Fresh organic root ginger has an intense fiery flavour.

Above: Organic dried chillies are free from harmful pesticide residues.

Fry dried spices before adding them to a dish. Heat a pan with or without oil and fry or toast the spices for about 1 minute, until they release their aroma. Shake the pan often to prevent them from sticking. Most spices should be toasted whole, then crushed with a pestle in a mortar or whizzed in a coffee blender. However such spices as nutmeg and cinnamon are too large or bulky to be heated whole. Crush cinnamon bark or grate whole nutmeg just before toasting it. These spices retain more flavour when they are stored whole.

Fresh organic root ginger is smaller and has a more intense flavour than the swollen and sometimes watery non-organic spice. Ginger and galangal add a hot yet refreshing flavour to sweet and savoury dishes, including marinades, stir-fries, fresh vegetables, poached fruit and cakes and bakes.

The five spices most often used in Indian cooking are coriander, cumin, turmeric, pepper and chilli. Many other spices are used alongside this quintet, including star anise and fenugreek. Try adding nutmeg to savoury dishes such as pumpkin soup and baked fish as well as more traditional sweet dishes such as Christmas pudding or rice pudding. The powerful essential oils in this spice have slightly euphoric properties, so they lift the spirits. No wonder nutmeg is a popular spice in mulled wine and other festive Christmas

treats. Add caraway seeds to sauerkraut or bean stews, as they help to ease flatulence. Coriander seeds can help to cool an otherwise hot and spicy dish, as well as adding their distinctive flavour. Chilli powder acts like cornflour (cornstarch), thickening stews and curries, and pepper adds accent to almost everything, including strawberries.

SALT

The main flavouring used in cooking throughout the world is salt. At one time this was guaranteed to be a natural product extracted from seawater. Table salt is now almost exclusively over-refined, with magnesium carbonate

PREPARING FRESH GINGER

1 You don't need to peel fresh organic root ginger. Using a small, sharp paring knife, simply chop to the size specified in the recipe.

2 Alternatively, grate ginger finely. Special bamboo graters can be found in many Asian stores, but an ordinary box grater will do the job equally well. Freshly grated ginger can be squeezed with the fingers to release the juice, if required.

Left: Sea salt contains a variety
of minerals and salts.

Right:
Wholegrain
organic
mustard.

added to ensure
it flows freely. Sea
salt, whether organically
certified or not, has a much
broader spectrum of taste because it
contains a variety of different minerals
and salts alongside the sodium chloride
that is its main component. Keep your
salt usage low, as using too much of this
mineral compound can lead to high
blood pressure. One benefit of using
good-quality salt is that it has a stronger
flavour, so you do not need to use as
much salt. Organically certified salts
are particularly delicious and it is most
reassuring to know that such salts are
routinely inspected by the certifier
whose logo they bear.

Right: Organic light and dark shoyu
(soy sauce) adds flavour.

are plenty of organic varieties, including
balsamic and Japanese mirin rice vinegar.
Some non-organic vinegars are good-
quality products, with fine flavours and
good fragrances. However, many non-
organic vinegars are horrible. The
vinegar in most of England's famous fish
and chip shops bears little resemblance
to good, old-fashioned malt vinegar.

chickens. Vegan organic mayonnaise is
also readily available, made from soy or
pea protein. The taste of some
organic full grain mustards puts regular
non-organic mustards to shame. While
many non-organic commercial salad
dressings threaten to drown your healthy
leaves in refined, sugary oils, organic
salad dressings have been known to
outshine a home-made mixture.
Although the best chutneys and pickles
are made in your kitchen, there are
plenty of excellent ones available in
supermarkets, farmers' markets and
good organic stores.

SOY SAUCES

Many organic cooks use organic soy
sauces such as tamari and shoyu to add
saltiness and depth to their meals. These
products will enhance the flavour of
most savoury dishes, but should be
added in moderation, at the end of the
cooking process. High temperatures
destroy the delicate proteins and enzymes
that are so beneficial in these products.

VINEGARS

Organic vinegars are made by fermenting
ingredients such as organic apples and
grapes. Over time, these fine ingredients
will develop into zesty condiments to be
drizzled over fish or added to salad
dressings, pickles and marinades. There

At the opposite end of the
spectrum is organic cider
vinegar. This raw, unfiltered,
non-distilled, undiluted product
is aged in wooden barrels and
contains no preservatives, and has
superb health benefits. It is antibacterial,
antiseptic, anti-inflammatory and
detoxifying. It also helps to keep blood
thin, which is useful for people who eat
meat and dairy products.

OTHER CONDIMENTS

Many condiments contain vinegar as a
major ingredient, including mustard,
prepared salad dressings, mayonnaise,
chutneys, pickles and olives. The benefits
of buying organic versions of these
products are obvious, since you can be
sure that a good vinegar has been used
as a base. Other ingredients will be
organic, too, so whatever you buy is
likely to be flavoursome and of good
quality. The eggs in organic mayonnaise
will have come from free-range organic

Above: Cider vinegar is antibacterial.

DRINKS

Over the past decade or so, the demand for organic drinks has grown enormously. From a niche market, the beverage industry has burgeoned, producing drinks that are often so delicious that even those who are not yet fully committed to the organic ideal seek them out. From table water to gin, an organic certification mark on the bottle is a sign of fine quality and sustainable ingredients.

Below, left to right: Organic biodynamic white and red wines and elderflower wine

WINE

Organic wine is an explosion of flavours. Very often produced by small artisan vineyards, the organic grapes used in organic wines are much more diverse than those found in the majority of standard non-organic wines. Hangovers are usually caused by sulphites, which can also provoke asthma and migraines. Levels of sulphur are much lower in organic wines, so you really can feel the difference the next day. Organic vineyards recycle their waste grape skins by composting them, and they often plant flowering plants among the vines to attract pollinating insects and predators.

Prizewinning organic and biodynamic red and white wines are produced all over the world, including in France, Italy, Australia and California. Red wine is full of health-promoting antioxidants, so it is good for preventing heart disease as well as relieving stress if drunk in moderation.

To find a good supplier of organic wine, contact an independent wine dealer. The Internet is an invaluable tool for finding such retailers; simply make a search for organic wine dealers and look for one in your area. Alternatively, buy the wines direct from the vineyard.

Fruit wines can also be delicious. Organic stores sell several varieties, but the best way to investigate the many delights of elderberry, elderflower and blackcurrant wine is to make your own. Home wine-making kits can be used with organic ingredients to produce excellent results.

Store organic wine on its side in a cool, dark place to keep the cork moist. Try adding your favourite wines to sauces and fruit salads, or organic sherry and port to trifles and cakes.

SPIRITS

Wines are not the only prizewinning organic drinks. Some incredible spirits are available, including industry award winners such as Del Meguey mezcal. This organic mezcal is produced by traditional artisans in Mexico who have had the craft passed down to them through countless generations. Del Meguey produce five kinds of organic mezcal, with their top-of-the-range product achieving international status as one of the finest spirits in the world.

Organic gin and vodka have also reached a fine quality now, with Juniper Green gin and UK5 vodka made in London, England. Distilled from organic raw ingredients, you will find that these spirits have a clean, round taste, with lots of warm flavours in the gin. You can also buy organic Scotch whisky, plus more unusual spirits including Grappa and Calvados.

BEER AND CIDER

Organic beer and lager microbreweries have sprung up and begun to flourish all over the world, from North America to Belgium and Germany. The intensity that organic hops impart to the flavour of organic beers and lagers has encouraged the general trend towards high quality traditional brews. There are dark stouts and light lagers, bronze bitters and extra strong Belgian beers. There is even a German hemp beer, Cannabia, based on an ancient Roman recipe.

Organic ciders are made from organic apples, and often contain much less added sulphur dioxide than non-organic ciders. This makes them less likely to provoke hangovers in the morning. The largest range of organic cider is currently produced in England, but they are also brewed commercially in France.

Serve cider cold with a hot pork dinner or ham lunch. Alternatively, add a little to the pan when roasting lamb for additional flavour and acidity.

WATER

The ultimate soft drink is water. Essential for human health, it is undeniably the most thirst-quenching drink of them all. Add a squeeze of lemon juice or a sprig of fresh mint, and it becomes even more enjoyable. Although bottled water cannot be certified as organic, the label can state that it was sourced from organically farmed land. This is important if you want to avoid pesticides that may have run off agrochemical farmland into the water table beneath.

Tap water quality varies hugely between regions, depending on the geology of the area and its filtration capabilities. At best, it is pure and full of beneficial minerals such as calcium. At worst, it can contain pesticides, hormones and heavy metals.

Water Filters The best way to ensure that the water you drink is as pure as possible is to invest in a good-quality water filter. There are many variations on three basic types. The most common is the carbon filter, which is good at cleaning most impurities, including fluoride. An even better version incorporates a built-in reverse osmosis system that guarantees absolute purity from all heavy metals and other pollutants. Distillers are

Left to right: Organic Juniper Green gin, made in London, and German hemp beer, Cannabia

Above: Fresh organic lemonade

also available, but the water they produce must be supplemented carefully with minerals from foods or supplements. Choosing organic drinks is a good way of avoiding additives, but drinking pure water is even better.

FIZZY DRINKS

If you want to enjoy fizzy drinks or sodas as part of an organic diet it is essential that the drinks you buy are also organic. Non-organic colas are universally bad for your health. Although it is usual for both organic and non-organic fizzy drinks to contain a very high proportion of sugar, the non-organic drinks are full of artificial chemical additives that are seriously undermining. The phosphoric acid in colas is directly related to loss of calcium in bone. This can lead to osteoporosis, a disease that is becoming more common throughout the industrialized world.

Non-organic diet drinks usually contain synthetic sweeteners such as aspartame and saccharine. These artificial additives are strictly banned in organic foods, with very good reason. Aspartame is a neurotoxin that affects the appetite control centres in the brain. As a result, serotonin levels in the brain drop, often leading to depression. Consumers of artificially sweetened drinks often have difficulty dieting.

FRUIT CORDIALS

Not only are organic cordials better
than non-organic ones in terms of taste
and sweetness, but they are also more
nutritious. They contain no artificial
colourings or flavourings, refined sugars
or artificial sweeteners. Made from real
fruit juices, they taste much more like
the fruit pictured on the label than the
highly processed alternatives. However,
many organic cordials are still high in
sugar, so check the ingredients, especially
if you are preparing the drink for
a child. Organic sugar is almost as
unhealthy as non-organic sugar, and
just as destructive to teeth.

FRUIT AND VEGETABLE JUICES

Commercially available organic juices
vary considerably in terms of flavour,
but all score over non-organic ones
because they are free of pesticide
residues. It takes a lot of fruit and
vegetables to make a relatively small
amount of juice. If the produce contains
pesticide residues, these will be
concentrated when the fruit or vegetable
is juiced. Drinking organic juice means
that you are getting more concentrated
vitamins, minerals and phytonutrients
instead.

If you buy fruit or vegetable
juices, try to ensure that they
come from freshly pressed

*Right: Organic fruit and
vegetable juices are a fabulous
source of vitamins, minerals
and phytonutrients.*

*Right: Vanilla spice tea leaves, fair-trade
breakfast and Japanese nagata kukicha teas*

produce rather than concentrates.
Minimal processing results in a more
natural taste and higher nutrient content.
Some juices now include natural healers
and energizers such as ginseng,
chlorophyl-rich spirulina and wheatgrass.

Juicing The best juices are freshly made,
either squeezed manually from citrus
fruits or processed with the aid of a
juice machine, or juicer. Most juicers are
based on the centrifugal system. The
fresh produce is grated and sieved at
high speed to separate the juice from the
pulp. Other juicers work by effectively
"chewing" the produce. The juice that
is released comes from
between the plant's
cell walls and is
extremely high
in nutrients and

flavour. These machines are called
masticating juicers, and although
expensive, they are the best on the
market. Hard and soft fruits and
vegetables, leafy greens and fresh herbs
can all be juiced in machines.

If you do not own a juicer, make fruit
juices in a food processor or blender.
Peel, stone (pit), core or seed the fruit
before blending. Juices made in this way
tend to be thicker and have a higher fibre
content than regular juices because the
pulp has not been removed. Soft
fruits, such as melon and grapes,
are ideal for blended juices.

TEAS, FRUIT TEAS AND TISANES

Organic teas are grown with
respect for the land and the people
who tend it. The teas are generally
fairly traded, with communities far
away from the end beverage gaining
real benefits whenever a packet is sold.
Pesticide residues are at issue here.
Although these are not high in
agrochemically grown teas, the crop is
generally sprayed intensively throughout
its growth. This pollutes the land and

poses a serious health threat to the workers. Organic teas are full of flavour, and are readily available in lots of different varieties, including loose leaves and tea bags containing either single estate varieties or blends. Flavoured or spiced teas are also on sale. All these products contain vitamins and minerals as well as powerful antioxidants that protect the heart and help to prevent cancer. When you buy organic, even the tea bags are better for the environment, because unlike non-organic tea bags, they have to be chlorine-free.

There are hundreds of organic fruit teas, spice teas and herbal tisanes available, generally with much better flavour than the non-organic equivalents.
Fruit teas Organic fruit teas rely on natural fruit for their flavour and colour, whereas non-organic fruit teas are often boosted with synthetic and "nature-identical" flavourings and colours. This results in overpoweringly strong rather than less subtle tastes.
Herbal tisanes and spice teas These have direct healing benefits as well as delicate flavours. The herbs and spices they contain are often pharmacoepial grade, meaning that they are of the same quality as herbs prescribed by herbalists.

Some blends are available specifically formulated for medicinal purposes as well as flavour, including mixes to help you sleep, to aid digestion, to ward off colds or to ease stress.

Lavender, hyssop, thyme and marjoram infused together are taken as a remedy for cold symptons. Hops, chamomile and lime flower are used to beat insomnia. Rosemary is said to stimulate the circulation and improve concentration while thyme boosts the immune system and helps fight infections. Elderflower tisane can ease painful sinuses and bronchial conditions.

Almost any herb and its flowers can be used to make tea, and the method is generally the same. Place several sprigs of the freshly picked herb in a cup and pour over hot, but not boiling, water and leave for several minutes to infuse. Strain the liquid to remove the leaves and drink it hot or cold with honey, lemon or sugar to taste. Spices require

Above: Organic drinking chocolate powder

greater heat to extract the constituents, so they need to be placed in a pan of cold water, heated and simmered for 10 to 15 minutes.

COFFEE AND COCOA

Organic coffee and cocoa are grown in hot, tropical, mountainous regions such as South and Central America, East Africa and Indonesia. It is essential to have faith in the producer's trading practices. The cultivation of agrochemical coffee often involves heavy pesticide use, especially in developing countries. There are health and safety concerns, too, about conditions for workers on the plantations. The confidence that comes from buying organically grown, fairly traded coffee doubles the pleasure of drinking this beverage. Look out for organic instant coffee granules or powder as well as ground coffee or whole roasted beans. Store whole or ground beans in the refrigerator and they will retain their freshness for longer.

Organic drinking chocolate is available as an instant powder. Although organic coffee and drinking chocolate powder are not the healthiest organic products, organic drinking chocolate is much better for you than the non-organic version because it contains only natural ingredients, including antioxidant-rich organic cocoa. Intensively produced non-organic drinking chocolate contains dried non-organic milk, hydrogenated fats, refined sweeteners and artificial flavourings.

Above: Buying and grinding fair-traded organic coffee beans can double the pleasure of drinking coffee.

SPRING

As the weather starts to get warmer, the fresh organic ingredients traditionally associated with this time of year start to appear in the shops and markets. The season's vegetables require little cooking to bring out their sweet flavour: try asparagus with a tangy lemon sauce, or young carrots and leeks. Brightly coloured spring vegetables also taste great when served with pasta or added to soups. Light fish dishes are a popular choice after winter – salmon fish cakes or fillets of sea bream in filo pastry are served simply with spring vegetables, and this is the time of year to enjoy tender, organic lamb. For dessert, nothing beats delicate spring rhubarb served with ginger ice cream, or made into a delicious meringue pie.

CHICKEN, AVOCADO and SPRING ONION SOUP

Organic avocados ripen naturally over a longer period of time than non-organic, producing really rich-flavoured fruit. Combined here with chicken and spring onions they add a creaminess to this delicious soup.

SERVES SIX

1.5 litres/2½ pints/6¼ cups chicken stock
½ fresh chilli, seeded
2 skinless, boneless chicken breast fillets
1 avocado
4 spring onions (scallions), finely sliced
400g/14oz can chickpeas, drained
sea salt and freshly ground black pepper

1 Pour the chicken stock into a large pan and add the chilli. Bring to the boil, add the whole chicken breast fillets, then lower the heat and simmer for about 10 minutes, or until the chicken is cooked.

COOK'S TIP
Handle chillies with care as they can irritate the skin and eyes. It is advisable to wear rubber gloves when preparing them.

2 Remove the pan from the heat and lift out the chicken breasts with a slotted spoon. Leave to cool a little, then, using two forks, shred the chicken into small pieces. Set the shredded chicken aside.

3 Pour the chicken stock into a food processor or blender and add the chilli. Process the mixture until smooth, then return to the pan.

4 Cut the avocado in half, remove the skin and stone (pit), then slice the flesh into 2cm/¾in pieces. Add it to the stock, with the spring onions and chickpeas.

5 Return the shredded chicken to the pan, with salt and pepper to taste, and heat gently. When the soup is heated through, spoon into warmed bowls and serve.

PASTA and CHICKPEA SOUP

A simple, country-style soup. The shapes of the pasta and the beans complement one another beautifully. Look out for really large pasta shells, which you can find in farmers' markets and good organic stores.

SERVES FOUR TO SIX

1 onion
2 carrots
2 celery sticks
60ml/4 tbsp olive oil
400g/14oz can chickpeas, rinsed
   and drained
200g/7oz can cannellini beans,
   rinsed and drained
150ml/¼ pint/⅔ cup passata (bottled
   strained tomatoes)
120ml/4fl oz/½ cup water
1.5 litres/2½ pints/6¼ cups chicken stock
2 fresh or dried rosemary sprigs
200g/7oz dried giant conchiglie
sea salt and ground black pepper
freshly grated Parmesan cheese or
   premium Italian-style vegetarian
   cheese, to serve

1 Chop the onion, carrots and celery sticks finely, either in a food processor or by hand.

2 Heat the olive oil in a large pan, add the chopped vegetable mixture and cook over a low heat, stirring frequently, for 5 minutes, or until the vegetables are just beginning to soften.

3 Add the chickpeas and cannellini beans, stir well to mix, then cook for 5 minutes. Stir in the passata and water, then cook, stirring, for 2–3 minutes.

4 Add 475ml/16fl oz/2 cups of the stock and one of the rosemary sprigs. Bring to the boil, cover, then simmer gently, stirring occasionally, for 1 hour.

5 Pour in the remaining stock, add the pasta and bring to boil, stirring. Lower the heat slightly and simmer, stirring frequently, until the pasta is *al dente*: 7–8 minutes or according to the instructions on the packet.

6 When the pasta is cooked, taste the soup for seasoning. Remove the rosemary and serve the soup hot in warmed bowls, topped with grated cheese and a few rosemary leaves from the rosemary sprig.

COOK'S TIP
Organic passata is a must for this recipe as most non-organic tomato products contain genetically modified tomatoes.

TAPENADE with QUAIL'S EGGS and CRUDITÉS

*This olive-based spread or dip makes a sociable start to a meal. Serve the tapenade
with hard-boiled quail's eggs or small organic hen's eggs and a selection of mixed spring
vegetable crudités and let everyone help themselves.*

SERVES SIX

225g/8oz/2 cups pitted black olives
2 large garlic cloves, peeled
15ml/1 tbsp salted capers, rinsed
6 canned or bottled anchovy
    fillets, drained
50g/2oz good-quality canned tuna
5–10ml/1–2 tsp Cognac (optional)
5ml/1 tsp chopped fresh thyme
30ml/2 tbsp chopped fresh parsley
30–60ml/2–4 tbsp extra virgin olive oil
a dash of lemon juice
30ml/2 tbsp crème fraîche or
    fromage frais (optional)
12–18 quail's eggs
ground black pepper

For the crudités
bunch of spring onions (scallions),
    halved if large
bunch of radishes, trimmed
bunch of baby fennel, trimmed and halved
    if large, or 1 large fennel bulb, cut into
    thin wedges

To serve
French bread
unsalted (sweet) butter or olive oil and
    sea salt to dip

1 Process the olives, garlic cloves,
capers, anchovies and tuna in a food
processor or blender. Transfer to a
mixing bowl and stir in the Cognac, if
using, the thyme, parsley and enough
olive oil to make a paste. Season to taste
with pepper and a dash of lemon juice.
Stir in the crème fraîche or fromage frais,
if using, and transfer to a serving bowl.

2 Place the quail's eggs in a pan of cold
water and bring to the boil. Cook for
only 2 minutes, then immediately drain
and plunge the eggs into iced water to
stop them from cooking any further and
to help make them easier to shell.

3 When the eggs are cold, carefully
part-shell them.

4 Serve the tapenade with the eggs
and crudités and offer French bread,
unsalted butter or oil and sea salt to
accompany them.

COOK'S TIPS
• Crème fraîche or fromage frais softens
the distinctive flavour of the olives for a
milder tapenade.
• In Provence, where tapenade comes
from, it is traditional to serve it with
crudités of celery, fennel and tomato.
• Tapenade is also delicious spread on
toast and served with pre-dinner drinks.

OYSTERS ROCKEFELLER

This is the perfect dish for those who prefer to eat their oysters lightly cooked. As a cheaper alternative, for those who are not "as rich as Rockefeller", give mussels or clams the same treatment; they will also taste delicious.

SERVES SIX

450g/1lb/3 cups coarse sea salt,
   plus extra to serve
24 oysters, opened
115g/4oz/½ cup butter or
   non-hydrogenated margarine
2 shallots, finely chopped
500g/1¼lb spinach leaves, finely chopped
60ml/4 tbsp chopped fresh parsley
60ml/4 tbsp chopped celery leaves
90ml/6 tbsp fresh white or wholemeal
   (whole-wheat) breadcrumbs
10–20ml/2–4 tsp vodka
cayenne pepper
sea salt and ground black pepper
lemon wedges, to serve

COOK'S TIP

If you prefer a smoother stuffing, whizz it to a paste in a food processor or blender at the end of step 3.

1 Preheat the oven to 220°C/425°F/ Gas 7. Make a bed of coarse salt on two large baking sheets. Set the oysters in the half-shell in the bed of salt to keep them steady. Set aside.

2 Melt the butter or margarine in a frying pan. Add the chopped shallots and cook them over a low heat for 2–3 minutes until they are softened. Stir in the spinach and let it wilt.

3 Add the parsley, celery leaves and breadcrumbs to the pan and fry gently for 5 minutes. Season with salt, pepper and cayenne pepper.

4 Divide the stuffing among the oysters. Drizzle a few drops of vodka over each oyster, then bake for about 5 minutes until bubbling and golden brown. Serve on a heated platter on a shallow salt bed with lemon wedges.

LEEK and MUSSEL TARTLETS

Wild mussels are easily harvested and are simply gathered off rocks in shallow water by hand. Serve these vividly coloured little tarts as a first course, with a few salad leaves, such as watercress, rocket and frisée.

3 Preheat the oven to 190°C/375°F/ Gas 5. Roll out the pastry and line six 10cm/4in tartlet tins (quiche pans). Prick the bases and line the sides with foil. Bake for 10 minutes. Remove the foil and bake for 5–8 minutes. Reduce the temperature to 180°C/350°F/Gas 4.

4 Soak the saffron in 15ml/1 tbsp hot water for 10 minutes. Fry the leeks in the oil in a pan over a medium heat for 6–8 minutes. Add the peppers and cook for 2 minutes.

SERVES SIX

large pinch of saffron threads
2 large leeks, sliced
30ml/2 tbsp olive oil
2 large yellow (bell) peppers, halved, seeded, grilled (broiled), peeled and cut into strips
900g/2lb mussels
2 large eggs
300ml/½ pint/1¼ cups single (light) cream or soya cream
30ml/2 tbsp finely chopped fresh parsley
sea salt and ground black pepper
salad leaves, to serve

For the pastry
225g/8oz/2 cups plain (all-purpose) flour
115g/4oz/½ cup chilled butter, diced
45–60ml/3–4 tbsp chilled water

1 To make the pastry, sift the flour into a mixing bowl and add the butter. Rub the butter in with your fingertips until the mixture resembles fine breadcrumbs.

2 Sprinkle 45ml/3 tbsp of the water over and mix with a round-bladed knife until the mixture comes together and a soft dough is formed. Add more water if necessary. Wrap the dough in clear film (plastic wrap) and chill for 30 minutes.

COOK'S TIP
Use soya cream instead of the single cream and soya margarine instead of butter for a non-dairy option.

5 Bring 2.5cm/1in depth of water to the boil in a large pan and add 10ml/2 tsp salt. Scrub the mussels and remove the beards. Discard any mussels that stay open when tapped, then throw the rest into the pan. Cover and cook over a high heat, shaking the pan occasionally, for 3–4 minutes, or until the mussels open. Discard any unopened mussels. Shell the remainder.

6 Beat the eggs, cream and saffron liquid together. Season with salt and pepper and whisk in the parsley. Arrange the leeks, peppers and mussels in the cases, add the egg mixture and bake for 20–25 minutes. Serve with salad leaves.

DEEP-FRIED TOFU BALLS

*Tofu is a wonderfully healthy and versatile ingredient and is flavoured to perfection in
this Japanese dish, known as hiryozu, which means flying dragon's head. The tangy lime
sauce provides a lovely contrast to the savoury tofu balls.*

SERVES FOUR

2 × 285g/10¼oz packets firm tofu
20g/¾oz carrot, peeled
40g/1½oz green beans
2 large (US extra large) eggs, beaten
30ml/2 tbsp sake
10ml/2 tsp mirin
5ml/1 tsp sea salt
10ml/2 tsp shoyu
pinch of unrefined caster (superfine) sugar
    or rapadura
sunflower oil, for deep-frying

For the lime sauce
45ml/3 tbsp shoyu
juice of ½ lime
5ml/1 tsp rice vinegar or mirin

To garnish
300g/11oz mooli (daikon), peeled
2 dried red chillies, halved and seeded
4 chives, finely chopped

1 Drain the tofu and wrap in a dishtowel
or kitchen paper. Set a chopping board
on top and leave for 2 hours, or until it
loses most of its liquid.

2 Cut the mooli for the garnish into
about 4cm/1½in thick slices. Make 3–4
small holes in each slice with a skewer
or chopstick and insert chilli pieces into
the holes. Leave for 15 minutes, then
grate the daikon and chilli finely.

3 To make the tofu balls, chop the
carrot finely. Trim and cut the beans into
5mm/¼in lengths. Cook both vegetables
for 1 minute in boiling water.

4 In a food processor, blend the tofu,
eggs, sake, mirin, salt, shoyu and sugar
until smooth. Transfer to a bowl and
mix in the carrot and beans.

5 Fill a wok or pan with oil 4cm/1½in
deep, and heat to 185°C/365°F.

6 Soak a piece of kitchen paper with a
little vegetable oil, and lightly moisten
your hands with it. Scoop 40ml/2½ tbsp
of the mixture in one hand and shape
into a ball between your hands.

7 Carefully slide the ball into the oil and
deep-fry until crisp and golden brown.
Drain on kitchen paper. Repeat with the
remaining mixture.

8 Arrange the tofu balls on a plate and
sprinkle with chives. Put 30ml/2 tbsp
grated mooli in each of four bowls. Mix
the lime sauce ingredients in a small
serving bowl. Serve the hot tofu balls
with the lime sauce to be mixed with
grated daikon by each guest.

ASPARAGUS with LEMON SAUCE

*This is a good spring dish as the asparagus gives the immune system a kick start to help
detoxify after winter. The sauce has a light, fresh taste and brings out the best in asparagus.*

SERVES FOUR AS A FIRST COURSE

675g/1½lb asparagus, tough ends removed,
   and tied in a bundle
15ml/1 tbsp cornflour (cornstarch)
10ml/2 tsp unrefined sugar or rapadura
2 egg yolks
juice of 1½ lemons
sea salt

COOK'S TIP

Use tiny asparagus spears for an elegant
appetizer for a special dinner party.

1 Cook the bundle of asparagus in
boiling salted water for 7–10 minutes.

2 Drain the asparagus well (reserving
200ml/7fl oz/scant 1 cup of the cooking
liquid) and arrange the spears
attractively in a serving dish. Set aside.

3 Blend the cornflour with the cooled,
reserved cooking liquid and place in a
small pan. Bring to the boil, stirring all
the time with a wooden spoon, then
cook over a gentle heat until the sauce
thickens slightly. Stir in the sugar, then
remove the pan from the heat and allow
to cool slightly.

4 Beat the egg yolks thoroughly with the
lemon juice and stir gradually into the
cooled sauce. Cook the sauce over a
very low heat, stirring all the time, until
it thickens. Be careful not to overheat
the sauce or it may curdle. Once the
sauce has thickened, remove the pan
from the heat and continue stirring for
1 minute. Season with salt or sugar if
necessary. Allow the sauce to cool slightly.

5 Stir the cooled lemon sauce, then
pour a little over the cooked asparagus.
Cover and chill for at least 2 hours
before serving accompanied by the rest
of the lemon sauce.

PENNE with CREAM and SMOKED SALMON

This modern classic uses just three essential ingredients, which combine together
beautifully to make a quick and easy dish. Accompany with a green salad, ciabatta bread
and sparkling wine for a simple but nutritious and tasty meal.

SERVES FOUR

350g/12oz/3 cups dried penne or
    other pasta tubes
115g/4oz thinly sliced smoked salmon
2–3 fresh thyme sprigs
30ml/2 tbsp extra virgin olive oil
150ml/¼ pint/⅔ cup extra-thick
    single (light) cream or
    soya cream
sea salt and ground black pepper

1 Cook the dried pasta in a large pan of
lightly salted boiling water for 10 minutes
until it is just tender, or according to the
instructions on the packet.

2 Meanwhile, using sharp kitchen
scissors, cut the smoked salmon slices
into thin strips, about 5mm/¼in wide.
Strip the leaves from the thyme sprigs
and rinse them thoroughly in cold water.

3 Drain the pasta and return it to the
pan. Add the oil and heat gently, then
stir in the cream with about one-quarter
of the smoked salmon and thyme leaves,
then season with pepper. Heat gently
for 3–4 minutes, stirring all the time.
Check the seasoning. Divide the pasta
among four warmed bowls, top with
the remaining salmon and thyme leaves
and serve immediately.

VARIATION
Although white penne is the traditional pasta
to serve with this sauce, it also goes very
well with fresh wholemeal penne or ravioli
stuffed with spinach and ricotta cheese.

CHICKEN and ASPARAGUS RISOTTO

Use fairly thick asparagus in this classic springtime risotto, as fine spears tend to overcook. The thick ends of the asparagus are full of flavour and they become beautifully tender in the time it takes for the rice to absorb the stock.

SERVES FOUR

75ml/5 tbsp olive oil
1 leek, finely chopped
115g/4oz/1½ cups oyster or brown cap
   (cremini) mushrooms, sliced
3 skinless, boneless chicken breast
   fillets, cubed
350g/12oz asparagus
250g/9oz/1¼ cups risotto rice
900ml/1½ pints/3¾ cups simmering
   chicken stock
sea salt and ground black pepper
fresh Parmesan or premium
   Italian-style vegetarian cheese curls,
   to serve

1 Heat the olive oil in a pan. Add the finely chopped leek and cook gently until softened, but not coloured. Add the sliced mushrooms and cook for 5 minutes. Remove the vegetables from the pan and set aside.

2 Increase the heat and cook the cubes of chicken until golden on all sides. Do this in batches, if necessary, and then return them all to the pan.

3 Meanwhile, discard the woody ends from the asparagus and cut the spears in half. Set the tips aside. Cut the thick ends in half and add them to the pan. Return the leek and mushroom mixture to the pan and stir in the rice.

4 Pour in a ladleful of boiling stock and cook gently, stirring occasionally, until the stock is completely absorbed. Continue adding the stock a ladleful at a time, simmering until it is absorbed, the rice is tender and the chicken is cooked.

COOK'S TIP
To thoroughly remove all the soil from organic leeks, slice in half along their length and rinse under running water.

5 Add the asparagus tips with the last ladleful of boiling stock for the final 5 minutes and continue cooking the risotto very gently until the asparagus is tender. The whole process should take about 25–30 minutes.

6 Season the risotto to taste with salt and freshly ground black pepper and spoon it into individual warm serving bowls. Top each bowl with curls of cheese, and serve.

HERB-CRUSTED RACK of LAMB with PUY LENTILS

This lamb roast is quick and easy to prepare but looks impressive when served – it is the perfect choice when entertaining. Puy lentils are a favourite ingredient in the south of France. Their delicate flavour is the perfect complement to the rich meat.

SERVES FOUR

2 × 6-bone racks of lamb, chined
50g/2oz/1 cup fresh white or wholemeal (whole-wheat) breadcrumbs
2 large garlic cloves, crushed
90ml/6 tbsp chopped mixed fresh herbs, plus extra sprigs to garnish
50g/2oz/¼ cup butter, melted or 50ml/3½ tbsp olive oil
sea salt and ground black pepper
new potatoes, to serve

For the Puy lentils
1 red onion, chopped
30ml/2 tbsp olive oil
400g/14oz can Puy lentils, rinsed and drained
400g/14oz can chopped tomatoes
30ml/2 tbsp chopped fresh flat leaf parsley

1 Preheat the oven to 220°C/425°F/ Gas 7. Trim any excess fat from the lamb, and season with salt and pepper.

2 Mix together the breadcrumbs, garlic, herbs and butter or oil, and press on to the fat-sides of the lamb. Place in a roasting pan and roast for 25 minutes. Cover with foil; stand for 5 minutes before carving.

3 Cook the onion in the olive oil until softened. Add the lentils and tomatoes and cook gently for 5 minutes, or until the lentils are piping hot. Stir in the parsley and season to taste.

4 Cut each rack of lamb in half and serve with the lentils and new potatoes. Garnish with herb sprigs.

LAMB BURGERS with RED ONION and TOMATO RELISH

A sharp-sweet red onion relish works well with burgers based on Middle Eastern style lamb. Serve with pitta bread and tabbouleh for an authentic taste, though baked potatoes and a crisp green salad are also good.

SERVES FOUR

25g/1oz/3 tbsp bulgur wheat
500g/1¼lb lean minced (ground) lamb
1 small red onion, finely chopped
2 garlic cloves, finely chopped
1 green chilli, seeded and finely chopped
5ml/1 tsp ground toasted cumin seeds
2.5ml/½ tsp ground sumac (optional)
15g/½oz/¼ cup chopped fresh flat
    leaf parsley
30ml/2 tbsp chopped fresh mint
olive oil, for frying
sea salt and ground black pepper

For the relish
2 red (bell) peppers, halved and seeded
2 red onions, cut into 5mm/¼in thick slices
75–90ml/5–6 tbsp extra virgin olive oil
350g/12oz cherry tomatoes, chopped
½–1 fresh red or green chilli, seeded
    and finely chopped (optional)
30ml/2 tbsp chopped fresh mint
30ml/2 tbsp chopped fresh parsley
15ml/1 tbsp chopped fresh oregano
    or marjoram
2.5–5ml/½–1 tsp each ground toasted
    cumin seeds
2.5–5ml/½–1 tsp sumac (optional)
juice of ½ lemon
unrefined caster (superfine) sugar
    or rapadura, to taste

1 Pour 150ml/¼ pint/⅔ cup hot water over the bulgur wheat in a mixing bowl and leave to stand for 15 minutes, then drain the wheat in a sieve and squeeze out the excess moisture.

2 To make the relish, grill (broil) the peppers, skin side up, until the skin chars and blisters. Place in a bowl, cover and leave to stand for 10 minutes. Peel off the skin, dice the peppers finely and place in a bowl.

3 Brush the onions with 15ml/1 tbsp oil and grill for 5 minutes on each side, until browned. Leave to cool.

4 Place the bulgur in a bowl and add the minced lamb, onion, garlic, chilli, cumin, sumac, if using, parsley and mint. Mix the ingredients thoroughly together by hand, then season with 2.5ml/½ tsp salt and plenty of black pepper and mix again. Form the mixture into eight small burgers.

5 Chop the onions for the relish. Add with the tomatoes, chilli to taste, herbs and 2.5ml/½ tsp each of the cumin and sumac, if using, to the peppers. Stir in 60ml/4 tbsp of the remaining oil and 15ml/1 tbsp of the lemon juice. Season with salt, pepper and sugar and leave to stand for 20–30 minutes.

6 Heat a heavy frying pan over a high heat and grease lightly with olive oil. Cook the burgers for about 5–6 minutes on each side, or until just cooked at the centre.

7 While the burgers are cooking, taste the relish and adjust the seasoning, adding more pepper, sugar, oil, chilli, cumin, sumac, if using, and lemon juice to taste. Serve the burgers with the relish.

LAMB STEW with NEW POTATOES and SHALLOTS

This fresh lemon-seasoned stew is finished with an Italian mixture of chopped garlic, parsley and lemon rind known as gremolata, the traditional topping for osso bucco.

SERVES SIX

1kg/2¼lb boneless shoulder of lamb,
   trimmed of fat and cut into
   5cm/2in cubes
1 garlic clove, finely chopped
finely grated rind of ½ lemon and
   juice of 1 lemon
90ml/6 tbsp olive oil
45ml/3 tbsp wholemeal (whole-wheat) flour
1 large onion, sliced
5 anchovy fillets in olive oil, drained
2.5ml/½ tsp unrefined caster (superfine)
   sugar or rapadura
300ml/½ pint/1¼ cups fruity white wine
475ml/16fl oz/2 cups lamb stock or half
   stock and half water
1 fresh bay leaf
fresh rosemary sprig
fresh parsley sprig
500g/1¼lb small new potatoes
250g/9oz shallots, peeled but left whole
45ml/3 tbsp double (heavy) cream or
   soya cream (optional)
sea salt and ground black pepper

For the gremolata
1 garlic clove, finely chopped
finely shredded rind of ½ lemon
45ml/3 tbsp chopped fresh flat leaf parsley

1 Mix the lamb with the garlic and the rind and juice of ½ lemon in a non-metallic container. Season with pepper and mix in 15ml/1 tbsp olive oil, then leave to marinate in the refrigerator for 12–24 hours.

2 Drain the lamb carefully, reserving the marinade, and pat the lamb dry with kitchen paper. Preheat the oven to 180°C/350°F/Gas 4.

COOK'S TIP
A mezzaluna (double-handled, half-moon shaped, curved chopping blade) makes a very good job of chopping gremolata ingredients. If using a food processor or electric chopper, take care not to over-process the mixture as it is easy to mince the ingredients to a paste.

3 Heat 30ml/2 tbsp olive oil in a large, heavy frying pan. Season the flour with salt and pepper and toss the drained, dried lamb in it to coat it lightly, shaking off any excess flour. Add the lamb to the pan, in small batches, and seal it on all sides in the hot oil stirring constantly with a wooden spoon.

4 As each batch of lamb becomes brown, transfer it to an ovenproof pan or flame-proof casserole. You may need to add an extra 15ml/1 tbsp olive oil to the pan.

5 Reduce the heat, add another 15ml/1 tbsp oil to the pan and cook the sliced onion gently over a very low heat, stirring frequently, for 10 minutes until softened and golden but not browned. Add the drained anchovy fillets and the sugar, and cook, mashing the anchovies into the onion with a wooden spoon.

6 Add the reserved marinade, increase the heat a little and cook for 1–2 minutes, then pour in the fruity white wine and lamb stock or lamb stock and water, and bring to the boil. Simmer the sauce gently for about 5 minutes, then pour the sauce over the lamb in the pan or casserole.

7 Tie the bay leaf, rosemary and parsley together to make a bouquet garni and add to the lamb. Season the stew, then cover tightly and cook in the oven for 1 hour. Add the potatoes to the stew and stir well, then return the stew to the oven and cook for a further 20 minutes.

8 Meanwhile, to make the gremolata, chop the garlic, lemon rind and parsley together finely. Place in a dish, then cover and set aside.

9 Heat the remaining olive oil in a frying pan and brown the shallots on all sides, then stir them into the lamb stew. Cover and cook the stew for a further 30–40 minutes until the lamb is tender. Transfer the lamb and vegetables to a warmed serving dish and keep hot. Discard the bunch of herbs.

10 Boil the remaining cooking juices to reduce, then add the double cream or soya cream, if using, and simmer for 2–3 minutes. Adjust the seasoning, adding a little lemon juice to taste if liked. Pour this sauce over the lamb, scatter the gremolata mixture over the top and serve immediately.

SALMON FISH CAKES

The secret of a good fishcake is to make it with freshly prepared fish and potatoes,
home-made breadcrumbs and plenty of fresh herbs, such as dill and parsley or tarragon.
Serve simply with rocket leaves and lemon wedges.

SERVES FOUR

450g/1lb cooked salmon fillet
450g/1lb freshly cooked potatoes, mashed
25g/1oz/2 tbsp butter, melted or
    30ml/2 tbsp olive oil
10ml/2 tsp wholegrain mustard
15ml/1 tbsp each chopped fresh dill and
    chopped fresh parsley or tarragon
grated rind and juice of ½ lemon
15g/½oz/2 tbsp wholemeal
    (whole-wheat) flour
1 egg, lightly beaten
150g/5oz/2 cups dried breadcrumbs
60ml/4 tbsp sunflower oil
sea salt and ground black pepper
rocket (arugula) leaves and chives, to garnish
lemon wedges, to serve

1 Flake the cooked salmon, discarding any skin and bones. Put it in a bowl with the mashed potato, melted butter or oil and wholegrain mustard, and mix well. Stir in the herbs and the lemon rind and juice. Season to taste with plenty of sea salt and ground black pepper.

2 Divide the mixture into eight portions and shape each into a ball, then flatten into a thick disc. Dip the fish cakes first in flour, then in egg and finally in breadcrumbs, making sure that they are evenly coated with crumbs.

3 Heat the oil in a frying pan until it is very hot. Fry the fish cakes in batches until golden brown and crisp all over. As each batch is ready, drain on kitchen paper and keep hot. Garnish with rocket and chives and serve with lemon wedges.

COOK'S TIP
Any fresh white or hot-smoked fish is suitable. Always buy organically farmed fish, or sustainably caught wild fish.

FILLETS of SEA BREAM in FILO PASTRY

Any firm fish fillets can be used for this dish – bass, grouper and red mullet or snapper are particularly good – and, as the number of organic seawater fish farms grows, an increasing variety of breeds is becoming available. Each parcel is a meal in itself and can be prepared several hours in advance.

3 Thinly slice the potatoes lengthways. Brush a baking sheet with a little of the oil. Lay a sheet of filo pastry on the sheet, brush it with oil, then lay a second sheet crossways over the first. Repeat with two more pastry sheets. Arrange a quarter of the sliced potatoes in the centre, season and add a quarter of the shredded sorrel. Lay a bream fillet on top, skin-side up. Season.

4 Loosely fold the filo pastry up and over to make a neat parcel. Make three more parcels; place on the baking sheet. Brush with half the melted butter or oil. Bake for about 20 minutes until the filo is puffed up and golden brown.

SERVES FOUR

8 small waxy salad potatoes,
  preferably red-skinned
200g/7oz sorrel, stalks removed
30ml/2 tbsp olive oil
16 filo pastry sheets, thawed if frozen
4 sea bream fillets, about 175g/6oz each,
  scaled but not skinned
50g/2oz/¼ cup butter, melted or
  60ml/4 tbsp olive oil
120ml/4fl oz/½ cup fish stock
250ml/8fl oz/1 cup whipping cream
  or soya cream
sea salt and ground black pepper
finely diced red (bell) pepper and
  salad leaves, to garnish

VARIATION

Use small spinach leaves or baby chard in place of the sorrel.

1 Preheat the oven to 200°C/400°F/ Gas 6. Cook the potatoes in a pan of lightly salted boiling water for about 20 minutes, or until just tender. Drain and leave to cool.

2 Set about half the sorrel leaves aside. Shred the remaining leaves by piling up six or eight at a time, rolling them up like a fat cigar and slicing them.

5 Meanwhile, make the sorrel sauce. Heat the remaining butter or oil in a pan, add the reserved sorrel and cook gently for 3 minutes, stirring, until it wilts. Stir in the stock and cream. Heat almost to boiling point, stirring so that the sorrel breaks down. Season to taste and keep hot until the fish parcels are ready. Serve garnished with red pepper and salad leaves. Hand round the sauce separately.

SEARED SCALLOPS with CHIVE SAUCE on LEEK and CARROT RICE

Scallops are one of the most delicious shellfish. Organically farmed scallops feed on naturally occurring plankton and are a healthy food whose cultivation has a low environmental impact.

SERVES FOUR

12–16 shelled scallops
45ml/3 tbsp olive oil
50g/2oz/⅓ cup wild rice
65g/2½oz/5 tbsp butter or
   75ml/5 tbsp olive oil
4 carrots, cut into long thin strips
2 leeks, cut into thick, diagonal slices
1 small onion, finely chopped
115g/4oz/⅔ cup long grain rice
1 fresh bay leaf
200ml/7fl oz/scant 1 cup white wine
450ml/¾ pint/scant 2 cups fish stock
60ml/4 tbsp double (heavy) cream or
   soya cream
a little lemon juice
25ml/1½ tbsp chopped fresh chives
30ml/2 tbsp chervil sprigs
sea salt and ground black pepper

1 Lightly season the shelled scallops, brush with 15ml/1 tbsp of the olive oil and set aside.

2 Cook the wild rice in a pan in plenty of boiling water for about 30 minutes or according to the packet instructions, until tender, then drain.

3 Heat half the butter or oil in a small frying pan and cook the carrot strips fairly gently for 4–5 minutes. Add the leek slices and fry for another 2 minutes. Season with sea salt and black pepper and add 30–45ml/2–3 tbsp water, then cover and cook the vegetables for a few minutes more. Uncover the pan and cook until the liquid has reduced. Set aside off the heat.

4 Melt half the remaining butter with 15ml/1 tbsp of the remaining oil in a heavy pan. Add the onion and fry for 3–4 minutes, until softened but not browned.

5 Add the long grain rice and bay leaf to the pan and cook, stirring constantly, until the rice looks translucent and the grains are coated with oil.

6 Pour in half the wine and half the stock. Season to taste with salt and bring to the boil. Stir, then cover and cook very gently for 15 minutes, or until the liquid is absorbed and the rice is cooked and tender.

7 Reheat the carrots and leeks gently, then stir them into the long grain rice with the wild rice. Taste and adjust the seasoning, if necessary.

8 Meanwhile, pour the remaining wine and stock into a small pan and boil it rapidly until reduced by half.

COOK'S TIP
Choose fresh rather than frozen scallops as the frozen ones tend to exude water on cooking. Have the pan very hot as scallops need only the briefest cooking at high heat – just until they turn opaque and brown on each side.

VARIATION
Use organic brown rice instead of the white long grain rice – it has a longer cooking time so check the packet for instructions.

9 Heat a heavy frying pan over a high heat. Add the remaining butter or oil. Add the scallops, and lightly sear them for 1–2 minutes on each side, then set aside and keep warm.

10 Pour the reduced stock and wine into the pan and heat until bubbling, then add the cream and boil until thickened. Season with lemon juice, sea salt and plenty of ground black pepper. Stir in the chopped chives and seared scallops.

11 Stir the chervil sprigs into the mixed rice and vegetables and pile it on to individual serving plates. Arrange the scallops on top and spoon the sauce over the rice. Serve immediately.

FROZEN CLEMENTINES

These pretty, sorbet-filled fruits store well in the freezer, so make them well in advance and they will be perfect for an impromptu dinner party. Organic citrus fruit has a matt skin — evidence that they have not been coated with shiny anti-fungal wax.

MAKES TWELVE

16 large clementines or small oranges
175g/6oz/scant 1 cup unrefined caster (superfine) sugar or rapadura
105ml/7 tbsp water
juice of 2 lemons
a little fresh orange juice (if necessary)
fresh mint leaves, to decorate

1 Carefully slice the tops off 12 of the clementines to make lids. Place the lids on a baking sheet. Loosen the clementine flesh with a sharp knife then carefully scoop it out into a mixing bowl, keeping the shells intact. Scrape out as much of the membrane from the shells as possible. Place the shells on the baking tray and place the tray in the freezer.

2 Put the sugar and water in a heavy pan and heat gently, stirring until the unrefined caster sugar or rapadura dissolves. Boil for 3 minutes without stirring, then leave the syrup to cool. Stir in the lemon juice.

3 Grate the rind from the remaining four clementines. Squeeze the fruits and add the juice and rind to the lemon syrup.

4 Process the clementine flesh in a food processor or blender, then press it through a sieve placed over a bowl to extract as much juice as possible. Add this to the syrup. You need about 900ml/1½ pints/3¾ cups of liquid. Make up to the required amount with fresh orange juice if necessary.

5 If making by hand, pour the mixture into a shallow plastic container and freeze for 3–4 hours, beating twice as the sorbet thickens to break up the ice crystals. If using an ice cream maker, churn the mixture until it holds its shape.

6 Gently pack the citrus sorbet into the clementine shells, mounding them up slightly in the centre. Position the lids on top and return the fruit to the freezer for several hours, or until the sorbet is frozen solid.

7 Transfer the frozen clementines to the refrigerator about 30 minutes before serving, to allow the sorbet to soften a little. Serve on individual plates and decorate with fresh mint leaves.

RHUBARB and GINGER ICE CREAM

The tangy combination of gently poached rhubarb and chopped ginger is blended with
mascarpone to create this pretty blush-pink ice cream. Look for tender slim stalks of
forced rhubarb in spring – it has a delicate pink colour and a delicious flavour.

SERVES FOUR TO SIX

5 pieces of preserved stem ginger
450g/1lb trimmed rhubarb, sliced
115g/4oz/generous ½ cup unrefined
    caster (superfine) sugar or rapadura
30ml/2 tbsp water
150g/5oz/⅔ cup mascarpone cheese
150ml/¼ pint/⅔ cup whipping cream
    or soya cream
wafer baskets, to serve (optional)

1 Using a sharp knife, roughly chop the
preserved stem ginger and set it aside.
Put the rhubarb slices into a pan and
add the sugar and water. Bring to the
boil, then cover and simmer for about
5 minutes until the rhubarb is just tender
and still bright pink.

2 Tip the mixture into a food processor
or blender, process until smooth, then
leave to cool. Chill if time permits.

3 If making by hand, in a bowl, mix
together the mascarpone, cream and
stem ginger with the rhubarb purée.
Pour the mixture into a plastic tub and
freeze for 6 hours, or until firm, beating
the mixture once or twice during the
freezing time to break up the ice crystals.

COOK'S TIP
Rapadura is an alternative to refined sugar.
It is made by sun-drying organic sugar
cane juice and has a similar colour and
texture to soft brown sugar, but has more
flavour and is more nutritious.

4 If using an ice cream maker, churn
the purée for 15–20 minutes until it is
thick. Put the mascarpone into a bowl,
soften it with a wooden spoon, then
beat in the cream. Add the stem ginger,
then churn in the ice cream maker until
firm. Serve scoops of the ice cream in
bowls or wafer baskets.

BANANA and APRICOT CARAMEL TRIFLE

Organic bananas are an excellent source of potassium and very good for the digestion –
making this an irresistible dessert for a special occasion. Ginger cake makes an ideal
base, adding sharpness to the creamy flavours.

SERVES SIX TO EIGHT

300ml/½ pint/1¼ cups milk or
    soya milk
1 vanilla pod (bean), or 4–5 drops
    vanilla essence (extract)
45ml/3 tbsp unrefined caster (superfine)
    sugar or rapadura
20ml/4 tsp cornflour (cornstarch)
3 egg yolks
60ml/4 tbsp apricot conserve (jam)
175–225g/6–8oz ginger cake, cubed
3 bananas, sliced, with one reserved
    for topping
115g/4oz/generous ½ cup granulated sugar
    or rapadura
300ml/½ pint/1¼ cups double (heavy)
    cream or soya cream
a few drops of lemon juice

1 Pour the milk into a small pan.
Carefully split the vanilla pod (if using)
down the middle and scrape the tiny
seeds into the pan.

2 Add the vanilla pod, or vanilla
essence, to the milk and bring just to
the boil, then remove the pan from the
heat and set aside. When the milk has
cooled slightly, remove the vanilla pod.

VARIATION
For an adult-only version of this trifle,
substitute a plainer sponge cake for the
ginger cake and moisten the sponge with
a little apricot brandy and a small glass
of sweet dessert wine in step 6.

3 Whisk together the sugar, cornflour
and eggs until pale and creamy. Whisk in
the milk and return the mixture to the
pan. Heat to simmering point, stirring
all the time, and cook gently over a low
heat until the custard coats the back of
a wooden spoon thickly.

4 Leave to cool, covered tightly with
clear film (plastic wrap). Ensure the clear
film is pressed against the surface of the
custard to prevent a skin forming.

5 Put the apricot conserve and 60ml/
4 tbsp water in a pan and heat gently
for 2–3 minutes, stirring.

COOK'S TIP
Use whatever type of cake you prefer in
the base of the trifle. Leftover Madeira
cake, with its tangy citrus flavour, makes a
perfect choice. Choose a jam or conserve
with flavours that complement those of
your chosen cake: strawberry and
raspberry conserve are good with lemon
cake, or try peach conserve with a
chocolate sponge.

6 Put the cubed cake in a deep serving
bowl or dish and pour on the apricot
preserve. Cover with sliced bananas,
then the custard. Chill for 1–2 hours.

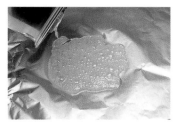

7 Melt the sugar in a small pan with
60ml/4 tbsp water and, when it has
dissolved, cook until it is just turning
golden. Immediately pour on to a sheet
of foil and leave to harden, then break
the caramel into pieces.

8 Whip the cream until it forms soft
peaks and spread it evenly over the
custard. Chill the trifle for 2–3 hours,
then top with the remaining sliced
banana, dipped into lemon juice, and the
cracked caramel pieces.

CITRUS and CARAMEL CUSTARDS

Make these Spanish-style custards with organic milk as it is the only type of milk guaranteed to be free of GMOs and excess added antibiotics and hormones. Wonderfully smooth, the custards are delicately scented with tangy citrus flavours and aromatic cinnamon.

2 Preheat the oven to 160°C/325°F/ Gas 3. Whisk the egg yolks, cornflour and sugar together. Remove the rinds and cinnamon from the hot milk and cream and discard. Whisk the hot milk and cream into the egg yolk mixture.

3 Add the grated citrus rind to the custard mixture and stir through. Pour into four individual dishes, each 13cm/ 5in in diameter. Place in a roasting pan and pour warm water into the pan to reach three-quarters of the way up the sides. Bake for 25 minutes, or until the custards are just set. Remove the dishes from the water; leave to cool, then chill.

4 Preheat the grill (broiler) to high. Sprinkle the custards liberally with icing sugar and place under the grill until the tops turn golden brown and caramelize.

COOK'S TIPS
• Prepare the grated rind first, then cut a few strips of rind from the ungrated side using a swivel-bladed vegetable peeler.
• You can use a special cook's blowtorch or salamander to caramelize the tops instead of grilling (broiling) them.

SERVES FOUR

450ml/¾ pint/scant 2 cups milk or soya milk
150ml/¼ pint/⅔ cup single (light) cream
    or soya cream
1 cinnamon stick, broken in half
thinly pared rind of ½ lemon
thinly pared rind of ½ orange
4 egg yolks
5ml/1 tsp cornflour (cornstarch)
40g/1½oz/3 tbsp unrefined caster
    (superfine) sugar or rapadura
grated rind of ½ lemon
grated rind of ½ orange
unrefined icing (confectioner's) sugar,
    to dust

1 Place the milk and cream in a pan. Add the cinnamon stick halves and the strips of pared lemon and orange rind. Bring to the boil, then reduce the heat and simmer for 10 minutes.

RICOTTA CHEESECAKE

This Sicilian-style cheesecake makes good use of ricotta's firm texture. Here, the cheese is enriched with eggs and cream and enlivened with the unwaxed grated rind of organic orange and lemon producing an irresistible, tangy dessert cheesecake filling.

SERVES EIGHT

450g/1lb/2 cups ricotta cheese
120ml/4fl oz/½ cup double (heavy) cream
   or soya cream
2 eggs
1 egg yolk
75g/3oz/6 tbsp unrefined caster (superfine)
   sugar or rapadura
finely grated rind of 1 orange and 1 lemon,
   plus extra to decorate

For the pastry
175g/6oz/1½ cups plain (all-purpose) flour
45ml/3 tbsp unrefined caster (superfine)
   sugar or rapadura
115g/4oz/½ cup chilled butter, diced
1 egg yolk

1 To make the pastry, sift the flour and sugar on to a cold work surface. Make a well in the centre and add the butter and egg yolk. Work the flour into the butter and egg yolk.

2 Gather the dough together, reserve a quarter of it and press the rest into a 23cm/9in fluted flan tin (quiche pan) with a removable base, and chill.

3 Preheat the oven to 190°C/375°F/ Gas 5. Put the cheese, cream, eggs and egg yolk, sugar and citrus rinds in a large bowl and beat well.

4 Prick the bottom of the pastry case, then line with foil and fill with baking beans. Bake for 15 minutes, transfer to a wire rack, remove the foil and beans and allow the pastry to cool in the tin.

5 Spoon the cheese and cream filling into the pastry case and level the surface. Roll out the reserved dough and cut into long, even strips. Arrange the strips on the top of the filling in a lattice pattern, sticking them in place with water.

6 Bake the cheesecake for 30–35 minutes until golden and set. Transfer to a wire rack and leave to cool, then carefully remove the side of the tin. Use a palette knife (metal spatula) to transfer the tart to a serving plate. Decorate with citrus rind before serving.

VARIATIONS
• Add 50g/2oz/⅓ cup plain chocolate chips to the filling in step 3.
• Scatter 75g/3oz sultanas (golden raisins) into the pastry case before adding the filling.

RHUBARB MERINGUE PIE

The sharp tang of tender forced rhubarb with its sweet meringue topping will really tantalize the taste buds. This pudding is delicious hot or cold with cream or vanilla ice cream.

SERVES SIX

200g/7oz/1¾ cups plain (all-purpose) flour, plus extra for flouring
25g/1oz/¼ cup ground walnuts
115g/4oz/½ cup chilled butter or non-hydrogenated magarine, diced
275g/10oz/generous 1½ cups unrefined caster (superfine) sugar or rapadura
4 egg yolks
675g/1½lb rhubarb, cut into small pieces
grated rind and juice of 3 oranges
75ml/5 tbsp cornflour (cornstarch)
3 egg whites
whipped cream or soya cream, to serve

1 Sift the flour into a bowl and add the ground walnuts. Rub in the butter until the mixture resembles fine breadcrumbs. Stir in 30ml/2 tbsp of the sugar with 1 egg yolk beaten with 15ml/1 tbsp water. Mix to a firm dough. Turn out on to a floured surface and knead. Wrap in a plastic bag and chill for 30 minutes.

2 Preheat the oven to 190°C/375°F/ Gas 5. Roll out the pastry on a floured surface and use to line a 23cm/9in fluted flan tin (quiche pan). Prick the base with a fork. Line with foil and fill with baking beans. Bake for 15 minutes.

3 Put the rhubarb, 75g/3oz/6 tbsp of the remaining sugar and the orange rind in a pan. Cover and cook gently until the rhubarb is tender.

4 Remove the foil and beans from the pastry case, then brush with a little of the remaining egg yolk. Bake for 10–15 minutes until the pastry is crisp.

5 Blend together the cornflour and the orange juice in a small bowl. Remove from the heat, stir the cornflour mixture into the cooked rhubarb, then bring back to the boil, stirring constantly until thickened. Cook for a further 1–2 minutes. Allow the mixture to cool slightly, then beat in the remaining egg yolks. Pour into the cooked pastry case, spreading it evenly.

6 Whisk the egg whites in a large mixing bowl until they form soft peaks, then gradually whisk in the remaining sugar, 15ml/1 tbsp at a time, whisking well after each addition.

7 Spoon the meringue over the filling to cover completely. Bake for 25 minutes until golden. Serve warm, or leave to cool for about 30 minutes and serve with whipped cream.

TUSCAN CITRUS SPONGE

This tangy cake comes from the little Tuscan town of Pitigliano. It is a light and airy
whisked sponge made with matzo and potato flours rather than traditional wheat flour.

SERVES SIX TO EIGHT

12 eggs, separated
300g/11oz/1½ cups unrefined caster
    (superfine) sugar or rapadura
120ml/4fl oz/½ cup fresh orange juice
grated rind of 1 orange
grated rind of 1 lemon
50g/2oz/½ cup potato flour, sifted
90g/3½oz/¾ cup fine matzo meal or
    matzo meal flour, sifted
unrefined icing (confectioner's) sugar,
    for dusting
orange juice and segments of orange,
    to serve

1 Preheat the oven to 160°C/325°F/
Gas 3. Whisk the egg yolks until pale
and frothy, then whisk in the sugar,
orange juice, orange rind and lemon rind.

2 Fold the sifted flours or flour and
meal into the egg and sugar mixture. In
a clean bowl, whisk the egg whites until
stiff, then fold into the egg yolk mixture.

VARIATION
Omit the lemon and replace the orange
with two blood oranges for a really
fresh fruity flavour.

3 Pour the cake mixture into a deep,
ungreased 25cm/10in cake tin (pan) and
bake for about 1 hour, or until a cocktail
stick (toothpick), inserted in the centre,
comes out clean. Leave to cool in the tin.

4 When cold, turn out the cake and
invert on to a serving plate. Dust with
a little icing sugar and serve in wedges
with orange segments, moistened with a
little fresh orange juice.

COOK'S TIPS
• When testing to see if the cake is
cooked, if you don't have a cocktail stick to
hand, use a strand of raw dried spaghetti
instead – it will work just as well.
• If you cannot find organic matzo meal,
try fine polenta instead.

RUSSIAN POPPY SEED CAKE

This plain and simple cake is based on my mother's recipe. Flavoured with lemon and vanilla, and studded with tiny black organic poppy seeds, it has a nutty, distinctive taste that is utterly delicious.

SERVES ABOUT EIGHT

130g/4½oz/generous 1 cup self-raising
   (self-rising) flour
5ml/1 tsp baking powder
2 eggs
225g/8oz/generous 1 cup unrefined caster
   (superfine) sugar or rapadura
5–10ml/1–2 tsp vanilla essence (extract)
200g/7oz/scant 1½ cups poppy
   seeds, ground
15ml/1 tbsp grated lemon rind
120ml/4fl oz/½ cup milk or soya milk
130g/4½oz/generous ½ cup unsalted
   (sweet) butter or non-hydrogenated
   margarine, melted and cooled
30ml/2 tbsp sunflower oil
unrefined icing (confectioners') sugar,
   sifted, for dusting
whipped cream or soya cream, to serve

1 Preheat the oven to 180°C/350°F/ Gas 4. Grease a deep 23cm/9in round springform cake tin (pan). Sift together the flour and baking powder.

2 Using an electric whisk, beat together the eggs, sugar and vanilla essence for 4–5 minutes until pale and fluffy. Stir in the poppy seeds and the lemon rind.

VARIATION
To make a poppy seed tart, pour the cake mixture into a par-cooked pastry crust, then bake for 30 minutes, or until the filling is firm and risen.

3 Gently fold the sifted ingredients into the egg and poppy seed mixture, in three batches, alternating with the milk, then fold in the melted butter or margarine and sunflower oil.

4 Pour the mixture into the tin and bake for 40 minutes, or until firm. Cool in the tin for 15 minutes, then invert on to a wire rack. Leave until cold, dust with icing sugar and serve with cream.

DOUBLE-GINGER CAKE

Preserved stem ginger and organic root ginger, which is smaller and has a more intense
flavour than the non-organic variety, are used in this tasty tea bread.

SERVES EIGHT TO TEN

3 eggs
225g/8oz/generous 1 cup unrefined caster
  (superfine) sugar or rapadura
250ml/8fl oz/1 cup sunflower oil
5ml/1 tsp vanilla essence (extract)
15ml/1 tbsp syrup from a jar of preserved
  stem ginger
225g/8oz courgettes (zucchini), grated
2.5cm/1in piece fresh root ginger, peeled
  and finely grated
350g/12oz/3 cups unbleached plain
  (all-purpose) flour
5ml/1 tsp baking powder
5ml/1 tsp ground cinnamon
2 pieces preserved stem ginger, drained
  and finely chopped
15ml/1 tbsp unrefined demerara (raw)
  sugar or rapadura
butter, to serve (optional)

1 Preheat the oven to 190°C/375°F/
Gas 5. Beat together the eggs and sugar
until light and fluffy. Slowly beat in the
oil until the mixture forms a batter.
Mix in the vanilla essence and ginger
syrup, then stir in the grated courgettes
and fresh ginger.

2 Sift together the flour and baking
powder into a large bowl. Add the
cinnamon and mix well, then stir
the dried ingredients into the
courgette mixture.

COOK'S TIP
There is no need to peel fresh organic
root ginger. Special bamboo graters can be
found in many Asian stores, but a simple
box grater will do the job equally well.

3 Lightly grease a 900g/2lb loaf tin (pan)
and pour in the courgette mixture,
making sure it fills the corners. Smooth
and level the top.

4 Mix together the chopped stem ginger
and demerara sugar in a small bowl, then
sprinkle the mixture evenly over the
surface of the courgette mixture.

5 Bake for 1 hour, or until a skewer
comes out clean when inserted into the
centre. Leave the cake to cool in the
tin (pan) for 20 minutes, then turn out
on to a wire rack and leave to cool
completely. Serve in slices with butter,
if you like.

SUMMER

The abundance of fresh produce at this time of year makes summer a

wonderful time for any cook. With sunny days and long, balmy

evenings for picnics and barbecues, summer eating is a sheer delight.

Take your pick from a wide selection of colourful salads to make

the most of the dazzling array of organic fruit and vegetables

available now. If you fancy cooking outside, try barbecueing

marinated beef with onion rings, and accompany with organic bread

and a simple green salad. With a wide selection of mouthwatering

fruits in season, summer desserts are something special. Try a

refreshing watermelon granita or, for something really indulgent,

coffee crêpes with peaches and cream.

VICHYSSOISE

*This classic, chilled summer soup is based on the flavourful combination of leeks and
potatoes, made luxuriously velvety by adding dairy or soya cream.*

SERVES FOUR TO SIX

50g/2oz/¼ cup unsalted (sweet) butter or
    50ml/3½ tbsp olive oil
450g/1lb leeks, white parts only, sliced
3 large shallots, sliced
250g/9oz floury potatoes (such as
    Maris Piper), peeled and cut
    into chunks
1 litre/1¾ pints/4 cups light chicken stock
    or water
300ml/½ pint/1¼ cups double (heavy)
    cream or soya cream
a little lemon juice (optional)
sea salt and ground black pepper
fresh chives, to garnish

1 Heat the butter or oil in a heavy pan.
Add the leeks and shallots and cook
gently, covered, for 15–20 minutes, stirring
once or twice, until soft but not browned.

2 Add the potato chunks to the pan
and cook, uncovered, for a few minutes,
stirring occasionally.

3 Stir in the light chicken stock or water,
5ml/1 tsp sea salt and ground pepper to
taste. Bring to the boil, then reduce the
heat and partly cover the pan. Simmer
for 15 minutes, or until the potatoes
are soft.

4 Cool, then process the soup until
smooth in a food processor or blender.
Pour the soup into a bowl and stir in the
cream. Season to taste.

5 Chill the soup for at least 4 hours or
until very cold. Taste the chilled soup for
seasoning and add a squeeze of lemon
juice, if required. Pour the soup into
bowls and garnish with chives.

COLD SOMEN NOODLES

At the height of summer, cold somen noodles served immersed in ice cold water
and accompanied by sauces and relishes make a refreshing and exotic meal.

SERVES FOUR

300g/11oz dried somen or soba noodles

For the dipping sauce
105ml/7 tbsp mirin
2.5ml/½ tsp sea salt
105ml/7 tbsp shoyu
20g/¾oz kezuri-bushi
400ml/14fl oz/1⅔ cups water

For the relishes
2 spring onions (scallions), trimmed and
    finely chopped
2.5cm/1in fresh root ginger, peeled and
    finely grated
2 shiso or basil leaves, finely
    chopped (optional)
30ml/2 tbsp toasted sesame seeds

For the garnishes
10cm/4in cucumber
5ml/1 tsp sea salt
ice cubes or a block of ice
ice-cold water
115g/4oz cooked, peeled small
    prawns (shrimp)
orchid flowers or nasturtium flowers
    and leaves (optional)

1 To make the dipping sauce, put the mirin in a pan and bring to the boil to evaporate the alcohol. Add the salt and shoyu and shake the pan gently to mix. Add the kezuri-bushi and mix with the liquid. Add the water to the pan and bring to the boil over a vigorous heat for 3 minutes without stirring. Remove from the heat and strain through a muslin bag. Leave to cool, then chill for at least an hour.

2 Prepare the cucumber garnish. If the cucumber is bigger than 4cm/1½in in diameter, cut in half and scoop out the seeds, then slice thinly. For a smaller cucumber, first cut into 5cm/2in lengths, then use a vegetable peeler to remove the seeds and make a hole in the centre. Slice thinly. Sprinkle with the salt and leave in a sieve for 20 minutes, then rinse in cold water and drain.

3 Bring at least 1.5 litres/2½ pints/ 6¼ cups water to the boil in a large pan. Meanwhile, untie the bundle of somen. Have 75ml/2½fl oz/⅓ cup cold water to hand. Somen only take 2 minutes to cook. Put the somen in the rapidly boiling water. When it foams again, pour the glass of water in. When the water boils again, the somen are ready. Drain into a colander. Rinse under cold running water, and rub the somen with your hands to remove the starch. Drain well.

4 Put some ice cubes or a block of ice in the centre of a chilled, large glass bowl, and add the somen. Gently pour on enough ice-cold water to cover the somen, then arrange cucumber slices, prawns and flowers, if using, on top.

5 Prepare all the relishes separately in small dishes or small sake cups.

6 Divide approximately one-third of the dipping sauce among four small cups. Put the remaining sauce in a jug (pitcher) or gravy boat.

7 Serve the noodles cold with the relishes. The guests are invited to put any combination of relishes into their dipping-sauce cup. Hold the cup over the somen bowl, pick up a mouthful of somen, then dip them into the sauce and eat. Add more dipping sauce from the jug and more relishes as required.

PROVENÇAL AIOLI with SMOKED HADDOCK

This substantial salad is a meal on its own and perfect for summer entertaining. Choose
organic vegetables and vary them according to what is in season as the summer progresses.

SERVES SIX

1kg/2¼lb smoked haddock
bouquet garni
18 small new potatoes, scrubbed
1 large or 2 small fresh mint sprigs, torn
225g/8oz French (green) beans, trimmed
225g/8oz broccoli florets
6 eggs, hard-boiled
12 baby carrots, with leaves if possible,
    scrubbed
1 large red (bell) pepper, seeded and cut
    into strips
2 fennel bulbs, cut into strips
18 red or yellow cherry tomatoes
sea salt
6 large whole cooked prawns (shrimp)
    or langoustines, in the shell,
    to garnish (optional)

For the aioli
600ml/1 pint/2½ cups home-made or
    good-quality bought mayonnaise
2 fat garlic cloves (or more if you
    prefer), crushed
cayenne pepper

1 Put the smoked haddock into a sauté
pan and pour in enough water to barely
cover the fish. Add the bouquet garni.
Bring the water to the boil, then cover
and poach very gently for about
10 minutes until the fish flakes quite
easily when tested with the tip of a sharp
knife. Drain the fish, discard the bouquet
garni and set aside until required.

2 Cook the potatoes with the mint in a
pan of lightly salted boiling water until
just tender. Drain and set aside.

3 Cook the beans and broccoli in
separate pans of lightly salted boiling
water for about 5 minutes. They should
still be very crisp. Refresh the vegetables
under cold water and drain again, then
set aside.

4 Remove the skin from the haddock
and break the flesh into large flakes. Shell
the eggs and halve them lengthways.

5 Pile the haddock in the middle of a
large serving platter and arrange the eggs
and all the vegetables round the edges
or randomly. Garnish with the prawns or
langoustines if you are using them.

6 To make the aioli, put the mayonnaise
in a bowl and stir in the crushed garlic
and cayenne pepper to taste. Serve in
individual bowls or one large bowl to
hand round.

GRILLED SKEWERED CHICKEN

Organic chicken has a superb flavour and these fabulous little skewers make great finger food. Cook on the barbecue or grill and serve sizzling hot.

SERVES FOUR

8 chicken thighs with skin, boned
8 large, thick spring onions (scallions), trimmed
oil, for greasing
lemon wedges, to serve

For the yakitori sauce
60ml/4 tbsp sake
75ml/5 tbsp shoyu
15ml/1 tbsp mirin
15ml/1 tbsp unrefined caster (superfine) sugar or rapadura

1 First, make the *yakitori* sauce. Mix all the ingredients together in a small pan. Bring to the boil, then reduce the heat and simmer for 10 minutes.

2 Cut the chicken into 2.5cm/1in cubes. Cut the spring onions into 2.5cm/1in long sticks.

3 To cook the chicken on a barbecue, soak eight bamboo skewers overnight in water. This prevents the skewers from burning during cooking. Prepare the barbecue. Thread about four pieces of chicken and three spring onion pieces on to each of the skewers. Place the *yakitori* sauce in a small bowl and have a brush ready.

4 Cook the skewered chicken on the barbecue. Keep the skewer handles away from the fire, turning them frequently. Brush the chicken with sauce. Return to the coals and repeat this process twice more until the chicken is well cooked.

5 Alternatively, to grill (broil), preheat the grill (broiler) to high. Oil the wire rack and spread out the chicken cubes on it. Grill both sides of the chicken until the juices drip, then dip the pieces in the sauce and put back on the rack. Grill for 30 seconds on each side, repeating the dipping process twice more.

6 Set aside and keep warm. Gently grill the spring onions until soft and slightly brown outside. Do not dip. Thread the chicken and spring onion pieces on to skewers as above.

7 Arrange the skewered chicken and spring onions on a serving platter and serve accompanied by lemon wedges.

COURGETTE FRITTERS with PISTOU

A wide variety of different organic courgettes are available, ranging in colour from pale yellow to deep green. The pistou sauce, made with fresh basil, provides a lovely contrast in flavour, but you could substitute other sauces, such as a tomato and garlic one or a herb dressing.

SERVES FOUR

450g/1lb courgettes (zucchini), grated
75g/3oz/⅔ cup plain (all-purpose) or
   wholemeal (whole-wheat) flour
1 egg, separated
15ml/1 tbsp olive oil
oil for shallow frying
sea salt and ground black pepper

For the pistou sauce
15g/½oz/½ cup basil leaves
4 garlic cloves, crushed
90g/3½oz/1 cup finely grated
   Parmesan cheese or premium
   Italian-style vegetarian cheese
finely grated rind of 1 lemon
150ml/¼ pint/⅔ cup olive oil

1 To make the pistou sauce, crush the basil leaves and garlic in a mortar with a pestle to make a fine paste. Transfer the paste to a bowl and stir in the grated cheese and lemon rind. Gradually blend in the oil, a little at a time, until combined, then transfer to a serving dish.

2 To make the fritters, put the grated courgettes in a sieve over a bowl and sprinkle with plenty of salt. Leave for 1 hour then rinse thoroughly. Dry well on kitchen paper.

3 Sift the flour into a bowl and make a well in the centre, then add the egg yolk and oil. Measure 75ml/5 tbsp water and add a little to the bowl.

4 Whisk the egg yolk and oil, gradually incorporating the flour and water to make a smooth batter. Season and set aside for 30 minutes.

5 Stir the grated, rinsed courgettes into the batter. Whisk the egg white until stiff, then fold into the batter.

6 Heat 1cm/½in of oil in a frying pan. Add dessertspoons of batter to the oil and fry for about 2 minutes until golden brown and crispy. Remove from the pan, using a slotted spoon. Place the fritters on kitchen paper and keep warm while frying the rest. Serve the hot fritters with the pistou sauce.

GRILLED AUBERGINE PARCELS

This is a great organic recipe – little Italian bundles of tomatoes, mozzarella cheese and basil, wrapped in slices of aubergine. The parcels are naturally low in saturated fat, sugar and salt but are indulgent and delicious, too.

SERVES FOUR

2 large, long aubergines (eggplant)
225g/8oz buffalo mozzarella cheese
2 plum tomatoes
16 large basil leaves
30ml/2 tbsp olive oil
sea salt and ground black pepper

For the dressing
60ml/4 tbsp olive oil
5ml/1 tsp balsamic vinegar
15ml/1 tbsp sun-dried tomato purée (paste)
15ml/1 tbsp lemon juice

For the garnish
30ml/2 tbsp toasted pine nuts
torn basil leaves

1 Remove the stalks from the aubergines and then cut the aubergines lengthways into thin, even slices – the aim is to get 16 slices in total (each about 5mm/¼in thick), disregarding the first and last slices.

2 Bring a large pan of water to the boil and cook the aubergine slices for 2 minutes. Drain, then dry on kitchen paper.

3 Cut the mozzarella cheese into eight slices. Cut each tomato into eight slices, not counting the first and last slices.

4 Take two aubergine slices and place on a flameproof tray, in a cross. Place a slice of tomato in the centre, season lightly, add a basil leaf, then a slice of mozzarella, another basil leaf, a slice of tomato and more seasoning.

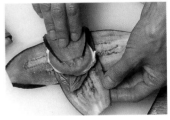

5 Fold the ends of the aubergine slices around the mozzarella and tomato filling to make a parcel. Repeat with the rest of the ingredients to make eight parcels. Chill the parcels for 20 minutes.

6 To make the tomato dressing, whisk together all the ingredients and season to taste with salt and pepper.

7 Preheat the grill (broiler). Brush the parcels with oil and cook for 5 minutes on each side. Serve hot, with the dressing, sprinkled with pine nuts and basil.

TABBOULEH

This is a wonderfully refreshing, tangy salad of soaked bulgur wheat and masses of fresh organic mint and parsley. Increase the amount of fresh herbs for a greener salad.

SERVES FOUR TO SIX

250g/9oz/1½ cups bulgur wheat
1 large bunch spring onions (scallions),
    thinly sliced
1 cucumber, finely chopped or diced
3 tomatoes, chopped
1.5–2.5ml/¼–½ tsp ground cumin
1 large bunch fresh flat leaf
    parsley, chopped
1 large bunch fresh mint, chopped
juice of 2 lemons, or to taste
60ml/4 tbsp extra virgin olive oil
cos or romaine lettuce leaves
olives, lemon wedges, tomato wedges,
    cucumber slices and mint sprigs,
    to garnish (optional)
natural (plain) yogurt, to serve (optional)

1 Pick over the bulgur wheat to remove any dirt. Place it in a bowl, cover with cold water and leave to soak for about 30 minutes. Tip the bulgur wheat into a sieve and drain well, shaking to remove any excess water, then return it to the bowl.

2 Add the spring onions to the bulgur wheat, then mix and squeeze together with your hands to combine.

3 Add the cucumber, tomatoes, cumin, parsley, mint, lemon juice and oil to the bulgur wheat and toss well.

4 Heap the tabbouleh on to a bed of lettuce leaves and garnish with olives, lemon wedges, tomato, cucumber and mint sprigs, if you like. Serve with a bowl of natural yogurt, if you like.

VARIATION
Use couscous soaked in boiling water in place of the bulgur wheat and use fresh coriander (cilantro) instead of parsley.

TOMATO and MOZZARELLA SALAD

Sweet naturally ripened organic tomatoes and fresh basil capture the essence of summer
in this simple salad. Choose plum or beefsteak tomatoes for this dish.

SERVES FOUR

5 ripe tomatoes
2 × 225g/8oz buffalo mozzarella cheeses,
    drained and sliced
1 small red onion, chopped

For the dressing
½ small garlic clove, peeled
15g/½oz/½ cup fresh basil leaves
30ml/2 tbsp chopped fresh flat
    leaf parsley
25ml/1½ tbsp small salted capers, rinsed
2.5ml/½ tsp mustard
75–90ml/5–6 tbsp extra virgin olive oil
5–10ml/1–2 tsp balsamic vinegar
ground black pepper

For the garnish
fresh basil leaves
fresh parsley sprigs

1 First make the dressing. Put the garlic, basil, parsley, half the capers and the mustard in a food processor or blender and process briefly to chop. Then, with the motor running, gradually pour in the olive oil through the feeder tube to make a smooth purée with a dressing consistency. Add the balsamic vinegar to taste and season with plenty of ground black pepper.

2 Slice the tomatoes. Arrange the tomato and mozzarella slices on a plate. Scatter the onion over and season with a little ground black pepper.

3 Drizzle the dressing over the salad, then scatter a few basil leaves, parsley sprigs and the remaining capers on top as a garnish. Leave for 10–15 minutes before serving.

SUMMER SALAD

*Ripe organic tomatoes, mozzarella and olives make a good base for a fresh and tangy
pasta salad that is perfect for a light summer lunch.*

SERVES FOUR

350g/12oz/3 cups dried penne
150g/5oz packet buffalo mozzarella,
    drained and diced
3 ripe tomatoes, diced
10 pitted black olives, sliced
10 pitted green olives, sliced
1 spring onion (scallion), thinly sliced on
    the diagonal
1 handful fresh basil leaves

For the dressing
90ml/6 tbsp extra virgin olive oil
15ml/1 tbsp balsamic vinegar or
    lemon juice
sea salt and ground black pepper

COOK'S TIP
Mozzarella made from buffalo milk
has more flavour than the type made
with cow's milk. Look for *mozzarella de
buffalo* in your organic store.

1 Cook the pasta for 10–12 minutes,
or according to the instructions on the
packet. Tip it into a colander and rinse
briefly under cold running water, then
shake the colander to remove as much
water as possible and leave to drain.

VARIATION
Make the salad more substantial by adding
sliced peppers, flaked tuna, anchovy fillets
or diced ham. Always choose sustainably
caught tuna and anchovies.

2 Make the dressing. Whisk the olive oil
and balsamic vinegar or lemon juice in a
jug (pitcher) with a little salt and pepper
to taste.

3 Place the pasta, mozzarella, tomatoes,
olives and spring onion in a large bowl,
pour the dressing over and toss together
well. Taste for seasoning before serving,
sprinkled with basil leaves.

COUNTRY PASTA SALAD

*Colourful, tasty and nutritious, this is the ideal pasta salad for a summer picnic. A variety
of organic pasta is available – any medium-size shapes are suitable for this salad.*

SERVES SIX

300g/11oz/2¾ cups dried fusilli
150g/5oz fine green beans,
    trimmed and cut into
    5cm/2in lengths
1 potato, about 150g/5oz, diced
200g/7oz cherry tomatoes, halved
2 spring onions (scallions),
    finely chopped
90g/3½oz/scant 1¼ cups Parmesan
    cheese or premium Italian-style
    vegetarian cheese, coarsely shaved
6–8 pitted black olives, cut into rings
15–30ml/1–2 tbsp capers, to taste

For the dressing
90ml/6 tbsp extra virgin olive oil
15ml/1 tbsp balsamic vinegar
15ml/1 tbsp chopped fresh flat leaf parsley
sea salt and ground black pepper

1 Cook the pasta according to the
instructions on the packet. Drain it into
a colander, rinse under cold running
water until cold, then shake the colander
to remove as much water as possible.
Leave to drain and dry.

2 Cook the beans and diced potato in a
pan of boiling water for 5–6 minutes or
steam for 8–10 minutes. Drain and let cool.

3 To make the dressing, put all the
ingredients in a large bowl with a little
sea salt and ground black pepper to
taste and whisk well to mix.

4 Add the tomatoes, spring onions,
Parmesan, olive rings and capers to the
dressing then stir in the cold pasta, beans
and potato. Toss well to mix. Cover and
leave to stand for about 30 minutes.
Taste for seasoning before serving.

VARIATIONS
Use other pasta shapes, such as penne or
conchigli, instead of fusilli. Try wholemeal
pasta shapes for a nuttier taste. Other
summer vegetables – steamed courgettes
(zucchini) or mangetouts (snow peas), or
roasted red (bell) peppers – all taste
wonderful in this salad.

THAI BEEF SALAD

Meat does not need to dominate a meal, as this light Thai salad shows. Especially when cooking with good-quality organic meat, a little adds a lot of flavour.

SERVES FOUR

675g/1½lb fillet (tenderloin) or rump
    (round) beef steak
30ml/2 tbsp olive oil
2 small mild red chillies, seeded and sliced
225g/8oz/3¼ cups shiitake mushrooms,
    finely sliced

For the dressing
3 spring onions (scallions), finely chopped
2 garlic cloves, finely chopped
juice of 1 lime
15–30ml/1–2 tbsp fish or oyster sauce,
    to taste
5ml/1 tsp unrefined soft light brown sugar
    or rapadura
30ml/2 tbsp chopped fresh coriander (cilantro)

To serve
1 cos or romaine lettuce, torn into strips
175g/6oz cherry tomatoes, halved
5cm/2in piece cucumber, peeled, halved
    and thinly sliced
45ml/3 tbsp toasted sesame seeds

1 Preheat the grill (broiler) until hot, then cook the steak for 2–4 minutes on each side depending on how well done you like steak. (In Thailand, the beef is traditionally served quite rare.) Leave the beef to cool for at least 15 minutes.

2 Use a very sharp knife to slice the meat as thinly as possible and place the slices in a bowl.

VARIATION
If you can find them, yellow chillies make a colourful addition to this dish. Substitute one for one of the red chillies.

3 Heat the olive oil in a small frying pan. Add the seeded and sliced red chillies and the sliced mushrooms and cook for 5 minutes, stirring occasionally. Turn off the heat and add the grilled steak slices to the pan, then stir well to coat the beef slices in the cooked chilli and mushroom mixture.

4 Stir all the ingredients for the dressing together, then pour it over the meat mixture and toss gently.

5 Arrange the salad ingredients on a serving plate. Spoon the warm steak mixture in the centre and sprinkle the sesame seeds over. Serve at once.

FRESH TUNA SALAD NIÇOISE

This classic colourful salad is transformed into something really special by using fresh tuna. When buying tuna make sure it is line-caught tuna that is certified as sustainably caught by the Marine Stewardship Council (MSC).

SERVES FOUR

4 tuna steaks, about 150g/5oz each
30ml/2 tbsp olive oil
225g/8oz fine green beans, trimmed
1 small cos or romaine lettuce or
　2 little gem lettuces
4 new potatoes, boiled
4 ripe tomatoes, or 12 cherry tomatoes
2 red (bell) peppers, seeded and cut
　into thin strips
4 hard-boiled eggs, sliced
8 drained anchovy fillets in oil,
　halved lengthways (optional)
16 large black olives
sea salt and ground black pepper
12 fresh basil leaves, to garnish

For the dressing
15ml/1 tbsp red wine vinegar
90ml/6 tbsp olive oil
1 fat garlic clove, crushed

3 Separate the lettuce leaves and rinse them thoroughly under cold running water and dry them on kitchen paper. Arrange them on four individual serving plates. Slice the cooked potatoes and tomatoes, if large (leave cherry tomatoes whole or halve them) and divide them among the plates. Arrange the beans and red pepper strips over the potatoes and tomatoes.

4 Shell the hard-boiled eggs and cut them into thick slices. Place a few slices of egg on each plate with the anchovy fillets, if using, and olives.

5 To make the dressing, whisk together the vinegar, olive oil and garlic and season to taste. Drizzle over the salads, arrange the tuna steaks on top, scatter over the basil and serve.

1 Brush the tuna on both sides with a little olive oil and season. Heat a ridged griddle or the grill (broiler) until very hot, then grill the tuna steaks for 1–2 minutes on each side; the flesh should be pink and juicy in the middle.

2 Cook the beans in a pan of lightly salted boiling water for 4–5 minutes, or until crisp-tender. Drain, refresh under cold water and drain again.

COOK'S TIP
To intensify the flavour of the peppers, grill (broil) them until the skins are charred, place in a bowl and cover with kitchen paper. Leave for 10–15 minutes, then rub off the skins.

SPICED VEGETABLE COUSCOUS

This tasty vegetarian main course is easy to make and can be prepared with any number of seasonal organic vegetables such as spinach, peas, broad beans or corn.

SERVES SIX

45ml/3 tbsp olive oil
1 large onion, finely chopped
2 garlic cloves, crushed
15ml/1 tbsp tomato purée (paste)
2.5ml/½ tsp ground turmeric
2.5ml/½ tsp cayenne pepper
5ml/1 tsp ground coriander
5ml/1 tsp ground cumin
225g/8oz/1½ cups cauliflower florets
225g/8oz baby carrots, trimmed
1 red (bell) pepper, seeded and diced
225g/8oz courgettes (zucchini), sliced
400g/14oz can chickpeas, drained
   and rinsed
4 beefsteak tomatoes, skinned and sliced
45ml/3 tbsp chopped fresh coriander
   (cilantro)
sea salt and ground black pepper
coriander sprigs, to garnish

For the couscous
2.5ml/½ tsp sea salt
450g/1lb/2⅔ cups couscous
50g/2oz/¼ cup butter or
   50ml/3½ tbsp sunflower oil

1 Heat 30ml/2 tbsp oil in a large pan, add the onion and garlic and cook until soft and translucent. Stir in the tomato purée, turmeric, cayenne, coriander and cumin. Cook, stirring, for 2 minutes.

2 Add the cauliflower, baby carrots and pepper, with enough water to come halfway up the vegetables. Bring to the boil, then lower the heat, cover and simmer for 10 minutes.

3 Add the courgettes, chickpeas and tomatoes to the pan and cook for 10 minutes. Stir in the fresh coriander and season. Keep hot.

4 To cook the couscous, bring about 475ml/16fl oz/2 cups water to the boil in a large pan. Add the remaining olive oil and the salt. Remove from the heat and add the couscous, stirring. Allow to swell for 2 minutes.

5 Add the butter or sunflower oil, and heat through gently, stirring to separate the grains.

6 Turn the couscous out on to a warm serving dish, and spoon the cooked vegetables on top, pouring over any liquid. Garnish with coriander and serve immediately.

GRILLED VEGETABLE PIZZA

You really can't go too far wrong with this classic mixture of Mediterranean grilled vegetables on home-made pizza dough. It is filling and healthy, and is a favourite with children.

3 Place the pizza dough on a sheet of baking parchment on a baking sheet and roll or gently press it out to form a 25cm/10in round, making the edges slightly thicker than the centre.

4 Lightly brush the pizza dough with any remaining oil, then spread the chopped plum tomatoes evenly over the dough.

SERVES SIX

1 courgette (zucchini), sliced
2 baby aubergines (eggplant) or
   1 small aubergine, sliced
30ml/2 tbsp olive oil
1 yellow (bell) pepper, seeded and sliced
115g/4oz/1 cup corn meal
50g/2oz/½ cup potato flour
50g/2oz/½ cup soya flour
5ml/1 tsp baking powder
2.5ml/½ tsp sea salt
50g/2oz/¼ cup non-hydrogenated margarine
about 105ml/7 tbsp milk
4 plum tomatoes, skinned and chopped
30ml/2 tbsp chopped fresh basil
115g/4oz buffalo mozzarella cheese, sliced
sea salt and ground black pepper
fresh basil sprigs, to garnish

1 Preheat the grill (broiler). Brush the courgette and aubergine slices with a little oil and place on a grill rack with the pepper slices. Cook under the grill until lightly browned, turning once.

2 Meanwhile, preheat the oven to 200°C/400°F/Gas 6. Place the corn meal, potato flour, soya flour, baking powder and salt in a mixing bowl and stir to mix. Lightly rub in the margarine until the mixture resembles coarse breadcrumbs, then stir in enough of the milk to make a soft but not sticky dough.

VARIATION

Top the pizza with 115g/4oz sliced goat's cheese instead of the mozzarella for a creamy alternative.

5 Sprinkle with the chopped basil and season with salt and pepper. Arrange the grilled vegetables over the tomatoes and top with the cheese.

6 Bake for 25–30 minutes until crisp and golden brown. Garnish the pizza with fresh basil sprigs and serve immediately, cut into slices.

COOK'S TIP

This recipe uses a combination of different types of flours to give an interesting flavour and texture to the base. If you prefer, use 225g/8oz/2 cups of plain (all-purpose) flour or a combination of half plain and half wholemeal (whole-wheat) flours.

OLIVE OIL ROASTED CHICKEN with SUMMER VEGETABLES

This is a delicious alternative to a traditional roast chicken. Organic chicken can be so much tastier and more tender than intensively reared poultry, especially if the birds are raised biodynamically.

SERVES FOUR

1.8–2kg/4–4½lb roasting chicken
150ml/¼ pint/⅔ cup extra virgin olive oil
½ lemon
few sprigs of fresh thyme
450g/1lb small new potatoes
1 aubergine (eggplant), cut into
    2.5cm/1in cubes
1 red (bell) pepper, seeded and quartered
1 fennel bulb, trimmed and quartered
8 large garlic cloves, unpeeled
coarse sea salt and ground black pepper

1 Preheat the oven to 200°C/400°F/ Gas 6. Rub the chicken all over with olive oil and season with pepper. Place the lemon half inside the bird, with a sprig or two of thyme. Put the chicken breast side down in a large roasting pan. Roast for about 30 minutes.

2 Remove the chicken from the oven and season with salt. Turn the chicken right side up, and baste. Surround the bird with the potatoes, roll them in the pan juices, and return to the oven.

3 After 30 minutes, add the aubergine, red pepper, fennel and garlic cloves to the pan. Drizzle with the remaining oil, and season with salt and pepper. Add any remaining thyme to the vegetables. Return to the oven, and cook for about 40 minutes more, basting and turning the vegetables occasionally.

4 To find out if the chicken is cooked, push the tip of a sharp knife between the thigh and breast. If the juices run clear, it is done. The vegetables should be tender and just beginning to brown. Serve the chicken and vegetables from the pan, or transfer the vegetables to a serving dish, joint the chicken and place it on top. Serve the skimmed juices in a gravy boat.

VARIATION
Serve rosemary potato wedges with the chicken. Heat 60ml/4 tbsp olive oil for 10 minutes in a roasting pan in an oven preheated to 200°C/400°F/Gas 6. Cut the potatoes into wedges and add to the oil. Sprinkle over 10ml/2 tsp dried rosemary. Season and bake for 50–60 minutes.

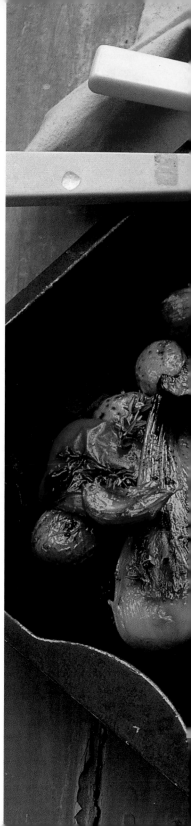

GRIDDLED CHICKEN with TOMATO SALSA

This simple meal is a great way to enjoy the flavour, colour and health benefits of organic ingredients. For the best result, marinate the chicken overnight.

SERVES FOUR

4 boneless, skinless chicken breast fillets,
   about 175g/6oz each
30ml/2 tbsp fresh lemon juice
30ml/2 tbsp olive oil
10ml/2 tsp ground cumin
10ml/2 tsp dried oregano
15ml/1 tbsp coarse black pepper

For the salsa
1 green chilli
450g/1lb plum tomatoes, seeded
   and chopped
3 spring onions (scallions), chopped
15ml/1 tbsp chopped fresh parsley
30ml/2 tbsp chopped fresh coriander
   (cilantro)
30ml/2 tbsp fresh lemon juice
45ml/3 tbsp olive oil

1 With a meat mallet, pound the chicken between two sheets of clear film (plastic wrap) until thin.

2 In a shallow dish, combine the lemon juice, oil, cumin, oregano and pepper. Add the chicken and turn to coat. Cover and leave to marinate for at least 2 hours, or in the refrigerator overnight.

3 To make the salsa, char the chilli skin either over a gas flame or under the grill (broiler). Leave to cool for 5 minutes. Carefully rub off the charred skin, taking care to wash your hands afterwards. For a less hot flavour, discard the seeds.

4 Chop the chilli very finely and place in a bowl. Add the seeded and chopped tomatoes, the chopped spring onions, chopped fresh parsley and coriander, lemon juice and olive oil and mix well. Set aside until ready to serve.

5 Remove the chicken from the marinade. Heat a ridged griddle. Add the chicken fillets and cook on one side until browned, for about 3 minutes. Turn over and cook for a further 4 minutes. Serve with the chilli salsa.

COOK'S TIP
The hottest part of the chilli is the white membrane that connects the seeds to the flesh. By charring the flesh, the natural sweetness is released and the heat is moderated.

MARINATED BEEF with ONION RINGS

Mexican chillies combine well with garlic in this marinade for grilled steak. Organic beef is
tastier and has a better balance of cholesterol than the non-organic kind.

SERVES FOUR

20g/³⁄₄oz large mild dried red chillies
    (such as mulato or pasilla)
2 garlic cloves, plain or smoked,
    finely chopped
5ml/1 tsp ground toasted cumin seeds
5ml/1 tsp dried oregano
60ml/4 tbsp olive oil
4 × 175–225g/6–8oz beef steaks, rump
    (round) or rib-eye
sea salt and ground black pepper

For the onion rings
2 onions, sliced into rings
250ml/8fl oz/1 cup milk or soya milk
75g/3oz/³⁄₄ cup coarse corn meal
2.5ml/¹⁄₂ tsp dried red chilli flakes
5ml/1 tsp ground toasted cumin seeds
5ml/1 tsp dried oregano
sunflower or safflower oil,
    for deep-frying

1 Cut the stalks from the dried red chillies and discard the seeds. Toast the chillies in a dry frying pan over a high heat, stirring constantly, for 2–4 minutes, until they give off their aroma. Place the chillies in a bowl, cover with warm water and leave them to soak for 20–30 minutes. Drain the chillies and reserve the soaking water.

2 Process the soaked, drained chillies to a paste with the finely chopped garlic, toasted cumin seeds, oregano and oil in a food processor. Add a little of the soaking water, if needed. Season with ground black pepper.

3 Wash and dry the steaks, place them in a non-metallic container, rub the chilli paste all over them and leave to marinate in the refrigerator for up to 12 hours.

4 To make the onion rings, soak the onion slices in the milk for 30 minutes. Mix the corn meal, chilli, cumin and oregano, and season with salt and pepper.

5 Heat the oil for deep-frying in a deep pan to 160–180°C/325–350°F, or until a cube of day-old bread turns brown in about a minute.

6 Drain the onion rings and dip each one into the corn meal mixture, coating it thoroughly. Fry for 2–4 minutes until browned and crisp. Do not overcrowd the pan, but cook in batches. Lift the onion rings out of the pan with a slotted spoon and drain on kitchen paper.

7 Heat a barbecue or cast-iron griddle. Season the steaks with salt and cook for about 4 minutes on each side for a medium result; reduce or increase this time according to how rare or well done you like steak. Serve the steaks with the onion rings.

MOROCCAN FISH TAGINE with COUSCOUS

Fish is a staple food for the organic cook, with its balance of amino acids and oils. Always ensure that it is either organically farmed or sustainably caught in the wild.

SERVES EIGHT

1.3kg/3lb firm fish fillets such as monkfish or
   hoki, skinned and cut into 5cm/2in cubes
60ml/4 tbsp olive oil
4 onions, chopped
1 large aubergine (eggplant), cut into
   1cm/½in cubes
2 courgettes (zucchini), cut into
   1cm/½in cubes
400g/14oz can chopped tomatoes
400ml/14fl oz/1⅔ cups passata (bottled
   strained tomatoes)
200ml/7fl oz/scant 1 cup fish stock
1 preserved lemon, chopped
90g/3½oz/scant 1 cup olives
60ml/4 tbsp chopped fresh coriander (cilantro)
sea salt and ground black pepper
couscous, to serve
coriander sprigs, to garnish

For the harissa
3 large fresh red chillies, seeded and chopped
3 garlic cloves, peeled
15ml/1 tbsp ground coriander
30ml/2 tbsp ground cumin
5ml/1 tsp ground cinnamon
grated rind of 1 lemon
30ml/2 tbsp sunflower oil

4 Heat the remaining olive oil in a separate pan. Add the aubergine cubes and fry for 10 minutes, or until they are golden brown. Add the cubed courgettes and fry the vegetables for a further 2 minutes, stirring occasionally.

5 Tip the aubergine mixture into the shallow pan and combine with the onions, then stir in the chopped tomatoes, the passata and fish stock. Bring to the boil, then lower the heat and simmer the mixture for about 20 minutes.

6 Stir the fish cubes and preserved lemon into the pan. Add the olives and stir gently. Cover and simmer over a low heat for about 15–20 minutes until the fish is just cooked through. Season to taste. Stir in the chopped coriander. Serve with couscous and garnish with coriander sprigs.

COOK'S TIP
To make the fish go further, you could add 225g/8oz/1¼ cups cooked chickpeas to the tagine.

1 To make the harissa, whizz everything in a food processor to a smooth paste.

2 Put the fish in a wide bowl and add 30ml/2 tbsp of the harissa. Toss to coat, cover and chill for at least 1 hour.

3 Heat half the oil in a shallow pan. Cook the onions for about 10 minutes. Stir in the remaining harissa; cook for 5 minutes, stirring occasionally.

HAKE AU POIVRE with RED PEPPER RELISH

Use South African hake rather than hake from European waters, where stocks are low due to overfishing. Or try line-caught tuna or haddock from Icelandic waters.

3 Make the relish. Cut the red peppers in half lengthways, remove the core and seeds from each and cut the flesh into 1cm/½in wide strips. Heat the olive oil in a wok or a shallow pan that has a lid. Add the peppers and stir them for about 5 minutes, or until they are slightly softened. Stir in the chopped garlic, tomatoes and the anchovies, then cover the pan and simmer the mixture very gently for about 20 minutes, until the peppers are very soft.

4 Tip the contents of the pan into a food processor and whizz to a coarse purée. Transfer to a bowl and season to taste. Stir in the capers, balsamic vinegar and basil. Keep the relish hot.

SERVES FOUR

30–45ml/2–3 tbsp mixed peppercorns
    (black, white, pink and green)
4 hake steaks, about 175g/6oz each
30ml/2 tbsp olive oil
sea salt and ground black pepper

For the relish
2 red (bell) peppers
15ml/1 tbsp olive oil
2 garlic cloves, chopped
4 ripe tomatoes, peeled, seeded
    and quartered
4 drained canned anchovy fillets,
    roughly chopped
5ml/1 tsp capers
15ml/1 tbsp balsamic vinegar,
    plus a little extra to serve
12 fresh basil leaves, shredded, plus
    a few extra to garnish

1 Put the peppercorns in a mortar and crush them coarsely with a pestle. Alternatively, put them in a plastic bag and crush them with a rolling pin.

2 Season the hake fillets lightly with salt, then coat them evenly on both sides with the crushed peppercorns. Set the coated fish steaks aside while you make the red pepper relish.

5 Heat the olive oil in a shallow pan, add the hake steaks and fry them, in batches if necessary, for 5 minutes on each side, turning them once or twice, until they are just cooked through.

6 Place the fish on individual plates and spoon a little red pepper relish on to each plate. Garnish with basil leaves and a little extra balsamic vinegar. Serve the rest of the relish separately.

WATERMELON GRANITA

Pastel pink flakes of ice, subtly blended with the citrus freshness of lime and the delicate,
refreshing flavour of organic watermelon, make this granita a treat for the eye and the tastebuds.

2 Bring the sugar and water to the boil in a small pan, stirring constantly until the sugar has dissolved. Pour the syrup into a bowl. Allow the syrup to cool, then chill until needed.

3 Strain the purée through a sieve into a large plastic container. Discard the melon seeds. Pour in the chilled syrup, lime rind and juice and mix well.

4 Cover and freeze for 2 hours until the granita mixture around the sides of the container is mushy. Mash the ice finely with a fork and return to the freezer.

5 Freeze for a further 2 hours, mashing the mixture every 30 minutes, until the granita has a slushy consistency. Scoop it into individual dishes and serve with the wedges of lime.

SERVES SIX

1 whole watermelon,
   about 1.8–2kg/4–4½lb
150g/5oz/¾ cup unrefined caster
   (superfine) sugar or rapadura
150ml/¼ pint/⅔ cup water
finely grated rind and juice
   of 2 limes
lime wedges, to decorate

COOK'S TIP
If you are using another melon, such as cantaloupe or Charentais, you may not need as much lime juice. Add half in step 3, then taste the mixture and adjust as necessary.

1 Cut the watermelon into quarters. Discard most of the seeds, scoop the flesh into a food processor and process briefly until smooth. Alternatively, use a blender, and process the watermelon quarters in small batches.

VARIATION
To serve this granita cocktail-style, dip the rim of each glass serving dish in a little water, then dip it into a little unrefined caster (superfine) sugar. Spoon in the granita, pour over a little Tequila and decorate with lime wedges.

FROZEN MELON

Freezing sorbet in hollowed out fruit, which is then cut into icy wedges, is an excellent idea. The refreshing flavour makes this dessert irresistible on a hot summer's day.

SERVES SIX

50g/2oz/¼ cup unrefined caster (superfine) sugar or rapadura
30ml/2 tbsp clear honey
15ml/1 tbsp lemon juice
60ml/4 tbsp water
1 medium cantaloupe melon or Charentais melon, about 1 kg/2¼lb
crushed ice, cucumber slices and borage flowers, to decorate

1 Put the sugar, honey, lemon juice and water in a heavy pan, and heat gently until the sugar dissolves. Bring to the boil, and boil for 1 minute, without stirring, to make a syrup. Leave to cool.

2 Cut the cantaloupe or Charentais melon in half and discard the seeds. Carefully scoop out the flesh using a metal spoon or melon baller and place in a food processor, taking care to keep the halved shells intact.

3 Blend the melon flesh until very smooth, then transfer to a mixing bowl. Stir in the cooled sugar syrup and chill until very cold. Invert the melon shells and leave them to drain on kitchen paper for a few minutes, then transfer them to the freezer while making the sorbet.

4 If making by hand, pour the mixture into a container and freeze for 3–4 hours, beating well twice with a fork, a whisk or in a food processor, to break up the ice crystals and produce a smooth texture. If using an ice cream maker, churn the melon mixture in the ice cream maker until the sorbet holds its shape.

5 Pack the sorbet into the melon shells and level the surface with a knife. Use a dessertspoon to scoop out the centre of each filled melon shell to simulate the seed cavity. Freeze the prepared fruit overnight until firm.

6 To serve, use a large knife to cut each melon half into three wedges. Serve on a bed of ice on a large platter or individual serving plates, and decorate with the cucumber slices and borage flowers.

COOK'S TIP
If the melon sorbet is too firm to cut when taken straight from the freezer, let it soften in the refrigerator for 10–20 minutes. Take care when slicing the frozen melon shell into wedges. A serrated kitchen knife is easier to work with.

CHOCOLATE MERINGUES with MIXED FRUIT COMPOTE

Mini-chocolate meringues are sandwiched with crème fraîche and served with a compote of mixed summer berries to make this impressive dessert.

SERVES SIX

105ml/7 tbsp unsweetened red
  grape juice
105ml/7 tbsp unsweetened apple juice
30ml/2 tbsp clear honey
450g/1lb/4 cups mixed fresh summer
  berries, such as blackcurrants, redcurrants, raspberries and blackberries

For the meringues
3 egg whites
175g/6oz/¾ cup unrefined caster
  (superfine) sugar or rapadura
75g/3oz good-quality plain chocolate,
  finely grated
175g/6oz/scant 1 cup crème fraîche

1 Preheat the oven to 110°C/225°F/
Gas ¼. Grease and line two large baking
sheets with baking parchment, cutting
the paper to fit.

2 To make the meringues, whisk the
egg whites in a large mixing bowl until
stiff. Gradually whisk in half the sugar,
then fold in the remaining sugar, using a
metal spoon. Gently fold in the grated
plain chocolate.

3 Carefully spoon the meringue mixture
into a large piping (pastry) bag fitted
with a large star nozzle. Pipe small round
whirls of the mixture on to the prepared
baking sheets.

4 Bake the meringues for 2½–3 hours
until they are firm and crisp. Remove
from the oven. Carefully peel the
meringues off the paper, then transfer
them to a wire rack to cool.

5 Meanwhile, make the compote. Heat
the fruit juices in a small pan with the
honey until almost boiling.

COOK'S TIP
Organic chocolate has a slightly higher
proportion of cocoa and less sugar than
non-organic equivalents. And, as organic
cocoa is naturally high in tannins and
antioxidant flavonoids as well as B vitamins
and iron, organic chocolate consumed in
moderation is actually good for you. Look
for chocolate that has 70 per cent cocoa
solids for the best flavour and higher
nutritional content.

6 Place the mixed fresh berries in a
large bowl and pour over the hot fruit
juice and honey mixture. Stir gently to
mix, then set aside and leave to cool.
Once cool, cover the bowl with clear
film (plastic wrap) and chill until required.

7 When ready to serve, gently sandwich
the cold meringues together with the
crème fraîche and arrange them on a
serving plate or dish.

8 Serve the meringues immediately on
individual plates with the mixed fruit
compote to accompany.

VARIATION
Packs of frozen mixed berries are
available and can be used in place of
fresh in this recipe. Allow the berries
to defrost thoroughly in a sieve over a
mixing bowl, then use as in step 6.

FRAGRANT FRUIT SALAD

Organic summer fruits make a delicious seasonal fruit salad. Any combination of fruits can be used, although this exotic choice is particularly suitable for a dinner party.

SERVES SIX

130g/4½oz/scant ¾ cup unrefined sugar
    or rapadura
thinly pared rind and juice of 1 lime
60ml/4 tbsp brandy
5ml/1 tsp instant coffee granules or powder
    dissolved in 30ml/2 tbsp boiling water
1 small pineapple
1 papaya
2 pomegranates
1 medium mango
2 passion fruits or kiwi fruit
fine strips of lime peel, to decorate

COOK'S TIP
Allow the salad to stand at room temperature for an hour before serving so the flavours can blend.

1 Put the sugar and lime rind in a small pan with 150ml/¼ pint/⅔ cup water. Heat gently until the sugar dissolves, then bring to the boil and simmer for 5 minutes. Leave to cool, then strain into a large serving bowl, discarding the lime rind. Stir in the lime juice, brandy and dissolved coffee.

2 Using a sharp knife, cut the plume and stalk ends from the pineapple. Peel and cut the flesh into bitesize pieces. Add to the bowl. Discard the central core.

3 Halve the papaya and scoop out the seeds. Cut away the skin, then slice the papaya. Halve the pomegranates and scoop out the seeds. Add to the bowl.

4 Cut the mango lengthways into three pieces, along each side of the stone. Peel the skin off the flesh. Cut into chunks and add to the bowl.

5 Halve the passion fruits and scoop out the flesh using a teaspoon or peel and chop the kiwi fruit. Add to the bowl and serve, decorated with lime peel.

SUMMER BERRIES in WARM SABAYON GLAZE

*This luxurious combination of summer berries under a light and fluffy alcoholic sauce is
lightly grilled to form a crisp, caramelized topping.*

SERVES FOUR

450g/1lb/4 cups mixed summer berries,
  or soft fruit
4 egg yolks
50g/2oz/¼ cup unrefined caster (superfine)
  sugar or rapadura
120ml/4fl oz/½ cup white dessert wine,
  plus extra to serve (optional)
a little unrefined icing (confectioner's)
  sugar, sifted, and mint leaves,
  to decorate (optional)

COOK'S TIP

If you want to omit the alcohol, use a
pure fruit juice instead, such as grape,
mango or apricot.

1 Arrange the fruit in four flameproof
dishes. Preheat the grill (broiler).

2 Whisk the egg yolks in a large bowl
with the sugar and wine. Place the bowl
over a pan of hot water and whisk
constantly until thick, fluffy and pale.

3 Pour equal quantities of the sabayon
sauce into each dish. Place under the
grill for 1–2 minutes until just turning
brown. Sprinkle the fruit with icing sugar
and scatter with mint leaves just before
serving, if you like. Add an extra splash
of wine to the dishes, if you like.

COFFEE CRÊPES with PEACHES and CREAM

Juicy golden organic peaches and cream conjure up the sweet taste of summer. Here they are delicious as the filling for these light coffee-flavoured buckwheat crêpes.

SERVES SIX

75g/3oz/⅔ cup plain (all-purpose) flour
25g/1oz/¼ cup buckwheat flour
1 egg, beaten
200ml/7fl oz/scant 1 cup milk or
   soya milk
15g/½oz/1 tbsp butter, melted
100ml/3½fl oz/scant ½ cup brewed
   coffee, cooled
sunflower oil, for frying

For the filling
6 ripe peaches
300ml/½ pint/1¼ cups double
   (heavy) cream
15ml/1 tbsp brandy
225g/8oz/1 cup crème fraîche
65g/2½oz/generous ¼ cup unrefined caster
   (superfine) sugar or rapadura
30ml/2 tbsp unrefined icing (confectioner's)
   sugar, for dusting (optional)

1 Sift the flours into a mixing bowl. Make a well in the middle and add the beaten egg, half the milk and the melted butter. Gradually mix in the flour, beating until the mixture is smooth, then beat in the remaining milk and the coffee.

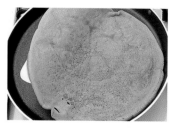

2 Heat a drizzle of sunflower oil in a 15–20cm/6–8in crêpe pan. Pour in just enough batter to cover the base of the pan thinly, swirling the pan to spread the mixture evenly. Cook for 2–3 minutes until the underneath is golden brown, then flip the crêpe over using a metal spatula and cook the other side.

3 Slide the crêpe out of the pan on to a plate. Continue making crêpes until all the mixture is used, stacking and interleaving them with baking parchment.

4 To make the filling, halve the peaches and carefully remove the stones. Cut the peaches into thick slices. Whip the cream and brandy together until soft peaks form. Beat the crème fraîche with the sugar until smooth. Beat 30ml/2 tbsp of the cream into the crème fraîche, then fold in the remainder.

5 Place six of the crêpes on individual serving plates. Spoon a little of the brandy cream on to one half of each crêpe and top with peach slices. Gently fold the crêpe over and dust with a little sifted icing sugar, if you like. Serve immediately.

BLUEBERRY FRANGIPANE FLAN

A tangy lemon pastry case is filled with a nutty sweet almond filling dotted with ripe blueberries. Their wonderful colour and taste are a seasonal favourite.

SERVES SIX

30ml/2 tbsp ground coffee
45ml/3 tbsp milk or soya milk
50g/2oz/¼ cup unsalted (sweet) butter
50g/2oz/¼ cup unrefined caster (superfine)
    sugar or rapadura
I egg
115g/4oz/1 cup ground almonds
15ml/1 tbsp plain (all-purpose)
    flour, sifted
225g/8oz/2 cups blueberries
30ml/2 tbsp jam
15ml/1 tbsp brandy
crème fraîche or sour cream, to serve

For the pastry
175g/6oz/1½ cups plain (all-purpose) flour
115g/4oz/½ cup unsalted (sweet) butter or
    non-hydrogenated margarine
25g/1oz/2 tbsp unrefined caster sugar
    or rapadura
finely grated rind of ½ lemon
15ml/1 tbsp chilled water

I Preheat the oven to 190°C/375°F/
Gas 5. To make the pastry, sift the flour
into a bowl and rub in the butter. Stir in
the sugar and lemon rind, then add the
water and mix to a firm dough. Wrap
the dough in clear film (plastic wrap) and
chill for 20 minutes.

2 Roll out the pastry on a lightly floured
work surface and use to line a 23cm/9in
loose-based flan tin (quiche pan). Line
the pastry with baking parchment and
baking beans and bake for 10 minutes.
Remove the paper and beans and bake
for a further 10 minutes. Remove from
the oven.

3 Meanwhile, to make the filling, put the
ground coffee in a bowl. Bring the milk
almost to the boil, then pour over the
coffee and leave to infuse for 4 minutes.
Cream the butter and sugar until pale.
Beat in the egg, then add the almonds
and flour. Strain in the coffee-flavoured
milk through a fine sieve and fold in.

4 Spoon the coffee mixture into the
pastry case and spread evenly. Scatter
the blueberries over the top and push
them down slightly into the mixture.
Bake for 30 minutes, until firm, covering
with foil after 20 minutes.

5 Remove the tart from the oven and
allow to cool slightly. Heat the jam and
brandy in a small pan until melted.
Brush over the flan and remove from
the tin. Serve warm with crème fraîche
or sour cream.

APRICOT and ALMOND TART

This rich tart relies on a simple but perfect combination of apricots and almond filling.
Fresh apricots are only available during the summer months so make the most of them.

SERVES SIX

115g/4oz/½ cup butter or
    non-hydrogenated margarine
115g/4oz/scant ½ cup unrefined caster
    (superfine) sugar or rapadura
1 egg, beaten
50g/2oz/⅓ cup ground rice
50g/2oz/½ cup ground almonds
few drops of almond essence (extract)
450g/1lb fresh apricots, halved and stoned
sifted unrefined icing (confectioners')
    sugar, for dusting (optional)
apricot slices and fresh mint sprigs,
    to decorate (optional)

For the pastry
115g/4oz/1 cup brown rice flour
115g/4oz/1 cup corn meal
115g/4oz/½ cup butter or
    non-hydrogenated margarine
25g/1oz/2 tbsp unrefined caster (superfine)
    sugar or rapadura
1 egg yolk

1 To make the pastry, place the rice
flour and corn meal in a large mixing
bowl and stir to mix. Lightly rub in
the butter or margarine with your
fingertips until the mixture resembles
fine breadcrumbs.

VARIATIONS
For a change, use ground hazelnuts and
vanilla essence (extract) in place of the
ground almonds and almond essence.
Pears, peaches or nectarines can be used
in this recipe instead of the apricots. Or
use a combination of the three fruits to
make a mixed fruit tart.

2 Add the sugar, stir in the egg yolk and
add enough chilled water to make a
smooth, soft but not sticky dough. Wrap
the dough in clear film (plastic wrap) and
chill for 30 minutes.

3 Preheat the oven to 180°C/350°F/
Gas 4. Line a 24cm/9½in loose-bottomed
flan tin (quiche pan) with the pastry by
pressing it gently over the base and up
the sides of the tin, making sure that
there are no holes in the pastry. Trim the
edge of the pastry with a sharp knife.

4 To make the almond filling, place the
butter or margarine and sugar in a
mixing bowl and cream together, using
a wooden spoon, until the mixture is
light and fluffy.

5 Gradually add the beaten egg to the
mixture, beating well after each addition.
Fold in the ground rice and almonds and
the almond essence and mix well to
incorporate them.

6 Spoon the almond mixture into the
pastry case, spreading it evenly with
the back of a spoon, then arrange the
apricot halves cut side down on top.

7 Place the tart on a baking sheet and
bake for 40–45 minutes until the filling
and pastry are cooked and lightly
browned. Serve warm or cold, dusted
with icing sugar and decorated with
apricots and sprigs of mint, if you like.

COOK'S TIP
Organic apricots are often smaller and
are more intensely coloured than non-
organic fruit. They have a sweeter, juicier
flavour too. Organic apricots, like organic
peaches and figs, help regulate the body's
digestive system. Try substituting organic
peaches and figs in this recipe.

BLUEBERRY MUFFINS

Light and fruity, these well-known American muffins are delicious at any time of day.
Serve them warm for breakfast or brunch, or as a tea-time treat.

MAKES TWELVE

180g/6¼oz/generous 1½ cups plain
   (all-purpose) flour
60g/2¼oz/¼ cup unrefined sugar or rapadura
10ml/2 tsp baking powder
2 eggs
50g/2oz/¼ cup butter or
   non-hydrogenated margarine, melted
175ml/6fl oz/¾ cup milk or soya milk
5ml/1 tsp vanilla essence (extract)
5ml/1 tsp grated lemon rind
175g/6oz/1½ cups fresh blueberries

1 Preheat the oven to 200°C/400°F/
Gas 6. Grease a 12-cup muffin tin or
arrange 12 paper muffin cases on a
baking tray.

2 Sift the plain flour, sugar and baking
powder into a large mixing bowl.

3 In another bowl, whisk the eggs until
blended. Add the melted butter, milk,
vanilla essence and grated lemon rind to
the whisked eggs, and stir thoroughly
to combine.

4 Make a well in the dry ingredients and
pour in the egg mixture. With a large
metal spoon, stir until the flour is just
moistened, but not smooth.

5 Add the blueberries to the muffin
mixture and gently fold in, being careful
not to crush the berries.

6 Spoon the batter into the muffin tin
or paper cases, leaving enough room
for the muffins to rise.

7 Bake for 20–25 minutes until the tops
spring back when touched lightly. Leave
the muffins in the tin, if using, for about
5 minutes before turning out on to a
wire rack to cool a little before serving.

VARIATION
Muffins are delicious with all kinds of
different fruits. Replace the blueberries
with the same weight of bilberries,
blackcurrants, stoned cherries
or raspberries.

COOK'S TIP
If you want to serve these muffins for
breakfast, prepare the dry ingredients
the night before to save time.

STRAWBERRY JAM and SCONES

There is not much that can beat freshly made scones with good-quality jam. Making your own is not difficult and their flavour really will be much better than shop-bought varieties.

MAKES ABOUT 1.3KG/3LB JAM
AND 10–12 SCONES

For the strawberry jam
1kg/2¼lb/9 cups small strawberries
900g/2lb/4½ cups unrefined granulated sugar
juice of 2 lemons

For the scones
225g/8oz/2 cups plain (all-purpose) flour
15ml/1 tbsp baking powder
50g/2oz/¼ cup butter or
    non-hydrogenated margarine, diced
1 egg, beaten, plus extra to glaze
75ml/5 tbsp milk or soya milk
clotted or double (heavy) cream, to serve

1 Layer the strawberries and sugar in a large bowl. Cover and leave overnight.

2 The next day, tip the strawberries and their juice into a large heavy pan. Add the lemon juice. Bring to the boil, stirring until the sugar has dissolved.

3 Boil steadily for 10–15 minutes. Spoon a small amount on to a chilled saucer. Chill for 3 minutes, then push the jam with your finger; if wrinkles form, it is ready. Cool for 10 minutes.

4 Pour the strawberry jam into warm, sterilized jars, filling them right to the top. Cover the jam with a disc of waxed paper, waxed side down, and seal the jar with a damp cellophane round and secure with an elastic band while the jam is still hot. Label when the jars are cold. The jam can be stored in a cool dark place, and it should keep for up to 1 year.

5 To make the scones, preheat the oven to 220°C/425°F/Gas 7. Butter a baking sheet. Sift the flour and baking powder together, then rub in the butter or margarine. Make a well in the centre of the flour mixture, add the egg and milk and mix to a soft dough using a fork or a round-bladed knife.

6 Turn out the scone dough on to a floured surface, and knead very lightly until smooth. Roll out the dough to about a 2cm/¾in thickness and cut into 10 or 12 rounds using a 5cm/2in plain or fluted cutter dipped in flour.

7 Transfer to the baking sheet, brush the tops with egg, then bake for about 8 minutes, until risen and golden. Cool slightly on a wire rack then serve with the jam and clotted or double cream.

AUTUMN

As the nights start to draw in, make the most of hearty organic vegetables with warming soups and stews. Try roasted garlic squash soup with tomato salsa or potatoes and parsnips baked with garlic and cream. Delicious fish dishes include sole with wild mushrooms, served simply with roasted root vegetables. Autumn orchards provide a wonderful array of fruits – organic apples, plums and pears are popular in both sweet and savoury dishes: try duck sausages with spicy plum sauce. Sticky pear pudding is the ultimate comfort food, while individual blackberry and apple soufflés are just right for a dinner party. Freshly baked cakes are especially satisfying at this time of year – serve them warm for a real taste of autumn.

CLAM, MUSHROOM and POTATO CHOWDER

Members of the same family as mussels, scallops and oysters, clams have a sweet flavour and firm texture, which combine beautifully with wild mushrooms in this filling soup.

SERVES 4

48 clams, scrubbed
50g/2oz/¼ cup unsalted (sweet) butter
    or non-hydrogenated margarine
1 large onion, chopped
1 celery stick, sliced
1 carrot, sliced
225g/8oz/3¾ cups assorted wild and
    cultivated mushrooms
225g/8oz floury potatoes (such as
    Maris Piper or King Edward),
    thickly sliced
1.2 litres/2 pints/5 cups boiling light
    chicken or vegetable stock
1 thyme sprig
4 parsley stalks
sea salt and ground black pepper
thyme sprigs, to garnish

1 Place the clams in a large, heavy pan, discarding any that are open. Add 1cm/½in of water to the pan, then cover and bring to the boil. Cook the clams over a medium heat for 6–8 minutes, shaking the pan occasionally, until the clams open (discard any clams that do not open).

2 Drain the clams over a bowl and remove most of the shells, leaving some in the shells as a garnish. Strain the cooking juices into the bowl, add all the clams and set aside.

3 Add the butter, onion, celery and carrot to the pan and cook gently until just softened but not coloured. Add the wild and cultivated mushrooms and cook for 3–4 minutes until their juices begin to appear. Add the potato slices, the clams and their juices, the stock, thyme and parsley stalks.

4 Bring to the boil, then reduce the heat, cover and simmer for 25 minutes. Season to taste, ladle into soup bowls, and garnish with thyme sprigs.

ROASTED GARLIC and SQUASH SOUP

This is a wonderful, richly flavoured dish. A spoonful of hot and spicy tomato salsa gives
bite to this sweet-tasting butternut squash and garlic soup.

SERVES FOUR TO FIVE

2 garlic bulbs, outer papery
   skin removed
75ml/5 tbsp olive oil
a few fresh thyme sprigs
1 large butternut squash, halved
   and seeded
2 onions, chopped
5ml/1 tsp ground coriander
1.2 litres/2 pints/5 cups vegetable or
   chicken stock
30–45ml/2–3 tbsp chopped fresh oregano
   or marjoram
sea salt and ground black pepper

For the salsa
4 large ripe tomatoes, halved and seeded
1 red (bell) pepper, halved and seeded
1 large fresh red chilli, halved and seeded
30–45ml/2–3 tbsp extra virgin olive oil
15ml/1 tbsp balsamic vinegar

3 Heat the remaining oil in a large, heavy pan and cook the onions and ground coriander gently for about 10 minutes, or until softened.

4 Skin the pepper and chilli and process in a food processor or blender with the tomatoes and 30ml/2 tbsp olive oil. Stir in the vinegar and seasoning to taste. Add the remaining oil if you think the salsa needs it.

5 Squeeze the roasted garlic out of its papery skin into the onions. Scoop the squash out of its skin and add it to the pan. Add the vegetable or chicken stock, 2.5ml/½ tsp salt and plenty of black pepper. Bring to the boil and simmer for 10 minutes.

6 Stir in half the chopped fresh oregano or marjoram and allow the soup to cool slightly, then process it in batches if necessary, in a food processor or blender until smooth. Alternatively, press the soup through a fine sieve.

7 Reheat the soup in a clean pan without allowing it to boil, then taste for seasoning before ladling it into individual warmed bowls. Top each with a spoonful of the tomato salsa and sprinkle over the remaining chopped fresh oregano or marjoram. Serve immediately.

1 Preheat the oven to 220°C/425°F/ Gas 7. Place the garlic bulbs on a piece of foil and pour over half the olive oil. Add the thyme sprigs, then fold the foil around the garlic bulbs to enclose them completely. Place the foil parcel on a baking sheet with the butternut squash and brush the squash with 15ml/1 tbsp of the remaining olive oil. Add the halved and seeded tomatoes, red pepper and fresh chilli for the salsa.

2 Roast the vegetables for 25 minutes, then remove the tomatoes, pepper and chilli. Reduce the temperature to 190°C/ 375°F/Gas 5 and cook the squash and garlic for 20–25 minutes more, or until the squash is tender.

ROAST GARLIC with GOAT'S CHEESE PÂTÉ

The combination of sweet, mellow roasted garlic and goat's cheese is a classic one. The pâté is flavoured with walnuts and herbs and is particularly good made with the new season's walnuts, sometimes known as "wet" walnuts, which are available in the early autumn.

SERVES FOUR

4 large garlic bulbs
4 fresh rosemary sprigs
8 fresh thyme sprigs
60ml/4 tbsp olive oil
sea salt and ground black pepper
thyme sprigs, to garnish
4–8 slices sourdough bread and
    walnuts, to serve

For the pâté
200g/7oz/scant 1 cup soft goat's cheese
5ml/1 tsp finely chopped fresh thyme
15ml/1 tbsp chopped fresh parsley
50g/2oz/⅓ cup walnuts, chopped
15ml/1 tbsp walnut oil (optional)
fresh thyme, to garnish

1 Preheat the oven to 180°C/350°F/Gas 4. Strip the papery skin from the garlic bulbs. Place them in an ovenproof dish large enough to hold them snugly. Tuck in the fresh rosemary sprigs and fresh thyme sprigs, drizzle the olive oil over and season with a little sea salt and plenty of ground black pepper.

2 Cover the garlic tightly with foil and bake in the oven for 50–60 minutes, opening the parcel and basting once halfway through the cooking time. Set aside and leave to cool.

3 Preheat the grill (broiler). To make the pâté, cream the cheese with the thyme, parsley and chopped walnuts. Beat in 15ml/1 tbsp of the cooking oil from the garlic and season to taste with plenty of ground black pepper. Transfer the pâté to a serving bowl and chill until ready to serve.

4 Brush the sourdough bread slices on one side with the remaining cooking oil from the garlic bulbs, then grill (broil) until lightly toasted.

5 Divide the pâté among four individual plates. Drizzle the walnut oil, if using, over the goat's cheese pâté and grind some black pepper over it. Place some garlic on each plate and serve with the pâté and some toasted bread. Garnish the pâté with a little fresh thyme and serve a few freshly shelled walnuts with each portion.

SLOW-COOKED SHIITAKE with SHOYU

Shiitake mushrooms cooked slowly are so rich and filling, that some people call them "vegetarian steak". This Japanese dish, known as Fukumé-ni, can last a few weeks in the refrigerator, and is a useful and flavourful addition to other dishes.

SERVES FOUR

20 dried shiitake mushrooms
45ml/3 tbsp sunflower or safflower oil
30ml/2 tbsp shoyu
15ml/1 tbsp toasted sesame oil

VARIATION
You can make a delicious rice dish using the slow-cooked shiitake to serve with grilled fish or chicken. Cut the slow-cooked shiitake into thin strips. Mix with 600g/1lb 5oz/5¼ cups cooked brown rice and 15ml/1 tbsp finely chopped chives. Serve in individual rice bowls and sprinkle with toasted sesame seeds.

1 Start soaking the dried shiitake the day before. Put them in a large bowl almost full of water. Cover the shiitake with a plate or lid to stop them floating to the surface of the water. Leave to soak overnight.

2 Measure 120ml/4fl oz/½ cup liquid from the bowl. Drain the shiitake into a sieve. Remove and discard the stalks.

3 Heat the oil in a wok or a large frying pan. Stir-fry the shiitake over a high heat for 5 minutes, stirring continuously.

4 Reduce the heat to the lowest setting, then add the measured liquid and the shoyu. Cook the mushrooms until there is almost no moisture left, stirring frequently. Add the toasted sesame oil and remove from the heat.

5 Leave to cool, then slice and arrange the shiitake on a large plate.

RED ONION and MUSHROOM TARTLETS with GOAT'S CHEESE

Crisp and savoury, these attractive little tarts are delicious served with a few mixed salad leaves drizzled with a garlic-infused French dressing.

SERVES SIX

60ml/4 tbsp olive oil
25g/1oz/2 tbsp butter or
   non-hydrogenated margarine
4 red onions, thinly sliced
5ml/1 tsp unrefined soft light brown sugar
15ml/1 tbsp balsamic vinegar
15ml/1 tbsp soy sauce
200g/7oz/3 cups button (white)
   mushrooms, sliced
1 garlic clove, finely chopped
2.5ml/½ tsp chopped fresh tarragon
30ml/2 tbsp chopped fresh parsley
250g/9oz goat's cheese log (chèvre)
sea salt and ground black pepper
mixed salad leaves, to serve

For the pastry

200g/7oz/1¾ cups plain (all-purpose) flour
pinch of cayenne pepper
90g/3½oz/scant ½ cup butter or
   non-hydrogenated margarine
40g/1½oz/½ cup freshly grated Parmesan
   cheese or premium vegetarian cheese
45–60ml/3–4 tbsp iced water

1 To make the pastry, sift the flour and cayenne into a bowl, add the butter, and rub in with the fingertips.

2 Stir in the grated cheese, then bind the pastry with the iced water. Press the pastry into a ball, then wrap it in clear film (plastic wrap) and chill.

3 Heat 15ml/1 tbsp of the oil and half the butter in a heavy frying pan, then add the onions. Cover and cook gently for 15 minutes, stirring occasionally.

4 Uncover the pan, increase the heat slightly and sprinkle in the sugar. Cook, stirring frequently, until the onions begin to caramelize and brown. Add the balsamic vinegar and soy sauce and cook briskly until the liquid evaporates. Season to taste then set aside.

5 Heat another 30ml/2 tbsp of the oil and the remaining butter or margarine in a pan, then add the sliced mushrooms and chopped garlic and cook fairly briskly for 5–6 minutes, or until the mushrooms are browned and cooked.

6 Set a few cooked mushrooms and onion rings aside, then stir the rest of the mushrooms into the onions with the fresh tarragon and parsley. Adjust the seasoning to taste. Preheat the oven to 190°C/375°F/Gas 5.

COOK'S TIP

Shortcrust pastry is traditionally made with all plain (all-purpose) flour. For a healthier, higher fibre pastry use half plain and half wholemeal (whole-wheat) flour. This gives a nutty, slightly textured result.

7 Roll out the pastry and use to line six 10cm/4in tartlet tins (quiche pans). Prick the pastry bases with a fork and line the sides with strips of foil. Bake for 10 minutes, remove the foil and bake for another 5–7 minutes, or until the pastry is lightly browned and cooked. Remove the tartlets from the oven and increase the temperature to 200°C/400°F/Gas 6.

8 Remove the pastry shells from the tins and arrange them on a baking sheet. Divide the onion mixture equally among the pastry shells. Cut the goat's cheese into six equal slices and place one slice on each tartlet. Distribute the reserved mushrooms and onion rings, drizzle with the remaining oil and season with pepper.

9 Return the tartlets to the oven and bake for 5–8 minutes, or until the goat's cheese is just beginning to turn brown. Serve with mixed salad leaves.

VARIATION

For a milder flavour sliced buffalo mozzarella cheese can be used to top the tartlets instead of the goat's cheese.

FLORETS POLONAISE

Simple steamed organic vegetables become something very special with this pretty egg topping. They make a perfect dinner party side dish or are great with a weekday supper.

SERVES SIX

500g/1¼lb mixed vegetables,
   such as cauliflower, broccoli,
   romanesco and calabrese
50g/2oz/¼ cup butter or 60ml/4 tbsp extra
   virgin olive oil
finely grated rind of ½ lemon
1 large garlic clove, crushed
25g/1oz/½ cup fresh breadcrumbs, lightly
   baked or grilled (broiled) until crisp
2 eggs, hard-boiled
sea salt and ground black pepper

VARIATION
Use wholemeal (whole-wheat) breadcrumbs
instead of the white crumbs. They will give
a nuttier flavour and crunchier texture.

1 Trim the vegetables and break into equal-size florets. Place the florets in a steamer over a pan of boiling water and steam for 5–7 minutes, until just tender.

2 Toss the steamed vegetables in butter or oil and transfer to a serving dish.

3 While the vegetables are cooking, mix together the lemon rind, garlic, seasoning and baked or grilled breadcrumbs. Finely chop the eggs and mix together with the remaining ingredients. Sprinkle the chopped egg mixture over the cooked vegetables and serve at once.

ORANGE CANDIED SWEET POTATOES

Organic sweet potatoes are free of the fungicides sprayed on non-organic tubers and
are an excellent source of vitamins, including cancer-preventing betacarotene.

SERVES EIGHT

900g/2lb sweet potatoes
250ml/8fl oz/1 cup orange juice
50ml/2fl oz/¼ cup maple syrup
5ml/1 tsp freshly grated root ginger
7.5ml/1½ tsp ground cinnamon
6.5ml/1¼ tsp ground cardamom
2.5ml/½ tsp salt
ground black pepper
ground cinnamon and orange segments,
    to garnish

COOK'S TIP
This popular American dish is traditionally
served with roast turkey at Thanksgiving
and Christmas. Serve with extra orange
segments to make it really special.

1 Preheat the oven to 180°C/350°F/
Gas 4. Peel and dice the potatoes and
then steam them for 5 minutes.

2 Meanwhile, stir the remaining
ingredients together. Spread out on to
a non-stick shallow baking tin (pan).

3 Scatter the potatoes over the baking
tin. Cook for 1 hour, stirring every
15 minutes, until they are tender and
well coated in the spicy syrup.

4 Serve garnished with orange segments
and ground cinnamon.

GARLIC CHIVE RICE with MUSHROOMS

A wide range of organic mushrooms is readily available. They combine well with rice and garlic chives to make a tasty accompaniment to vegetarian dishes, fish or chicken.

SERVES FOUR

350g/12oz/generous 1¾ cups
   long grain rice
60ml/4 tbsp groundnut (peanut) oil
1 small onion, finely chopped
2 green chillies, seeded and finely chopped
25g/1oz garlic chives, chopped
15g/½oz fresh coriander (cilantro)
600ml/1 pint/2½ cups vegetable or
   mushroom stock
2.5ml/½ tsp sea salt
250g/9oz mixed mushrooms, thickly sliced
50g/2oz cashew nuts, fried in 15ml/1 tbsp
   olive oil until golden brown
ground black pepper

1 Wash and drain the rice. Heat half the oil in a pan and cook the onion and chillies over a gentle heat, stirring occasionally, for 10–12 minutes until soft.

2 Set half the garlic chives aside. Cut the stalks off the coriander and set the leaves aside. Purée the remaining chives and the coriander stalks with the stock in a food processor or blender.

VARIATION

For a higher-fibre alternative make this dish with brown rice. Increase the cooking time in step 3 to 25–30 minutes or follow the packet instructions.

3 Add the rice to the onions and fry over a low heat, stirring frequently, for 4–5 minutes. Pour in the stock mixture, then stir in the salt and a good grinding of black pepper. Bring to the boil, then stir and reduce the heat to very low. Cover tightly with a lid and cook for 15–20 minutes, or until the rice has absorbed all the liquid.

4 Remove the pan from the heat and lay a clean, folded dishtowel over the pan, under the lid, and press on the lid to wedge it firmly in place. Leave the rice to stand for a further 10 minutes, allowing the towel to absorb the steam while the rice becomes completely tender.

5 Meanwhile, heat the remaining oil in a frying pan and cook the mushrooms for 5–6 minutes until tender and browned. Add the remaining garlic chives and cook for another 1–2 minutes.

6 Stir the cooked mushroom and chive mixture and chopped coriander leaves into the rice. Adjust the seasoning to taste, then transfer to a warmed serving dish and serve immediately, scattered with the fried cashew nuts.

ROASTED SHALLOT and SQUASH SALAD

This is especially good served with a grain or starchy salad, based on rice or couscous,
for example. Serve with plenty of hand-made organic bread to mop up the juices.

SERVES FOUR TO SIX

75ml/5 tbsp olive oil
15ml/1 tbsp balsamic vinegar, plus a little
    extra, if you like
15ml/1 tbsp sweet soy sauce
350g/12oz shallots, peeled but left whole
3 fresh red chillies
1 butternut squash, peeled, seeded
    and cut into chunks
5ml/1 tsp finely chopped fresh thyme
15g/½oz flat leaf parsley
1 small garlic clove, finely chopped
75g/3oz/¾ cup walnuts, chopped
150g/5oz feta cheese
sea salt and ground black pepper

1 Preheat the oven to 200°C/400°F/
Gas 6. Beat the olive oil, balsamic
vinegar and soy sauce together in a large
bowl, then season with a little salt and
plenty of freshly ground black pepper.

2 Toss the shallots and two of the
chillies in the oil mixture and tip into a
large roasting pan or ovenproof dish. Roast
for 15 minutes, stirring once or twice.

3 Add the butternut squash chunks and
roast for a further 30–35 minutes,
stirring once, until the squash is tender
and browned. Remove from the oven,
stir in the chopped fresh thyme and set
the vegetables aside to cool.

4 Chop the parsley and garlic together
and mix with the walnuts. Seed and
finely chop the remaining chilli.

5 Stir the parsley, garlic and walnut
mixture into the vegetables. Add
chopped chilli to taste and adjust the
seasoning, adding a little extra balsamic
vinegar, if you like. Crumble the feta and
add to the salad. Transfer to a serving
dish and serve immediately.

POTATOES and PARSNIPS BAKED with GARLIC and CREAM

As the potatoes and parsnips cook, they gradually absorb the garlic-flavoured cream, while the cheese browns to a crispy finish.

SERVES FOUR TO SIX

3 large potatoes, total weight
   about 675g/1½lb
350g/12oz small–medium parsnips
200ml/7fl oz/scant 1 cup single (light)
   cream or soya cream
105ml/7 tbsp milk or soya milk
2 garlic cloves, crushed
butter or olive oil, for greasing
about 5ml/1 tsp freshly grated
   nutmeg
75g/3oz/¾ cup coarsely grated
   Cheddar cheese
sea salt and ground black pepper

1 Peel the potatoes and parsnips and cut them into thin slices using a sharp knife. Place them in a steamer and cook for 5 minutes. Leave to cool slightly.

2 Meanwhile, pour the cream and milk into a heavy pan, add the crushed garlic and bring to the boil over a medium heat. Remove the pan from the heat and leave to stand at room temperature for about 10 minutes to allow the flavour of the garlic to infuse into the cream and milk mixture.

3 Lightly grease a 25cm/10in long, shallow rectangular earthenware baking dish with butter or oil. Preheat the oven to 180°C/350°F/Gas 4.

4 Arrange the thinly sliced potatoes and parsnips in layers in the greased earthenware dish, sprinkling each layer of vegetables with a little freshly grated nutmeg and a little salt and plenty of ground black pepper.

VARIATIONS

• Use sweet potatoes in place of some or all of the ordinary potatoes – choose orange-fleshed ones for a pretty colour contrast with the parsnips. Other root vegetables such as Jerusalem artichokes, carrots, swede (rutabaga) or turnips would also work well.
• Other hard cheeses would be equally good in this recipe – try Red Leicester or Gruyère, or go for the even more strongly flavoured Parmesan, premium Italian-style vegetarian cheese or Pecorino.

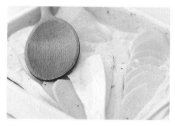

5 Pour the garlic-flavoured cream and milk mixture into the dish and then press the sliced potatoes and parsnips down into the liquid. The liquid should come to just underneath the top layer of vegetables. Cover the dish with a piece of lightly buttered foil or baking parchment and bake for 45 minutes.

6 Remove the dish from the oven and remove the foil or paper from the dish. Sprinkle the grated Cheddar cheese over the vegetables in an even layer.

7 Return the dish to the oven and bake uncovered for a further 20–30 minutes, or until the potatoes and parsnips are tender and the topping is golden brown.

COOK'S TIPS

• If you have one, use a mandolin or a food processor fitted with a slicing blade to slice the potatoes and parsnips thinly and evenly for this gratin.
• At the end of the cooking time, to test if the vegetables are tender, insert a sharp knife through the middle of the potatoes and parsnips. The knife should slide in easily and the vegetables feel soft.

TOFU and VEGETABLE THAI CURRY

Non-organic soya products, including tofu, are often made from genetically modified beans that are resistant to pesticides. By using organic tofu in this fragrant curry you benefit from its great texture and superior nutritional value whilst helping to protect the Earth.

SERVES FOUR

175g/6oz tofu, drained
45ml/3 tbsp dark soy sauce
15ml/1 tbsp sesame oil
5ml/1 tsp chilli sauce
2.5cm/1in piece fresh root ginger,
    finely grated
225g/8oz cauliflower
225g/8oz broccoli
30ml/2 tbsp sunflower oil
1 onion, sliced
400ml/14fl oz/1⅔ cups coconut milk
150ml/¼ pint/⅔ cup water
1 red (bell) pepper, seeded and chopped
175g/6oz green beans, halved
115g/4oz/1½ cups shiitake or button
    (white) mushrooms, halved
shredded spring onions (scallions),
    to garnish
boiled brown rice or noodles, to serve

For the curry paste
2 chillies, seeded and chopped
1 lemon grass stalk, chopped
2.5cm/1in piece fresh galangal or
    fresh root ginger, chopped
2 kaffir lime leaves
10ml/2 tsp ground coriander
a few sprigs fresh coriander (cilantro),
    including the stalks

1 Cut the drained tofu into 2.5cm/1in cubes and place in an ovenproof dish. Mix together the soy sauce, sesame oil, chilli sauce and ginger and pour over the tofu. Toss gently to coat all the cubes evenly, then leave to marinate for at least 2 hours or overnight if possible, turning and basting the tofu occasionally.

2 To make the curry paste, place the chopped chillies, lemon grass, galangal, kaffir lime leaves, ground coriander and fresh coriander in a food processor, and process for a few seconds until well blended. Add 45ml/3 tbsp water and process to a thick paste.

3 Preheat the oven to 190°C/375°F/Gas 5. Using a large sharp knife, cut the cauliflower and broccoli into small florets and cut any stalks into thin slices.

4 Heat the sunflower oil in a frying pan, add the sliced onion and gently fry for about 8 minutes, or until soft and lightly browned. Stir in the prepared curry paste and the coconut milk.

5 Add the water and bring to the boil, then stir in the red pepper, green beans, cauliflower and broccoli. Transfer to an earthenware casserole or Chinese sand pot. Cover and place in the oven.

6 Stir the tofu and marinade, then place the dish in the top of the oven and cook for 30 minutes. After 30 minutes, stir the tofu and marinade into the curry with the mushrooms.

7 Reduce the oven temperature to 180°C/350°F/Gas 4 and cook for about 15 minutes more, or until the vegetables are tender. Garnish with spring onions and serve with boiled rice or noodles.

COOK'S TIP

Organic tofu or beancurd is made from organic soya beans and is sold in blocks. It is a creamy white colour and has a solid gel-like texture. Tofu has a bland flavour and its absorbent nature means that it takes on the flavours of marinades or any other food that it is cooked with.

SPAGHETTI with EGGS and BACON

Organic ingredients really enhance the flavours of simple, classic dishes such as this Italian favourite, which makes a great last-minute supper.

SERVES FOUR

30ml/2 tbsp olive oil
1 small onion, finely chopped
1 large garlic clove, crushed
8 pancetta or rindless smoked streaky
   (fatty) bacon rashers (strips), cut into
   1cm/½in strips
350g/12oz fresh or dried spaghetti
4 eggs
90–120ml/6–8 tbsp reduced-fat
   crème fraîche
60ml/4 tbsp freshly grated Parmesan
   cheese or premium Italian-style
   vegetarian cheese, plus extra
   to serve
sea salt and ground black pepper

1 Heat the oil in a large pan, add the onion and garlic and fry gently for about 5 minutes until softened.

2 Add the pancetta or bacon to the pan and cook for 10 minutes, stirring.

3 Meanwhile, cook the spaghetti in a large pan of salted boiling water for 10 minutes or according to the instructions on the packet until *al dente*.

4 Put the eggs, crème fraîche and grated Parmesan in a bowl. Stir in plenty of black pepper, then beat together well.

5 Drain the pasta thoroughly, tip it into the pan with the pancetta or bacon and toss well to mix.

6 Turn off the heat under the pan, then immediately add the egg mixture and toss thoroughly so that it cooks lightly and coats the pasta.

7 Season to taste, then divide the spaghetti among four warmed bowls and sprinkle with freshly ground black pepper. Serve immediately, with extra grated cheese handed separately.

COOK'S TIP
You can replace the crème fraîche with double (heavy) cream, sour cream or soya cream, if you prefer.

CHICKEN with CASHEW NUTS

This popular Chinese dish is quick and easy to make and can be enjoyed to the full by using good-quality organic products that are full of flavour.

SERVES FOUR

350g/12oz skinless chicken
   breast fillets
pinch of ground white pepper
15ml/1 tbsp dry sherry
300ml/½ pint/1¼ cups chicken stock
15ml/1 tbsp sunflower oil
1 garlic clove, finely chopped
1 small carrot, cut into cubes
½ cucumber, about 75g/3oz, cut into
   1cm/½in cubes
50g/2oz/½ cup drained canned bamboo
   shoots, cut into 1cm/½in cubes
   (optional)
5ml/1 tsp cornflour (cornstarch)
15ml/1 tbsp soy sauce
25g/1oz/¼ cup dry-roasted cashew nuts
2.5ml/½ tsp sesame oil
noodles, to serve

1 Cut the chicken into 2cm/¾in cubes. Place the cubes in a bowl, stir in the white pepper and sherry, cover and marinate for 15 minutes.

2 Bring the stock to the boil in a large pan. Add the chicken and cook, stirring, for 3 minutes. Drain, reserving 90ml/ 6 tbsp of the stock, and set aside.

3 Heat the sunflower oil in a large non-stick frying pan until it is very hot, add the finely chopped garlic and stir-fry for a few seconds. Add the cubed carrot, cucumber and bamboo shoots, if using, and continue to stir-fry the vegetables over a medium heat for 2 minutes.

4 Stir in the chicken and reserved stock. Mix the cornflour with the soy sauce and add the mixture to the pan. Cook, stirring, until the sauce thickens slightly. Finally, add the cashew nuts and sesame oil. Toss to mix thoroughly, then serve with noodles.

MOUSSAKA

This is a traditional eastern Mediterranean dish, popular in both Greece and Turkey.
Layers of minced mutton, aubergines, tomatoes and onions are topped with a creamy
yogurt and cheese sauce in this delicious, authentic recipe.

SERVES FOUR

450g/1lb aubergines (eggplant)
150ml/¼ pint/⅔ cup olive oil
1 large onion, chopped
2–3 garlic cloves, finely chopped
675g/1½lb lean minced (ground) mutton
15ml/1 tbsp plain (all-purpose) flour
400g/14oz can chopped tomatoes
30ml/2 tbsp chopped mixed fresh herbs,
    such as parsley, marjoram and oregano
sea salt and ground black pepper

For the topping
300ml/½ pint/1¼ cups natural
    (plain) yogurt
2 eggs
25g/1oz feta cheese, crumbled
25g/1oz/⅓ cup freshly grated Parmesan
    cheese or premium Italian-style
    vegetarian cheese

1 Slice the aubergines and layer them in
a colander, sprinkling with salt. Cover the
aubergines with a plate and a weight,
then leave to drain for about 30 minutes.

2 Drain the aubergines, rinse well, then
pat dry with kitchen paper.

3 Heat 45ml/3 tbsp of the oil in a large,
heavy pan. Fry the onion and garlic until
softened, but not coloured. Add the
mutton and cook over a high heat,
stirring often, until browned.

4 Stir in the flour until mixed, then stir
in the tomatoes, herbs and seasoning.
Bring to the boil, reduce the heat and
simmer gently for 20 minutes.

5 Meanwhile, heat a little of the
remaining olive oil in a large frying pan.
Add as many aubergine slices as can be
laid in the pan in a single layer. Cook
until golden on both sides then remove
from the pan. Heat more oil and
continue frying the aubergines in
batches, adding olive oil as necessary.

COOK'S TIP
Many kinds of organic aubergines do not
taste bitter; therefore it is not usually
necessary to salt them before cooking.
However, if they are to be fried, as in this
recipe, salting and drying them reduces
the amount of fat that they absorb and
helps them to brown during cooking.

6 Preheat the oven to 180°C/350°F/
Gas 4. Arrange half the aubergine slices
in a large, shallow ovenproof dish.

7 Top the aubergine slices with about
half of the meat and tomato mixture,
then add the remaining aubergine slices.
Spread the remaining meat mixture
over the aubergines.

8 To make the topping, beat together
the yogurt and eggs, then mix in the feta
and Parmesan or Italian-style cheeses.
Pour the mixture over the meat and
spread it evenly.

9 Transfer the moussaka to the oven
and bake for 35–40 minutes, or until
golden and bubbling.

VARIATION
Use large courgettes (zucchini) in place
of the aubergines, if you like, and cut
them diagonally into fairly thick slices.
There is no need to salt the courgettes
before frying them.

DUCK SAUSAGES with SPICY PLUM SAUCE

A variety of organic sausages is available direct from farmers and small butchers, and any pork or game sausages would work in this dish. Rich duck sausages are best baked in their own juices.

SERVES FOUR

8–12 duck sausages

For the sweet potato mash
1.5kg/3¼lb sweet potatoes, cut
   into chunks
25g/1oz/2 tbsp butter or
   30ml/2 tbsp olive oil
60ml/4 tbsp milk
sea salt and ground black pepper

For the plum sauce
30ml/2 tbsp olive oil
1 small onion, chopped
1 small red chilli, seeded and chopped
450g/1lb plums, stoned and chopped
30ml/2 tbsp red wine vinegar
45ml/3 tbsp clear honey

1 Preheat the oven to 190°C/375°F/ Gas 5. Arrange the duck sausages in a single layer in a large, shallow ovenproof dish. Bake the sausages, uncovered, in the oven for 25–30 minutes, turning the sausages two or three times during cooking, to ensure that they brown and cook evenly.

2 Meanwhile, put the sweet potatoes in a pan and add water to cover. Bring to the boil, then reduce the heat and simmer for 20 minutes, or until tender.

3 Drain and mash the potatoes, then place the pan over a low heat. Stir frequently for about 5 minutes to dry out the mashed potato. Beat in the butter or oil and milk, season to taste.

4 Make the plum sauce. Heat the oil in a small pan and fry the onion and chilli gently for 5 minutes. Stir in the plums, vinegar and honey, then simmer gently for 10 minutes.

5 Serve the freshly cooked sausages with the sweet potato mash and plum sauce.

SPICY VENISON CASSEROLE

Being high in flavour but low in saturated fat, organic venison is a good choice for healthy,
yet rich, casseroles. Cranberries and orange bring a delicious fruitiness to this spicy recipe.

SERVES FOUR

15ml/1 tbsp olive oil
1 onion, chopped
2 celery sticks, sliced
10ml/2 tsp ground allspice
15ml/1 tbsp plain (all-purpose) or
    wholemeal (whole-wheat) flour
675g/1½lb stewing venison, cubed
225g/8oz fresh or frozen cranberries
grated rind and juice of 1 orange
900ml/1½ pints/3¾ cups beef or
    venison stock
sea salt and ground black pepper

1 Heat the oil in a flameproof casserole.
Add the onion and celery and fry for
about 5 minutes, or until softened.

2 Meanwhile, mix the ground allspice
with the flour and either spread the
mixture out on a large plate or place
in a large plastic bag. Toss a few pieces
of venison at a time (to prevent them
becoming soggy) in the flour mixture
until they are all lightly coated. Spread
the floured venison out on a large plate
until ready to cook.

3 When the onion and celery are
just softened, remove them from the
casserole using a slotted spoon and set
aside. Add the venison pieces to the
casserole in batches and cook until well
browned and sealed on all sides.

COOK'S TIP
Freshly made home-made stock is always
best, but if you are short of time, look
for cartons or tubs of fresh stock in the
chilled food cabinets of organic stores.

4 Add the cranberries and the orange
rind and juice to the casserole along
with the stock and stir well. Return the
vegetables and the browned venison to
the casserole and heat until simmering.
Cover tightly and reduce the heat.

5 Simmer for about 45 minutes, or until
the venison is tender, stirring occasionally.
Season the venison casserole to taste
with a little salt and plenty of ground
black pepper before serving.

VARIATIONS
Farmed organic venison is increasingly
easy to find and is available from many
good butchers and organic meat delivery
companies. It makes a rich and flavourful
stew, but lean pork or braising steak
could be used in place of the venison, if
you prefer. You could also replace the
cranberries with pitted and halved prunes
and, for extra flavour, use either ale or
stout instead of about half the stock.

STUFFED ROAST LOIN of PORK with APPLE SAUCE

The secret of a good roast with apple sauce is simple, good-quality ingredients, such as organic pork and traditionally made cider.

SERVES SIX

15ml/1 tbsp light olive oil
2 leeks, chopped
150g/5oz/⅔ cup ready-to-eat dried
    apricots, chopped
150g/5oz/scant 1 cup dried dates, stoned
    and chopped
75g/3oz/1½ cups fresh white or wholemeal
    (whole-wheat) breadcrumbs
2 eggs, beaten
15ml/1 tbsp fresh thyme leaves
1.5kg/3¼lb boned loin of pork
sea salt and ground black pepper

For the apple sauce
450g/1lb cooking apples
30ml/2 tbsp cider or water
25g/1oz/2 tbsp butter or 30ml/2 tbsp
    olive oil

1 Preheat the oven to 220°C/425°F/ Gas 7. Heat the oil in a large pan and cook the leeks until softened. Stir in the apricots, dates, breadcrumbs, eggs and thyme, and season with salt and pepper.

2 Lay the pork skin side up, and use a sharp knife to score the rind crossways.

3 Turn the meat over and cut down the centre of the joint to within 1cm/½in of the rind and fat, then work from the middle outwards towards one side, cutting most of the meat off the rind but keeping a 1cm/½in layer of meat on top of the rind. Cut to within 2.5cm/1in of the side of the joint. Repeat on the other side of the joint.

4 Spoon half the stuffing over the joint, then fold the meat over it.

5 Tie the joint back into its original shape, then place in a roasting pan and rub the skin with salt. Roast the pork for 40 minutes, then reduce the oven temperature to 190°C/375°F/Gas 5 and cook for a further 1½ hours, or until the meat is tender and cooked through.

6 Meanwhile, shape the remaining stuffing into walnut-size balls. Arrange on a tray, cover with clear film (plastic wrap) and chill until 20 minutes before the pork is cooked. Then add the stuffing balls to the roasting pan and baste them with the cooking juices from the meat.

7 When cooked, cover the meat closely with foil and leave to stand in a warm place for 10 minutes before carving.

8 To make the apple sauce, peel, core and chop the apples, then place in a small pan with the cider or water and cook for 5–10 minutes, stirring occasionally, or until very soft. Beat well or process in a food processor or blender to make smooth apple sauce. Beat in the butter or oil. Reheat the apple sauce just before serving, if necessary.

9 Carve the joint into thick slices. If the crackling is very hard, you may find that it is easier to slice the crackling off the joint first, before carving the meat, then cut the crackling into serving pieces using poultry shears or a heavy, sharp chef's knife or cleaver. Serve the stuffed loin of pork with the crackling, stuffing balls, apple sauce and a selection of seasonal autumn vegetables.

COOK'S TIP
The resting time before carving is very important, so don't be tempted to skip it.

SALMON and RICE GRATIN

This all-in-one supper dish is ideal for informal autumn entertaining as it can be made in advance and reheated for about half an hour before being served with a tossed salad.

4 Remove the pan from the heat and, without lifting the lid, allow the rice to stand, undisturbed, for 5 minutes.

5 Meanwhile, make the sauce. Mix the milk, flour and butter or margarine in a pan. Bring to the boil over a low heat, whisking constantly until the sauce is smooth and thick. Stir in the curry paste with salt and pepper to taste. Simmer for 2 minutes.

6 Preheat the grill (broiler). Remove the sauce from the heat and stir in the chopped parsley and rice, with half the cheese. Using a large metal spoon, fold in the flaked fish and eggs. Spoon into a shallow gratin dish and sprinkle with the rest of the cheese. Cook under the grill until the topping is golden brown and bubbling. Serve in individual dishes, garnished with chopped parsley.

SERVES SIX

675g/1½lb fresh salmon fillet, skinned
1 bay leaf
a few parsley stalks
1 litre/1¾ pints/4 cups water
400g/14oz/2 cups basmati rice, soaked
    and drained
30–45ml/2–3 tbsp chopped fresh parsley,
    plus extra to garnish
175g/6oz/1½ cups grated Cheddar cheese
3 hard-boiled eggs, chopped
sea salt and ground black pepper

For the sauce
1 litre/1¾ pints/4 cups milk or soya milk
40g/1½oz/⅓ cup plain (all-purpose) flour
40g/1½oz/3 tbsp butter or
    non-hydrogenated margarine
5ml/1 tsp mild curry paste

1 Put the salmon fillet in a wide, shallow pan. Add the bay leaf and parsley stalks, with a little salt and plenty of black pepper. Pour in the water and bring to simmering point. Poach the fish for about 12 minutes until just tender.

2 Lift the salmon fillet out of the pan using a slotted spoon, then strain the cooking liquid into a large pan. Leave the fish to cool, then remove any visible bones and flake the flesh gently into bitesize pieces with a fork.

3 Add the soaked and drained rice to the pan containing the fish-poaching liquid. Bring the liquid to the boil, then lower the heat, cover tightly with a lid and simmer gently for 10 minutes without lifting the lid.

VARIATIONS
Organically farmed prawns (shrimp) could be substituted for the salmon, and other hard cheeses, such as Gruyère or Red Leicester, could be used instead of the Cheddar cheese.

POTATO-TOPPED FISH PIE

This traditional Scottish dish should be prepared from wild fish such as hoki, caught
sustainably. Always ensure you buy wild fish bearing the MSC logo.

SERVES FOUR

675g/1½lb hoki fillets (or other sustainably
   caught white fish)
300ml/½ pint/1¼ cups milk or soya milk
½ lemon, sliced
1 bay leaf
1 fresh thyme sprig
4–5 black peppercorns
50g/2oz/¼ cup butter or
   non-hydrogenated margarine
25g/1oz/¼ cup plain (all-purpose) flour
30ml/2 tbsp chopped fresh parsley
5ml/1 tsp anchovy essence
150g/5oz/2 cups shiitake or chestnut
   mushrooms, sliced
sea salt, ground black pepper and
   cayenne pepper

For the topping
450g/1lb potatoes, cooked and mashed
   with milk or soya milk
50g/2oz/¼ cup butter or
   non-hydrogenated margarine
2 tomatoes, sliced
25g/1oz/¼ cup grated Cheddar cheese

3 Heat the remaining butter in a frying
pan, add the sliced mushrooms and
sauté until tender. Season and add to the
flaked fish. Mix the sauce into the fish
and stir gently to combine. Transfer the
mixture to an ovenproof casserole.

4 Preheat the oven to 200°C/400°F/
Gas 6. Beat the mashed potato with the
butter until very creamy. Season, then
spread the topping evenly over the fish.
Fork up the surface and arrange the
sliced tomatoes around the edge.
Sprinkle the exposed topping with the
grated cheese.

5 Bake for 20–25 minutes until the
topping is browned. If you prefer, finish
the browning under a hot grill (broiler).

VARIATION
Instead of using plain mashed potatoes, try
a mixture of mashed potato and mashed
swede (rutabaga) or sweet potato.

1 Put the fish skin side down in a
shallow pan. Add the milk, lemon slices,
bay leaf, thyme and peppercorns. Bring
to the boil, then lower the heat and
poach gently for about 5 minutes until
just cooked. Strain off and reserve the
milk. Remove the fish skin and flake
the flesh, discarding any bones.

2 Melt half the butter in a small pan, stir
in the flour and cook gently for 1 minute.
Add the reserved milk and boil, whisking,
until smooth and creamy. Stir in the parsley
and anchovy essence and season to taste.

GRILLED MACKEREL with SPICY DHAL

Oily fish such as mackerel are nutritious and great for your nervous system. They are complemented by a tart or sour accompaniment, like these delicious tamarind-flavoured lentils or split peas. Serve with chopped fresh tomatoes, onion salad and flat bread.

SERVES FOUR

250g/9oz/generous 1 cup red lentils, or
   yellow split peas (soaked overnight)
1 litre/1¾ pints/4 cups water
30ml/2 tbsp sunflower oil
2.5ml/½ tsp each mustard seeds,
   cumin seeds, fennel seeds and
   fenugreek or cardamom seeds
5ml/1 tsp ground turmeric
3–4 dried red chillies, crumbled
30ml/2 tbsp tamarind paste
30ml/2 tbsp chopped fresh coriander
   (cilantro)
4 mackerels
ground black pepper
fresh red chilli slices and finely chopped
   coriander, to garnish
flat bread and tomatoes, to serve

1 Rinse the lentils or split peas, drain them thoroughly and put them in a pan. Pour in the water and bring to the boil. Lower the heat, partially cover the pan and simmer the lentils or split peas for 30–40 minutes, stirring occasionally, until they are tender and mushy.

2 Heat the oil in a wok or shallow pan. Add the mustard seeds, then cover and cook for a few seconds until they pop. Remove the lid, add the rest of the seeds, with the turmeric and chillies and fry for a few more seconds.

3 Stir in the lentils or split peas and the tamarind paste and mix well. Bring to the boil, then simmer for 10 minutes until thick. Stir in the coriander.

4 Clean the fish then heat a ridged griddle or the grill (broiler) until very hot. Make six diagonal slashes on either side of each fish and remove the head. Season, then grill for 5–7 minutes on each side. Serve, garnished with red chilli and chopped coriander, accompanied by the dhal, flat bread and tomatoes.

SOLE with WILD MUSHROOMS

If possible, use organic chanterelles for this dish; their glowing orange colour combines really wonderfully with the intensely golden sauce. Otherwise, use any pale-coloured or oyster mushrooms that you can find instead.

SERVES FOUR

4 Dover sole fillets, about 115g/4oz
    each, skinned
50g/2oz/¼ cup butter or
    non-hydrogenated margarine
500ml/17fl oz/generous 2 cups fish stock
150g/5oz/2 cups chanterelles or
    oyster mushrooms
a large pinch of saffron threads
150ml/¼ pint/⅔ cup double (heavy) cream
    or soya cream
1 egg yolk
sea salt and ground white pepper
flat leaf parsley sprigs, to garnish
boiled new potatoes and steamed broccoli
    florets, to serve

1 Preheat the oven to 200°C/400°F/ Gas 6. Cut the sole fillets in half lengthways and place them on a board with the skinned side uppermost. Season, then roll them up. Use a little of the butter to grease a baking dish just large enough to hold all the sole fillets in a single layer. Arrange the rolls in it, then pour over the fish stock. Cover tightly with foil and bake for 12–15 minutes until cooked through.

2 Meanwhile, pick off any bits of fern or twig from the chanterelles and wipe the mushrooms with a damp cloth. Halve or quarter any large ones. Heat the remaining butter in a frying pan until foaming and sauté the mushrooms for 3–4 minutes until just tender. Season with salt and pepper and keep hot.

3 Lift the cooked sole fillets out of the cooking liquid and place them on a heated serving dish. Keep hot. Strain the liquid into a small pan, add the saffron, set over a very high heat and boil until reduced to about 250ml/8fl oz/1 cup. Stir in the cream and let the sauce bubble gently for a few seconds.

4 Lightly beat the egg yolk in a small bowl, pour on a little of the hot sauce and stir well. Stir the mixture into the remaining sauce in the pan and cook over a very low heat for 1–2 minutes until slightly thickened. Season to taste. Stir the chanterelles into the sauce and pour it over the sole fillets. Garnish with parsley sprigs and serve at once. Boiled new potatoes and steamed broccoli florets make the perfect accompaniment.

HONEY BAKED FIGS with HAZELNUT ICE CREAM

Organic figs have a deliciously intense flavour. They are smaller than non-organic fruit as they are not forced to absorb water during growing, so you may need three per person.

SERVES FOUR

1 lemon grass stalk, finely chopped
1 cinnamon stick, roughly broken
60ml/4 tbsp clear honey
200ml/7fl oz/scant 1 cup water
8 large or 12 small figs

For the hazelnut ice cream
450ml/¾ pint/scant 2 cups double (heavy)
   cream or soya cream
50g/2oz/¼ cup unrefined caster (superfine)
   sugar or rapadura
3 egg yolks
1.5ml/¼ tsp vanilla essence (extract)
75g/3oz/¾ cup hazelnuts

1 To make the ice cream, place the cream in a pan and heat slowly until almost boiling. Place the sugar and egg yolks in a bowl and whisk until creamy.

2 Pour a little cream on to the egg yolk mixture and stir. Pour into the pan and mix with the rest of the cream. Cook over a low heat, stirring constantly, until the mixture lightly coats the back of the spoon – do not allow it to boil. Pour into a bowl, stir in the vanilla and leave to cool.

3 Preheat the oven to 180°C/350°F/ Gas 4. Place the hazelnuts on a baking sheet and roast for 10–12 minutes, or until they are golden brown. Leave the nuts to cool, then place them in a food processor or blender and process until they are coarsely ground.

4 Transfer the ice cream mixture to a metal or plastic freezer container and freeze for 2 hours, or until the mixture feels firm around the edge. Remove the container from the freezer and whisk the ice cream to break down the ice crystals. Stir in the ground hazelnuts and freeze the mixture again until half-frozen. Whisk again, then freeze until firm.

COOK'S TIPS
• If you prefer, rather than whisking the semi-frozen ice cream, tip it into a food processor and process until smooth.
• There are several different types of organic figs available and they can all be used in this recipe. Choose from green-skinned figs that have an amber-coloured flesh, dark purple-skinned fruit with a deep red flesh or green/yellow-skinned figs with a pinky-coloured flesh.

5 Place the lemon grass, cinnamon stick, honey and water in a small pan and heat slowly until boiling. Simmer the mixture for 5 minutes, then leave the syrup to stand for 15 minutes.

6 Preheat the oven to 200°C/400°F/ Gas 6. Meanwhile, carefully cut the figs into quarters, leaving them intact at the bases. Place the figs in an ovenproof baking dish and pour over the honey-flavoured syrup.

7 Cover the dish tightly with foil and bake the figs for about 15 minutes, or until tender.

8 Take the ice cream from the freezer about 10 minutes before serving, to soften slightly. Transfer the figs to serving plates. Strain a little of the cooking liquid over the figs and then serve them with a scoop or two of hazelnut ice cream.

VARIATION
This recipe also works well with halved, stoned organic nectarines or peaches – cook as from step 6 and serve with the home-made ice cream.

STICKY PEAR PUDDING

Pears are at their best in autumn and, combined with other organic ingredients such as cloves, coffee and maple syrup, they form the basis of this indulgent dessert.

SERVES SIX

30ml/2 tbsp ground coffee
15ml/1 tbsp near-boiling water
4 ripe pears
juice of ½ orange
50g/2oz/½ cup toasted hazelnuts
115g/4oz/½ cup butter or
   non-hydrogenated margarine, softened
115g/4oz/generous ½ cup unrefined caster
   (superfine) sugar or rapadura, plus an
   extra 15ml/1 tbsp for baking
2 eggs, beaten
50g/2oz/½ cup self-raising (self-rising)
   flour, sifted
pinch of ground cloves
8 whole cloves (optional)
45ml/3 tbsp maple syrup
fine strips of orange rind, to decorate

For the orange cream
300ml/½ pint/1¼ cups whipping cream
15ml/1 tbsp unrefined icing
   (confectioners') sugar, sifted
finely grated rind of ½ orange

1 Preheat the oven to 180°C/350°F/
Gas 4. Lightly grease a 20cm/8in loose-based sandwich tin (shallow cake pan). Put the ground coffee in a small bowl and pour the water over. Leave to infuse for 4 minutes, then strain through a fine sieve.

2 Peel, halve and core the pears. Thinly slice across the pear halves part of the way through. Brush the pears with orange juice. Grind the hazelnuts in a coffee grinder until fine.

3 Beat the butter and the caster sugar together until very light and fluffy. Gradually beat in the eggs, then fold in the flour, ground cloves, hazelnuts and coffee.

4 Spoon the mixture into the prepared sandwich tin and level the surface with a spatula.

5 Pat the pears dry on kitchen paper, then arrange them carefully in the sponge mixture, flat side down.

6 Lightly press two whole cloves, if using, into each pear half. Brush the pears with 15ml/1 tbsp maple syrup.

7 Sprinkle 15ml/1 tbsp caster sugar over the pears. Bake for 45–50 minutes, or until firm and well-risen.

8 While the sponge is cooking, make the orange cream. Whip the cream, icing sugar and orange rind until soft peaks form. Spoon into a serving dish and chill until needed.

9 Allow the sponge to cool for about 10 minutes in the tin, then remove and place on a serving plate. Lightly brush with the remaining maple syrup before decorating with orange rind and serving warm with the orange cream.

COOK'S TIP
Organic pears are a good source of soluble fibre and are great at lowering cholesterol and easing constipation. Buy slightly underripe fruit and leave them to ripen on a sunny windowsill for a few days – overripe pears go off quickly.

VARIATION
Apple and cinnamon could be used in this pudding instead of pears and cloves, with a lemon cream in place of orange cream.

CUSTARD TART with PLUMS

When this tart is made with really ripe, organic sweet plums, it makes a wonderful hot or cold weekend dessert. Serve it with thick cream, ice cream or Greek yogurt.

2 Flour a deep 18cm/7in square or 20cm/8in round loose-bottomed flan tin (tart pan). Roll out the pastry and use to line the tin. This pastry is soft at this stage, so don't worry if you have to push it into shape. Chill for another 10–20 minutes.

3 Preheat the oven to 200°C/400°F/ Gas 6. Line the pastry case with baking parchment and fill with baking beans, then bake for 15 minutes. Remove the paper and baking beans, reduce the oven temperature to 180°C/350°F/Gas 4 and bake for a further 5–10 minutes until the base is dry.

4 Halve and stone the plums, and arrange them neatly in the pastry case. Whisk together the remaining egg and egg yolks with the sugar, the milk and vanilla essence and pour over the fruit.

5 Return the tart to the oven and bake for 25–30 minutes, or until the custard is just firm to the touch. Remove the tart from the oven and allow to cool. Sprinkle with flaked almonds and dredge with icing sugar before serving with cream, ice cream or Greek yogurt.

SERVES FOUR TO SIX

175g/6oz/1½ cups plain (all-purpose) flour, sifted
pinch of salt
45ml/3 tbsp unrefined caster (superfine) sugar or rapadura
115g/4oz/½ cup unsalted (sweet) butter or non-hydrogenated margarine
2 eggs, plus 2 egg yolks
350g/12oz ripe plums
300ml/½ pint/1¼ cups milk or soya milk
few drops of vanilla essence (extract)
toasted flaked (sliced) almonds and sifted unrefined icing (confectioners') sugar, to decorate

1 Place the flour, salt, 15ml/1 tbsp of the sugar, the butter and one of the eggs in a food processor or blender and process until thoroughly combined. Tip out the mixture on to a clean, lightly floured surface and bring it together into a ball. Wrap the pastry in clear film (plastic wrap) and chill for 10 minutes to rest.

VARIATIONS
• This tart is equally delicious made with organic apricots, peaches or nectarines.
• Make a nutty pastry by replacing 15ml/ 1 tbsp of the flour with ground almonds.

BUTTERNUT SQUASH and MAPLE PIE

This American-style pie has a rich shortcrust pastry case and a creamy filling, sweetened
with maple syrup and flavoured with fresh organic ginger and a dash of brandy.

SERVES TEN

1 small butternut squash
60ml/4 tbsp water
2.5cm/1in piece of fresh root ginger,
    peeled and grated
beaten egg, to glaze
120ml/4fl oz/½ cup double (heavy) cream
    or soya cream, plus extra to serve
90ml/6 tbsp maple syrup
45ml/3 tbsp unrefined light muscovado
    (brown) sugar or rapadura
3 eggs, lightly beaten
30ml/2 tbsp brandy
1.5ml/¼ tsp grated nutmeg

For the pastry
175g/6oz/1½ cups plain (all-purpose) flour
115g/4oz/½ cup butter or
    non-hydrogenated margarine, diced
10ml/2 tsp unrefined caster (superfine)
    sugar or rapadura
1 egg, lightly beaten

1 To make the pastry, sift the flour into
a mixing bowl. Rub in the butter or
margarine until the mixture resembles
fine breadcrumbs. Add the sugar and the
egg. Mix to a dough. Wrap in clear film
(plastic wrap). Chill for 30 minutes.

2 Cut the butternut squash in half, then
peel and scoop out the seeds. Cut the
flesh into cubes and put in a pan with
the water. Cover and cook gently for
15 minutes. Remove the lid, stir in the
ginger and cook for a further 5 minutes
until all the liquid has evaporated and
the squash is tender. Cool slightly, then
purée in a food processor until smooth.

3 Roll out the pastry and use to line a
23cm/9in flan tin (tart pan). Gather up
the trimmings, re-roll them thinly, then
cut them into maple-leaf shapes. Brush
the edge of the pastry case with beaten
egg and attach the maple leaf shapes at
regular intervals to make a decorative
rim. Cover with clear film and chill for
30 minutes.

4 Put a heavy baking sheet in the oven
and preheat to 200°C/400°F/Gas 6.
Prick the pastry base with a fork, line
with foil and fill with baking beans. Bake
on the hot baking sheet for 12 minutes.

5 Remove the foil and beans and bake
the pastry case for a further 5 minutes.
Brush the base of the pastry case with
beaten egg and return to the oven for
about 3 minutes. Reduce the oven
temperature to 180°C/350°F/Gas 4.

6 Mix 200g/7oz/scant 1 cup of the
butternut purée with the cream, syrup,
sugar, eggs, brandy and grated nutmeg.
(Discard any remaining purée.) Pour
into the pastry case. Bake for about
30 minutes, or until the filling is lightly
set. Cool slightly, then serve with cream.

BAKED APPLE DUMPLINGS

A wonderful way to make the most of apples in season. The sharpness of the fruit contrasts perfectly with the maple syrup drizzled over this delightful pastry parcel.

SERVES EIGHT

8 firm cooking apples, peeled
1 egg white
130g/4½oz/⅔ cup unrefined caster
   (superfine) sugar or rapadura
45ml/3 tbsp double (heavy) cream or
   soya cream, plus extra whipped cream,
   to serve
2.5ml/½ tsp vanilla essence (extract)
250ml/8fl oz/1 cup maple syrup

For the pastry
475g/1lb 2oz/4½ cups plain
   (all-purpose) flour
350g/12oz/1½ cups butter or
   non-hydrogenated margarine, diced

1 To make the pastry, sift the flour into a large bowl. Rub in the butter until the mixture resembles fine breadcrumbs.

2 Sprinkle over 175ml/6fl oz/¾ cup water and mix until the dough holds together, adding more water if necessary. Gather into a ball. Wrap in clear film (plastic wrap) and chill for 10 minutes. Preheat the oven to 220°C/425°F/Gas 7.

3 Cutting from the stem end, core the apples without cutting through the base. Roll out the pastry thinly. Cut squares almost large enough to enclose the apples; brush with egg white and set an apple in the centre of each.

4 Cut pastry rounds to cover the tops of the cored apples. Reserve the pastry trimmings. Combine the unrefined sugar, cream and vanilla essence in a small bowl. Spoon one-eighth of the mixture into the hollow of each apple.

5 Place a pastry round on top of each apple, then bring up the sides of the pastry square to enclose it, pleating the larger piece of pastry to make a snug fit around the apple. Moisten the joins with cold water where they overlap and press down so they stick in place.

6 Make apple stalks and leaves from the pastry trimmings and use to decorate the dumplings. Set them in a large greased baking dish, at least 2cm/¾in apart. Bake for 30 minutes, then reduce the oven temperature to 180°C/350°F/Gas 4 and continue baking for 20 minutes more, or until the pastry is golden brown and the apples are tender.

7 Transfer the dumplings to a serving dish. Mix the maple syrup with the juices in the baking dish and drizzle over the dumplings. Serve the dumplings hot with whipped cream.

HOT BLACKBERRY and APPLE SOUFFLÉS

*The deliciously tart autumn flavours of blackberry and apple complement each other
perfectly to make a light, mouthwatering hot pudding.*

MAKES SIX

butter or non-hydrogenated margarine,
    for greasing
150g/5oz/¾ cup unrefined caster (superfine)
    sugar or rapadura, plus extra for dusting
350g/12oz/3 cups blackberries
1 large cooking apple, peeled and finely diced
grated rind and juice of 1 orange
3 egg whites
unrefined icing (confectioner's) sugar,
    for dusting

1 Preheat the oven to 200°C/400°F/
Gas 6. Generously grease six 150ml/
¼ pint/⅔ cup individual soufflé dishes
with butter and dust with caster sugar,
shaking out the excess sugar.

2 Put a baking sheet in the oven to
heat. Cook the blackberries, diced apple
and orange rind and juice in a pan for
about 10 minutes or until the apple has
pulped down well. Press through a sieve
into a bowl. Stir in 50g/2oz/¼ cup of the
caster sugar. Set aside to cool.

3 Put a spoonful of the fruit purée into
each prepared soufflé dish and spread
evenly. Set the dishes aside.

4 Place the egg whites in a grease-free
bowl and whisk until they form stiff
peaks. Very gradually whisk in the
remaining caster sugar to make a stiff,
glossy meringue mixture.

5 Fold in the remaining fruit purée and
spoon the flavoured meringue into the
prepared dishes. Level the tops with a
palette knife, and run a table knife
around the edge of each dish.

6 Place the dishes on the hot baking
sheet and bake for 10–15 minutes until
the soufflés have risen well and are
lightly browned. Dust the tops with
icing sugar and serve immediately.

COOK'S TIP
Running a table knife around the inside
edge of the soufflé dishes before baking
helps the soufflés to rise evenly without
sticking to the rim of the dish.

PLUM CHARLOTTES with FOAMY CALVADOS SAUCE

A variety of different types of organic plums are available at this time of year – from tangy yellow greengages to sweet and juicy Victorias.

SERVES FOUR

115g/4oz/½ cup butter or
    non-hydrogenated margarine, melted
50g/2oz/¼ cup demerara (raw) sugar
    or rapadura
450g/1lb ripe plums, stoned (pitted) and
    thickly sliced
25g/1oz/2 tbsp unrefined caster (superfine)
    sugar or rapadura
30ml/2 tbsp water
1.5ml/¼ tsp ground cinnamon
25g/1oz/¼ cup ground almonds
8–10 large slices of white or wholemeal
    (whole-wheat) bread

For the Calvados sauce
3 egg yolks
40g/1½oz/3 tbsp unrefined caster
    (superfine) sugar or rapadura
30ml/2 tbsp Calvados

1 Preheat the oven to 190°C/375°F/ Gas 5. Line the base of four individual 10cm/4in-diameter deep, earthenware ramekin dishes with baking parchment. Brush evenly and thoroughly with a little of the melted butter or margarine, then sprinkle each dish with a little of the demerara sugar, rotating the dish in your hands to coat each dish evenly.

VARIATIONS
• Slices of peeled pear or eating apples can be used in this recipe instead of the stoned, sliced plums.
• If you cannot find organic Calvados any organic fruit-based spirit will work in this dish.

2 Place the stoned plum slices in a pan with the caster sugar, water and ground cinnamon and cook gently for 5 minutes, or until the plums have softened slightly. Leave the plums to cool, then stir in the ground almonds.

3 Cut the crusts off the bread and then use a plain pastry cutter to cut out four rounds to fit the bases of the ramekins. Dip the bread rounds into the melted butter and fit them into the dishes. Cut four more rounds to fit the tops of the dishes and set aside.

4 Cut the remaining bread into strips, dip into the melted butter and use to line the sides of the ramekins completely.

5 Divide the plum mixture among the lined dishes and level the tops with the back of a spoon. Place the bread rounds on top and brush with the remaining butter. Place the ramekins on a baking sheet and bake for 25 minutes.

6 Make the sauce just before the charlottes are ready. Place the egg yolks and caster sugar in a large bowl, and whisk them together until pale. Place the bowl over a pan of simmering water and whisk in the Calvados. Continue whisking until the mixture is very light and frothy.

7 Remove the charlottes from the oven and turn out on to warm serving plates. Pour a little sauce over and around the charlottes and serve immediately.

COOK'S TIP
For an extra creamy dessert, serve the puddings with Greek (US strained plain) yogurt or crème fraîche.

PARSNIP CAKE with ORANGE ICING

This fabulous vegan cake is similar to the ever-popular carrot cake, but uses non-dairy alternatives to margarine and cream cheese.

SERVES TEN

250g/9oz/2¼ cups wholemeal (whole-
    wheat) self-raising (self-rising) flour
15ml/1 tbsp baking powder
5ml/1 tsp ground cinnamon
5ml/1 tsp freshly ground nutmeg
130g/4½oz/9 tbsp vegan margarine
130g/4½oz/scant ½ cup unrefined soft
    light brown sugar or rapadura
250g/9oz parsnips, coarsely grated
1 banana, mashed
finely grated rind and juice of 1 orange

For the topping
225g/8oz/1 cup organic soya
    cream cheese
45ml/3 tbsp unrefined icing
    (confectioner's) sugar
juice of 1 small orange
fine strips of orange peel

1 Preheat the oven to 180°C/350°F/
Gas 4. Lightly grease and line the base
of a 900g/2lb loaf tin (pan).

2 Sift the flour, baking powder and
spices into a large bowl. Add any bran
remaining in the sieve.

COOK'S TIP
If you can't find self-raising wholemeal
flour, use ordinary wholemeal flour and
add an extra 15ml/1 tbsp baking powder.

VARIATION
Serve the cake as a dessert with a
generous spoonful of organic natural
(plain) yogurt, crème fraîche or soya
cream, flavoured with grated orange rind
or a little Calvados.

3 Melt the margarine in a pan, add the
sugar and stir until dissolved. Make a well
in the flour mixture, then add the
melted margarine and sugar. Mix in the
parsnips, banana and orange rind and
juice. Spoon the mixture into the
prepared tin and level the top with the
back of a spoon.

4 Bake for 45–50 minutes until a skewer
inserted into the centre of the cake
comes out clean. Allow the cake to
cool slightly before removing from the
tin, then transfer to a wire rack to
cool completely.

5 To make the topping, beat together the
cream cheese, icing sugar, orange juice
and strips of orange peel until smooth.
Spread the topping evenly over the cake.

COUNTRY APPLE CAKE

This perennial favourite is a great way to take advantage of the season's apple harvest.
There are any number of organic apples available nowadays, including heirloom and
almost-lost local varieties, which makes cooking and eating this cake a real treat.

MAKES ONE 18CM/7IN CAKE

115g/4oz/½ cup soft non-hydrogenated
   margarine
115g/4oz/½ cup unrefined soft light brown
   sugar or rapadura
2 eggs, beaten
115g/4oz/1 cup self-raising (self-rising)
   flour, sifted
50g/2oz/½ cup rice flour
5ml/1 tsp baking powder
10ml/2 tsp mixed (apple-pie) spice
1 cooking apple, cored and chopped
115g/4oz/scant 1 cup raisins
about 60ml/4 tbsp milk or soya milk
15g/½oz/2 tbsp flaked (sliced) almonds

1 Preheat the oven to 160°C/325°F/
Gas 3. Lightly grease and line a deep 18cm/
7in round, loose-bottomed cake tin (pan).

2 Cream the margarine and sugar in a
mixing bowl. Gradually add the eggs,
then fold in the flours, baking powder
and spice.

3 Stir in the chopped apple, raisins and
enough of the milk to make a soft,
dropping consistency.

4 Turn the mixture into the prepared tin
and level the surface. Sprinkle the flaked
almonds over the top. Bake the cake for
1–1¼ hours until risen, firm to the touch
and golden brown.

5 Cool the apple cake in the tin for
about 10 minutes, then turn out on to a
wire rack to cool. Cut into slices when
cold. Alternatively, serve the cake warm,
in slices, with custard or ice cream. Store
the cold cake in an airtight container or
wrapped in foil.

VARIATIONS
• Use sultanas (golden raisins) or
chopped dried apricots or pears instead
of the raisins.
• A wide variety of organic ice creams
is available from independent dairies and
supermarkets – vanilla goes particularly
well with this cake.

OAT and RAISIN DROP SCONES

Serve these easy-to-make organic scones at tea time or as a dessert – or even a special breakfast or brunch – with real maple syrup or clear honey.

MAKES ABOUT SIXTEEN

75g/3oz/⅔ cup self-raising (self-rising) flour
2.5ml/½ tsp baking powder
50g/2oz/scant ½ cup raisins
25g/1oz/¼ cup fine oatmeal
25g/1oz/2 tbsp unrefined caster (superfine)
    sugar or rapadura
grated rind of 1 orange
2 egg yolks
10g/¼oz/½ tbsp unsalted (sweet) butter
    or non-hydrogenated margarine, melted
200ml/7fl oz/scant 1 cup single (light)
    cream or soya cream
200ml/7fl oz/scant 1 cup water
sunflower oil, for greasing
icing (confectioner's) sugar, for dusting

1 Sift the self-raising flour and baking powder together into a large mixing bowl.

COOK'S TIP
Wrap the cooked scones in a clean dishtowel to keep them soft.

2 Add the raisins, oatmeal, sugar and orange rind. Gradually beat in the egg yolks, butter, cream and water to make a creamy batter.

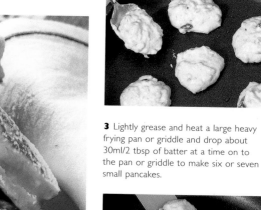

3 Lightly grease and heat a large heavy frying pan or griddle and drop about 30ml/2 tbsp of batter at a time on to the pan or griddle to make six or seven small pancakes.

4 Cook over a moderate heat until bubbles show on the scones' surface, then turn them over and cook for a further 2 minutes until golden.

5 Transfer to a plate and dust with icing sugar. Keep warm while cooking the remaining mixture. Serve warm.

CARAMELIZED ONION and WALNUT SCONES

These scones are very good buttered and served with mature Cheddar cheese. Make small
scones to use as a base for cocktail savouries, served topped with a little soft goat's cheese.

4 Add the cooked onion and cumin mixture, chopped walnuts and chopped fresh thyme, then bind to make a soft, but not sticky, dough with the buttermilk.

5 Roll or pat out the mixture to an even thickness of just over 1cm/½in. Stamp out 10–12 scones using a 5–6cm/ 2–2½in plain round cutter.

6 Place the scones on a floured baking tray, glaze with the milk or soya milk and scatter with a little salt and the remaining cumin seeds. Bake the scones for 12–15 minutes until well-risen and golden brown. Allow to cool for a few minutes on a wire rack and serve warm spread with butter, non-hydrogenated margarine or goat's cheese.

MAKES TEN TO TWELVE

90g/3½oz/7 tbsp butter or
    non-hydrogenated margarine
15ml/1 tbsp olive oil
1 Spanish onion, chopped
5ml/1 tsp cumin seeds, lightly crushed
200g/7oz/1¾ cups self-raising
    (self-rising) flour
5ml/1 tsp baking powder
25g/1oz/¼ cup fine oatmeal
5ml/1 tsp light unrefined muscovado
    (brown) sugar
90g/3½oz/scant 1 cup chopped walnuts
5ml/1 tsp chopped fresh thyme
120–150ml/4–5fl oz/½–⅔ cup buttermilk
a little milk or soya milk
sea salt and ground black pepper

1 Melt 15g/½oz/1 tbsp of the butter with the oil in a small pan and cook the onion gently, covered, for 10–12 minutes. Uncover, then continue to cook gently until it begins to brown.

2 Add half the cumin seeds and increase the heat slightly. Continue to cook, stirring occasionally, until the onion begins to caramelize. Cool. Preheat the oven to 200°C/400°F/Gas 6.

3 Sift the flour and baking powder into a large bowl and add the oatmeal, sugar, 2.5ml/½ tsp salt and black pepper. Add the remaining butter or margarine and rub in until the mixture resembles fine breadcrumbs.

FRUIT, NUT AND SEED TEABREAD

Cut into slices and spread with a little butter or non-hydrogenated margarine,
jam or honey, this teabread makes an ideal breakfast bread. The dried fruit,
nuts and seeds mean it is a fine source of fibre.

MAKES ONE 900G/2LB LOAF

115g/4oz/⅔ cup dried dates, chopped
115g/4oz/½ cup dried apricots, chopped
115g/4oz/1 cup sultanas (golden raisins)
115g/4oz/½ cup unrefined soft light brown
  sugar or rapadura
225g/8oz/2 cups self-raising (self-rising)
  flour
5ml/1 tsp baking powder
10ml/2 tsp mixed (apple pie) spice
75g/3oz/¾ cup chopped mixed nuts
75g/3oz/¾ cup mixed seeds, such as
  linseed, sunflower and sesame seeds
2 eggs, beaten
150ml/¼ pint/⅔ cup semi-skimmed
  (low-fat) milk or soya milk

COOK'S TIPS
• Use wholemeal (whole-wheat) self-raising (self-rising) flour for an unbeatable nutty flavour.
• Organic dates have an extremely sweet taste, which makes them wonderful to bake with.
• Try adding hemp seeds to the seed mixture for a really nutritious touch.

1 Preheat the oven to 180°C/350°F/ Gas 4. Lightly grease a 900g/2lb loaf tin (pan). Place the chopped dates and apricots and sultanas in a large mixing bowl and stir in the sugar.

2 Place the flour, baking powder, mixed spice, mixed nuts and seeds in a separate bowl and mix well.

3 Stir the eggs and milk into the fruit mixture, then add the flour mixture and beat together until well mixed.

4 Spoon the mixture into the prepared tin and level the surface. Bake for about 1 hour until the teabread is firm to the touch and lightly browned.

5 Allow to cool in the tin for a few minutes, then turn out on to a wire rack to cool completely. Serve warm or cold, cut into slices. Wrap the teabread in foil to store.

HUNGARIAN FRUIT BREAD

When dried, many of the nutrients and sugars in fruit are concentrated but so, unfortunately, are any pesticide residues. So, to ensure a clear conscience as you tuck into a slice of this delightful light bread, always use organic dried fruits – a much healthier choice.

SERVES EIGHT TO TEN

sunflower oil, for greasing
7 egg whites
175g/6oz/scant 1 cup unrefined caster
   (superfine) sugar or rapadura
115g/4oz/1 cup flaked (sliced)
   almonds, toasted
115g/4oz/¾ cup sultanas (golden raisins)
grated rind of 1 lemon
165g/5½oz/1⅓ cups plain (all-purpose)
   flour, sifted, plus extra for flouring
75g/3oz/6 tbsp butter or
   non-hydrogenated margarine, melted

1 Preheat the oven to 180°C/350°F/ Gas 4 and grease and flour a 1kg/2¼lb loaf tin (pan). Whisk the egg whites until they are very stiff, but not crumbly. Fold in the sugar gradually, then the flaked, toasted almonds, sultanas and lemon rind.

2 Fold the flour and butter into the mixture and tip it into the prepared tin. Bake for about 45 minutes until well risen and pale golden brown. Cool for a few minutes in the tin, then turn out and serve warm or cold, in slices.

WINTER

Warming comfort food helps keep out winter chills. Root vegetables such as swede (rutabaga), carrots, turnips and parsnips are readily available and can be included in hearty soups, stews and casseroles. For vegetarians, substantial main courses include wholesome pulses and spices – try parsnips and chickpeas in garlic, onion, chilli and ginger paste. Rich, meaty dishes include traditional chilli con carne and irresistible boeuf bourguignonne – delicious served with mashed root vegetables and organic red wine. Winter fish dishes feature strong-flavoured ingredients: try smoked haddock with mustard cabbage. Satisfying winter treats include mouthwatering orange marmalade chocolate loaf.

WINTER FARMHOUSE SOUP

Root vegetables form the base of this chunky, minestrone-style main meal soup.
Always choose organic vegetables and vary according to what you have to hand.

SERVES FOUR

30ml/2 tbsp olive oil
1 onion, roughly chopped
3 carrots, cut into large chunks
175–200g/6–7oz turnips, cut into
    large chunks
about 175g/6oz swede (rutabaga), cut into
    large chunks
400g/14oz can chopped Italian tomatoes
15ml/1 tbsp tomato purée (paste)
5ml/1 tsp dried mixed herbs
5ml/1 tsp dried oregano
50g/2oz dried (bell) peppers, washed and
    thinly sliced (optional)
1.5 litres/2½ pints/6¼ cups vegetable
    stock or water
50g/2oz/½ cup dried macaroni
400g/14oz can red kidney beans, rinsed
    and drained
30ml/2 tbsp chopped fresh flat leaf parsley
sea salt and ground black pepper
freshly grated Parmesan cheese or premium
    Italian-style vegetarian cheese, to serve

1 Heat the olive oil in a large pan, add the onion and cook over a low heat for about 5 minutes until softened. Add the carrot, turnip and swede chunks, canned chopped tomatoes, tomato purée, dried mixed herbs, dried oregano and dried peppers, if using. Stir in a little salt and plenty of pepper to taste.

2 Pour in the vegetable stock or water and bring to the boil. Stir well, cover the pan, then lower the heat and simmer for 30 minutes, stirring occasionally.

3 Add the pasta to the pan and bring quickly to the boil, stirring. Lower the heat and simmer, uncovered, for about 8 minutes until the pasta is only just tender, or according to the instructions on the packet. Stir frequently.

4 Stir in the kidney beans. Heat through for 2–3 minutes, then remove the pan from the heat and stir in the parsley. Taste the soup for seasoning. Serve hot in warmed soup bowls, with grated cheese handed separately.

MOROCCAN SPICED MUTTON SOUP

Classic north African spices – ginger, turmeric and cinnamon – are combined with chickpeas and mutton to make this hearty, warming main-course soup.

SERVES SIX

75g/3oz/½ cup chickpeas, soaked overnight
15g/½oz/1 tbsp butter or 15ml/1 tbsp
    olive oil
225g/8oz mutton, cut into cubes
1 onion, chopped
450g/1lb tomatoes, peeled and chopped
a few celery leaves, chopped
30ml/2 tbsp chopped fresh parsley
15ml/1 tbsp chopped fresh coriander
    (cilantro)
2.5ml/½ tsp ground ginger
2.5ml/½ tsp ground turmeric
5ml/1 tsp ground cinnamon
1.75 litres/3 pints/7½ cups water
75g/3oz/scant ½ cup green lentils
75g/3oz/¾ cup vermicelli or soup pasta
2 egg yolks
juice of ½–1 lemon, to taste
sea salt and ground black pepper
fresh coriander (cilantro), to garnish
lemon wedges, to serve

1 Drain the chickpeas and set aside. Heat the butter or oil in a large pan and fry the mutton and onion for 2–3 minutes, stirring, until the mutton is just browned.

2 Add the chopped tomatoes, celery leaves, herbs and spices and season well with ground black pepper. Cook for about 1 minute, then stir in the water and add the green lentils and the soaked, drained and rinsed chickpeas.

3 Slowly bring to the boil and skim the surface to remove the froth. Boil rapidly for 10 minutes, then reduce the heat and simmer very gently for 2 hours, or until the chickpeas are very tender.

4 Season with salt and pepper, then add the vermicelli or soup pasta to the pan and cook for 5–6 minutes until it is just tender. If the soup is very thick at this stage, add a little more water.

5 Beat the egg yolks with the lemon juice and stir into the simmering soup. Immediately remove the soup from the heat and stir until thickened. Pour into warmed serving bowls and garnish with plenty of fresh coriander. Serve the soup with lemon wedges.

COOK'S TIP
If you have forgotten to soak the chickpeas overnight, place them in a pan with about four times their volume of cold water. Bring very slowly to the boil, then cover the pan, remove it from the heat and leave to stand for 45 minutes before using as described in the recipe.

CHICKEN, LEEK and CELERY SOUP

This makes a substantial main course soup with fresh crusty bread. You will need nothing more than a mixed green salad or fresh winter fruit to follow, such as satsumas, tangerines or apricots.

SERVES FOUR TO SIX

1.3kg/3lb chicken
1 small head of celery, trimmed
1 onion, coarsely chopped
1 fresh bay leaf
a few fresh parsley stalks
a few fresh tarragon sprigs
2.5 litres/4 pints/10 cups cold water
3 large leeks
65g/2½oz/5 tbsp butter or 75ml/5 tbsp
   olive oil
2 potatoes, cut into chunks
150ml/¼ pint/⅔ cup dry white wine
30–45ml/2–3 tbsp single (light) or soya
   cream (optional)
sea salt and ground black pepper
90g/3½oz pancetta, grilled until crisp,
   to garnish

1 Cut the breasts off the chicken and set aside. Chop the rest of the chicken carcass into 8–10 pieces and place in a large pan or stockpot.

2 Chop 4–5 of the outer sticks of the head of celery and add them to the pan with the coarsely chopped onion. Tie the bay leaf, parsley stalks and tarragon sprigs together to make a bouquet garni and add to the pan. Pour in the cold water to cover the ingredients and bring to the boil. Reduce the heat and cover the pan with a lid, then simmer for 1½ hours.

3 Remove the chicken from the pan using a slotted spoon and cut off and reserve the meat. Strain the stock through a sieve, then return it to the cleaned pan and boil rapidly until it has reduced in volume to about 1.5 litres/2½ pints/6¼ cups.

4 Meanwhile, set about 150g/5oz of the leeks aside. Slice the remaining leeks and the remaining celery, reserving any celery leaves. Chop the celery leaves and set them aside to garnish the soup or reserve a few of the leek pieces.

5 Heat half the butter or oil in a large, heavy pan. Add the sliced leeks and celery, cover and cook over a low heat for about 10 minutes, or until the vegetables are softened but not browned. Add the potatoes, wine and 1.2 litres/2 pints/5 cups of the stock.

6 Season with a little salt and plenty of black pepper, bring to the boil and reduce the heat. Part-cover the pan and simmer the soup for 15–20 minutes, or until the potatoes are cooked.

COOK'S TIP
There are a vast number of different varieties of organic potatoes but all fall into two main types: floury and waxy. Floury potatoes such as Maris Piper and Estima are ideal for soups, mashing or baking. Waxy potatoes such as Charlotte or Pink Fir Apple are delicious simply boiled and served with butter.

7 Meanwhile, skin the reserved chicken breasts and cut the flesh into small pieces. Melt the remaining butter or oil in a frying pan, add the chicken and fry for 5–7 minutes until cooked.

8 Thickly slice the reserved leeks, add to the frying pan and cook, stirring occasionally, for a further 3–4 minutes until they are just cooked.

9 Process the soup with the cooked chicken from the stock in a food processor or blender. Taste and adjust the seasoning, and add more stock if the soup is very thick.

10 Stir in the cream, if using, and the chicken and leek mixture. Reheat the soup gently. Serve in warmed bowls. Crumble the pancetta over the soup and sprinkle with the chopped celery leaves or reserved leek slices.

VARIATIONS
• If you prefer, use ready-cut chicken portions instead of jointing a whole chicken.
• Streaky (fatty) bacon can be used instead of pancetta to add a delicious flavour to the soup.

SPICED ONION KOFTAS

These delicious Indian onion fritters are made with chickpea flour, otherwise known as gram flour or besan, which has a distinctive nutty flavour. Serve with chutney or a yogurt dip.

3 Add the chickpea flour and baking powder to the onion mixture in the bowl, then use your hand to mix all the ingredients thoroughly.

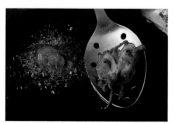

4 Shape the mixture by hand into 12–15 koftas about the size of golf balls.

MAKES TWELVE TO FIFTEEN

675g/1½lb onions, halved and thinly sliced
5ml/1 tsp sea salt
5ml/1 tsp ground coriander
5ml/1 tsp ground cumin
2.5ml/½ tsp ground turmeric
1–2 green chillies, seeded and
    finely chopped
45ml/3 tbsp chopped fresh coriander
    (cilantro)
90g/3½oz/¾ cup chickpea flour
2.5ml/½ tsp baking powder
sunflower oil, for deep-frying

To serve
lemon wedges (optional)
fresh coriander sprigs
yogurt and herb dip (see Cook's Tip)

1 Place the onions in a colander, add the salt and toss. Place on a plate and leave to stand for 45 minutes, tossing once or twice. Rinse the onions, then squeeze out any excess moisture.

2 Place the onions in a bowl. Add the ground coriander, cumin, turmeric, finely chopped chillies and chopped fresh coriander. Mix well.

COOK'S TIP
To make a yogurt and herb dip to serve with the koftas, stir 30ml/2 tbsp each of chopped fresh coriander (cilantro) and mint into about 225g/8oz/1 cup set natural (plain) yogurt. Season with salt, ground toasted cumin seeds and a pinch of muscovado (brown) sugar

5 Heat the sunflower oil for deep-frying to 180–190°C/350–375°F, or until a cube of day-old bread browns in about 30–45 seconds. Fry the koftas, four to five at a time, until deep golden brown all over. Remove with a slotted spoon and drain each batch on kitchen paper and keep warm until all the koftas are cooked. Serve the koftas warm with lemon wedges (if using), coriander sprigs and a yogurt and herb dip.

LENTIL DHAL with ROASTED GARLIC

This spicy lentil dhal makes a sustaining and comforting meal when served with brown rice or Indian breads and any dry-spiced dish, particularly a cauliflower or potato dish.

SERVES FOUR TO SIX

40g/1½oz/3 tbsp butter or ghee
1 onion, chopped
2 green chillies, seeded and chopped
15ml/1 tbsp chopped fresh root ginger
225g/8oz/1 cup yellow or red lentils
900ml/1½ pints/3¾ cups water
45ml/3 tbsp roasted garlic purée (paste)
5ml/1 tsp ground cumin
5ml/1 tsp ground coriander
200g/7oz tomatoes, peeled and diced
a little lemon juice
sea salt and ground black pepper
30–45ml/2–3 tbsp coriander (cilantro) sprigs, to garnish

For the spicy garnish

30ml/2 tbsp sunflower oil
4–5 shallots, sliced
2 garlic cloves, thinly sliced
15g/½oz/1 tbsp butter or ghee
5ml/1 tsp cumin seeds
5ml/1 tsp mustard seeds
3–4 small dried red chillies
8–10 fresh curry leaves

1 First begin the spicy garnish. Heat the oil in a large, heavy pan. Add the shallots and fry them over a medium heat for 5–10 minutes, stirring occasionally, until they are crisp and browned. Add the garlic and cook, stirring frequently, for a moment or two until the garlic colours slightly. Remove the pan from the heat and use a slotted spoon to remove the shallots and garlic from the pan and set aside.

COOK'S TIP

Ghee is clarified butter that has had all the milk solids removed by heating – it was originally made to extend the keeping qualities of butter in India. It is the main cooking fat used in Indian cooking. Because the milk solids have been removed, ghee has a high smoking point and can therefore be cooked at higher temperatures than ordinary butter. Look for organic ghee in whole food stores.

2 Melt the 40g/1½oz/3 tbsp butter or ghee for the dhal in the pan, add the onion, chillies and ginger, and cook for 10 minutes until golden.

3 Stir in the yellow or red lentils and water, then bring to the boil, reduce the heat and part-cover the pan. Simmer, stirring occasionally, for 50–60 minutes until it is the same consistency as a very thick soup.

4 Stir in the roasted garlic purée, cumin and ground coriander, then season with salt and pepper to taste. Cook the dhal for a further 10–15 minutes, uncovered, stirring frequently.

5 Stir in the tomatoes and then adjust the seasoning, adding a little lemon juice to taste if necessary.

6 To finish the spicy garnish: melt the butter or ghee in a frying pan. Add the cumin and mustard seeds and fry until the mustard seeds begin to pop. Stir in the small dried red chillies and fresh curry leaves, then immediately swirl the mixture into the cooked dhal. Garnish with coriander and the spicy fried shallots and garlic and serve.

JERUSALEM ARTICHOKES with GARLIC

The slightly smoky and earthy flavour of Jerusalem artichokes is excellent with garlic, shallots and smoked bacon. These are good with chicken, pork or a classic nut roast.

SERVES FOUR

50g/2oz/¼ cup butter or 50ml/3½ tbsp
  olive oil
115g/4oz smoked bacon, chopped
800g/1¾lb Jerusalem artichokes
8–12 garlic cloves, peeled
115g/4oz shallots, chopped
75ml/5 tbsp water
30ml/2 tbsp olive oil
25g/1oz/½ cup fresh white or wholemeal
  (whole-wheat) breadcrumbs
30–45ml/2–3 tbsp chopped fresh parsley
sea salt and ground black pepper

1 Melt half the butter or heat half the olive oil in a heavy frying pan, add the chopped bacon and cook until it is brown and just beginning to crisp. Remove half the bacon from the frying pan and set aside.

COOK'S TIP
If you are unable to find organic shallots, try using another mild and sweet allium instead, such as red onions. Their dark colour also complements the creamy artichokes in this dish.

2 Add the artichokes, garlic and shallots to the pan, and cook, stirring frequently, until the artichokes and garlic begin to brown slightly.

3 Season with salt and black pepper to taste and stir in the water. Cover and cook for a further 8–10 minutes, shaking the pan occasionally.

4 Uncover the pan, increase the heat and cook for 5 minutes, or until all the moisture has evaporated and the artichokes are tender.

5 In another frying pan, heat the remaining butter or oil with the 30ml/ 2 tbsp olive oil. Add the white or wholemeal breadcrumbs and fry over a moderate heat, stirring frequently with a wooden spoon, until crisp and golden. Stir in the chopped parsley and the reserved cooked bacon.

6 Combine the artichokes with the crispy breadcrumb and bacon mixture, mixing well. Season to taste with a little salt and plenty of ground black pepper, if necessary. Transfer to a warmed serving dish and serve immediately.

BRAISED RED CABBAGE with BEETROOT

Cook this vibrantly coloured dish in the oven at the same time as a pork casserole or joint of meat for a simple, easy-to-prepare meal.

SERVES SIX TO EIGHT

675g/1½lb red cabbage
1 Spanish onion, thinly sliced
30ml/2 tbsp olive oil
2 tart eating apples, peeled,
   cored and sliced
300ml/½ pint/1¼ cups vegetable stock
60ml/4 tbsp red wine vinegar
375g/13oz raw beetroot (beet), peeled
   and coarsely grated
sea salt and ground black pepper

COOK'S TIP

When buying any type of cabbage, choose one that is firm and heavy for its size. The leaves should look healthy – avoid any with curling leaves or blemishes.

1 Cut the red cabbage into fine shreds, discarding any tough outer leaves and the core, and place in an ovenproof dish.

2 Place the thinly sliced onion and the olive oil in a frying pan and sauté until the onion is soft and golden.

3 Preheat the oven to 190°C/375°F/ Gas 5. Stir the apple slices, vegetable stock and wine vinegar into the onions, then transfer to the dish. Season with salt and pepper, and cover.

4 Cook the cabbage for 1 hour. Stir in the beetroot, re-cover the dish and cook for a further 20–30 minutes, or until the cabbage and beetroot are tender.

PARSNIPS and CHICKPEAS in GARLIC, ONION, CHILLI and GINGER PASTE

Organic root vegetables, such as parsnips, often have a knobbly appearance that makes them interesting and individual, and their flavours are sweeter and more intense.

SERVES FOUR

200g/7oz/1 cup dried chickpeas, soaked
    overnight in cold water, then drained
7 garlic cloves, finely chopped
1 small onion, chopped
5cm/2in piece fresh root ginger, chopped
2 green chillies, seeded and finely chopped
450ml/¾ pint/scant 2 cups plus
    75ml/5 tbsp water
60ml/4 tbsp sunflower oil
5ml/1 tsp cumin seeds
10ml/2 tsp ground coriander seeds
5ml/1 tsp ground turmeric
2.5–5ml/½–1 tsp chilli powder
    or mild paprika
50g/2oz/½ cup cashew nuts, toasted
    and ground
250g/9oz tomatoes, peeled and chopped
900g/2lb parsnips, cut into chunks
5ml/1 tsp ground roasted cumin seeds
juice of 1 lime, to taste
sea salt and ground black pepper

To serve
fresh coriander (cilantro) leaves
a few cashew nuts, toasted
natural (plain) yogurt
naan bread or chapatis

1 Put the soaked chickpeas in a pan, cover with cold water and bring to the boil. Boil vigorously for 10 minutes, then reduce the heat so that the water boils steadily. Cook for 1–1½ hours, or until the chickpeas are tender. (The cooking time depends on how long the chickpeas have been stored.) Drain and set aside.

2 Set 10ml/2 tsp of the finely chopped garlic aside, then place the remainder in a food processor or blender with the onion, ginger and half the chopped chillies. Add the 75ml/5 tbsp water and process to make a smooth paste.

COOK'S TIP
Do not add salt to the water when cooking dried chickpeas, as this will toughen them.

3 Heat the oil in a frying pan and cook the cumin seeds for 30 seconds. Stir in the coriander seeds, turmeric, chilli powder or paprika and the ground cashew nuts. Add the ginger paste and cook, stirring frequently, until the water begins to evaporate. Add the tomatoes and stir-fry for 2–3 minutes.

4 Mix in the cooked chickpeas and parsnip chunks with the 450ml/¾ pint/ scant 2 cups water, a little salt and plenty of black pepper. Bring to the boil, stir, then simmer, uncovered, for 15–20 minutes until the parsnips are completely tender.

5 Reduce the liquid, if necessary, by bringing the sauce to the boil and then boiling fiercely until the sauce is thick. Add the ground roasted cumin with more salt and/or lime juice to taste. Stir in the reserved garlic and green chilli, and cook for a further 1–2 minutes. Scatter the fresh coriander leaves and toasted cashew nuts over and serve straight away with yogurt and warmed naan bread or chapatis.

BARLEY RISOTTO with ROASTED SQUASH and LEEKS

This is more like a pilaff made with slightly chewy, nutty-flavoured pearl barley than a classic risotto. Sweet organic leeks and roasted squash are superb with this earthy grain.

SERVES FOUR TO FIVE

200g/7oz/1 cup pearl barley
1 butternut squash, peeled, seeded and
    cut into chunks
10ml/2 tsp chopped fresh thyme
60ml/4 tbsp olive oil
25g/1oz/2 tbsp butter
4 leeks, cut into fairly thick diagonal slices
2 garlic cloves, finely chopped
175g/6oz/2½ cups chestnut mushrooms, sliced
2 carrots, coarsely grated
about 120ml/4fl oz/½ cup vegetable stock
30ml/2 tbsp chopped fresh flat leaf parsley
50g/2oz/⅔ cup Parmesan cheese or
    premium Italian-style vegetarian cheese,
    grated or shaved
45ml/3 tbsp pumpkin seeds, toasted, or
    chopped walnuts
sea salt and ground black pepper

1 Rinse the barley, then cook it in simmering water, keeping the pan part-covered, for 35–45 minutes, or until tender. Drain. Preheat the oven to 200°C/400°F/Gas 6.

2 Place the squash in a roasting pan with half the thyme. Season with pepper and toss with half the oil. Roast, stirring once, for 30–35 minutes, until the squash is tender and beginning to brown.

3 Heat half the butter with the remaining olive oil in a large frying pan. Cook the leeks and garlic gently for 5 minutes. Add the mushrooms and remaining thyme, then cook until the liquid from the mushrooms evaporates and they begin to fry.

4 Stir in the carrots and cook for about 2 minutes, then add the barley and most of the vegetable stock. Season well and part-cover the pan. Cook for a further 5 minutes. Pour in the remaining stock if the mixture seems dry.

5 Stir in the parsley, the remaining butter and half the cheese, then stir in the squash. Add seasoning to taste and serve immediately, sprinkled with the toasted pumpkin seeds or walnuts and the remaining cheese.

VARIATIONS
• Make the risotto with organic brown rice instead of the barley – cook following the packet instructions and continue from step 2.
• Any type of organic mushrooms can be used in this recipe – try sliced field (portabello) mushrooms for a hearty flavour.

PEPPERS FILLED with SPICED VEGETABLES

Indian spices season the potato and aubergine stuffing in these colourful baked peppers.
They are good with brown rice and a lentil dhal. Alternatively, serve them with a salad,
Indian breads and a cucumber or mint and yogurt raita.

SERVES SIX

6 large evenly shaped red (bell) or
    yellow (bell) peppers
500g/1¼lb waxy potatoes
1 small onion, chopped
4–5 garlic cloves, chopped
5cm/2in piece fresh root ginger, chopped
1–2 fresh green chillies, seeded
    and chopped
105ml/7 tbsp water
90–105ml/6–7 tbsp sunflower oil
1 aubergine (eggplant), diced
10ml/2 tsp cumin seeds
5ml/1 tsp kalonji seeds
2.5ml/½ tsp ground turmeric
5ml/1 tsp ground coriander
5ml/1 tsp ground toasted cumin seeds
pinch of cayenne pepper
about 30ml/2 tbsp lemon juice
sea salt and ground black pepper
30ml/2 tbsp chopped fresh coriander
    (cilantro), to garnish

1 Cut the tops off the red or yellow peppers, then remove and discard the seeds. Cut a thin slice off the base of the peppers, if necessary, to make them stand upright.

2 Bring a large pan of lightly salted water to the boil. Add the peppers and cook for 5–6 minutes. Drain and leave them upside down in a colander.

COOK'S TIP
The hottest part of a chilli is the white membrane that connects the seeds to the flesh. Removing the seeds and membrane before cooking gives a milder flavour.

3 Cook the potatoes in lightly salted, boiling water for 10–12 minutes until just tender. Drain, cool and peel, then cut into 1cm/½in dice.

4 Put the onion, garlic, ginger and green chillies in a food processor or blender with 60ml/4 tbsp of the water and process to a purée.

5 Heat 45ml/3 tbsp of the sunflower oil in a large, deep frying pan and cook the diced aubergine, stirring occasionally, until it is evenly browned on all sides. Remove from the pan and set aside. Add another 30ml/2 tbsp of the sunflower oil to the pan, add the diced potatoes and cook until lightly browned on all sides. Remove the potatoes from the pan and set aside.

6 If necessary, add another 15ml/1 tbsp sunflower oil to the pan, then add the cumin and kalonji seeds. Fry briefly until the seeds darken, then add the turmeric, coriander and ground cumin. Cook for 15 seconds. Stir in the onion and garlic purée and fry, scraping the pan with a spatula, until the onions begin to brown.

7 Return the potatoes and aubergine to the pan, season with salt, pepper and 1–2 pinches of cayenne. Add the remaining water and 15ml/1 tbsp lemon juice and then cook, stirring, until the liquid evaporates. Preheat the oven to 190°C/375°F/Gas 5.

8 Fill the peppers with the spiced vegetable mixture and place on a lightly greased baking tray. Brush the peppers with a little oil and bake for 30–35 minutes until they are cooked. Allow to cool a little, then sprinkle with a little more lemon juice, garnish with the coriander and serve.

COOK'S TIP
Kalonji, or nigella as it is also known, is a tiny black seed. It is widely used in Indian cookery, especially sprinkled over breads or in potato dishes. It has a mild, slightly nutty flavour and is best toasted for a few seconds in a dry or lightly oiled frying pan over a medium heat before using in a recipe. This helps to bring out its flavour, as with most spices.

MARMALADE-GLAZED GOOSE

Succulent roast goose is the classic centrepiece for a traditional British winter family lunch. Red cabbage cooked with leeks, and braised fennel are tasty accompaniments.

SERVES EIGHT

4.5kg/10lb goose
1 cooking apple, peeled, cored and
    cut into eighths
1 large onion, cut into eighths
bunch of fresh sage, plus extra to garnish
30ml/2 tbsp ginger marmalade, melted
sea salt and ground black pepper

For the stuffing
25g/1oz/2 tbsp butter or 30ml/2 tbsp
    olive oil
1 onion, finely chopped
15ml/1 tbsp ginger marmalade
450g/1lb/2 cups ready-to-eat
    prunes, chopped
45ml/3 tbsp Madeira
225g/8oz/4 cups fresh white or wholemeal
    (whole-wheat) breadcrumbs
30ml/2 tbsp chopped fresh sage

For the gravy
1 onion, chopped
15ml/1 tbsp plain (all-purpose) or
    wholemeal (whole-wheat) flour
150ml/¼ pint/⅔ cup Madeira
600ml/1 pint/2½ cups chicken stock

1 Preheat the oven to 200°C/400°F/Gas 6. Prick the skin of the goose all over and season it inside and out.

COOK'S TIP
Red cabbage goes well with goose. Cook 1 small leek, sliced, in 75g/3oz/6 tbsp butter or 90ml/6 tbsp olive oil, add 1kg/2¼lb/9 cups shredded red cabbage, with the grated rind of 1 orange, and cook for 15 minutes.

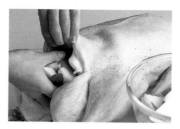

2 Mix the apple, onion and sage leaves together and spoon the mixture into the parson's nose end of the goose.

3 To make the stuffing, melt the butter or oil in a large pan and cook the onion for about 5 minutes, or until softened but not coloured. Remove the pan from the heat and stir in the marmalade, chopped prunes, Madeira, breadcrumbs and chopped sage.

4 Stuff the neck end of the goose with some of the stuffing, and then set the remaining stuffing aside in the refrigerator. Sew up the bird or secure it with skewers to prevent the stuffing from escaping during cooking.

5 Place the goose in a large roasting pan. Butter a piece of foil and use to cover the goose loosely, then roast in the preheated oven for 2 hours.

6 Baste the goose frequently during cooking and remove any excess fat from the pan as necessary, using a small ladle or serving spoon. (Strain, cool and chill the fat in a covered container: it is excellent for roasting potatoes.)

7 Remove the foil from the goose and brush the melted ginger marmalade over the goose, then roast for 30–40 minutes more, or until cooked through. To check if the goose is cooked, pierce the thick part of the thigh with a metal skewer; the juices will run clear when the bird is cooked. Remove from the oven and cover with foil, then leave to stand for 15 minutes before carving.

8 While the goose is cooking, shape the remaining stuffing into walnut-size balls and place them in an ovenproof dish. Spoon 30ml/2 tbsp of the goose fat over the stuffing balls and bake for about 15 minutes before the goose is cooked.

9 To make the gravy, pour off all but 15ml/1 tbsp of fat from the roasting pan, leaving the meat juices behind. Add the onion and cook for 3–5 minutes, or until softened but not coloured. Sprinkle in the flour and then gradually stir in the Madeira and stock. Bring to the boil, stirring continuously, then simmer for 3 minutes, or until thickened and glossy. Strain the gravy and serve it with the carved goose and stuffing. Garnish with fresh sage leaves.

CHICKEN CASSEROLE with WINTER VEGETABLES

A casserole of wonderfully tender organic chicken, winter root vegetables and lentils, finished with crème fraîche, mustard and tarragon.

SERVES FOUR

350g/12oz onions
350g/12oz leeks
225g/8oz carrots
450g/1lb swede (rutabaga)
30ml/2 tbsp olive oil
4 chicken portions, about 900g/2lb
   total weight
115g/4oz/½ cup green lentils
475ml/16fl oz/2 cups chicken stock
300ml/½ pint/1¼ cups apple juice
10ml/2 tsp cornflour (cornstarch)
45ml/3 tbsp crème fraîche
10ml/2 tsp wholegrain mustard
30ml/2 tbsp chopped fresh tarragon
sea salt and ground black pepper
fresh tarragon sprigs, to garnish

1 Preheat the oven to 190°C/375°F/ Gas 5. Prepare and chop the vegetables.

2 Heat the oil in a large flameproof casserole. Season the chicken portions and brown them in the hot oil until golden. Remove the chicken from the pan.

3 Add the onions to the casserole and cook for 5 minutes, stirring, until they begin to soften and colour. Add the leeks, carrots, swede and lentils to the casserole and stir over a medium heat for 2 minutes.

4 Return the chicken to the pan, then add the stock, apple juice and seasoning. Bring to the boil and cover tightly. Cook in the oven for 50–60 minutes, or until the chicken and lentils are tender.

5 Place the casserole on the hob (stovetop) over a medium heat. In a small bowl, blend the cornflour with about 30ml/2 tbsp water to make a smooth paste and add to the casserole with the crème fraîche, wholegrain mustard and chopped tarragon. Adjust the seasoning, then simmer gently for about 2 minutes, stirring, until thickened slightly, before serving, garnished with tarragon sprigs.

COOK'S TIP
Chop the vegetables into similarly sized pieces so that they cook evenly. Organic vegetables do not need to be peeled.

BRAISED SHOULDER of MUTTON with PEARL BARLEY and BABY VEGETABLES

A wonderful variety of organic grains is readily available. In this tasty winter stew, pearl barley absorbs all the juices to become full-flavoured with a nutty texture when cooked.

SERVES FOUR

60ml/4 tbsp olive oil
1 large onion, chopped
2 garlic cloves, chopped
2 celery sticks, sliced
a little plain (all-purpose) or wholemeal
   (whole-wheat) flour
675g/1½lb boned shoulder of mutton,
   cut into cubes
900ml–1 litre/1½–1¾ pints/3¾–4 cups
   mutton stock
115g/4oz/½ cup pearl barley
225g/8oz baby carrots
225g/8oz baby turnips
sea salt and ground black pepper
30ml/2 tbsp chopped fresh marjoram,
   to garnish
warm, crusty bread, to serve

1 Heat 45ml/3 tbsp of the oil in a flameproof casserole. Cook the onion and garlic until softened, add the celery, then cook until the vegetables brown.

2 Season the flour and toss the mutton in it. Use a draining spoon to remove the vegetables from the casserole. Add the remaining oil to the juices in the casserole and heat. Brown the mutton in batches until golden.

3 When all the meat is browned, return it to the casserole with the vegetables. Stir in 900ml/1½ pints/3¾ cups of the stock and the pearl barley. Cover, then bring to the boil, reduce the heat and simmer for 1 hour, or until the pearl barley and mutton are tender.

4 Add the baby carrots and turnips to the casserole for the final 15 minutes of cooking. Stir the meat occasionally during cooking and add the remaining stock, if necessary. Stir in seasoning to taste, and serve piping hot, garnished with marjoram, with warm, crusty bread as an accompaniment.

MUTTON SHANKS with BEANS and HERBS

In this hearty winter dish, full-flavoured organic mutton shanks are slowly cooked in the oven until tender on a bed of tasty cannellini beans and mixed vegetables.

SERVES FOUR

175g/6oz/1 cup dried cannellini, butter
   (lima) or haricot (navy) beans, soaked
   overnight in cold water
150ml/¼ pint/⅔ cup water
45ml/3 tbsp olive oil
4 large mutton shanks, 225g/8oz each
1 large onion, chopped
450g/1lb carrots or swede (rutabaga),
   cut into thick chunks
2 celery sticks, cut into thick chunks
450g/1lb tomatoes, quartered
250ml/8fl oz/1 cup vegetable or
   mutton stock
4 fresh rosemary sprigs
2 bay leaves
sea salt and ground black pepper

1 Drain and rinse the soaked cannellini beans and place them in a large pan of unsalted boiling water. Bring back to the boil and boil rapidly for 10 minutes, then drain again.

2 Place the 150ml/¼ pint/⅔ cup water in a large casserole and then add the drained cannellini beans. Preheat the oven to 220°C/425°F/Gas 7.

3 Heat 30ml/2 tbsp of the olive oil in a large frying pan, add the mutton shanks and cook over a high heat, turning them occasionally until brown on all sides. Remove the mutton shanks from the pan and set aside.

4 Add the remaining oil to the pan, then add the onion, and sauté for 5 minutes until soft and translucent.

5 Add the carrots or swede and celery to the pan and cook for 2–3 minutes. Stir in the quartered tomatoes and the vegetable or mutton stock and mix well. Transfer the vegetable mixture to the casserole and season well with salt and pepper. Add the fresh rosemary and bay leaves and stir again to combine.

6 Place the mutton shanks on top of the beans and vegetables. Cover the casserole and cook in the preheated oven for about 30 minutes, or until the liquid is bubbling.

7 Reduce the oven temperature to 160°C/325°F/Gas 3 and continue cooking for about 1½ hours, or until the meat is tender. Check the seasoning and serve on deep, warmed plates, placing each mutton shank on a bed of beans and vegetables.

COOK'S TIP

Mutton shanks are small joints cut from the lower end of the leg. One shank is an ideal-size portion for one. Until recently you would have had to order them from the butcher, but they are now becoming increasingly available, especially from good farmers' markets and home delivery services. To obtain a tender result, shanks should be cooked for a long time at a low temperature.

VARIATIONS

• If you prefer, two 400g/14oz cans cannellini beans can be used in this dish – simply place the drained beans in the casserole with the water and continue from step 3.
• A variety of other organic root vegetables would work well in this recipe – try sweet potatoes, butternut squash, parsnips or celeriac instead of the carrots or swede. In spring, replace the mutton with spring lamb and add a mixture of baby turnips and baby carrots.

CHILLI CON CARNE and RICE

Originally made with finely chopped beef, chillies and kidney beans by hungry labourers working on the Texan railroad, this famous Tex-Mex stew has become an international favourite. Be authentic by using organic ingredients.

SERVES EIGHT

1.2kg/2½lb lean braising steak
30ml/2 tbsp sunflower oil
1 large onion, chopped
2 garlic cloves, finely chopped
15ml/1 tbsp plain (all-purpose) or
    wholemeal (whole-wheat) flour
300ml/½ pint/1¼ cups red wine
300ml/½ pint/1¼ cups beef stock
30ml/2 tbsp tomato purée (paste)
sea salt and ground black pepper
fresh coriander (cilantro) leaves, to garnish
boiled white or brown rice, to serve

For the beans
30ml/2 tbsp olive oil
1 onion, chopped
1 red chilli, seeded and chopped
2 × 400g/14oz cans red kidney beans,
    drained and rinsed
400g/14oz can chopped tomatoes

For the topping
6 tomatoes, peeled and chopped
1 green chilli, seeded and chopped
30ml/2 tbsp chopped fresh chives
30ml/2 tbsp chopped fresh coriander
150ml/¼ pint/⅔ cup sour cream

1 Cut the meat into thick strips and then cut it crossways into small cubes. Heat the oil in a large, flameproof casserole. Add the chopped onion and garlic, and cook, stirring occasionally, for 5–8 minutes until softened but not coloured. Meanwhile, season the flour with a little salt and plenty of pepper and place it on a plate, then toss a batch of meat in it.

2 Use a draining spoon to remove the onion from the pan, then add the floured beef and cook over a high heat, stirring occasionally with a wooden spoon until browned on all sides. Remove from the pan and set aside, then flour and brown another batch of meat.

3 When the last batch of meat is browned, return the first batches with the onion to the pan. Stir in the wine, stock and tomato purée. Bring to the boil, reduce the heat and simmer for 45 minutes, or until the beef is tender.

4 Meanwhile, to make the beans, heat the olive oil in a frying pan and cook the onion and chilli until softened. Add the kidney beans and tomatoes and simmer gently for 20–25 minutes.

5 Mix the tomatoes, chilli, chives and coriander for the topping. Ladle the meat on to plates, then add the beans and the tomato topping. Top with sour cream and coriander leaves and serve with rice.

BOEUF BOURGUIGNONNE

*The classic French dish of beef cooked in Burgundy style, with red wine, small pieces of
bacon, baby onions and mushrooms, is traditionally cooked for several hours at a low
temperature. Using organic top rump or braising steak reduces the cooking time.*

SERVES SIX

175g/6oz rindless streaky (fatty) bacon
    rashers (strips), chopped
900g/2lb lean braising steak, such as top
    rump of beef or braising steak
30ml/2 tbsp plain (all-purpose) or
    wholemeal (whole-wheat) flour
45ml/3 tbsp sunflower oil
25g/1oz/2 tbsp butter or 30ml/2 tbsp
    olive oil
12 shallots
2 garlic cloves, crushed
175g/6oz/2½ cups mushrooms, sliced
450ml/¾ pint/scant 2 cups robust red wine
150ml/¼ pint/⅔ cup beef stock
    or consommé
1 bay leaf
2 sprigs each of fresh thyme, parsley
    and marjoram
sea salt and ground black pepper
mashed root vegetables, such as celeriac
    and potatoes, to serve

1 Preheat the oven to 160°C/325°F/
Gas 3. Heat a large flameproof casserole,
then add the bacon and cook, stirring
occasionally, until the pieces are crisp
and golden brown.

2 Meanwhile, cut the meat into
2.5cm/1in cubes. Season the flour and
use to coat the meat. Use a draining
spoon to remove the bacon from the
casserole and set aside. Add and heat
the sunflower oil, then brown the beef
in batches and set aside with the bacon.

COOK'S TIP

Boeuf Bourguignonne freezes very well.
Freeze for up to 2 months. Thaw
overnight in the refrigerator, then transfer
to a flameproof casserole and add 150ml/
¼ pint/⅔ cup water. Stir well, bring to
the boil, stirring occasionally, and simmer
steadily for at least 10 minutes, or until
the meat is piping hot.

3 Add the butter or olive oil to the
casserole. Cook the shallots and garlic
until just starting to colour, then add
the mushrooms and cook for 5 minutes.
Replace the bacon and meat, and stir in
the wine and stock or consommé. Tie the
herbs together and add to the casserole.

4 Cover and cook for 1½ hours, or
until the meat is tender, stirring once
or twice. Season to taste before serving
with mashed root vegetables.

STEAK, MUSHROOM and ALE PIE

Organic steak has a great quality and fine texture and flavour – it is delicious in this Anglo-Irish dish. Creamy mashed potatoes or parsley-dressed boiled potatoes and slightly crunchy carrots and green beans or cabbage are perfect accompaniments. For a bar-style meal, French fries and a side salad can be served with the pie.

SERVES FOUR

30ml/2 tbsp olive oil
1 large onion, finely chopped
115g/4oz/1½ cups chestnut or button (white) mushrooms, halved
900g/2lb lean beef in one piece, such as rump or braising steak
30ml/2 tbsp plain (all-purpose) wholemeal (whole-wheat) flour
45ml/3 tbsp sunflower oil
300ml/½ pint/1¼ cups stout or brown ale
300ml/½ pint/1¼ cups beef stock or consommé
500g/1¼lb puff pastry, thawed if frozen
beaten egg, to glaze
sea salt and ground black pepper
steamed organic vegetables, to serve

1 Heat the olive oil in a large, flameproof casserole, add the onion and cook gently, stirring occasionally, for about 5 minutes, or until it is softened but not coloured. Add the halved mushrooms and continue cooking for a further 5 minutes, stirring occasionally.

2 Meanwhile, trim the meat and cut it into 2.5cm/1in cubes. Season the flour and toss the meat in it.

COOK'S TIP
To make individual pies, divide the filling among four individual pie dishes. Cut the pastry into quarters and cover as above. If the dishes do not have rims, press a narrow strip of pastry around the edge of each dish to seal the lid in place. Cook as above, reducing the cooking time slightly.

3 Use a draining spoon to remove the onion mixture from the casserole and set aside. Add and heat the oil, then brown the steak in batches over a high heat to seal in the juices.

4 Replace the vegetables, then stir in the stout or ale and stock or consommé. Bring to the boil, reduce the heat and simmer for about 1 hour, stirring occasionally, or until the meat is tender. Season to taste and transfer to a 1.5 litre/2½ pint/6¼ cup pie dish. Cover and leave to cool. If you have time, chill the meat filling overnight as this allows the flavour to develop. Preheat the oven to 230°C/450°F/Gas 8.

5 Roll out the pastry in the shape of the dish and about 4cm/1½in larger all around. Cut a 2.5cm/1in strip from around the edge of the pastry. Brush the rim of the pie dish with water and press the pastry strip onto it. Brush the pastry rim with beaten egg and cover the pie with the pastry lid. Press the lid firmly in place and then trim the excess pastry from around the edge of the dish.

6 Use the blunt edge of a knife to tap the outside edge of the pastry rim, pressing it down with your finger as you seal the steak and mushroom filling into the dish. (This sealing technique is known as knocking up.)

7 Pinch the outside edge of the pastry between your fingers to flute the edge. Roll out any remaining pastry trimmings and cut out five or six leaf shapes to garnish the centre of the pie. Brush the shapes with a little beaten egg before pressing them lightly in place.

8 Make a hole in the middle of the pie using the point of a sharp knife to allow the steam to escape during cooking. Brush the top carefully with beaten egg and chill for 10 minutes in the refrigerator to rest the pastry.

9 Bake the pie for 15 minutes, then reduce the oven temperature to 200°C/400°F/Gas 6 and bake for a further 15–20 minutes, or until the pastry is risen and golden brown. Serve the pie hot with steamed organic vegetables.

FILLETS of BRILL in RED WINE SAUCE

Forget the old maxim that red wine and fish do not go well together. The robust sauce
adds colour and richness to this excellent dish.

SERVES FOUR

4 fillets of brill, about 175–200g/6–7oz
   each, skinned
150g/5oz/10 tbsp chilled butter or
   non-hydrogenated margarine, diced,
   plus extra for greasing
115g/4oz shallots, thinly sliced
200ml/7fl oz/scant 1 cup robust
   red wine
200ml/7fl oz/scant 1 cup fish stock
salt and ground white pepper
fresh chervil or flat leaf parsley leaves,
   to garnish

COOK'S TIP

If your baking dish is not flameproof,
then tip the liquid into a pan to cook
on the stove.

1 Preheat the oven to 180°C/350°F/
Gas 4. Season the fish on both sides
with a little salt and plenty of pepper.
Generously butter a flameproof dish,
which is large enough to take all the
brill fillets in a single layer without
overlapping. Spread the shallots over the
base and lay the fish fillets on top. Season.

2 Pour in the red wine and fish stock,
cover the dish and bring the liquid to
just below boiling point. Transfer the dish
to the oven and bake for 6–8 minutes,
or until the brill is just cooked.

3 Using a fish slice, carefully lift the fish
and shallots on to a serving dish, cover
with foil and keep hot.

4 Transfer the dish to the hob and bring
the cooking liquid to the boil over a high
heat. Cook it until it has reduced by half.
Lower the heat and whisk in the chilled
butter or margarine, one piece at a time,
to make a smooth, shiny sauce. Season
with salt and ground white pepper, set
aside and keep hot.

5 Divide the shallots among four
warmed plates and lay the brill fillets on
top. Pour the sauce over and around the
fish and garnish with the chervil or flat
leaf parsley.

VARIATION

Turbot, halibut or John Dory fillets can
also be cooked in this way. Make sure
that your fish is caught sustainably.

SMOKED HADDOCK with MUSTARD CABBAGE

A wide range of organic mustards are available – wholegrain is used in this warming winter dish, but any type can be used instead.

2 Meanwhile put the smoked haddock fillet in a large shallow pan with the milk, onion rings and bay leaves. Add the lemon slices and white peppercorns. Bring to simmering point, cover and poach until the fish flakes easily when tested with the tip of a sharp knife. This will take 8–10 minutes, depending on the thickness of the fillets. Take the pan off the heat and set aside until needed. Preheat the grill (broiler).

3 Cut the tomatoes in half horizontally, season them with a little salt and plenty of pepper and grill (broil) until lightly browned. Drain the cabbage, refresh under cold water and drain again.

SERVES FOUR

I Savoy or pointu cabbage
675g/1½lb undyed smoked haddock fillet
300ml/½ pint/1¼ cups milk or
   soya milk
½ onion, peeled and sliced into rings
2 bay leaves
½ lemon, sliced
4 white peppercorns
4 ripe tomatoes
50g/2oz/¼ cup butter or 50ml/3½ tbsp
   olive oil
30ml/2 tbsp wholegrain mustard
juice of 1 lemon
sea salt and ground black pepper
30ml/2 tbsp chopped fresh parsley,
   to garnish

I Cut the Savoy or pointu cabbage in half, remove the central core and thick ribs, then shred the cabbage. Cook in a pan of lightly salted boiling water, or steam over boiling water for about 10 minutes until just tender. Leave in the pan or steamer until required.

4 Heat the butter or oil in a shallow pan or wok, add the cabbage and toss over the heat for 2 minutes. Mix in the mustard and season to taste, then tip the cabbage into a warmed serving dish.

5 Drain the haddock. Skin and cut the fish into four pieces. Place on top of the cabbage with some of the cooked onion rings and grilled tomato halves. Pour on the lemon juice, then sprinkle with chopped fresh parsley and serve.

SEAFOOD LASAGNE

This dish can be as simple or as elegant as you like. For an elegant dinner party, you can dress it up with scallops, mussels or prawns; for a casual family supper, you can use simple fish such as haddock and hoki. Whatever fish or shellfish you choose, ensure it comes from a sustainable source.

SERVES EIGHT

350g/12oz haddock
350g/12oz salmon fillet
350g/12oz undyed smoked haddock
1 litre/1¾ pints/4 cups milk or
    soya milk
500ml/17fl oz/2¼ cups fish stock
2 bay leaves
1 small onion, peeled and halved
75g/3oz/6 tbsp butter or
    non-hydrogenated margarine,
    plus extra for greasing
45ml/3 tbsp plain (all-purpose) or
    wholemeal (whole-wheat) flour
150g/5oz/2 cups mushrooms, sliced
225–300g/8–11oz fresh lasagne
60ml/4 tbsp freshly grated Parmesan
    cheese or premium Italian-style
    vegetarian cheese
sea salt, ground black pepper, freshly
    grated nutmeg and paprika
rocket (arugula) leaves, to garnish

For the tomato sauce
30ml/2 tbsp olive oil
1 red onion, finely chopped
1 garlic clove, finely chopped
400g/14oz can chopped tomatoes
15ml/1 tbsp tomato purée (paste)
15ml/1 tbsp torn fresh basil leaves

1 Make the tomato sauce. Heat the oil in a pan and fry the onion and garlic over a low heat for 5 minutes, until softened and golden. Stir in the tomatoes and tomato purée and simmer for 20–30 minutes, stirring occasionally. Season with a little salt and plenty of black pepper and stir in the basil.

VARIATION
A good selection of organic pastas are available, including a variety of types of lasagne. Choose from classic lasagne, lasagne all'uovo (rich egg pasta sheets) or lasagne verdi (spinach lasagne), which is an attractive dark green colour.

2 Put all the fish in a shallow flameproof dish or pan with the milk, stock, bay leaves and onion. Bring to the boil over a moderate heat; poach for 5 minutes, until almost cooked. Leave to cool.

3 When the fish is almost cold, strain it, reserving the liquid. Remove the skin and any bones, and flake the fish.

4 Preheat the oven to 180°C/350°F/ Gas 4. Melt the butter in a pan, stir in the flour; cook for 2 minutes, stirring. Gradually add the poaching liquid and bring to the boil, stirring. Add the mushrooms and cook for 2–3 minutes. Season with salt, pepper and nutmeg.

5 Lightly grease a shallow rectangular ovenproof dish. Spoon a thin layer of the mushroom sauce over the base of the dish and spread it out evenly with a spatula. Stir the flaked fish into the remaining mushroom sauce in the pan.

6 Add a layer of lasagne, then a layer of fish and sauce. Add another layer of lasagne, then spread over all the tomato sauce. Continue to layer the lasagne and fish, finishing with a layer of fish.

7 Sprinkle over the grated cheese, then bake for 30–45 minutes until golden. Before serving, sprinkle with paprika and garnish with rocket leaves.

SPICY PUMPKIN and ORANGE BOMBE

*In this fabulous ice cream dessert, the subtle flavour of organic pumpkin is transformed
with the addition of citrus fruits and spices. The delicious ice cream mixture is then
encased in syrupy sponge and served with an orange and whole-spice syrup.*

SERVES EIGHT

115g/4oz/½ cup unsalted (sweet) butter or
   non-hydrogenated margarine, softened
115g/4oz/generous ½ cup unrefined caster
   (superfine) sugar or rapadura
115g/4oz/1 cup self-raising
   (self-rising) flour
2.5ml/½ tsp baking powder
2 eggs

For the ice cream
450g/1lb fresh pumpkin, seeded and cubed
1 orange
300g/11oz/scant 1½ cups unrefined
   granulated sugar or rapadura
300ml/½ pint /1¼ cups water
2 cinnamon sticks, halved
10ml/2 tsp whole cloves
30ml/2 tbsp orange flower water
300ml/½ pint/1¼ cups extra thick double
   (heavy) cream or soya cream
2 pieces preserved stem ginger, grated
unrefined icing (confectioners') sugar,
   for dusting

1 Preheat the oven to 180°C/350°F/
Gas 4. Grease and base-line a 450g/1lb
loaf tin (pan).

2 To make the sponge, beat the butter
or margarine, caster sugar, flour, baking
powder and eggs in a bowl until creamy.

3 Spoon the mixture into the prepared
tin, then level the surface and bake in
the preheated oven for 30–35 minutes
until firm in the centre. Leave in the tin
for a few minutes then turn out on to a
wire rack to cool.

4 Make the ice cream. Steam the cubes
of pumpkin for about 15 minutes, or
until tender. Drain and blend in a food
processor to form a smooth purée.
Leave to cool.

5 Pare thin strips of rind from the
orange, scrape off any white pith, then
cut the strips into very fine shreds.
Squeeze the orange and set the juice
aside. Heat the unrefined sugar and water
in a small, heavy pan until the sugar
dissolves. Bring the syrup to the boil and
boil rapidly without stirring for 3 minutes.

6 Stir in the orange shreds, orange juice,
cinnamon and cloves and heat gently for
5 minutes. Strain the syrup, reserving
the orange shreds and spices. Measure
300ml/½ pint/1¼ cups of the syrup
and reserve. Return the spices to the
remaining syrup and stir in the orange
flower water. Pour into a jug (pitcher)
and set aside to cool.

COOK'S TIP
If you prefer a smooth syrup, strain to
remove the cinnamon sticks and cloves
before spooning it over the bombe.

7 Beat the pumpkin purée with 175ml/
6fl oz/¾ cup of the measured strained
syrup until evenly combined. Stir in the
cream and ginger. Cut the cake into 1cm/
½in slices. Dampen a 1.5 litre/2½ pint/
6¼ cup deep bowl and line it with clear
film (plastic wrap). Pour the remaining
strained syrup into a shallow dish.

8 Dip the cake slices one at a time
briefly in the syrup and use to line the
prepared bowl, placing the syrupy
coated sides against the bowl.

9 To freeze the ice cream by hand, pour
the pumpkin mixture into a shallow
container and freeze until firm. Scrape
the ice cream into the sponge-lined bowl,
level the surface and freeze until firm,
preferably overnight. If using an ice cream
maker, churn the pumpkin mixture until
very thick, then spoon it into the
sponge-lined bowl. Level the surface and
freeze until firm, preferably overnight.

10 To serve, invert the bombe on to a
plate. Lift off the bowl and clear film.
Dust with the icing sugar and serve
with the spiced syrup spooned over.

CHOCOLATE MOUSSE with GLAZED KUMQUATS

Bright orange kumquats balance this rich, dark mousse perfectly. There are some excellent organic chocolates available. It is worth spending a little more on them because they have such a luxurious taste and texture, and good fair-trade values.

SERVES SIX

225g/8oz dark (bittersweet) chocolate,
　broken into squares
4 eggs, separated
30ml/2 tbsp brandy
90ml/6 tbsp double (heavy) cream
　or soya cream

For the glazed kumquats
275g/10oz kumquats
115g/4oz/generous ½ cup unrefined
　granulated sugar or rapadura
150ml/¼ pint/⅔ cup water
15ml/1 tbsp brandy

I Make the glazed kumquats. Slice the fruit lengthways and place cut side up in a shallow serving dish.

2 Place the sugar in a pan with the water. Heat gently, stirring constantly, until the sugar has dissolved, then bring to the boil and boil rapidly, without stirring, until a golden-brown caramel forms.

VARIATION
If you can't find kumquats, then use peeled and sliced small, seedless organic oranges, pink-fleshed grapefruit or satsumas instead.

3 Remove the pan from the heat and very carefully stir in 60ml/4 tbsp boiling water to dissolve the caramel. Stir in the brandy, then pour the caramel over the kumquats and leave to cool. Once completely cold, cover and chill.

4 Line a shallow 20cm/8in round cake tin (pan) with clear film (plastic wrap). Melt the chocolate in a bowl over a pan of barely simmering water, then remove the bowl from the heat.

5 Add the egg yolks and brandy to the chocolate and beat well, then fold in the cream, mixing well. In a separate clean bowl, whisk the egg whites until stiff, then gently fold them into the chocolate mixture.

6 Pour the mixture into the prepared tin and level the surface with a spatula. Chill for several hours until set.

7 To serve, turn the mousse out on to a plate and cut into slices or wedges. Serve the chocolate mousse on serving plates and spoon some of the glazed kumquats and syrup alongside.

CHRISTMAS ICE CREAM TORTE

This fruity ice cream cake makes an exciting alternative to traditional Christmas pudding, but don't feel that you have to limit it to the festive season. Packed with dried organic fruit and nuts, it is perfect for any special occasion and tastes sensational.

SERVES EIGHT TO TEN

75g/3oz/¾ cup dried cranberries
75g/3oz/scant ½ cup pitted prunes
50g/2oz/⅓ cup sultanas (golden raisins)
175ml/6fl oz/¾ cup port
2 pieces preserved stem ginger, chopped
25g/1oz/2 tbsp unsalted (sweet) butter or
    non-hydrogenated margarine
45ml/3 tbsp light muscovado (brown) sugar
90g/3½oz/scant 2 cups fresh white or
    wholemeal (whole-wheat) breadcrumbs
600ml/1 pint/2½ cups double (heavy)
    cream or soya cream
30ml/2 tbsp unrefined icing
    (confectioners') sugar
5ml/1 tsp mixed (apple pie) spice
75g/3oz/¾ cup brazil nuts, finely chopped
2–3 bay leaf sprigs, egg white, caster
    (superfine) sugar or rapadura and
    fresh cherries, to decorate

1 Put the dried fruit in a food processor and process briefly to chop roughly. Tip the fruit into a bowl and add the port and ginger. Leave to marinate for 2 hours.

2 Melt the butter in a frying pan. Add the muscovado sugar and heat gently until dissolved. Tip in the breadcrumbs and fry gently for 5 minutes. Leave to cool.

3 Tip the breadcrumbs into a food processor and process to finer crumbs. Sprinkle a third into an 18cm/7in loose-based springform tin (pan) and freeze.

4 Whip the cream with the icing sugar and mixed spice to soft peaks. Fold in the nuts and dried fruit mixture.

5 To make sugared bay leaves for decoration, wash and dry the sprigs, then paint both sides with beaten egg white. Dust evenly with sugar. Leave to dry for 2–3 hours.

6 Spread a third of the spiced fruit cream mixture over the frozen breadcrumb base in the tin, taking care not to dislodge any of the crumbs. Sprinkle the cream mixture with another layer of the fine, crispy breadcrumbs. Repeat the layering, finishing with a layer of the spiced fruit cream mixture. Cover the torte with clear film (plastic wrap) and freeze it overnight.

7 Remove the torte from the freezer and place in the refrigerator for about 1 hour before serving, decorated with sugared bay leaves and fresh cherries.

DRIED FRUIT COMPOTE

Compotes made with dried fruit are just as wonderful as those made with fresh fruits, especially in winter when fewer organic fresh fruit varieties are in season.

SERVES FOUR

225g/8oz/1⅓ cups mixed dried fruit
75g/3oz/⅔ cup dried cherries
75g/3oz/⅔ cup sultanas (golden raisins)
10 dried prunes
10 dried apricots
hot, freshly brewed fragrant tea, such as
  Earl Grey or jasmine, to cover
15–30ml/1–2 tbsp unrefined caster
  (superfine) sugar or rapadura
¼ lemon, sliced
60ml/4 tbsp brandy

1 Put the dried fruits in a bowl and pour over the hot tea. Add sugar to taste and the lemon slices. Cover with a plate, set aside and leave to cool to room temperature.

2 When the fruits are cool, cover the bowl with clear film (plastic wrap) and chill in the refrigerator for at least 2 hours and preferably overnight. Just before serving, pour in the brandy and stir well.

MOROCCAN RICE PUDDING

*A simple and delicious alternative to a traditional British rice pudding. The rice is cooked
in almond-flavoured milk and delicately flavoured with cinnamon and orange flower water.*

SERVES SIX

25g/1oz/¼ cup almonds, chopped
450g/1lb/2¼ cups pudding rice
25g/1oz/¼ cup unrefined icing
    (confectioners') sugar or rapadura
1 cinnamon stick
50g/2oz/¼ cup butter or
    non-hydrogenated margarine
1.5ml/¼ tsp almond essence (extract)
175ml/6fl oz/¾ cup milk or soya milk
175ml/6fl oz/¾ cup single (light) cream or
    soya cream
30ml/2 tbsp orange flower water
toasted flaked (sliced) almonds and ground
    cinnamon, to decorate

1 Put the almonds in a food processor
or blender with 60ml/4 tbsp of very hot
water. Process until the almonds are
finely chopped, then push through a
sieve into a bowl. Return the almond
mixture to the food processor or
blender, add a further 60ml/4 tbsp very
hot water, and process again. Push the
almond mixture through the sieve into
a pan.

2 Add 300ml/½ pint/1¼ cups water and
bring the mixture to the boil. Add the
rice, icing sugar or rapadura, cinnamon
stick, half the butter, the almond
essence, half the milk and half the cream.

3 Bring to the boil, then simmer,
covered, for about 30 minutes, adding
more milk and cream as the rice mixture
thickens. Continue to cook the rice,
stirring, and adding the remaining milk
and cream, until the pudding becomes
thick and creamy. Stir in the orange
flower water, then taste the rice pudding
for sweetness, adding a little extra sugar,
if necessary.

4 Pour the rice pudding into a serving
bowl and sprinkle with the toasted
flaked almonds. Dot with the remaining
butter and dust with a little ground
cinnamon. Serve the pudding hot.

BAKED MAPLE and PECAN CROISSANT PUDDING

This variation of the classic English bread and butter pudding uses rich, flaky croissants, topped with a delicious mixture of organic fruit and nuts. Maple-syrup-flavoured custard completes this mouthwatering dessert.

SERVES FOUR

75g/3oz/scant ½ cup sultanas
   (golden raisins)
45ml/3 tbsp brandy
4 large croissants
50g/2oz/¼ cup butter or non-hydrogenated
   margarine, plus extra for greasing
40g/1½oz/⅓ cup pecan nuts,
   roughly chopped
3 eggs, lightly beaten
300ml/½ pint/1¼ cups milk or soya milk
150ml/¼ pint/⅔ cup single (light) cream
   or soya cream
120ml/4fl oz/½ cup maple syrup
25g/1oz/2 tbsp demerara (raw) sugar
maple syrup and pouring (half-and-half)
   cream or soya cream, to serve (optional)

1 Lightly grease the base and sides of a small, shallow ovenproof dish. Place the sultanas and brandy in a small pan and heat gently, until warm. Leave to stand for 1 hour.

2 Cut the croissants into thick slices and then spread with butter on one side.

3 Arrange the croissant slices butter side uppermost and slightly overlapping in the greased dish. Scatter the brandy-soaked sultanas and the roughly chopped pecan nuts evenly over the buttered croissant slices.

4 In a large bowl, beat the eggs and milk together, then gradually beat in the single or soya cream and maple syrup.

COOK'S TIPS
• The main sweetener in this recipe is maple syrup. It is made by tapping the sap of the maple tree. Organic maple syrup is not overprocessed so it retains its natural richness.
• Pecan nuts are an elongated nut in a glossy red oval-shaped shell, but are usually sold shelled. They are native to the USA and have a sweet, mild flavour. Pecans are most commonly used in pecan pie but are also popular in ice creams and cakes. Walnuts can be substituted for pecans in most recipes, and they would be perfect in this one if you don't have any pecan nuts.

5 Pour the egg custard through a sieve, over the croissants, fruit and nuts in the dish. Leave the pudding to stand for 30 minutes so that some of the custard is absorbed by the croissants. Preheat the oven to 180°F/350°C/Gas 4.

6 Sprinkle the demerara sugar evenly over the top, then cover the dish with foil. Bake the pudding for 30 minutes, then remove the foil and continue to cook for about 20 minutes, or until the custard is set and the top is golden brown.

7 Leave the pudding to cool for about 15 minutes before serving warm with extra maple syrup and a little pouring cream or soya cream, if you like.

VARIATION
Thickly sliced one-day-old bread, large slices of brioche or fruit bread could be used instead of the croissants. Slightly stale one-day-old croissants are easier to slice and butter; they also soak up the custard more easily.

ORANGE MARMALADE CHOCOLATE LOAF

Do not be alarmed at the amount of cream in this recipe – it's naughty but necessary, and replaces butter to make a deliciously mouthwatering moist dark chocolate cake, finished with a bitter-sweet sticky marmalade filling and topping.

SERVES EIGHT

115g/4oz dark (bittersweet) chocolate
3 eggs
175g/6oz/scant 1 cup unrefined caster
   (superfine) sugar or rapadura
175ml/6fl oz/¾ cup sour cream
200g/7oz/1¾ cups self-raising
   (self-rising) flour

For the filling and topping
200g/7oz/⅔ cup bitter orange marmalade
115g/4oz dark (bittersweet) chocolate
60ml/4 tbsp sour cream
shredded orange rind, to decorate

1 Preheat the oven to 190°C/375°F/ Gas 5. Grease a 900g/2lb loaf tin (pan) lightly, then line the base with a piece of baking parchment. Break the chocolate into pieces. Melt the chocolate in a heatproof bowl placed over hot water.

2 Combine the eggs and sugar in a separate bowl. Using a hand-held electric mixer, beat the mixture until it is thick and creamy, then stir in the sour cream and melted chocolate. Fold in the flour evenly using a metal spoon.

3 Pour the mixture into the prepared tin and bake for about 1 hour, or until well risen and firm to the touch. Cool for a few minutes in the tin, then turn out onto a wire rack and let the loaf cool completely.

4 Make the filling. Spoon two-thirds of the marmalade into a small pan and melt over a low heat. Break the chocolate into pieces. Melt the chocolate in a heatproof bowl placed over hot water. Stir the chocolate into the marmalade with the sour cream.

5 Slice the cake across into three layers and sandwich back together with about half the marmalade filling. Spread the rest over the top of the cake and leave to set. Spoon the remaining marmalade over the cake and scatter with shredded orange rind, to decorate.

COOK'S TIP
A fantastic variety of different types of organic marmalades are available, including farmhouse and hand-made regional varieties.

SEMOLINA and NUT HALVA

In Eastern Mediterranean cooking semolina is used in many desserts.
Here it provides a spongy base for soaking up a deliciously fragrant spicy syrup.

SERVES TEN

For the halva
115g/4oz/½ cup unsalted (sweet) butter or
    non-hydrogenated margarine, softened
115g/4oz/generous ½ cup unrefined caster
    (superfine) sugar or rapadura
finely grated rind of 1 orange, plus
    30ml/2 tbsp juice
3 eggs
175g/6oz/1 cup semolina
10ml/2 tsp baking powder
115g/4oz/1 cup ground hazelnuts
natural (plain) yogurt, to serve

To finish
350g/12oz/1¾ cups unrefined caster
    (superfine) sugar or rapadura
2 cinnamon sticks, halved
juice of 1 lemon
60ml/4 tbsp orange flower water
50g/2oz/½ cup unblanched hazelnuts,
    toasted and chopped
50g/2oz/½ cup blanched almonds, toasted
    and chopped
shredded rind of 1 orange, to decorate

1 Preheat the oven to 220°C/425°F/
Gas 7. Grease and line the base of a deep
23cm/9in square solid-based cake tin (pan).

2 Lightly cream the butter in a large
bowl. Add the sugar or rapadura, orange
rind and juice, eggs, semolina, baking
powder and hazelnuts and beat the
ingredients together until smooth.

3 Tip into the prepared tin and level the
surface. Bake for 20–25 minutes until
just firm and golden. Leave to cool in
the tin.

4 To make the syrup, put the unrefined
caster sugar in a small heavy pan with
550ml/18fl oz/2½ cups water and the
halved cinnamon sticks. Heat gently,
stirring occasionally with a wooden spoon,
until the sugar has dissolved completely.

5 Bring to the boil and boil fast, without
stirring, for 5 minutes. Measure half the
boiling syrup and add the lemon juice
and orange flower water to it. Pour over
the halva. Reserve the remainder of the
syrup in the pan.

6 Leave the halva in the tin until the
syrup is absorbed, then turn it out on to
a plate and cut diagonally into diamond-
shaped portions. Scatter with the nuts.

7 Boil the remaining syrup until slightly
thickened then pour it over the halva.
Scatter the shredded orange rind over
the cake to decorate and serve with
natural yogurt.

GREEK FRUIT and NUT PASTRIES

These aromatic sweet pastry crescents are packed with walnuts, which are a really rich source of nutrients. Serve with a cup of organic coffee.

3 Meanwhile, to make the filling, mix the honey and coffee. Add the fruit, walnuts and nutmeg. Stir well, cover and leave to soak for at least 20 minutes.

4 Roll out a portion of dough on a lightly floured surface until about 3mm/ 1/8in thick. Stamp out rounds using a 10cm/4in round cutter.

5 Place a heaped teaspoonful of filling on one side of each round. Brush the edges with a little milk, then fold over and press the edges together to seal. Repeat with the remaining pastry until all the filling is used.

6 Put the pastries on lightly greased baking sheets, brush with milk and sprinkle with caster sugar.

7 Make a steam hole in each with a skewer. Bake for 35 minutes, or until lightly browned. Cool on a wire rack.

VARIATIONS
Any dried fruit can be used in this recipe – try a combination of the following: sultanas (golden raisins), raisins, currants, apricots, cherries or prunes.

MAKES SIXTEEN

60ml/4 tbsp clear honey
60ml/4 tbsp strong brewed coffee
75g/3oz/1/2 cup mixed dried fruit, chopped
175g/6oz/1 cup walnuts, chopped
1.5ml/1/4 tsp freshly grated nutmeg
milk, to glaze
caster (superfine) sugar or rapadura,
    for sprinkling

For the pastry
450g/1lb/4 cups plain (all-purpose) flour
2.5ml/1/2 tsp ground cinnamon
2.5ml/1/2 tsp baking powder
150g/5oz/10 tbsp unsalted (sweet) butter
    or non-hydrogenated margarine
1 egg
120ml/4fl oz/1/2 cup chilled milk
    or soya milk

1 Preheat the oven to 180°C/350°F/ Gas 4. To make the pastry, sift the flour, ground cinnamon and baking powder into a bowl. Rub in the butter until the mixture resembles fine breadcrumbs. Make a well in the middle.

2 Beat the egg and chilled milk or soya milk together and add to the well in the dry ingredients. Mix to a soft dough. Divide the dough into two equal pieces and wrap each in clear film (plastic wrap). Chill for 30 minutes.

COOK'S TIP
These traditional Greek pastries are known as *moshopoungia* in Greece. Serve them warm with morning coffee or afternoon tea with a dollop of whipped cream or crème fraîche.

ORANGE and CORIANDER BRIOCHES

The warm spicy flavour of coriander combines particularly well with orange.
Serve these little buns with marmalade for a lazy weekend breakfast.

MAKES TWELVE

225g/8oz/2 cups strong white bread flour
15g/½oz fresh yeast
2.5ml/½ tsp salt
15ml/1 tbsp unrefined caster (superfine)
    sugar or rapadura
10ml/2 tsp coriander seeds, coarsely ground
grated rind of 1 orange
2 eggs, beaten
50g/2oz/¼ cup unsalted (sweet) butter or
    non-hydrogenated margarine, melted
1 small egg, beaten, to glaze
shredded orange rind, to decorate (optional)

1 Grease 12 individual brioche tins.
Blend the yeast with 25ml/1½ tbsp tepid
water in a bowl until smooth. Sift the
flour into a mixing bowl and stir in the
yeast, salt, sugar, coriander seeds and
orange rind. Make a well in the centre,
pour in 30ml/2 tbsp hand-hot water, the
eggs and melted butter and beat to
make a soft dough. Turn the dough on
to a lightly floured surface and knead for
5 minutes. Return to the clean, lightly
oiled bowl, cover with clear film (plastic
wrap) and leave in a warm place for
about 1 hour, or until doubled in bulk.

2 Tip the dough out on to a floured
surface, knead briefly and roll into a
sausage shape. Cut into 12 pieces. Break
off a quarter of each piece and set aside.
Shape the larger pieces of dough into
balls and place in the prepared tins.

VARIATION
If you prefer, use 10ml/2 tsp easy-blend
(rapid-rise) dried yeast instead of fresh
yeast, and add to the flour in step 1.

3 With a floured wooden spoon handle,
press a hole in each dough ball. Shape
each small piece of dough into a little
plug and press into the holes.

COOK'S TIP
These little brioches look particularly
attractive if they are made in special
brioche tins. However, they can also be
made in bun or muffin tins.

4 Place the brioche tins on a baking
sheet. Cover with lightly oiled clear film
and leave in a warm place until the
dough rises almost to the top of the tins.
Preheat the oven to 220°C/425°F/Gas 7.
Brush the brioches with beaten egg and
bake for 15 minutes until golden brown.
Scatter over extra shreds of orange rind
to decorate, if you like, and serve the
brioches warm with butter.

SPICED POACHED KUMQUATS

Kumquats are not available throughout the year, but they are undoubtedly at their best just before the Christmas season. These fruits can be bottled and given as presents. Their marvellous spicy-sweet citrus flavour complements both sweet and savoury dishes.

SERVES SIX

450g/1lb/4 cups kumquats
115g/4oz/generous ½ cup unrefined caster
    (superfine) sugar or rapadura
150ml/¼ pint/⅔ cup water
1 small cinnamon stick
1 star anise
a bay leaf, to decorate (optional)

COOK'S TIP
To prepare jars for home preserves,
preheat the oven to 160°C/325°F/Gas 3.
Wash the jars in hot soapy water, rinse and
dry thoroughly. Place the jars in the oven
for 10 minutes, then turn off the oven.

1 Cut the kumquats in half and discard
the pips. Place the kumquats in a pan
with the sugar, water and spices. Cook
over a gentle heat, stirring until the
sugar has dissolved.

2 Increase the heat, cover the pan and
boil the mixture for 8–10 minutes until
the kumquats are tender. To bottle the
kumquats, spoon them into warm,
sterilized jars, seal and label. Decorate
the kumquats with a bay leaf before
serving, if you like.

COOK'S TIP
Serve these delectable treats with baked
ham, roast turkey or venison steaks.
They would also make a perfect
accompaniment for moist almond or
chocolate cake; or serve with organic
vanilla or chocolate ice cream.

THREE-FRUIT MARMALADE

*Seville oranges have a fine flavour and are the best variety for marmalade.
They are only available for a limited time in winter so make the most of them then.*

MAKES 2.25KG/5LB

2 Seville oranges
2 lemons
1 grapefruit
1.75 litres/3 pints/7½ cups water
1.5kg/3¼lb/7½ cups unrefined
    granulated sugar
croissants, to serve (optional)

1 Wash the fruit, halve and squeeze their
juice. Pour into a large heavy pan. Tip
the pips and pulp in a square of muslin
(cheesecloth), gather into a bag and tie
tightly with string. Tie the bag to the pan
handle so it dangles in the juice.

2 Cut the citrus skins into thin wedges;
scrape off and discard the membranes
and pith. Cut the rinds into slivers and
add to the pan with the measured water.
Bring to a simmer and cook gently for
2 hours until the rinds are very tender
and the water has reduced by half. Test
the rinds for softness by pressing a
cooled piece with a finger.

3 Remove the muslin bag from the pan,
squeezing out the juice into the pan. Discard
the bag. Stir the unrefined granulated
sugar into the pan and heat very gently,
stirring occasionally with a wooden
spoon, until all the sugar has dissolved.

4 Bring the mixture to the boil and then
boil vigorously for 10–15 minutes, or
until the marmalade reaches 105°C/220°F.

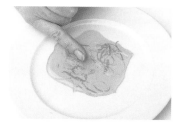

5 Alternatively, test the marmalade for
setting by pouring a small amount on to
a chilled saucer. Chill for 2 minutes, then
push the marmalade with your finger;
if wrinkles form on the surface, it is
ready. Cool for 15 minutes.

6 Stir the marmalade and pour it into
warm, sterilized jars. Cover with waxed
paper discs. Seal and label when cold.
Store in a cool dark cupboard. Serve
with warm croissants, if you like.

SAUCES, SALSAS, CHUTNEYS AND BREADS

Home-made sauces, salsas and breads, made with fresh, seasonal

produce, often taste much better than ready-made versions. As

fruits and vegetables come into season, start making large

quantities of sauces and chutneys, such as chilli sauce and apple

and tomato chutney, or delicious accompaniments such as garlic

mayonnaise or onion sauce, which can transform simple dishes.

Take your pick from a wide range of organic flavoured breads; try

pumpkin and walnut bread or cheese and onion cornbread, and

serve with delicious organic cheeses and cold meats.

TAHINI SAUCE

Made of sesame seeds, spiced with garlic and lemon juice, this is Israel's most famous
sauce. It makes a delicious dip and, when thinned with water, can be spooned over falafel.

SERVES FOUR TO SIX

150–175g/5–6oz/²⁄₃–¾ cup tahini
3 garlic cloves, finely chopped
juice of 1 lemon
1.5ml/¼ tsp ground cumin
small pinch of ground coriander
small pinch of curry powder
50–120ml/2–4fl oz/¼–½ cup water
cayenne pepper
sea salt

For the garnish
15–30ml/1–2 tbsp extra virgin olive oil
chopped fresh coriander (cilantro) or
    flat leaf parsley leaves
handful of olives and/or pickled vegetables
a few chillies or a hot pepper sauce

1 Put the tahini and garlic in a bowl
and mix together well. Stir in the lemon
juice, cumin, ground coriander and
curry powder.

COOK'S TIP
Tahini sauce forms the basis of many of
the salads and dips popular in Middle
Eastern cuisine.

2 Slowly add the water to the tahini,
beating all the time. The mixture will
thicken, then become thin. Season with
cayenne pepper and salt.

3 To serve, spoon the tahini on to a
serving plate, individual plates or into a
shallow bowl. Drizzle over the oil and
sprinkle with the other garnishes.

CHILLI SAUCE

Hot with chillies, pungent with garlic, and fragrant with exotic cardamom, this spicy sauce can be served with rice, couscous, soup and roast chicken or vegetable dishes.

MAKES ABOUT 475ML/16FL OZ/2 CUPS

5–8 garlic cloves, chopped
2–3 medium-hot chillies, such as jalapeño,
    seeded and chopped
5 tomatoes, diced
1 small bunch coriander (cilantro),
    roughly chopped
1 small bunch flat leaf parsley, chopped
30ml/2 tbsp extra virgin olive oil
10ml/2 tsp ground cumin
2.5ml/½ tsp ground turmeric
2.5ml/½ tsp curry powder
seeds from 3–5 cardamom pods
juice of ½ lemon
sea salt
a few sprigs of parsley or coriander,
    to garnish

COOK'S TIP
There is simply no comparison between the flavour of a freshly picked organic tomato that has been allowed to ripen naturally and the taste of an artificially ripened tomato. Organic growers select the sweetest, tastiest varieties, and whether you buy tiny cherry tomatoes or big beefsteaks, you will not be disappointed.

VARIATIONS
• To make a spicy dip, put 400g/14oz chopped fresh tomatoes, or a mixture of chopped fresh and canned tomatoes, in a bowl. Stir in 120ml/4fl oz/½ cup of the chilli sauce, or to taste, and season with salt, if necessary. Spread the dip on to wedges of flat bread, such as pitta bread, or serve in a bowl with strips of raw vegetables for dipping.
• To make a spicy tomato relish, soak 30ml/2 tbsp fenugreek seeds in cold water for at least 2 hours and preferably overnight. Drain, then grind the seeds in a spice grinder or pound them in a mortar with a pestle until they form a smooth paste. In a bowl, combine the paste with 15ml/1 tbsp of the chilli sauce and 2 diced tomatoes. Season with salt and black pepper to taste.

1 Put all the sauce ingredients except the salt in a food processor or blender. Process until finely chopped, then season with salt if necessary.

2 Pour the sauce into a bowl, cover and chill. Garnish with chopped herbs before serving. The sauce can be stored in the refrigerator for 3–4 days.

PEANUT SAUCE

Organic peanuts are an especially good source of iron, protein and fibre.
This peanut sauce goes well with Indonesian meat or seafood satay.

2 Add the shallots, garlic, ginger, most of the sliced chillies and the ground coriander to the pan and cook over a low heat, stirring occasionally, for 4–5 minutes, until the shallots are softened but not at all browned.

3 Transfer the spice mixture to a food processor or blender and add the peanuts, lemon grass, 5ml/1 tsp of the sugar, the soy sauce, and 105ml/3fl oz of the coconut milk and the fish sauce. Blend to form a fairly smooth sauce.

4 Taste the mixture and add more fish sauce, tamarind purée, seasoning, lime juice and/or more sugar as necessary.

5 Stir in the extra coconut milk and a little water if the sauce seems very thick, but do not make it too runny.

6 Serve the sauce cool or reheat it gently, stirring all the time to prevent it from spitting. Garnish with the remaining sliced chilli before serving.

SERVES FOUR TO SIX

30ml/2 tbsp groundnut (peanut) oil
75g/3oz/¾ cup unsalted peanuts, blanched
2 shallots, chopped
2 garlic cloves, chopped
15ml/1 tbsp chopped fresh root ginger
1–2 green chillies, seeded and
   thinly sliced
5ml/1 tsp ground coriander
1 lemon grass stalk, tender base only, chopped
5–10ml/1–2 tsp unrefined light muscovado
   (brown) sugar or rapadura
15ml/1 tbsp dark soy sauce
105–120ml/3–4fl oz/scant ½ cup canned
   coconut milk
15–30ml/1–2 tbsp Thai fish sauce
15–30ml/1–2 tbsp tamarind purée (paste)
lime juice
sea salt and ground black pepper

1 Heat the oil in a small, heavy frying pan and gently fry the peanuts, stirring frequently, until they are lightly browned. Use a slotted spoon to remove the nuts from the pan and drain them thoroughly on kitchen paper. Set aside to cool.

COOK'S TIP
To make tamarind purée, soak 25g/1oz tamarind pulp in 120ml/4fl oz/½ cup boiling water in a non-metallic bowl for about 30 minutes, mashing the pulp occasionally with a fork. Then press the pulp through a stainless steel sieve. This purée will keep for several days in a covered container in the refrigerator.

ONION SAUCE

This delicious, dark onion sauce goes really well with organic meat or vegetarian sausages.
It is also good with mashed potatoes, swede or turnip.

SERVES FOUR

45ml/3 tbsp olive oil
450g/1lb onions, halved and thinly sliced
45ml/3 tbsp plain (all-purpose) or
  wholemeal (whole-wheat) flour
400–500ml/14–17fl oz/1²/₃–2 cups
  vegetable stock
1 fresh thyme sprig
10ml/2 tsp dark soy sauce
sea salt and ground black pepper

2 Increase the heat slightly and cook for another 20–30 minutes, stirring occasionally, until the onions are a dark, golden brown.

3 Stir in the flour, then cook for a few minutes, stirring all the time. Gradually stir in 400ml/14fl oz/1²/₃ cups of the hot stock. Simmer, stirring, for a few minutes until thickened, adding a little more stock if the gravy is too thick.

4 Add the thyme, season with salt and pepper, then cook very slowly, stirring frequently, for 10–15 minutes.

5 Stir in the soy sauce and a little more seasoning, if necessary. Add a little more stock if the gravy is too thick, remove the thyme, and serve immediately.

1 Put the oil in a small, heavy pan and heat gently. Add the sliced onions and fry, stirring occasionally, for 15–20 minutes until the onions are soft and beginning to brown.

VARIATIONS
• The onions can be browned in the oven instead of on the stove-top. This is best done in sunflower or olive oil rather than butter, which would burn. Place the sliced onions in an ovenproof dish and toss with 45ml/3 tbsp oil. Cook in an oven preheated to 190°C/375°F/Gas 5 for 20 minutes, stirring once or twice, then raise the oven temperature to 220°C/425°F/Gas 7 and cook for a further 15–25 minutes.
• Part of the vegetable stock may be replaced with red wine or dark beer. You may need to add a little extra sugar to balance the acidity of the wine or beer.

GUACAMOLE

Many different types of organic onion are available; this chunky guacamole uses
sweet red onion for flavour and colour. Serve as a dip or sauce.

SERVES FOUR

2 large ripe avocados
1 small red onion, very finely chopped
1 red or green chilli, seeded and very
    finely chopped
½–1 garlic clove, crushed with a little
    sea salt
finely shredded rind of ½ lime and juice
    of 1–1½ limes
225g/8oz tomatoes, seeded
    chopped
30ml/2 tbsp roughly chopped fre
    coriander (cilantro)
2.5–5ml/½–1 tsp ground toasted
    cumin seeds
15ml/1 tbsp olive oil
15–30ml/1–2 tbsp sour cream (option
sea salt and ground black pepper
lime wedges dipped in sea salt (optional),
    and fresh coriander sprigs,
    to garnish

1 Cut one of the avocados in half and
lift out and discard the stone (pit).
Scrape the flesh from both halves into a
bowl and mash it roughly with a fork.

2 Add the onion, chilli, garlic, lime rind,
~~~~~~~~~~ der and stir well
                              d
seasoning to taste, then stir in the
olive oil.

3 Halve and stone (pit) the remaining
avocado. Dice the flesh and stir it into
the guacamole.

4 Squeeze in fresh lime juice to taste,
mix well, then cover and leave to stand
for 15 minutes so that the flavour

Serve with lime wedges dipped in sea
salt, if you wish, and garnish with fresh
coriander sprigs.

GARLIC MAYONNAISE

Fresh wet organic garlic is available in spring and summer, but try to use dried, cured
bulbs as they have a more pungent flavour for this mouthwatering creamy mayonnaise.

SERVES FOUR TO SIX

2 large egg yolks
pinch of dried mustard
about 300ml/½ pint/1¼ cups mild olive oil
15–30ml/1–2 tbsp lemon juice, white wine
   vinegar or warm water
2–4 garlic cloves
sea salt and ground black pepper

1 Make sure the egg yolks and oil have
come to room temperature before you
start. Place the yolks in a bowl with the
mustard and a pinch of salt, and whisk
together to mix.

2 Gradually whisk in the oil, one drop at
a time. When almost half the oil has
been fully incorporated, start to add it
in a slow, steady stream, whisking all
the time.

3 As the mayonnaise starts to thicken,
thin it down with a few drops of lemon
juice or vinegar, or a few teaspoons of
warm water.

4 When the mayonnaise is as thick as
soft butter, stop adding oil. Season the
mayonnaise to taste and add more
lemon juice or vinegar as required.

5 Crush the garlic with the blade of a
knife and stir it into the mayonnaise. For
a slightly milder flavour, blanch the garlic
twice in plenty of boiling water, then
purée the cloves before beating them
into the mayonnaise.

WATCHPOINT

The very young, the elderly, pregnant
women and those in ill-health or with a
compromised immune system are advised
against consuming raw eggs or dishes
containing them.

VARIATIONS

• To make Provençal aioli, crush 3–5
garlic cloves with a pinch of salt in a
bowl, then whisk in the egg yolks. Omit
the mustard but continue as above.
• For spicy garlic mayonnaise, omit the
mustard and stir in 2.5ml/½ tsp harissa or
red chilli paste and 5ml/1 tsp sun-dried
tomato purée (paste) with the garlic.
• Use roasted garlic purée or puréed
smoked garlic to create a different flavour.
• Beat in about 15g/½oz mixed fresh
herbs such as tarragon, parsley, chervil
and chives.

CONFIT of SLOW-COOKED ONIONS

This jam of caramelized onions will keep for several days in a sealed jar in the refrigerator.
You can use red, white or yellow onions, but yellow onions will give the sweetest result.

2 Season with salt and plenty of pepper, then add the thyme, bay leaf and sugar. Cook slowly, uncovered, for another 15–20 minutes, or until the onions are very soft and dark.

3 Add the prunes, vinegar and wine with 60ml/4 tbsp water and cook over a low heat, stirring frequently, for a further 20 minutes, or until most of the liquid has evaporated. Add a little water and reduce the heat if the mixture dries too quickly.

4 Adjust the seasoning, adding more sugar and/or vinegar to taste. Leave the confit to cool, then stir in the remaining 5ml/1 tsp oil. The confit is best stored for 24 hours before eating. Serve either cold or warm.

SERVES SIX TO EIGHT

30ml/2 tbsp olive oil
15g/½oz/1 tbsp butter or
    non-hydrogenated margarine
500g/1¼lb onions, sliced
3–5 fresh thyme sprigs
1 fresh bay leaf
30ml/2 tbsp unrefined light muscovado
    (brown) sugar or rapadura,
    plus a little extra
50g/2oz/¼ cup prunes, chopped
30ml/2 tbsp balsamic vinegar,
    plus a little extra
120ml/4fl oz/½ cup red wine
sea salt and ground black pepper

1 Reserve 5ml/1 tsp of the oil, then heat the rest with the butter in a small, heavy pan. Add the onions, cover and cook gently for 15 minutes, stirring occasionally.

VARIATION
Baby onions with tomato and orange
Gently fry 500g/1¼lb peeled pickling (pearl) onions or small *cipollini* in 60ml/4 tbsp olive oil until lightly browned, then sprinkle in 45ml/3 tbsp of unrefined soft light brown sugar or rapadura. Let the onions caramelize a little, then add 7.5ml/1½ tsp crushed coriander seeds, 250ml/8fl oz/1 cup red wine, 2 bay leaves, a few thyme sprigs, 3 strips orange zest and 45ml/3 tbsp tomato purée (paste) and the juice of 1 orange. Cook very gently, uncovered, for 1 hour, stirring occasionally until the sauce is thick and reduced. Uncover for the last 20 minutes of cooking time. Sharpen with 15–30ml/1–2 tbsp sherry vinegar and serve cold, sprinkled with chopped fresh parsley.

APPLE and TOMATO CHUTNEY

This mellow, golden, spicy chutney makes the most of fresh autumn produce.
Any type of organic tomatoes can be used successfully in this recipe.

MAKES ABOUT 1.8KG/4LB

1.3kg/3lb cooking apples
1.3kg/3lb tomatoes
2 large onions
2 garlic cloves
250g/9oz/1¾ cups pitted dates
2 red (bell) peppers
3 dried red chillies
15ml/1 tbsp black peppercorns
4 cardamom pods
15ml/1 tbsp coriander seeds

5ml/1 tsp sea salt
600ml/1 pint/2½ cups distilled malt vinegar
1kg/2¼lb/5¼ cups unrefined granulated
  sugar or rapadura

3 Pour in the vinegar and sugar and then leave to simmer for 30 minutes, stirring more frequently as the chutney becomes thick and pulpy.

4 Spoon the chutney into warm, dry, sterilized jars. Seal each jar with a waxed and store in a cool, dry place.

1 Peel and chop the apples. Peel and chop the tomatoes, onions and garlic. Quarter the dates. Core and seed the peppers, then cut into chunky pieces. Put all the prepared ingredients, except the red peppers, into a preserving pan.

2 Slit the chillies. Put the peppercorns and remaining spices into a mortar and roughly crush with a pestle. Add the chillies, spices and salt to the pan.

FOCACCIA

This is a flattish bread, originating from Genoa in Italy, made with flour, olive oil and salt.
There are many variations from many regions but this is the traditional type.

MAKES I ROUND 25CM/10IN LOAF

25g/1oz fresh yeast
400g/14oz/3½ cups unbleached strong
　white bread flour
10ml/2 tsp sea salt
75ml/5 tbsp olive oil
10ml/2 tsp coarse sea salt

I Dissolve the yeast in 120ml/4fl oz/
½ cup warm water. Allow to stand for
10 minutes. Sift the strong white bread
flour into a large bowl, make a well in
the centre, and add the yeast, salt and
30ml/2 tbsp oil. Mix in the flour and add
more water to make a dough.

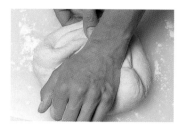

2 Turn out on to a floured work surface
and knead the dough until smooth and
elastic. Return to the bowl, cover with a
cloth, and leave to rise in a warm place
for 2–2½ hours until doubled in bulk.

3 Knock back the dough and knead
again for a few minutes. Press into an
oiled 25cm/10in tart tin, and cover with
a damp cloth. Leave the dough to rise
again for 30 minutes.

4 Preheat the oven to 200°C/400°F/
Gas 6. Poke the dough all over with your
fingers, to make little dimples in the
surface. Pour the remaining oil over the
dough, using a pastry brush to take it to
the edges. Sprinkle with the salt.

5 Bake for 20–25 minutes, until the
bread is a pale gold. Carefully remove
from the tin and leave to cool on a rack.
The bread is best eaten on the same
day, but it also freezes very well.

VARIATIONS
Focaccia is often baked with a selection
of different toppings. Before baking, lightly
sprinkle over any or a combination of the
following: chopped pitted olives, slices of
red or yellow (bell) pepper, sprigs of fresh
rosemary or diced sun-dried tomatoes.

OLIVE BREAD

Variations of this strongly flavoured bread are popular all over the Mediterranean.
For this Greek recipe use rich, oily olives or those marinated with herbs.

MAKES TWO 675G/1½LB LOAVES

2 red onions, thinly sliced
30ml/2 tbsp olive oil
225g/8oz/2 cups pitted black
   or green olives
50g/2oz fresh yeast
800g/1¾lb/7 cups strong white bread flour
7.5ml/1½ tsp salt
45ml/3 tbsp each roughly chopped parsley,
   coriander (cilantro) or mint

1 Fry the onions in the oil until soft.

2 Dissolve the yeast in 250ml/8fl oz/
1 cup warm water. Allow to stand for
10 minutes. Put the flour, salt and herbs
in a large bowl with the olives and fried
onions and add the yeast mixture.

3 Mix with a round-bladed knife, adding
as much warm water as is necessary to
make a soft dough.

4 Turn out on to a lightly floured surface
and knead for about 10 minutes. Put in a
clean bowl, cover with clear film (plastic
wrap) and leave in a warm place until
doubled in bulk.

5 Preheat the oven to 220°C/425°F/
Gas 7. Lightly grease two baking sheets.
Turn the dough on to a floured surface
and cut in half. Shape into two rounds and
place on the baking sheets. Cover the
dough loosely with lightly oiled clear film
and leave until doubled in size.

VARIATION
Shape the dough into 16 small rolls. Slash
the tops as in step 6 and reduce the
cooking time to 25 minutes.

6 Slash the tops of the loaves two or
three times with a knife, then bake for
about 40 minutes, or until the loaves
sound hollow when tapped on the
bottom. Transfer to a wire rack to cool.

CHAPATIS

More and more types of organic bread are available, but chapatis simply have to be made by hand. These chewy, unleavened breads are eaten throughout Northern India. They are usually served as an accompaniment to spicy dishes.

2 Knead for 5–6 minutes until smooth. Place in a lightly oiled bowl, cover with a damp dishtowel and leave to rest for 30 minutes. Turn out on to a floured surface. Divide the dough into six equal pieces. Shape each piece into a ball.

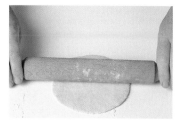

3 Press the dough into a larger round with the palm of your hand, then roll into a 13cm/5in round. Stack, layered between clear film (plastic wrap), to keep moist.

4 Heat a griddle or heavy frying pan over a medium heat for a few minutes until hot. Take one chapati, brush off any excess flour, and place on the griddle. Cook for 30–60 seconds, or until the top begins to bubble and white specks appear on the underside.

5 Turn the chapati over using a metal spatula and cook for a further 30 seconds. Remove from the pan and keep warm, layered between a folded dishtowel, while cooking the remaining chapatis. If you like, the chapatis can be brushed lightly with melted ghee or butter immediately after cooking. Serve warm.

MAKES SIX CHAPATIS

175g/6oz/1½ cups *atta* or wholemeal (whole-wheat) flour
2.5ml/½ tsp sea salt
120ml/4fl oz/about ½ cup water
5ml/1 tsp sunflower oil
melted ghee, butter or non-hydrogenated margarine, for brushing (optional)

COOK'S TIP

Atta or *ata* is a very fine wholemeal flour, which is only found in Indian stores and supermarkets. It is sometimes simply labelled chapati flour. *Atta* can also be used for making rotis and other Indian flat breads.

1 Sift the flour and salt into a large mixing bowl. Add the water and mix to a soft dough using your hand or a round-bladed knife. Knead in the oil, then turn the dough out on to a lightly floured surface.

PITTA BREAD

There are many different types of pitta bread, ranging from very flat ones, to those with pockets, to a thicker cushiony one, as here. They are fun to make, and look all the better for a little wobbliness around the edges.

MAKES TWELVE

25g/1oz fresh yeast
500g/1¼lb/5 cups unbleached strong white
   bread flour, or half white and
   half wholemeal (whole-wheat)
15ml/1 tbsp sea salt
15ml/1 tbsp olive oil
250ml/8fl oz/1 cup water

1 Dissolve the yeast in 120ml/4 fl oz/
½ cup warm water. Allow to stand for
10 minutes. Put the bread flour and salt

and stir enough liquid into the flour
mixture to make a stiff dough.

2 Place the dough in a clean bowl, cover
with a clean dishtowel and leave in a
warm place for at least 30 minutes and
up to 2 hours.

3 Knead the dough for 10 minutes, or
until smooth. Lightly oil the bowl, place
the dough in it, cover again and leave to
rise in a warm place for about 1 hour, or
until doubled in size.

4 Divide the dough into 12 equal-size
pieces. With lightly floured hands,
measuring about 20cm/8in and about
5mm–1cm/¼–½in thick. Keep the rolled
breads covered with a clean dishtowel.

5 Heat a large, heavy frying pan over a

in the pan and cook for 15–20 seconds.
Carefully turn it over and cook the
second side for about 1 minute.

6 When large bubbles start to form on
the bread, turn it over again. It should
puff up. Using a folded clean dishtowel,
gently press on the bread where the
bubbles have formed. Cook for a total of
3 minutes, then remove the pitta from
the pan. Repeat with the remaining dough
until all the pittas have been cooked.

7 Wrap the pitta breads in a clean
dishtowel, stacking them as each one is
cooked. Serve the pittas hot while they
are soft and moist.

VARIATION
To cook the breads in the oven, preheat
the oven to 220°C/425°F/Gas 7. Fill an
unglazed or partially glazed dish with hot
water and place in the bottom of the
oven. Alternatively, soak a handful of
unglazed tiles in hot water and arrange
them in the bottom of the oven. Use
either a non-stick baking sheet or a lightly
oiled ordinary baking sheet and heat in
the oven for a few minutes. Place two or
three pieces of flattened dough on to the
hot baking sheet and place in the hottest
part of the oven. Bake for 2–3 minutes.
They should puff up. Repeat with the
remaining dough until all the pittas have
been cooked.

SAN FRANCISCO SOURDOUGH BREAD

There are many sourdough bread recipes, but this is a great one to start with. The bread is leavened using a flour and water paste, which is left to ferment with the aid of airborne yeast. Use unbleached organic flour and the finished loaves will have a moist crumb and crispy crust, and will keep for several days.

MAKES TWO ROUND LOAVES

For the starter
50g/2oz/½ cup wholemeal (whole-wheat) flour
pinch of ground cumin
15ml/1 tbsp milk or soya milk
15–30ml/1–2 tbsp water
1st refreshment
60ml/4 tbsp water
115g/4oz/1 cup strong white bread flour
2nd refreshment
60ml/4 tbsp water
115g/4oz/1 cup strong white bread flour

For the bread: 1st refreshment
75ml/5 tbsp very warm water
75g/3oz/⅔ cup unbleached plain
   (all-purpose) flour
2nd refreshment
175ml/6fl oz/¾ cup lukewarm water
200–225g/7–8oz/1¾–2 cups unbleached
   plain (all-purpose) flour

For the sourdough
280ml/9fl oz/scant 1¼ cups warm water
500g/1¼lb/5 cups unbleached white bread flour
15ml/1 tbsp sea salt
flour, for dusting
ice cubes, for baking

1 Sift the flour and cumin for the starter into a bowl. Add the milk and sufficient water to make a firm but moist dough. Knead for 6–8 minutes. Return the dough to the bowl, cover with a damp dishtowel and leave in a warm place, 24–26°C/75–80°F, for about 2 days. When it is ready the starter will appear moist and wrinkled and will have developed a crust.

2 Pull off the hardened crust and discard. Scoop out the moist centre (about the size of a hazelnut), which will be aerated and sweet smelling, and place in a clean bowl. Mix in the water for the 1st refreshment. Gradually add the flour and mix to a dough.

3 Cover with clear film (plastic wrap) and return to a warm place for 1–2 days. Discard the crust and gradually mix in the water for the 2nd refreshment to the starter, which by now will have a slightly sharper smell. Gradually mix in the white flour, cover and leave in a warm place for 8–10 hours.

4 For the bread, mix the sourdough starter with the water for the 1st refreshment. Gradually mix in the flour to form a firm dough. Knead for 6–8 minutes until firm. Cover with a damp dishtowel and leave in a warm place for 8–12 hours, or until doubled in bulk.

5 Gradually mix in the water for the 2nd refreshment, then gradually mix in enough flour to form a soft, smooth elastic dough. Re-cover and leave in a warm place for 8–12 hours. Gradually stir in the water for the sourdough, then gradually work in the flour and salt. This will take 10–15 minutes. Turn out on to a lightly floured surface and knead until smooth and very elastic. Place in a large lightly oiled bowl, cover with lightly oiled clear film and leave to rise, in a warm place, for 8–12 hours.

6 Divide the dough in half and shape into 2 round loaves by folding the sides over to the centre and sealing.

7 Place seam side up in flour-dusted *couronnes* bowls or baskets lined with flour-dusted dishtowels. Re-cover and leave to rise in a warm place for 4 hours.

8 Preheat the oven to 220°C/425°F/Gas 7. Place an empty roasting pan in the bottom of the oven. Dust two baking sheets with flour. Turn out the loaves seam side down on the prepared baking sheets. Using a sharp knife, cut a criss-cross pattern by slashing the top of the loaves 4–5 times in each direction.

9 Place the baking sheets in the oven and immediately drop the ice cubes into the hot roasting pan to create steam. Bake the bread for 25 minutes, then reduce the oven temperature to 200°C/400°F/Gas 6 and bake for a further 15–20 minutes, or until it sounds hollow when tapped on the base. Transfer to wire racks to cool.

COOK'S TIP
If you'd like to make sourdough bread regularly, keep a small amount of the starter covered in the refrigerator. It will keep for several days. Use the starter for the 2nd refreshment, then continue as directed.

PUMPKIN and WALNUT BREAD

*Walnuts, nutmeg and pumpkin combine to yield a moist, tangy and slightly sweet bread
with an indescribably good flavour. Serve partnered with meats or cheese.*

MAKES ONE LOAF

500g/1¼lb pumpkin, peeled, seeded and
  cut into chunks
75g/3oz/6 tbsp caster (superfine) sugar
5ml/1 tsp grated nutmeg
50g/2oz/¼ cup butter, melted
3 eggs, lightly beaten
350g/12oz/3 cups unbleached strong white
  bread flour
10ml/2 tsp baking powder
2.5ml/½ tsp sea salt
75g/3oz/¾ cup walnuts, chopped

1 Grease and neatly base-line a loaf tin
(pan) measuring 21 × 12cm/8½ × 4½in.
Preheat the oven to 180°C/350°F/
Gas 4.

2 Place the pumpkin in a pan, add water
to cover by about 5cm/2in, then bring to
the boil. Cover, lower the heat and
simmer for about 20 minutes, or until
the pumpkin is very tender. Drain well,
then purée in a food processor or
blender. Leave to cool.

3 Place 275g/10oz/1¼ cups of the purée
in a large bowl. Add the sugar, nutmeg,
melted butter and eggs and mix. Sift the
flour, baking powder and salt into a large
bowl and make a well in the centre.

4 Add the pumpkin mixture to the
centre of the flour and stir until smooth.
Mix in the walnuts.

5 Transfer to the prepared tin and bake
for 1 hour, or until golden and starting
to shrink from the sides of the tin. Turn
out on to a wire rack to cool.

COOK'S TIP
If you have more pumpkin purée than you
need, use the remainder in soup.

WHOLEMEAL SUNFLOWER BREAD

Organic sunflower seeds give a nutty crunchiness to this hearty wholemeal loaf.
Serve with a chunk of cheese and a rich tomato chutney.

3 Cover the bowl with a damp dishtowel and leave the dough to rise in

4 Preheat the oven to 200°C/400°F/ Gas 6. Turn out the dough on to a lightly floured work surface and knead for about 10 minutes until elastic – the dough will still be quite sticky, but resist the temptation to add more flour.

5 Form the dough into a rectangle and place in the loaf tin. Sprinkle the top with sunflower seeds. Cover with a damp dishtowel and leave to rise again for a further 15 minutes.

6 Bake for 40–45 minutes until golden. When ready, the loaf should sound hollow when tapped underneath. Leave for 5 minutes, turn out of the tin and cool on a wire rack.

MAKES ONE LOAF

25g/1oz fresh yeast
450g/1lb/4 cups strong wholemeal
 (whole-wheat) flour
2.5ml/½ tsp sea salt
50g/2oz/scant ½ cup sunflower seeds,
 plus extra for sprinkling

1 Dissolve the yeast in 120ml/4fl oz/ ½ cup warm water. Allow to stand for 10 minutes. Grease and lightly flour a 450g/1lb loaf tin (pan).

2 Put the flour, salt and sunflower seeds in a large mixing bowl and stir to combine the ingredients. Make a well in the centre and gradually stir in the yeast mixture. Mix vigorously with a wooden spoon, adding sufficient extra warm water to form a soft, sticky dough.

VARIATION

Other seeds would be good in this bread – try sesame seeds, pumpkin seeds or a mixture of sesame, pumpkin, hemp and sunflower seeds.

CHEESE and ONION CORNBREAD

Full of flavour, this tasty organic cornbread is delicious served freshly baked, warm or cold in slices, either on its own or spread with a little butter. It makes an ideal accompaniment to soups, stews and chillies.

MAKES ONE 900G/2LB LOAF

15ml/1 tbsp sunflower oil
1 onion, thinly sliced
175g/6oz/1½ cups corn meal
75g/3oz/⅔ cup rice flour
25g/1oz/¼ cup soya flour
15ml/1 tbsp baking powder
5ml/1 tsp unrefined caster (superfine)
    sugar or rapadura
5ml/1 tsp sea salt
115g/4oz/1 cup coarsely grated mature
    Cheddar cheese
200ml/7fl oz/scant 1 cup tepid milk or
    soya milk
2 eggs
40g/1½oz/3 tbsp non-hydrogenated
    margarine, melted

1 Preheat the oven to 190°C/375°F/ Gas 5. Lightly grease a 900g/2lb loaf tin (pan). Heat the oil in a frying pan, add the onion and cook gently for 10–15 minutes until softened, stirring occasionally. Remove the pan from the heat and set aside to cool.

2 Place the corn meal, rice flour, soya flour, baking powder, sugar and salt in a large mixing bowl and combine thoroughly. Stir in the grated cheese, mixing well.

3 In a jug (pitcher), beat together the milk, eggs and melted margarine. Add to the flour mixture and mix well using a wooden spoon.

4 Stir the cooled, cooked onions into the corn meal mixture and stir well until the onions are evenly incorporated.

5 Spoon the onion mixture into the prepared tin, level the surface and bake for about 30 minutes until the bread has risen and is golden brown.

6 Run a knife around the edge to loosen the loaf. Turn out on to a wire rack to cool slightly and serve warm. Alternatively, leave it on the rack until completely cold, then cut into slices. To store the loaf, wrap it in foil or seal in a plastic bag.

VARIATIONS
• A wide selection of organic flours is available. In addition to a range of wheat flours, you can choose from buckwheat, rice, rye or maize.
• Reserve a little of the grated cheese and cooked onion and scatter it over the top of the bread before baking.

COOK'S TIP
A loaf tin that has drop-down sides is useful when making corn bread. Because it has a much softer texture than conventional yeast breads, you need to take care when turning out the cooked bread onto the wire rack.

GLOSSARY

As in every specialist area, organics has its own language. The following is a guide to some of the specialist terms in common usage.

Agriculture The cultivation of crops and raising of livestock for the production of food and other products.

Agrochemical A chemical or chemical compound used in farming. Also an adjective to describe produce derived from farms that extensively use these chemicals, or the method of agriculture that utilizes agrochemicals.

Aquaculture The farming of fish and other creatures that live in fresh or sea water e.g. salmon and prawns.

Artificial additives Chemicals and chemical compounds added to foods in order to manipulate their taste, colour, texture or shelf life. These include powerful toxins such as tartrazine, a neurotoxin that is used in cordials and soft drinks (sodas) to dye them orange. Only seven of the seven thousand additives used in non-organic food may be used in organic food.

Biodiversity The wide diversity of plants and creatures that occurs in nature. Also the ideal of organic systems of farming, biodiversity is a term to describe farms rich in different species of plants and animals, whether intentionally cultivated and bred, or those which occur naturally.

Biodynamics Based on the work of the early twentieth century theosophist Rudolph Steiner, biodynamic farming relies on companion planting, homeopathic preparations and a seven-year cycle of crop rotation to remain entirely chemical-free. Biodynamic farms are completely self-contained, integrating different crops and livestock to create a mini-ecosystem. The lunar calendar is used as a guide to planting and harvesting crops, with different star constellations signalling the most fruitful times for these activities. Biodynamics is part of the family of organic farming styles.

Certification Each organic certification board has a different code of standards. However, the basic organic standards are legally defined in international law, so every certification board throughout the world must at least comply with these standards. Check details with each certifier if you want to know if they enforce standard organic standards or stricter ones.

Companion planting A method of growing plants in combinations that optimize their beneficial effects while minimizing their negative effects on each other. For example, growing potatoes near tomatoes weakens their resistance to potato blight, so this should be avoided. Growing chamomile and peppermint in proximity is beneficial, as both plants produce more active essential oils in combination. Companion planting is a practical way of conserving and utilizing biodiversity.

Compost Vegetable and animal matter that has been purposefully decomposed (aerobically fermented) to create a natural source of nutrients for growing crops. Encourages good soil quality and beneficial enzyme production. Organic farmers must follow strict procedures to produce composts and

manures. They compost for lengthy periods to ensure that e-coli and other bugs are killed off. Also extensively manufactured and utilised by organic home gardeners.

Crop rotation A traditional method of effectively managing soil fertility on a farm by systematically rotating crops between different fields. This method often includes leaving fields to lie fallow, meaning that they are rested from production to regain their naturally fertile soil.

Fair trade The concept that a fair price will be paid for goods produced by farmers and workers in the developing world. Many poorer farmers are forced to sell their products for much less than is just if there is no other outlet for them. Fair trade means that a buyer from the developed world will not exploit this opportunity to pay less money than a commodity is worth. Effectively, honourable behaviour rather than exploitation. The official Fairtrade Mark prohibits child and forced labour, and

guarantees that workers receive a decent standard of housing, health and safety protection and employment rights. It also promotes programmes for environmental sustainability.

Fertilizers Generally refers to synthetic chemicals and chemical compounds based on synthetic nitrates used by farmers to give plants extra nutrients for growth. An excess of nitrates is known to cause cancer in humans and animals. Organic farming uses natural fertilizers instead, such as manure, seaweed, clays and rockdust.

Free range A term to describe farm animals and birds that have been able to gain some access to open pastures and skies. When applied to chickens and their eggs, it may simply mean that the chicken house has "popholes" but does not guarantee that the birds will have used these exits, especially if they have been bred in confinement. In the UK the Soil Association has the highest standards for free range poultry and eggs – prohibiting debeaking and overcrowding, and ensuring that all birds range properly in daylight. If in doubt, check with your local certification board for details of their guidelines.

Fungicides Chemicals and chemical compounds used to prevent moulds growing on crops or food products by killing fungal spores. Organic farming prohibits their use. However, where the whole crop might otherwise be lost to something like potato blight or mildew, small amounts of

traditional chemicals, such as copper and sulphur compounds may be used by organic farmers. This practice is restricted to extreme cases, and permission must be granted from an organic certifier.

Gardening The practice of organic gardening is an extremely valuable activity. The United Nations' Food and Agriculture Organisation has calculated that small biodiverse gardens can produce thousands of times more food per acre than large intensive monocultures. Home gardening in Indonesia provides around 40 per cent of all food, and in Eastern Nigeria, the 2 per cent of land cultivated as domestic gardens provides 50 per cent of the food. Gardening provides people in industrialised nations with a connection to the food they eat, whether it is growing herbs in a window box or fruit and vegetables in a garden.

Genetic modification The manipulation of genetic material between different unrelated species of living entities. In agriculture, the creation of crops known as Genetically Modified Organisms (GMOs) or Transgenic Organisms by extracting genes from one species and inserting them in another. GM farming is part of the family of farming styles that makes up agrochemical farming.

GMOs Genetically Modified Organisms (see previous entry).

Herbicides Chemicals and chemical compounds used to kill weeds. Organic farming prohibits their use.

Hydroponics A modern method of agrochemical farming that grows plants in a purely synthetic environment. The plants are suspended in a liquid mixture of nutrient compounds in a medium of sand or gravel. Bright lights are often used to stimulate plant growth. Many non-organic potato and tomato crops are now routinely grown without soil.

Insecticides Chemicals and chemical compounds used to kill insects.

Irradiation The passing of food through a radiation field to preserve it beyond its natural shelf life. The use of ionizing irradiation to preserve food is prohibited under organic standards.

Legumes Crops related to the bean family. Planted extensively in organic agriculture to maintain beneficial levels of nitrogen in the soil. Legumes have the capacity to fix nitrogen from the air into the soil through nodules in their roots. They are often planted as part of the crop rotation system in fallow fields.

Monocultures Agrochemical farms that continually grow only one kind of crop over a vast area. Monocultures are the antithesis of biodiversity, and they are the prevalent form of agriculture in most industrialized nations at the beginning of the 21st century. Four per cent of all farms in the USA produce half of the food grown there on huge swathes of land growing only a single species.

Organic A method of farming based on the cultivation of good soil quality and biodiversity. The use of agrochemicals is strictly regulated and kept to the absolute minimum. It prohibits GMOs (even in animal feed), and is a legally binding term defined in international law. The rearing of organic animals must be according to strict welfare standards, and they may only be treated with chemicals such as antibiotics as a last resort to cure illness. When the term is used to describe a food product or item, at least 95 per cent of its ingredients must be certified organic and it may not be irradiated.

Permaculture This is the design and maintenance of food growing systems which have the diversity, stability, and resilience of natural ecosystems. It is the harmonious integration of the landscape with people, in cities or rural areas. Permaculture can be as small as a city balcony or as large as a forest. It is a way of providing food, energy, shelter and other material and non-material needs in a sustainable way.

Pesticides Chemicals and chemical compounds used by farmers and gardeners to kill pests. These products often contain organophosphates, which belong to the same family of chemicals as nerve gases. Synthetic pesticides are applied to crops and livestock as a matter of course in agrochemical agriculture for the prevention and treatment of pests. In organic farming, they may only be applied to crops if all other non-chemical actions to tackle a pest problem have failed, and then only with permission from a certifier. Organic farming relies on biodiversity to provide natural predators to control pests, or uses natural plant-based pesticides. Standards are rigorous and organic farms unfortunate enough to be affected by pesticide drift from neighbouring agrochemical properties have on occasion had their licences revoked.

Prevention The method utilised by organic farmers to minimise the use of agrochemicals, hormones and antibiotics in farming practices. Pesticide use is minimised by careful management, from companion planting to the use of satellite technology to detect potential parasites. Chemical use for livestock is minimised by keeping numbers of animals and fish lower per pen, and encouraging more freedom of movement within the farm or fish tank.

Processed food Food that has been ready prepared from its raw state for consumption. This can be through a great variety of processes, including boiling, slicing, and baking. Processing food by its very nature removes nutrients and vitality. 70 per cent of all food grown in the USA is processed before it reaches the shops. Only 1 per cent of food grown in India is processed before it is retailed. Indian citizens do not eat their produce raw, but simply process the ingredients themselves at home.

Selective breeding A traditional genetic technique that produces plants or animals with a particular genetic profile. Reasons may include creating a distinctive taste, unusual colour or hardier variety. It is unrelated to modern genetic modification, as selective breeding takes part between plants of the same species through interbreeding rather than between differing species using DNA displacement technology.

SUPPLIERS & INFORMATION SOURCES

UK & EIRE

Architectural Salvage, Index,
Hutton and Rostron,
admin@handr.co.uk
www.handr.co.uk

Biodynamic Agricultural
Association
Tel: +44 (0)1453 759501

British Nutrition Foundation
Tel: +44 (0)20 7404 6504

British Trust for Conservation
Volunteers
information@btcv.org.uk
www.btcv.org.uk

Cambrian Organics
Tel: +44 (0)1559 363151
www.cambrianorganics.com

Centre for Alternative
Technology
Tel: +44 (0)1654 702400
www.cat.org.uk

Circaroma Organic Skincare
Tel: +44 (0)20 7249 9392
www.circaroma.com

Clearspring
Tel: +44 (0)20 8740 1781
rudkin@dircon.co.uk

Community Composting
Network

ccn@gn.apc.org
www.othas.org.uk/cnn/

Compassion in World
Farming
Tel: +44 (0)1730 264208
www.ciwf.co.uk

Fairtrade Foundation
Tel: +44 (0)20 7405 5942
www.fairtrade.org.uk

Farmers' World Network
www.fwn.org.uk

Food and Agricultural
Organization (United Nations)
www.fao.org

Fresh and Wild
Tel: +44 (0)800 9175 175
www.freshandwild.com

Friends of the Earth
Tel: +44 (0)20 7490 1555
www.foe.co.uk

Graig Farm
Tel: +44 (0)1597 851655
www.graigfarm.co.uk

Green Endings
Tel: +44 (0)20 7424 0345
www.greenendings.co.uk

Greenfibres
Tel: +44 (0)1803 868001
www.greenfibres.com

Green Gardener
Tel: +44 (0)1603 715096
www.greengardener.co.uk

Greenhouse Supply
Tel: +44 (0)800 018 7889
www.greenhousesupply.co.uk

Green People
Tel: +44 (0)1444 401444
www.greenpeople.co.uk

Hambledon Herbs
Tel: +44 (0)1823 401104
www.hambledonherbs.co.uk

HDRA, the Organic
Organisation
Tel: +44 (0)24 7630 3517
Fax: +44 (0)24 7663 9229
enquiry@hdra.org.uk
www.hdra.org.uk

Himalayan Green Tea
Tel: +44 (0)1895 632409
www.nvspharmacy.co.uk

Irish Organic Farmers and
Growers Association
Tel: +353 (0)506 32563
Fax: +353 (0)506 32063
info@irishorganic.ie
www.irishorganic.ie

Kinvara Irish Organic Smoked
Salmon
Tel: +353 (0)916 37489

Llain Farm Fresh Meats
Tel: +44 (0)1348 831210

Marine Stewardship Council
Tel: +44 (0)20 7350 4000
www.msc.org

National Association of Farmers'
Markets
Tel: +44 (0)1225 787914

Neal's Yard Bakery
Tel: +44 (0)20 7836 5199
www.nealsyardbakery.co.uk

NHR Organic Oils
Tel: +44 (0)845 310 8066
www.nhr.kz

Organic Delivery Company
(London)
Tel: +44 (0) 20 7739 8181
www.organicdelivery.co.uk

www.organicfood.co.uk –
Ysanne Spevack's organic food
and lifestyle website.
The Organic Garden catalogue
chaseorg@aol.com
www.OrganicCatalog.com

Organic Wine Company
Tel: +44 (0)1494 446557
www.organicwinecompany.com

Permaculture Magazine
Tel: +44 (0)845 458 4150
info@permaculture.co.uk
www.permaculture.co.uk

Pero Organic Pet Foods
Tel: +44 (0)1690 710457
pero@perofsbusiness.co.uk

Pesticide Action Network UK
Tel: +44 (0)20 7274 8895
www.pan-uk.org

Planet Organic
Tel: +44 (0)20 7221 7171
deliveries@planetorganic.com
www.planetorganic.com

Plants for a Future
Tel: +44 (0)1208 872963
pfaf@scs.leeds.ac.uk
www.scs.leeds.ac.uk/pfaf

Race and Race Artisan Foods
Tel: +44 (0)1647 277454
raceorganic@aol.com

Ravens Oak Dairy
Tel: +44 (0)1270 524210
www.ravensoakdairy.co.uk

Rocombe Farm Organic
Ice Cream
Tel: +44 (0)1482 575884
icecreamcentre@netscape
online.co.uk

Royal Society for the Protection
of Birds
Tel: +44 (0)1767 680551
www.rspb.org.uk

Scarletts PlantCare
Tel: +44 (0)1206 240466
www.scarletts.co.uk

Scottish Quality Salmon
Tel: +44 (0)1738 587000
www.scottishsalmon.co.uk

Seasoned Pioneers
Tel: +44 (0)800 0682348
www.seasonedpioneers.co.uk

Sheepdrove Organic Farm
Tel: +44 (0)1488 71659
www.sheepdrove.com

Simply Soaps
Tel: +44 (0)1603 720869
www.simplysoaps.com

Slow Food Movement (UK)
c/o The Village Bakery
Tel: +44 (0)1768 881515
www.slow-food.com

The Soil Association
Tel: +44 (0)117 929 0661
info@soilassociation.org
www.soilassociation.org

Solar Homes
Tel: +44 (0)1275 540112
www.solarsense-uk.com

Special Diets News
Tel: +44 (0)20 7722 2866
www.inside-story.com

Sustain
Tel: +44 (0)20 7837 1228
Fax: +44 (0)20 7837 1141
www.sustainweb.org

Swaddles Green Farm
Tel: +44 (0)1460 234387
www.swaddles.co.uk

Triodos Bank
Tel: +44 (0)117 973 9339
mail@triodos.co.uk
www.triodos.co.uk

UK Register of Organic Food
Standards (UKROFS)
Tel: +44 (0)20 7238 5915

Vintage Roots
Tel: +44 (0)800 980 4992
www.vintageroots.co.uk

Well Hung Meats
Tel: +44 (0)1752 830282
www.carswellfarm.co.uk

Wiggly Wigglers
Tel: +44 (0)1981 500391
www.wigglywigglers.co.uk

The Wildlife Trusts UK Office
Tel: +44 (0)870 036 7711
arawson@wildlife-trusts.cix.co.uk
www.wildlifetrusts.org

Willing Workers on Organic
Farms (WWOOF)
Tel: +44 (0)1273 476286
www.phdc.com/wwoof

Windrush Willow
Tel: +44 (0)1395 233669
www.windrushwillow.com

Women's Environmental
Network
Tel: +44 (0)20 7247 3327
www.gn.apc.org/wen

USA & CANADA

Alternative Farming Systems
Information Center
Tel: +1 301 504 6559
www.nal.usda.gov/afsic

Biodynamic Farming and
Gardening Association, Inc.
Tel: +1 415 561 7797
www.biodynamics.com

Canadian Organic Growers
Tel: +1 506 375 7383
info@cog.ca
www.cog.ca

Diamond Organics
Tel: +1 888 ORGANIC

Ecological Agriculture Projects
http://eap.mcgill.ca/general/
home_frames.htm

Extremely Green Gardening
Company LLC
Tel: +1 781 878 5397
info@extremelygreen.com
www.extremelygreen.com

Gardens Alive! Inc.
Tel: +1 812 537 8650
www.gardensalive.com

Institute for Agriculture &
Trade's National Organic
Program
Tel: +1 202 720 3252

Nanaimo Community Gardens
Society
Tel: +1 250 753 9393
www.communitygardens.tripod.com
/nanaimo

The National Information
Network for Organic Farmers,
Gardeners & Consumers
Tel: +1 613 767 0796
www.cog.ca

Northeast Organic Farming
Association
info@nofa.org
www.nofa.org

Northwest Coalition for
Alternatives to Pesticides
Tel: +1 541 344-5044
www.pesticide.org

Nova Scotia Organic Growers
Association
NSOGA@gks.com
www.gks.com/NSOGA

Organic Grapes into Wine Alliance
www.isgnet.com/ogwa

Organic Style Magazine
www.organicstyle.com

Organic Trade Association
Tel: +1 413 774 7511
info@ota.com
www.ota.com

Organic Trading and
Information Center
www.organicfood.com

Peaceful Valley Farm Supply, Inc.
Tel: +1 530 272 4769
contact@groworganic.com
www.groworganic.com

Planet Natural
Tel: +1 406 587 5891
Fax: +1 406 587 0223
info@planetnatural.com
www.planetnatural.com

Rodale Institute
Tel: +1 610 967 5171
info@rodale.com
www.rodale.com

Seeds of Change
Tel: +1 888 762 7333
www.seedsofchange.com

Terra Viva Organics
Tel: +1 866 599 2847
Fax: +1 604 448 9374
info@tvorganics.com
www.tvorganics.com

Transfair
Tel: +1 510 663 5260
Fax: +1 510 663 5264
info@transfairusa.org
www.transfairusa.org

Whole Foods
Tel: +1 512 477 4455
www.wholefoods.com

Wild Oats
Tel: +1 800 494 9453
www.wildoats.com

AUSTRALIA

Biodynamic Marketing
Company Ltd
Tel: +61 (3) 5966 7370

Biological Farmers of Australia
Co Op Ltd
Tel: +61 (7) 4639 3299

Eden Seeds
Tel: +61 (7) 5533 1107
Fax: +61 (7) 5533 1108

Excel-Crop
Tel: +61 (3) 9802 0307
Fax: +61 (3) 9802 1502
kssspr@tig.com.au

NASSA (National Association
for Sustainable Agriculture)
Tel: +61 (8) 8370 8455
www.nassa.com.au

Organic Federation of
Australia Inc.
Tel: +61 (2) 9299 8016
Fax: +61 (2) 9299 0189
info@ofa.org.au
www.ofa.org.au

Organic Herb Growers of
Australia Inc.(OHGA)
Tel: +61 (2) 6622 0100
Fax: +61 (2) 6622 0900
admin@organicherbs.org
www.organicherbs.org

Organic Retailers and Growers
Association of Australia
Tel: +61 (3) 9737 9799
www.orgaa.org.au

The Organic Super Site
Tel: +61 (2) 9523 6134
Fax: +61 (2) 9523 6134
dom@organicsupersite.com
www.organicsupersite.com

Robinvale Organic &
Bio-Dynamic Wines Australia
Tel: +61 (3) 5026 3955
Fax: +61 (3) 5026 1123
demeter1@iinet.net.au
www.organicwines.com.au

NEW ZEALAND

Bio-Gro New Zealand
www.biogro.co.nz

Certified Organics Ltd.
Tel: +64 (9) 525 3432
Fax: +64 (9) 525 3462
info@certified-organics.com
www.certified-organics.com

Deeweed
Tel: +64 (9) 292 4143
www.deweed.co.nz

Eco-Store
Tel: +64 (9) 360 8477
www.ecostore.co.nz

Greenearths Garden Landscaping
Tel: +64 (9) 443 6486
www.greenearth.co.nz

New Zealand Organics
Tel: +64 (9) 376 1330
Fax: +64 (9) 361 0082
www.nzorganics.co.nz

Organic Products Exporters of
New Zealand, Inc. (OPENZ)
Tel: +64 (3) 365 6806
Fax: +64 (3) 365 6308
info@organicsnewzealand.org.nz
www.organicsnewzealand.org.nz

ACKNOWLEDGEMENTS

Christine and Michael Lavelle would like to thank the following people who worked as models for the photography: Joe Lovell. Debbie Hart for her willow weaving skills, Jane Dobson for her graft unions and Ian Gandy and Stewart Brown for the lawn maintenance shots. A big thank you to Writtle College and their staff for allowing the use of their grounds and glasshouses to take many of the photographs.

Ysanne Spevack would like to thank the following people for their assistance. Without people like you, this book could never have happened …

John Barrow at Organic Delivery Company
Peter Bradford at Fresh & Wild
Lynda Brown
Steve Chandra
Charles, Prince of Wales
Carol Charlton
Caroline Conran
Gilli Davies
The Dkiks
Julie Edgar at Scottish Quality Salmon
The Finelli-Blowers
Dido Fisher
Jenni Fleetwood
Lou Gibbs
Patrick Holden, Sue Flook and Sarah Jeffs at the Soil Association
Peter Kindersley at Sheepdrove Farm
Guy Lafayette and David Lee at Consultancy for Corporate Change
Margaret Malone
Mia Manners
Vini Medley
Kate Pengelly
Miriam Polunin
Sarah Ratty
Anita Roddick
Craig Sams
Howard-Yana Shapiro
Brian Spevack
Michael van Straten
Amy Williams at Marine Stewardship Council
Antony Worrall-Thompson
Joy Wotton

The publisher would like to thank the following for kindly allowing photography to take place in their gardens:

t = top   b = bottom   l = left
r = right   c = centre

The Centre for Alternative Technology, Wales 12t; 21b; 38t; 39t; 67br; 110;120c; 127bc and br; 128t; 136t; 147bl; Dean Court, Dorset 22; 32b; 42; 43c; 71bl; Edmondsham Manor, Dorset 10; 13t; 14bl; 16t; 36t; 69t; 82c; 84; 98t; 102t; 112t; 115tl; 129t; 135tl; 143bl; 212; 499; Fardel Manor, Devon 5, 36c; 61t; 68bl; 107tl; 113b; 119b; 121tl; 146c; 148bl; Valerie Ferguson, Bath 13b; 37t; 44bl; 48tr; 49t (all pictures in sequence); 62t and c; 78t; 81br; 83tl; 83cl; 120t 131b; 135tr; 135b; 139b; 152t; HDRA, the Organic Organisation, Coventry 8t; 9bc; 12b; 15; 16br; 18c; 20b; 21t; 34tr; 62b; 66; 67bl; 79br; 80t; 80c; 80b; 83br; 111c; 113tl and tr; 115tr; 120b; 121tr; 128b; 129t; 131t; 136b; 147t; 162bl; 249; 503; 505; Adrian Penrose 46t; 81t; RHS Rosemoor, Devon 6; 11c; 14br; 23bl; 27br; 68t; 86; 102b; 114t; 132; 134t; 134b; 158br; 155br; 156t; 206t; 506; RHS Wisley, Surrey 68b; 126; Peter Robinson 16bl; 111r; The Royal Society for the Protection of Birds, Bedfordshire 78c; Writtle College, Chelmsford 9tl; 9b; 18b; 23br; 25tr; 32t; 35 (all pictures); 43br; 46br; 82t; 83bl; 87 (all pictures in sequence); 88; 90t; 90bl; 91bl and br; 92c; 93 (all pictures in sequence); 97t; 102c; 106t; 106-107 (all pictures in sequence); 107tr; 114b; 115b; 116t; 116bl and br; 117b; 138t

PICTURE CREDITS

The publisher would also like to thank the following for allowing their photographs to be reproduced:

The Garden Picture Library 73r (three from top; Sunniva Harte); 74t (Janet Sorrell); 75 (ten from top; Lamontagne); 172bl (Howard Rice); 175cr (Jerry Pavia); 175b (Sunniva Harte); 176t (Sunniva Harte); 176b (Brian Carter); 181t (David Askham); 185t (Neil Holmes); 185c (Michael Howes); 185b (Michael Howes); 190t (Philippe Bonduel); 190c (Mayer/Le Scanff); 230t (Howard Rice); 230r (Vaughn Fleming); 233t (Neil Holmes); 247 (John Glover); Holt Studios International 73l (four from top; Nigel Cattlin); 73l (13 from top; Nigel Cattlin); 73r (four from top; Nigel Cattlin); 73r (eight from top; Nigel Cattlin); 75 (seven from top; Nigel Cattlin); 75 (11 from top; Nigel Cattlin); 77 (four from top; Nigel Cattlin); 124 (three from top; Primrose Peacock); 124 (four from top; Nigel Cattlin); 125 (six from top; M. Szadzuik/R. Zinck); NHPA 72br; 73tl; 73l (seven from top); 73l (eight from top); 73l (nine from top); 73l (ten from top); 73r (five from top); 75 (three from top); 73r (two from top); 73r (six from top) Anthony Blake Photo Library: 256t, 256b, 257, 258t, 308bl; A-Z Botanical Collection Ltd 262r (Bjorn Svensson); 264r (Sylvia Sroka); Science Photo Library 296l (Simon Fraser); Fletcher & Baylis 298r. Ysanne Spevack's portrait on jacket by Lou Gibbs.

BIBLIOGRAPHY

Bissell, Frances – The Organic Meat Cookbook (Ebury Press, 1999)
Boyd, Hilary – Banishing the Blues (Mitchell Beazley, 2000)
Brown, Edward Espe – Tassajara Bread Book (Shambhala, 1970)
Brown, Edward Espe – Tomato Blessings and Radish (Riverhead Books, 1997)
Brown, Lynda – Organic Living (Dorling Kindersley, 2000)
Charlton, Carol – Organic Café Cookbook (David and Charles, 1999)
Clayton, Dr Paul – Health Defence (Accelerated Learning Systems, 2001)
Elliot, Rose – Beanfeast (White Eagle Publishing Trust, 1975)
Elliott, Renée and Trevillé, Eric – Organic Cookbook (Dorling Kindersley, 2000)
Heaton, Shane – Organic Farming, Food Quality and Human Health (Soil Association, 2001)
Lifespan Community Collective – Full of Beans (L C C Ltd, 1982)
Lucas, Dr Caroline MEP – Stopping the Great Food Swap (Earthscan, 2000)
Miller, Mark – Red Sage (Ten Speed Press, 1999)
Shapiro, Howard-Yana and Harrisson, John – Gardening for the Future of the Earth (Bantam, 2000)
van Straten, Michael – Superfoods (Dorling Kindersley, 1990)
van Straten, Michael – Organic Superfoods (Mitchell Beazley, 1999)

GARDENING INDEX

RECIPE INDEX